T0141897

Lecture Notes in Information Systems and Organisation

Volume 35

Lecture Notes in Information Systems and Organization—LNISO—is a series of scientific books that explore the current scenario of information systems, in particular IS and organization. The focus on the relationship between IT, IS and organization is the common thread of this collection, which aspires to provide scholars across the world with a point of reference and comparison in the study and research of information systems and organization. LNISO is the publication forum for the community of scholars investigating behavioral and design aspects of IS and organization. The series offers an integrated publication platform for high-quality conferences, symposia and workshops in this field. Materials are published upon a strictly controlled double blind peer review evaluation made by selected reviewers. LNISO is abstracted/indexed in Scopus

More information about this series at http://www.springer.com/series/11237

Youcef Baghdadi · Antoine Harfouche ·
Marta Musso
Editors

ICT for an Inclusive World

Industry 4.0—Towards the Smart Enterprise

 Springer

Editors
Youcef Baghdadi
Department of Computer Science
Sultan Qaboos University
Muscat, Oman

Antoine Harfouche ⓘ
Business Department
University Paris Nanterre
Nanterre, France

Marta Musso
Department of Economics
and Business Science
University of Cagliari
Cagliari, Italy

ISSN 2195-4968 ISSN 2195-4976 (electronic)
Lecture Notes in Information Systems and Organisation
ISBN 978-3-030-34268-5 ISBN 978-3-030-34269-2 (eBook)
https://doi.org/10.1007/978-3-030-34269-2

This Springer imprint is published by the registered company Springer Nature Switzerland AG
The registered company address is: Gewerbestrasse 11, 6330 Cham, Switzerland

Preface

The fourth ICTO conference (ICTO2018) took place in Paris on March 22 and 23, 2018. Like the previous editions (ICTO2017, ICTO2016, and ICTO2015), this edition focused on the impact of information and communication technologies (ICTs) on organizations and society, specifically how could such technologies be used for an inclusive world. ICTO2018 has been led jointly with MENACIS2018.

Both conferences dealt with newer innovative technologies for an inclusive world, social media, and the impacts of ICT on developing countries. These issues can be addressed both in the private and public sector either national or international, mainly through technology innovations. The conferences were also concentered on how such innovative ICTs impact organizations and societies.

ICTO2018 and MENACIS2018 received 92 submissions in all areas of ICTs and information systems. ICTO2018 and MENACIS2018 accepted 65 papers from 43 countries: Algeria, Australia, Austria, Belgium, Cameroon, Canada, Egypt, France, Germany, Greece, India, Indonesia, Iran, Iraq, Ireland, Italy, Japan, Latvia, Lebanon, Liechtenstein, Luxembourg, Malaysia, Mexico, Morocco, Netherlands, New Zealand, Nigeria, Oman, Portugal, Qatar, Romania, Russia, Saudi Arabia, Singapore, Slovakia, Spain, Sudan, Switzerland, Tunisia, Turkey, United Arab Emirates, UK, and USA.

Several innovative and rigorously developed contributions raised interesting debates at the conference. This book includes 41 chapters that have been selected through a double-blind review process as the best and most interesting ICTO2018 and MENACIS2018 submissions.

The 41 contributions have been clustered around three headings from ICTO2018: (1) Innovative technologies for an inclusive word, (2) Social media, and (3) Use of innovative technologies in developing countries. In addition, a special heading presents the selected papers from MENACIS2018

Innovative Technologies for an Inclusive Word: In this part, 11 chapters show how newer technologies improve the life of individuals, organizations, and societies.

1. Chapter "Business Process Mining for Service Oriented Architecture" by A. Al Sheriqui and Y. Baghdadi presents a process to mine services from running business processes. These services are then transformed into a complete set of sound Web services. The objective is to make business processes more flexible through the compositions of Web services.

2. Chapter "A Multi-step Approach for Managing Intellectual Capital Inside Communities of Practice" by C. Meret, M. Iannotta, D. Giacomelli, and M. Gatti aims at refining and implementing a multi-step approach of intellectual capital management and assessment. Intellectual capital can be seen as a set of intangible assets commonly grouped into three dimensions (1) human capital as a set of individual knowledge, (2) structural capital as the knowledge and capabilities stored in the organizational structure, and (3) relational capital as the internal and external relationships with stakeholders.

3. Chapter "The Influence of ICT Adoption on the Development of Managerial Modes of Consulting Firms in France" by N. Raissi seeks to understand the nature of relationships between components of ICT adoption and managerial modes. The paper focuses on the experience of consulting firms, namely how they perceive the role of ICT on the management fashion. Participants in this study consisted of 30 consultants of a major management-consulting firm in France. The analysis was conducted with the qualitative method, which is the correspondence factor analysis (CFA) using SPSS software.

4. Chapter "Organizational Agility and the Complementary Enabling Role of IT and Human Resources: Proposition of a New Framework" by M. A. Marhraoui and A. El Manouar explores how IT infrastructure and human resources practices can have a direct and complementary effect through IT acceptance and developed IT skills. The chapter highlights also the role of using and mastering human resource information systems (HRIS) in enhancing organizational agility, which plays an intermediary role for the firm's sustainable performance.

5. Chapter "Creating Shared Value Through Information Technologies" by A. El Manouar and W. El Hilali attempts to revisit the concept of shared value, namely its definition, the motivation behind adopting it, and what makes it different from corporate social responsibility and sustainability. The chapter summarizes three ways to create shared value and discusses how ICT could bring a contribution to create and capture this kind of value. The chapter introduces a framework that summarizes and shows the necessary steps to create shared value through IT.

6. Chapter "Web Platform and Corporate Welfare: An Inclusive Organizational Solution" by S. Bonomi, N. Piccinelli, C. Rossignoli, and F. Ricciardi presents a case of a welfare platform created by a non-profit Italian organization, where ICT has a fundamental role in coordinating the supply of corporate welfare services and include SMEs, allowing them to catch opportunities that otherwise would be a prerogative of big ones.

7. Chapter "Information Technology Infrastructure: A Source of Entrepreneurs' Economic Challenges" by W. Palmer presents a study that would serve as a catalyst to bring awareness to the effect of technological change on nascent entrepreneurs and may lead to a strategy to provide resources to affected entrepreneurs.

8. Chapter "Regional Binding in Information Networks of Open Data Promotion in Local Governments of Japan" by A. Yoshida, T. Noda, and M. Honda presents a study that aims to obtain findings about information flow contributing to the open data promotion in Japanese local governments. A Web questionnaire survey is conducted to obtain information networks of open data promotion in local governments. The survey showed that network in the open data personnel had different characteristics from those of the Web reference relationship network in social network analysis.

9. Chapter "Handover and QoS Parameters a Performance Assessment on 3G Based SDN" by F. Laassiri, M. Moughit, and N. Idboufker presents a performance implementation of multi-criteria algorithm decisions in software-defined network to improve the performance under third-generation networks. The work is based on the UMTS mobility, which is adopted by the interface S1, with a macro-mobility of level 3 based on MIPv6. SIP protocol is used between two end users to evaluate the performance of 3G networks with SDN network paradigm applied.

10. Chapter "Towards Cities as Communities" by M. Romanelli presents a study that aims at identifying a path in order to rethink cities as communities oriented toward sustainability, driving cities to becoming smart and sustainable, designing citizen-centered services relying on building smart governance. Sustaining infrastructures for innovation, knowledge, and development helps cities to evolve as communities by continuously reinventing the patterns of sustainable development within urban ecosystems, improving the wealth and quality of life for people, and sustaining urban business and innovation for learning and knowledge opportunities.

11. Chapter "Innovative Approaches to Work Organization and New Technologies. First Insight from the Italian Context" by T. Torre and D. Sarti focuses on the role played by ICTs in supporting the development of new ways to work and perform, promising a better balance between work and life. Through the experiences of three Italian enterprises, which are among the first users of these approaches and, more precisely of smart working (SW), the chapter analyzes conditions and implications of this deep change in work organization.

Social Media: In this part, six chapters address issues such as how social media can drive fundamental business changes, as their innovative nature allows for interactive communication between customers and businesses.

12. Chapter "Internet for Supporting and Promoting Accessible Tourism: Evidence from Italy" by G. Perna, L. Varriale, and M. Ferrara presents a conceptual study that provides a deep analysis of "accessible tourism" phenomenon through a description of the evolution process of the regulatory system. The chapter investigates the role of the Internet and new technologies to the dissemination of information analyzing tourist Web sites with a focus on the Italian context.

13. Chapter "Assistive Technology for the Social Inclusion at School: A Portrait of Italy" by G. Perna, L. Varriale, and M. Ferrara focuses on two main objectives: (1) to present the main aids for the various types of disabilities (cognitive, sensory, motoric) offered by the computer and multimedia technologies in the field of didactics; and (2) to analyze the use of technology in Italian schools to foster the integration process of students with disabilities.

14. Chapter "Social Media Communication in Hospitality: The Case of Parisian Hotels" by B. Boubaker and T. P. Dauxert presents a study to understand the expert's point of view on social media communication strategies, adopted or that could be adopted by French hotels (in Paris region), especially in terms of customer engagement. The chapter presents the theoretical and managerial implications of the study, its limitations, and future research ideas.

15. Chapter "Antecedent Factors in Adolescents Consumer Socialization Process Through Social Media" by C. Aarthy and J. Nair presents an attempt to find the antecedent factors that influence adolescents' consumer socialization process through social media and its impact on family purchase. Socialization process framework is adopted to investigate among 254 respondents. The results show there is a positive influence of antecedent variables like age, social media, and peer identification on purchase intention, and the variable social media also influence product involvement in family decision making. The outcome of this research is expected to benefit the academicians and marketers to explore the impact of social media on adolescent in their family decision making.

16. Chapter "Social Media Patient Engagement in Healthcare: An Italian Case Study" by R. Pinna, M. Musso, P. Carrus, and G. Melis aims to analyze how health organizations use social media to engaging patients in the process of their health, care, and treatment; and how this platform can facilitate the value co-creation processes in healthcare context. The findings of the study have important implications for public healthcare organizations in order to understand how to implement social media engagement and establish procedures to facilitate the process.

17. Chapter "Adoption of Social Media for Public Relations Professionals in Oman" by A. Al-Badi, A. Tarhini, and H. Al-Bolushi presents a study that aims to identify the main factors that encourage Omani public relations professionals to adopt and use social media based on the Unified Theory of Acceptance and Use of Technology. The proposed model of social media acceptance by public relations consists of seven variables, namely six (demographic information, performance expectancy, effort expectancy, social influence, facilitating conditions, and perceived enjoyment), which are independent variables and a seventh (behavioral intention) as a dependent variable. Data was collected

using an online survey from public relations professionals from both the public and private sectors in Oman. The findings show that the tendency and general awareness of social media by public relation professionals are high, and many organizations use or plan to use social media for the purpose outreaching target audience.

Impact of Innovative Technologies in Developing Countries: In this part, 14 chapters address issues such as how newer technologies affect organizations in developing countries.

18. Chapter "An Insight into Concepts of Technology Transfer and Its Role in the National Innovation System of Latvia" by V. Stepanova aims at evaluating relevant concepts of technology transfer, as well as its role in the national innovation system of Latvia. Through the research conducted and the results obtained, the authors of the research have substantiated the need to develop a new information technology model based on information technology standards, marketing and commercialization processes, as well as technology transfer handbooks.

19. Chapter "Moderating Effects of Age and Gender on Social Commerce Adoption Factors the Cameroonian Context" by P. C. N. Tcheuffa, J. R. K. Kamdjoug, and S. F. Wamba aims to determine the factors that influence the adoption of social commerce in Cameroon. To this effect, the authors have designed a research model inspired by TAM2 and the trust theory. Data was collected from 404 Internet users in Cameroon. The results found that the perceived ease of use, perceived usefulness, and trust have a significant effect on the intention to use social commerce. In contrast, concerning the moderating effect, only the group age is being proved to have a significant effect specifically on the relationship between perceived usefulness and the intention to use social commerce. This study ends with the implications for practice and research.

20. Chapter "Mobile Commerce Adoption in a Developing Country: Driving Factors in the Case of Cameroon" by F. W. N. Dongmo1, J. R. K. Kamdjoug, and S. F. Wamba seeks to investigate factors predicting the consumer's intention to adopt m-commerce in Cameroon, but also the moderating effects of the demographic variables on such prediction. Data was collected from 262 Cameroonian respondents aged less than 45, as this age category accounts for the bulk of unconditional IT users in the country. Findings of this research are expected to help companies and organizations dealing with m-commerce to better develop marketing strategies, applications, and services likely to attract more users.

21. Chapter "The Information and Communication Technologies (ICT) in Leadership—Case of Lebanese Public Sector" by D. Sidani and B. Harb seeks to analyze how the role of the leaders of the public sector evolves in view of technological transformations resulting from the adoption and the diffusion of ICT in their institutions. To face these new technological challenges, the person in charge of the public sector must exceed the role of a traditional

manager to the role of a transformational leader. Hence organizations are adapting their structure to this data era so it gives an intermediary role to data scientists in the public institutions.

22. Chapter "E-Banking Users' Profiles in Lebanon Exploration of the Role of Socio-Demographic Factors" by B. Harb and M. Saleh aims to explore and identify the role of the socio-demographic factors in the adoption of e-banking by the clientele of a big commercial bank operating in Lebanon. The analysis and processing of data emanating from the bank through the SPSS software allow us to draw representative profiles of customers based on their socio-demographic criteria. The obtained results are consistent with previous researches and confirmed the impact of age, income, educational level, and profession on the adoption of e-banking by the Lebanese consumer. These results provide an in-depth understanding of the role of socio-demographic characteristics in the use of electronic distribution channels and help Lebanese banking institutions better establish strategies for promoting online banking services in the future.

23. Chapter "The FDI-Economic Growth Nexus: A Human Resource Management Perspective—The Case of the ICT Sector in Sub-Saharan Africa" by A. Hammami and C. Dal Zotto assesses how human resource management can contribute to the success of foreign direct investment (FDI) in ICT in Sub-Saharan Africa in terms of human capital development and economic development. The chapter provides a human resource management perspective on the FDI-economic growth nexus in that empirical context.

24. Chapter "Traditional Banks and Fintech: Survival, Future and Threats" by N. M. Boustani assesses the different conditions and requirements for the survival of the banking sector amidst the emergence of the Fintech startups worldwide and specifically in Lebanon. The chapter explains the emergence and positioning of Fintech firms before developing a research model for this end. The model shall be based on the behavioral and innovation theories in finance, will be tested on-site using structured interviews with banking specialists and officials, and will finally quantitatively be analyzed for research purposes.

25. Chapter "ICT and the Performance of Lebanese Banks: A Panel Data Analysis" by A. Dabbous explores the impact of ICT on the performance of 25 Lebanese commercial banks for the period between 2000 and 2014. The study uses a panel data analysis to assess the effect of the number of Internet users and domain registrations in Lebanon on the performance of the banks. Results reveal that there is a positive statistical significant relationship between ICT and the performance of the banks. Moreover, the capital adequacy ratio, the size of the bank, the growth rate of the gross domestic product, and the lending interest rates were found to have a positive impact on the performance. The chapter concludes that a higher level of ICT use is an important factor that determines commercial banks' profitability as it supports the commercial work of the banks and enables them to achieve better performance.

26. Chapter "The Challenges Faced During the Implementation of Smart Schools in Oman" by A. Al-Badi, A. Tarhini, and H. Al-Mawali aims to (1) explore the challenges faced during the implementation of smart schools from the perspectives/viewpoints of the service provider, teachers, and school IT administrators; and (2) provide a set of recommendations to minimize such challenges. Two case studies were conducted among schools that had already started implementing the process of becoming smart schools. Both case studies included a set of interviews with schoolteachers, the people in charge of the proposed project, school IT administrators, and a service provider. In addition, there were sets of classroom observations conducted in the respective schools. Study results and the examination of data analysis revealed that there are many challenges faced by the perspective parties, and these challenges are discussed in some detail. The researchers then provided a set of recommendations to minimize, or indeed to overcome the challenges encountered in becoming a smart school in Oman.

27. Chapter "Big Data in the Banking Sector from a Transactional Cost Theory (TCT) Perspective—The Case of Top Lebanese Banks" by C. Chedrawi, Y. Atallah, and S. Osta discusses challenges and role of big data in the banking sector through the transaction cost theory approach of Williamson (1985). The chapter reveals the actions currently undertaken by the two leading banks in the Lebanese market in order to optimize big data integration in their internal and external transactions.

28. Chapter "Urban Concentration in Lebanon: The Need for Urban Observatories" by A. Nassereddine and A. Dabbous shows that poor data collection in Lebanon and the lack of serious plan to calculate, monitor, and improve urban indicators put the future of urban quality of life in Lebanon at risk. The chapter uses as a case study in Lebanon, the Tripoli Economic and Development Observatory (TEDO). Using original visual maps from TEDO, the case shows how urban observatories can be used to detect critical problems and their underlying causes and how they help in delivering effective solutions leading to better sustainability assessment.

29. Chapter "Cloud Computing and the New Role of IT Service Providers in Lebanon: A Service Dominant Logic Approach" by B. El Zoghbi and C. Chedrawi discusses the cloud computing value co-creation opportunity for IT service providers in Lebanon by identifying their new role in fixing the cloud computing roadmap from a service-dominant logic.

30. Chapter "Success and Failure of the Institutionalization of IS Dispositives Within Organizations: The Effect of External Pressures and the Role of Actors" by A. Harfouche, J. Arida, M. A. B. El Rassi, P. Bou Saba, and M. Saba presents a study that investigates the actor's role when faced with a change by examining the differences in their reactions to it and how they could influence the success or failure of a new IS dispositive adoption in three different types of organizations.

31. Chapter "Transformational Process of the Implementation of an Information System Dispositive in an Organization: The Role of Power and Interests from an Institutional Perspective" by A. Harfouche, J. Arida, and G. Aoun addresses the role of power and interests in implementing a new information system (IS) in an organization. It examines how responses to external pressures and expectations can be led by powerful agents that can use resources and their membership to relevant social and institutional groupings in order to generate a transformational process in their organization.

The *MENACIS 2018* part includes ten chapters:

32. Chapter "Individual Intention to Become an Entrepreneur: Technological Perspective" by M. Albashrawi and T. Alashoor sheds light on the technological perspective and develops a theoretical model that extends the theory of planned behavior by incorporating IT factors into established entrepreneurial models. The developed model explains how general computer self-efficacy and computer anxiety can determine entrepreneurial intention. SEM is used to test the developed model, and preliminary results are presented.

33. Chapter "Developing an IT Risk Management Culture Framework" by N. Azizi and B. Rowlands develops an IT risk management (IT-RM) framework based on Cameron and Quinn's model involving four dimensions of culture. Each cultural dimension is described in terms of how they relate to the implementation of IT-RM initiatives. The chapter illustrates the utility of the framework by linking the four general cultural dimensions to propose a conceptual model of IT-RM values and beliefs. The chapter presents a necessary step in developing the concept of IT-RM culture and moving frameworks such as COBIT5 toward a more comprehensive framework based on systemic empirical research.

34. Chapter "Industry 4.0: Impact of New Technologies on Logistics Management" by S. Elfirdoussi, H. Hrimech, F. Fontane, and H. Kabaili presents a study on the impact of new technologies on logistics issues in the context of Industry 4. 0. We have relied on a set of works aimed at transforming the logistic process into a smart process, with a capacity for communication, perception, action, and management of the information available locally or through a network.

35. Chapter "Using Immersive Virtual Reality in Ancient Egypt's Giza Plateau" by D. Rateb, H. Hosny, and F. Haikal aims to adopt an innovative IT means for presenting the ancient Egyptian heritage to both the academics and tourists, remotely. Academic staff and students, tourists, tour agents/guides, and historians can all benefit from online access to major Egyptian monuments using an advanced Immersive Virtual Reality (IVR) package, such as Second Life (SL). IVR is a form of technology that creates computer-generated worlds or immersive environments, which people can explore and interact with. SL is a virtual game environment that has been used successfully in education and tourism.

36. Chapter "Governance of IS Security in a Cloud Computing Ecosystem: A Longitudinal Approach" by W. Bouaynaya proposes an analysis of IS governance in three phases: pre-adoption, adoption, and post-adoption of cloud

computing. The approach aims to highlight the different artifacts and key concepts of security governance in a cloud computing ecosystem. The chapter differentiates between three key artifacts: data as an asset, the cloud solution as a system, and the service provider as an actor to understand their relationships with the enterprise.

37. Chapter "Rate of Penetration (ROP) Prediction in Oil Drilling Based on Ensemble Machine Learning" by D. Rezki, L. H. Mouss, A. Baaziz, and N. Rezki presents the prediction of the rate of progression in oil drilling based on random forest algorithm, which is part of the family of ensemble machine learning. The ROP parameter plays a very important role in oil drilling, which has a great impact on drilling costs, and its prediction allows drilling engineers to choose the best combination of input parameters for better progress in drilling operations. The chapter shows that the random forest algorithm chosen for the proposed model is better than the other MLS techniques in speed or precision, following what we found in the literature and tests done with the open source machine learning tool on historical oil drilling logs from fields of Hassi Terfa located in southern Algeria.

38. Chapter "A New Model for Information Security Risk Management" by A. Shirazi and M. Kazemi introduces a new risk management method for information security risk management, proposed and applied for the first time in the IT department of a telecommunication company in Iran. According to law requirements and security strategic plan, the mentioned company implemented information security risk management (ISMS). So one of the main phases of ISMS is the risk management. The results show that the methodology of the information security risk management, containing the risk identification, risk analysis, risk evaluation, and risk treatment, uses the frameworks of ISO 27005, ISO 27002, ISO 27011, OCTAVE and NIST 800-30, and OWASP standards. This new method is practical and accurate and is suitable for large-scale organizations.

39. Chapter "Using Process Mining for Process Analysis Improvement in Pre-hospital Emergency" by P. Badakhshan and A. Alibabaei uses process mining techniques to analyze pre-hospital processes in the emergency room. The process discovery phase is implemented based on four different states, which are introduced in this study to increase the accuracy of process analysis. After discovering the process model, conformance checking and enhancement are the following steps that were done in this study. The data is extracted from the automation system of a pre-hospital emergency room, which is used as input event logs for process mining. Statistical records including control sheet of one year were provided by the organization. Control sheet and in consequence the P-control chart are used as a supplement of conformance checking phase. Enhancement phase is based on two states and used performance analysis by considering factors of output, cycle time/duration, and costs, which helps the pre-hospital emergency room to improve their processes.

40. Chapter "Digital Innovation in Manufacturing Firms: Why Smart Connected Products Become a Challenge?" by M. Ivanov examines the emerging role of digital innovation in the context of traditional manufacturing firms. Throughout this chapter, digital innovation refers to the innovation of smart connected products evolved from the symbiosis of physical products and digital components (digitization). The chapter follows a case-study design with in-depth analysis of how manufacturing firms react on and define digital innovation. The study is exploratory and interpretative in nature and adopts the grounded theory approach. This research provides an important opportunity to advance the understanding of how digital innovation emerges in manufacturing firms.

41. Chapter "A Dynamic System for Instabilities Prediction" by M. A. Issami aims to develop a dynamic system able to detect instantly different instabilities using ABM models. It consists of implementing a strategy-based prevention holistic and integrated.

Muscat, Oman   Youcef Baghdadi
Nanterre, France   Antoine Harfouche
Cagliari, Italy   Marta Musso
August 2019

Acknowledgements

We would like to express our gratitude to the Paris Nanterre University for hosting ICTO2018 and MENACIS2018 and allowing us to use the facilities of the university.

ICTO2018 and MENACIS2018 would never have seen the day and gather this quality researcher without the huge efforts of the tireless and extremely patient Prof. Antoine Harfouche, the general organization chair, to whom we extend here our warm thanks.

We extend our gratitude to Prof. Marco de Marco, Uninettuno University, Italy, Prof. Alice Robbin, Indiana University Bloomington, USA, Prof. Cinzia Dal Zotto, Neuchâtel University, Switzerland, Prof. Youcef Baghdadi, Sultan Qaboos University, Oman, Prof. Teresina Torre, Università di Genova, Italy, and Prof. Tetsuo Noda, Shimane University, Japan.

Special thanks to Prof. Frantz Rowe, who received the ICTO Golden Medal for his lifetime achievement during the ICTO2018 conference.

Last but not least, we want to thank the 120 members of the scientific committee and reviewers who generously gave of their time and knowledge, especially: Abbas Tarhini, Abdallah Nassereddine, Abdullah Azhari, Adebowale Ojo, Adebowale Owoseni, Adekunle Afolabi, Adnan Albar, Ahmad Alibabaei, Akio Yoshida, Alain Osta, Amal Dabbous, Ananth Chiravuri, Anne-Céline Ginoux, Antoine Chollet, Bessem Boubaker, Bissane Harb, Céline Averseng, Charbel Chedrawy, Chiara Meret, Christine Abdalla Mikhaeil, Cinzia Dal Zotto, Daniel Phelps, Daniele Pederzoli, Daria Plotkina, Dina Rateb, Dina Sidani, El Kebir Ghandour, Elie Nasr, François Deltour, G. Leah Davis, Georges Aoun, Hafiz Imtiaz Ahmad, Hassan Dennaoui, Heba Tannous, Héctor M. Pérez-Feijoo, Ibrahim Eskandar Ibrahim Fadhel, Ibrahim Osman, Iman Taani, Jamil Arida, Jessy Nair, Karine Aoun, Kassem Danach, Kichan Nam, Maria Menshikova, Mario Saba, Mary Ann Barbour El Rassi, May Sayegh, Mohamed Amine Issami, Mohammad Alsharo, Mousa Albashrawi, Nabil Georges Badr, Nada Mallah Boustani, Nadia Tebourbi, Nikos

Vasilakis, Nizar Raissi, Nooredin Etezady, Norshidah Mohamed, Pierrette Howayeck, Sabrina Bonomi, Salam Abdallah, Samuel Fosso Wamba, Sana Rouis, Selwa Elfirdoussi, Sola Oni, Soraya Ezzeddine, Sumayya Banna, Wadi Tahri, Wail El Hilali, and Yinka Oyerinde.

Contents

MENACIS 2018

Innovative Technologies for an Inclusive World

Business Process Mining for Service Oriented Architecture

Amna Al Shereiqi and Youcef Baghdadi

Abstract Service Oriented Architecture (SOA) is an architectural style that uses loosely coupled services, which have separate concerns, as the primary constituents to build software solutions as compositions of services. It emphasizes loosely coupling and interoperability of services, required for agility and flexibility of business processes (BPs), hence allowing current BPs as well as future BPs to be integrated. To design such SOA-compliant software that supports BPs, the service identification is a critical phase. Indeed, the form under which the service is located may impact the effectiveness of the SOA. More particularly, the granularity of the entire services is very crucial in attaining the flexibility. The main objective of this research is to mine BPs for SOA by introducing a new service identification approach. The approach first uses a BP mining discovery technique to discover the BP model. Then, it clusters the activities into tasks, and finally organizes tasks into an initial set of services. And checks the compliance of the resulted services against the service orientation principles. The proposed approach is validated by a case study. The approach helps large enterprises to mine their BPs, develop them, and identify services. Finally, we recommend an automation of the proposed service identification approach to making it more effective and useful BPs.

Keywords Business process · Business process mining · Service oriented architecture · Web service · Service orientation · Service identification

1 Introduction

An enterprise usually has a large and complex information system (IS) that consists of a huge number of BPs. Some are well modeled and others are not. Enterprises need to continuously adapt their BPs to cope up with business requirement changes,

A. Al Shereiqi · Y. Baghdadi (✉)
Department of Computer Science, Sultan Qaboos University, Muscat, Oman
e-mail: ybaghdadi@squ.edu.om

A. Al Shereiqi
e-mail: m084074@student.squ.edu.om

© Springer Nature Switzerland AG 2020
Y. Baghdadi et al. (eds.), *ICT for an Inclusive World*,
Lecture Notes in Information Systems and Organisation 35,
https://doi.org/10.1007/978-3-030-34269-2_1

which requires more agility and flexibility of their BPs [1]. This agility is difficult to achieve because: (i) BP modeling considers that all the instances of the same BP run in the same way, and (ii) the tightly coupled components of the architecture of the legacy IS supporting the BP do not enable the loose coupling and interoperability required for flexibility and agility [2].

It is proven that SOA enables the agility of the enterprise through more flexibility of its BPs.

However, moving to SOA requires re-engineering the BPs in order to transform their activities into reusable, loosely coupled services [3].

One of the most used techniques toward reengineer running BPs is known as BP mining, which allows the extraction of the knowledge about BPs from the event logs of existing IS [4]. It is concerned with the discovery, monitoring, and improvement of the BPs by obtaining the wider knowledge from the event logs that is generated from existing ISs.

However, how to extract the activities from running BPs that are not modeled and present them as services is still an issue?

In this research, we propose a novel approach that will assist enterprises to mine their BPs in order to reengineer them in new technologies such as SOA. It is based on service identification methods. the new suggested service identification approach that mines BPs, clustering their activities into tasks, initialing a set of services, listing the services, and verifying the service candidates against the service orientation principles.

The remainder of this chapter is organized as follows. Section 2 presents the concepts related to this research. Section 3 presents some related works. Section 4 details the research methodology and the proposed approach. Section 5 applies the approach to a case study. Finally, a conclusion section provides some future work.

2   Background

In this chapter, key concepts related to the research are reviewed, including BP, BP mining, BP reengineering, SOA, and service identification techniques.

Business Process Management
Business Process Management (BPM) concerns with seven phases as proposed by Mathiesen et al. [5]. These are: identification, modeling (as-is), analysis, improvement (to-be), implementation, execution (to-do), and monitoring/controlling.

Business Process Modeling

BP modeling is defined as description of the activities in a diagrammatic manner. It shows the events and the variables from one place to another [6]. It is the most important step in BPM.

There are many techniques that are used by BPM such as UML diagrams, Business Process Modeling Notation (BPMN), data flow diagrams, flowchart technique, role activity diagrams, role interaction diagrams, Gantt charts, integrated definition for function modeling, colored petri-nets, object oriented methods, workflow technique, and simulation model.

Business Process Mining

Business process mining is an extraction of the knowledge about the running BPs from the event logs of the running IS. The goal of BP mining is to discovering, monitoring, and improving real BPs by extracting them from event logs of running IS [4]. Indeed, more and more events are being recorded, thus, providing detailed information about the history of the running BPs, and there is a need to improve and support BPs in the competitive and rapidly changing environment.

The main components of BP mining are event logs and process model. An event log is defined as "a collection of events used as input for process mining. Events do not need to be stored in a separate log file" [7]. Event logs comprise information about the start and completion of process steps together with related context data [8]. Every log entry holds an identifier of the case, an activity name, a timestamp, a user identifier, a booking code and a notification [9]. It is used as starting point in mining [10]. The process model is generated from the event logs [11].

Tools for BP Mining

BP mining are performed by various software tools. There are about fifteen commercial process mining tools. This research uses Disco because it is free for academia (by using academic credentials). In addition, it provides an automatic process discovery modeling as the event logs are imported into the system. This allows a simply filtering and examining the attributes in parallel with the exposed fuzzy model. Furthermore, it provides a filtering mechanism that is more transparent and obviously introduced in comparison to the other tools. Moreover, it imports log size capacity up to five million events. It is supported by standalone desktop version platform and it is easy to use. It enables animation of processes, which makes it easy to discover bottlenecks on the flow of processes and the animation of processes can be stored as video format. This approach uses a Disco to mine BP, as it introduces a large number of cases [12]. Disco uses as input an event log in CSV, MXML, XLS, XES or FXL format and produces as-is BP model as output. In addition, it produces the frequency of each activity and the frequency of each edge in the BP model. Disco imports the event log which fulfills the minimum requirement for analysis, including case ID, activity, and timestamp.

Business Process Reengineering

Business Process Reengineering (BPR) was defined early in 1997 by Blyth as "the fundamental re-thinking and radical redesign of BP to achieve dramatic improvement in critical, contemporary measures of performance, such as cost, quality, service, and speed" [13]. The goal of BPR is to radically improve the BPs. It needs the organizational restructuring with the aid of simplification and standardization and IT. Hammer [14] defined seven principles for BPR.

Service Oriented Architecture

SOA is defined as "an architectural paradigm for developing and integrating hetero-geneous ISs with strict message-driven communication paradigm" [15]. It provides a set of guidelines, principles, and techniques in which BPs, information, and enterprise assets can be effectively re-organized and re-deployed to support and enable strategic plans and productivity levels that are required by competitive business environments [16].

The improvement of flexibility, interoperability, and abstraction level of software components are the major aim of SOA. Loose coupling and discoverability are the two key principles of SOA [17].

3   Related Work

Several service identification methods (SIMs) are proposed. These methods use different inputs, strategies, and techniques, and produce different types of output. The artifacts used as input include BP, application domain, legacy system, mix, data, feature, or use cases. They generally produce one of the six types of services: business process service, data service, composite service, IT service, web service, and partner service.

In this research, we are interested in the SIMs that use the BP as input artifact. Wang et al. proposed a method to identify the normalized service from the BP model. This method has three stages: (1) identify some normalized services from BPs and design the containment relationship between service and business activities, (2) design service ports in the business aspect, and (3) design the component set that constitutes a service and message mapping between service ports and component interfaces in the technical aspect. It is based on BP decomposition and algorithm techniques. However, it has not been validated by a case study [18]. Inaganti and Behara [19] concentrated on recognizable proof of big business level services and built up the choreography of the services through BP. They use BP decomposition strategy and some guidelines techniques to identify services. Their technique for service identification is restricted to the service identification procedure. Although the proposed method is clear for service identification, the measures for identification of business activities are not introduced. Besides, it is not approved with any useful case study and does not propose standard displaying documentations for process modeling and SOA. Amsden [20] focused on the description of service elements that should be located in service form of the specification phase. The method uses BP decomposition strategy and analysis technique to determine services. It has been validated by real example. Mani et al. [21] presented a method that focuses on the design specification of the user interface. It captures the unified user interface design specification from the business procedure and the information display. It uses the BP decomposition and user interface strategies to identify services. A shopping cart of Amazon case study has been used to validate this method. Jamshidi et al. [22] proposed a method that consists of four steps: (1) modeling of BP, (2) identification or the location of service model elements, (3) grouping or the categorization of services, (and 4) proper documentation of service. It is uses BP decomposition and business entity strategies and algorithm technique to determine services. This method is evaluated based on its use, users' form of analysis, and strength or power over the existing methods. Dwivedi and Kulkarni [23] introduced a method that uses some heuristics for identifying service candidates along with model driven development. It is uses BP model (with UML) as input. As techniques, it is uses BP decomposition strategy and algorithm technique to identify a list of services. It has been validated by a real example. Bianchini et al. [24] presented a method that focuses on identifying services from a collaborative BP. It is divided into four phases: (1) semantic form of the process annotation, (2) proper identification of candidate services, (3) evaluation and analysis of service strong cohesion/coupling, and (4) refinement of the entire process decomposition. It uses BP decomposition strategy and an ontology technique to determine candidate services. It has been validated by a case study. Yousef et al. [25] proposed a method called BPAOntoSOA that uses ontology technique and BP decomposition strategy to identify services. It is based on BP understanding and analysis, taking into account functional and non-functional requirements. It is uses clustering algorithm to improve the correctness of mapping business functions to services in the resulting service oriented model. It is validated by a case study of healthcare sector. Azevedo et al. [26] introduced a method that applies heuristics to characterize services from the semantic investigation of process components and from a syntactic examination of process models. It consists of three stages: (1) selection of activities, (2) identification and classification of candidate services, and (3) consolidation of candidate services. Kim and Doh [27] proposed a method that uses the concept of graph clustering. It considers activities as service identification and bunches activities with high cooperation to maximize the cohesion of local tasks. It uses BP decomposition strategy and algorithm technique to determine services. It is validated by case study. Ren and Wang [28] proposed a method that uses a BP as input and produces a service model as output. It uses a clustering algorithm. It is validated by a case study. Nikravesh et al. [29] presented a method called 2PSIM. It uses as a BP as input to generate a service model. It identifies services by applying graphic form of partitioning algorithms. Kazemi et al. [30] exhibited an automated technique to generate business services by using a BP decomposition strategy. Jamshidi et al. [31] introduced an automated method that uses the best practices and the core principles of the form of model driven software development. It uses as starting input an enterprise business model and produces a service model. It determines services by implementing a meta-heuristic algorithm. It was evaluated against enterprise scale study. Soltani and Benslimane [32] developed a method called an Automatic Model-Driven Service Identification (AMSI) that uses a high level of BP model as input to specify service model artifacts. It identifies services by applying multi-objective evolutionary. Birkmeier et al. [33] proposed a method to determine services from BP models. The general impacts of this approach are to illustrate how the form of the business architecture can be utilized to drive the organization of the IS architecture and to make a proper confirmation of the alignment with business needs. El Amine and Benslimane [34] exhibited a type of a mechanized approach to generate business services by actualizing a few outline measurements based on process decomposition strategy. It takes a BP as input information and produces a list of business services by applying a multi-objective combinatorial particle swarm optimization algorithm. Bianchini et al. [35] acquainted a Process with Service approach (P2S). It is a computer-aided methodology to permit the recognizable proof of services that consolidates a collaborative BP. Mohamed et al. [36] proposed an automated method. It identifies services from BPs. It applies for bunching a hybrid particle swarm optimization algorithm and several design metrics for delivering reusable services with appropriate granularity and a satisfactory level of coupling and cohesion. Leopold et al. [37] proposed a mechanized service identification technique that distinguishes a list of positioned service candidates from BP models. Specifically, it creates a list of atomic services, composite services, and inheritance hierarchy services.

All of the above-mentioned SIMs use as input a business process model. Since, it plays an important part wrapping the phase's form of the BP design and system implementation. However, in most cases, the BP model could not introduce all possible essential tasks and interrelated control flows in the design phase. Moreover, the BP model is not sufficiently adaptive to respond at a runtime to the dynamic environments [38].

4   The Proposed Approach

This section presents the proposed approach along with the used research methodology. The research methodology mainly consists of two steps: (1) study the BP mining approaches, and (2) selection of a suitable SIM. The proposed approach is based on the service identification phase of a service oriented development.

4.1   The Research Methodology

This section details the steps of the research methodology that is used to design the proposed approach. As shown in Fig. 1, the methodology consists mainly in surveying the BP mining techniques and the existing SIMs to select a suitable SIM,

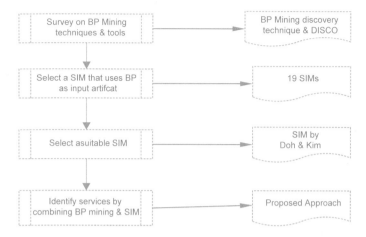

Fig. 1 Steps and output of the research methodology

then combining the BP mining techniques with the SIM method to identify services from the running BPs.

Step 1: Study the BP mining

BP mining focuses on the analysis of the BP by using an event log. It aims at discovering, monitoring, and improving the BPs by extracting knowledge from the event logs that are generated automatically in the IS [4]. It consists of three types of techniques: discovery, conformance checking, and enhancement.

However, the proposed approach is limited to the discovery technique. A discovery technique uses an event log as input and produces a BP model without using any prior information. Figure 2 depicts the BP mining discovery technique process. It starts

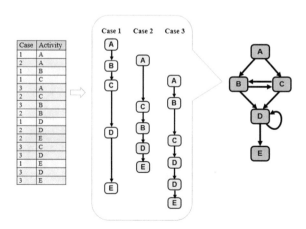

Fig. 2 The process of BP mining discovery technique

Fig. 3 Methodology of selected SIMs

from the event log, then extract each case or process instance, and finally combine them to produce the BP model.

Step 2: Selecting a suitable SIM

This step consists mainly in searching for existing SIMs that use as input a BP to select a suitable SIM by comparing the existing, as shown in Fig. 3.

SIMs are divided into three scenarios: top down, bottom up, and hybrid. This research focuses on the top-down scenario and starts from the input-output matrix introduced by Gu and Lago [39] to select SIMs. According to this research, there are about thirty SIMs based on the top-down scenario. They use various inputs artifacts such as BP, application domain, legacy system, data, feature model, use case, and/or a mix of them. These SIMs use strategies such as BP decomposition, business functions, business entity, ownership and responsibility, goal driven, component based, existing supply, front office application usage analysis, infrastructure, non-functional requirement, and user interface. They are based on techniques used such as algorithm, guideline, analysis, ontology, pattern, and information manipulation. Finally, these methods produce output in various formats such as informal service specification, service model, formal service specification, service implementation, or a list of services.

This research focuses only on the SIMs that use as input a BP. Table 1 depicts an example of comparison between SIMs that use BP as input: authors, publication year, type of input, strategy used to understand the type of input, type of output, technique, and the validation.

Table 1 SIMs that use a BP as input to get a service as output

Author	Year	Type of input	Strategy	Type of output	Technique	Validation
Mani et al.	2008	Business process	Business process decomposition and user interface	Service implementation	Algorithm	Case study
Kim & Doh	2009	Business process	Business process decomposition	Service implementation	Algorithm	Evaluated

Table 2 Comparison between Mani et al. method and Kim and Doh method

Service identification method criteria	Mani et al. [21]	Kim and Doh [27]
Scenario	Top-down	Top-down
Strategy	BP decomposition and user interface	BP decomposition
Input	BP	BP
Input format	BP model and data model	Model
Service classification scheme	Two service hierarchies: Service and human task	Three service hierarchies: Service, task, and activity
Covering of SOA design phases	Service identification, specification, and realization	Service identification and specification
Characteristics	WSDL description and case study	WSDL description and case study
Application of process models for service identification	Process model and data model are decomposed to generate user interface model than maps to service candidates	Process model divided into service candidates

This research compares between two SIMs that use a BP as input and produce services as output. It uses different criteria introduced by Klose et al. [40] and Kim and Doh [27] as shown in Table 2. These criteria are: scenario, strategy, input, input format, service classification scheme, covering of SOA design phases, characteristics, and application of process models for service identification.

Both methods are analyzed in the top-down scenario that starts with the high-level artifacts as input to identify services. While, both of them start with BP as input, the format of an input differs in each method. Mani et al. method starts with the BP model and data model, but Kim and Doh method starts with the BP model only. In addition, both methods produce as output service implementation written in Web Service Description Language (WSDL). The other comparison criteria are approximately similar. Thus, the proposed approach will be based on Kim and Doh method, because BP model is produced by only a BP only mining software tool.

The SIM introduced by Kim and Doh in 2009 has three activities: clustering of activities into tasks, organizing tasks into initial set of services, and describing the services.

4.2 The Proposed Approach Described

The proposed approach uses as input an event log and produces a list of services as output.

First, a BP mining discovery technique allows the extraction of the BP model from the event log of running IS. Next, the obtained BP model is used as an input in the clustering activity, whereby, each cluster is mapped into a task. These tasks are then organized into an initial set of services by allocating the activities to the corresponding task and defining operations for each task. Then, each task becomes a service and is inserted into its corresponding list. Finally, the resulted services are verified to comply with the principles SOA.

The approach consists of seven activities: collect an event log of the BP, convert an event log file into a suitable format that is understood by a BP mining software tool, use the BP mining discovery technique tool and produce a BP, cluster the activities of the BP model into tasks, organize tasks into initial a set of services, check the compliance of the resulting services with SOA principles. These activities are performed sequentially, as shown in Fig. 4.

Step 1. Collecting an event log of the BP
An event log contains information about events referring to an activity and a case of the running BP. Each event represents an activity name and is related to the particular case (case identifier). In addition, an event log introduces more information about events such as resource executing or initiating the activity, the timestamp of event and data elements recorded with the event [41].

Event logs can be automatically generated from different business systems such as ERP systems, CRM or Workflow Management systems. The two common formats of event logs are Mining eXtensible Markup Language (MXML) and eXtensible Event Stream (XES) [42].

Since, most legacy systems of the large enterprises are not documented or explicitly presented, they have very limited information about what is actually happening in their organization. In practice, there is often a significant gap between what is

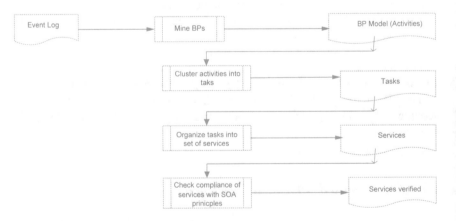

Fig. 4 The proposed approach illustrated

prescribed or supposed to happen, and what actually happens. The event log contains more valuable and embedded knowledge. It is used as a starting point of this approach, i.e. as an input artifact for BP mining.

Step 2. Converting an event log file into a suitable format that is understood by a BP mining software tool
Each software tool uses different formats of event logs. For instance, CSV, XLS, MXML, XES, and FXL formats are understood by Disco.

Step 3: Using the BP mining discovery technique tool to produce a BP model
In this appraoch, we use Disco as the BP mining discovery technique software tool. The following steps depict how to use it:

Step 4: Clustering the activities into tasks
The BP model generated by Disco will be the starting input in this step with the frequency of each activity and the frequency of each edge in the model. Each activity in the BP model maps into a task. It clusters tasks which have edge with high frequency into a new task through hierarchical clustering algorithm to minimize the coupling of tasks and to maximize the cohesion of tasks. Then, the following rules depict how to cluster tasks and how to calculate the frequency of new tasks:

Rule 1: When two adjacent tasks are merged, one of their incident edges having the highest frequency is selected first.
Rule 2: Once an edge is selected, the edge cannot be selected again in each repetition.
Rule 3: When tasks are merged, a new task is generated and its frequency is calculated.
Rule 4: When adjacent two tasks are combined into a new task, the frequency of new task is the maximum frequency of two tasks.

Rule 1 and Rule 2 are used to determine which tasks are merged. On the other hand, the model is reconstructed by adjusting edges based on Rule 3 and the frequencies of new tasks are assigned based on Rule 4.

The edges linked to two tasks, which are merged into a new cluster, are connected to a new task. Tasks are then repeatedly combined in the same manner.

The termination of the clustering of tasks is based on the preferred size of services and the reasonable number of services desired for business domain. Since, the number of services directly affects the performance and network overheads.

Step 5. Organizing tasks into an initial set of services
The objective of this step is to organize tasks into services, where the cohesion within the service is maximized and the coupling between services is minimized. Service specification is derived by organizing identified tasks into services. Graph clustering provides a good way for grouping the vertices in the graph according to their connections. A structure of tasks is generated and activities in the task are suggested to be included in a service. This method provides a potential design with different levels of inter-service coupling, where activities are organized into services and smaller services are successively integrated into bigger ones.

Step 6. Listing of services
For an identified service, a set of attributes to describe and document the capability of each service is defined. The rich description of the capabilities can be passed to development teams who can use the information to help select the appropriate implementation technologies, hosts, deployment topologies. The list of services is easily derived from tasks and activities are provided by the BP model.

Step 7. Verifying service candidates against the service orientation principles
The identified services need to be evaluated against service orientation principles, while performing service identification phase.

5 Case Study

5.1 Presentation

The Road Traffic Fine Management sector was formed due to a great urge for a professional interface in between the motoring public and municipalities who gives out traffic fines. An Italian Local Police Force presents an IS that handles Road Traffic Fine Management process.

The Road Traffic Fine Management process has eleven activities: create fine, send fine, insert fine notification, insert date appeal to the prefecture, appeal to judge, add a penalty, send for credit collection, send the appeal to the prefecture, receive appeal result from the prefecture, notify result appeal to an offender, and payment.

This research uses the event log that was recorded by the IS that manages the Road Traffic Fine Management process, as a case study. The event log contains about 150,370 cases and 561,470 events.

The Road Traffic Fine Management process requires implementation in SOA to be more efficient, effective, and flexible.

5.2 Application

The event log has been collected from the internet, as a real event log of road traffic fine management process. It consists of 150,370 events. It contains all information of the road traffic fine management process for instance case ID, activity, complete timestamp, resource, total payment, notification type, expense, vehicle class. However, the needed fields are case ID, activity, and timestamp (Fig. 5).

The event log format has been converted to CSV (Comma-Spread Values) format to be acceptable.

In this step, Disco takes an event log with the various format such as CSV, XLS, MXML, XES, and FXL as input and produces a BP model as output. Moreover, it

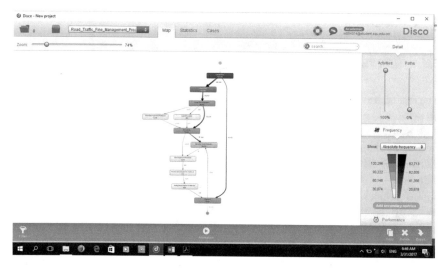

Fig. 5 A road traffic fine management process model

presents the frequency of each activity and edge in the model. The format of Road Traffic Fine Management process event log is CSV.

Firstly, all activities are converted into tasks. Secondly, the edge between two tasks with the highest frequency is selected. The new task is generated by merging those two tasks, where the frequency of this new task is the maximum frequency of two tasks. The connections to new task are updated.

The generated tasks are mapped into an initial set of services, as shown in Table 3.

Service	Task	Activity
Service 1	Task 7	Create fine Receive fine Insert fine notification Add penalty Send for credit collection Payment Insert date appeal to prefecture Send appeal to prefecture
Service 2	Task 8	Receive result appeal from prefecture Notify result appeal to offender
Service 3	Appeal to judge	Appeal to judge

Table 3 Set of services, tasks and activities

6   Conclusion

6.1   Summary

The research aimed at mining BPs in order to reengineer them in SOA. It concentrated on service identification based on running BPs in order to improve their flexibility with SOA.

The literature review has shown that the existing SIMs do not use event logs of the running BPs as input, though they contain valuable information of the running BPs.

The project has proposed a new top-down approach to identify service candidates by using the running BPs. The proposed approach uses as input an event log of a running BP to produce a list of services. It is a step-wise process that consists of: (1) collecting the event log of a running BP, (2) converting the event log file into a suitable format that is understood by a BP mining software tool, (3) using the BP mining discovery technique tool to produce a BP model, (4) clustering of activities into tasks, (5) organizing tasks into an initial set of services, (6) listing the services, and (7) verifying the resulting service against service orientation principles.

The proposed approach has been applied to a real BP, where the event log for Road Traffic Fine Management process was used as input to generate a set of services that would support the process in an SOA.

This research has theoretical and practical impacts. From a theoretical perspective, the research contributes to service technology by introducing new service identification approach. From a practical perspective, the proposed approach can assist the enterprises to mine their BPs in order to model them with services with respect to SOA and make them more flexible.

This approach still needs additional improvement, as it does not categorize the resulting services into various types, such as business services, IT services, data services, or composite services, based on the nature of the logic these services encapsulate and the manner the services are usually used within SOA.

6.2 Future Work

The proposed approach can be further:

- Refined in order to identify high quality services.
- Extended to cover all phases of SOA software development.
- Automated by using a tool in order to perform the service identification process faster and easier.

References

1. Baghdadi, Y.: A business model for B2B integration through Web services. In IEEE International Conference on e-Commerce Technology, pp. 187–194, IEEE (2004)
2. Baghdadi, Y.: Modelling business process with services: towards agile enterprises. Int. J. Bus. Inf. Syst. 15(4), 410–433 (2014)
3. Baghdadi, Y., Al-Bulushi, W.: A guidance process to modernize legacy applications for SOA. Serv. Oriented Comput. Appl. 9(1):41–58 (2015)
4. Van Der Aalst, W.: Process mining: overview and opportunities. ACM Trans. Manage. Inf. Syst. (TMIS) 3(2), 7 (2012)
5. Mathiesen, P., Watson, J., Bandara, W., Rosemann, M.: Applying social technology to business process lifecycle management. In: International Conference on Business Process Management, pp. 231–241. Springer, Heidelberg (2011, August)
6. Chapman, A.: Business Process Modeling. Accessed in March 2016. Retrieved from: http://www.businessballs.com/business-process-modelling.htm
7. Daniel, F., Barkaoui, K., Dustdar, S.: Business Process Management Workshops: BPM 2011 International ..., Part 1 (2012)
8. Mans, R.S., Schonenberg, M.H., Song, M., van der Aalst, W.M., Bakker, P.J.: Application of process mining in healthcare—a case study in a Dutch hospital. In: International Joint Conference on Biomedical Engineering Systems and Technologies, pp. 425–438. Springer, Heidelberg (2008, January)
9. Rubin, V.A., Mitsyuk, A.A., Lomazova, I.A., van der Aalst, W.M.: Process mining can be applied to software too! In: Proceedings of the 8th ACM/IEEE International Symposium on Empirical Software Engineering and Measurement, p. 57 (2014, September)
10. Van Dongen, B.F., de Medeiros, A.K.A., Verbeek, H.M.W., Weijters, A.J.M.M., Van Der Aalst, W.M.: The ProM framework: a new era in process mining tool support. In: International Conference on Application and Theory of Petri Nets, pp. 444–454. Springer, Heidelberg (2005, June)
11. Kalenkova, A.A., van der Aalst, W.M., Lomazova, I.A., Rubin, V.A.: Process mining using BPMN: relating event logs and process models. Software & Systems Modeling, 1–30 (2015)
12. Kebede, M.: Comparative Evaluation of Process Mining Tools (2015)
13. Blyth, A.: Business process re-engineering. ACM SIGGROUP Bulletin 18(1), 4–6 (1997)
14. Hammer, M., Champy, J.: Re-engineering the Corporation: A Manifesto for Business Revolution. Harper Business, New York (1993)
15. Fung, B.C., Trojer, T., Hung, P.C., Xiong, L., Al-Hussaeni, K., Dssouli, R.: Service-oriented architecture for high-dimensional private data mashup. IEEE Trans. Serv. Comput. 5(3), 373–386 (2012)
16. Papazoglou, M.P., Van Den Heuvel, W.J.: Service-oriented design and development methodology. Int. J. Web Eng. Technol. 2(4), 412–442 (2006)

17. Dai, W., Vyatkin, V., Christensen, J.H., Dubinin, V.N.: Bridging service-oriented architecture and IEC 61499 for flexibility and interoperability. IEEE Trans. Ind. Inform. **11**(3), 771–781 (2015)
18. Wang, Z., Xu, X., Zhan, D.: Normal forms and normalized design method for business service. In: IEEE International Conference on e-Business Engineering, ICEBE 2005, pp. 79–86 (2005, October)
19. Inaganti, S., Behara, G.K.: Service Identification: BPM and SOA Handshake. BPTrends **3**, 1–12 (2007)
20. Amsden, J.: Modeling SOA: Part 1. Service specification. IBM Dev. Works (2007)
21. Mani, S., Sinha, V.S., Sukaviriya, N., Ramachandra, T.: Using user interface design to enhance service identification. In: IEEE International Conference on Web Services, ICWS'08, pp. 78–87 (2008, September)
22. Jamshidi, P., Sharifi, M., Mansour, S.: To establish enterprise service model from enterprise business model. In: IEEE International Conference on Services Computing, SCC'08, vol. 1, pp. 93–100. IEEE (2008, July)
23. Dwivedi, V., Kulkarni, N.: A model driven service identification approach for process centric systems. In: Congress on Services Part II, 2008. SERVICES-2. IEEE, pp. 65–72 (2008, September)
24. Bianchini, D., Cappiello, C., De Antonellis, V., Pernici, B.: P2S: a methodology to enable inter-organizational process design through web services. In International Conference on Advanced Information Systems Engineering, pp. 334–348. Springer, Heidelberg (2009, June)
25. Yousef, R., Odeh, M., Coward, D., Sharieh, A.: BPAOntoSOA: a generic framework to derive software service oriented models from business process architectures. In: Second International Conference on the Applications of Digital Information and Web Technologies, ICADIWT'09, pp. 50–55 (2009, August)
26. Azevedo, L.G., Santoro, F., Baião, F., Souza, J., Revoredo, K., Pereira, V., Herlain, I.: A method for service identification from business process models in a SOA approach. In: Enterprise, Business-Process and Information Systems Modeling, pp. 99–112. Springer, Heidelberg (2009)
27. Kim, Y., Doh, K.G.: Formal identification of right-grained services for service-oriented modeling. In: International Conference on Web Information Systems Engineering, pp. 261–273. Springer, Heidelberg (2009, October)
28. Ren, M., Wang, Y.: Rule based business service identification using UML analysis. In: 2nd IEEE International Conference on Information Management and Engineering (ICIME), pp. 199–204 (2010, April)
29. Nikravesh, A., Shams, F., Farokhi, S., Ghaffari, A.: 2PSIM: two phase service identifying method. In: On the Move to Meaningful Internet Systems: OTM 2011, pp. 625–634 (2011)
30. Kazemi, A., Rostampour, A., Azizkandi, A.N., Haghighi, H., Shams, F.: A metric suite for measuring service modularity. In: Proceedings of the 2011 CSI International Symposium on Computer Science and Software Engineering (CSSE 2011). IEEE, USA, pp. 95–102 (2011)
31. Jamshidi, P., Mansour, S., Sedighiani, K., Jamshidi, S., Shams, F.: An Automated Service Identification Method, p. 2. Technical Report, TR-ASER-2012-01, Automated Software Engineering Research Group, Shahid Beheshti University (2012)
32. Soltani, M., Benslimane, S.M. From a High Level Business Process Model to Service Model Artifacts-A Model-Driven Approach. In: ICEIS, vol. 3, pp. 265–268 (2012)
33. Birkmeier, D.Q., Gehlert, A., Overhage, S., Schlauderer, S.: Alignment of business and it architectures in the german federal government: a systematic method to identify services from business processes. In: 2013 46th Hawaii International Conference on System Sciences (HICSS), pp. 3848–3857 (2013, January)
34. El Amine, C.M., Benslimane, S.M.: Using combinatorial particle swarm optimization to automatic service identification. In: 13th International Arab Conference on Information Technology ACIT, pp. 17–19 (2013)
35. Bianchini, D., Cappiello, C., De Antonellis, V., Pernici, B.: Service identification in interorganizational process design. IEEE Trans. Serv. Comput. **7**(2), 265–278 (2014)

36. Mohamed, M., Mohamed, B.S., Chergui, M.E.A.: A hybrid particle swarm optimization for service identification from business process. In: 2014 Second World Conference on Complex Systems (WCCS), pp. 122–127 (2014, November)
37. Leopold, H., Pittke, F., Mendling, J.: Automatic service derivation from business process model repositories via semantic technology. J. Syst. Softw. **108**, 134–147 (2015)
38. Jiang, L., Wang, J., Shah, N., Cai, H., Huang, C., Farmer, R.: A process-mining-based scenarios generation method for SOA application development. Serv. Oriented Comput. Appl. **10**(3), 303–315 (2016)
39. Gu, Q., Lago, P.: Service identification methods: a systematic literature review. In: European Conference on a Service-Based Internet, pp. 37–50. Springer, Berlin, Heidelberg (2010)
40. Klose, K., Knackstedt, R., Beverungen, D.: Identification of Services-A Stakeholder-Based Approach to SOA Development and its Application in the Area of Production Planning. In: ECIS, Vol. 7, pp. 1802–1814
41. Van der Aalst, W.M.P.: Process Mining: Discovery, Conformance and Enhancement of Business Processes. Springer, Heidelberg (2011)
42. AlShathry, O.: Process mining as a business process discovery technique. Computer Engineering & Information Technology (2016)
43. Paszkiewicz, Z.: Process mining techniques in conformance testing of inventory processes: an industrial application. In: International Conference on Business Information Systems, pp. 302–313. Springer, Heidelberg (2013, June)

A Multi-step Approach for Managing Intellectual Capital Inside Communities of Practice

Chiara Meret, Michela Iannotta, Desiree Giacomelli and Mauro Gatti

Abstract The increasingly pervasive use of social online services has contributed to raising interest in studying the active participation of individuals to business development processes. Starting from a validated framework for intellectual capital analysis, the aim of this research project is to refine and implement a multi-step approach of intellectual capital management and assessment. Intellectual capital (IC) can be seen as a set of intangible assets commonly grouped into three dimensions: (1) human capital (HC), as a set of individual knowledge; (2) structural capital (SC), as the knowledge and capabilities stored in the organizational structure; and (3) relational capital (RC), as the internal and external relationships with stakeholders. The unit of analysis upon which the integrated step-by-step methodology is based is an online community of practice, operating within one of the most important Italian telecommunication company. The basic assumption underlying this study is that communities of practice (CoPs) play a fundamental role in innovation dynamics because of their ability to shape the organizational knowledge base. An integrated approach will provide both academics and practitioners an effective tool for assessing intellectual capital and its related dimensions, its creation and the effectiveness of implementation plans conceived as a result of its application.

Keywords Intellectual capital · Communities of practice · Intellectual capital assessment · Multi-Step approach

C. Meret (✉) · M. Iannotta · D. Giacomelli · M. Gatti
Department of Management, Sapienza University of Rome, Via Del Castro
Laurenziano, 9, 00161 Rome, Italy
e-mail: chiara.meret@uniroma1.it

M. Iannotta
e-mail: michela.iannotta@uniroma1.it

D. Giacomelli
e-mail: desiree.giacomelli@uniroma1.it

M. Gatti
e-mail: mauro.gatti@uniroma1.it

© Springer Nature Switzerland AG 2020
Y. Baghdadi et al. (eds.), *ICT for an Inclusive World*,
Lecture Notes in Information Systems and Organisation 35,
https://doi.org/10.1007/978-3-030-34269-2_2

1 Introduction

According to Hislop [1, 2], communities of practice (CoPs) rely on two central premises: (1) an activity-based nature of knowledge and (2) a group-based character of the organizational activity. In this sense, it is possible to define the learning value of CoPs as the ability to develop a shared commitment among its participants [3]. In line with Brown and Duguid [4], CoPs consist of four main features: (1) a stock of knowledge shared by the participants, (2) shared values and attitudes among the members, (3) common group identity, and (4) a flow of relationships and interrelations between the abovementioned variables. Shared values emphasize interdependent contribution over devotion to duty, based on a common purpose toward which employees together are working, understanding the strategic challenges and opportunities of collaborating [5, 6]. In line with the abovementioned considerations, the aim of this research project is to refine and implement a multi-step approach of intellectual capital management and assessment within an online CoP.

Intellectual Capital (IC) in CoPs have been recently analyzed by both researchers and practitioners [7, 8]. However, there are still insufficient empirical contributions, due both to a non-univocal conception of the meaning of intellectual capital, and to different contexts in which it has been applied. Moreover, there is still a necessity of in-depth exploring and empirically assessing the impact of IC components to the contribution of CoPs to the value creation process.

To fulfill this gap, qualitative and quantitative methods can be combined to provide a tool to assess and manage IC implementation within CoPs [9–14]. In line with Grimaldi et al. [10] and Cricelli et al. [11], it is possible to analyze IC and its internal factors through a stock and flow analysis of its variables. According to their work, it is possible to trace a comprehensive methodology by including members, sponsors, internal and external leaders of CoPs. Thus, the attributed meaning of value creation of online CoPs relies on when they are used for social learning activities, such as sharing information, tips and documents, learning from each other's experience, helping each other with challenges, co-creating knowledge, and offering new kinds of development opportunities [3]. Therefore, it is possible to identify a common path of conceptual foundations for both IC and Knowledge Management, such as the resource-based view, the dynamic capabilities, and the knowledge-based view of the firm, for which the organizational ability to develop, use, and benefit from its knowledge and IC supports the building of a sustainable competitive advantage [3, 12, 15–17].

The paper is structured as follows: the second paragraph is dedicated to the theoretical background; the third paragraph includes the four-step methodology with related sub-steps; the fourth section illustrates the state of the project and first relevant aids.

2 Theoretical Background

2.1 Communities of Practice and Intellectual Capital

CoPs represent an "interdependent process management" [5:2] in which people orient their interests and actions beyond physical or vertical organizational boundaries. This horizontal process arises within the community aspect of a shared identity around a set of topics and represents the collective intention of members to manage a domain of knowledge and to sustain learning around it [3, 5]. In this sense, community members "need to recognize their own experience of participation in the results and the process of evaluation if they are to use it for reflection and guidance" [3:7]. Accordingly, CoPs are implemented in the so-called learning organizations to lead change and complexity by fostering informal relations and encouraging a free, horizontal flow of knowledge, both inside and outside their borders [11]. This translates into the attributed meaning of value creation of CoPs, at the heart of our research.

IC can be seen as a set of intangible assets commonly grouped into three components: (1) Human Capital (HC), as a set of individual knowledge; (2) Structural Capital (SC), representing the knowledge and capabilities stored in the organizational structure; and (3) Relational Capital (RC), as the internal and external relationships with stakeholders [12, 18–21]. Research on IC grew "as a natural corollary of the resource and knowledge based views of the firm" [9:16]. Furthermore, Marr [22] defines HC as the intangible resources that are related to the individual, such as employees' values and attitudes, know-how and skill sets and competences. SC represents the organizational internalized knowledge, such as its values, culture, procedures, systems and intellectual property [9, 23]. RC consists of valuable relationships with customers, suppliers and other relevant internal and external stakeholders [24].

Originally developed by Lave and Wenger [25], CoPs are systems of relationships between people, activities, and the rest of the world. They are vital places of negotiation, learning, meaning, and identity [25, 26]. "The learning value of community derives from the ability to develop a collective intention to advance learning in a domain. This shared commitment to a domain and to the group of people who care about it is a learning resource" [3:10]. CoPs, therefore, have a horizontal and informal membership, since members use each other's experience around a topic or set of challenges as a learning resource, enhancing the level of IC in all of its articulations [3, 27]. As in knowledge-based organizations the phenomenon of value creation refers to intangible assets, IC elements should be assessed and managed as catalysts for product and process innovation success [9, 12].

2.2 Intellectual Capital Assessment

Several authors suggest assessing the firm value creation by making use of IC concept and its characterizing factors; however, measuring intangible assets is difficult, since traditional measures (e.g. financial measures or profit and loss statement) are inadequate [10–12, 28–30]. Skandia was the first company introducing a dynamic

IC report, by highlighting hidden factors of human and structural capital [19, 29]. In its model, IC is the multiplication of an overall IC value and its coefficient of efficiency. By reducing the number of available indices, Edvnisson and Malone [19] already note cross-references between measures. Roos et al. [31] derive an IC-Index to overcome previous anchoring to monetary measurements, requiring organizations to understand the underlying relationships between measures. Accordingly, it also focuses on flows and dynamics of IC. Then, Bontis et al. [32] suggest the necessity to develop a process model for selecting the correct indicators, based on the sources of company value coming from IC, key success factors, identity, strategy and long term-goals. In a similar vein is Brooking's Technology Broker IC audit [30]. By assuming the four components of market assets, intellectual property assets, human-centered assets and infrastructure assets, she developed 20 questions and related question-naires, in a first attempt of combining both qualitative and quantitative measures of IC. Finally, Sveiby [33] claims that money must no longer be used as a proxy for human efforts in his Intangible Assets Monitor model, believing that by correctly leveraging IC, financial capital will follow.

Despite these previous efforts, a methodology for capturing all the aspects related to this new paradigm is still hard to be found. Given the twofold nature of CoPs (formal and informal), it is necessary that decision makers participate directly in assessing and managing the value creation process, together with directly involved people (members).

3   A Four-Step Methodology

In line with Binder and Clegg [13], assessing the strategic impact to the value creation process requires combining both qualitative and quantitative methods, and consid-ering people's opinions besides the specificity of the context. Starting from a need of deepening the combined analysis of IC components, the purpose of this research project is to implement a step-by-step methodology to assess the factual contribution of IC components of a CoP, for defining its value creation and development strate-gies. It consists of a sequence of four steps firstly implemented for the MindSh@re project [10–13]. The applied framework not only considers the quantity (stock), but also the quality (flows) of the IC components, given the twofold nature of knowledge assets (static and dynamic) [10, 19, 33]. The reason behind is that IC comprehends both resources that exist at a certain point of time (a stock of IC) and the interac-tion between physical and intangible resources (a flow of IC) [10]. Most of the step requires a combined analysis of outcomes for the detection and implementation of the results.

Step 1 is the result of 7 preliminary meetings between the researchers and 3 managers of the one most important Italian telecommunication company. The project group defined the materials and the selection of 12 subject matter experts (SMEs) of the designated CoP, basing on their participation to discussion, promotion of topics and previous knowledge with Network Leaders. The sample consists of both managerial and professional staff, contacted via email. Figure 1 synthesizes the steps.

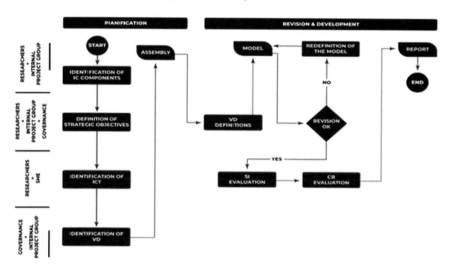

Fig. 1 Project flowchart. Own elaboration

3.1 Step 1

The first step consists in identifying the IC components. The related sub-steps are: (a) definition of the CoP's strategic objectives with the project group, in relation to the company's strategy; (b) definition of knowledge assets (IC Factors), such as IC components that affect the effectiveness of the CoP. The identification of the IC Factors is derived by using the Nominal Group Technique (digital version), involving a group of 12 selected SMEs of the CoP [34, 35]. Community members need to recognize their own participation in the results and in the process of evaluation to support the value creation [10]; (c) identification of a number ranging from 3 to 5 Value Drivers (VD), defined as a homogeneous set of IC Factors [10, 36, 37], by the project group and two Network Leaders of the CoP. This sub-step and the following three ones were defined within a focus group; (d) clustering of the identified VD into 3 strategic objectives of the CoP to verify their consistency with the company's strategic goals; (e) assemblage into homogeneous groups of IC Factors in a minimum of 3 and a maximum of 5 VD, based on pertinence, in turn assigned to the three components of HC, SC, RC; (f) definition of each VD, to be shared with the SMEs; and (e) assemblage into a comprehensive model for IC value creation, to be shared with and evaluated by the involved SMEs.

3.2   Step 2

The second step consists in the evaluation of the strategic impact (SI) of each VD. It represents the relevance of IC Factors/VD to the achievement of the goals of the CoP. Step 2 is divided into: (a) assigning a score from 1 to 5 (low-medium-high impact) to each IC Factor by SMEs of the selected CoP, which measures the influence of each of the VD; (b) the Impact Score of each VD is obtained by averaging its scores assigned to the IC Factors; (c) the strategic impact (SI) of each VD (low-medium-high scale) denotes the interval in which the Impact Score falls.

The present step, as well as the following one, was entirely developed within a one-day focus group, moderated by the project promoters. The focus group was fully recorded, transcribed and analyzed by one of the researchers.

3.3   Step 3

The third step consists in evaluating Performances (stock variables) pertaining to each VD and possible Cross-Relationships (CR) between them (flow variable). The sub-steps required are: (a) VD Performance Analysis and assignment of a value ranging from 1 to 9 by the SMEs; (b) C-R Analysis to assess the influence that each VD has on the others. Participants in this process are called upon to express a judgment on the nature of the influence of each VD on the remaining, whether direct or indirect; (c) calculation of the average value of each row that provides the Performance Score of each VD; (d) calculation of the Performance Level of each VD, based on a qualitative evaluation low-medium-high; (e) assignment of a value of 0.5 for indirect and 1 for direct influences identified, with the goal of identifying the number of relationships; (f) calculation of the C-R level of each VD, based on a low-medium-high qualitative assessment.

3.4   Step 4

In the fourth step, relevant information from previous stages are elaborated for data analysis, with the aim of interpreting the results and identifying priorities and actions to be included in the Improvement Strategy. It is articulated as follows: (a) process-ing of the "CR-Performance" Matrix, which represents the synthesis between the results of step 3. The comparison between these two aspects makes it possible to identify critical VD, as an evolution of the static component of stock. It also allows to identify VD initially considered critical, but showing no impact on performance. Placement within the matrix paves the way for formulating corrective actions and implementation strategies for achieving strategic goals; (b) development of the first IC Report synthesizing the results obtained from the whole analysis, to be shared with the Hubs of knowledge; (c) definition of the Improvement Strategy based on a preliminary analysis of strengths and weaknesses of VD, possible corrective actions and priorities assigned to actions (values 1–3), in line with the strategic objectives; (d) sharing a Final Report with all participants.

4 Analysis and Discussion of Findings

Adopting a systemic-dynamic approach, this project aims to identify the factual contribution of each constituent element of intellectual capital and its direct and indirect influence on the creation of value and on the performance of the community under investigation. To achieve this goal, it is necessary to identify the IC value drivers (VD), and the intellectual capital factors (ICF) that compose it. This methodological approach also makes it possible to implement a strategic guide to their management, in relation to the strategic objectives of the community.

The creation of value as understood, is presented as an effect of the connections between human, structural (or organizational) and relational capital.

This research project is an integral part of a wider project for the evaluation of intellectual capital generated by the communities of one of the major Italian telecommunications companies.

4.1 The Nominal Group Technique: Main Results

As part of the project, a total of 54 ICFs have been submitted to the 12 SMEs judgment. The list is the result of a mixture of ICF prevalently present in the academic and managerial literature and of the data emerging from direct analysis on the field and from the documental analysis of reports made available by the company.

Each participant was contacted by email and had a week to select 27 of the 54 ICF presented, and assign a unique score from 1 to 27, based on their relevance to the community. A score equal to 1 represented minimal importance, up to the 27-indicative score of maximum relevance. Once the contributions were received, one of the authors proceeded to weight and order all the answers, as shown in Table 1.

Table 1 Ordered list of ICF

Problem solving	Team working
Competence growth	Emotional intelligence
Internal collaboration	Trust
Development of a shared technical culture within the group	On job training
Previous experience	Social net interaction
Motivation	Proactivity
Shared values	Influence and weight of the community
Information management	Sense of belonging to the company
Knowledge sharing procedures	Community building
Diversity of skills	Consistency with company strategy
Organizational identity	Customer relations
Best practice	Informal relations
Lateral thinking	Members' satisfaction
Flexibility	

4.2 The Focus Group with the Governance: Main Results

Given that the process of value creation depends largely on how the IC components interact, its evaluation should fundamentally begin with the identification and categorization of its essential components of HC, SC, and RC. From the analysis of the prevailing literature on the taxonomy of the IC categorization, VDs representing the categories with the highest frequency of occurrence in recent publications and in company practices, in knowledge intensive sectors, have been extrapolated. These were subsequently reclassified into 15 macro-categories following the criterion of non-intersection, to make them as exclusive and exhaustive as possible, as shown in Table 2.

The focus group with the governance lasted around 3 hours. Participants were asked to review the available documents to: (1) define the strategic objectives; (2) identify the community VDs, for each category of HC, SC and RC; (3) grouping in homogeneous sets of ICFs; (4) develop a definition for each VD; and (5) elaborate the community IC creation model. The meeting was crucial to decide working simultaneously on two different models: a first model called "As-Is" and a second model called "To-Be". Figures 2 and 3 respectively show the two models.

Table 2 List of VDs

Knowledge skills	Customer relations
Management skills	Inter-firm relations
Creativity and innovation	Intra-firm relations
Work attitude	Supplier relations
Education and training	Financial relations
Intangible infrastructural assets	Institution relations
Information technology	Brand and image
Intellectual property	

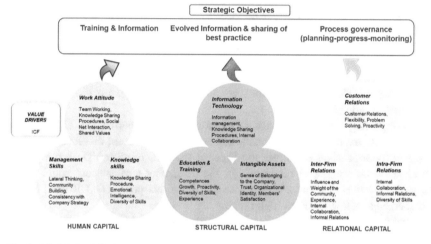

Fig. 2 Model "As-Is". Own elaboration

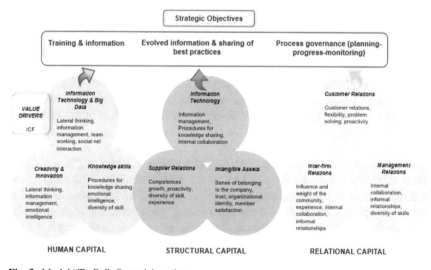

Fig. 3 Model "To-Be". Own elaboration

4.3   The Focus Group with the SMEs: Main Results

The focus group with the SMEs lasted about 3 h and a half and was led by one of the authors with the presence of two other project members. The purpose of the meeting was to obtain the three evaluations of: (a) strategic impact; (b) cross-relationships; and (c) performance, on the different components of the first models identified by the governance, given the objectives of the community. Therefore, using a bottom-up approach, the same members had the opportunity to discuss the contents critically.

In order to evaluate the strategic impact (SI) of VDs, the 12 SMEs were asked to assess the influence of the ICF on the VDs to achieve the strategic objectives. A numerical value was associated with each ICF, on a scale ranging from 1 to 2 for a weak impact, equal to 3 for an average impact, from 4 to 5 for a strong impact. In order to proceed with the evaluation, the definitions associated to each VD by the governance have been made available to the SMEs. The researcher subsequently calculated the impact score of each VD, obtained by estimating the average of the relative scores. Hence, the SI expresses the interval in which each impact score (low-medium-high) falls.

Subsequently, a cross-relationship evaluation (CR) was performed. This analysis allowed us to examine the interrelations between the different elements of IC, to evaluate the modalities of influence (direct or indirect) of each VD on the others. To identify the number of relationships, the researcher gave a score equal to 0.5 for indirect influences, and a score equal to 1 for direct ones. The CR level is also represented as a low-medium-high range.

Finally, participants were asked to evaluate the level of performance of VDs, representative of the current level of "stock" of the community under analysis. Each SME has expressed a qualitative evaluation on each ICF, assigning a value from 1 (min) to 9 (max).

For reasons of space, it is not possible to include in their entirety all six tables relating to the two models "As-Is" and "To-Be". However, Figs. 4 and 5 summarize the comparison of the results within the SI-Performance and CR-Performance matrices of both the models.

Each VD is positioned within the array based on the respective SI and Performance values. The positioning leads us to reflect on possible corrective actions or improvement strategies to achieve the strategic objectives, in light of the discrepancies between the expected model and the real/current one. The upper right quadrant suggests that the greatest impacts (not only on a strategic level, but also on a performance level) are currently linked to the VD5 of Education & Training. The remaining VDs would seem to have an average SI, with a notable exception represented by the Customer Relations VD. The latter is not understood by the SMEs, neither in reference to the definition provided by the governance, nor in reference to their *modus operandi*. Overall, VDs of HC perform better than all others in both models.

These matrices represent the synthesis between CR and Performance. By comparing these two aspects, the graphical representation allows to recognize which are critical and influential VDs. As a consequence, the matrix graphically expresses the

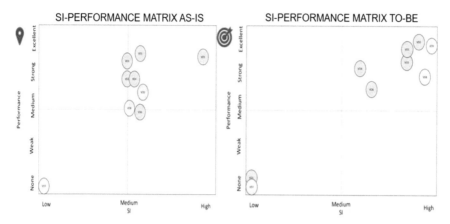

Fig. 4 SI-Performance matrices. Own elaboration

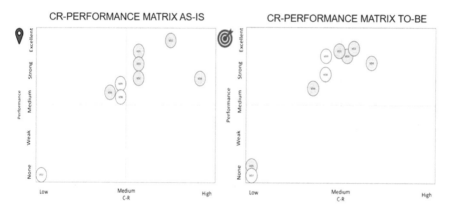

Fig. 5 CR-Performance matrices. Own elaboration

"flows" of knowledge between VDs to be exploited for the achievement of the strategic objectives. Based on the methodology adopted, the final objective of this analysis is to understand which VD need investments, before establishing strategic actions. From the analysis of the CR-Performance of the "As-Is" model, it is evident that the most influential VD was the VD4 (Information Technology), followed by the VD1 (Work Attitude). However, the VD4 (Information Technology) had a very low level of performance above the average level of other VDs. This result suggests the need to intervene in the strengthening of the VD4 (Information Technology), in order to have a positive effect on all the other VDs.

Furthermore, it is important to highlight that although the VD5 (Education & Training) has the highest Performance value, this impacts on an average high level on the other VDs. A possible explanation may be linked to the cessation of interventions and training programs provided by the SMEs themselves. Two possible alternatives for the governance of the community could be: (a) reintroducing the VD5 into the "To-Be" model; or (b) reconsider the articulation in ICF of the VD5 of the "As-Is" model and insert a new reference in the "To-Be" model. Moreover, on the basis of the content analysis of the two context-specific definitions attributed to VD5 and VD7, these would appear to be overlying. As an alternative, it has been suggested to intervene with a new formulation and communication of the definition, also in the case of VD5. It is interesting to note that all the components of HC behave homogeneously, comparing the different models.

4.4   The Improvement Strategy

In the formulation of the final Improvement Strategy, the governance of the community decided to work exclusively on the results of the "To-Be" model, but in light of the revelations linked to the "As-Is" model.

Table 3 is a summary of the previous sub-steps, while the last two columns on the right contain the implementation actions and their priority

Table 3 Improvement strategy

Improvement strategy			SI	CR	Perf	Actions	Priority
VD1	HC	Information technology and big data	High	Med	High	New communication of the definition; follow-up within a year to evaluate changes and results; clarification of the importance of the tool	1
VD2		Creativity & innovation	High	Med	High	No actions	
VD3		Knowledge skills	High	Med	High	Offer training to best performers; engage the community to suggest self-candidatures for 2 Network Supporters *pro tempore*; participation in a community knowledge management workshop event	1
VD4	SC	Information technology	Med	Med	High	Clarification of the importance of the tool	1
VD5		Supplier relations	NA	NA	NA	NA	NA

(continued)

Table 3 (continued)

Improvement strategy			SI	CR	Perf	Actions	Priority
VD6		Intangible assets	Med	Med	Med	Net learning; News intranet/Smart Corner webinar on the recognition of best practices developed by the community	2
VD7	RC	Customer relations	NA	NA	NA	NA	NA
VD8		Inter-firm relations	High	Med	High	New communication of the definition; strengthening the role of the Network Supporter in explaining the interdependencies among the participants' works, given the difficulties in understanding internal and external relations with respect to their community	3
VD9		Management relations	High	Med	High	No actions	

(from 1 = high to 3 = low). The actions are the result of a preliminary focus group with the governance, subsequently discussed in the final workshop together with the SMEs.

5 Conclusions and Further Insights

The purpose of the research project is to provide an integrated methodology to evaluate strategic IC components of a CoP, grounded in theory to ensure relevance, and data-oriented -directly derived by involving relevant stakeholders- to provide validity and reliability. In fact, in line with relevant literature, community members participate to the results and the process of evaluation [3, 10–12, 26, 35].

Potentialities of CoPs have already attracted attention both in management literature and practice, also influencing debates on the knowledge economy [26]. This means that managing distributed online communities involves much more than choosing the correct technological tools, if human dimension is neglected [26, 38, 39]. The choice of the methodology is, in fact, consistent with the very nature of CoPs, and allows to take into account the relevant stakeholders opinions besides the specificity of the context of analysis [11, 13].

Accordingly, our approach does not focus so much on what the organization or people know, but on the process through which they learn and create knowledge and therefore, value. Starting from the central premise that CoPs represent the privileged *locus* of analysis of learning on an individual and collective level, we analyzed and presented the creation of value as an effect of the connections between human, structural (or organizational) and relational capital. Their interaction can be productive only if bonds between them become strong.

This research is an integral part of a wider project for the evaluation of intellectual capital generated by the online communities of practice of one of the major Italian telecommunications companies. Overall, results provide guidelines to efficient management and development of online communities inside the organization. The first strength of the project lies in the use of a multi-step methodology [40]. The integrated approach provides both academics and practitioners with an effective tool for proactively promoting, assessing and managing the creation of value of a CoP. As a result of its application, it is not only possible to value the stock and flow variables of IC, but also to analyze its factual contributions in order to propose an action plan for its effective functioning, furthermore contributing to broadening the definition proposed by Brown and Duguid [4, 10, 11]. This will allow for a further exploration in the assessment of the strategic impact to the value creation process of online communities [5]. We are aware of the limits related to the presentation of a single case study. However, the easy replicability of the steps and methods do not make this a *taylor made* work. The analysis conducted in full can produce results with a strong impact for the investigation and management of all the communities within the organization.

References

1. Hislop, D.: The complex relations between communities of practice and the implementation of technological innovations. Int. J. Innov. Manage. 7(2), 163–188 (2003)
2. Hislop, D.: Knowledge Management in Organizations. A Critical Introduction, 2nd edn. Oxford University Press, Oxford (2009)
3. Wenger, E., Trayner, B., de Laat, M.: Promoting and Assessing Value Creation in Communities and Networks: A Conceptual Framework. Rapport 18, Ruud de Moor Centrum (2011)
4. Brown, J.S., Duguid, P.: Knowledge and organization: a social-practice perspective. Organ. Sci. 12(2), 198–213 (2001)
5. Adler, C., Hecksher, B.: The Firm as a Collaborative Community. Reconstructing Trust in the Knowledge Economy. Oxford University Press, Oxford (2007)
6. Barnes, J.: Methods of measuring community characteristics. Child Psychol. Psychiatry Rev. 2(4), 163–169 (1997)
7. Alcaniz, L., Gomez-Bezares, F., Roeslender, R.: Theoretical perspectives on intellectual capital: a backward look and a proposal for going forward. Account. Forum 35(2), 104–117 (2011)
8. Purani, K., Satish, N.: Knowledge community: integrating ICT into social development in developing economies. Ai Soc. 21(3), 329–345 (2007)
9. Costa, R.V., Ramos, A.P.: Designing an AHP methodology to prioritize critical elements for product innovation: an intellectual capital perspective. Int. J. Bus. Sci. Appl. Manage. 10(1), 15–34 (2015)

10. Grimaldi, M., Cricelli, L., Rogo, F.: A theoretical framework for assessing managing and indexing the intellectual capital. J. Intellect. Capital **14**(4), 501–521 (2013)
11. Grimaldi, M., Cricelli, L., Rogo, F.: A methodology to assess value creation in communities of innovation. J. Intellect. Capital **13**(3), 305–330 (2012)
12. Grimaldi, M., Cricelli, L., Rogo, F., Iannarelli, A.: Assessing and managing intellectual capital to support open innovation paradigm. World Acad. Sci. Eng. Technol. **6**(1), 93–103 (2012)
13. Binder, M., Clegg, B.: Enterprise management: a new frontier for organisations. Int. J. Prod. Econ. **106**(2), 409–430 (2007)
14. Zheng, S., Zhang, W., Du, J.: Knowledge-based dynamic capabilities and innovation in networked environments. J. Knowl. Manage. **15**(6), 1035–1051 (2001)
15. Seleim, A.A.S., Khalil, O.E.M.: Understanding the knowledge management intellectual capital relationship: a two-way analysis. J. Intellect. Capital **12**(4), 586–614 (2011)
16. Lin, C., Liu, A., Hsu, M.L., Wu, J.C.: Pursuing excellence in firm core knowledge through intelligent group decision support system. Ind. Manage. Data Syst. **108**(3), 277–296 (2008)
17. Spender, J.C.: Making knowledge the basis of a dynamic theory of the firm. Strateg. Manage. J. **17**, 45–62 (1996)
18. Bontis, N., Chua, W., Richardson, S.: Intellectual capital and the nature of business in Malaysia. J. Intellect. Capital **1**(1), 85–100 (2000)
19. Edvinsson, L., Malone, M.S.: Intellectual Capital: Realizing your Company's True Value by Finding its Hidden Brainpower. Harper Business, New York, NY (1997)
20. Sveiby, K.E.: The New Organizational Wealth: Managing and Measuring Knowledge-based Assets. Berrett-Koehler Publishers, San Francisco, CA (1997)
21. Kaplan, R.S., Norton, D.P.: The balanced scorecard—measures that drives performance. Harvard Bus. Rev. **70**(1), 71–79 (1992)
22. Marr, B.: Impacting Future Value: How to Manage your Intellectual Capital. Canada: The Society of Management Accountants of Canada, the American Institute of Certified Public Accountants and the Chartered Institute of Management Accountants (2008)
23. Bueno, E., Salmador, M.P.: Perspectivas sobre Dirección del Conocimiento y Capital Intelectual. Instituto Universitario Euroforum Escorial, Madrid (2000)
24. Roos, G., Bainbridge, A., Jacobsen, K.: Intellectual capital analysis as a strategic tool. Strategy Leadersh. **29**(4), 21–26 (2001)
25. Lave, J., Wenger, E.: Situated Learning: Legitimate Peripheral Participation. Cambridge University Press, Cambridge (1991)
26. Amin, A., Roberts, J.: Communities of Practice? Varieties of Situated Learning. EU Network of Excellence Dynamics of Institutions and Markets in Europe (DIME) (2008)
27. Lesser, E.L., Prusak, L.: Communities of practice, social capital and organizational knowledge. In: Lesser, E.L., Fontaine, M.A., Slusher, J.A. (eds.) Knowledge and Communities, pp. 123–131. Butterworth Heinemann, Boston (2000)
28. Marr, B., Spender, J.C.: Measuring knowledge assets–implications of the knowledge economy for performance measurement. Measuring Bus. Excellence **8**(1), 18–27 (2004)
29. Bontis, N.: Assessing knowledge assets: a review of the models used to measure intellectual capital. Int. J. Manage. Rev. **3**(1), 41–60 (2001)
30. Brooking, A.: Intellectual Capital: Core Assets for the Third Millennium Enterprise. Thomson Business Press, London (1996)
31. Roos, J., Roos, G., Dragonetti, N.C., Edvinsson, L.: Intellectual Capital: Navigating in the New Business Landcape. Mcmillan, London (1997)
32. Bontis, N.: Managing an Organizational Learning System by Aligning Stocks and Flows of Knowledge: An Empirical Examination of Intellectual Capital, Knowledge Management and Business Performance. University of Western Ontario, London, Canada (1999)
33. Sveiby, K.E.: The New Organizational Wealth: Managing and Measuring Knowledge-Based Assets. Barrett-Kohler, San-Francisco (1997)
34. Delbecq, A.L., van de Ven, A.H.: A group process model for problem identification and program planning. J. Appl. Behav. Sci. **7**(4), 466–492 (1971)

35. Randall, B.D.: Nominal Group Technique: A User's Guide. University of Wisconsin (2006).
    http://instruction.bus.wisc.edu/obdemo/readings/ngt.html
36. Andreou, A.N., Green, A., Stankosky, M.: A framework of intangible valuation areas and
    antecedents. J. Intellect. Capital 8(1), 52–75 (2007)
37. Chu, P.Y., Lin, Y.L., Hsiung, H.H., Liu, T.Y.: Intellectual capital: an empirical study of ITRI.
    Technol. Forecast. Soc. Change 73, 886–902 (2006)
38. Meret, C., Iannotta, M., Gatti, M.: The power of Web 2.0 storytelling to overcome knowledge
    sharing barriers. In: Harfouche, A., Cavallari, M. (eds.) ICT for a Better Life and a Better
    World. Springer, Berlin (in print)
39. Riege, A.: Three-dozen knowledge-sharing barriers managers must consider. J. Knowl.
    Manage. 9(3), 18–35 (2005)
40. Amatura, E., Punziano, G.: I Mixed Methods nella ricerca sociale. Carocci Editore (2016)

The Influence of ICT Adoption on the Development of Managerial Modes of Consulting Firms in France

Nizar Raissi and Henda Matoussi

Abstract This study seeks to understand the nature of relationships between components of information and communications technology (ICT) adoption and managerial modes. The paper focuses on the experience of consulting firms, how they perceived the role of ICT tools on the management fashion. Participants in this study consisted of 30 consultants of a major management consulting firm in France. The analysis was conducted with qualitative method which is the correspondence factor analysis (CFA) using SPSS software. From the study, firstly, we found that reengineering influenced by internet, software and website access more than other ICT tools. Secondly, the innovation has a high correlation with communications technology. Thirdly, the coaching connects more with EDI, cloud computing, transactions and Data. Finally, partnership as managerial fashion determinants has very strong relationships with hardware and procedures.

Keywords ICT · Managerial modes · EDI · Cloud computing · Coaching · Reengineering

1 Introduction

Using information technology has become one of the necessary elements to improve the efficiency of organization. It offers great opportunities to facilitate strategy and its development to services with high added-value rather emphasis on daily tasks and routine. The modern organization has become dependent on rapidly changing

N. Raissi (✉)
College of Islamic Economics and Finance, Umm al Qura University, Mecca, Kingdom of Saudi Arabia
e-mail: raissinizar1510@gmail.com

Laboratory ARBRE (Applied Research in Business Relationships & Economics), University of Tunis, Tunis, Tunisia

H. Matoussi
Deanship of Educational Services, IT Department, Taibah University, Madina, Kingdom of Saudi Arabia

© Springer Nature Switzerland AG 2020
Y. Baghdadi et al. (eds.), *ICT for an Inclusive World*,
Lecture Notes in Information Systems and Organisation 35,
https://doi.org/10.1007/978-3-030-34269-2_3

information in all stages, starting with information relevant on enterprise functions as production size, investment, quality management system (QMS), management of information system (MIS), taking into account the needs of employees, activities and competitors' products [1]. It can be said that technology is the driving goal in which seen as weapons face to the difficulties of communication and transition information in various forms inside and outside organization and to understand how much is expected to convert jobs and paper files to electronic files. So, owning IT is required, but not controlling the latter loses its meaning because the goal of any path is to obtain the information in a timely manner and the extent of its accuracy and credibility, if the condition is violated by its terms it will lose its meaning [2]. Then, the access to new and useful information requires the practice of high skills to run the institution functions in addition to modern technology in this area. The common motivation to integrate these technologies is that may empower the management practices by providing the tools to support and enhance their integration in organizations' functions [3, 4]. The goal of any company is to ensure continuous improvement and market leading. In order to satisfy this objective, the adoption of ICT tools presented as a real necessity for organisations. Thus, many studies proved that managers thought that employees in any level of administrative hierarchy must be able to dealing with technology [5–8]. Also, Information and communication technology (ICT) contribute each day to promote the management practices. The relevance of this paper consists to study the relationship between ICT and management practices which derives from the needs of organization to improve their techniques and modes of management by following the technology evolution. Various factors have been identified as determinants of this association. The components of ICT defined as software, cloud computing, internet access, data, communications technology, transactions, hardware, website, EDI (Electronic Data Interchange) and procedures [9–11]. In the other side, the determinants of managerial modes presented by innovation, partnership, coaching, reengineering [12–19].

2 Literature Review

It is widely known that ICTs have evolved dramatically in transforming communities, cultures and economies. The countries' economies have perceived changes resulting from speedy improvements in ICTs such as social media and big data. The Internet, mobile technology and broadband connectivity, already widespread in developed countries, are rapidly embedded in the global markets. Social networks have made insightful changes and citizens cooperate with each other and with their governments [20–22]. Open government data, cloud computing, e-administration and mobile device utilization have developed the world network. Therefore, we argue that the managerial competencies of a firm as articulated by its creativity and innovation efforts are likely to significantly affect choices of ICT implementation in organisations. Hence, the first hypothesis to test can be written as follows:

Hypothesis 1: A firm's innovation competency is positively associated with ICT adoption.

According to [23], the joint venture is a fundamental strategy for entrepreneurial cooperation that operates to own high-tech tools. Indeed, the participation in partnerships policy has many benefits and costs. For the benefits way, partnerships are typical when ensure technological alliances, cost sharing and entrance to stakeholders complementary know-hows and assets. Nonetheless, this strategy has many costs as the search of suitable partners, risk of convenience, project application and negotiation, [24]. The Partnership continues to raise awareness on ICT adoption that is why the second hypothesis was formulated to clarify this relationship:

Hypothesis 2: A partnership as organizational strategy is positively associated with ICT adoption.

Another important element was that reengineering can be made to catch up or maintain ICT practices. The business process reengineering (BPR) reveals radical changes with high efficiency when the ICT support their operations. Also, significant BPR movement allows a continuous improvement (Kaizen) in firms by rethink business processes, new strategic vision, and IT adoption [25]. Many advocates of BPR practices agreed that in order to maintain breakthroughs, organizations require ICT tools and other management fashion as total quality of management (TQM). Management should involve ICT to obtain performance and competitiveness. In addition, BPR and ICT can be used as leverage for transformational change framework through changes of strategies, support and tools [26, 27]. To verify this relationship, the hypothesis H3 was designed as follows:

Hypothesis 3: Reengineering process is positively associated with ICT adoption.

Technology and internet have become a fundamental ICT tools to help managers to making-decision and strategy through the investigation of useful information which is expanding. The e-coaching defined as an online communication system that provides assistance to managers at firms [28]. The overriding aim of coaching is to optimize and motivate the teamwork through conversation (active listening, asking open questions, skillful use of paraphrase, reflection, feedback, etc.) [29]. The e-coaching allows increasing of organizational-commitment to technology and internet [30]. Moreover, the consultants' learning trajectories in the consulting practice go through adoption of ICT tools and online business coaching as a managerial fashion waves. The managers (coaches) used e-coaching to reduce complexity of workplace and to manage diversity of skills and knowledge that need employees to improve their productivity [31]. Therefore, based on hypothesis 4, we test the relationship between coaching and ICT as follows:

Hypothesis 4: Online business coaching is positively associated with ICT adoption.

Finally, to review this topic, the hypotheses argued below need test to be confirmed or rejected. That is why in next sections we are called to explain methodology and discuss our findings.

3 Methodology

The aim of study was to identify and analyze the factors that define the relationships between ICT components and managerial modes. The study conducting with a survey based on questionnaire distributed to 30 consulting firms in France in order to collecting qualitative data. The research method was the correspondence factor analysis (CFA) which is qualitative method that allows us to study the association between two qualitative variables. This method is based on inertia and it purposes to characterize on the one hand a maximum of the total inertia on the first factorial axis and on the other hand a maximum of the residual inertia on the second axis. The research variables presented in final step of analysis on plot of row and column points. Furthermore, to refine our analysis, we proposed to study the correspondences that may exist between the variables representing the determinants of ICT adopted within consulting firms in France and the managerial modes (MM). To this end, a contingency table has been constructed (Table 1)which makes it possible to study the distribution of the workforce according to two qualitative variables namely ICT and MM. The use of the correspondence analysis technique, subsequently CFA, well suited to the analysis of qualitative data is therefore the most appropriate. As well as CFA deals with contingency tables (dependency tables) in which a pair (i, j) corresponds to a positive number k_{ij} which is usually the result of enumeration. The master data is usually grouped in a table. We study simultaneously, on a population, two qualitative variables I and J which can take respectively n and p values (or modalities). We denote by k_{ij} the number of individuals belonging simultaneously to the categories i and j of the variables I and J. In table k_{ij}, are associated two tables with one dimension each: the table of margins in line k_I and the table of margins in column k_J. The contingency table (Table 1) and marginal tables (Tables 2 and 3) are shown below:

The Table 1 (4 × 10) below crosses 4 Variables of MM with 10 variables of ICT. The results of this analysis are shown in the tables and graphs below:

In this table, rows and columns play similar roles: they are two partitions of the same population. To make the distances between line-points and column-points meaningful, line and column profiles should be used, that is to say percentage distributions within a row and a column. Indeed, two observations i and i' will be considered identical if the corresponding lines are proportional. Indeed, the distance between, for example, the point "innovation" and the point "procedures", calculated from the raw numbers of correspondences table, would only reflect the differences in numbers, considerable, between these two variables. On the other hand, calculated on the line profiles of the row profiles table, it will reflect differences of risk towards the variables, by comparing the percentages of each of these variables, without taking into account the total numbers of variables. In the same way, to compare two variables, we will consult the column profiles of the table column profiles. We will therefore define the table of profiles of I on J by posing:

Table 1 Correspondence Table

MM	ICT components										Active Margin
	IAC	SOF	CCO	Data	CT	TRA	HAD	WEB	EDI	PRO	
INO	19	15	13	9	12	14	13	17	10	20	142
PAT	12	7	13	10	17	10	20	12	7	20	128
COA	12	7	19	15	14	16	5	9	17	10	124
REG	20	12	17	10	20	12	7	20	12	4	134
Active margin	63	41	62	44	63	52	45	58	46	54	528

Innovation (INO), Partnership (PAT), Coaching (COA), Reengineering (REG), Internet access (IAC), Software (SOF), Cloud computing (CCO), Communications technology (CT), Transactions (TRA), Hardware (HAD), Website (WEB), Procedures (PRO)

$$P_{ij} = Ki / \sum_i Kij = Kij/Ki$$

We also create MM profiles (row profiles) as follows: $(100 \times Kij/Ki)$

The ICT profiles (column profiles) presented as follows: $(100 \times Kij/Ki)$

It is the RP and CP tables that define the coordinates in the two spaces (in the form of frequencies and not percentages: total rows or columns equal to 1 instead of 100) (Tables 2 and 3).

We note that:

- total size in the table $k = 528 = \sum_i \sum_j Kij$,
- With: $i = $ Total lines
  $j = $ total number of columns
- relative frequencies $f_{ij} = kij/k$
- relative frequencies marginal lines $f_{i.} = \sum_J f_{ij}$
- relative frequencies marginal columns $f_{.j} = \sum_I f_{ij}$

According to [32]:

- In the space R_p, we construct a cloud of n points, each point i having coordinates for the quantities: $\{f_{ij}/f_i; \ j = 1, 2, \ldots, p\}$ and being assigned the mass $(f_{i.})$.
- These n points will be located in a subspace with p-1 dimensions, their n coordinates verifying the relation $\sum_J (f_{ij}/f_i) = 1$ for all $i = 1, \ldots, n$.
- In the space R_n, we construct a cloud of p points, each point j having for coordinates the quantities: $\{f_{ij}/f_i; \ i = 1, 2, \ldots, n\}$ and being assigned the mass $(f_{.j})$.
- These p points will be located in a subspace with $n - 1$ dimensions, their p coordinates verifying the relation $\sum_I (f_{ij}/f_j) = 1$ for all $j = 1, \ldots, p$.

Then, proximities between points are interpreted in terms of proximities between profiles. The starting dimension is the one corresponding to the smallest dimension of table. In our case, we will place ourselves in R_n where $n = 4$.

Choice of distances:

To work on profiles, in the spaces R_p and R_n these spaces are given a distance different from the usual Euclidean distance: the Chi-square distance (weighted distance). The distance between two risk categories i and i' will be given by:

$$d_2(i, i') = \sum_{j=1}^{p} (1/f_j) \times \left((f_{ij}/f_i) - (f_{ij}/f_j) \right)^2 \tag{1}$$

The distance between two variables j and j' will be:

$$d_2(j, j') = \sum_{i=1}^{n} (1/f_i) \times \left((f_{ij}/f_j) - (f_{ij}/f_i) \right)^2 \tag{2}$$

Table 2 Table of Row Profiles (RP)

MM	ICT components										Active margin
	IAC	SOF	CCO	Data	CT	TRA	HAD	WEB	EDI	PRO	
INO	0.134	0.106	0.092	0.063	0.085	0.099	0.092	0.120	0.070	0.141	1.000
PAT	0.094	0.055	0.102	0.078	0.133	0.078	0.156	0.094	0.055	0.156	1.000
COA	0.097	0.056	0.153	0.121	0.113	0.129	0.040	0.073	0.137	0.081	1.000
REG	0.149	0.090	0.127	0.075	0.149	0.090	0.052	0.149	0.090	0.030	1.000
Mass	0.119	0.078	0.117	0.083	0.119	0.098	0.085	0.110	0.087	0.102	

Table 3 Table of Column Profiles (CP)

MM	ICT components											
	IAC	SOF	CCO	Data	CT	TRA	HAD	WEB	EDI	PRO	Mas
INO	0.302	0.366	0.210	0.205	0.190	0.269	0.289	0.293	0.217	0.370	0.269
PAT	0.190	0.171	0.210	0.227	0.270	0.192	0.444	0.207	0.152	0.370	0.242
COA	0.190	0.171	0.306	0.341	0.222	0.308	0.111	0.155	0.370	0.185	0.235
REG	0.317	0.293	0.274	0.227	0.317	0.231	0.156	0.345	0.261	0.074	0.254
A-M	1.000	1.000	1.000	1.000	1.000	1.000	1.000	1.000	1.000	1.000	

The Chi-square distance verifies the principle of distributional equivalence.

Principle of distributional equivalence:
If two line-points i_1 and i_2 are merged in R_p and if we consider them as a single point affected by the sum of the masses of i_1 and i_2 (replaced by i_0), then the distances between all the pairs of points in R_p and in R_n remain unchanged. It is the same for two column points' j_1 and j_2 of R_n having the same properties. This distance must make points "close" to I whose associations to J, whose behaviors on J (thus the profiles) are close or similar. In the same way, this distance will make appear "distant" points differing substantially according to J.

4 Results and Discussion

The results delivered by the machine include eigenvalues, percentages of inertia, factorial coordinates, relative and absolute contributions.

- The cloud support is a space at $n - 1 = 4 - 1 = 3$ dimensions.
- The trace of the matrix $= 0.096$ (it is the sum of the eigenvalues other than 1).
- Eigenvalues occur through the coefficient $1/\sqrt{\lambda\alpha}$ to characterize the quality of the simultaneous representation.
- The "eigenvalue" represents, for each factor, the value of the inertia of the cloud on this factor compared to the sum of all the eigenvalues which represents 100% of this inertia (Tables 4 and 5).
- i = variable identifier.
- **Mass fi** = marginal weight associated with point I.
- $\psi\alpha i$ = coordinate of the individual i on the rank axis α.
- $ca\alpha i = f_i \psi_{\alpha i}^2 / \lambda\alpha$ = absolute contribution of the individual i to the variance of the axis α.
- $cr\alpha i$ = relative contribution of α to the eccentricity of $i = \psi_{\alpha i}^2 / \rho_{(i)}^2$ = square cosine of the angle formed by i and the axis α = explanation of the individual i by the row axis α (Table 6).

Table 4 Findings Summary

Dimension	Singular value	Inertia	Chi square	Sig.	Proportion of inertia		Confidence singular value	
					Accounted for	Cumulative	Standard deviation	Correlation
								2
1	0.240	0.058			0.600	0.600	0.042	0.020
2	0.163	0.026			0.276	0.875	0.043	
3	0.109	0.012			0.125	1		
Total		0.096	50.64	0.004[a]	1	1		

[a]27 degrees of freedom

Table 5 Overview row points[a] (Variables MM)

Managerial modes		Mass	Score in dimension		Inertia	Contribution				Of dimension to inertia of point		
						Of point to inertia of dimension		Of point to inertia of				
			1	2		1	2			1	2	Total
dimension0	INO	0.269	−0.281	0.214	0.014	0.088	0.076			0.366	0.145	0.511
	PAT	0.242	−0.659	−0.174	0.03	0.439	0.045			0.85	0.04	0.89
	COA	0.235	0.498	−0.593	0.028	0.243	0.508			0.507	0.487	0.994
	REG	0.254	0.466	0.488	0.025	0.23	0.371			0.534	0.396	0.93
Active Total		1			0.096	1	1					

[a]Symmetrical normalization

Table 6 Overview Column Points[a] (Variables ICT)

ICT components	Mass	Score in dimension		Inertia	Contribution				
					Of point to inertia of dimension		Of dimension to inertia of point		
		1	2		1	2	1	2	Total
Internet access	0.119	0.136	0.451	0.005	0.009	0.15	0.113	0.84	0.953
Software	0.078	0.026	0.555	0.006	0	0.147	0.002	0.629	0.631
Cloud computing	0.117	0.348	−0.243	0.005	0.059	0.043	0.708	0.234	0.942
Data	0.083	0.286	−0.535	0.006	0.028	0.147	0.292	0.694	0.986
Communications technology	0.119	0.114	0.104	0.005	0.006	0.008	0.073	0.041	0.114
Transactions	0.098	0.244	−0.281	0.003	0.024	0.048	0.407	0.365	0.772
Hardware	0.085	−1.026	−0.034	0.023	0.374	0.001	0.925	0.001	0.926
Website	0.11	0.081	0.634	0.007	0.003	0.271	0.023	0.973	0.996
EDI	0.087	0.602	−0.441	0.011	0.132	0.104	0.718	0.262	0.98
Procedures	0.102	−0.923	−0.361	0.025	0.363	0.082	0.838	0.087	0.925
Active total	1			0.096	1	1			

[a]Symmetrical normalization

- **j** = variable identifier
- **Mass** = weight associated with the point j = fj
- $\varphi\alpha j$ = coordinate of the variable j on the rank axis α
- **caαj** $= f_j \varphi_{\alpha j}^2 / \lambda\alpha$ = absolute contribution of the variable j to the variance of the axis α.
- **crαj** = relative contribution of α to the inertia of j $= \varphi_{\alpha j}^2 / \rho_{(j)}^2$ = square cosine of the angle formed by j and the axis α = explanation of the variable j by the rank axis α.

According to [32] the absolute contributions, caαi and caαj express the part taken by a given element in the variance explained by a factor. They make it possible to know which variables intervene strongly in the construction of a factor.

$Ca_\alpha(i) = f_i \psi_{\alpha i}^2 / \lambda\alpha$: It measures the part of the element i in the explained variance of the axis α. We will have: $\sum_{i=1}^{n} Ca_\alpha(i) = 1$.

The absolute contribution of the element j to the axis α is: $Ca_\alpha(j) = f_j \varphi_{\alpha j}^2 / \lambda\alpha$. The points with strong absolute contributions on an axis α are those that contribute to defining the meaning of this factorial axis. These are the explanatory points of the axis. The relative contributions, $Cr_\alpha(i)$ and $Cr_\alpha(j)$ express the part taken by a factor in explaining the dispersion of an element.

$Cr_\alpha(i) = \psi_{\alpha i}^2 / d_p^2(i, G)$: This is the cosine square of the point i with the axis α. It is interpreted as the square of a correlation coefficient. The relative contribution of the element j to the axis α is: $Cr_\alpha(j) = \varphi_{\alpha j}^2 / d_n^2(j, H)$.

G and H are the centers of gravity of the points clouds in R_p and R_n; d is the distance from point i to the center of gravity. Points with strong relative contributions on an axis α are the points explained in the axis (Tables 7 and 8).

Graphical representation in the first factorial plan:
According to [32], one of the interests of the CFA is to allow a graphical representation of I and J points clouds in a space of small dimension, allowing to highlight elements (correspondences) that the numerical computation does not allow to appreciate instantly. Traditionally, the representation is in 2 dimensions (2 axes), successively drawing the factorial planes F1/F2, F1/F3 and F2/F3 (and more, if more factors are required in the interpretation). For representations, the coordinates are

Table 7 Confidence row points

Managerial modes		Standard deviation in dimension		Correlation
		1	2	1–2
Dimension0	Innovation	0.226	0.349	0.197
	Partnership	0.182	0.308	−0.302
	Coaching	0.267	0.171	0.803
	Reengineering	0.221	0.24	−0.59

Table 8 Confidence column points

ICT components	Standard deviation in dimension		Correlation
	1	2	1–2
Internet access	0.221	0.117	−0.349
Software	0.335	0.361	0.005
Cloud computing	0.132	0.153	0.63
Data	0.252	0.13	0.662
Communications technology	0.222	0.406	0.003
Transactions	0.16	0.201	0.271
Hardware	0.192	0.43	−0.044
Website	0.294	0.097	−0.309
EDI	0.215	0.216	0.785
Procedures	0.225	0.408	−0.496

those calculated in the tables parameters of points-rows and columns. The proximities observable on the first factorial plan are shown schematically in Figs. 1 and 2.

The proximity between two MM line points reflects a similarity of ICT variable profiles (hardware and procedures). The proximity between two points-columns (ICT) reflects a similarity of risk profiles MM (innovation and partnership). The simultaneous representation of the row points and the column points makes it possible to identify the variables responsible for certain proximities. The proximities between profiles are interpreted by reference to the average profile. Proximities are

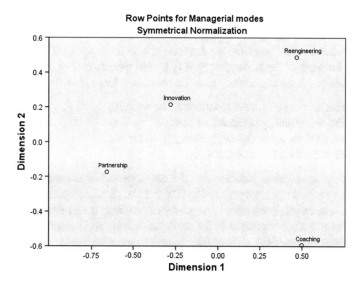

Fig. 1 Row points of managerial modes

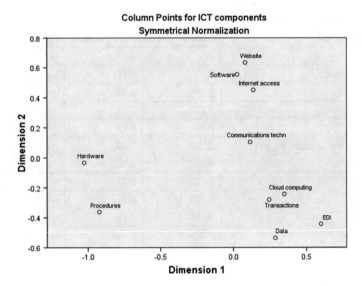

Fig. 2 Column points of ICT components

easier to interpret at the periphery of the graph. The variables responsible for the construction of the axes (strong absolute contributions) are for the first axis: "partnership", "hardware", "EDI" and "procedures" (which explain 92.3% of the variance in absolute value). The variable "innovation" participates little because its mass is 3 times weaker than "partnership". For axis 2, the variable "website" has a strong contribution (63.4%) while "communications technology" is only 10.4%. For MM variables, "partnership" defines the first axis (65.9%) and the variable "coaching" for the second axis for (59.3%). Based on their relative contributions, these two variables characterize the first and the second axis. For ICT variables "procedures" for the first axis with (92.3%) and "website" for the second axis for (63.4%). The graph should be read in the light of the tables that qualify its interpretation (Fig. 3).

From this graph we notice that there are correspondences between:

- Reengineering, internet access, software and website,
- Innovation and communications technology.
- Coaching, EDI, cloud computing, transactions and data,
- Partnership, hardware and procedures.

These correspondences indicate that the development of the managerial modes (MM) is determined by factors related to ICT as EDI, cloud computing, transactions and data. These factors contribute to improve the coaching used by leader such as his ability to involve the consultants in the decision-making and the strategic choice of the missions as well as his engagement in the firm to solve the conflicts of interests and improve its Strategic Business Area (SBA) with its professional environment. Then, the hypothesis 4 which argued that online business coaching is positively associated with ICT adoption was confirmed. These findings are coherent with previous studies

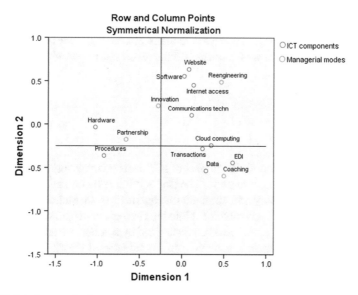

Fig. 3 Biplot of row and column points

[28]. Other organizational factors determine the mode partnership as determinant of management fashion, namely the collaboration of the members of the company and their participation in the resolution of the company's problems. In addition, it has been shown that involving the company members in the missions by adopting ICT tools as procedures and hardware; and working in consensus with the client system is a factor in the development of MM. Also, the results confirmed the hypothesis 2 which argued that a partnership as organizational strategy is positively associated with ICT adoption. This result is consistent with several researches [23]. The use of the services of external providers through internet access is dominated by a symbolic function according to which the leaders try to pass their own decisions, to legitimize their actions and to influence members' behaviors in organization by pushing them to the conformity. Thus, several contradictions exist in the consulting market making it inefficient. These contradictions are manifested in the disconnect between the speeches and the actions of the stakeholders (internal and external consultants). The adoption of software and website by consultants and the monitoring of anomalies and malfunctions throughout their missions considered a guarantee of success. This allows us to say that the procedures of the profession of consultant make it possible to improve the managerial techniques and gives the most to the MM. Thus, the results confirmed the hypothesis 3 which argued that reengineering process is positively associated with ICT adoption was confirmed. This result is consistent with researches [26]. Indeed, the communication technology of the intellectual services market (determinants of the consulting or best practice of consulting) depends on several variants one of the organizational order, the other one of managerial and technical order. As a result, the evolution of best practice consulting is strongly correlated

with the adoption of managerial techniques in fashion and ICT adoption. Therefore, the hypothesis 1 which argued that a firm's innovation competency is positively associated with ICT adoption was confirmed. This result consistent with the researches [20–22].

5 Conclusions

This research aims to identify the impact of ICT tools on managerial fashion, where the subject is divided into two parts. The first section is theoretical, dealing with a topic Knowledge economy and strategic management of institutions and key concepts related to ICT and its involvement into the strategic management of companies through their strategic roles which is characterized by competitive advantage, investment of strategic intelligence, activation of organizational development, adoption of quality management and the engineering of strategic alliances and partnership. The second part is applied to study the impact of information technology on the management modes of consulting firms in France. The study concluded that ICT is fundamental to promote the management fashion of consulting firms. The benefits of ICT in terms of continuous improvement for firms could be presented through 4 main relationships. The first between reengineering, internet access, software and website. The second between innovation and communications technology. The third one between coaching, EDI, cloud computing, transactions and data. And the fourth one between partnership, hardware and procedures. Also, the traditional management has become unable to make the organization able to cope with the intense competition known by the consulting sector in France, especially after the opening of this sector to foreign competition and the solution lies in the transition to use technologies and new methods of management. In addition, this study interest researcher, but especially to scientists in field of management information system (MIS). The difficulties encountered throughout this research are the heterogeneity of managerial modes that our study selected only 4 modes which are reengineering, innovation, partnership and coaching. Nonetheless, in reality there are many modes which present high interest to be tested like total quality of management and lean management, etc. We suggest as perspectives to test this study in other sectors as government institutions and to compare findings with our results with the aim to conclude about the role of ICT in development of management fashion in both private and public sector.

References

1. Fullan, M., Smith, G.: Technology and the problem of change. Paper presented at the International Educational Conference, 27–28 August, Petaling Jaya, Malaysia (2001)
2. Hu, Q., Kapucu, N.: Information communication technology utilization for effective emergency management networks. Pub. Manage. Rev. **18**(3), 323–348 (2016)

3. Kimberling, E.: Key Findings From the 2015 ERP Report. Panorama Consulting Solutions (2015)
4. Raissi, N.: The impact of ERP application on employees' performance and working process agility in higher education sector. J. Internet Bank. Commer. **22**(S8:026), 1–10 (2017)
5. Hilbert, M., Lopez, P.: The world's technological capacity to store, communicate, and compute information. Science **332**(6025), 60–65 (2011)
6. Zuppo, C.M.: Defining ICT in a boundaryless world: the development of a working hierarchy. Int. J. Manag. Inf. Technol. **4**(3), 13–23 (2012)
7. Groysberg, B.: The seven skills you need to thrive in the C-suite. Harvard Bus. Rev. (2014)
8. Anthopoulous, L., Reddick, C., Giannakidou, I., Mavridis, N.: Why e-government projects fail? An analysis of the Healthcare.gov website. Govern. Inf. Quart. **33**, 161–173 (2016)
9. Chaudhuri, A.: ICT for development: solutions seeking problems & quest. J. Inf. Technol. **27**(4), 326–338 (2012)
10. Edvinsson, L.: IC 21: reflections from 21 years of IC practice and theory. J. Intellect. Capital **14**(1), 163–172 (2013)
11. Khalifa, B.A.: Determinants of information and communication technologies adoption by Tunisian firms. J. Innov. Econ. **20**(2), 151 (2016)
12. Abrahamson, E.: Management fashion. Acad. Manage. Rev. **21**(1), 254–285 (1996)
13. Marr, B.: Management consulting practice on intellectual capital. J. Intellect. Capital **6**(4), 469–473 (2005)
14. Baldwin, C., Heinerth, C., Von Hippel, E.: How user innovations become commercial products: a theoretical investigation and case study. Res. Policy **5**(9), 1291–1313 (2006)
15. Bardon, T.: Quel est le rôle des cabinets de conseil en management dans la dynamique du savoir collectif managérial? Une approche néo-institutionnelle. XVIème Conférence Internationale de Management Stratégique, 1–27 (2007)
16. Asimakou, T.: The knowledge dimension of innovation management. Knowl. Manage. Res. Pract. **7**(1), 82–90 (2009)
17. Akram, K., Siddiqui, S.H., Nawaz, M.A., Ghauri, T.A., Cheema, A.K.H.: Role of knowledge management to bring innovation: an integrated approach. Int. Bull. Bus. Adm. **11**, 121–134 (2011)
18. Barney, J.B., Hesterly, W.S.: Strategic Management and Competitive Advantage. Pearson, London (2012)
19. Florian, B., Julia, H., Kurt, M.: Unveiling the myths of M&A integration: challenging general management and consulting practice. J. Bus. Strategy **36**(2), 16–24 (2015)
20. Ghobakhloo, M., Sadegh Sabouri, M., Sai Hong, T., Zulkifli, N.: Information technology adoption in small and medium-sized enterprises; an appraisal of two decades literature. Interdisc. J. Res. Bus. **1**(7), 53–80 (2011)
21. Ongori, H., Migiro, S.O.: Information and communication technologies adoption in SMEs: literature review. J. Chin. Entrepreneurship **2**(1), 93–104 (2013)
22. Tan, K.S., Chong, S.C., Lin, B., Eze, U.C.: Internet-Based ICT Adoption (2010)
23. Erdiaw-Kwasie, M.O., Khorshed, A., Shahiduzzaman, M.: Bettering corporate social responsibility through empowerment and effective engagement practices: an Australian mining perspective. In: Higgins, C., Hendry, J.R. (eds.), Proceedings of the Twenty-fifth Annual Meeting of the International Association for Business and Society, pp. 140–150 (2014)
24. Colombo, M.G., Giannangeli, S., Grilli, L.: Public subsidies and the employment growth of high-tech start-ups: assessing the impact of selective and automatic support schemes. Ind. Corp. Change **22**, 1273–1314 (2013)
25. Klievink, B., Janssen, M.: Realizing joined-up government. Dynamic capabilities and stage models for transformation. Gov. Inf. Quart. **26**(2), 275–284 (2009)
26. Weerakkody, V., Janssen, M., Dwivedi, Y.K.: Transformational change and business process reengineering (BPR): lessons from the British and Dutch public sector. Gov. Inf. Quart. **28**(3), 320–328 (2011)
27. Weerakkody, V., Dhillon, G.: Moving from E-Government to T-Government: a study of process re-engineering challenges in a UK local authority perspective. Int. J. Electron. Gov. Res. **4**(4), 1–16 (2008)

28. Afshin, A., Babalola, D., Mclean, M., Yu, Z., Ma, W., Chen, C.Y., Arabi, M., Mozaffarian, D.: Information technology and lifestyle: a systematic evaluation of internet and mobile interventions for improving diet, physical activity, obesity, tobacco, and alcohol use. J. Am. Heart Assoc. **31**, e003058 (2016). http://doi.org/10.1161/JAHA.115.003058
29. Szmidt, H.: Coaching Line. Nowe wyzwania dla kadr, menedżerów i dla Ciebie Wydawnictwo Oświatowe FOSZE, Rzeszów, p. 19 (2012)
30. Ghorob, A., Vivas, M.M., De Vore, D., Ngo, V., Bodenheimer, T., Chen, E., Thom, D.H.: The effectiveness of peer health coaching in improving glycemic control among low-income patients with diabetes: protocol for a randomized controlled trial. BMC Public Health, 11–208 (PMCID: PMC3082244) (2011)
31. Chao, C.: Toward Full Participation in Management Consulting Practice. Education + Training **47**(1), 18–30 (2005)
32. Evrard, Y. Pras, B., Roux, E.: Market: Etudes et Recherches en Marketing, Nathan, 3ème Edition (2003)

Organizational Agility and the Complementary Enabling Role of IT and Human Resources: Proposition of a New Framework

Mohamed Amine Marhraoui and Abdellah El Manouar

Abstract Nowadays, companies' environment is characterized by a rapid and continuous change. This includes economic, social, political and environmental aspects. Firms should then be able to sense risks and opportunities in their environments, and to act adequately in a rapid and efficient manner. Changes become thus a main source of sustainable competitive advantage. Organizational agility is a key dynamic capability, which allows the firm to cope with new market orientations, to take advantage of risks and to seize opportunities. The agile characteristics are enabled by a set of facilitators including particularly information technology and human resources. In this work, we explore through our proposed Framework, how IT infrastructure and human resources practices can have a direct and complementary effect through IT acceptance and developed IT skills. We highlight also the role of using and mastering human resources information systems (HRIS) in enhancing organizational agility, which plays an intermediary role for firm's sustainable performance.

Keywords Information technology resources · Human resources practices · HRIS · IT acceptance · IT skills · Organizational agility · Sustainable performance

1 Introduction

The pace of change in firms' environment has increased rapidly in the last ten years. This is driven essentially by digital disruption, new ways of working and mass production.

Indeed, during the last ten years, the global economy has shifted rapidly to a knowledge-based one. This revolution is accelerated by a rapid production of knowledge due to the scientific and technological progress. Also, the immaterial capital has

M. A. Marhraoui (✉) · A. El Manouar
ENSIAS Engineering School, Mohammed V University, Rabat, Morocco
e-mail: mohamed-amine_marhraoui1@um5.ac.ma

A. El Manouar
e-mail: a.elmanouar@um5s.net.ma

© Springer Nature Switzerland AG 2020
Y. Baghdadi et al. (eds.), *ICT for an Inclusive World*,
Lecture Notes in Information Systems and Organisation 35,
https://doi.org/10.1007/978-3-030-34269-2_4

become more important as the natural resources are rare and the information is more abundant thanks to investments in R&D, education, collaboration and innovation. Consequently, the digital era allows producing, reconfiguring and processing large amount of data.

Thus, companies should be aware of these changes and be well prepared to act consequently in order to maintain a sustainable competitive advantage. Organizational agility helps companies to sense rapid changes in their environment and to respond adequately [1]. The capacities, enabling organizational agility, belong to different groups including: process, knowledge management, human resources, organizational structure, innovation and information technology [2].

In this work, we focus on information technologies and human resources as agility providers. This study is original as previous research has focused only on the impact of IT on organizational agility, or on the human side of organizational agility. Through our proposed model, we also aim to focus on complementary effects of using and adopting IT resources on the improvement of organizational agility. We differentiate the HRIS from the other IT resources as we tackle particularly the impact of the use and the adoption of HRIS in comparison to the other IT resources.

Regarding the adoption of IT resources, we've chosen the TAM (Technology Acceptance Model) as it is the most reliable and robust Framework in the literature modeling how IT users perceive systems' usefulness and ease of use, and how these influence the attitude toward the use of IT.

This article is structured as follow. Section 2 is devoted to a literature review presenting human resource practices, information technology resources and their complementary effects (IT acceptance, IT skills). Section 3 describes the proposed Framework and the main hypothesis linking IT acceptance and IT skills to firm's sustainable performance by highlighting the intermediary role of organizational agility. Finally, Sect. 4 provides a brief conclusion of this article and the future research perspectives.

2 Literature Review: Organizational Agility, HR Practices, IT Resources and Their Complementary Effects

2.1 Organizational Agility from a Dynamic Capabilities Perspective

According to (Teece 2007), competitive advantage is not only linked to the acquisition of unique knowledge and skills that are difficult to imitate, but also to dynamic capabilities. These allow the company to continually adapt to its environment and equip itself with the appropriate levers to maintain a competitive advantage [3].

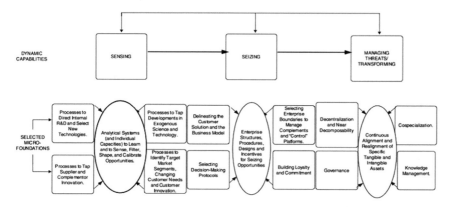

Fig. 1 Dynamic capabilities theory (Teece 2007)

Teece proposes a Framework (Fig. 1) based on three capacities and related micro-foundations:

(1) **Sensing**: it is the ability to quickly detect threats and opportunities. The company provides the means to study the evolution of the market, the internal and external environment and advanced technology through R&D initiatives.

(2) **Seizing**: as detecting opportunities and threats is not sufficient, Teece offers levers to seize them through the second ability.

(3) **Managing threats/transforming**: this last capacity is the continuous alignment of the tangible and intangible assets of the company in order to obtain a sustainable competitive advantage.

Organizational agility is a key dynamic capability of the company. Agile organizations are dynamic and adaptable. Having a loosely coupled structure, they can be competitive in the era of rapid change. These organizations combine harmoniously the characteristics of fluidity and flexibility with a minimum of order, control and predictability [4, 5]. Organizational agility enables the company to maintain competitive leadership by quickly meeting customer expectations and responding to international competition, to fragmented markets and to increasing external cooperation relationships [6]. According to [7], agility is the ability of a company to grow in an environment of continuous and unpredictable change while ensuring high-quality, lower costs and consumer-responsive products.

The two following examples are used to illustrate the agility concept. The 1st example is related to ING bank. In 2015, ING has adopted an agile way of working which consists not only on changing the IT functions but also on forming multi-disciplinary teams, inculcating agile culture and using new hiring/communicating methods [8]. The 2nd example is related to Kodak which was the leading photography film producer in the 80/90. Kodak was bankrupted because it didn't deal with the rise of digital photography. Kodak wasn't open to change and didn't take the adequate decisions in order to adapt to evolving conditions [9].

2.2 HR Practices

From a resource based view of the firm, human resources are a strategic asset [10]. Thus, developing human resource practices is related to employees' mindset and their behaviors.

The employees' mindset, when empowered [11], drives innovation throughout the organization [12]. Employees' behavior is related to resistance or support to change [13]. Resistance to change can be driven by a lack of company's vision of the future, a low motivation among employees and a lack of creativeness when looking for appropriate change strategy [14]. In addition, employees' pro-activity is another desired behavior. It is related to personal initiative [15] and commitment at work [16].

Also, employees should in the current complex and turbulent environment, work on self-development through continuous learning. This is driven by self-determination and motivation [17]. The proactive/innovative mindset and the adequate employees' behaviors require an efficient and adaptable human resource management strategy. This latter includes training and development, performance appraisal/rewarding systems, talent recruitment, job design and employees benefits [18].

2.3 IT Resources

IT resources include the infrastructure related to applications, communications, data management, security and channels [19]. The IT infrastructure offers the capabilities upon which the business processes depend [20]. Moreover, the application infrastructure can be either firm-wide (intranet, electronic mail, customer database …), or local when it is customized for a specific business unit [21]. On one hand, local applications change more regularly and are related to sales processes, support systems or order processing. On the other hand, wide applications change less regularly such as budgeting, accounting, operations management, purchasing and HRIS (human resources information systems) [22].

More particularly, HRIS as defined by (Kovach et al. 1999) [23] allow collecting, maintaining, retrieving and validating pertinent information about organization's human resources and personnel activities. HRIS allow the firm not only to manage administrative functions but also to have strategic advantages as HRIS provide managers with a decision making tool based on the collected data (return on training, turnover rates and costs …) [24]. The HRIS functions contain human resources analysis, strategic integration, knowledge management, planning, personnel development, communication and record/compliance [25] (Fig. 2).

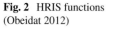

Fig. 2 HRIS functions
(Obeidat 2012)

2.4 HR Complementarities: IT Acceptance and IT Skills

The use of IT resources requires adequate human resources practices in order to adopt and to master available IT infrastructure (and HRIS).

2.4.1 IT Acceptance

The technology acceptance model (TAM) measures how stakeholders perceive and use available information within the organization [26]. The perceived ease of use and perceived usefulness play an intermediary role in their relation between system characteristics and the probability of system use (as a measure of success) (Fig. 3).

This IT acceptance varies according to the culture of the organization [27]. A second update of this model called TAM2 added social influence processes (subjective norm, image) and cognitive instrumental processes (job relevance, output quality and results demonstrability) [28].

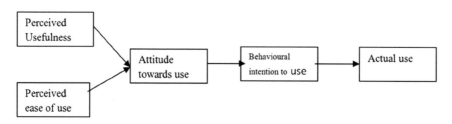

Fig. 3 Technology acceptance model (Davis 1985)

2.4.2 IT Skills

The ability of employees to master IT resources helps the company to deploy information systems quickly. By training and development, firms can build key technical competencies, which are either general or specific [29]. The adoption of new information technologies requires a new set of skills for employees [30]. The IT skills include both traditional technical skills related to infrastructure/IT management; and new skills related to IT innovative hardware (data centers, IoT, data storage), to the capability to manage flexible applications and to the need for standardization [31].

3 The Conceptual Framework

3.1 Framework Description

The proposed Framework (Fig. 4) describes how companies which invest in IT resources and HR practices can be more agile. They can achieve this goal by having employees who are able to adopt IT applications more rapidly (IT acceptance), and can easily use new IT tools and applications (IT skills). The Framework states also that these agile companies are more competitive.

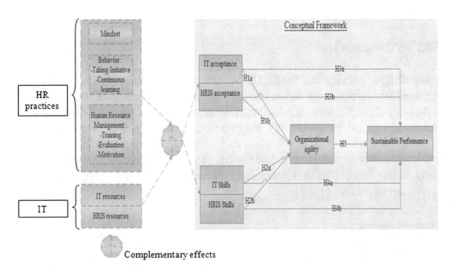

Fig. 4 Our proposed framework

Table 1 Our proposed Framework hypothesis description

Hypothesis	Description
H1a	IT acceptance have a positive impact on organizational agility
H1b	The more employees adopt HRIS the more the firm is agile
H2a	Firms which develop their employees' IT skills are more agile
H2b	The more employees master HRIS the more the firm is agile
H3a	IT acceptance have a positive impact on firm's performance
H3b	The more employees adopt HRIS the more the firm is performing
H4a	Firms which develop their employees' IT skills are more performing
H4b	The more employees master HRIS the more the firm is performing
H5	The more the firm is agile the more it is performing

3.2 Main Hypothesis

Table 1 describes the main hypothesis of our proposed Framework.

H1a: IT acceptance has a positive impact on organizational agility

The study conducted by (Zain et al. 2004) confirms that IT acceptance have a positive impact on organizational agility [32]. Indeed, the study is based on the technology acceptance model (TAM) [18] that measures how stakeholders perceive and use the available information within the organization. This IT acceptance depends on the organization culture, top management support and HR involvement/experience. These latter parameters influence positively the firm's organizational agility. Another study conducted by (Almahamid 2013) [33] has found that IT acceptance (especially e-government systems acceptance) drives positively firm's agile capabilities. It includes responsiveness, competency, flexibility and speed.

H1b: The more employees adopt HRIS the more the firm is agile

HRIS adoption can be influenced by three groups of factors: organizational (top management support, organizational size), technology readiness and environmental (competitors, regulations and social development) [34]. The use of HRIS can help the company to be more agile. Indeed, HRIS implementation evolves through three phases: publication of information, automation of transactions and finally a change in human resource management inside the company so as to deal with change [35].

H2a: Firms which develop their employees' IT skills are more agile

The ability of employees to acquire and develop new IT skills allows the firm to enhance its organizational agility [36]. Moreover, employees when trained on existing applications and up-to-date technologies are well prepared to change in work conditions and are able to collaborate more effectively [37].

H2b: The more employees master HRIS the more the firm is agile

HR professionals rely on HRIS in order to gather accurate and up-to-date information about human capital [38]. This allows the HR department to deal with social, organizational and rapidly evolving technologies. Thus, the firm is more agile regarding its environment.

H3a: IT acceptance have a positive impact on firm's performance

The concept of IT acceptance is inspired from the theory of innovation diffusion. Indeed, a technological innovation starts with an invention before a large-scale use [39]. Information technology acceptance enhances performance either on the individual or on the organizational level [40]. On the individual level, the IT user satisfaction and the actual use of systems have a positive impact on individual performance and productivity [40]. On the organizational level, the use of IT, especially decision support systems, is associated to higher organizational performance [41].

H3b: The more employees adopt HRIS the more the firm is performing

The acceptance of HRIS by employees can enhance their development and hence firm's performance. A survey conducted by (Ball, 2001) confirms that small organizations are less likely to use HRIS, and focus only on the administrative part rather than analytical/strategic modules [42]. The barriers of HRIS adoption include inadequate knowledge, lacks of managers' commitment, the organization culture and the non-perception of HRIS advantages [43]. However, HRIS, when adopted, can provide companies with valuable information which can help for strategic decision making [23].

H4a: Firms which develop their employees' IT skills are more performing

T.A. Byrd has studied this question in detail, especially for employees working in the IT department. Indeed, he argues that these employees should master, in addition to the technical IT skills, the soft skills including organizational, functional and managerial skills [44]. Moreover, from a resource-based view of the firm, (Gautam et al. 2005) confirms that IT technical skills can provide the company with a competitive advantage if knowledge is shared across business and support units [45].

H4b: The more employees master HRIS the more the firm is performing

Technical training on human resources information systems (HRIS) is needed in order to allow managers to acquire the required knowledge and to develop their HRIS skills [46]. Consequently, HR information systems, when mastered, allow collecting reliable/useful data, decreasing paperwork, reducing cost per hire and making accurate decisions on employees' raises/promotions/career management [34]. A survey conducted by [47], confirms that companies, where employees master HRIS, can attain more considerably a sustainable competitive advantage [46].

H5: The more the firm is agile the more it is performing

Agile firms can respond effectively to unexpected changes, increase execution speed and optimize the performance of the supply chain [48]. Moreover, on the organizational level, an agile company identifies market needs, opportunities for improvement of its products and implements the necessary actions to seize these opportunities in order to be more effective. Also, as stakeholders' requirements of sustainability change overtime, agile capabilities are needed. Agile companies are thus more performing on the economic, social and environmental levels. Indeed, on the economic level, agile capabilities help companies to maximize the value delivered to customers. The design and the implementation of products can adapt easily to changing customers' expectations [49]. In addition, on the social level, agile companies share easily information across processes and enhance thus their social and relational capital [50]. Finally, on the environmental level, agility allows companies to adapt to environmental changes. Thus, they can comply easily with environmental regulation [51].

4 Conclusion and Perspectives

In this paper, we have focused on an unexplored area, which is related to IT acceptance and developed IT skills as a complementary effect of IT infrastructures and human resources practices.

We proposed a new model linking the adoption/mastery of IT resources and firm's agility. We supposed also that agility has a positive effect on firm's sustainable performance.

As this paper describes an ongoing project, future research will focus on verifying the different hypothesis through a quantitative study. As we want to focus on the Moroccan context of using IT, we will use a survey in order to collect data from managers in different companies or in the same company through time. We will adopt a regression analysis, which will allow verifying the relationships between the constructs of our model. Another perspective will be to study the feedback effect of organizational agility on the companies' HR practices and IT infrastructure.

References

1. Sambamurthy, V., Bharadwaj, A., Grover, V.: Shaping agility through digital options: reconceptualizing the role of information technology in contemporary firms. MIS Q. **27**(2), 237–263 (2003)
2. Marhraoui, M.A., El Manouar, A.: IT-enabled organizational agility-proposition of a new Framework. J. Theor. Appl. Inf. Technol. **95**(20), 5431–5442 (2017)
3. Teece, D.J.: Explicating dynamic capabilities: the nature and microfoundations of (sustainable) enterprise performance. Strateg. Manage. J. **28**(13), 1319–1350 (2007)

4. Dyer, L., Shafer, R.: Dynamic Organizations: Achieving Marketplace and Organizational Agility with People, (CAHRS Working Paper 03-04). Cornell University, School of Industrial and Labor Relations, Center for Advanced Human Resource Studies, Ithaca, NY (2003)
5. Wouter, A., De Smet, A., Weerda, K.: Agility: It Rhymes with Stability McKinsey Q. (2015)
6. Charbonnier, A.: L'agilité organisationnelle: un nouveau défi pour la GRH, Congrès de l'AGRH (2006)
7. Breu, K., Christopher, J.H., Strathern, M., Bridger, D.: Workforce agility: the new employee strategy for the knowledge economy. J. Inf. Technol. **17**(1), 21–31 (2002)
8. Jacobs, P., Schlatmann, B.: ING's agile transformation. McKinsey Q. (2017)
9. Mui, C.: How Kodak Failed, Forbes (2012)
10. Dunford, B.B., Snell, S.A., Wright, P.M.: Human Resources and the Resource Based View of the Firm (CAHRS Working Paper #01-03). Cornell University, School of Industrial and Labor Relations, Center for Advanced Human Resource Studies, Ithaca, NY (2001). http://digitalcommons.ilr.cornell.edu/cahrswp/66
11. Boudrias, J.S., Gaudreau, P., Savoie, A., Morin, A.J.: Employee empowerment: from managerial practices to employees' behavioral empowerment. Leadersh. Organ. Dev. J. **30**(7), 625–638 (2009)
12. Jung, D.D., Wu, A., Chow, C.W.: Towards understanding the direct and indirect effects of CEOs' transformational leadership on firm innovation. Leadersh. Q. **19**(5), 582–594 (2008)
13. Shin, J., Taylor, M.S., Seo, M.-G.: Resources for change: the relationships of organizational inducements and psychological resilience to employees' attitudes and behaviors toward organizational change. Acad. Manage. J. **55**(3), 727–748 (2012)
14. Pardo del Val, M., Martínez Fuentes, C.: Resistance to change: a literature review and empirical study. Manage. Decis. **41**(2), 148–55 (2003)
15. Frese, M., Fay, D., Hilburger, T., et al.: The concept of personal initiative: operationalization, reliability and validity in two German samples. J. Occup. Organ. Psychol. **70**(2), 139–161 (1997)
16. Den Hartog, D.N., Belschak, F.D.: Personal initiative, commitment and affect at work. J. Occup. Organ. Psychol. **80**(4), 601–622 (2007)
17. London, M., Smither, J.W.: Empowered self-development and continuous learning. Human Resour. Manage. **38**(1), 3–15 (1999)
18. Pauwe, J., Boon, C., Collings, D.G., Wood, G.: Strategic HRM: a critical review. In: Human Resource Management: A Critical Approach, pp. 38–54 (2009)
19. Weill, P., Subramani, M., Broadbent, M.: IT Infrastructure for Strategic Agility (2002)
20. McKay, D.T., Brockway, D.W.: Building IT Infrastructure for the 1990 s. Stage by Stage, vol. 9, vol. 3, pp. 1–11 (1989)
21. Weill, P., Vitale, M.: What IT infrastructure capabilities are needed to implement e-business models? MIS Q. **1**(1), 17 (2002)
22. Weill, P., Broadbent, M.: Leveraging the New Infrastructure: How Market Leaders Capitalize on Information Technology. Harvard Business Press (1998)
23. Kovach, K.A., Cathcart Jr., C.E.: Human resource information systems (HRIS): providing business with rapid data access, information exchange and strategic advantage. Public Pers. Manage. **28**(2), 275–282 (1999)
24. Kovach, K.A., Hughes, A.A., Fagan, P., Maggitti, P.G.: Administrative and strategic advantages of HRIS. Employ. Relat. Today **29**(2), 43–48 (2002)
25. Obeidat, B.Y.: The relationship between human resource information system (HRIS) functions and human resource management (HRM) functionalities. J. Manage. Res. **4**(4), 192–211 (2012)
26. Davis, F.D.: A Technology Acceptance Model for Empirically Testing New End-user Information Systems: Theory and Results (Doctoral dissertation, Massachusetts Institute of Technology) (1985)
27. Gefen, D., Straub, D.W.: Gender differences in the perception and use of e-mail: an extension to the technology acceptance model. MIS Q., 389–400 (1997)
28. Venkatesh, V., Davis, F.D.: A theoretical extension of the technology acceptance model: four longitudinal field studies. Manage. Sci. **46**(2), 186–204 (2000)

29. Dyer, L., Shafer, R.A.: From human resource strategy to organizational effectiveness: lessons from research on organizational agility. In: CAHRS Working Paper Series, 125 (1998)
30. Bartel, A., Ichniowski, C., Shaw, K.: How does information technology affect productivity? Plant-level comparisons of product innovation, process improvement, and worker skills. Q. J. Econ. **122**(4), 1721–1758 (2007)
31. IDC Trends 2020: Main Trends for ICT and Their Implications for e-leadership Skills, August 2014
32. Zain, M., Rose, R.C., Abdullah, I., Masrom, M.: The relationship between information technology acceptance and organizational agility in Malaysia. Inf. Manage. **42**(6), 829–839 (2005)
33. Almahamid, S.M.: E-government system acceptance and organizational agility: theoretical framework and research agendas. Int. J. Inf. Bus. Manage. **5**(1) (2013)
34. Beadles, I.I., Aston, N., Lowery, C.M., Johns, K.: The impact of human resource information systems: an exploratory study in the public sector. Commun. IIMA **5**(4), 6 (2005)
35. Lengnick-Hall, M.L., Moritz, S.: The impact of e-HR on the human resource management function. J. Labor Res. **24**(3), 365–379 (2003)
36. Tallon, P.P.: Inside the adaptive enterprise: an information technology capabilities perspective on business process agility. Inf. Technol. Manage. **9**(1), 21–36 (2008)
37. Powell, T.C., Dent-Micallef, A.: Information technology as competitive advantage: the role of human, business, and technology resources. Strateg. Manage. J., pp. 375–405 (1997)
38. Hendrickson, A.R.: Human resource information systems: backbone technology of contemporary human resources. J. Labor Res. **24**(3), 382–394 (2003)
39. Dillon, A., Morris, M.G.: User acceptance of new information technology: theories and models. In: Annual Review of Information Science and Technology. Information Today, Medford, NJ (1996)
40. Igbaria, M., Tan, M.: The consequences of information technology acceptance on subsequent individual performance. Inf. Manage. **32**(3), 113–121 (1997)
41. Devaraj, S., Kohli, R.: Performance impacts of information technology: is actual usage the missing link? Manage. Sci. **49**(3), 273–289 (2003)
42. Ball, K.S.: The use of human resource information systems: a survey. Pers. Rev. **30**(6), 677–693 (2001)
43. Ngai, E.W.T., Wat, F.K.T.: Human resource information systems: a review and empirical analysis. Pers. Rev. **35**(3), 297–314 (2006)
44. Byrd, T.A., Lewis, B.R., Turner, D.E.: The impact of IT personnel skills on IS infrastructure and competitive IS. Inf. Resour. Manage. J. **17**(2), 38 (2004)
45. Ray, G., Muhanna, W.A., Barney, J.B.: Information technology and the performance of the customer service process: a resource-based analysis. MIS Q., 625–652 (2005)
46. De Sanctis, G.: Human resource information systems: a current assessment. MIS Q., 15–27 (1986)
47. Hannon, J., Jelf, G., Brandes, D.: Human resource information systems: operational issues and strategic considerations in a global environment. Int. J. Human Resour. Manage. **7**(1), 245–269 (1996)
48. Baskerville, R. (ed.): Business Agility and Information Technology Diffusion: IFIP TC8 WG 8.6 International Working Conference, 8–11 May 2005, Atlanta, Georgia, USA, vol. 180. Springer Science & Business Media (2005)
49. Kapoor, V., van Solingen, R.: The Responsive Enterprise, White Paper. Prowareness (2016)
50. Tarafdar, M., Qrunfleh, S.: Agile supply chain strategy and supply chain performance: complementary roles of supply chain practices and information systems capability for agility. Int. J. Prod. Res. **55**(4), 925–938 (2017)
51. Melville, N.P.: Information systems innovation for environmental sustainability. MIS Q. **34**(1), 1–21 (2010)

Creating Shared Value Through Information Technologies

Abdellah El Manouar and Wail El Hilali

Abstract Shared Value is a concept that incites business corporations to invest in solving social and societal needs while seeking to increase their revenues. The concept is based on finding a win-win situation that will create a value for both society and economy, hence the term of "shared value". This paper is an attempt to revisit this business concept. It reviews its definition, the motivation behind adopting it, and what makes it different from corporate social responsibility and sustainability. Further, it summarizes three ways to create shared value and discusses how information technologies (IT) could bring a contribution to create and capture this kind of value. The paper introduces a framework that summarizes and shows the necessary steps to create a shared value through IT.

Keywords Shared value · Information technologies · Social and societal needs

1 Introduction

Shared value is one of those feel-good and attractive words that are used a lot nowadays in situations relating business to society. This concept seeks to drive companies to prioritise solving social and societal problems while still doing business [1]. Betting on shared value is a business strategy that companies craft in order to achieve a competitive advantage through social impacts [2].

Identifying and targeting social and societal needs could give birth to new opportunities that companies should seize in order to create new markets and capture more value. Novartis for example saw rural India as a shared value opportunity. The pharmaceutical giant invested in both training health-care providers and equipping local clinics in order to get access to a new potential market [3].

A. El Manouar · W. El Hilali (✉)
Mohammed V University, Rabat, Morocco

A. El Manouar
e-mail: a.elmanouar@um5s.net.ma

© Springer Nature Switzerland AG 2020   67
Y. Baghdadi et al. (eds.), *ICT for an Inclusive World*,
Lecture Notes in Information Systems and Organisation 35,
https://doi.org/10.1007/978-3-030-34269-2_5

Some companies saw it as an opportunity to lower their costs. Johnson & Johnson for example [4] had, as a return, $2.7 for each dollar invested on health-care programmes, reducing its global bill of its employees' health-cares by $250 million.

Other businesses took the creation of shared value a way to shine their brand image. Incorporating social dimensions into the value proposition enables differentiation from the competitors. Switching from thinking 'product' to 'purpose' helped some companies to redefine their positioning. Nestlé for example, by adopting this way of thinking, has positioned itself as a "Nutrition" company instead of a "Food and beverage" company [5]. In a similar vein, Nike started to define itself as a "Health and wellness" company instead of a "Footwear" business.

2   The Concept of Shared Value

The business concept of shared value was introduced first in 2007 [6]. A clear definition of this philosophy appeared in 2011, defined it as "policies and operating practices that enhance the competitiveness of a company while simultaneously advancing the economic and social condition in the communities in which it operates" [7]. Shared value is a state of mind that looks for a win-win situation between the two stakeholders. It differs from corporate social responsibility (CSR) and sustainability concepts that try to identify and handle a win-lose or a lose-lose situation created by the neoclassical way of doing business in a capitalism system.

The literature on shared value considers it as a social innovation [8]. Adopting this concept has given birth to new business models such as "Social freemium" and "buy one give one" [9].

3   Shared Value: Literature Review

Numerous researches have been done around the concept of shared value. Reference [10] linked the creation of shared value to five elements that are social purpose, a defined social need, measurement, the right innovation structure, and co-creation with external stakeholders. Others discussed the importance of adopting new business models in order to create and capture a shared value [11]. The importance of measurement in creating shared value was also highlighted in the report [12].

On the other hand, Ref. [13] published a critical review of this concept, judging it to be unoriginal, naïve, ignoring the tensions between social and economic goals and based on a narrow conception of the role of business in society.

This paper comes to revisit the concept and tries to discuss how to deliver it in the digital era, fully benefiting from the possibilities that IT offers nowadays.

Philanthropy
- Donations to worthy social causes
- Volunteering

Corporate social responsibility
- Compliance with community standards
- Good corporate citizenships

Sustainability
- Equilibrium between Economy, society and environment

Shared value
- Integrating societal improvement into economic value creation itself
- Driving social improvement with a business model

Fig. 1 The role of business in society: evolving approaches, adapted from [5]

4 Shared Value, Corporate Social Responsibility and Sustainability

As stated in the first paragraph, Shared Value, CSR and Sustainability are different concepts that deal, more or less, with the same issues. CSR was defined by the Commission of the European Communities as "a concept whereby companies integrate social and environmental concerns in their business operations and in their interaction with their stakeholders on a voluntary basis" [14]. Sustainability however is more about finding a sort of equilibrium between three dimensions, which are economy, society and environment while taking into consideration the prosperity and the well-being of future generations [15]. Mark Kramer associates shared value creation with seizing new business opportunities that "create new markets, improve profitability and strengthen competitive positioning" [16].

The role of business in society has evolved overtime (see Fig. 1), from a cost centre to a profit centre:

5 Creating Shared Value

Reference [7] introduces three different and distinct ways to create shared value. These roads could be followed in both advanced and developing economies. The following section is a try to analyse the three ways to create a shared value supported by the use of IT.

5.1 Reconceiving Products and Markets Through IT

To answer unmet needs, products and markets should be reconceived and redesigned. Understanding customers' societal benefits and harms will be the starting point for any change or adaptation. We believe that IT could play a major role at this stage.

Social media solutions represent a gold mine of information to gather. Understanding potential customers' needs has never been as easier as today. Companies should exploit this opportunity in order to fill any gap.

Furthermore, IT has given birth to new Internet Based Service companies that pioneered the emergence of sharing economy, creating by that a shared value. Uber for example, has succeeded in opening opportunities for people to generate income in more than 250 cities [17] using underutilized resources.

Cisco, the giant network service provider has used IT to create new markets. By investing a lot in the "Networking Academy" program based on an e-learning solution, the company has helped to train more than four million students worldwide [18]. On one hand, the graduated talents have accessed to new and better jobs improving by that their living standards. On the other hand, Cisco succeeded in creating a pool of loyal and talented workforces that will, for sure, prefer to adopt Cisco solutions and products. Cisco has created a win-win situation, giving birth to a new business opportunity that could lead to a sustainable growth, which should be the ultimate quest of every company [19]. Cisco succeeded in integrating a social dimension into its core business.

To sum up, in the two different cases, IT has played a major role in both the conception of the product and the creation of new markets.

5.2   Redefining Productivity in the Value Chain Through IT

The value chain is the set of activities that a given company should perform in order to deliver a product or a service [20]. The efficiency in the value chain is reliant on reducing externalities such as pollution, which will decrease the aggregate costs regarding the firm and the society. Redefining the value chain could lead in this case to the creation of a shared value.

Information technology has for sure its word to say in this case. The evolution of IT solutions has allowed companies to implement many concepts in order to be more efficient and competitive in the way they handle their supply chains. The Just-in-time/Lean approach [21] for example has never been as affordable as today thanks to IT.

Furthermore, IT could play a major role in creating a shared value by reducing its own carbon footprints. Adopting a green IT approach could reduce the consumption of energy throughout the value chain [22].

5.3   Enable Local Cluster Development Through IT

No firm could create and deliver value without the involvement of external stake-holders. Reference [7] argues that productivity and innovation are strongly influenced by supporting companies, such as suppliers. Deficiencies in any member of the influencing stakeholders could impact the efficiency of the company.

IT could be a way to accompany the improvement of efficiency of suppliers. Sharing of information, knowledge and skills has been trivialized thanks to IT.

Educating customers also could be doable through some massive open online course (MOOC) websites. Lack of education limits the demand for products and leads to environmental degradation, unhealthy workers, and high security costs [7].

6   Framework for Creating Shared Value Based on IT

Following the three ways discussed in part 5 from an IT perspective, we can conclude that creating shared value starts by discovering and knowing social needs of communities. We agree with [10] that it is a key step and we believe that collecting data (through social media, Big data…) and communicating effectively with the community is the first thing to do. We refer to this step as "Perception".

Accessing and storing data is no longer a constraint. Reference [23] sees that companies are faced with a "data deluge" in the digital era. Data should be turned into strategic assets to be used over time. With the possibilities that IT offer (through big data tools for example), companies are allowed nowadays to "unlock new sources of value" by analysing and treating the unstructured data collected. New kind of analysis and predictions are now possible thanks to the advance of IT. Analysis is the second step in our framework.

Data-driven decision-making is the next step in our framework. We distinguish between internal and external actions to be adopted, linked to IT, and that could lead to create a shared value:

- Internal actions could concern either the value chain or the human capital. Exploiting the potential of IT could lead to more efficiency in the value chain, reducing by that some negative externalities such as pollution. IT solutions could also improve the wellbeing of workforces by providing them online training sessions and open online courses to improve their skills.
- External actions concern activities that will improve the wellbeing of communities. The advance of IT has given citizens a possibility to earn an income through sharing economy solutions. Companies could also sponsor some MOOC solutions in order to promote education, creating by that future potential customers.

Bellow our framework that summarizes the necessary steps to deliver shared value through IT (Fig. 2).

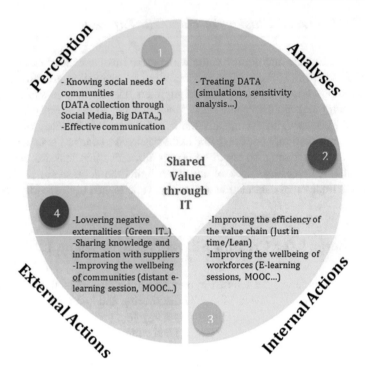

Fig. 2 The necessary steps to create shared value through IT

7 A Case Study: Creating Shared Value by a Telecom Operator Through IT

The following is an application of the framework explained in the previous paragraph in the telecom context. In fact, in an industry characterized by a fierce competition, finding a way to shine and reinforce the brand image becomes a must that could lead to a competitive advantage. Creating shared value vis-à-vis customers might be how to achieve the Holy Grail of strategic competitiveness.

As affirmed, creating shared value through IT starts by knowing and understanding exactly the social needs of customers. Operators have access to tremendous volume of data, daily generated by clients. Analyzing these unstructured data through Big Data tools for example should give Telcos real information about social and societal needs of the community.

Let's focus on the educational needs of society. Operators could know exactly the educational websites and on-line encyclopedias that are accessed the most by students. Telcos could adopt a courageous action by making the access to these websites free of charge for students, from their mobile phones. This will not just shine the brand image of the operator as a sponsor of education; it will also drive

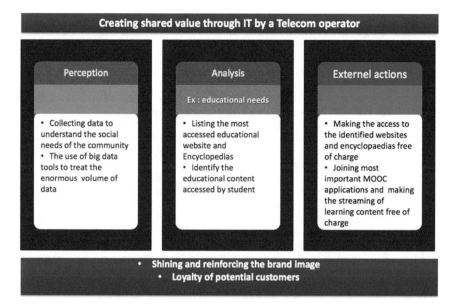

Fig. 3 Creating shared value through IT: case of a telecom operator

both students and parents to transfer their phone subscriptions to the operator. A win-win situation and a shared value are created.

Operators could also join some of the most well known and most used MOOC solutions such as Coursera and EdX in order to make the streaming of the learning videos free. Sponsoring education will also give birth to a new generation of loyal customers, which will increase both the market share and the revenue of the operator (Fig. 3).

8 Conclusion

Shared value is a state of mind that should be incorporated into the business decision-making process of every corporation. Companies should see the solving of social and societal needs a pool of new opportunities to seize instead of cost centers. Shared value comes to widen the "invisible hands" concept of Adam Smith [24] by impacting voluntarily the society.

In this article, we discussed the concept of shared value and we tried to analyse the contribution of IT in spreading out this positive win-win mind-set. We proposed after a framework to adopt in order to create shared value using IT.

This framework has a limitation as not all the social needs could be addressed through IT. But if it is the case, IT will help for sure in the creation of a shared value.

References

1. Cunningham, J., Harney, B.: Strategy and Strategists. OUP Oxford, Oxford, UK (2012)
2. INSEAD Knowledge: https://knowledge.insead.edu/strategy/converting-social-impact-into-competitive-advantage-5105
3. Better Ways of Doing Business: Creating Shared Value. https://www.theguardian.com/sustainable-business/blog/creating-shared-value-social-progress-profit
4. Lundström, A., Zhou, C.: Rethinking social entrepreneurship and social enterprises: a three-dimensional perspective. In: Lundström, A., Zhou, C., von Friedrichs, Y., Sundin, E. (eds.) Social Entrepreneurship: Leveraging Economic, Political, and Cultural Dimensions, pp. 71–89. Springer International Publishing, Cham (2014)
5. Harvard Business Review. http://www.hbs.edu/faculty/Publication%20Files/20130523%20-%20FSG%20Shared%20Value%20Leadership%20Summit%20-%20MEP%20Keynote%20-%20FINAL%20FINAL_d18ef7ea-e736-4da0-b3b4-e9eac61b87a8.pdf
6. Kramer, M.R., Porter, M.E.: Strategy and society: the link between competitive advantage and corporate social responsibility. Harvard Bus. Rev. **84**(12), 78–92 (2006)
7. Kramer, M.R., Porter, M.: Creating shared value. Harvard Bus. Rev. **89**(1/2), 62–77 (2011)
8. Michelini, L.: Innovation for social change. In: Social Innovation and New Business Models: Creating Shared Value in Low-Income Markets, pp. 1–18. Springer, Heidelberg (2012)
9. Lüdeke-Freund, F., Massa, L., Nancy, N., Brent, A., Musango, J.: Business Models for Shared Value. University of Cape Town, South Africa (2017)
10. Pfitzer, M., Bockstette, V., Stamp, M.: Innovating for shared value. Harvard Bus. Rev. **91**(9), 100–107 (2013)
11. Michelini, L., Fiorentino, D.: New business models for creating shared value. Soc. Responsib. J. **8**(4), 561–577 (2012)
12. Harvard Business Review. https://www.hbs.edu/faculty/Publication%20Files/%20Measuring_Shared_Value_57032487%20-9e5c-46a1-9bd8-90bd7f1f9cef.pdf
13. Crane, A., Palazzo, G., Spence, L.J., Matten, D.: Contesting the Value of "Creating Shared Value". University of California, Berkeley, vol. 56, no. 2 (2014)
14. Commission of the European Communities. https://ec.europa.eu/europeaid/sites/devco/files/communication-corporate-social-responsibility-sustainable-development-com2002347-20020702_en.pdf
15. Martinet, V.: Economic Theory and Sustainable Development: What Can We Preserve for Future Generations?, 1st edn. Routledge, Oxon (2012)
16. FSG Creating Shared Value Blog. https://Creation shared value through IT-ICTO2018 Article16.docx
17. Lacy, P., Rutqvist, J.: Waste to Wealth: The Circular Economy Advantage, 1st edn. Palgrave Macmillan, UK (2016)
18. FSG. https://sharedvalue.org/examples/networking-academy-creating-clusters-technological-ly-advanced-workers-key-markets-worldwide
19. Zenger, T.: Beyond Competitive Advantage: How to Solve the Puzzle of Sustaining Growth While Creating Value. Harvard Business Review Press, USA (2016)
20. Porter, M.E.: Competitive Advantage: Creating and Sustaining Superior Performance, Illustrated edn. Free Press, USA (2004)
21. Ward, P., Zhou, H.: Impact of information technology integration and lean/just-in-time practices on lead-time performance. Decis. Sci. **37**(2), 177–203 (2006)
22. Tomlinson, B.: Greening Through IT. MIT Press, Massachusetts (2012)
23. Rogers, D.L.: The Digital Transformation Playbook: Rethink Your Business for the Digital Age. Columbia University Press, New York (2016)
24. Smith, A.: The Invisible Hand. Penguin Group USA, USA (2009)

Web Platform and Corporate Welfare: An Inclusive Organizational Solution

Sabrina Bonomi, Nicola Piccinelli, Cecilia Rossignoli
and Francesca Ricciardi

Abstract The latest economic trend necessitates a reconsideration of welfare as a place where public authorities and private companies collaborate to satisfy social needs, that are growing in quantities and varieties. Enterprises have a pivotal role in this new welfare system, the so-called "Second Welfare", by adopting for their workers a win-win model that combines their corporate social responsibility with a welfare society. By corporate welfare, indeed, the Government can meet citizens' needs more efficiently and effectively, people can increase their well-being and companies can improve performances and productivity. Firstly, those practices seemed a privilege for bigger companies but recently also workers of smaller companies have been included. At this aim, a case of a welfare platform created by an Italian non-profit organization is presented. ICT has a fundamental role to coordinate the supply of corporate welfare services and include SMEs, allowing them to catch opportunities that otherwise would be a prerogative of big ones.

Keywords Corporate welfare · Web platform · Information systems · Collaborative innovation · Organizational change · Better life

S. Bonomi (✉)
eCampus University, via Isimbardi 10, 22060 Novedrate, CO, Italy
e-mail: sabrina.bonomi@uniecampus.it

N. Piccinelli
Garda vita e BCC del Garda, Montichiari, BS, Italy
e-mail: nicola.piccinelli@garda.bcc.it

C. Rossignoli
University of Verona, via dell'Artigliere, 8, 37139 Verona, Italy
e-mail: cecilia.rossignoli@univr.it

F. Ricciardi
University of Turin, via Giuseppe Verdi, 8, 10124 Turin, Italy
e-mail: francesca.ricciardi@unito.it

© Springer Nature Switzerland AG 2020
Y. Baghdadi et al. (eds.), *ICT for an Inclusive World*,
Lecture Notes in Information Systems and Organisation 35,
https://doi.org/10.1007/978-3-030-34269-2_6

1 Introduction

Over the last few decades, Italy has progressively shifted from a welfare model handled in complete autonomy from the Government to a welfare community [1]. The collaboration between public authorities and private subjects, indeed, was necessary to provide answers to this community in order to satisfy social needs that are increasing in quantities and varieties. This process originated a new welfare model, in which companies fulfil an important role. Due to their economic and organizational abilities, they adopt social and environmental sustainability policies, in Corporate Social Responsibility (CSR) logic, for example the corporate welfare (CW) model [2, 3]. CW regards services provided by a company to its employees in order to improve both their working conditions and their personal lives, by offering several options to sustain their family income, safeguarding health, parenthood, studies and free time, etc. that welfare state is not able to guarantee anymore [4]. CW is an important tool for enterprises, it strengthens a bond between companies and employees, allowing them to appeal and to keep talented people. CW also provides considerable tax benefits and it is incentivized by law and contracts. Nonetheless, CW cannot be improvised; it requires study, attention, time, and it is difficult to realize, especially for small companies [5, 6]. CW providers can be helpful. They are enterprises that support others in all phases of design, implementation, and monitoring of welfare plans. In Italy, welfare plans had a considerable growth only in the last two years, thanks to the reduction of taxes introduced by the Stability Law (S.L.) in 2016 [7] and confirmed by the one in 2017 [8], despite welfare plans allowing companies to solidify their specific competitive advantages [9]. Furthermore, technology 4.0., encouraged by the Italian government too, is spreading through all industrial sectors as well as the overall vision of the operators in health services and those supporting welfare more generally. In particular, non-profit organizations, more and more involved in social and health area, due to the government financial difficulties, thanks to information and communication technologies (ICT), compete with organizations traditionally outside their range of expertise. CW, indeed, arises from negotiation with unions and it is a prerogative of big companies. Recently, also small and medium enterprises (SMEs) can access to welfare, since it is possible to introduce it as a liberality [7].

The purpose of this work is to understand if and how an ICT platform, especially if offered by non-profit organizations, can be helpful to include more people, even workers of SMEs, in CW. After a literature review about the welfare community and Italian context, organizational change, and web platforms, a case study is presented. The so-called *"Creawelfare"* is a platform for CW, created by a network of Mutual aid societies and a group of local cooperative banks, in order to meet the welfare needs including, in particular, their employees, young people, and SMEs. Finally, the conclusions of authors and future developments are presented.

2 Theoretical Background

2.1 The Italian "Second Welfare"

The recent relevant social and economic changes increased and diversified social needs, thus the traditional organization of welfare shook. Several causes, like globalization and economic crisis, demographic drop and the increasing in the average life of the population, made welfare unsustainable for many States, unable to provide for the community needs [1, 10]. Therefore, these States, Italy included, had to transform their welfare state model into a welfare society one [11], providing necessary services to the community through collaboration between public administration (PA) and private companies. Italian deficit increased and the cut of public expenditure was necessary despite heavy taxation. Hence, a paradox has been reached: public system, conceived to pursue the realization of social equity, determined instead an increase of inequalities. Italian people, indeed, spend 34 billion euros for their health, using private services, that are on the rise. Most of the expenses (87%) are "out of pocket" [1, 12], i.e. took place without help of mutual aid society or additional health care [13]. The so-called "second welfare" [1] aims to use rationally and efficiently resources, involving new players (business, private insurance, banking foundations, associations and local authorities etc.), necessary to address more and more complicated needs, in a highly constrained public finance context and in a political climate of resistance to increased fiscal pressure [14]. The term originates from two reasons: a temporal reason, since it is a successive model to be integrated into the traditional welfare state, and a functional one, since it is added to the schemes of the former to break the gap and experiment with new organizational, managerial and financial models [14].

2.2 The Evolution of Italian Corporate Welfare

The 2009 crisis and reduction of welfare stimulated many enterprises to, compensate, fostering their workers' well-being, in order to increase their work performance and, therefore, business productivity [15]. CW is the set of actions that employers shall put in place for its workers and their families, from health care assistance to payments in kind [16]. The origin of CW logic actually dates back to the mid-nineteenth century, with the development of industrialization and urbanization, when mutual aid societies (MAS) were born, and their members could receive free care in case of illness, and when industrial owners worked to build houses and structures for their workers [17] next to factories. While these actions were considered in a paternalistic view, now they are part of corporate contracts [4], and a real collective "welfare society". In the 1970s, CW slowed down due to new welfare reforms and the establishment of National Health Service. The reasons why this topic has become very topical, include the crisis as mentioned above and the social and demographic changes, especially the ageing population and the increase in working women [18].

Initially, only large companies embraced CW, simply based on the employer's will. In recent years, even SMEs began to implement CW [17], mainly due to the provisions of the Stabilization Act in 2016 [7] and later extended by the one in 2017 [8]. Articles 51 and 100 of TUIR [19, 20], provided strong incentives for SMEs to support workers and their families. Innovations mainly concern four aspects: the elimination of the requirement of volunteering in the provision of welfare services; the deduction for performance premiums; the extension of facilities to new services; the use of vouchers. CW measures can differ depending on the source of regulation. If CW initiative is promoted through a direct relationship between enterprise and workers (or some categories of them), it is named "one-sidedness". If it is promoted through brokering by trade unions, is called "bilateral". Benefits will not be taxed even if they are provided after bargaining, as long as they are listed in TUIR [20] (i.e. education, teaching, recreation, social and health care or worship) and have a clear and immediate economic savings on performance premiums [21]. "Performance premium" is the amount of money, or alternatively, the set of welfare services provided to a worker for increasing performance (productivity, efficiency, quality of work, etc.), i.e. forms of salary flexibility linked to business performance indicators [15, 21, 22]. Workers may freely choose whether to receive their premium in the form of wage increase or in its transformation into fully untaxed welfare services [22].

In "second welfare", enterprises become the "*trait d'union*" between Government and community. They meet the social needs of workers and their families, giving an impulse to a CW model in CSR perspective. Due to the benefits granted by PA, companies undertake to offer various products, services and benefits to their staffs. Nonetheless, making a welfare plan does not only mean gaining economic benefits but also enhancing specific benefits that make enterprises competitive in their market. Implementing a CW policy is more feasible for large businesses that can afford to spend a lot of time and resources in structuring a project to provide for the health of workers and their families. Although recent regulations gave a strong boost to the development of these techniques, they appear applicable mostly in solid and complex contexts. SMEs instead does not seem to have been sufficiently taken into account [6, 17, 23]. Resources allocated to a welfare plan are not taxable if assigned to a homogeneous category worker, i.e. with the same structure (employees, executives, senior executives, etc.), level of contracts or income (i.e. all employees with a lower income than "X"). *Ad personam* plans or addressed to a few employees, such as company directors or CEO, are excluded. CW initiatives must be collected into TUIR areas [19, 20]:

1. Supplementary pension schemes, i.e. how workers invest in their future retirement, thanks to additional contributions paid by the company in which they operate.
2. Integrative healthcare; it is the area of CW that provides supplementary health services to staff and can be extended to families as well. It is made up of both

compulsory funds provided by the National Health Service (Italian acronym SSN) and voluntary mutuality practices promoted by management.

3. Assistance services to facilitate work-life balance; the main initiatives concern pension and assistance services for elderly and non-self-sufficient people. This area of welfare is destined to grow, given the increase in the average age of the population and the evolution of the family unit.

4. Insurance policies: it is the area with the highest initiative rate among companies. A compulsory component of accident-related casualties is provided by national labour agreements. Companies, however, may negotiate with workers other types of policies (e.g. casualty insurance, life-assurance insurance, etc.).

5. Work-life balance for equal opportunities: it is a fast-growing area in recent years. Enterprises undertake to give flexibility on working hours, in addition to other minor work-related measures (maternity allowance, bureaucratic practices, business transport services, company nursery services, kindergartens convention, schools, playgrounds...).

6. Economic support for workers and families: they are initiatives aimed at providing economic assistance to employees and their family members (free accommodation or low-priced accommodation, canteen service, meals or restaurants arrangements, agreements on the purchase of consumer goods, reimbursement of subscription to public transport, loans granted on favourable terms, etc.).

7. Training, a welfare service for a better qualification of the human capital by specialized advanced vocational courses, as well as language courses and other tools. Workers upgrade and/or develop new skills.

8. Support for the education of workers' children and family members; this area is still in its early stages, mainly through the reimbursement of school expenses.

9. Culture, recreation, and leisure: this area doesn't have an adequate initiative rate but it is a good practice of CW with initiatives that foster a climate of well-being between staff (corporate cultural events, products such as cinemas and theatres, conventions with gyms and sports centres, travel, artistic training, etc.).

10. Support for weaknesses and social integration: these are initiatives to encourage the inclusion, in the life of a company, of weak people such as disabled people or to help non-EU citizen to be integrated into society, delivering a variety of services (assistance in bureaucracy, housing, language training, cultural mediation, etc.).

11. Safety and accident prevention, i.e. voluntary education and training initiatives for prevention, codes of conduct to be respected and safety certifications.

12. Welfare extension to environment and community: many enterprises are actively involved in the community in which they are located, through contributions to volunteering and services in support of cultural and recreational events, homes and housing, schools and kindergartens, transport, and so on.

The 2016 S.L. [7] included benefits for children (pre-school education and training services, including supplementary and related services, summer and winter centre attendance services, scholarship services, etc.) and services for the care of elderly and not self-sufficient families. The 2017 S.L. [8] included insurance for non-self-sufficiency and serious illness. The employer may provide goods, assistance, works, and services by a legitimate document, in paper or electronic form, with a nominal value [19], called "vouchers". It can be used by the employer to promote the provision of company welfare services; these documents made an impetus to the adoption of policies to protect the well-being of staff even among SMEs. Vouchers may not be used by a person other than the holder, they cannot be transferred to third parties and are entitled to the performance indicated for the total of their nominal value without any supplement to the holder of the document. CW is based on the implicit assumption that employment relationship must include satisfying needs that are not efficiently or insufficiently met by monetary compensation.

2.3 A Win-Win Model

The implementation of CW policies links State with the community, represented by all workers and their families. All components of the system benefit from this situation, therefore the CW model is classified as a win-win-win situation.

First, the Government established a public-private collaboration that allows a fundamental transition to second welfare. Through facilities provided for in recent years, in particular through provisions of the S.L. 2016 and 2017 [7, 8], Government implemented decision-making and executive decentralization process of welfare plans. By streamlining the tasks of the PA and by shifting from a traditional welfare state model to an integrative scheme, in which companies are called to play a role of primary importance, the State has implemented a more sustainable and effective project to satisfy social needs [10].

Secondly, workers engaged in companies that adopt CW practices, enjoy numerous benefits resulting from various initiatives within the company. The main benefits are increasing real wages and purchasing power, supplying goods and services selected by workers themselves among the proposed ones; increasing of welfare, guaranteed by business initiatives, both at individual and household level, the good organizational climate within companies; work-life balance. Thanks to CW services, employees can optimally harmonize, manage and organize their time.

Finally, employers find several positive results stemming from a company welfare policy, such as the increase of labour productivity, the main goal pursued by businesses adopting CW practices. Workers' performance improves, boosted by performance premiums and favoured by incentives provided for both entrepreneurs and workers [15, 22]. Company's climate and employee satisfaction improve, favoured by benefits offered to the staff who creates greater corporate well-being. The workers' loyalty increases; CW implementation makes them feel important and appreciated, avoiding high turnover rates and the escape of best talents. Absenteeism and associated costs decrease through initiatives aimed at work-life balance. Corporate image improves; enterprises need to be more and more attentive to ethical and social implications of their activities, from a CSR point of view, therefore welfare projects can only improve their image and reputation. Labour costs are reduced by tax advantage renewed by S.Ls. [7, 8] on all benefits provided to workers.

2.4 Organizational Change

Implementation of welfare plans generates a lot of advantages for all parties involved, but requires some organizational changes, both internal and external to the enterprise [16]. The main and most important change within enterprises, is related to employee relations, especially in case of "distance to power" [24]. In fact, enterprises must be clearer and more transparent while communicating with employees, explaining welfare plans and benefits brought to them, and knowing the real needs of its staff, in order to choose from the wide range of Welfare services available. Both internal stakeholders and middle management must be involved.

Human resources management is already involved in the design of Welfare plans, in order to perceive the needs of a company and create a staff segmentation by homogeneous categories, to better analyse requests and expectations of employees. Needs, indeed, range from individual to individual and depend on many factors, including age and place of residence. It is also important to have a long-term vision and to try predicting how the enterprises' population will evolve over the next few years.

Trade unions are also involved, and they have to change both their point of view and their way of action: they must no longer base their action and goals on the well-being of the individual, or of a part of the corporate population, but must look—and aim—at the well-being of the whole community of workers [25]. Work relationships are evolving; they are not a simple exchange of work performance and cash compensation, but worker's well-being is a key point behind relationships, and through which more attention is given to a person as the bearer of individual interests and values [18].

Further changes can be found in legal, administrative and financial offices. First of all, it should be pointed out how companies are extremely clear about performance premiums, proving that they are actually linked to incremental factors; if not, it would lose the opportunity to benefit from the tax disregard recognised to premiums [22]. In other words, enterprises must demonstrate that factors used in premiums calculations are actually incremental compared to a time frame defined on the basis of indexes and data. Given that welfare benefits are not included in contributory calculations (in contrast to cash prizes) companies must provide plans with a supplementary pension. For this reason, in fact, some companies are considering a premium to the supplementary pension [1]. ICT is another area that must change to introduce Welfare plans, helping to identify the best systems of welfare services once they have been selected according to the needs of both workers and company [26].

Finally, two key steps must be taken to implement welfare plans and their assessment: the first is the training of managers involved; the second is the implementation of monitoring activities, which may identify corrective actions. Managers are a key figure of enterprises and of this process so they must be educated to be an example, to involve and to stimulate employees to use the offered services, to explain to the staff that the company implements welfare plans for their well-being and to clarify what these plans consist of, how to implement them and in which way.

About evaluation systems, enterprises must monitor the achieved results, in order to see if the efforts are producing the expected results or whether corrective forms are needed [27]. It is necessary to monitor both the qualitative elements, such as the workers' satisfaction and their perception of services quality and quantitative elements, as time and economic savings.

Companies can use different approaches to implement welfare plans. A first selection can be made by complexity: they can make individual interventions, meeting the needs of employees in the short-term, or more articulated ones, with various suitable activities and actions to different collaborators. Size of company also affects the choice [6]; small companies hardly offer workers a wide range of services and conventions to choose, but they have more direct and close relationships with them in order to optimize interventions, or to get into network with other companies to offer shared services at lower prices [17, 27, 28]. It is also necessary to consider the economic and organizational resources that can be used: simple interventions aimed at modifying the organizational structure or working times; less content-based investments, which generate benefits through tax incentives; or even more significant investments with a medium to long-term horizon. Implementing Welfare plans, especially before competitors, can help companies in many ways, as a CSR action [29]. In fact, investing in both human and economic resources as well as in time becomes tolerable if it helps to achieve productivity, competitiveness and sustainability goals in the short, medium and long-term [15]. To deal with today's increasingly growing competitiveness, to attract and retain talented people, motivating and involving them in company's mission, is a key condition and all of this is facilitated by Welfare's plans [9]. To be able to differentiate in terms of supply of these plans, then, represents a competitive distinction. Designing a Welfare strategy to workers' needs, allows companies to reach goals only if they first reach those of their employees. Welfare Business Plan may be voluntary, occasional—due to the employer's liberty—or provided through business regulation (employer is engaged, through this voluntary document, towards employees), and negotiable. If it concerns performance and productivity premiums, it is derived from a company union agreement and it's mandatory; if the object of negotiation is the supply of goods and services, it derives form a company union agreement and it is optional.

Employer must consider several factors, in order to understand the best method, such as needs expressed by employees in order to decide which services should be included in this plan; consequences, taxes and contributions produced by selected services; degree of involvement of employees and trade unions in the choice of benefits; budget of the employer's sustainable costs and their relative distribution to employees (per worker or per homogeneous category) [22]. Welfare strategy, indeed, can be directed to a single person; in this case, only certain types of benefit generate tax advantages. Enterprises should focus primarily on the normative, economic and cultural aspects, in addition to the organizational ones, in order to implement welfare plans. It should be important to know and to study norms in all their risks and opportunities, in order to find out also limits of action, and estimate costs and benefits of the plan. Starting or improving a restructuration of welfare plan requires long-term financial vision, but also a vision of short-term savings prospects. Secondarily, employers can analyse organizational aspects, such as the choice of suppliers and technologies to be used; company must be aware of the consequences of its choices and of their impact on the organization. It is essential, as shown, to investigate and to know the needs of collaborators, cultural vision is indeed fundamental. It is often enough to carry out a socio-demographic survey that does not generate too many expectations but that helps to define the needs of people involved and suggests the best services. At present, there are a lot of welfare providers: service companies, software houses and on-site platforms, insurance brokerage companies, and some companies that can be defined as "spurious". To build effective Welfare plans, we often rely on external consultants or we use service providers and/or consulting firms because of organizational difficulties, but an actual focus on needs reduces the risk of failure [30].

2.5   Web Platforms

Web platforms allow the creation of a welfare system, sharing experiences and thus the best practices can be extended to less-experienced companies, especially if they are medium or small. SMEs are thus able to take advantage of opportunities that would not be exploited otherwise [17, 31]. Connecting with big business, SMEs can gain economies of scale, scope, and experience [6, 17]. Welfare Sharing is a service offering help to all the enterprises employees.

Jointly is an example of a platform, a start-up created in 2014, which guarantees efficiency through the use of advanced technology, and ensures the management of Welfare Plans in each stage. Another example is Easy Welfare (EW), a company that, through its platform, focuses on the well-being of employees and their families, offering EW for education and funding, well-being, leisure and so on. We can also find Well Work, a company with a twenty-year experience in services, which through a web platform organizes purchases and redemptions with an easy, fast and convenient system; it offers facilities for parents, studying plans related to flexible work and timetables, work permits, teleworking and nursery creation; services to health with corporate physicians, indoor gyms and nutritionists; for the resolution of small problems through a corporate minimarket, good housekeeping and take-away; for leisure with good expenses, conventions with shops and cinemas, libraries, travel agencies and others. A third example is Day, a leader in the Italian meal vouchers-market that, through a digital ecosystem, provides a full service to suppliers, who can publish their offerings and meet new customers, as well as customer companies that can create welfare plans for their employees and their families. Day also deals with employees that, through the platform, can make their welfare plan according to their specific needs, because the portal allows them to choose among a lot of services and opportunities. Edenred, a well-known company in the sector of meal vouchers and services, launched FlexBenefit [32]; it is a new web-based platform that allows each employee to choose and freely plan their own package of benefits, always under a budget limit assigned by the employer [30].

3 Method

The research question proposed by this study is to try to understand if and how the ICT platform can be helpful to include more people, even if workers of PMI, in CW. Due to the explorative nature of this study, a process of qualitative data collection and analysis [33] has been chosen as the most appropriate.

The case study is a new centralized platform to help mutual aid societies to give their usual services (providential and assistance services, social and health services, educational, recreational and training activities) in a more effective and efficient way in the CW sector. This platform can be a good instrument to networked organizational form that leverages ICTs to mobilize resources for higher territorial system resilience, sustainability and/or quality of life.

The research builds upon both a participant and a non-participant observation [34]. The data collection process started in September when the project was launched, and it is still in progress. One of the authors was directly involved in the project since the beginning, whilst other authors could witness some meetings where the project was discussed and could ask questions as some participating observers. Thanks to the reflective practice and the discussion of the experiences, all the authors achieved a direct and in-depth understanding of the concrete opportunities and problems, as implied by a project "in action". The research activities provided the authors with a multi-faceted experience of the phenomenon under study, as well as rich and diverse text and data archives, resulting from reports, website texts, social network texts, interview recordings, and researchers' field notes. These contents are collected with a word processor, in order to have a homogeneous archive for the analysis. The analyses of these archives allowed to yield a shared interpretation of the case, and to compare it to the extant literature.

4 *Creawelfare Case*: An Inclusive Platform for Welfare Services

4.1 *Mutual Aid Societies and COMIPA*

COMIPA is the acronym of "Consortium of Italian mutual aid societies in Pension and Assistance"; it was constituted in 1989 as a cooperative society. COMIPA operates at a national level for the promotion and development of associative mutuality, especially in the health and the social sphere [35].

A Mutual aid society (MAS) is a non-profit organization that provides health care and welfare services to its associates, as well as social protection services tailored to their needs and to the needs of their families. MAS is based on the principles of mutual help and reciprocal assistance, only working in favour of its members and their families, involving them to participate benefits of solidarity. It guarantees, by statute, a transparent administration: the association allows its members to determine its functioning, through the election of directors and management control. MASs, in Italy, can have different legal structures, particularly in the form of simple or registered association and that of a mutual aid company. As an association, they can take initiatives, organize events, and provide benefits and assistance beyond the sphere of social and health care. In this case, their utility reaches the highest level as they can be useful to members at every stage of their life (Fig. 1).

If a MAS adopts the recognized form of association, enjoys the perfect balance of autonomy (thanks to the acquisition of legal personality in accordance with Presidential Decree 361/2000) and, at the same time, it benefits from facilities provided by the law, within the limits and with respect to the constraints imposed by the same law. MAS can pursue one or more purposes between securing subsidies and assistance in cases of illness, impotence at work or retirement age, assisting families of deceased members, cooperating in the education of members and their families and giving assistance to its members for the purchase of goods and services and to exercise other offices of the economic security institutions [35]. The mutual sector is growing: for this year a 5.5% increase of associated people is foreseen of 5.5%, up to 600,000 members [12].

COMIPA through "Creawelfare" project seeks to transfer its welfare experience, gained over 25 years, to enterprises. COMIPA's goal is to help companies to improve their organizational climate, which is considered more than an interest generator. The consortium does not have the purpose of selling products neither having a margin on offered services, it but wants to provide enterprises a lower cost compared to their competitors, thanks to already existing conventions that reduce "commercial time". A MAS does not need a commercial network, thanks to the presence of the cooperative credit banks (BCCs) and other MASs, which further reduces management costs. COMIPA also aims to facilitate use of services, to collect any statistical information that will enable a study of needs to develop new conventions, where necessary, and to

Fig. 1 The bridging role of MAS. *Source* Authors

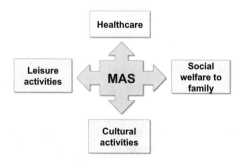

create an ecosystem of actions of social protection for people, enterprises, territory, and local communities by recovering the true dimension of well-being, which is satisfaction of people's primary needs along their entire life, not only a provision of services.

4.2   The "Creawelfare" Platform

Creawelfare (*CW*) is based on a centralized platform that allows economies of scale on the technological side while providing a simple, local and flexible service [36]. The purpose is, in fact, to enable the access to healthcare facilities and prevention centres, services and cultural activities already organized by individual MAS, but which can be networked and thus become a common asset. In other words, it wants to create a simpler and broader access to welfare services on the Italian territory, for mutual partners' customers, and for employees who benefit from a CW plan. The centralized platform, indeed, is able to create connections of mutual agreements between companies and service providers, developing specific packages for their employees, dedicating vouchers spendable at agreed centres, refund of expenses incurred by other centres or for specific activities envisaged by the legislation. On the date of our studies, this is the only platform that can customize every type of use according to workers' needs. Finally, the platform enables internal administrative management of the association.

A stimulus to its development was given by incentives for CW and in particular for smaller companies, including them in CW services, starting from places in which MASs are present and close, thanks to the BCCs of the same territory (representing a number of members of about 175,000 people involved). At the same time, however, it was attempted to develop a new product/service to expand the range of territorial welfare beneficiaries of individual MAS, even outside of bank member-customers.

The first step was an organizational analysis to identify the features of the company, which made it possible to adequately represent the criticalities detected and to check for any corrective actions. It was very important to deepen the knowledge of corporate population, through meetings with business representatives and employees, in order to better carry out in the first two steps. The choice, in fact, must be made in com-participation and, once it is done, it must be shared with the whole organization and supported by appropriate training.

4.2.1   Operation

The access to the platform is confidential and it is possible to have a direct interface on the corporate portal [36]. The first access obviously involves the acceptance of use of personal data by the platform; otherwise, the user will not be able to print the relevant vouchers or refund requests. The company can see the list of its active employees on the platform and all of their personal information, as they are not

Fig. 2 The way of working on the platform called "Creawelfare". *Source* Authors

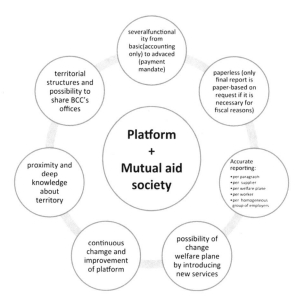

sensitive data. To take full advantage of the regulatory possibilities, every employee is carefully profiled, including dependents. On the platform some operators and services are pre-loaded and they can be integrated or adapted according to company requests. Therefore, the company can plan the welfare campaign by loading the ceilings for each employee. The worker has access to the dashboard; he can see the "welfare purse" according to the campaign and view the relevant services, based on agreements with the company. A choice is possible, depending on the ratings of other users, the owner who validates his/her voucher. It is important for the company to define the choice between the basic or the advanced solution, to evaluate proposals and possible packages, to verify—if it is considered a useful internal choice—the proposal with trade unions (RSUs), to share a report as well as to communicate and explain to employees the choices that have been made. The ideal would be a multi-annual agreement (Fig. 2).

4.2.2 Comparisons with Competitors

The mutualistic nature of COMIPA and MAS, and their practice in providing or facilitating access to cultural services, leisure, health and prevention services for our associates for the past 25 years, is a great help to juggle in the competitive environment. The platform, in fact, is a digitization of a process that allows benefiting, through CW from the same services thanks to whom a great experience has been gained, together with many others. MASs keep doing whatever they did before, innovating and simplifying through ICT. This allows them to open up to new people, albeit at less favourable conditions than those enjoyed by mutual partners (which support a cost of membership), but also guaranteeing workers, especially SMEs and social enterprises, the possibility to access the agreed services and agreements [17].

The development of CW is an opportunity to produce a positive marginality that can enable MAS and consortium not only to cover the costs of IT development and its commercial proposal, but to invest the profits derived from an expanded "welfare" network that grows beyond the neighbouring territory. The idea of covering the entire national territory has stimulated innovation; ICTs facilitate the use, improve management, automate bureaucratic aspects, thus allowing to have more time to invest in studying and proposing health, cultural and leisure activities and/or improving relationships with territorial partners, traders, and companies.

There is also the possibility to have immediate monitoring of welfare services delivered throughout the territory and this allows COMIPA to carry out a series of analysis and statistics that can be used for the improvement, expansion and enjoyment of new services, thus continuing to grow the advantage compared to its competitors.

At this moment, bank federations are involved to incentivize their Banks to use this platform. It is developing a specific plan about a conversion of performance premiums [22], in order to distribute throughout the year, the bureaucratic part in order to avoid the overload of offices in December. 86 national conditions were stipulated, particularly useful for the young people who have the most disparate needs; special agreements with local operators are being also stipulated, to channel all the wellbeing in the area where companies operate. In this way, national agreements are useful only for some particular needs. On a commercial basis, two packages have been created:

- "welfare base", a package of refunds with national vouchers. Enterprises with small amounts to manage have limited costs of a prevention plan or a special exam package;
- "complete well-being", is the complete use of the platform that includes benefits, vouchers, local conventions, prevention and customized smart packages. For this package, all employees are interviewed by an online survey and their needs are analysed to structure a "tailor-made" wellness plan.

5 Discussions and Conclusion

In the current economic scenario, it is necessary re-think the welfare concept, changing the role of Public Authority to move from a welfare state to a welfare society [11]. In this so-called "second welfare", no one of the three-major kind of organizations (Public Administration, Profit, and non-profit organizations) can be excluded from taking part in the construction of a welfare society [14]. According to Mallone [4], especially enterprises can assume a pivotal role in answering the ever-increasing needs for public goods, that the growth in population numbers and the simultaneous shortage of natural resources make this more difficult to achieve. The Italian Government, thanks to the last two years' S.L. [7, 8], incentivized enterprises, through fiscal benefits, to join to the CW plans. A win-win model arises, in which benefits are extended to all subjects involved (Public Authority, enterprises, and workers). For this reason, and especially for all the advantages at the organizational level that CW produces inside and outside of enterprises [37], it should be very important that all kind of enterprises should adopt welfare plans, despite their role, positions or dimensions. The role of ICT is fundamental to trigger this positive change and also to manage the process, because it provides an easy access to CW for all enterprises, including also SMEs and their workers, especially thanks to non-profit welfare providers. In the researchers' opinion, the case analysed is a perfect demonstration of this phenomenon. Encouraged by Authority's incentive, a consortium of mutual aid societies, which has a big experience in health care and welfare services, created an innovative organizational solution that allows to offer the core services to a lot of enterprises and their workers. The "creawelfare" platform, in fact, develops as a simple proposition, with no software to be installed locally, totally digital that, combined with spatial proximity of MASs and capillarity of the BCCs, to which they rely on, allows a large number of SMEs to access welfare plans by involving many workers; in this way, SMEs are included in CW, and can seize opportunities that otherwise would be prerogative of the bigger one [17, 31].

The study is only at the beginning and it can still be very much developed, also thanks to available materials, especially interviews, that will be revised to understand the MASs', the company's and workers' point of view; they are starting to use it regularly and it can suggest possible improvements. Even in this embryonic stage, we have already been able to see the remarkable potential that is stimulating the researchers' interest.

References

1. Ferrera, M., Maino, F.: Il secondo welfare in Italia: sfide e prospettive. (eng.trad. Second welfare in Italy: challenges and perspectives) Italianieuropei (3), 17–22 (2011)
2. Sacconi, L.: Guida critica alla responsabilità sociale e al governo d'impresa (eng.trad. Critical guide for corporate social responsibility and for business management) Bancaria Editrice, Roma, pp. 20, 162, 453–459 (2005)
3. Galtry, J.: The impact on breastfeeding of labour market policy and practice in Ireland, Sweden, and the USA. Soc. Sci. Med. **57**(1), 167–177 (2003)
4. Mallone, G.: Il welfare aziendale in Italia: una risposta ai nuovi bisogni sociali? (eng.trad. Corporate welfare in Italy: an answer to new social needs?). In: Bray, M., Granata, M. (a cura di): L'economia sociale: una risposta alla crisi, Roma, Solaris, 2012 (2013)
5. Perrini, F., Russo, A., Tencati, A.: Small business champions for corporate social responsibility. J. Bus. Ethics **74**(3), 285–300 (2007)
6. Lepoutre, J., Heene, A.: Investigating the impact of firm size on small business social responsibility: a critical review. J. Bus. Ethics **67**(3), 257–273 (2006)
7. Legge di Stabilità 2016 (eng. trad. Stability Law), disponibile all'indirizzo http://www.gazzettaufficiale.it/eli/id/2015/12/30/15G00222/sg
8. Legge di Stabilità 2017 (eng. trad. Stability Law), disponibile all'indirizzo http://www.gazzettaufficiale.it/eli/id/2016/12/21/16G00242/sg
9. Cerica, R.: Cultura organizzativa e performance economico-finanziarie (eng. trad. Organizational culture and economic – financial performance), Firenze University Press, Firenze, vol. 56, pp. 9–10 (2009)

10. Taylor-Gooby, P.: New Risks, New Welfare: The Transformation of the European Welfare State. Oxford University Press, Oxford (2004)
11. Titmuss, R.M.: Welfare state and welfare society. Nurs. Mirror Midwives J. **126**(10), 25 (1968)
12. Avitabile, C., Jappelli, T.: L'assicurazione sanitaria in Italia e in Europa, (eng.trad. Health insurance in Italy and Europe). In: Brugiavini, A., Jappelli, T. (a cura di), Verso un nuovo sistema di architettura sociale per la famiglia, Il Mulino, Bologna (2010)
13. Merico, C.: Società di mutuo soccorso. (eng. trad. Mutual aid societies) La Verità, virtualnwespaper.it 7/16 (2017)
14. Maino, F., Ferrera, M.: Primo rapporto sul secondo welfare in Italia (eng. trad. First report on Second welfare in Italy). Centro di Ricerca e D Luigi Einaudi, Torino (2013)
15. SWG Research: Creare valore con gli Employee Benefit (eng.trad. Creating value through employees' benefits) (2016). http://www.zurich.it
16. Treu, T.: Welfare aziendale. Migliorare la produttività e il benessere dei dipendenti (eng.trad. Corporate welfare. Improving productivity and well-being of employees) – Ipsoa, Milano (2013)
17. Massagli, E.: Il welfare aziendale territoriale per la micro, piccola e media impresa italiana (eng. trad. Corporate welfare for Italian SMEs) – ADAPT labour studies e-Book series n. 31 (2014)
18. Sobrero, R.: L'importanza delle risorse umane, focus sul welfare aziendale – (eng. trad. The importance of human resources, focus on corporate welfare) Pubblicazione e progetti speciali Unioncamere Piemonte (2012). http://www.csrpiemonte.it
19. Testo unico delle imposte sui redditi (TUIR). Articolo 51, Determinazione del reddito di lavoro dipendente (eng. trad. Determination of employees's income). http://www.altalex.com
20. Testo unico delle imposte sui redditi (TUIR). Articolo 100, Oneri di utilità sociale (eng. trad. Obligations of social utility). http://www.altalex.com
21. Pini, P.: Innovazione, relazioni industriali e risultati d'impresa. Un'analisi per il sistema industriale di Reggio Emilia (eng.trad. Innovation, industrial relationships and businesses' results), vol. 25, Franco Angeli ed. (2004)
22. Fabbri, R., Pini, P.: La recente contrattazione aziendale sul premio di risultato nelle imprese del territorio di Udine, in "Lavoro e diritto, Rivista trimestrale" 2/1999, pp. 297–330. https://doi.org/10.1441/4458
23. Grandi, D., Moriconi, A.: Legge di stabilità e reti di imprese: un "ponte" tra welfare e PMI (Stability Law and network of enterprises: a bridge between welfare and SMEs) – Bollettino Adapt n. 5 (2016)
24. Hofstede, G.: Comparing Values, Behaviors, Institutions, and Organizations Across Nations, pp. 1–40. Sage Publications, Thousand Oaks (2002)
25. Hofstede, G., McCrae, R.: Personality and Culture Revisited: Linking Traits and Dimensions of Culture, Cross-Cultural Research, pp. 38, 52 (2004)
26. Bollinger, D., Hofstede, G.: Inter nazionalità, Edizioni Angelo Guerini e Associati Srl, Milano, pp. 87–103, 117–130 (1989)
27. Moruzzi, M.: Reti del nuovo welfare: la sfida dell'e-care (eng.trad. New welfare networks), vol. 13. FrancoAngeli (2005)
28. Rapporto Welfare Index PMI (2016). Available on http://www.welfareindexpmi.it/rapporto-welfare_index-pmi-2016.pdf
29. McCartht, K.J.: Internationalisation Theory & Practice, University of Groningen Lecture Series (2017)
30. Boni, M., Finzi, E., Gatti, S., Gavezotti, G., Ongaretti, M., Risciotti,C., Vultaggio, A.: Perchè i progetti di welfare falliscono? (Eng. trad. Why welfare plans fail?) Red paper, Astra ricerche per Edenred italia (2011)
31. Maino, F., Mallone, G.: Le nuove regole sul welfare aziendale: cosa cambia per imprese e lavoratori? (eng.trad. The new rules about corporate welfare), pp. 16–19. Sviluppo & organizzazione (2016)
32. http://www.flexiblebenefit.eu

33. Yin, R.K.: Case Study Research: Design and Methods. Sage publications (2013)
34. Bryman, A., Bell, E.: Business Research Methods. Oxford University Press (2011)
35. https://www.comipa.org
36. https://www.creawelfare.it/
37. Gatti, M.: Welfare aziendale. La risposta organizzativa ai bisogni delle persone (eng.tr. Corporate Welfare. An organizational answer to people's needs) – Este, Milano (2014)

Information Technology Infrastructure: A Source of Entrepreneurs' Economic Challenges

Wesley Palmer

Abstract This qualitative study involved exploring the meaning of the experiences of entrepreneurs in New York State who faced economic challenges due to rapid changes in the information technology infrastructure. The basis of this research was Laudon and Laudon's management information theory. The first research question related to the experiences and dynamics of entrepreneurs whose businesses require adequate technological infrastructure, and the second question related to the ways entrepreneurs experience economic challenges due to rapid changes in business technology. Data collection took place through unstructured face-to-face interviews with 20 entrepreneurs in New York State using a purposive sampling method. Analyzing the data helped to develop participants' experiences into themes. Forty-five percent of participants did not have updated business technology. This study may serve as a catalyst to bring awareness to the effect of technological change on nascent entrepreneurs and may lead to a strategy to provide resources to affected entrepreneurs.

Keywords Information · Infrastructure · Technology · Entrepreneur · Innovation · Venture capitalist · Competitive advantage · Economic

1 Introduction

Access to business technology and the ability to acquire and use innovative systems to bolster economic activities are essential aspects of entrepreneurs' economic advancement. Many entrepreneurs are investing in high-technology office suites and online social networks to gain competitive advantage, but many have lagged behind [1–3]. This research was necessary because of the integral role entrepreneurs play in national and global economic development. Innovative technology serves as the driver for 24% of entrepreneurial enterprises [4]. Information technology is a critical component of business technology.

W. Palmer (✉)
Department of Business and Economics, York College,
City University of New York, New York, USA
e-mail: wpalmer@york.cuny.edu

© Springer Nature Switzerland AG 2020
Y. Baghdadi et al. (eds.), *ICT for an Inclusive World*,
Lecture Notes in Information Systems and Organisation 35,
https://doi.org/10.1007/978-3-030-34269-2_7

This exploratory study involved evaluating entrepreneurs' experiences with innovative business technology, such as computer hardware, computer software, data management technology, online social networks, and computer network systems, to gain insights into the effect on entrepreneurs [5]. Many entrepreneurial firms have outsourced some of their business activities to firms with advanced technology in an effort to cope with changing technology [3, 6]. Business technology changes every 18 months, and the rapid change poses a burden on entrepreneurial businesses. Although entrepreneurs have access to highly trained technology providers who are able to walk them through the operating process, troubleshoot, and provide answers, those services may not be beneficial after 18 months. The pervasive change of business technology has affected entrepreneurial product and service output [7]. Advanced business technology helps to increase entrepreneurs' business exponentially; however, changes in technology are also a source of problems. The findings section includes remedies for the problems and the shortcomings of excessive change in business technology. Continued technology education might be a useful approach to encourage entrepreneurs to adapt to modern technology at a faster pace [4].

1.1   Purpose

The purpose of this research was to heighten awareness of the effect of rapid innovation change on entrepreneurs' information technology infrastructure. Innovative technology enhances entrepreneurs' business contributions, but the excessive changes and the costs associated with those changes are the underlying challenge [7]. This exploratory study involved searching for the meaning of the effect of technology on the lived experiences of entrepreneurs [8]. A qualitative phenomenological methodology was suitable because the author was able to express the universal essence of the lived experiences of the participating entrepreneurs rather than present my opinion based on data analysis [9, 10].

1.2   Problem Statement

The problem is the pervasive changes in innovative technology that have challenged the lived experiences of entrepreneurs who have been unable to keep pace with current technological systems that are necessary for economic advancement [11]. Sixty percent of business technology users used advanced technology, including mobile communications, to make purchases, schedule appointments, host web conferences, and monitor security systems [3]. Furthermore, 50% of business owners in the United States use advanced remote technology to conduct businesses.

Average technological innovation levels increased by 21% over the past five years and were influenced by national economic development factors; factors related to efficiency accounted for 24%, and 31% were driven by innovations [4]. The results of the statistical analysis highlighted the pervasive emergence of information and communication technology in the business environment and the many ways that advanced technology has changed business processes [12, 13].

Businesses that keep pace with technology are reluctant to conduct business with small and fledgling entrepreneurial businesses that operate with dated technology because of the inadequacy of their operations, lack of stability, weaknesses in financial positions, and inadequate social ties with established market players [14]. Entrepreneurs on the global horizon have similar elements of weaknesses and inadequacies that derived from the rapid pace of technological change [4].

1.3 Research Questions

Entrepreneurial enterprises account for more than 50% of new and innovative technology, yet many entrepreneurial firms remain behind the curve with regard to business technology [3]. Entrepreneurs are the leaders in modern technology [15, 16] who continue to set new standards and forge innovations. Entrepreneurial firms have been the largest developers of business technology for the past decades [please be more specific] [2], yet some entrepreneurs continue to struggle to maintain adequate technological resources to modernize their business operations. This research involved a phenomenological study of entrepreneurial technological experiences guided by two research questions:

1. What are the experiences of entrepreneurs who have not kept pace with the information technology infrastructure due to the rapid changes in technology?
2. In what ways do the pervasive changes in business technology affect entrepreneurial ventures and threaten their viability?

2 Theoretical Framework

Central to this study was Laudon and Laudon management information system theory [3]. Foundational concepts of management information system theory was used to guide the study in terms of the application of web-based technology, network connectivity, mobile devices, and the constant changes of the business technological system. Technological acquisition is one of the most essential considerations when establishing businesses; without the acquisition of technology, entrepreneurs cannot establish their businesses efficiently. The theoretical framework established measurable guide in understanding how outdated technology could hamper business potential; thus, technological assessment is necessary for a comprehensive business analysis [11]. System requirement assessments involve examining two types of technological proposals: (a) information technology infrastructure, which includes major computer hardware, software, data storage, input, and output technologies, as well as (b) capacity, sustainability, efficiency, and economic benefits.

Technology assessment also includes critical analysis to determine the value that a technological system would add to a business. The success of a business depends on the acquisition and installation of the appropriate system requirements. These fundamental concepts lay the groundwork for the research. Management information theory helps to explain the importance of technological assessment and technological requirements, as well as their effect on entrepreneurial businesses [3].

A wide range of social, academic, and business literature contains descriptions of the technological void that entrepreneurs experience. Scholars and practitioners have developed several conceptual arguments through an iterative process as an attempt to explain entrepreneurs' technological experiences [17]. The literature reviewed presented several mixed findings with regard to entrepreneurs' technological adaptation. Some of the findings attributed entrepreneurs' technological void to a lack of managerial skills, poorly trained staff, lack of technological talents, and resistance to change, as well as failure to budget for technological innovations [8]. This research was built on the premise that business technology is the root of entrepreneurs' success.

This phenomenological study followed a framework for collecting data, analyzing data, and addressing the research questions. The assessment of business technology is necessary to determine the right mix of technology and value for finite resources [14, 18]. The efforts to provide service to their communities while making a living have been the practice of many entrepreneurs. Small family-run community grocers are evidence of entrepreneurs' commitment to their local communities.

3 Literature Review

The literature review revealed that entrepreneurs are making significant efforts to use advanced technological systems; 50% of entrepreneurial businesses use high-technology connectivity [16, 19]. Notwithstanding these successes, many entrepreneurial businesses still lag behind due to the lack of appropriate budget, technical competence, adaptation refusal, and administrative leadership [20, 21]. Although all types of training and educational support are available, many entrepreneurs do not have the resources to keep pace with the inordinate change and multiple technological systems.

Whereas technical incompetence and other administrative inefficiencies affect entrepreneurs in some ways, the major challenge to technological adoption may be the reluctance to change due to economic reasons [22, 23]. American businesses invested approximately $600 billion in hardware for information and telecommunication technology in 2015 [15, 24, 25]. In the global technological market, businesses spend over $3.8 trillion annually. Despite those expenditures, leaders of nascent and small firms continue to use outdated business systems, primarily due to their inability to keep pace with technological trends [15, 26].

Wireless connectivity has led to the migration of many physical systems, such as newspapers, magazines, mail, and flyers, into the technological systems and has substantially increased the need for bigger, faster, and more secure technological equipment [17, 27]. Approximately 150 million people read their news on some form of online medium [3]. Additionally, the emergence of social media has exponentially increased the need for electronic storage capacity. Thus, the demand for storage and the efficient flow of information have led technological innovators to develop systems with megabytes, gigabytes, and zettabytes [15, 28–30]. Each innovation called for an upgrade and sometimes an entirely new system that creates an economic burden on small business entrepreneurs.

3.1 Gap in the Research

The gap in the research was the lack of understanding how changing technology was affecting the lived experiences of entrepreneurs. There were no known business technological systems designed to help small business entrepreneurs cope with the drastic changes in technology and to alleviate the economic burden caused by innovations. Furthermore, there existed no formal plan to assist entrepreneurs with technological training and adoption. Entrepreneurial businesses can keep pace with new business technology if there are concessional considerations for small business entrepreneurs [2, 15, 16].

3.2 Methodology

The purposive sampling method was the most effective way to solicit participants based on the characteristics of the population and the objective of the study [31, 32]. In this research, the author selected a large pool of potential participants through a referral process and randomly selected the participants for the study.

3.3 Research Design

The study involved investigating the lived experiences of small and new entrepreneurs in New York State as a social and economic phenomenon in terms of entrepreneurs' personal interest and the effect of technology on entrepreneurial businesses and the communities within which they operate. In many communities, leaders of entrepreneurial organizations are the only employers to provide opportunities for residents. Therefore, an understanding of technological impact warrants an investigation.

3.4 Sampling Procedure

This phenomenological research study involved investigating the experiences of entrepreneurs in New York to learn how web-based systems, computer networks, and mobile technology affected their experiences. The research involved comparing and contrasting the experiences of 20 entrepreneurs to identify patterns and similarities among the participants [33]. The researcher used patterns and similarities to gain insight into the participating entrepreneurs' lived experiences. The study involved employing a combined sampling strategy to select participants who would serve as a rich source of credible information.

3.5 Population

The entrepreneurs who participated in the study were New York business owners. The purposive sampling strategy was the most suitable method due to the characteristics of the population. Because of its unique approach, the purposive sampling method allowed me to select participants who were typical of the entrepreneurial population by exercising professional judgment [31]. The sample size was broken down into numbers and percentage for easy calculation.

3.6 Data Collection and Analysis

The integrity of a study depends on the quality and strategy of the data collected. The larger the pool of participants in a scientific study is, the greater is the chance of producing a substantial theory that reflects the lived experiences of the participants [33]. Thus, the researcher engaged 20 small business entrepreneurs willing to participate in interviews. Each interview lasted for 45–60 min.

Data collection took place in New York, which was the designated area for the research. New York has a business community comprised of a large number of small and new businesses; these businesses have tremendous data sources to facilitate empirically designed research. The population included a diverse group of people, including Caucasians, African Americans, Jews, Hispanics, Asians, Caribbeans, and others.

In organizing and analyzing the vast volume of unstructured interviews collected using electronic media and written notes, NVivo 10 software helped to classify the data and establish patterns, themes, and similarities among the participants' responses. By using NVivo, the researcher was able to identify trends, patterns, and similarities in the data that were common in the experiences of the participants. The personal interviews of the participants served an essential role in this qualitative phenomenological research. Interviews are important elements in phenomenological studies because they help researchers to collect experiential stories that develop a richer and deeper understanding about human lived experiences [10].

3.7 Entrepreneurs' Demographics

Eight of 20 participants (40%) were female and the remaining 12 (60%) were male. Both male and female participants engaged in a wide variety of business activities, such as restaurants, supermarkets, podiatry-foot care centers, hair and beauty centers, business technologies, event planners, eye care centers, special education services, dry cleaning services, real estate services, retail stores, importation, and financial services. Educational attainment included high school diplomas and associate of applied science, Bachelor of Arts, Master of Science, medical doctor, doctor of education, and doctor of philosophy degrees. Seven of the participants had master degrees, one had md, one got a doctor in philosophy, eight got bachelors, and three got high school diplomas. The ages of the participants who engaged in the study ranged between 36 and 72.

3.8 Significant Themes

Table 1 contains the themes that answered the questions based on the identification of significant categories from more than 30% of participants' responses.

Table 1 Significant themes that answer the research questions

Themes	No. of participants ($N = 20$)	% of participants who experienced the themes
1. Technology infrastructure outdated	9	45
2. Technology systems up to date	11	55
3. Difficult to keep pace with technology	10	50
4. Significant economic impact	8	40
5. Experienced operational inefficiencies	7	35

3.9   Credibility and Validity

Qualitative research is credible if the results are satisfactory to the participants [32, 33]. The participants were the only ones capable of judging the correctness of the results because their lived experiences served as the basis of the results. The purposively selected sample was from a diverse group of entrepreneurs who produced thick and rich data. The researcher ensured this study was internally valid in terms of research design, operational definition, instrumentation, and conclusions [34]. The experiences shared by the research participants in New York were similar to the experiences of other entrepreneurs worldwide [4], which served as an indication of external validity.

4   Results

A brief discussion with the participants took place before the interviews to reiterate the procedures, protocols, and purpose of the study. The intent of the preliminary discussion was to allow the participants to share or clarify any concern they had regarding their role in the study. The research questions solicited answers based on the lived experiences of the phenomenon through the lens of a phenomenological approach.

Data analysis is a dynamic process in which researchers collect and organized texts, transcripts, electronic data, images and reduce them into statements, themes, meaning units, as well as descriptions [33, 34]. NVivo software served to organize and analyze the vast volume of unstructured data in media and written forms to classify the data, and to examine relationships between the participants. By using NVivo, the researcher was able to identify similarities in the data that were common in entrepreneurs' experiences.

To engage in the analysis process, the author created files for the interviews and organized them in alphabetical order for efficient processing. The researcher read margin notes and interview transcripts to identify trends in the research results; used the data collected to write a description of the essence of entrepreneurs' lived experiences; and organized, transcribed, and cross-examined the data for evidence that supported the authenticity of the research findings [9, 10, 33].

Discrepant, contradictions and variations from the general experiences of the studied phenomenon were observed. Participants with outdated technological infrastructure and those with updated technological systems varied markedly. Nine participants reported that they were operating with outdated systems and found it difficult to maintain competitive advantage in the market, while 11 of the participants reported that they had updated systems which helped them to operate efficiently and did not have any challenges maintaining updated technological systems.

Participant eight stated it was difficult keeping pace with modern technological systems during the early phase of the business. However, the business was able to acquire some financial assistance that was used to acquire updated technological infrastructure. Participant 10 stated that the business is still using outdated techno-logical system due to the business inability to keep pace with the rapid technological changes. Participant eight and 12 remarked that they could not use operational funds to acquire new technology; thus, their businesses were lagging behind the competi-tion. Participant four and 20 reported that old technological systems have resulted in loss of revenues as customers switched to new technological method of payments.

Variation is a significant component of iterative qualitative research. Variations reflect the integrity and the independent collection of the data. Although the intent of a phenomenological study is to find commonality among the lived experiences of the participants, a small variation does not alter the results significantly. The variation of this research was relatively small; nevertheless, it offered authenticity to the research process and content.

5   Discussion

Seven entrepreneurs who were unable to maintained adequate business technology for their business have experienced operations deficiencies that have resulted in slow sales and unsustainable profitability [35]. Further, the lack of new technology resulted in operations inefficiencies, such as improper inventory control, poor cash management accountability, inaccurate accounts receivable, and ineffective customer service.

The research revealed that 45% of entrepreneurs were operating with outdated technological systems. Fifty-five percent had modern technological systems and were operating successfully. Fifty percent of the participants interviewed were unable to keep pace with technology. Forty percent of entrepreneurs indicated that the rapid change in business technology was having significant economic hardship on their businesses, and 35% of participants revealed that they were experiencing opera-tion inefficiencies due to the rapid changes in information and the technological infrastructure. Eight of the participants reported that their businesses were suffering economically due to the pervasive change of business technology.

5.1   Recommendations

The need for technological resources in the small entrepreneurial sector was the cen-tral theme for the entrepreneurs who were engaged in the study; all the participants (100%) reported that a concessional system that would help finance entrepreneurs based on their individual business revenues might lead to a greater number of tech-nologically efficiency for entrepreneurial business operations. Small entrepreneurs' interest might be better served if an organization was established to assess the techno-logical needs of small entrepreneurs and provide assistance. In addition, an institution established to provide technological training and funding of small entrepreneurial businesses may help to keep entrepreneurs business on the technological frontier. Thus, a future study could examine why it is necessary for entrepreneurs to change or implement new technological systems every 18 months. Further study could be to examine the new technologies to see if they provide significant value beyond the previous version and can old technology be modified. Also, a future study could review the Small Business Administration program and policies to see in what ways that organization could assist entrepreneurs acquire modern technology.

5.2 Implications for Social Change

Entrepreneurs have made significant contributions nationally and globally. Some of their contributions included jobs generators, innovators, and stakeholders of the local communities in which they operated. Despite their technological challenges, many small business entrepreneurs support local schools and community centers as a way to improve the quality of life for local residents [2, 36]. Entrepreneurs are determined individuals who do not become discouraged easily. Thus, entrepreneurs have the ability to overcome technological barriers and build successful businesses despite technological challenges.

6 Conclusion

The emergence of multiple technological innovations and rapid changes in some business operations technologies have presented tremendous challenges for many entrepreneurs who lacked financial and technical resources. Despite those challenges, some entrepreneurs have been able to use their creativity to build successful business enterprises. Many small business entrepreneurs have discovered that they could leverage their limited resources by employing business technology and survive in a digital-, Internet-, and online-driven marketplace.

Entrepreneurs on the global business horizon have experienced various technological challenges, including the use of outdated technological systems that threaten to undermine their business efforts. Forty-five percent of the entrepreneurs who participated in the study operated with substandard technology which caused them to lag behind innovative business practice. Consequently, they had technological limitations that negatively affected business growth and limited their ability to take advantage of new market opportunities. In the light of this study, entrepreneurs can overcome the technological challenge if they formed a cooperative organization for technology funding and fund this organization through membership.

References

1. Blake, C., Kane, G.C.: How Facebook is delivering personalization on a whole new scale. MIT Sloan. Manage. Rev. **55**(4), 1–9 (2014)
2. Kaplan, J.M., Warren, A.C.: Patterns of Entrepreneurship Management. Wiley, Hoboken (2013)
3. Laudon, K.C., Laudon, J.P.: Essentials of Management Information System. Pearson, New York (2017)
4. Global Entrepreneurship Monitor: Funding and Sponsoring Institutions (2016). Retrieved from http://www.gemconsortium.org/report/49480
5. Butler, B.S., Patrick, J.B., Bateman, J.P., Gray, P.H., Diamant, E.I.: An attraction-selection-attrition theory of on-line community size and resilience. MIS Q. **38**(3), 699–728 (2014)
6. National Economic Council: Moving America's Small Businesses & Entrepreneurs Forward: Creating an Economy Built to Last (2012). http://whitehouse.gov/administration/eop/nec
7. Chapman, S.N., Arnold, T.J.R., Gatewood, A.K., Clive, M.L.: Introduction to Materials Management. Pearson, New York (2017)
8. Dedrick, J., Kraemer, K.L., Shih, E.: Information technology and productivity in developed and developing countries. J. Manage. Syst. **30**(1), 1–26 (2013)
9. Moustakas, C.: Phenomenological Research Methods. Sage, Thousand Oaks, CA (1994)
10. Van Manen, M.: Researching Lived Experience: Human Science for Action Sensitive Pedagogy. State University of New York Press, Albany (1990)
11. Feng, T., Xu, X.: How do enterprise resource planning systems affect firm risk: post-implementation impact? MIS Q. **39**(1), 39–60 (2015)
12. Anthony, V., Lowry, P.B., Eggett, D.: Using accountability to reduce access policy violations information systems. J. Manage. Inf. Syst. **29**(4), 263–290 (2013)
13. Panko, R.R., Panko, J.: Business Data Network and Security. Prentice Hall, Upper Saddle River (2015)
14. Wong, C.W.Y., Lai, K., Cheng, T.C.E.: Value of information integration to supply chain management: role of internal and external contingencies. J. Manag. Inf. Syst. **39**(1), 161–200 (2014)
15. Gartner, G.: Hype cycle for emerging technologies. Technology, 1–2. (2015). https://www.gartner.com/doc/3100227/hype-cycle-emerging-technologies
16. Raskino, M., Waller, G.: Digital to the Core: Remastering Leadership for Your Industry, Your Enterprise and Yourself. Brookline, Biblio Motion (2015)
17. Regis, P.L., Miley, C., Sengupta, S.: Multi-hop mobile wireless mesh network testbed developments and measurements. Int. J. Innovative. Res. Comput. Commun. Eng. **5**(8), 1 (2017)
18. Han, K., Sunil, M.: Information technology outsourcing and Non-IT operating costs: an empirical investigation. MIS Q. **37**(1), 315–331 (2013)
19. Liu, C.Z., Yoris, A.A., Hoon, S.C.: The effects of freemium strategy in the mobile app market: an empirical study of Google Play. J. Manage. Inf. Syst. **31**(3), 326–354 (2014)
20. Chen, J., Jan, S.: An economic analysis of on-line advertising using behavioral targeting. MIS Q. **38**(2), 429–449 (2014)
21. Chen, Y., Ramamurthy, K., Wen, K.: Organizations' information security policy compliance: stick or carrot approach. J. Manage. Inf. Syst. **29**(3), 157–188 (2013)
22. Brigham, E.E., Ehrhardt, M.C.: Financial Management: Theory and Practice. South-Western, Mason (2005)
23. Sullivan, D., Marvel, M.: How entrepreneur's knowledge and network ties relate to the number of employees in new SMEs. J. Small Bus. Manage. **49**, 185–206 (2011). https://doi.org/10.1111/j.1540-627x.2011.00321
24. Martens, D., Foster, P.: Explaining data-driven document classification. MIS Q. **38**(1), 73–99 (2014)
25. Mitter, C.: Business angel: issues, evidence, and implications for emerging markets. J. Int. Bus. Econ. **12**(3), 1–11 (2012). Retrieved from http://www.iabe.org/domains/iabex/journal.aspx?journalid=9

26. Chiang, I.R., Jhang-Li, J.: Delivery consolidation and service competition among internet service providers. J. Manag. Inf. Syst. **34**(3), 254–286 (2014)
27. Stallings, W.H., Lawrie, B.: Computer Security: Principles and Practice. Prentice Hall, Upper Saddle River (2015)
28. Gediminas, A., Bockstedt, J., Curley, S.P.: Bundling effects and variety seeking for digital information good. J. Manage. Inf. Syst. **31**(4), 182–212 (2015)
29. Maruping, L.M., Massimino, M.: Motivating employees to explore collaboration technology in team context. MIS Q. **35**(1), 1–3 (2015)
30. Tallon, P.P., Ramirez, V.R., Short, J.E.: The information artifact in IT governance: toward a theory of information governance. J. Manage. Inf. Syst. **30**(3), 141–178 (2014)
31. Singleton Jr., R., Straits, B.: Approaches to Social Research. Oxford University Press, New York (2010)
32. Trochim, W.M.K., Donnelly, J.P.: The Research Methods Knowledge Base. Cengage Learning, Mason (2008)
33. Creswell, J.W.: Qualitative Inquiry & Research Design. Sage, Thousand Oaks (2007)
34. Corbin, J., Strauss, A.: Basics of Qualitative Research. Sage, Thousand Oaks (2008)
35. Xia, Z., Xue, L., Whinston, A.B.: Managing independent information security risks: cyber insurance, managed security services and risk pooling arrangements. J. Manage. Inf. Syst. **30**(1), 123–152 (2013)
36. Hoffer, J.A., Ramesh, V., Heikki, T.: Modern Database Management. Prentice Hall, Upper Saddle River (2015)

Regional Binding in Information Networks of Open Data Promotion in Local Governments of Japan

Akio Yoshida, Tetsuo Noda and Masami Honda

Abstract With the development of information and communication technology, the way how certain knowledge, idea and concept spread in the society has become different from the past. The purpose of this study is to obtain findings about information flow contributing to the Open Data promotion in Japanese local governments. We conducted WEB questionnaire survey and obtained information networks of Open Data promotion in local governments. Network in the open data personnel had different characteristics from those of the WEB reference relationship network in Social Network Analysis. It shows those two networks have different structures. This result can be indicative that the regional binding plays an important role in the information network.

Keywords Local governments · Open data · Information network · Regional binding

1 Introduction

With the development of information and communication technology, the way how certain knowledge, idea and concept spread in the society has become different from the past. Knowledge of how information is propagated in an information society is one of the most important concerns. The concept of scale-free network is popular in social network analysis, in which popularity concentrates on some nodes, and those who obtain a lot of information get information more [1]. On the other hand, it has been pointed out that social studies in Japan should pay attention to the role played by social groups, and that social networks online and offline can be very different

A. Yoshida (✉)
Jawaharlal Nehru University, New Delhi, India
e-mail: akio.yoshida@gmail.com

T. Noda
Shimane University, Matsue, Japan

M. Honda
Tokyo Institute of Technology, Tokyo, Japan

© Springer Nature Switzerland AG 2020
Y. Baghdadi et al. (eds.), *ICT for an Inclusive World*,
Lecture Notes in Information Systems and Organisation 35,
https://doi.org/10.1007/978-3-030-34269-2_8

[2]. Although many researches are expected in this area, it is very difficult to extract networks in society and to capture the state of information propagation there.

In the survey project covering all of the Japanese local governments which implement Open Data, we got an opportunity to ask questions about the state of information propagation among local governments. How is the local governments' information network connected? Is there any differences in networks between online and offline? The findings obtained in this research will not only contribute to the consideration of the spread process of Open Data and future promotion activities, but also contribute to the theory of social networks. We will show in what kind of the project this study was done in the following parts.

Open Data is to publish the data possesed by an organization in the form easy-to-secondary-use. Among them, those data which are collected and held by governmental agencies are expected to contribute to solving regional problems. On 20th Jan 2017, Saitama prefecture in Japan has created a common format of Open Data in cooperation with 58 municipalities in the prefecture [3]. The common format is very important in both promotion and utility of Open Data, for it leads the resolution of local problems widely [4]. Though there is also a research on platform types of Open Data with a focus on network aspect [5], Japan is on the way of Open Data promotion.

In the view of network effect [6], the more local governments provide these public data, the values and utilities of each data sets will increase. Open Data initiatives in advanced municipalities bring about certain economic effects, and Open Data can spread to various places throughout the network. In this process, the following local governments get information from advanced ones. Both the estimation of economic effects and findings in the way of spread can help to promote Open Data.

With respect to economic effects by using Open Data, some estimates have been carried out by the governments including the EU Commission [7] and private research institutions, there are also the estimates made in Japan [8]. Noda carried out a study of the relevant prior research [9]. Subsequently, on the basis of the study results, a questionnaire survey for local governments of Japan was conducted [10]. A comparison of the major previous studies and this study are shown in Table 1. First, this survey also aims to estimate the economic effect in line with the current situation of Open Data in Japan. Second, the investigation object is the local government which is a provider of data. Third, the estimation process of the economic effects become clear by using a uniform question of WEB questionnaire. Fourth, there was no prior research on economic effects which treated the solution of regional issues and examined the existence of locality. There is an investigation about Open Data on major 20 municipalities in the vast Australia [11]. But it was not a research for economic effect or social network.

This study is included in the project about economic effect of Open Data. The purpose of this study in the project is to obtain the knowledge how Open Data spread in local governments of Japan by the network analysis on the answers in the questionnaire on how the local governments refer information of each other. Honda et al. have already pointed out the role of advanced cities in Open Data promotion [13]. Especially Sabae city in Fukui Prefecture, which is the first city that had started

Table 1 Comparison with previous surveys

	Tasman [12] 2008	Vickery [7] 2011	Jitsuzumi [8] 2013	This project [9] 2016
Area:	Oceania	EU	Japan	Japan
Investigation object:	Use operators	Use operators	Use operators	Data provider
Data provider:	All	Public agencies	Public agencies	Local governments
Kind of data:	Spatial information	All	All	All
Method:	Interview	Applying parameters from Tasman	Applying parameters from Tasman	Questionnaire (Web)

Source Noda et al. [4]

open data in Japanese local government, was referred well by other municipalities. In this study, total structures of information networks are analyzed. Municipalities can learn the ways of Open Data on websites by others. They can also get information about Open Data from personnel in other municipalities. Therefore, this study is going to clarify the difference. It will help us to know how to promote Open Data efficiently.

2 Method

WEB questionnaire were requested to the persons in charge of Open Data at local governments of Japan which have already implemented Open Data. WEB site for answer were constructed and e-mails of the request for answer were delivered using the SPIRAL of Piped Bits Co., Ltd. Period was up to 22nd February from 9th February, 2016. The investigation objects were extracted from Open Data municipality list of Fukuno [14] at the time of survey added Atsugi city, 182 local governments of Japan (Table 2). Response rate is at 57.1%, up to 63.5% excluding the administrative districts of major cities.

The main questions in this survey were, percentages and progress degrees of Open Data, the cost at the time of implementation of Open Data, the reduction cost of the past business, and the feeling of personnel. In addition, the use of the data, the possibility of private use, and the network of information propagation about Open Data in the inter-local government were asked. In the question of the information network, the 182 local governments made up of all subjects presented to the respondents by pull-down menu, to select the appropriate other local government in the order. Specific questions are as follows. If we asked them to answer all informants,

Table 2 Summary of survey on local government with open data

	All	Prefecture	City	Major city	Administrative district
All:	1963	47	1721	20	175
Request for survey (LG with OD):	182	23	115	18	26
Rate of LG with OD: (%)	9.3	48.9	6.7	90.0	14.9
Number of respondent:	104	14	75	10	5
Rate of recovery: (%)	57.1	60.9	65.2	55.6	19.2

*Included major cities in city, the number of all Cities is 1741
Source Yoshida et al. [9]

it would be too much a load for respondents. It might decrease response rate. Therefore, respondents were asked to select five municipalities in this survey, based on the name generator method in 1985 GSS [15].

- "Do you access the following other municipalities' WEB sites, in the reference of the state of Open Data? Please select five in the order you refer the most." … (A)
- "Do you get information about Open Data from personnel of public information at the following other municipalities? Please select five in the order you get the most, including the case you attended a seminar." … (B).

Information networks obtained from the two questions of the respondents were compared by Clustering Coefficient.

3   Results

The information network in WEB sites (A) is shown in Fig. 1. And the information network in persons in charge of information policy (B) is shown in Fig. 2. Node numbers were given to local governments from north to south. The numeral closeness also shows geographical closeness in Japan. Some core cities in those networks were shown in their names, not numbers. They are Sabae, Yokohama, Fukuoka, Shizuoka prefecture and Fukui prefecture. Degree centralization is 0.25 in information network in the WEB site (A), 0.23 in Information network in the persons in charge of public information (B). Density is 0.009 in (A), 0.005 in (B). Those results indicate that certain cities have more centrality in (A) than (B), and (A) has almost twice density of (B). They also can be seen in those figures.

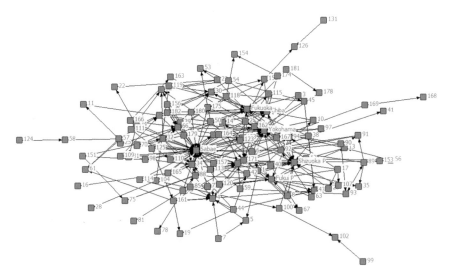

Fig. 1 Information network in WEB sites (A)

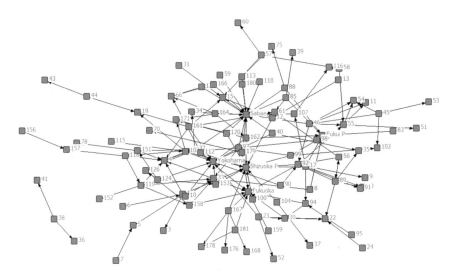

Fig. 2 Information network in persons in charge of information policy (B)

4 Discussion

What is the reason for the difference? As one of them, there exists a regional binding in the Open Data of the municipalities [13]. Sabae city in Fukui Prefecture which won the large number of nomination in this study is a pioneering local government in Open Data and has also grabbed nationwide attention. When other local governments are going to implement the Open Data, it is a very natural flow to check the WEB site of Sabae city trying to refer to their efforts. There also would be many local governments that participated in lectures and trying to listen to the person in charge directly. Such reference relationship like scale-free network is considered to exist [1]. Early adaptor like Sabae city, which is the first city in Open Data, has more chances to be referred.

On the other hand, 17 other municipalities in Fukui Prefecture has conducted Open Data at the time of this survey. Municipalities which has already implemented Open Data are at most 182, of the nationwide 1963 local governments as seen in Table 2. Municipalities with Open Data in Fukui Prefecture are 18 including Sabae city. This number is the most in Japan except the administrative district of Osaka City. On the flip side, it does not mean that the impact of Sabae city uniformly delivered across the country. Municipality around Sabae city implemented Open Data. It can be said that the influence of regional bindings appeared. Sabae city is linked nationwide in Fig. 1, but it is not in Fig. 2. These results are consistent with the analysis by degree distributions which showed the difference from scale-free network and suggested the existence of another networking structure [16].

5   Conclusion

This study only showed the difference of whole information networks between online and offline, and pointed out the possibility that regional bonds work well. But aiming to further promotion of Open Data, we should also remember that the regional peer pressure plays one of the important roles, and should not limit ourselves by following the success stories of some pioneering local governments.

In the formation of the social network, considering human constraints of time and money, it is also necessary to focus on familiar and homogeneous relationship. Findings of this study may not stay only in the range of Open Data promotion. Future task is to generate them considering peculiarity of Open Data.

References

1. Barabási, A.-L., Albert, R.: Emergence of scaling in random networks. Science **286**, 509–512 (1999)
2. Yoshida, A.: Factors influencing the size of personal networks. J. Socio-Inf. Stud. **14**(2), 171–180 (2010) (in Japanese)
3. The Nikkei.: Saitama prefecture makes it easy to use open data in a common form with municipalities., http://www.nikkei.com/article/DGXLASFB20HBQ_Q7A120C1L72000/ (in Japanese)
4. Noda, T., Honda, M., Yoshida, A.: Economic effect by open data in local government in Japan. In: Baghdadi, Y., Harfouche, A. (eds.) ICT for a Better Life and a Better World, The Impact of Information and Communication Technologies on Organizations and Society, pp. 165–173. Springer, Heidelberg (2019)

5. Danneels, L., Viaene, S., Van den Bergh, J.: Open data platforms: discussing alternative knowledge epistemologies. Gov. Inf. Q. **34**(3), 365–378 (2017)
6. Katz, M.L., Shapiro, C.: Network externalities, competition, and compatibility. Am. Econ. Rev. **75**(3), 424–440 (1985)
7. Vickery, G.: CReview of recent studies on PSI re-use and related market developments. http://ec.europa.eu/newsroom/dae/document.cfm?doc_id=1093 (2011)
8. Jitsuzumi, T., Hatta, M., Noda, T., Watanabe, T.: Innovation Nippon Study Group report Economic effect estimation of open data. http://innovation-nippon.jp/reports/2013StudyReport_OpenData.pdf (in Japanese)
9. Noda, T.: A consideration about the method of economic effect estimation by using Open Data. Shimane Univ. Fac. Law Lett. Bull. J. Econ. **41**, 33–52 (2015)
10. Yoshida, A., Noda, T., Honda, M.: A research of economic effects created by using open data in local governments. In: Proceedings of the Conference on Society of Socio-Informatics 2016 (2016) (in Japanese)
11. Chatfield, A.T., Reddick, C.G.: A longitudinal cross-sector analysis of open data portal service capability: the case of Australian local governments. Gov. Inf. Q. **34**(2), 231–243 (2017)
12. ACIL Tasman.: The value of spatial information: the impact of modern spatial information technologies on the Australian economy. Report Prepared for the CRC for Spatial Information and ANZLIC, Australia, the Spatial Information Council. http://www.crcsi.com.au/assets/Resources/7d60411d-0ab9-45be-8d48-ef8dab5abd4a.pdf (2008)
13. Honda, M., Noda, T., Yoshida, A.: Positioning of the precedent local government in the influence of open data promotion. In: Information Processing Society of Japan 137th, Information System and Social Environment research workshop (2016)
14. Fukuno, T.: Japan of Open Data City Map. http://fukuno.jig.jp/2013/opendatamap
15. Smith, T.W., Marsden, P., Hout, M., Kim, J.: General Social Surveys, 1972–2014: Cumulative Codebook. Chicago: NORC at the University of Chicago. (National Data Program for the Social Sciences Series, No. 22). http://gss.norc.org/get-documentation/questionnaires (2015)
16. Yoshida, A., Noda, T., Honda, M.: Information networks of open data promotion in local governments of Japan. J. Socio-Inform. **10**(1) (2018)

Handover and QoS Parameters a Performance Assessment on 3G Based SDN

Fatima Laassiri, Mohamed Moughit and Noureddine Idboufker

Abstract This paper presents a performance implementation of Multi-criteria algorithm decision in Software Defined Network (SDN) Controller to improve the performance under Third Generation (3G) networks. This work is based on the UMTS mobility, which is adopted by the interface S1, with a macro mobility of level 3 based on MIPv6. SIP protocol is used between two end users to evaluate the performance of 3G networks with SDN network paradigm applied.

Keywords SDN · 3G · QoS · OpenFlow · MIPv6

1 Introduction

Software Defined Network (SDN) [1] is a new network paradigm that is used to simplify network management and lower complexity in network technology. In this work QoS parameters are investigated on third generation (3G) cellular networks using SDN approach. The implementation is based on a simulation performance evaluation comparison between SDN-based and SDN-free 3G [2] network.

The communication between the two topologies is done with the Session Initiation Protocol (SIP) [3], with intra-UMTS mobility, that it is S1 and a macro-mobility of high quality that it is Mobile IPv6 (MIPv6).

F. Laassiri (✉) · M. Moughit
IR2M Laboratory, FST, Univ Hassan 1 UH1-Settat, Settat, Morocco
e-mail: laassiri.fati@gmail.com

M. Moughit
EEA & TI Laboratory, FST, Univ Hassan 2, Mohammedia, Morocco

N. Idboufker
National Schools of Applied Sciences, Univ Cadi Ayyad, Marrakech, Morocco

M. Moughit
National Schools of Applied Sciences Khouribga, Univ Hassan 1 UH1-Settat, Settat, Morocco

© Springer Nature Switzerland AG 2020
Y. Baghdadi et al. (eds.), *ICT for an Inclusive World*,
Lecture Notes in Information Systems and Organisation 35,
https://doi.org/10.1007/978-3-030-34269-2_9

2 Problem and Solution

3G cellular networks must provide high quality planning and organizations for their subscribers, while respecting traffic demands. Currently, 3G networks face various limitations, which can be classified as: Limited scalability, complex network management, manual network configuration, complex and expensive network devices, high cost, inflexibility, and network virtualization [4, 5].

Current QoS performance parameters in 3G networks are: end-to-end delay (~49 ms), latency (~9.9 ms), jitter (~84.1 ms), percentage of packets lost (20%), and MOS (2.8). Moreover, handover travel time is around (~45 ms). To improve QoS over 3G network we propose to add SDN technology with centralized control to the UMTS architecture.

The software defined mobile network (SDMN) concept is proposed as an extension of the SDN paradigm to support network specific mobile functionality. In addition, it has a higher degree of service awareness and optimal use of network resources than the original network concepts.

3 SDN and SDMN Networks

The SDN and virtualization concept adaptation to the mobile network domain will solve the aforementioned problems. The SDN concept not only solves these problems, but also improves the flexibility, scalability, and performance of a telecommunications network. SDN is initially designed for fixed networks.

However, mobile networks have different requirements than fixed networks such as mobility management, the valuable traffic transport, effective protection of the air interface, strong use of the tunnel in the transport of packages and more. Therefore The SDMN architecture is consists of three layers [6–8] as shown in Fig. 1.

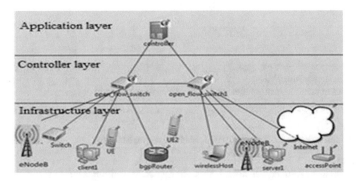

Fig. 1 SDN network architecture

The infrastructure layer: this layer is also known by the data plane (DP) layer, it is the physical part of the network that encompasses all the physical equipment. DP layer composed of network elements such as switches, base stations and other devices [9].

Network Controller: the logically centralized controller provides the consolidated control functionality of the DP switches. OpenFlow is the protocol that it is used to communicate with DP elements. Fundamentally, OpenFlow is used to install the flow rules in each switch to route long-distance network traffic. The limit between the network controller and the DP layer is traversed by the south bound application programming interface (API).

Application layer: this layer includes applications and programs that communicate the behaviour with SDN controller resources through north bound APIs.

Protocol OpenFlow: it provides an open and standard way for a controller to communicate with an OpenFlow switch [10]. It is a protocol standard open to researchers to run experimental protocols in networks they use [11]. It allows a logically centralized controller to install packet management rules in the underlying switches [12]. The OpenFlow specification also provides an excellent source of information. Because there are three types of messages supported by the OpenFlow protocol:

The controller-to-switch messages: controller-to-Switch messages are initiated by the controller to configure the switch, exchanging switching capability in the OpenFlow switch and managing the flow table [13].

The asynchronous messages: The asynchronous messages are sent by the Open-Flow switch to the controller, they announce a change in the network or the state of the switch. This change can be called an event [14].

The symmetric messages: symmetric messages are sent back and forth without any request to diagnose problems in a controller-switch connection [15].

4   Global Architecture of UMTS

Universal Mobile Telecommunication System (UMTS) is a third generation mobile networks that are part of the International Mobile Telecommunications (IMT-2000) family [16]. The UMTS network responds to the expected saturation of existing 2G networks and the need for new services with enhanced QoS [17].

The UMTS network is divided into three main parts:
The core network.
UMTS Terrestrial Radio Access Network (UTRAN).
The terminal or the user equipment (UE).

These three major domains are separated by different radio interfaces. Figure 2 shows the general architecture of UMTS, and Fig. 3 shows a typical SDN-free realization of the UMTS network topology while Fig. 4 shows a UMTS SDN-based topology realization.

Fig. 2 3G network
architecture

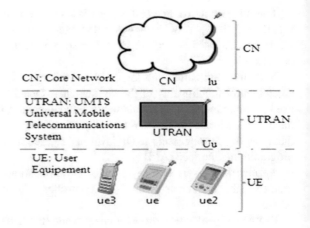

CN: Core Network

UTRAN: UMTS
Universal Mobile
Telecommunications
System

UE: User
Equipement

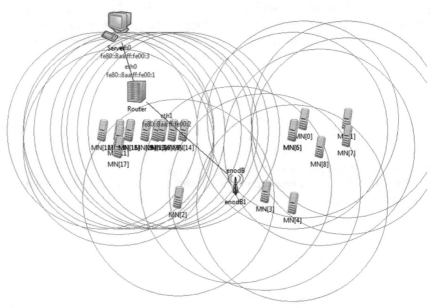

Fig. 3 Scenarios 1: 3G network architecture without SDN

The SDN architecture consists of a group of six packets, as described in the following modules (OpenFlow, ControllerApps, HostApps, HyperFlow, Kandoo, Utility).

This section describes the topologies of the simulation settings implemented under network simulator OMNeT++. The simulation has two scenarios: 3G SDN-fee and 3G SDN-based scenarios. In both scenarios we used the SIP protocol as the underlying protocol for communication between two users. We have used mobility under intra-UMTS with the interface S1 which occurs when user equipment moves from

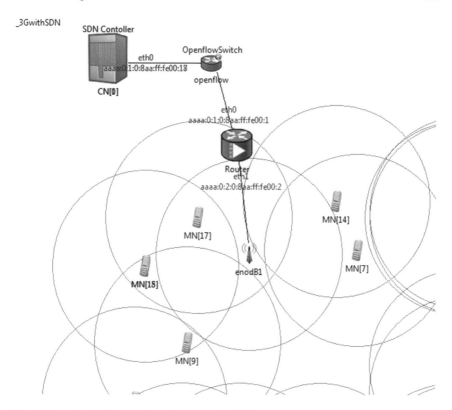

Fig. 4 Scenarios 2: 3G network architecture with SDN

one NodeB to another, with a manipulation of a macro-mobility of level 3 taking advantage of the MIPv6 protocol for mobile nodes to move randomly across the Internet while still receiving their datagrams at a fixed address. A brief description of UMTS 3G network architecture without and with SDN network is introduced.

4.1 Functional Architecture of UMTS SDMN

The UMTS architecture consists of the several functional components [17] such as Core Network, Radio Access Network UTRAN, User equipment (UE).

4.1.1 Core Network (CN)

CN [18] provides the connection between the different access networks of UMTS and other networks such as: telephone network, GSM network, RNIS network, etc.

It provides support for UMTS communication services; it also manages the location information of mobile users [19]. It consists of three parts including two areas:

Domain Packet Switched (PS): it allows the switching of packets [20]. The PS domain is composed of several modules:

- Serving GPRS Support Node (SGSN): responsible for registering users in a geographical area under a routing area (RA).
- Gateway GPRS Support Node (GGSN): it is gateway for UMTS packet service to external data networks such as Internet.
- Domain Circuit Switched (CS): it is used for telephony, and ISDN networks. The CS domain is composed of several modules:
- Mobile-services Switching Center (MSC): responsible for establishing communication with the user equipment. Its role is to switch the data.
- Gateway MSC (GMSC): is a gateway between the UMTS network and the public switched telephone network (PSTN). If user equipment contacts another device from a network outside the UMTS network, the communication goes through the GMSC which interrogates the HLR to retrieve the information of the user. Then, it routes the communication to the MSC on which the recipient user depends.
- Visitor Location Register (VLR): it is a database, quite similar to the HLR, attached to one or more MSCs. The VLR stores the temporary identity of the user equipment in order to prevent the interception of the identity of a user. The VLR is in charge of registering users in a geographical area LA (Location Area).

4.1.2   Radio Access Network UTRAN

The UTRAN access network allows several features [20]. These features include: network congestion control, allocation of radio resources, confidentiality, integrity, handover, paging, channel coding and decoding, synchronization between the NodeB and the radio network controller (RNC) and between the RNC and the core network. The main function of UTRAN is to transfer the data generated by the user. It acts as a bridge between the user equipment and the core network via the Uu and Iu interfaces. UTRAN is composed of two entities:

NodeB: it is an antenna that is distributed geographically throughout the country; it is equivalent of the BTS in GSM network. It manages the physical layer of the radio interface. It governs channel coding, interleaving, debit adaptation, and spreading. It communicates directly with the mobile under the interface named Uu, and with the RNC via the interface IU. Its main role is to provide radio reception and transmission functions for one or more cells of the UMTS access network with the user equipment. It works at the level of the physical layer of the OSI model (coding and decoding) [21]. Radio Network Controller (RNC): The main role of RNC is to manage the communications between the NodeB and the core network of UMTS.

It constitutes the access point for all services vis-a-vis the core network.

There are two types of RNCs to manage EU mobility when it moves from one cell to another with handover and macro-diversity mechanisms:

Serving RNC (SRNC): it manages radio connections with the mobile and serves as a point of attachment to the core network via IuPS and IuCS interfaces. It executes the handover and it executes the power control.

Drift RNC (DRNC): it allows you to manage other cells outside the SRNC, it also used by the mobile, to transfer data seamlessly between the mobile and the SRNC.

4.1.3   User Equipment (UE)

The user equipment (UE) is a major part of the overall 3G network architecture. It forms the final interface with the user. It has a higher number of applications and installations. It is essentially the device (in the broader terminology), although it has access to much faster data communications, it can be much more versatile because it contains applications. It consists of a variety of different elements, including RF circuits, processing, antenna, battery, etc.

5   SDN Components

SDN is a concept based on the separation between the control plane and the data plane. The architecture involve two main modules (1) the controller and (2) Switches:

SDN Controllers: its mission is to provide an abstraction layer of the network and present it as a system. It allows to quickly implementing a change on the network by translating a global request (for example: Prioritize the X application) in a series of operations on the network equipment (Netconf requests, additions of OpenFlow states, configuration in CLI...) Orders are given to the controller by an application via a so called northbound API. Controller software vendors publish the API documentation to enable interfacing applications. The controller communicates with the equipment via one or more southbound APIs. OpenFlow is positioned as a southbound API acting directly on the data plane. Other APIs allow acting on the management or control plane. Netconf is for example a southbound API allowing the controller to configure a device. A controller can even speak directly in CLI with a device to activate a feature.

OpenFlow switch: It is a physical switching device contains a number of ports and queues; it is based on the OpenFlow protocol.

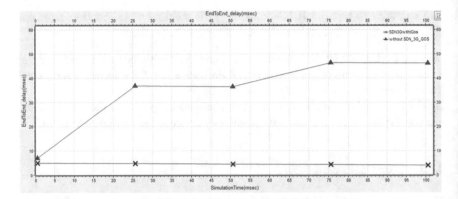

Fig. 5 End-to-end delay in 3G SDN-free and SDN-based scenarios

6 Simulation Results and Discussion

This paper presents a performance implementation of Multi-criteria algorithm decision in SDN Controller to improve the performance under 3G networks, in terms of QoS parameters such as end-to-end delay, latency, jitter, lost packet, MOS, under two network scenarios: 3G SDN-free and 3G SDN-based scenarios. It is worth mentioning that call setup time between two users in SDN-based approach was around 0.04 s while it was around 4 s in SDN-free approach.

6.1 End-to-End Delay Time Parameters

Figure 5 presents the end-to-end delay results, that the graph shows the 3G free scenario with a higher value of (49 ms) compared to the 3G based SDN scenarios that, it has a reliable delay of (9 ms) because it has the load balancing in SDN Controller, the one that it justifies as SDN adds a positive appreciation for 3G.

6.2 Jitter Parameters

Figure 6 illustrates the jitters, where the 3G scenario is based on SDN is about 0.03 ms, that it is low then half of 3G without SDN, it has the value of 0.15 ms, which results that the addition of a SDN network with multi-criterion algorithms in 3G is very low to be compared with the 3G without SDN.

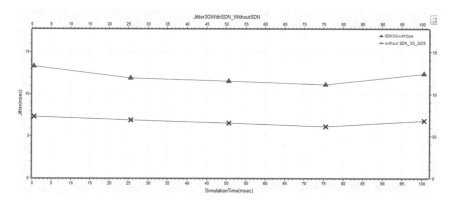

Fig. 6 Jitter in 3G SDN-free and SDN-based scenarios

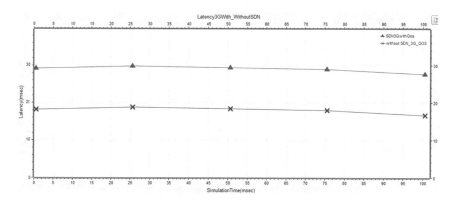

Fig. 7 Latency in 3G SDN-free and SDN-based scenarios

6.3 Latency Parameters

Figure 7 shows evolution of latency in 3G Networks without SDN is less (99 ms) but using SDN latency decrease to 80 ms.

6.4 Lost Packet Parameters

Figure 8 presents the 3G without SDN is 20%, so it is very high, compared to the 3G approach with SDN, it is about 0.5%. This shows the impact of adding SDN view to the 3G network.

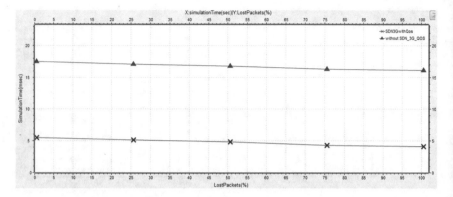

Fig. 8 Lost packets in 3G SDN-free and SDN-based scenarios

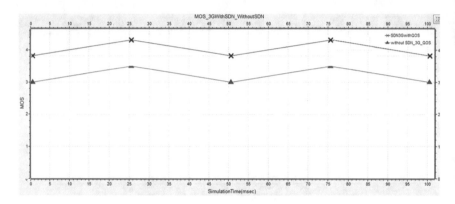

Fig. 9 MOS in 3G SDN-free and SDN-based scenarios

6.5 MOS Parameters

Figure 9 shows that the MOS offered by the 3G approach without SDN is 1, 9. Whereas the approach based on the 3G with SDN is about 2, 9. Which it presents an indicator of the increases in the quality of the vocal transmission.

7 Performance Synthessis

We can conclude that the 3G architecture with SDN is totally beneficial compared to without SDN.

8 Conclusion

This paper presents a performance implementation of Multi-criteria algorithm decision in Software Defined Network (SDN) Controller to improve the performance under Third Generation (3G) networks. This work is based on the UMTS mobility, which is adopted by the interface S1, with a macro mobility of level 3 based on MIPv6. SIP protocol is used between two end users to evaluate the performance of 3G networks with SDN network paradigm applied. It has been concluded that the implementation of the multi-criterion algorithm in SDN Controller for 3G has a high effect of performance parameters. The future work can focus on improving the Handover on 3G technology.

References

1. Laassiri, F., Moughit, M., Idboufker, N.: Evaluation of the QoS parameters in different SDN architecture using OMNeT 4.6++. In: International Conference STA'2017, IEEE (December 2017)
2. Dahlman, E., Parvall, S., Skold, J., Beming, P.: 3G Evolution, HSPA and LTE for Mobile Broadband, 2nd edn. Elsevier, First edition (2007)
3. Rosenberg, J., Schulzrinne, H., Camarillo, G., Johnston, A., Peterson, J., Sparks, R., Handley, M., Schooler, E.: SIP: session initiation protocol. https://www.rfc-editor.org/rfc/rfc3261.txt,Book (JUNE 2002)
4. Pentikousis, K., Wang, Y., Hu, W.: Mobile flow, toward software defined mobile networks. IEEE Commun. Mag. **51**(7), 44–53 (2013)
5. Li, L.E., Mao, Z.M., Rexford, J.: Toward software defined cellular networks. European Workshop on Software Defined Networking (EWSDN). IEEE, Darmstadt, Germany (2012)
6. Costa-Requena, J.: SDN integration in LTE mobile backhaul networks. SDN switches managed from the cloud together with the rest of LTE network elements. In: 2014 International Conference on InformationNetworking (ICOIN). IEEE
7. Hernandez, B.: (CEGO) LA T…L…"Phone sur IP, Réseau d'échange sur la gestion des centres de relations client le", p. 6 (February 2007)
8. Liu, Y., Ding, A.Y., Tarkoma, S.: Software Defined Networking in Mobile Access Networks. University of Helsinki, Helsinki (2013)
9. Scott-Hayward, S., O'Callaghan, G.: SakirSezer "Sdn Security: A Survey. IEEE (January 2014)
10. Tury, M.: 'Les risques d'OpenFlow et du SDN. maxence.tury@ssi.gouv.fr, ANSSI, May 2016
11. Gringeri, S., Bitar, N., Xia, T.J.: Extending software defined network principles to include optical transport. IEEE (March 2013)
12. McKeown, N., et al.: OpenFlow: enabling innovation in campus networks. SIGCOMM CCR, **38**(2) (March 2008)
13. Kumar, S., Kumar, T., Singh, G., Nehra, M.S.: Open flow switch with intrusion detection system. (IJSRET), 001–004 (October 2012)
14. Zangar Attia, N.: Intégration du Satellite dans les Réseaux Mobiles de 3G et B3G (April 2009)
15. Castellanos, C.U., Villa, D.L.: Performance of uplink fractional power control in UTRAN LTE. In: Vehicular Technology Conference, 2008. VTC Spring IEEE (May 2008)
16. Abousda, M.I., Bozed, K.A., Zerek, A.R.: Study the QoS and performance comparison of voice in MPLS and IP Networks. In: International Engineering Conference on Sustainability in Design and Innovation (ZEC Sustainability 2014), Amman, Jordan May 13–15 (2014)
17. Staehle, D., Mäder, A.: An analytic approximation of the uplink capacity in a UMTS network with heterogeneous traffic. Springer, vol. 5, pp. 81–90 (2003)

18. Khaoula, E.L.H.A.B.I.B.: 'Optimisation du réseau 3G en corrélation avec les statistiques et les KPI'S'. Mémoire de Fin d'Etudes, Juin (2011)
19. Naoui, K., Benahmed S.: Etude et mise en place de la solution VOIP over LTE, dimensionnement et mesure de la QoS. p. 16 (June 2015)
20. Ko, Y.-B., Shankarkumar, V., Vaidya, N.H.: Medium access control protocols using directional antennas in ad hoc networks. IEEE (August 2002)
21. http://www.radio-electronics.com/info/cellulartelecomms/umts/umts-wcdma-network-architecture.php (Decembre 2017)

Towards Cities as Communities

Mauro Romanelli

Abstract Cities should be communities that ensure high quality of life promoting effective services, sustaining knowledge acquisition and developing innovation, using technology to sustain urban growth and promote value creation. Cities becoming smart communities should adopt a smart approach to driving social and economic urban development employing information technology to promote innovation. Information and communication technologies (ICTs) help cities to achieve successful issues as smart communities within knowledge-based global and local economies and open societies. Sustaining smart growth relies on rethinking the city as a smart and sustainable community using technology to support collaboration between local government, businesses, education and research centres and people to change the city in a significant and positive way. Sustainable, inclusive and open cities should evolve as communities that use technology to support human capital value, to use knowledge sources encouraging public and private organizations to believe in cooperation for sustaining change through innovation.

Keywords Smart city · Smart community · Sustainable city

1 Introduction

Cities should become communities that ensure effective services and sustain social and economic innovation and growth within urban ecosystems identifying a smart and sustainable approach to development. Cities should support community development and encourage social interaction to promote opportunities for learning and knowledge sharing. Cities of the future should be knowledge oriented and technology-enabled communities. Cities should develop the smart city as a policy and managerial innovation, integrating services, technology and capabilities [1, 2]. Future smart communities should develop technology-enabled services platforms, promote urban development, sustain value creation for improving the quality of life and driving

M. Romanelli (✉)
University of Naples Parthenope, Via G. Parisi 13, 80132 Naples, Italy
e-mail: mauro.romanelli@uniparthenope.it

© Springer Nature Switzerland AG 2020
Y. Baghdadi et al. (eds.), *ICT for an Inclusive World*,
Lecture Notes in Information Systems and Organisation 35,
https://doi.org/10.1007/978-3-030-34269-2_10

processes of innovation and knowledge creation to enhance both service quality and supporting the education of people within the community [1–10].

Sustaining social, cultural and economic development relies more and more on revitalising economic and productive growth in urban and regional areas [11]. Technology helps cities to successful overcome issues as smart communities within knowledge-based global and local economies, and open societies. Sustaining smart growth relies on rethinking the city as a smart community that evolves towards sustainability by using technology to support collaboration between the local government, businesses, education and research centres and people to transform the city in a significant and positive way [8, 9].

This study aims at identifying a path in order to rethink cities as communities oriented towards sustainability, driving cities to becoming smart and sustainable, designing citizen-centred services relying on building smart governance. Sustaining infrastructures for innovation, knowledge and development helps cities to evolve as communities by continuously reinventing the patterns of sustainable development within urban ecosystems, improving the wealth and quality of life for people, sustaining urban business and innovation for learning and knowledge opportunities.

This study relies on literature review and analysis on the concepts of a city as smart community, innovation, development and sustainability of cities. Cities promoting a smart approach rediscover the city as a sustainable and smart-oriented community. The study is structured as follows. Following the introduction, the second section identifies how to define the city. In the third section, it is elucidated how to rethink the city as a smart community. The fourth section discusses how cities tend to become communities by reinventing as smart and sustainable cities, designing citizen-centred services and building smart governance, and promoting innovation systems and opportunities. The last section discusses and draws conclusions from the findings.

2 Defining Cities

There are several definitions about what a city is or should be. Thereby, cities are considered as social organisms that display internal and external forms of symbiosis and communication [12]. Cities are communities and places where people and businesses develop their activities to create value within an urban ecosystem. Cities exert influence on the quality of life and on the competitiveness of an urban business system. As meeting places and spaces, cities tend to develop as evolving organisms and learning systems, engendering creativity, encouraging social interaction and promoting the wealth of people within the community [13]. «Cities are economic and social systems in space. They are a product of deep-seated and persistent processes which enable and encourage people to amass in large numbers in small areas» [14]. Successful cities tend to achieve long-term results by relying on negotiation and organizational arrangements [15]. As places where the majority of people reside, cities are becoming the principal engines of economic growth and urban development evolving towards sustainability [16]. As meeting places and services providers, cities contribute to sustaining learning, education and culture driving social and economic innovation for change [10]. As service platforms and meeting places, cities contribute to creating and sharing knowledge by establishing objectives related to social and environmental issues [17].

3 Rethinking Cities as Smart Communities

Within knowledge-based economies cities should promote sustainable development by building smart communities as places for both life and work. Smart communities help promote economic development, job growth and ensure high quality of life [8].

Cities should use information technology to provide service ICT-enabled infrastructures and create digital platforms for advanced services to support businesses and facilitate public life [3]. Smart communities as cities use ICTs in order to better interact with their citizens using data and information and knowledge for problem solving [18]. Smart communities promote job growth and economic development. Smart communities contribute to improving the quality of life. Smart communities permit connectivity between local governments, schools, businesses, citizens and health and social services to address local objectives creating specific services and to help advance collective skills and capacities [19]. ICTs drive communities to become smart communities that revitalise local economies and to reduce the uncertainty emerging from the acceptance and implementation of ICTs [20]. Smart communities understand the potential of information technology driving private and public actors (local government, business, education, health care institutions and people) to cooperate and collaborate to change the community in a significant and positive way. Building smart and effective communities relies on active involvement and cooperation of businesses, education, government and individual citizens [8].

4 How to Drive Cities as Communities

Leading cities to becoming communities relies on driving social, economic and public value creation in the urban areas and implies to sustain a smart city approach, to design citizen-centred services by constructing smart governance and to promote innovation through continuous orientation to knowledge and learning.

4.1 Towards Smart and Sustainable Cities

Technology helps cities proceed towards sustainability by following a smart development approach. The adoption and implementation of ICT within an urban environment to ensure effective and efficient services helps to rethink and design a smart city as an innovative platform which integrates technology, services and social and urban systems [2]. A smart city is comprised of land, citizens, technology and a government [4]. Smart cities use information technology in order to develop smart industries and economies, promoting smart mobility, designing a smart government, relying on smart people and enhancing smart living and environments [21]. Cities tend to become smart cities sustaining human and social capital, participation, technological and transportation infrastructures for communication to promote sustainable economic development and growth and participatory governance ensuring high quality of life [5]. Within smart cities the quality of life is high due to the connections between the use of information technology within production processes, productivity, growth and human capital [22]. Sustaining smart growth relies on designing smart cities and communities that promote processes of innovation which improve the competitiveness of the urban system within knowledge-based economies [11, 23]. Developing a smart approach to governance and the economy by sustaining and increasing smart growth, developing smart cities communities helps ensure high quality of life for people living in urban areas [24]. Smart cities consider people as a critical resource to develop policies enabling the wealth of a community. A smart city is a centre of higher education which attracts creativity and a smart knowledge-oriented workforce in a dynamic learning environment. Smart city is a policy and managerial innovation. Technology, organisation and policies contribute to improving services, creating managerial capabilities and driving institutional urban problems [1]. Smart and sustainable cities use ICTs in order to identify new ways of addressing urban development for meeting the needs of future generations [25] and ensuring economic growth, employment opportunities and improving the quality of life, extending the wealth of people within a community and promoting sustainable urban development [26].

4.2 Designing Citizen-Centered Services by Constructing Smart Governance

Cities become efficient and effective service platforms following a smart approach to services innovation and delivery. Technology helps businesses, public bodies and citizens to build and improve services infrastructures to drive the urban development in geographical areas [4].

ICTs contribute to improving resilient cities as urban communities and can increase the city's ability to react to environmental, energy and economic pressures in ensuring a high quality of life as well as driving sustainable urban development

[27]. Cities should use information technology to provide ICT-enabled service infrastructures and create digital platforms for advanced services to support business and facilitate public life [3]. Cities becoming smart communities and sustainable cities tend to ensure efficient service delivery and infrastructures [26] by designing and implementing smart services that emphasise the citizen-centricity and services that are designed to follow the actual and specific demands and needs of their citizens [18]. City governments should use information technology to provide e-services, to promote e-partnering and e-democracy to sustain cooperation and foster citizens' participation in decision making. Cities should evolve leading citizens to become active agents participating in policy formulation and agenda (e-governance mode) and building a learning city where citizens are able to determine the rules for learning (learning city) [28, 29]. Sustaining smart governance should help both service delivery and innovation. Smart city governance refers to the use of ICT to achieve a successful outcome and build open governance processes. Engaging the community helps develop smart city initiatives that have a high impact on the quality of life of people [18]. Smarter cities should develop innovation for application as social, cultural environmental platforms rediscovering governance and community [30]. Sustaining smart governance helps both to define better policies and structure better forms of organisation between governments and other private and public organisations. Sustaining smart city governance helps the quality of the urban environment by influencing the nature of problem-domain and strengthening the local cooperative knowledge potential [31]. ICT helps to engage citizens in designing smart initiatives and project for ensuring better services and policies [32].

4.3 *Promoting Innovation Within Cities*

Cities of the future should actively promote urban development, sustaining learning and educational opportunities, driving social and economic innovation. Cities use technology and knowledge sources for engendering innovation and becoming knowledge-oriented cities that drive urban and sustainable development. Cities are engines of innovation systems and acquire intellectual capital [7].

Smart cities becoming smarter should create open 'digital citizen-developer' communities, smart open innovation urban ecosystems building new collaboration patterns and networks. Sustaining open innovation implies to design co-production and co-delivery of services and policies leading to more inclusive cities as platforms for efficient and effective services delivery and knowledge sharing [6]. Cities should drive knowledge-oriented, smart and inclusive growth. Cities should be « laboratories of knowledge development » [33] Within smart cities innovation helps improve the sustainability and resilience of communities [3]. The cities of tomorrow should offer higher education and training to attract and retain young, skilled and talented people who are searching for better employability, high income and quality of life. When becoming smart communities and drivers of economic growth, cities sustain open innovation through knowledge transfer among cities and supportive collaborations involving municipal governments, businesses citizenry and universities leading to co-creation, co-design and co-implementation of integrated and innovative solutions [9, 34]. Innovation processes and systems rely on managing knowledge sources. With regards to urban development, cities should employ knowledge sources involving private and public organizations, individuals and groups, people, professionals and social and cultural actors involved in co-creating innovation by using knowledge in urban environment. Developing knowledge-based cities relies on sustaining both a collective learning process and knowledge-based local development. Cities should support cooperation and integration to develop learning opportunities, support knowledge creation and sharing, driving human capital growth and designing the ways on how to reinforce knowledge and intellectual infrastructures within urban landscape and ecosystems [35].

5 Discussion and Conclusions

Rethinking cities as communities relies on sustaining smart city as a policy choice for building urban growth and ensuring efficient and effective services, developing innovation and opportunities for knowledge sharing. Cities as smart communities acquire human capital and sustainable sources for developing knowledge to support continuous organisational and individual learning in order to promote value creation.

Cities as communities tend to adopt a smart city approach when planning initiatives to involve city government, people, associations, businesses, educational and research centres to create public value. Cities following a smart city perspective proceed towards sustainability evolving as smart communities in the transition from ensuring services to developing innovation. The main contribution of this study is to provide a framework to identify how cities are becoming smart communities oriented to proceed towards sustainability in order to drive urban growth and development. Cities driving innovation by ensuring smart governance become communities oriented to sustainability as shown in Fig. 1.

Cities ensuring smart services tend to become service platforms by following a smart city approach to support the urban development and growth. Smart cities promoting smart governance initiatives and policies tend to design the city as a smart

	from Smart City	to Cities driving innovation
from ensuring services	Cities as Smart Platforms	Cities as Engine of innovation
to promoting smart governance	Cities as Smart Communities	Communities oriented to sustainability

Fig. 1 Cities as communities proceeding towards sustainability

community. Cities should be the engine of innovation by involving all the stake-holders of the urban ecosystem and sustain smart governance to proceed towards sustainability. People, businesses and organisations should cooperate in order to design the city as a community. Cities as smart services platforms drive urban development and growth. Smart cities developing innovation contribute to designing the city as an engine and driver of innovation for change. Sustainable cities design long-term policies, promote trust-based relationships with citizens encouraging people to participate in policy choices, develop smart governance driving change and sustaining continuous innovation. Cities should encourage partnerships between private and public organisations to develop knowledge creation for innovation and ensure a high quality of life in urban areas. As sustainable communities, cities should build an urban inclusive, cohesive, open and creative ecosystem engendering social, economic and public value co-creation and production relying on developing a smart city approach to drive growth, support smart governance, promoting opportunities for driving innovation and knowledge creation for education and learning. Sustainable, inclusive and open cities should evolve as communities using technology and sustaining human capital in order to create and use knowledge sources that encourage public and private organisations, industries, and to believe in cooperation to promote continuous change through innovation.

References

1. Nam, T., Pardo, T.A.: Smart city as urban innovation with dimensions of technology, people and institutions. In: Proceeding of the 5th In: International Conference on Theory and Practice of Electronic Governance, pp. 185–194. ACM (2011)
2. Albino, V., Berardi, U., Dangelico, R.M.: Smart cities: Definitions, dimensions, performance, and inititatives. J. Urban Technol. **22**, 3–21 (2015)
3. Anttiroiko, A.V., Valkama, P., Bailey, S.: Smart cities in the new service economy: building platforms for smart services. AI&Society. **29**, 323–334 (2014)
4. Dameri, R.P.: Searching for smart city definition: a comprehensive proposal. Int. J. Comput. Technol. **11**, 2544–2551 (2013)
5. Caragliu, A., Del Bo, C., Nijkamp, P.: Smart cities in Europe. J. Urban Technol. **18**, 65–82 (2011)
6. Paskaleva, K.A.: The smart city: a nexus for open innovation? Intell. Build. Int. **3**, 153–171 (2011)
7. Deakin, M.: Smart cities: state-of-the-art and governance challenge. Triple Helix. **1**, 1–16 (2014)
8. Lindskog, H.: Smart communities initiatives. In: Proceedings of the 3rd ISOne World Conference, vol. 16 (2004)
9. Eger, J.M.: Smart communities, universities, and globalizations: educating the workforce for tomorrow's economy. Metrop. Univ. **16**, 24–38 (2005)
10. Evans, B., Joas, S., Sundback, S., Theobald, K.: Governing Sustainable Cities. Earthscan, London (2005)
11. European Commission: Smart Cities and Communities—European Innovation Partnership. C(2012)4701 final, Brussels, 10.7.2012 (2012)
12. Schnore, L.F.: The city as a social organism. In: Bourne L.S. (ed.) Internal Structure of the City. Readings on space and environment, pp. 32–39. Oxford University Press, New York (1971)

13. Camagni, R.: Economia e pianificazione della città sostenibile. IlMulino, Bologna (1996)
14. Clark, D.: Urban world/global city. Routledge, London and New York (2004)
15. Czarniawska, B.: Remembering while forgetting: the role of automorphism in city management in Warsaw. Public Adm. **62**, 163–173 (2002)
16. Newman, P., Jennings, J.: Cities as sustainable ecosystems. Principles and practices. Island Press, Washington DC (2008)
17. Leon, R.D.: From the sustainable organization to sustainable knowledge-based organization. Econ. Insights—Trends Chall. **65**, 63–73 (2013)
18. Chourabi, H., Gil-Garcia, J.R., Pardo, T.A., Nam, T., Mellouli, S., Scholl, H.J., Walker, S., Nahon, K.: Understanding smart cities: an integrative framework. In: Proceedings of the 45th Hawaii International Conference on System Sciences, pp. 2289–2297. IEEE (2012)
19. Coe, A., Paquet, G., Roy, J.: E-governance and smart communities: a social learning challenge. Soc. Sci. Comput. Rev. **19**(1), 80–93 (2001)
20. Moser, M.A.: What is smart about the smart community movement. EJournal, 10, **11**(1), 1–11 (2001)
21. Giffinger, R., Fertner, C., Kramar, H., Kalasek, R., Pilchler-Milanović, N., Meijers, E.: Smart cities: ranking of European medium-sized cities. Vienna, Austria: Centre Centre of Regional Science (SRF), Vienna University of Technology. Available from http://www.smart-cities.eu/download/smart_cities_final_report.pdf
22. Shapiro, J.M.: Smart cities: quality of life, productivity and the growth. Effects of Human Capital. The Review of Economics and Statistics. **88**, 324–335 (2006)
23. Eger, J.M.: Smart growth, smart cities and the crisis at the pump. A Worldwide Phenomenon. I-Ways J. E-Gov. Ment Policy Regul. **32**, 47–53 (2009)
24. European Union: Cities of tomorrow. Challenges, visions, ways forward. European Commission, Directorate General for Regional Policy (2011)
25. Höjer, M., Wangel, J.: Smart sustainable cities: definition and challenges. In: Hilty, L., Aebischer, B. (eds.) ICT Innovations for Sustainability, pp. 333–349. Springer, Cham (2015)
26. Dhingra, M., Chattopadhyay, S.: Advancing smartness of traditional settlements-case analysis of Indian and Arab old cities. Int. J. Sustain. Built Environ. **5**, 549–563 (2016)
27. Papa, R., Galderisi, A., Majello, V., Cristina, M., Saretta, E.: Smart and resilient cities. A systematic approach for developing cross-sectoral strategies in the face of climate change. TeMA J. Land Use, Mobil. Environ. **8**, 19–49 (2015)
28. Michel, H.: e-administration, e-government, e-governance and the learning city: a typology of citizenship management using ICTs. Electron. J. E-Gov. Ment. **3**, 213–218 (2005)
29. Carrizales, T.: Functions of e-government. a study of municipal practices. State and Local Government Review, **40**, 12–26 (2008)
30. Allwinkle, S., Cruickshank, P.: Creating smart-er cities: an overview. J. Urban Technol. **18**, 1–17 (2011)
31. Meijer, A., Bolivar, M.P.R.: Governing the smart city: a review of the literature on smart urban governance. Int. Rev. Adm. Sci. **82**, 392–408 (2015)
32. Bolívar, M.P.R.: Smart cities: big cities, complex governance? In: Bolívar, M.P.R. (ed.) Transforming City Governments for Successful Smart Cities. pp. 1–8. Springer, Cham
33. Kunzmann, K.R.: Smart cities: a new paradigm of urban development. Crios **4**, 9–20 (2014)
34. European Commission: Report from the Commission to the Council on the Urban Agenda for the EU, COM(2017) 657 final, 20.11.2017 (2017)
35. Knight, R.V.: Knowledge-based Development: policy and Planning Implications for Cities. Urban Studies. **35**, 225–260 (1995)

Innovative Approaches to Work Organization and New Technologies. First Insight from the Italian Context

Teresina Torre and Daria Sarti

Abstract Innovative approaches to work organization find an essential basis in information and communication technologies (ICTs) and their most recent evolution. Our paper focuses on the role played by ICTs, in supporting the development of new ways to work and perform, promising a better balance between work and life. Through the experiences of three Italian enterprises, which are among the first users of these approaches and, more precisely of smart working (SW), the paper analyses conditions and implications of this deep change in work organization.

Keywords Information and communication technologies · Advances information technologies work organization · Innovative approaches to work organization · Smart working

1 Introduction

The relationship between work and technologies comprises a classic topic in the field of organization studies. In the past few decades, scholars interested in work organization and its evolution have been engaged in studying innovative approaches, which are diffusing to challenge the conventional models of work design and re-design, based on the traditional idea of hierarchy and on the classic managerial style focused on strict and direct control [1]. These methods are strongly connected with new technologies, deeply influencing work and its conditions.

Starting from the 1990s', we observe the introduction of new working solutions in parallel with the introduction of information and communication technologies (ICTs). Telework has received a particular attention, for its characteristic in nullifying physical distance (between worker and enterprise and among workers) and also in

T. Torre (✉)
Department of Economics and Business Studies, University of Genoa, Genoa, Italy
e-mail: teresina.torre@economia.unige.it

D. Sarti
Department of Economics and Management, University of Florence, Florence, Italy
e-mail: daria.sarti@unifi.it

© Springer Nature Switzerland AG 2020   133
Y. Baghdadi et al. (eds.), *ICT for an Inclusive World*,
Lecture Notes in Information Systems and Organisation 35,
https://doi.org/10.1007/978-3-030-34269-2_11

modifying the relationship that workers maintain with time [2–4]. Its diffusion has been less wide than it had been wished for and imagined [5–8], according to many observers, on account of the 'limits' of technologies and their inflexibility [9]. More recently, a great evolution has occurred, in parallel with the evolution and enrichment of technologies and of their tools. As a result, many different labels are now used to qualify the ways to organize work: some of these are explicitly related to the newness introduced by technologies—we think for example of mobile working [10]; others simply suggest that work can be done everywhere, like agile working [11] or nomadic working [12].

All these models share the idea that a different organization, inspired by discretion and flexibility, is required as the classic one no longer satisfies people. In any case, the role played by technologies is the determinant for the change: indeed, flexibility seems easier to be pursued using new technologies, which by definition are flexible.

Therefore, in other words, we can underline that it is the unexpected and quick acceleration in technologies, and especially in information and communication technologies (ICTs), and their intensive enforcement, which can play a fundamental role in work organization. With our research, we aim to deepen this relationship, looking to offer a contribution into this central debate in the organizational field.

The paper is organized in the following manner. First, some elements in respect of regarding the theoretical perspective that are useful to study the topic are proposed; then, the empirical in-depth analysis of one of these new approaches, viz. smart working, is presented and its more relevant results are discussed. Finally, considerations about the role of technologies in the evolution of work and its organization—so that future research activities could focus on it—are introduced.

2   The Theoretical Background

This paragraph will introduce the theoretical context in which our topic can be analysed. It represents the basis for the present study.

In greater detail, we consider three theoretical streams to be relevant. The first is the socio-technical perspective, which aids the understanding of the relationship between the two main parts in an organization, viz. the technical and the social one. Then, we introduce the technology acceptance model, the focus of which is the comprehension of the way in which people manage technologies. Finally, more recent considerations about the concept of ubiquity—related to the evolution of mobile systems and its portability—are introduced.

2.1   The Socio-Technical Perspective

The most appropriate theoretical context in which we can insert our reasoning is the concept of socio-technical system (STS), first proposed by a group of researchers of the Tavistock Institute [13–17]. This approach is still considered a useful framework to describe and understand organizations [18].

Historically, the STS approach emerged from the observation that the people worked in a different way compared to the procedures suggested by the Scientific Management, which emphasized specialization and division of labour, reducing the variety in working. The principal consequences of this method are that workers did not have the possibility to see the result of the work and that their role appeared minimized, as also their respective competences and ability in using working tools and instruments [13]. Moreover, it was observed that people worked together—and, so, relationships among workers were found to be important—and they cooperated and collaborated to use the available technologies [19].

According to the STS research stream, an organization has to be considered a system and, more precisely, as an open system, composed of two dimensions. The *social dimension* is composed by attributes of people—their attitudes, skills and values, the relationships among people, the authority structure—while the *technical dimension* is represented by processes, tasks and technology (e.g., materials, machinery, plants) that enable input to become output [18].

Central to this is the idea of *joint optimization*. The concept summarizes, on the one hand, the necessary dynamic equilibrium between key variances of the technical system for the organizational purposes and the variance control analysis developed by workers and, on the other hand, the need for job satisfaction on the part of a worker, which influences his/her behaviour in a working context [15]. In this perspective, the performance of a productive system is strictly connected with the interaction between the just-mentioned two coessential dimensions. Hence, the relevance of the relationship between technology, human beings and social aspects it is underscored and the need to consider these components together is explained for an effective organizational design.

The above mentioned systemic nature finds further relevance here: both subsystems are open and organic and regularly interact with the external environment, producing feedback and adaptive actions in order to face the necessary changes. At the same time, the two sub-systems interact each other, so that they have to be viewed as interdependent and complementary [20]. Hence, organizations might obtain positive performance only through actions devoted to their joint optimization [18]. In Fig. 1, the whole frame of relationships is described.

The strict and strong connection between right side and left side asks for a detailed and precise study of the technological component in the design of social systems (being tasks connected with their features). This is, indeed, the focus of this approach, which has much to say about our specific topic, offering evidence of a connection among all the variables in the system.

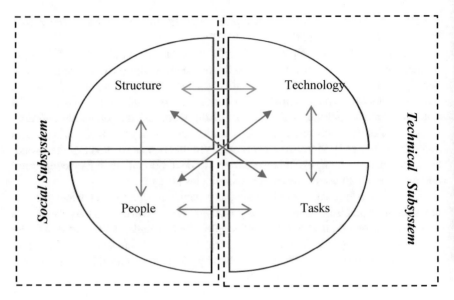

Fig. 1 The interacting variables within a work system (adapted from: Bostrom and Heinen [20])

2.2 The Technology Acceptance Model

Without the recent development in technologies and in the technological environment, any reasoning about innovative ways of work organization probably does not exist and surely not with the actually emphasis. Thus, the comprehension of the dynamics that intervene in the evolution of technologies and in the relationship people have with them and the way in which they are normally used is fundamental to understand the current evolution in the work context.

Much progress has been made in explaining and predicting the use of technology as work tools. A useful contribution in this direction has been offered by the seminal contribution of the technology acceptance model (TAM) [21, 22]. It studies the relationship between personal attitude towards technology and the real and effective use of the same technology in a working context, suggesting that individual intention to use technology depends on three dimensions [22]. The first is the perceived usefulness, which means how a person thinks that, in handling a particular technological support, his/her performance can be enhanced. It is evident that the incremental characteristic of more recent technologies plays an absolutely central role. The other is the perceived ease of use: it denotes how the same person thinks that, using the same support, his/her effort can be reduced. In this case, ICTS's evolution intervenes as a facilitating factor. The last is offered by social influences, which is the degree to which an individual perceives others' opinion as important in order to facilitate his/her adoption of the new system: the reference to managers and colleagues, to favourite and approve new work models based on technologies is immediate.

Close to the intention of use, another direct determinant of usage behaviour is represented by the facilitating conditions, which Venkatesch and colleagues [22] defines as the degree to which a person thinks that support towards the use of the technical system can help. This perception depends to a larger extent on the effort an organisation expends on facilitating the shifting towards innovative ways of working pledging any possible support (e.g., infrastructure and services). In this field, the role played by training is fundamental, because it is not only a technical problem (device, software and so on) but also an organizational one (appropriate knowledge and skills) and a cultural one (a new approach to relationships between managers and workers).

2.3 The Ubiquitous Media System and Its Portability

It is interesting to note that the model just presented helps the understanding of the behaviours of workers both in 'stationary' as well as in 'mobile' systems. The shift from a stationary concept to a mobile one represents an important step in the use of technologies in the working context (not only in it, of course) and, moreover, in the change of the way of working.

The mobile system is the combination of mobile and wireless technologies [23, 24], which represent two different technologies, recently converging and generating a totally new context: their contextual presence allows one to work without limitation of time and place. This is the central idea of ubiquitous media system.

As a matter of fact, work is possible when and where connection is available. Hence, in a mobile world work is possible wherever and always. A deep change has been observed exactly at this level: in the recent past, only some physical places were able to support work conditions with appropriate technology. In the present time, the enlargement of the wireless state, combined with the portability of the mobile tools, have produced an extension of the occasions of working.

Moreover, in order to understand how these new ways of work organisation can operate, in addition to hardware portability—which is mobile dimension—it is necessary to consider software portability, which means the ability of any software to adapt to mobile devices, which normally have reduced dimensions and which offer a larger opportunity to develop multitasking attitudes.

Indeed, what is important to underline is that ubiquity of ICTs in work settings has changed the behaviours of employees. This aspect introduces another relevant question, which is the individual relationship with ICT tools, which can become really very absorbing. Authors propose the concept of ICT self-discipline—a person's ability to regulate his/her behaviours towards ICTs, appropriately managing connectivity and information flows [25, 26]—to analyse how an individual relates him/herself to ICTs, managing the change in the nature of work caused by ICTs themselves. Portability plays a pivotal role in the development of innovative ways of working and the degree of ICT connectivity can create a positive or a negative impact on productivity, depending contemporaneously on the functioning of the whole system and the long-term perspective.

The emergence of new integrated forms of ubiquitous computing devices, allied with the proliferation of fluid multi-device platforms, enabled the development of Ubiquitous Media Systems (UMS) [24]. This new and complex form of connected IT artfacts encapsulates various functions and provides fluid information access across a variety of channels—enabling users to accomplish a multitude of tasks and interact fluidly in a ubiquitous digital ecosystem.

This significant technological evolution has engendered an urgent need to revisit our understanding of technology usage through the lens of theories that encompass the multifaceted nature of UMS.

3   Our Explorative Research

The present paper aims to deepen the relationship between technologies and new approaches to work organization. We consider the experience of smart working (SW), diffused in Italy for some years and recently introduced by a specific law (n. 81/2017), which describes what smart working is, its features and its conditions. According to its supporters, SW is defined by the possibility of working independently of time and place [27]: so, the typical variables such as office place, work conventions or work hours become very less relevant, compared to network and collaboration processes, which optimise work and its output. Many researches confirm that expectations and behaviours of workers are changing in the direction of smart working forms. A Cisco report [28] for example underlines the point that: 60% employees believe they do not need to be in the office to be productive, while 66% desire work flexibility and would accept a lower-paid job with more work flexibility than a higher-paid job with inflexibility. It seems a good and prolific field to study the role of technologies in work organization, through this innovative experience.

The need for an in-depth investigation in an under-researched field, such as the one of SW which lacks studies (in the Italian context, only Politecnico [29–31]—calls for an explorative approach using a multiple case-study technique [32] based on the experiences of three Italian enterprises which have adopted a SW implementation strategy. For the analysis a triangulation methodology was used, relying on different sources of data [33, 32] like face-to-face semi-structured interviews with the HR directors and the people in charge of developing the project of each firm involved in the research, phone conversations, organizational secondary data (e.g., website, press releases, internal documents). Interviews with the three organizations took place in different periods: the first phase has been developed between December 2015 and January 2016; the second between November 2016 and January 2017, the third between September and October 2018.

Anonymity was guaranteed to the companies, since this practice was suggested to favour candour and informational completeness [33]. Also, open ended questions

Table 1 Organizations involved in the analysis

Organization	Industry	Nr. of employees (end 2016)	Year of foundation
A	Engineering	5800	1988
B	Banking	600	2007
C	Technological services	165	2000

were used to give the informants the opportunity to express the wide scope of the concept they were questioned about [34].

Table 1 shows a synthetic overview of the organizations involved in the analysis.

3.1 Main Findings

The three enterprises here investigated share the same approach towards SW, which can be classified as a 'medium-soft' one. Participation by workers in this model is voluntary, approvals by the respective managers are requested, its use is envisaged for at the maximum of eight days per month and the larger than possible diffusion of this possibility among workers is favoured. For the days in SW, employees can work at home, in a hub or, following their specific activities, at a client's office. No limits are indicated, beyond the agreement of the boss.

The decision to implement SW, in all the three cases, is the consequence of the search to face complexity through an increase in organizational flexibility, the benefits of which are considered positive both for the enterprise and the worker. Indeed, SW is not itself the goal of a process of implementation but rather it is a 'mean' to reach a wider different objective, that is the strategic one. The organizational change realized by organizations has been a complex process because it has been conducted through participation of all workers involved and sharing ideas and decisions with the recipients and, further—when present within the organization—also trade unions' representatives were involved. We now focus our attention on the specific perspective of the technical system: as specified, we are interested in understanding the role of the two core parts of the technical subsystem (see Fig. 1): technology and tasks.

Technology

According to the STS approach, technical component concerns itself with any tools and techniques required to transform inputs into outputs. So, the first essential condition to develop SW is the attitude of the organization towards technology and its real positioning with regard to ICTs.

Two of the enterprises (Cases A and C) belong to the high-tech sector and they apparently work easily and in a friendly manner on the technological frontier. Hence, no problem in terms of inadequacy of tools available has been remarked on this side. The last case has met, indeed, some more difficulties in this direction, such as problems with connectivity, dysfunction with devices, and a certain lack of support when problems arise. It is also true that in this case, SW is foreseen by the client's site, too: in conditions, therefore, that can be controlled less by our enterprise.

Anyway, a few issues have to be considered with attention, because they can be sources of problems. Security is the top technical issue suggested by those interviewed. First of all, because workers do not seem too much careful and meticulous in their relationship with this source of risks (even if they meet difficulties). Enterprises are conscious that the principal challenge is to offer necessary support. The IT department has to organize a specifically devoted service for people working at distance, with mobile tools; this asks for specific resources, but also for an 'internal client orientation', so that a change in mind even for the staff of the IT department has to be carried out (and this point has been underlined in all the cases).

Also, problems connected with the functioning of technologies can be an obstacle for a positive development of the whole system. For example, incompatibility between older and newer technologies or between different devices used in office and out of office, or different configurations used by the workers of the same team are some of the examples proposed by those interviewed. These problems introduce us to another one. Sometimes it seems that the solution is to always have the last models of any tool. The quest for always up-to-dated ICT devices has to be attentively evaluated, if enterprises do not want to risk that these request expressed by smart workers (who by definition have a more developed inclination towards the adoption of any newness) introduce a continuous and unmanageable variability in the organizational interface and uncontrolled effects on the investment. This worry has been shown by Case C, but Case B, too, is attentive towards it.

Connectivity has been indicated as a possible limit for the diffusion of such forms of working. Wireless coverage is not guaranteed anywhere and this could be problematic for future evolution in SW (in Case A, agreements explicitly indicate places in which it is possible to work, preventing possible obstacles but limiting the possibilities of flexibility; cases B and C meet this problem, so that they ask insistently for more infrastructure as public service).

Task

As the question on which kinds of tasks that can be managed by distance, the positions of our enterprises are similar. They confirm the idea that, until now, most of the assignments can be done not in physical presence. The only real exception is represented by manufacturing activities (which are a large part of its business for Enterprise A, which indeed does not consider manufacturing as a department candidate for SW, even if deep changes are expected on this side in order to avoid a common sense of internal unfairness among workers in different job positions). Many tasks require for Pcs, in networking connections (by emails and by communication and sharing systems). Many tasks ask for participation in a team's activities, which can be developed in one's presence as is usually done, but also through conference systems and sharing platforms, which collect participants from everywhere and which allow people to work together independently with the help of the physical proximity. This means by consequence a new idea of control, a new way of interpreting leadership, a

Table 2 A synthesis of the mail elements about the technical side

	Technology	Task
Case A	Connectivity and devices (laptops) already available Necessary ICT support	All the tasks with a minimum of discretion (excluded manufacturing ones)
Case B	Connectivity and devices to implement Necessary ICT support	All the tasks directly related to customers
Case C	Connectivity and devices (laptops) already available Necessary ICT support	All the tasks related to customers and staff

new way of dividing activities among workers. Thus, it emerges that a new technical scenario introduces deep changes in the social scenario (Table 2).

In our analysis, the interdependence between the two subsystems—social and technological one—appears as the real critical point: the changes brought by SW can introduce misalignments and a new equilibrium could be found if the two subsystems continue in dialoguing. So, socially led changes are more easily managed with the help of technologies; equally, technology led changes ask for different approaches by involved people, in which acceptance doorstep gets down because conditions of acceptance are favourite through education and training and through empowerment, too. It is exactly here that the perspective of the acceptance model begins to play a relevant role in organizations wishing to change: people have to relate with ICT tools starting from their personal experience of usefulness and familiarity, which has to be helped and reinforced by the organizational context. At the same time, the quick evolution toward integrated forms of ubiquitous devices open new and important challenges from the individual perspective (the relationship between work and private life and expectation from job) and also from the enterprise's point of view (how to define the limits of work, how to support worker to be effective).

Participation becomes the key word for starting real change. It is interesting to remark that participation can be facilitated through technologies, but the goal which has to be pursued has to be clear which is: to support the integration process between technical and social system, focusing on the principal interactions and introducing innovations in the critical points. This means, for example, attention towards communication, as also care for a managerial style coherent with the new ways.

In Fig. 2, a graphical representation of our concluding remarks is presented.

4 Final Considerations

In this paper, we have analysed the relationships among the most relevant variables within a working system (to put in evidence if and how SW can be effective) and which is the role of new technologies in this scenario. We did this after taking into consideration the experience of three enterprises practising SW, which is one of the

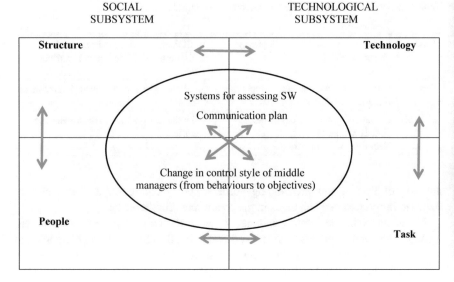

Fig. 2 The interacting variables within a work system and their relationships (Our elaboration based on the work by Chen and Nath [18])

most interesting innovative ways of organizing work, and being conscious of the limits related to the use of such a methodological approach.

By the way, SW is a typical portable system, both for the device hardware features and for software adaptability. Hence, system portability, which has a positive effect on effort expectancy, represent a condition for SW. The development and diffusion of these technologies, supporting communication, collaboration and social networking, along with the pervasive dissemination of powerful and easy-to-use mobile devices, can support organisations in developing a SW system [35]. While recent literature has analysed how ICT has made work more portable and ubiquitous [36], there is no a comprehensive understanding yet and no empirical evidence of the existence of complementarities among elements on which firms should focus in case they want to adopt an SW organizational model.

ICTs' solutions, especially the collaborative ones, allow a team to share in an easy and quick manner files, information and ideas [37]), because workers interact in real time in a flexible and effective way by contributing to a SW environment. Therefore, a deep change is working time and place is expected, a change that asks for different practices in managing co-workers, towards which the HR Department has to address middle managers. SW represents an occasion to transform internal culture radically.

The most interesting element, which has emerged from our research, is that the potentialities of ICTs play a dual-purpose role. On the one hand, they seem to enrich the social component in organization, allowing people to empower their work; and on the other hand, they put in evidence of a necessary change in the cultural approach towards work both by the managers and workers themselves. It is evident that this approach entails a focused organizational policy (which means a new culture, new styles of leadership, new jobs and skills, new attitudes and behaviours) together with digital supports. So, the two dimensions, which compose any organization according to the STS perspective, find a fundamental *raison d'être* in their reciprocal interactions.

In our analysis, the interdependence between the two subsystems appears as the real critical point: the changes brought by SW can introduce misalignments, if the two subsystems do not continue to dialogue. So, socially led changes are more easily managed with the help of technologies; equally, technology led changes ask for different approaches by the people involved, in which the acceptance threshold goes down because conditions of acceptance are made favourites through education and training and also through empowerment. Participation becomes the key word for starting real change.

The integration between the social system and the technical system is fundamental for SW, which is not understandable in its real dynamics from this perspective.

The STS approach helps one to understand how crucial the alignment between social and technical systems is. Each of these is pushed by different drivers, depending on their specific core and nature; but the reciprocal need for coordination, necessary for the functioning of any organization, has to act simultaneously. This seems really important, first of all with reference to our topic—born in times of technological dependence, when technologies makes unthinkable things possible: indeed, we have to consider the risk that the technological component prevails over the social one, which has been called simply to adapt itself. The real risk is the loss of relevance of the social component. At that point, the relational characteristics of modern technology could be useless. In future further research in this field has many challenging questions to answer.

References

1. Brewer, A.M.: Work design for flexible work scheduling: Barriers and gender implications. Gender, Work & Organization **7**(1), 33–44 (2000)
2. Di Martino, V., Wirth, L.: Telework: a new way of working and living. Int. Labour Rev. **5**, 529–554 (1990)
3. Torre, T.: Il lavoro a distanza: da flessibilità occasionale ad occasione di flessibilità. Persone & Imprese **1**, 74–84 (1998)
4. Torre, T.: Il lavoro a distanza. In: Cafferata, R. (ed.) Management e Organizzazione Aziendale. Aracne, Roma (1999)
5. Bailey, D.E., Kurland, N.B.: A review of telework research: findings, new directions and lessons for the study of modern work. J. Organ. Behav. **23**(4), 383–400 (2002)
6. Morganson, V.J., Major, D.A., Oborn, K.L.: Comparing telework location and traditional work arrangements, differences in work-life balance support, job satisfaction and inclusion. J. Manag. Psychol. **25**, 578–596 (2010)
7. Pyoria, P.: Managing telework: risks, fears and rules. Manag. Res. Rev. **34**(4), 386–399 (2011)
8. Welz C., Wolf F.: Telework in the European Union, European Foundation for the Improvement of living and working conditions, Report, Dublin (2010)

9. Taskin, L., Edwards, P.: The possibilities and limits of telework in a bureaucratic environment: lessons from the public sector. New Technol. Work. Employ. **22**(3), 195–207 (2007)
10. Cousins, K., Robey, D.: Managing work-life boundaries with mobile technologies: an interpretive study of mobile work practices. Inf. Technol. People **28**(1), 34–71 (2015)
11. Employers Network for Equality and Inclusion-ENEI: Agile Working, a guide for employers, Report, London
12. Chen, L. Corritore C.L.: A theoretical model of nomadic culture: assumptions, values, artifacts and the impact on employee job satisfaction. Commun. Assoc. Inf. Syst. **22**, article 13 (2008)
13. Emery, F.E., Trist, E.L.: Socio-technical Systems. In: Churchman, C.W., Verlust, M. (eds.) Management Science, Models and Techniques, vol. 2, Pergamon Press, Oxford (1960)
14. Emery, F.E.: Characteristics of Socio-Technical Systems. In Trist, E.E., Murray, H.E., Trist, B.E. (eds.) The Socio-Technical System Perspective University of Pennsylvania Press (1990)
15. Cherns, A.E.: Principles of sociotechnical design revisited. Hum. Relat. **40**, 153–162 (1987)
16. Appelbaum, S.H.: Socio-technical systems theory: an intervention strategy for organizational development. Manag. Decis. **35**(6), 452–463 (1997)
17. Mumford, E.: The story of socio-technical design: reflections on its successes, failures and potential. Info Syst. **16**, 317–342 (2006)
18. Chen, L., Nath, R.: A socio-technical perspective of mobile work. Inf. Knowl. Syst. Manag. **7**(1), 41–60 (2008)
19. Marchiori, M.: L'approccio socio-tecnico. In: Fabbri, T.M. (ed.) L'organizzazione: concetti e metodi, pp. 92–121. Carocci, Roma (2010)
20. Bostrom, R.P., Heinen, J.S.: MIS problems and failures: a socio-technical perspective, part II: the application of socio-technical theory. MIS Q. **1**(3), 11–28 (1977)
21. Venkatesh, V., Davis, F.D.: A theoretical extension of the technology acceptance model: four longitudinal field studies. Manage. Sci. **46**(2), 186–204 (2000)
22. Ventatesch, V., Morris, M.G., Gordon, B.D., Davis, F.D.: User acceptance of information technology: toward a unified view. Mis Quartely **27**(3), 425–478 (2003)
23. Scornavacca, E.: Incorporating system portability into technology acceptance models. In: ICMB, pp. 1–12 (2014)
24. Carillo, K., Scornavacca, E., Za, S.: The role of media dependency in predicting continuance intention to use ubiquitous media systems. Inf. Manag. **54**(3), 317–335 (2017)
25. Al-Dabbagh, B., Sylvester, A., Scornavacca, E.: To connect or disconnect–that is the question: ICT self-discipline in the 21st century workplace. ACIS (2014)
26. Al-Dabbagh, B., Scornavacca, E., Sylvester, A., Johnstone, D.: The effect of ICT self-discipline in the workplace. arXiv preprint arXiv:1606.00894 (2016)
27. Clapperton, G., Vanhoutte, P.: The Smarter Working Manifesto. Sunmakers Eldamar, Oxford (2014)
28. Boorsma, B., Bulchandani, R., Charles Jr, G., Drury, P., Grone, P., Kim, T., Spencer, P. Work-Life Innovation. Smart Work-A Paradigm Shift Transforming How, Where, and When Work Gets Done. San Jose, CA: Cisco Internet Business Solutions Group (IBSG) (2011). Retrieved April, 30 (2013)
29. di Milano, Politecnico: Smart Working: ripensare il lavoro, liberare energia. Rapporto Osservatorio Smart Working, Politecnico di Milano, Milano (2012)
30. di Milano, Politecnico: SmartWorking: scopriamo le carte!. Rapporto Osservatorio Smart Working, Politecnico di Milano, Milano (2015)
31. Politecnico di Milano: (Smart) Work in progress, Materials presented at the Conference on Smart Working, October 12^{ve} (2016)
32. Yin, R.K.: Case study Research Design and Methods Third Edition, Applied Social Research Methods Series, 5, Sage, Thousand Oaks, CA (2003)
33. Eisenhardt, K.M.: Building theories from case study research. Acad. Manag. Rev. **14**(4), 532–550 (1989)
34. Koriat, A., Goldsmith, M., Pansky, A.: Toward a psychology of memory accuracy. Annu. Rev. Psychol. **51**(2), 481 (2000)

35. Ahuja, M.K., Chudoba, K.M., Kacmar, C.J., McKnight, D.H., George, J.F.: IT Road War-riors: Balancing Work-family Conflict, Job autonomy, and work overload to mitigate turnover intentions. MIS Quarterly **31**(1), 1–17 (2007)
36. Yoo, Y., Henfridsson, O., Lyytinen, K.: Research commentary—the new organizing logic of digital innovation: an agenda for information systems research. Inf. Syst. Res. **21**(4), 724–735 (2010)
37. Chudoba, K.M., Lu, M., Watson-Manheim, M.B.: How virtual are we? Measuring virtuality and understanding its impact on a global organisation. Inf. Syst. J. **15**, 279–306 (2005)

Social Media

Internet for Supporting and Promoting Accessible Tourism: Evidence from Italy

Giuseppe Perna, Luisa Varriale and Maria Ferrara

Abstract In the last 10 years "accessible tourism" represents one topic that has been becoming more and more relevant, not only because of the increasing attention paid to civic and social values, but also because this tourism segment represents an undoubted economic opportunity able to create added value over time and, consequently, to increase profits. This conceptual study provides a deep analysis of "accessible tourism" phenomenon through a description of the evolution process of the regulatory system. Also, the role of the internet and new technologies to the dissemination of information analyzing tourist websites has been investigated with focus on the Italian context.

Keywords Accessible tourism · Disability · Technology · Internet · ICT · Italian tourism websites

1 Introduction

In the last fifty years, tourism has become a primary social need because it is a tool to know and discover the many realities that surround us. For this reason, it is essential to ensure access to the tourist experience to all citizens, regardless of personal, social, economic and any other conditions that may limit the use of this asset [1].

For accessibility it is intended to be able to use an asset in the absence of architectural, cultural and sensorial barriers [2]. In this regard, the Italian Committee for the Promotion and Support of Accessible Tourism provides a very clear definition: "*Accessibility, that is the absence of architectural, cultural and sensory barriers, is the indispensable condition to allow the*

G. Perna · L. Varriale (✉) · M. Ferrara
University of Naples "Parthenope", Naples, Italy
e-mail: luisa.varriale@uniparthenope.it

G. Perna
e-mail: giuseppe.perna@uniparthenope.it

M. Ferrara
e-mail: maria.ferrara@uniparthenope.it

© Springer Nature Switzerland AG 2020
Y. Baghdadi et al. (eds.), *ICT for an Inclusive World*,
Lecture Notes in Information Systems and Organisation 35,
https://doi.org/10.1007/978-3-030-34269-2_12

fruition of Italian tourism heritage. In terms of tourist usability this accessibility must be extended to the overall transport system, intermodality, medium-long haul, wheel, rail, aircraft and local transport systems. When we talk about a tourist destination, then, we refer to the local tourism system, that is to say all the services and the offer: catering, bathing, culture, food and wine, etc. but also to urban accessibility and the availability of information in different formats (e.g. tactile, braille, etc ...)" [1].

Ultimately, accessible tourism is understood as the set of services, structures and infrastructures that allow people with "particular needs" to live a holiday or enjoy moments of free time without obstacles [3].

People with "special needs" are those with physical disabilities (with reduced mobility), sensory (people who are blind, visually impaired, deaf, deaf, deaf and deaf), mental and psychic as well as all those with other disabilities or special needs such as example people with problems of orientation and communication, people with feeding problems, people with epilepsy, people with diabetes, people with allergies, pregnant women, etc. [4].

For the development of accessible tourism, it is crucial to understand the needs of people with disabilities and provide adequate support services for the specific needs of these individuals [5–7]. A tourist destination must meet the needs of any type of visitor and provide adequate incentives for a real enjoyment of the tourist experience. Communication and distribution of information are essential above all in the phase preceding the departure; for this reason, it is necessary to have tools that allow to reach a choice that satisfies one's desire for vacation [8, 9].

The presence of easily accessible structures is at the base of participation tourism [10] while the dissemination of information on currently accessible destinations is equally significant [11, 12] because it seems to be the most effective solution for expand the opportunities for tourism development for individuals with disabilities [8, 13]. In fact, it is possible to state that all changes in the physical environment will not bring any benefit to people with disabilities present in the world [14, 15] if information about their presence is not disseminated.

The paradigms of information on the needs that influence tourist choices and levels of tourist satisfaction have revealed the importance of two main conditions. Firstly, an awareness and understanding by society and tourism service providers of many different information needs [16–18] and secondly, the development of specific communication sources that meet individual needs [17, 19–22].

Previously, the provision of information on accessibility was very fragmented, inaccurate and incomprehensible [23]. As a result, over the past five years a number of approaches have emerged in Europe to encourage accessibility to tourism (cited in this document as accessibility schemes for tourism). These schemes, which act as a source of information communication to ensure the quality of the tangible resources provided in the destinations, have been set up by both the public and private sectors, with the main objective of encouraging greater assistance to overcome the information barriers of disabled tourists [17, 20, 22].

Through the Web, today, it is possible to satisfy any information need as it is possible to find information on any tourist destination, to receive advice from those who have already visited a particular tourist destination, to know before leaving a place that we do not actually have never seen but also book and buy holidays and tourist services. Therefore, it is important that access and understanding of such information is possible for any type of tourist regardless of whether it moves completely independently or not [8].

The objective of this study is to deepen the development of the concept of accessible tourism through the study of the normative evolution that concerned this issue and analyze the support that today the internet provides to the dissemination of information on the accessibility of a tourist destination. To this end, an online search was conducted of the Italian sites that provided this type of service, focusing our attention on the situation in Italy.

This paper is structured in the following chapters. Chapter 2 illustrates the initiatives, both at European and Italian level, undertaken over the years for the development of accessible tourism. Chapter 3 will analyze the relationship between tourism and the Web, for the dissemination of information on the accessibility of tourist destinations. Chapter 4 analyzes the situation, in Italy, of websites, blogs and networks that provide information on the accessibility in tourism to individuals with special needs.

2 Development and Regulations of Accessible Tourism

The international provision that for the first time put in evidence the difficult situation in which some individuals lived was represented by the proclamation, in 1981, of the UN International Year of Disabled Persons.

In the last twenty years great interest has been devoted to the theme of accessible tourism or to the difficulties that people with disabilities encounter when they decide to undertake a journey.

The first European country to intervene in the field of Accessible Tourism was Great Britain which, in 1981, created the European national information and counseling service for disabled people tourism, called "Holidays Care Service". In particular, a guide ("Providing for disabled visitors") was created with advice on the most appropriate structures and behaviors to be adopted to receive people with special needs [24].

Over the years, the European Union has shown increasing attention to accessible tourism and, in fact, in 1986, a commission was formed called the "Tourism Advisory Committee", to promote the dissemination of information on tourism between Member States. Europeans, while 1990 was proclaimed "European Year of Tourism", in order to make the most of all the initiatives related to this sector.

In 1988 the "Tourism for All" movement was born, which published a report with 63 recommendations to ensure compliance with the needs and needs of tourists with disabilities so that they were taken into consideration by tourism companies and integrated into their action policies [3].

With the growing interest of the European Union on this issue, in the 1990s, tourist facilities looking for adequate solutions to meet the needs of tourists with disabilities increased considerably in all states. In fact, all the European countries started a series of initiatives and, in particular Sweden to be considered, together with Great Britain, one of the most advanced countries in this sense, started a plan called "From patient to citizen" which had the objective to making Sweden a country accessible to all by 2010 [25].

Moreover, in Europe, in 2004, the CARE (Accessible Cities of European Regions) project was approved to realize, through common values and principles, a network of services and structures accessible through a common communication and detection methodology. The concept behind the birth of the CARE project was the awareness that people with disabilities are above all tourists and therefore must be able to choose a tourist destination according to their personal desires and not for the degree of accessibility of one place compared to another [26].

Among the works carried out during this project we mention the "Charter of the Hospitable City", a unique document for the whole European territory with the aim of disseminating the right practices to be implemented in a city to accommodate types of tourists with different needs. So, thanks to the launch of this project, the first steps were taken, at European level, to grow homogeneously the hospitality in different cities, creating a network of accessible structures and services and action plans for communication and information for tourists and residents [26].

Moreover, in 2006 ENAT (European Network for Accessible Tourism) was born, that is, a non-profit association that aims to promote the promotion and the practice of accessible tourism as well as exploit the knowledge and experience of the network to improve the accessibility of tourist information, transport, infrastructure and design services for all types of visitors with special access needs, providing models of excellence in tourism accessible to the entire tourism sector [27].

Finally, the most recent initiative proposed at European level, with a duration of three years, was the "Calypso project" undertaken by the European Commission for the Promotion of Social Tourism with the aim of bringing tourism to the less privileged categories such as the elderly, young people and 30, disabled people and low-income families [28].

In Italy, however, sensitivity on accessible tourism began to grow in 1989 when the report "Tourism for all" was drawn up; from that moment on many Italian companies such as cooperatives, associations, institutions, etc., started to develop campaigns to improve accessibility [24]. The first initiative took place in 1994 with the convention called "Tourism for All Networking" organized by CO.IN. (Cooperative Integrate Onlus) in Rome to improve the conditions of accessibility to tourism for people with special needs.

In 1999, a series of initiatives began to improve the following problems related to accessible tourism: lack of preparation for the reception of disabled persons by tour operators; absence of an information system regarding the availability of tourist facilities and infrastructures accessible to all; very few local information and assistance services for disabled people [29]. The initiatives promoted under the name of "Italy for all" led to the creation of a manual entitled "Quality in the tourist reception of clients with special needs" with a series of guidelines to implement concrete actions towards the development of a more accessible tourism for all [24].

At the beginning of the 2000 s, the ENEA (Agency for New Technologies, Energy and the Environment) developed the project "STARe—Tourist Services for Accessibility and Comfortable Residence". The project lasted 3 years in which they were realized: study on the demand and supply of accessible tourism in Italy; development methodology called IG-VAE (Guaranteed Information for the Assessment of Accessibility for its Needs) for the detection of the accessibility of tourist facilities and infrastructures; database containing information regarding the accessibility of 5000 tourist facilities in the area; "Vademecum for tourists with needs" for end users, containing information on transport services and tourism for those with special needs. The aim of the STARe project was to offer an ideal methodology for the realization of tourism projects aimed at everyone [24].

In 2000 the association "Si *può—Laboratorio Nazionale sul Turismo Accessible*" was born, which began, for the first time, to devote itself to communication, marketing and training for hospitality and tourism [30]. The interventions were mainly addressed to the operators involved in the tourism sector such as public administrations, promotion companies, tour operators, travel agencies, information services agencies, voluntary associations and social enterprises.

Between 2006 and 2010 several initiatives like "Turismabile" in Piedmont spread, an initiative to promote accessibility as a synonym of quality in the tourism offer, the Village for All project and the Accessible Tourism fair in Vicenza. In 2009, the Minister of Tourism, to promote initiatives aimed at improving the accessibility of Italian tourist facilities, set up a ministerial commission "For an accessible tourism". In the promotion of accessibility, the whole tourist supply chain must be involved (the transport system, the receptivity, the catering, the culture, the free time and the sport), above all through the training of the professional 7ures that are part of it and the quality of the welcome for all [4].

In May 2011, the Italian Government issued Legislative Decree 79/2011 which contains the Code of the state legislation on the issue of tourism regulation and market; this has the objectives of developing the tourism sector and giving greater protection to consumers and operators in the sector. In particular, Article 3 of the Code contains the principles on accessible tourism and it is also considered discriminatory act to prevent persons with disabilities from taking advantage of the tourist offer for reasons however referable to their disability.

In conclusion, it should be emphasized that the initiatives undertaken at European level but above all at the Italian level, for the last 10 years, have become increasingly frequent. This indicates how to make structures, services and infrastructures accessible to a multiplicity of people with different needs, is now essential.

3   The Need for Information for the Disabled Tourist: The Role of the Web

Tourist destinations offer a set of products and services designed to meet the needs of tourists [31], therefore, the dissemination of detailed information that covers in depth and in breadth all the components of the entire accessible structure, is of fundamental importance [7].

It is particularly important to inform potential customers about continuous accessible routes as accessible but isolated structures add nothing to the tourist experience [8]. Israeli (2002) has shown that as a result of the use of tourist facilities, disabled people have started to evaluate the accessible routes more and more positively [32].

Cavinato and Cuckovich (2002) found that not only the availability of complete information but also their reliability is an essential requirement for the disabled tourist [13]. The lack of reliable information is one of the main reasons preventing disabled people from traveling [8, 12, 33]. In a survey conducted by NOP Consumer (2003), survey participants said that the information needed to meet the needs of their trip, to be judged to be credible, must follow a 3-step process. Firstly, standards must be established by accredited disability organizations. Secondly, the evaluation of the structures with respect to these criteria should be carried out by an independent authoritative body and, thirdly, the subsequent dissemination of the information must also include the indications concerning the criteria that have led to the accreditation of the tourist facilities [34].

Moreover, to meet the needs of disabled tourists regarding the choice of a trip it is important that they can choose adequate information sources [8, 35, 36]. Many individuals follow a planning approach that involves multiple sources because the quality of information provided by a few sources is usually insufficient, only partially accurate or inaccessible [13, 33, 37–39]. However, this planning process takes a long time to research the necessary information and therefore can be discouraging for the choice of travel. Darcy (1998) argues that the amount and accuracy of information provided by a single source is the basic requirement for adequately meeting the planning needs of disabled people [8].

Cavinato and Cuckovich (2002) underline the importance of public bodies specialized in the dissemination of reliable information [13], while Cheng (2002), Burnett and Bender (2001) and Darcy (1998) stress that information on the accessibility of certain tourist destinations must be included in traditional channels to avoid isolating people with disabilities who would end up feeling the weight of their diversity for society [8, 40, 41]. Poor use of traditional channels, such as travel agencies, is a symbol of the lack of understanding of the true needs of disabled people [36].

In general, tourism requires the dissemination and exchange of information and the Web, today, appears to be the most effective means for their worldwide diffusion. Internet is a commercial and communication channel that allows the connection between service providers and consumers and through thousands of websites, tourists can get any kind of information for planning their trip. Hundreds of destinations, flights, rooms, activities are available today through a click [19].

As far as disabled users are concerned, websites must be characterized by the ability to display information in an intuitive and effective manner and must be easily accessible by any type of user. In these cases we talk about "Web without barriers" to identify a virtual world accessible to the disabled [17]. Unfortunately, many websites still present accessibility barriers that make it difficult if not impossible for millions of people with disabilities to navigate, understand and interact with the Web.

The removal of barriers is essential for all users (with speech, physical and cognitive disabilities) to use existing technologies. Very often the difficulties that disabled users encounter are due to deficiencies in the software design and content of sites that do not fully respect the design rules of devices designed specifically for the disabled such as: keyboards and mice for specific motor disabilities, Braile bar or synthesizers for the blind, Screen Reader, etc. [42].

In order to create accessible websites it is necessary to use: alternative texts for each type of multimedia content such as video or audio files, do not rely on a single color (the content must in fact be clear even if printed in black and white), separate the content from the presentation, use clear tables (which distinguish text and header), specify the language used (for Screen Reader), make reasonable pages even in the absence of scripts, avoid rapid and sudden movement of contents, ensure the use of an interface user also via keyboard commands (not necessarily scripts), guarantee independence from the device (mouse, keyboard...), do not require the use of additional technologies (eg to display pop-ups, etc.), provide information for contextualization and orientation (it must be easy to understand where you are and where you can go), to elaborate navigation mechanisms (menus, etc.) and document you clear and simple [43, 44].

Other elements that guarantee a good accessibility of the Web sites concern images and animations, in fact the use of the alt attribute is required, which provides the description of each graphic element. Multimedia files must have subtitles and transcriptions for audio and descriptions in the case of movies. Every web browsing device that allows a user with a disability to access the material he seeks, definitely improves his experience with the web world, reduces his frustration and makes him more willing to offer the service [45, 46].

With the advent of the Internet, therefore, disabled customers have access to a powerful and independent source of information with which to plan their holidays [9, 13, 38]. The Internet allows people with disabilities to look for detailed, reliable and up-to-date information because printed material is often not accurate enough. In addition, the Internet offers the possibility to reduce and simplify the search procedure [23, 33, 34] and can also provide an opportunity for sharing experiences among tourists. As with all travelers, people with disabilities benefit from the testimonies as they represent a valuable criteria for assessing the quality of the tourist destinations chosen or that we would like to visit [34, 38, 39].

Although the planning process differs from person to person, there are sets of special research tools divided according to the different types of disability [38, 47, 48], demonstrating the need for customer-oriented services [38, 41]. Based on the personal preferences of consumers, searches are possible according to the various types of disabilities or to the different levels of accessibility for each part of the destination [49]. The definition of the different research needs makes it possible to identify a more accurate target of potential customers [50].

We   can   therefore   conclude   that   tourism promotion campaigns are increasingly focusing on the formulation of offers aimed at the user, with the aim of transforming the potential customer into a true consumer. To do this, it is no longer enough to distribute information on traditional media, but it is also necessary to convey it to new channels and virtual spaces made available, such as social networks.

4   Web and Accessible Tourism: What Is the Situation in Italy?

For people with disabilities, the dissemination of information on the accessibility level of a given tourist destination is a key priority [7, 11, 12, 36, 39, 49, 51]. The fulfillment of this requirement becomes particularly crucial in that it establishes whether tourism remains an abstract concept or individuals, including those with a disability, can become active travelers [7, 10, 12]. Without sufficient information about accessible destinations, people with disabilities remain uncertain, that is, they do not know if their physical needs can be met and, consequently, they can decide to abstain from traveling and not meet important social and psychological needs. which: the desire to travel to rest and relax; try a feeling of freedom; have the opportunity to interact with society; have the opportunity to visit new places [48].

In Italy the subject of accessibility is very topical and sees more and more people engaged for more than 20 years. The state has committed itself a lot from the point of view of the regulations but also the associations and the private individuals have promoted several projects. Accessibility is no longer considered as a niche but an integral part of the tourism offer and contributes with other elements in creating a product with excellent quality.

In this period, thanks also to the fundamental contribution of inter-net and new technologies, information spreads faster and faster and the comparison between the various initiatives and the various projects is increasingly constructive. In our country we find that most of the sites and blogs that provide information on accessibility in tourism have been created for the most part within the private tourism sector by companies or coop-eratives. In this section of our paper we will report the analysis conducted on the situation in Italy concerning the presence of websites, blogs, networks that provide information on the accessibility of a tourist destination.

Web sites have been identified with greater visibility on the main search engine in the world, Google, or present in its first 5 pages and therefore more sought after by users. These sites are characterized by the presence of accessible multimedia guides and services offering information on accessibility in tourism. The research was conducted using the following keywords: "accessible tourism", "disability", "technology", "internet".

The research showed that, in Italy, the most "clicked" websites are: www.diversamenteagibile.it, www.superabile.it, www.anglat.it, www.disabili.com, www.superando.it.

Diversamenteagibile.it is a site/blog where everyone can share information and opinions about the structures and tourist attractions in which he spent the holidays. You can share photos, information and movies that are considered useful for other people [52].

Superabile.it offers help to disabled people and is promoted by INAIL (National Institute for Insurance against Accidents at Work). Those who need information can easily access it thanks to the thematic channel organization which facilitates the search; a section is also available in which press releases, photos, audio, video and books are available and consultable. Another good thing about this site is the fact that there is also a section where you can become part of a community, are in fact proposed a blog, the ability to write to the editors and the ability to receive answers directly from the experts [53].

A.N.G.L.A.T. (National Association Guide Handicapped Transport Legislation), it has been operating since the 80s in the field of mobility and public and private transport for people with disabilities. It is engaged in the tourism sector accessible for about 10 years providing a service of free certification of accessibility of the tourist facility. Within the dedicated site, in addition to information regarding the legislation, it is also possible to participate in a community and receive updated information whenever requested [54].

Disabili.com is an online journal that aims to provide all the information possible in relation to the issue of accessibility for both people who have a form of disability permeate that temporary. It is a site where you can find information about school and education, or even sport, family, car, travel and leisure, culture, work and mobility [55].

Superando.it is a consortium company commissioned by FISH (Italian Federation for the Overcoming of the Handicap) which groups together a series of associations such as the Telethon Foundation and also collaborates with important newspapers such as Corriere della Sera, Vita and Mattino di Padova. The main purpose is to provide information and to create a debate about any form of disability or necessity, and to do so at best seven reference sub-groups have been created linked to the main head: rights, autonomy, health, work, study, sport and tourism, society [56].

We can observe that most of the websites have been designed by companies or cooperatives, suggesting a greater sensitivity and interest towards the issues related to accessibility in the tourism sector among private operators rather than in public institutions. The creation of a unique information network for tourist accessibility and greater consistency in presenting them would be appropriate. The Region should create a database of tourist facilities and accessible itineraries and present them in a single site that could refer to one managed at the state level.

5 Concluding Remarks

Accessible tourism, understood as a set of services and facilities that allow customers with special needs to enjoy the holiday and leisure time without obstacles or difficulties, has developed over the last 15 years thanks to the initiatives promoted by numerous stakeholders (companies, private organizations and public, profit and non-profit) operating in the sector.

In the course of our discussion we have seen how technology is of paramount importance for improving accessibility. In particular, the new information technology can provide elements to make the websites of tourist structures in a fully accessible format allowing the communication and dissemination of information, fundamental for disabled people wishing to undertake a journey.

Although the authors mentioned in this paper stressed the importance of disseminating information to people with disabilities, research to date has not examined whether these needs have been met by the recent European production of tourism access schemes.

References

1. Presidenza del Consiglio dei Ministri: Qualità nell'accoglienza turistica di ospiti con esigenze specifiche, pp. 8–15, (2010)
2. Minuti, M.S.: Turismo sostenibile, turismo per tutti: l'accessibilità come elemento di qualità e volano di sviluppo dei sistemi turistici territoriali, Perugia, pp. 35–41. (2012)
3. Tourism For All. http://www.tourismforall.org
4. Presidenza del Consiglio dei Ministri. http://www.governo.it
5. Donoghue, C.: Challenging the authority of the medical definition of disability: an analysis of the resistance to the social constructionist paradigm. Disabil. Soc. **18**(2), 199–208 (2003)
6. Germ, P., Schleien, S.: Inclusive community leisure services: responsibilities of key players. Ther. Recreat. J. **31**, 22–37 (1997)
7. Yau, M., McKercher, B., Packer, T.: Travelling with a disability—more than an access issue. Ann. Tour. Res. **31**(4), 946–960 (2004)
8. Darcy, S.: Anxiety to Access: Tourism Patterns and Experiences of New South Wales People With a Physical Disability. Tourism New South Wales, Sydney (1998)
9. Buhalis, D.: eTourism: Information Technology for Strategic Tourism Management. Prentice Hall, Harlow (2003)
10. Pühretmair, F.: It's Time to make etourism accessible. In: Miesenberger, K., Klaus, J., Zagler, W., Burger, D. (eds.) Computers Helping People with Special Needs, pp. 272–279. Springer Verlag, Berlin (2004)
11. Shaw, G., Veitch, C., Coles, T.: Access, disability, and tourism: changing responses in the United Kingdom. Tour. Rev. Int. **8**(3), 167–176 (2005)
12. Stumbo, N., Pegg, S.: Travellers and tourists with disabilities: a matter of priorities and loyalties. Tour. Rev. Int. **8**(3), 195–209 (2005)
13. Cavinato, J., Cuckovich, M.: Transportation and tourism for the disabled: an assessment. Transp. J. **31**(3), 46–53 (2002)
14. Daruwalla, P., Darcy, S.: Personal and societal attitudes to disability. Ann. Tour. Res. **32**(2), 549–570 (2005)
15. Smith, R.: Leisure of disabled tourists—barriers to participation. Ann. Tour. Res. **14**, 376–389 (1987)

16. Fodness, D., Murray, B.: A model of information search behavior. J. Travel. Res. **37**(3), 220–230 (1999)
17. Gursoy, D., McCleary, K.: An integrative model of tourists' information search behavior. Ann. Tour. Res. **31**(2), 353–373 (2004)
18. Vogt, C., Fesenmaier. D.: Tourist and retailers' perceptions of services. Ann. Tour. Res. **22**(4), 763–780 (1995)
19. Allison, M.: Leisure, diversity and social justice. J. Leis. Res. **32**(1), 2–6 (2000)
20. Fodness, D., Murray, B.: Tourist information search. Ann. Tour. Res. **24**(3), 503–523 (1997)
21. Gursoy, D., Chen, J.: Competitive analysis of cross cultural information search behavior. Tour. Manag. **21**(6), 583–590 (2000)
22. Vogt, C., Fesenmaier, D.: Expanding the functional information search model. Ann. Tour. Res. **25**(3), 551–578 (1998)
23. Toerisme Vlaanderen: Tourism for All in the European Union. Status Report on Tourist Accommodation Schemes in Europe. "Tourism for all"—Meeting of EU Ministers of Tourism, 1–2 July 2001, Brugge
24. Laura, A.: Petrangeli, A: Viaggiare si può, pp. 21–47. Turismo e persone disabili, Deagostini, Novara (2003)
25. Manzo, A., Bravo, N.: Viaggiare senza limiti: il Turismo per Tutti in Europa, pp. 45–68. Istituto Italiano per il Turismo per Tutti, Torino (2010)
26. C.A.R.E.: Turismo Accessibile e bisogni speciali. Strumenti di comunicazione per il mercato, Associazione si può (a cura di), (2013)
27. European Network for Accessible Tourism. http://www.accessibletourism.org
28. European Commission: Calypso apre nuovi orizzonti di viaggio in Europa, Lussemburgo (2010)
29. Catena, D., Ligorio, D., Pansonlini, R., Rossetti, A.: Promozione e commercializzazione del prodotto turistico accessibile, Progetto Eu.For.Me. (2013)
30. Laboratorio Nazionale Turismo Accessibile. http://www.laboratoriosipuo.net
31. Leiper, N.: Tourism Management. RMIT Press, Melbourne (1995)
32. Israeli, A.: A preliminary investigation of the importance of site accessibility factors for disabled tourists. J. Travel. Res. **41**(1), 101–104 (2002)
33. Darcy, S., Daruwalla, P.: The trouble with travel: people with disabilities and travel. Soc. Altern. **18**(1), 41–46 (1999)
34. Consumer, N.O.P.: Holiday-Taking and Planning Amongst People with a Disability. NOP Consumer, London (2003)
35. Daniels, M., Drogin, E., Wiggins, B.: "Travel Tales": an interpretive analysis of constraints and negotiations to pleasure travel as experiences by persons with physical disabilities. Tour. Manag. **26**(6), 919–930 (2005)
36. McKercher, B., Packer, T., Yau, M., Lam, P.: Travel agents as facilitators or inhibitors of travel: perceptions of people with disabilities. Tour. Manag. **24**(4), 465–474 (2003)
37. McGuire, F., Dottavio, D., O'Leary, J.: Constraints to participation in outdoor creation across the life span: a nation-wide study of limitors and prohibitors. The Gerontologist **26**, 528–544 (1986)
38. Ray, N., Ryder, M.: "Ebilities" tourism. an exploratory discussion of the travel needs and motivations of the mobility disabled. Tour. Manag. **24**(1), 57–72 (2003)
39. Turco, D., Stumbo, N., Garncarz, J.: Tourism constraints for people with disabilities. Park. & Recreat. **33**(9), 78–84 (1998)
40. Cheng, K.: What Marketers should know about People with Disabilities. 28 October 2005
41. Burnett, J., Bender Baker, H.: Assessing the travel-related behaviors of the mobility-disabled consumer. J. Travel. Res. **40**(1), 4–11 (2001)
42. Medina, L.: Ecotourism and certification: confronting the principles and pragmatics of socially responsible tourism. J. Sustain. Tour. **13**(3), 281–295 (2005)
43. IsITT: Viaggiare senza limiti: il turismo per tutti in Europa. Torino, Tipografia Luca Ricci (2010)
44. Martini, U.: Internet e le imprese turistiche: un'analisi dell'impatto della rete sul funzionamento del mercato turistico leisure, in "Micro & Macro Marketing", a. X, n. 2 (2011)

45. Baroni, F., Lazzari, M.: Tecnologie informatiche e diritti umani per un nuovo approccio all'accessibilità. Ital. J. Disabil. Stud. **1**(1), 79–92 (2013)
46. Hampton, K.N., Sessions Goulet, L., Rainie, L., Purcell, K.: Social networking sites and our lives (2011)
47. BMWA: Economic Impulses of Accessible Tourism for All. Bundesministerium für Wirtschaft und Arbeit, Report, Berlin (2004)
48. Shaw, G., Coles, T.: Disability, holiday making and the tourism industry in the UK: a preliminary survey. Tour. Manag. **25**(3), 397–404 (2004)
49. Disability Now 2005 Disabled People's Needs. Unpublished Document
50. Gibson, H., Yiannakis, A.: Tourist roles—needs and the lifecourse. Ann. Tour. Res. **29**(2), 358–383 (2002)
51. Imrie, R., Kumar, M.: Focusing on disability and access in the built environment. Disabil. Soc. **13**(3), 357–374 (1998)
52. Diversamenteagibile.it. http://www.diversamenteagibile.it
53. Superabile—INAI. https://www.superabile.it
54. Associazione Nazionale Guida Legislazioni Andicappati Trasporti. http://www.anglat.it
55. Disabili.com. https://www.disabili.com
56. Superando.it. http://www.superando.it

Assistive Technology for the Social Inclusion at School: A Portrait of Italy

Giuseppe Perna, Luisa Varriale and Maria Ferrara

Abstract A modern and inclusive school has the primary goal of accepting and enhancing differences, ensuring that every student is fully involved in the learning process and social dynamics. New technologies, and in particular the so-called "Assistive Technologies", can provide a valuable contribution to responding appropriately to these needs. In particular, they can support and assist the full participation of students with disabilities in the learning process, either by allowing them to overcome the damage or impairment, and by overcoming the barriers created by traditional educational methods. Thus, Assistive Technologies are, or may become, one of the most important elements for the realization of truly inclusive pedagogy. This paper focuses on two main objectives: to present the main aids for the various types of disabilities (cognitive, sensory, motoric) offered by the computer and multimedia technologies in the field of didactics; analyse the use of technology in Italian schools to foster the integration process of students with disabilities.

Keywords Disability · School · Technology · Inclusive · ICT · Italian school · Educations · Pedagogy · Teaching · Assistive technology

1 Introduction

In normal daily activities, there has long been a rapid and constant evolution of new technologies (computers, internet, telematics networks and wireless networks): this has determined and continues to lead to a continuous transformation of the social, political, economic, productive, cultural and scientific. In addition, their diffusion in the various contexts of everyday life, from the world to the school, from leisure to

G. Perna (✉) · L. Varriale · M. Ferrara
University of Naples "Parthenope", Naples, Italy
e-mail: giuseppe.perna@uniparthenope.it

L. Varriale
e-mail: luisa.varriale@uniparthenope.it

M. Ferrara
e-mail: maria.ferrara@uniparthenope.it

© Springer Nature Switzerland AG 2020
Y. Baghdadi et al. (eds.), *ICT for an Inclusive World*,
Lecture Notes in Information Systems and Organisation 35,
https://doi.org/10.1007/978-3-030-34269-2_13

domestic use, from extracurricular education to the university, have transformed the habits and lifestyle of each of us, the way of learning, thinking, communicating and interacting [1]. For some years now, the interest in didactics towards new technologies has increased strongly; the applications of new technologies in the field of education have enabled the development of important pedagogical opportunities, not least in the integration of students with disabilities. In the debates on new technology applied to teaching only a dozen years ago, he doubted the utility of the computer in education, looking for pros and cons [2]. Today, the problem is to offer new technologies, recognized as a strategic tool whose general access is a crucial aspect of equal opportunities offered by the training system.

The diffusion of new technologies in classrooms, for the purpose of renewing the teaching methods, has benefited a crucial aspect of the Italian school, or the integration process. The concept of inclusion refers to principles of non-discrimination, equal dignity and social equity, with ideal life and society profiles: in this context, the role and use of technologies to support participation and acquisition of knowledge and skills of disabled students [3].

As is well known, *Information and Communication Technology* (ICT) at school can perform various functions: from those enabling to carry out basic school-based activities that otherwise could not be performed by disabled students, those that support advanced teaching design for the whole class (teaching software, internet, e-learning, etc.), or use of didactic software and didactic software use [4]. In particular, *Assistive Technologies* are instrumentation that integrate, replace, or enhance the person's abilities and can significantly change their lifestyle in the sense of improving levels of autonomy in carrying out manual activities, which at school, for disabled students, are represented by the so-called basic activities (read, write, draw, calculate, access teaching aids, etc.). Often, these activities occur through the use of personal computers and, depending on the degree and type of disability, any auxiliary hardware and software for the so-called "assisted access" to the computer, or the use of aids to enable the person with disabilities accessing the facilities that can offer a standard computer [5].

The role of Assistive Technologies at school is thus exhausted in the ability to provide students and teachers with the opportunity to improve the levels of early autonomy and the possibilities of expanding the range of work activities offered by the secondary, who have the specific task of organizing and designing teaching activities so that they can exploit the best Assistive Technologies [6]. In this context, teaching software, such as tutorials, exercises, and retrieval software are included, just to name a few, specially designed to encourage learning, the result of which, of course, depends on the teacher's methodological preparation much more than by the intrinsic quality of the instrument as they assist and do not replace the teaching itself. Otherwise, more simply, it can be understood as intelligent use of office software and ICT equipment (internet, scanners, MP3 players, digital cameras, digital cameras, smart phones, i-pads, tablets, etc.) to promote collaborative work among students with varying degrees of skill and between students and teachers who are encouraged to promote real inclusion experiences, such as the ability to attend e-learning courses with their own classroom in situations of impossibility to be present at school.

Therefore, in the field of didactics, despite the extensive debate within the recent Evidence Based research [7] on the effectiveness of school technology, they have acquired an increasing importance for the opportunities for learning and integration offered to students with disabilities to achieve that autonomy that would not have been possible in other ways. It has therefore become crucial to allow the widest possible dissemination of these tools, particularly in school contexts, so as to form an environment of school policies, practices and resources that will enable these students, including access to l integration, to achieve their training objectives [8].

The aim of this study is to present the main aids for the various types of disabilities (cognitive, sensory, motoric) offered by the informatics and multimedia technologies in the field of didactics, especially the special one, which can favor the processes of inclusion and of learning in a significant relational context. In addition, with reference to the Italian school context, we want to analyze the availability of assistive technologies for students with disabilities. To this end, reference was made to the data reported in the ISTAT survey on the integration of students with disabilities in primary and secondary schools.

This study is structured in the following sections. In Sect. 2 we analyze the evolution of Italian legislation on the recognition of the importance of full participation in school life by all students, especially those with disabilities, which must be equally valued, treated with respect and provided with the same opportunities at school. Based on this perspective, the topic of Special Educational Needs (BES) was introduced for the first time in the Warnock Report (1978) and that in Italy, with the Ministerial Directive of 27/12/2012, they were divided into three major sub-categories: disability; that of specific evolutionary disorders and that of socioeconomic, linguistic and cultural disadvantage. Section 3 introduced and defined the concept of Assistive Technologies and their use in the context of the integration of students with disabilities. In Sect. 4, based on the different types of student's disabilities, has described the main aids offered by computer science and multimedia technologies in the field of didactics. In Sect. 5, with reference to the Italian school, have been shown the main findings regarding the use of technology in teaching to meet the needs of students with disabilities. Finally, in Sect. 6 some final considerations are provided about the phenomenon investigated.

2 Disability and Inclusive Education: Analysis of Regulatory Developments

There are many conventions, statements, assertions and decisions on disability, integration and special education in the international sphere that guide the sociocultural and economic policies and strategies of the various countries concerned to make education real for everyone.

As part of the 48th International Conference on Education in UNESCO, dedicated to *Inclusive education: the way of the future* (Geneva, November 25–28,

2008), has been underlined the need to clarify with greater rigor the conceptual dimension of inclusion in relation to the concept of integration. Another important international document is represented by *Guidelines for Integration in Education* (2009) by UNESCO where convergence of all decisions regarding school integration comes from the *Universal Declaration of Human Rights* (1948), *Convention on Discrimination in Education* (1960), the *Convention on the Rights of the Child* (1989), the *Convention on the Protection and Promotion of Diversity in Cultural Expressions* (2005). More recently, the *Convention on the Rights of Persons with Disabilities* (2006), and specifically Article 24, highlighted the crucial importance of school integration [9].

In the 1970s, characterized by important and significant changes in politics, family, society, customs and culture, in Italy, by law n. 317 of August 4, 1977, the right to study and to the formation of the subject in difficulty is enshrined and fully integrated into the normal classes, with the consequent use of the support teacher (who therefore possesses specific professional and didactic skills). Since 1977, there have been continuous laws and ministerial circulars, all aimed at the effective integration of people with disabilities in the elementary school until the so-called "framework law" for social assistance, social integration and people's rights with handicap (law n. 104 of 5 February 1992), which welcomes all the relevant issues and disciplines both the integration of such subjects into schools (including secondary ones) and their inclusion in society and the world of work. By law 104, students are seen as subjects who, while being in *"learning difficulties, relationships..."*, are not marginalized either on the human or on the social level, as established by art. 3 of our Constitutional Charter which not only assures *"equal social dignity (...) without distinction (...) of personal conditions"*, but instructs the Republic to *"remove obstacles (...) which (...) prevent the full development of the person... and the effective participation of all workers in the political, economic and social organization of the country"*. Finally, with D.P.R., dated 24 February 1994, provision was made for *"addressing and coordinating the tasks of local health units in the field of students with handicap"*. The right of a person with disabilities to integration into ordinary classes is confirmed by law n. 53 (so-called *Moratti Reform*). This, in fact, governs the personalization of the teaching and learning method, that is, an adaptation of education to the understanding skills of each individual pupil. In each school, the G.I.O. (*Internal Operations Group*), with the fundamental task of elaborating P.E.P. (*Personalized Educational Plan*) in order to design the full integration of those in difficulty [10].

Finally, with law n. 170 of 2010, dyslexia, disorientation, dysgraphia and dyscalculia are recognized as *Specific Learning Disorders* (DSA) while with the Ministerial Directive of December 27, 2012 *"Intervention Tools for Students with Special Educational Needs and Territorial Organization for the Discipline, school enrolment"*, introduces the term *"Special Education Needs"* (BES). The latter, together with the application ministerial circular n. 8 of March 6, 2013, has begun a fundamental and difficult change in the structure and organization of the Italian school system.

The term "Special Educational Needs" is used, in the first place, in the Warnock Report drawn up in England in 1978. The latter stated the need to integrate students with disabilities and therefore be judged different using an inclusive teaching methodology equal for all students [10]. Subsequently, in 2001, the Special Educational Needs and Disability Act reiterates the need to prevent any feeling of discrimination against students with Special Educational Needs and affirms the need to promote their adherence to the school environment, also raising awareness among families.

It is with the worldwide recruitment of the *International Classification of Functioning* (ICF), which has spread a new way of considering health and disability. In fact, the ICF model is used to classify and describe both health and disability in order to create a single language that acts as a reference scheme. According to this model, the person must be assessed as "a complex and interconnected system that interacts with personal and environmental factors, from a health and non-disease perspective" [11]; with it the concept of handicap is replaced by that of "limit to social participation" and the disability of the individual is not necessarily physical but may also be due to disturbances or disturbances of other nature such as environmental factors.

In Italy, the emanation of the Ministerial Directive that introduced the concept of Special Educational Needs is the result of this cultural change that attributes a new meaning to the concepts of health and disability. Specifically, the Directive specifies that: "*the area of school disadvantage is much wider than the one explicitly referred to as the deficit. In each class there are students who demand special attention for a variety of reasons: social and cultural disadvantage, specific learning disabilities and/or specific evolutionary disorders, difficulties arising from the lack of knowledge of Italian culture and language because they belong to cultures different*".

In the 27/12/2012 Directive, Special Needs Education includes three major subclasses: disability, namely, cognitive delay, physical, psychological and sensory disabilities; specific learning disorders and/or specific evolutionary disorders, i.e., DSA, verbal and non-obstructions, difficulty in synchronism of movements, dyspraxia, mild autistic spectrum disorder, mixed specific evolutionary disorders, etc.); socioeconomic, cultural and linguistic disadvantage. In the Directive it is, in fact, specified that: "*In each class there are students who submit a request for special attention for a variety of reasons (...) each pupil with continuity or for certain periods may manifest Special Educational Needs or for psychological, social reasons with respect to which schools need to provide an adequate and personalized response*". Then, students with Special Educational Needs have the right to a specific and customized didactic program, which underlines the typical peculiarities of each student's non-standardizable understanding and the right to be followed for their complete realization. To this end, it is also possible to resort to compensatory instruments or dispensing measures provided for by the implementing provisions of law 170/2010 (DM 5669/11) [11].

The application circular of MIUR n. 8 of March 6, 2013 focuses on the need for an educational plan for all students with Special Educational Needs, stating that "*The Personalized Learning Plan can no longer be understood as mere explication of compensatory and dispensing tools for students with DSA; it is the tool that will include, for example, didactic-educational curricula calibrated on the minimum expected levels for outgoing skills (of which many students with BES, without any diagnostic certification), programmatic tools more useful than to compensations or dispensations, with exquisitely didactic-instrumental character*".

The Circular also clarifies the position of students who have a cultural, social, economic and personal disadvantage: "*Every student, for continuity or for certain periods, may manifest Special Educational Needs: either for physical, biological, physiological reasons or for psychological reasons, social, which requires that schools offer an adequate and personalized response. Such types of BES should be identified on the basis of objective elements (such as reporting social service providers), or well-founded psycho-educational and didactic considerations*".

The role of the International Classification of Functioning (ICF) developed by the World Health Organization (ICF) is crucial in this regard as it allows to identify the student's Special Educational Needs. In particular, unlike other European countries, this model has been very successful in Italy as it can be defined as: disability and handicap such as physical and sensory lesions, acute or chronic diseases, epilepsy; slow development; autism; inadequate vision, memory, hearing; defects in language and therefore in communication; difficulties in learning; DSA; difficulty in maintaining concentration, little intellectual capacity measured by intellectual quotient; bullying; economic difficulties and discrimination related to ethnic or social origin [11].

Ultimately, the ICF model allows to identify and describe the different conditions of students with Special Education Needs: some will fundamentally have biological complications or difficulties in personal activities; others will have problems with the environment, participation etc. The objective of this significant opening is to "*recognize all dignity in need, regardless of which combination of causal factors has produced their situation*" [12].

3 Inclusion Technology for Disabled Student

Technology is changing traditional teaching models. The school world is increasingly confronted with students chewing the languages of computer programming and knowing the dynamics of digitized interaction. Here, the systems offered by technological innovation are fully integrated into the process of building future teaching and also in the creation of personalized programs for children with disabilities.

Technologies for the educational needs of students with disabilities, called "*assistive technology*, have become an integral part of the life of every person who is in a state of disability. With this term, therefore, the tools used by people with disabilities are shown to be able to perform activities despite the presence of limitations due to functional deficits of various kinds [13].

As appropriately underlined in the European Study EUROSTAT "the term technology does not only refer to physical objects as instruments or *equipment; more generally, it refers to products, organizational arrangements, or ways to do things that include a number of technical principles and components. The term assistive applies to technology when used to compensate for functional limitation, to facilitate independent life, to allow disabled or elderly people to fully realize their potential*" [14].

In Italy, the term Assistive Technology appears officially in the text of law n. 4 of 2004, which limits its scope to the telematics scope until it comes to considering Assistive Technologies as synonyms for aids and therefore use their own definition in version 2007 of UNI EN ISO 9999 as *"any product (including devices, equipment, tools or technology systems, software) specializing in production or of common commercial activity, designed to prevent, compensate, control, alleviate or eliminate any impairment, activity limitations or obstacles to participation"*. In fact, these are instrumentalities that complement, add to or enhance the person's ability and can significantly change their lifestyle in the sense of improving levels of autonomy in carrying out manual activities [15]. Technological development has helped to refine technology aids and teaching aids, making them much more flexible and adaptable to the end user, and to make the Assistive Technologies in the field of education more and more important to the learning and integration opportunities of students with disabilities. In fact, by using them, it is possible to provide students with tools to improve their levels of autonomy, but also to expand the range of teaching staff activities that have the specific task of organizing and designing didactic activity in so as to make the best use of Assistive Technologies [6].

For disadvantaged students, especially in school, so-called basic activities (reading, writing, drawing, calculating, accessing educational aids etc.) often occur through the use of personal computers and, depending on the degree and type disability, support for any auxiliary hardware and software for so-called "assisted access" to the computer, that is, the use of aids to enable a person with disabilities to access the facilities that they can offer a standard computer. In this context, the didactic software is specially designed to facilitate learning, the result of which, of course, depends on the teacher's methodological preparation rather than by the intrinsic quality of the instrument. Educational software is technology that supports (and does not replace) teaching, or allows students to acquire disciplinary content such as: tutorial, exercise, recovery software, etc. [6].

The didactic/educational use of the software, on the other hand, refers to technologies that propose activities useful to educate general and transversal skills, such as: simulation software for environments; adventure-game; multimedia production tools; author software, etc. Otherwise, more simply, it can be understood as intelligent use of office software and ICT equipment (internet, scanners, MP3 players, cameras and digital cameras, smart phones, i-pads, tablets, etc.) to promote collaborative work among students with varying degrees of skill and between students and teachers who are encouraged to promote real inclusion experiences, such as the ability to attend e-learning courses with their own classroom in situations of impossibility to be present at school [16]. There are, however, no generalizable scientific evidence that demonstrates that the use of technology in didactics typically results in an improvement in learning. In particular, studies on cognitive load have shown that differences in learning levels with or without technologies are determined by the methodologies of use and the quality of the interactions they involve [17]. In essence, the use of new technologies does not automatically generate learning, but rather the processes and ways of using it to determine learning outcomes in the subject. There are contexts in which technologies lie with learning as tools of facilitation and stimulation for the activation of higher cognitive processes in which once again the didactic attitude is to make a difference. Moreover, in the area of special education and disability technologies are a priority instrument for ensuring in most cases access to knowledge, autonomy and social participation, contributing to the growth of people's quality of life.

The relevance of the use of technologies as an inclusive resource has also been analyzed by *Evidence Based Education* (EBE) research [18], in which multiple-time studies with quantitative broad spectrum methods have shown that the use of learning technologies does not involve any statistically significant difference in learning, as the effect size (ES) remains below a significant threshold in all types of technological use, excluding interactive video [19]. This data is present in Hattie's work by an author who has synthesized 800 800-meta-analysis of school-age learning outcomes.

Hattie's data also show that better results can be found in teaching strategies in highly interactive contexts, in which he emphasizes feed-back, peer learning, and student control over learning. the teachers have received adequate training beforehand.

Calvani within the conceptual framework of Evidence Based Education (EBE) claims that "... *it is not the technology that affects the internal forms of learning and it is not lawful to attribute that expectation. Differences are produced by the methodologies and in particular as Hattie says, by the quality of the interactions they involve...*" [20]. But within a generally modest average effectiveness, as evidenced by the fact that the use of learning technologies does not involve any statistically significant difference in learning, since the Effect Size (ES) remains below a significant threshold in all types of technological use, excluding interactive videos, are circumstances that make it more effective to use them: computer use is more useful when it comes to offering a variety of approaches and learning paths, when the instructor was formed on the use of the computer as a tool when the student has control of it, when peer learning is optimized and the use of feedback.

In addition to this, according to Calvani, "... *there are many reasons justifying the use of technologies, which go beyond their direct impact on the learning outcomes: they can be indispensable tools for individualizing paths, collecting resources, giving community life educators, to broaden the possibilities of access and expression, to stimulate new ideas on education...*" [20].

Particularly in the field of students with special educational needs there are areas where the use of technologies is of utmost priority, since access to knowledge, such as sensory deficits and motors, would in no way be possible. They can also help to improve independence, productivity, job placement and social participation by increasing forms of communication, exchanges and, in general, improving the quality of life and social inclusion. In such situations, therefore, the logic of experimental comparisons, the methodology on which EBE is based, presents some issues, such as the case of special education, since "... *experimental investigations with control groups have become more difficult, wide variability of the problems that subjects present, which complicates if it is not impossible to define homogeneous groups, making it necessary to resort to other methodologies, such as drawings centred on individual subjects or mixed methods...*" [20].

Beyond the specificities of the industry, according to Calvani, "...*if we can demonstrate that technologies contribute to improving some aspects of the context and school life without counter-productive effects on learning, it would be unwise to counteract employment...*" [20], especially from an inclusive policy perspective. In fact, the use of technologies can bring many benefits to the communication, sharing, conservation and management of teaching resources inside the school. The fact that content becomes manipulable, editable, individualizable in relation to the different levels of learning difficulties now appears to be one of the major opportunities that technology offers to school. Addition to the extension of networking and networking opportunities, a teacher can personally dialogue with his/her students via web 2.0 tools (blog, mobile…) and more generally didactic strategies based on e-learning 2.0 can achieve some results in favour of e-inclusion, e-participation, although at the moment the evidence is not decisive [19].

4 Analysis of the Technologies for the Educational Needs of Students with Disabilities

Assistive technologies are, therefore, the cornerstone of an educational process, modern and effective, aimed at disabled students. They can support and assist the full participation of these students in the learning process, either by allowing them to overcome the damage or impairment, and by overcoming the barriers created by traditional educational methods. This type of technology is, or may become, one of the most important elements for the realization of a truly inclusive pedagogy: it has a profound impact both in education and in work, and determines the possibility of integration in school and society. It includes any tool, system or service that supports disabled people in their daily lives, in education, in work, in leisure time [21].

The assistive technology sector is vast: they include simple and well-known products, such as the blind sticker or manual pushchair for disabled motorcyclists, but also sophisticated high tech products such as personal computers and electronic wheelchairs voice command. For the different types of disabilities, let us analyze the key technologies used in the field of teaching to facilitate students' learning and inclusion processes. Motor disability includes a variety of deficits such as inability to perform certain movements, parasitic movements such as tremor, difficulty in coordinating the eyepiece, lower precision and speed of movement and muscular strength, and assistive technologies can provide a great support for children who have such difficulties. For example, for students to write to the computer is easier and easier than writing a letter manually. In addition, you can adjust the keyboard and mouse sensitivity to reduce involuntary errors.

The main aids that can support students with motor deficiency in using the computer are: keyboards, pointing systems, voice recognition, scanning, and word prediction. Depending on the baby's needs (amplitude of motion travel, pressure force, etc.), keyboards that meet individual needs can be found on the market, such as:

enlarged keyboards, which have a small number of keys but with larger size than usual that facilitates the selection; reduced keyboards with smaller and closer keys, effective especially when the user cannot carry large movements and is subject to fatigue; keyboard emulators that reproduce the latter on the screen and can be controlled by the mouse or through a scanning technique; voice command, that is, the user's voice is recognized and transformed into commands for the computer [21].

The student with motor deficiency (but also children with visual disabilities) often finds the mouse to be laborious and complicated, as its use requires accurate and precise motor skills. To overcome this difficulty, you can replace the use of the mouse directly with the keyboard that replaces the mouse with the arrow keys.

Voice recognition is the process through which the computer, through a specific software, recognizes and stores the human voice. These are particularly useful software in the presence of particular deficiencies, thanks to the fact that these programs, using only voice, allow you to replace all the mouse functions, ensuring the possibility of widespread use of the computer, including navigation on Internet by the user with motor impairment. Scanning is a process that allows you to identify and choose an item belonging to a set through successive choices made in sub-sets smaller and smaller than the starting point. The choice of elements takes place through sensors that, depending on the child's ability, can be characterized by size, degree of sensitivity and be activated by hands, feet, head, voice, and muscle movements.

Finally, use of programs that make the writing process faster, suggesting, after writing a few letters, a list of words that begin in the same way. By doing so, the child is helped to reduce the writing time of writing with less energy. The blind and visually impaired students, however, can achieve complete autonomy in completing their schoolwork by means of multimodality, that is, the ability of an electronic document to be consulted in different ways while maintaining the same content [21].

The computer represents a blind pupil as an indispensable tool for achieving its independence, even in anticipation of a future labor outlet. There are a number of aids that can help students with visual impairment to use the computer autonomously. Among them, the screen reader (screen reader) has the task of communicating to the blind person what appears on the PC screen; This is a software that illustrates the contents of the screen and uses voice synthesis. Voice Sync is a program that automatically converts text into voice, reading the content. The Braille display (also called the Braille line or Braille bar) turns Braille data received from the screen reader. Reads line-by-line content on your PC screen [22]. The Braille printer allows you to print on a braille paper on a paper pad. There are Braille printers that allow you to print Braille text on both the front and back of the sheet. The ability to print Braille texts allows the teacher to personalize the blind eye of the blind student. The scanner with an OCR (*Optical Character Recognition*) program captures the image of printed text pages by turning them into multimodal digital documents.

For students with hypovision problems, a mouse with the scroll wheel (Intellimouse) should be used to calibrate the magnification based on the student's real needs. Zoom magnifiers and software allow you to expand the size of the items on the computer screen (both written and images text). Of crucial importance are the "*speaking or audio books*": these are texts read aloud recorded on a magnetic tape.

Book readers are tools that allow *"self-reading of printed texts and contain in a single device a system for capturing and recognizing texts and a vocal synthesis"* [22].

In general, the use of high resolution screens is forbidden for students who see little, as they reduce the size of all the elements on the screen. It is recommended to use low resolutions, for example 800 × 600 or 1024 × 768 [22]. Fundamental to the sighted students is *"the use of sharp and well-marked characters. In general, vision-lovers prefer stick-like ones (same profile throughout the stretch, e.g. Arial, Tahoma, Verdana) compared to variable-profile ones. Thick and other slender traits, such as Times New Roman"* [22].

For students with hearing impairment, the computer offers the ability to understand and understand; the use of video-writing programs represents a useful support for the audio-visual students in the difficult task of writing composition.

The educational software used for the particular needs of students with hearing impairment can be categorized into 4 types of systems: (a) *drill and practice teaching systems* for reading and writing techniques aimed at reducing specific language learning difficulties that manifest deaf children; (b) *multimedia systems* that allow the deaf student to come into contact with a certain amount of knowledge by accessing different ways of presenting the content and, more specifically, through the written language, movie clips in Sign Language, drawings and animations; (c) *Micromonde-based systems*, i.e. systems where students can deal with problem solving through the exploration and manipulation of concrete representations that deaf students can control through a motor-perceptual approach; (d) *general-purpose systems*, such as a network synchronous communication system (i.e., chat systems), which allows for the structuring of a communicative context that takes on a kind of dialogue based on the use of written language [23].

Students who are unable to adequately communicate through oral language (for example, children with physical disabilities, developmental delays, autism, apathy or other language disorders) may learn to express themselves in increasing mode.

The *Alternative Alternative Communication* (AAC) aims precisely to facilitate communication and to improve social skills, becoming a promoter of integration [24]. Alternative Alternative Communication is a form of assistive technology; it includes any device, word, image, sign language, symbol or gesture that compensates for the difficulties of expressive and receptive communication. The Alternative Alternative Communication may include drawings, photographs, symbols, words, letters, objects used alone or in combination with communication boards, voice output devices (*VOCAs, Voice Output Communication Aid*) or keyboards [25]. Vocal Output Communication Aids (VOCAs) are portable devices that allow the child to select and turn the iconic message into voice. If you are using a VOCAs, it is often effective to record messages from a child (or child) of the same age as the subject, so that he or she can identify with the voice. VOCAs represent an effective means of communication for students who no longer have or have never had the ability to communicate with the voice and who are unable to handle an alphabetical system [22].

Voice Entry Devices are effective tools for students with verbal expression difficulties, as they can increase expressive, language skills, and enhance cognitive skills.

Many Alternative Alternative Communication systems rely on iconic communication consisting of images or set of symbols to which a certain message is associated. Graphic systems can be used with both simple, non-technological tools such as paper tables, consultation books, aprons, etc., and through technologically advanced aids such as the computer or speech entry communicators. Communicating with an iconic system is by pointing or selecting images. The most popular iconic communication systems are Picture Communication Symbols (PCS), addressed to people who can only communicate elementarily and based on vocabulary limited, and a simple morphosyntactic structure, and Bliss, aimed at people who can communicate to a more complex level, and consists of a set of extended symbols that allows to construct sentences ex novo [22].

Finally, with assistive technologies, educational paths can be exploited that use information technology to achieve greater autonomy and school integration of students with cognitive problems. In the presence of a pupil with mental retardation, the computer can act as a way to foster a truly inclusive learning environment. In fact, the computer is often felt by children as an adult tool and therefore it can increase self-esteem and motivation [21]. If the use of the standard keyboard creates problems because of its complexity (the keys are too many and too similar to each other), it should be equipped with a special keyboard or an easy-to-use keyboard. They are originally designed for disabled motorcyclists, but their use is also being extended to cognitive impairments and disabilities as part of preschool children [22].

5 Technology and School Inclusion: Reports on the Situation in Italy

For over thirty years from the issuance of law n. 577/77 which has begun the process of integration of disabled children in public schools, it can be said that the results achieved show high levels of insertion in Italy. School integration, however, is a concept that goes beyond the mere increase of school enrollment: the degree of integration is measured by information describing the integrated service offering in terms of tools and people that state and non-state schools and local authorities set up in order to meet the needs of the disadvantaged population.

Based on the latest survey conducted by ISTAT (school year 2015/2016) on the level of integration of students with disabilities in primary and secondary primary and secondary schools, state and non-governmental organizations, we highlight the key findings below, focusing our attention on use of technology in special education.

School data is censored, while pupil information is of a sample nature. The population of interest of the investigation in question, that is, the set of statistical units around which it intends to investigate, is made up of students with disabilities present in schools in the school year 2015/2016. The overall size of the school sample was fixed at 3000 units, while the sample size of students to be interviewed was set at

13,751. The selection archive for the survey consists of the list of primary and secondary schools of grade I where there is at least one pupil with disabilities; that archive was provided by the Ministry of Education and contains for each school the number of students with disabilities. In the survey phase, several sample school drops occurred, bringing the sample from 3000 to 2552, for a total of 11,254 interviewed students [26].

In the school year 2015–2016 there are about 156,000 students with disabilities in Italy (3.4% of the total students), of which more than 88 thousand in the primary school (equal to 3.1% of the total students, were 2.1% in the 2001–2002 school year) and about 68 thousand in secondary school (3.9% of the total, 2.6% in 2001–2002). The highest percentage is found in Abruzzo and Sicily for the primary (3.6%) and still in Abruzzo for the first-degree secondary (4.8%), while the lowest percentage is recorded in Basilicata (2.3% of primary school students and 2.7% of secondary school students). Males represent more than 65% of students with disabilities in both school orders: 217 males per 100 females in primary school and 188 males per 100 females in secondary school. The average age is 8.7 years in the primary school and is 12.5 years for those attending secondary school, without pointing out appreciable territorial differences compared to the national average value. The data on the middle ages are more frequent in the school beyond the expected age.

The most common type of problem in all spatial segments is the one related to intellectual disability, which is about 42.5% of the population with disabilities in the primary school and 50.3% of the one in the secondary grade I grade. In primary school, this problem is followed by developmental and language disorders affecting 24.9% and 21.8% respectively of students with disabilities.

Secondary grade, after intellectual disability, the most common problems are related to learning disabilities and development disorders affecting respectively 22.1% and 21.4% of students with disabilities. Multiproblematic students represent on average 45% of the total students with disabilities with small variations between territorial breakdowns: 25% have two problems and the remaining 20% have three or more problems. To detect data on assistive technology, during the survey, schools were asked to point out the presence of computer workstations with special hardware peripherals and specific software for special education for students with different types of disabilities as well as use by the pupil with the support of educational aids provided by the school. The presence of the workstations, their daily availability (presence of classrooms), and the actual utilization of teaching technology in the teaching staff were measured. About one quarter of primary and secondary primary schools have no computer workstations for people with disabilities, with higher percentages in the South: 31.5% of primary schools and 26.4% of secondary schools, and lower in Center with 25.2% of primary schools and 20.3% of secondary schools. The region with more than one school equipped with computerized workstations is Emilia-Romagna with 84.5% of primary schools and 85.7% of secondary school students. Less-favored schools, both for primary and secondary schools, are those of Molise (with 57.7% and 52.5% respectively of the schools).

Adapted computerized workstations are mainly located in dedicated workshops (57.7% of primary schools and 54.8% of secondary schools of first degree). Less frequent was the presence of computerized workstations adapted to students with disabilities (40% in primary school and 36.7% in secondary school) and in supportive classrooms (34% of primary schools and 49.7% of the I grade secondary schools).

The percentage of schools in which none of the teaching teachers use technology in teaching, although available to them, is 5.8% of primary and 3.4% of first-degree secondary students. The Autonomous Province of Bolzano has the largest percentage of schools in which no support teacher uses technology in primary schools (23.8%); while in the first degree secondary is the autonomous province of Trento (12%).

Throughout the country, the proportion of schools in which no support teacher has attended specific courses on educational technologies for students with disabilities represents 17.9% in primary school and 15.2% in secondary school. This share is particularly high for both school orders in Valle d'Aosta, where they reach 42.9% of primary schools and 29.4% of secondary schools of I grade. More than a quarter of the schools, however, have all the support staff with specific courses with little territorial differences. Compensatory teaching instruments are highly heterogeneous in their use: the most used aids are the computer and multimedia devices used to customize teaching (e.g. PCs, tablets, recorders, cd/dvd players, cameras), in use for almost 47% of students with support. An important proportion, equal to 23.2% of the students, instead uses learning learning software, consistent with the significant presence of learning difficulties in the disadvantaged population. There is still a 34.6% share of the students who do not use any teaching aids. There are no significant differences between the two school orders in the use of teaching aids. In this context, the use of new technologies, emphasizes the ISTAT study, could be a real facilitator in the process of inclusion of students with disabilities, especially if the computer workstation is located within the classroom. In fact, there are specific software for performing didactic activities or hardware peripherals designed for various types of disabilities. Despite these premise, however, the survey reveals that more than a quarter of the schools under consideration do not yet have computer workstations for people with disabilities, with higher points in primary schools in Southern Italy.

6 Concluding Remarks

In our research we wanted to emphasize how using technology can be a valuable help in teaching for disabled students or with special educational needs.

However, effective use of new technology tools in inclusive education requires changes and modifications also in approaches and pedagogic strategies. In particular, teachers are considered to play a key role in making better use of the opportunities offered by new technologies in order to guarantee the right of people with disabilities to participate in education and to encourage full inclusion of all students in the main systems of instruction.

Teachers need to have helpful and comprehensive information on the accessibility features of software and hardware, whether they are created ad hoc for a particular pedagogic use, but not for ad hoc but usable use for pedagogical purposes, and industry-specific knowledge and good practice to support the elaboration, sharing and re-use of inclusive pedagogical programs with ICTs.

This exploratory study presents the limit to be focused on the Italian context. In a future research it would be interesting to compare the results of the use of assistive technology in Italian schools with those of other European countries related to the use of the same technologies.

References

1. Fiorucci, M.: La mediazione culturale. Strategie per l'incontro. Armando Editore, Roma, p. 8, (2007)
2. Richmond, K.W.: Il computer nell'educazione. Pro e contro, Armando Editore, Roma, p. 35 (1985)
3. Ianes, D., Cramerotti, S.: Alunni con BES. Bisogni Educativi Speciali, Erickson, Trento, pp. 14–27 (2013)
4. Ferlino, L.: Risorse digitali per l'integrazione scolastica: speciali o Designed for All?. In: Pardi, P., Simoneschi, G. (eds.) Studi e documenti degli annali della Pubblica Istruzione, vol. 127, pp. 99–107, Le Monnier, Firenze (2009)
5. Maragliano, R.: Nuovo manuale di didattica multimediale. Roma-Bari, Laterza (2007)
6. Guerreschi, M.: Autonomia, partecipazione, integrazione: il ruolo delle tecnologie. In: Pardi, P., Simoneschi, G. (eds.) Studi e documenti degli annali della Pubblica Istruzione, vol. 127, pp. 65–82. Le Monnier, Firenze, (2009)
7. Calvani, A., Vivanet, G.: Evidence Based Education e modelli di valutazione formativa per le scuole. J. Educ., Cult. Psychol. Stud. (ECPS) (2014)
8. Chiaro, M.: Didattica, Ricerca e Statistica. Strumenti teorico-operativi per la formazione degli insegnanti. Aracne Editore, Roma (2012)
9. Pavone, M.: Inserimento, Integrazione, Inclusione. In: d'Alonzo, L., Caldin R. (eds). Questioni, sfide e prospettive della Pedagogia Speciale. L'impegno della comunità di ricerca, pp. 145–148. Liguori Editore, Napoli (2012)
10. Chiappetta Cajola, L.: Fondamenti teorici e operativi per una didattica dell'inclusione, pp. 11–36. In: Ferrari, F., Santini, G. (eds.) Musiche inclusive. Modelli musicali d'insieme per il sostegno alla partecipazione e all'apprendimento nella secondaria di primo grado. Roma: MIUR–Universitalia (2014)
11. Ianes, D., Macchia, V.: La didattica per i Bisogni Educativi Speciali, pp. 33–50. Erickson, Trento (2008)
12. Favorini, A.M.: Pedagogia Speciale e formazione degli insegnanti, Verso una scuola inclusiva. Franco Angeli, Milano (2010)
13. Zambotti, F.: Tecnologie come risorsa inclusiva, Trento, Erickson, p. 28 (2013)
14. European Council: eAccessibility for people with disabilities—Council Resolution (2002)
15. Terzi, L.: L'approccio delle capacità applicato alla disabilità: verso la giustizia nel campo dell'istruzione. In: Borgnolo, G., De Camillis, R., Francescutti, C., Frattura, L., Troiano, R., Bassi, G, Tubaro, E. (eds.) ICF e Convenzione ONU sui diritti delle persone con disabilità, pp. 55–62. Trento, Erickson (2009)
16. Galliani, L.: Formazione degli insegnanti e competenze nelle tecnologie della comunicazione educativa. Giornale Italiano della Ricerca Educativa, SIRD 2(3), 93–99 (2009)
17. Hattie, J.: Visible learning: a synthesis of over 800 meta-analyses relating to achievement. Routledge, London-New York (2009)
18. Vivanet, G.: Evidence Based Education: un quadro storico. Form@re, Open J. Form. Rete, 13(2), 41–51 (2013)

19. Chiaro, M.: Le tecnologie nella progettazione didattica nella prospettiva ICF-CY. Ital. J. Educ. Res., numero **12** (2014)
20. Calvani, A.: Per un'istruzione evidence based. Analisi teorico-metodologica internazionale sulle didattiche efficaci e inclusive, pp. 20–55, Trento, Erickson (2012)
21. Besio, S.: Favorire la partecipazione e l'inclusione: tecnologie assistive e ICF. In: Pardi, P., Simoneschi, G. (eds.) Tecnologie educative per l'integrazione. Studi e Documenti degli Annali della Pubblica Istruzione (127/2009), pp. 103–123. Firenze, Le Monnier (2009)
22. Fogarolo, F.: Il computer di sostegno, pp. 65–80. Ausili informatici a scuola. Trento, Erickson (2012)
23. Chiappini, G.: Software Didattico e sordità, CNR—Genova, pp. 69–71 (2003)
24. Burkhart, L.J.: Comunicazione Aumentativa Totale nella scuola dell'infanzia. Isaac Italy, Omega (2007)
25. Cafiero, J.M.: Comunicazione aumentativa e alternativa, pp. 19–20. Gardolo, Erickson (2009)
26. ISTAT: Anno scolastico 2015–2016. L'integrazione degli alunni con disabilità nelle scuole primarie e secondarie di primo grado statali e non statali, http://www.istat.it (2016)

Social Media Communication in Hospitality: The Case of Parisian Hotels

Bessem Boubaker and Tatiana Pekarskaia Dauxert

Abstract Social media are a driver of fundamental business changes, as their innovative nature allows for interactive communication between customers and businesses. This communication is particularly important for hotels and tourism firms, because many consumers prepare their travel online and search information from a variety of sources, including social media. In this study, we realized twenty semi-structured exploratory interviews with hospitality experts and marketing, communication and social media professionals in France. The purpose of the study was to understand the expert's point of view on social media communication strategies, adopted or that could be adopted by French hotels (in Paris region), especially in terms of customer engagement. We also present theoretical and managerial implications of the study, its limitations and future research ideas.

Keywords Bloggers · Customer engagement · France · Hotel · Lurker · Social media

1 Introduction

Social media are a driver of fundamental business changes, as their innovative nature allows for interactive communication between customers and businesses [1–4]. Social media allow customers to comment, review, create and share content in the online networks. They also allow customers to communicate directly with organizations, brands and marketers [5]. This creates challenges and opportunities for marketers when they interact with customers in real time and have to manage the large amount of incoming customer data [6–9]. The communication via social media

B. Boubaker (✉)
UVSQ, Versailles, France
e-mail: bessem.boubaker@voltaire-business-school.com

Voltaire Business School—VBS Ferney Genève, Ferney-Voltaire, France

T. P. Dauxert
ATER, PRISM—Université Paris 1 Panthéon-Sorbonne, Paris, France
e-mail: Tatiana.Dauxert@univ-paris1.fr

© Springer Nature Switzerland AG 2020
Y. Baghdadi et al. (eds.), *ICT for an Inclusive World*,
Lecture Notes in Information Systems and Organisation 35,
https://doi.org/10.1007/978-3-030-34269-2_14

is particularly important for hotels and tourism properties because many consumers prepare their travel online and search for information from a variety of sources, including the social media [10–12].

In our study, we realized twenty semi-structured exploratory expert interviews with hotel, marketing, communication and social media professionals in France. The purpose of the study was to understand the experts' point of view on the social media communication strategies, already adopted or that could be adopted by French hotels (especially in Paris and Paris region). The interviews were fully transcribed, and we realized a thematic content analysis. In this research note, we will present the conceptual framework, the literature review, as well as the methodology adopted for our research. We will also discuss the first results of the interview analysis. Finally, the limitations of this study and future research ideas will be mentioned.

2   Conceptual Framework and Literature Review

Social media are defined as a "group of Internet-based applications that build on the ideological and technological foundations of Web 2.0 and that allow the creation and exchange of User-Generated Content" [13, p. 61]. This definition means that tourism sites like TripAdvisor, Booking.com, Airbnb, and Lonely Planet are considered as social media [14, 15]. They allow customers to comment, review, spread and create content online that appears even in search engine results. A customer can easily share his or her opinion with a multitude of people in only one click and, therefore, he/she plays the role of a "defender" of the brand and could help it to acquire new customers [16]. This acquisition is facilitated by the fact that these people often have similar needs and interests [17]. The combination of social networks with other advertising channels could further strengthen their effectiveness, although previous research demonstrates relatively low effectiveness of advertising [18].

The importance of social media as a means of engaging customers in the tourism industry can not be ignored [1, 14, 15, 19, 20]. Social media are a means of online communication and collaboration among interdependent networks [21]. The most omnipresent example is the Facebook social network that perfectly illustrates the possibilities of interaction between connected networks, with its nearly a billion members community. Web users have incorporated social media into their lives, they use social networks to talk with friends, share messages, ask for advice, publish creative results, follow news, search and organize information, develop social leisure activities and so on [21]. For example, Whole Foods, an upscale grocery chain in the United States, and Dell, a manufacturer and hardware retailer, use Twitter as an important customer service channel.

If we look at the many publications on the applications and the consequences of social media participation (for customers) and social media marketing (for companies) available today, we can note that the majority of the content relates to positive features of the social media. For customers, social media offer opportunities for social reinforcement, interpersonal interconnectivity, self-discovery, entertainment and functional value [e.g., 22]. For the marketers, the benefits include, among others, the accessibility to customer groups, the opportunities for engagement, cost savings on other media and the possibility of encouraging the word-of-mouth (WOM) [21]. Indeed, social media have brought many benefits that meet the needs of individuals, consumers, organizations and brands, but these advantages have also a counterpart: some negative consequences.

For brands, negative features associated with social media and social media marketing include security breaches, a loss of control of the content, a diffusion of negative word-of-mouth (as easily as of the positive WOM) and new forms of responsibility. It is necessary and important to take into consideration these negative features in order to assess the global value of the social media for the society and the preparation of customers and businesses for an effective use of the social media [21].

Social media are the dominant driver of customer engagement, and their technologies are very different from the previous customer-relation technology platforms. They are available to customers, they are transparent and facilitate bidirectional interactions between customers and organizations [e.g., 4, 7, 23, 24]. Goh et al. [24] have found that messages from engaged customers were 22 times more valuable than those from marketers, so they have highlighted the importance of customer engagement. The latter represents a more and more important objective in the recent literature. Indeed, engagement is linked to various significant performance indicators, including sales growth, customer participation in the product development, consumer reviews and recommendations [25–28]. Not surprisingly, a lot of this brand engagement is produced online via social media [29]. Customers that are engaged in online brand communities feel more connected to their brands, they also have more trust in their favorite brands, are more attached to them, have greater brand satisfaction and are more loyal [30].

Customer engagement is characterized by repeated interactions between a customer and a company. This reinforces the emotional, psychological or physical investment of a customer in the brand and the company [31, 32]. This notion of investment is supported by the social exchange theory, according to which individuals assess the tangible and intangible costs and benefits of engaging in relations [33]. In order that the engagement between a customer and a brand persists, customers must at least have a balance, or a positive imbalance for them, between these costs and benefits over time [2, 34]. For example, customers could invest enthusiasm and attention by engaging with a brand to get benefits such as news about products, special offers, through a feeling of belonging [35, 36].

In the tourism context, previous research has found that customer engagement stimulates loyalty, trust and brand assessment [37]. Social media make customer engagement easier, but none of these phenomena has been sufficiently studied yet in the tourism context. The use of social media is very important in hotels and tourism firms, including Facebook and Twitter [11]; Instagram and other social media like TripAdvisor, Airbnb and Booking.com that gain popularity and influence [14, 15, 38]. TripAdvisor is the most important travel rating platform in the world that achieved a turnover of 1.246 billion in 2014, with a growth of 32% from the previous year [39].

The "silent groups" in online communities, commonly known as "lurkers", constitute the majority of the members of an online community. The famous principle "90-9-1" stipulates that in a collaborative website, like an online community, 90% of the participants just read the content, 9% of participants contribute to modify the content and only 1% of the participants actively create new content [40]. The numbers may be different but it has been widely proven that the majority of the content in an online community is created by a minority of users. Even though lurkers represent a significant proportion of users, researchers have paid little attention to the analysis of this phenomenon until recently. Surveys on online communities [41], email discussion lists [42], social network services [43] and e-learning courses [44, 45] have been realized to discover the reasons that underly methods to encourage the lurkers to post. Different models have been proposed to explain the "clandestine" behavior, and these models have identified various factors that influence the online performance, such as the culture of the community, the user personality and the relationship between the users and the group [42, 46–49].

Some studies considered the lurkers as "stowaways" and conveyed a negative attitude towards them [50–53]. The durability of an online community requires new content and timely interactions, but lurkers are considered just "profiteers" who observe the interactions of others and contribute very little to the community, or not at all [54].

On the other hand, several studies have argued that most lurkers are not just selfish individuals that use the common good without making any contribution [55, 56]. On the contrary, to hide is not only normal, but it could also be a form of action, of participation, a valuable form of online behavior [57]. Many lurkers consider themselves as members of the community [55]. Lave and Wenger [58] determine the hidden behavior in a community as a form of cognitive learning, which can be seen as a legitimate peripheral participation. In an online community, peripheral members are less visible but they benefit from the exchange of knowledge and contributions at the same degree as non-peripheral members do [59].

The literature analysis above leads us to formulate our research questions as follows:

1. What are the communication strategies adopted by Parisian hotels using the social media?
2. How does this communication contribute to customer engagement?

3   Methodology

We conducted 18 semi-structured face-to-face expert interviews, one phone interview and one Skype interview (20 interviews in total, with a mean length of 40 min). Among the interviewed experts, there are professionals of the hospitality sector, and also marketing, communication and social media professionals from other sectors.

The main themes and sub-themes of the interview guide included the overall vision of the social media use of and the usefulness of communication via the social media, especially for hotels. Among the sub-themes, there were different types of social media and the reasons for the presence of a company in these media; types and regularity of messages published in the social media; estimated effects on consumers; types of consumers and their degree of engagement; evaluation of the efficiency of the communication in the social media; risks associated with this communication, particularly for the hotel sector.

The interview guide was based on the social media and communication literature review. We found useful to include in our expert sample some hospitality professionals and also some marketing, communication and social media professionals who had not necessarily previous experience in the hospitality industry, in order to have a broader view of the social media use in different sectors and possible applications in the hospitality. In interviews with non-hotel experts, we asked their opinion, from the point of view of their respective experiences, on the social media use in the hotel industry. The interviews were fully transcribed, and we realized a manual thematic content analysis, completed by a content analysis on NVivo 11.

4   First Results

As for the presence in the social media of hotels whose experts participated in our qualitative study, all the hotels are present but at different levels. For numerous companies in different fields, and especially in the hospitality industry, the importance of the image is obvious and becomes a strategic issue. Visual representations influence the imagination of future customers or recall memories to the regular customers. Some hotels also showcase their employees as the ambassadors of the corporate values and service quality (the example of a Parisian hotel that realized videos on various hospitality jobs involving its employees. This campaign has been deployed on Youtube and has had some success with many users who liked and shared the videos of this hotel).

Among the social networks that are the most suitable to share photos and videos, experts mostly cited Facebook, Instagram, Youtube and Pinterest. Twitter is less used, at least by the interviewed hotel professionals in our sample, and some of them noted a lack of engagement of the followers on this platform when compared to other social networks. Google + has been cited only twice, and the main purpose of the presence in this network is the search engine optimization (SEO) by Google which is important for hotels. In addition, to better reach foreign clients and to meet their needs, several hotels have created accounts in specific social networks of certain countries or geographical areas where their main customers come from (like Weibo and Wechat in China, or VKontakte in Russia and neighboring Russian-speaking countries).

Among the followers/fans of the pages and the profiles of the hotels, one can find regular customers, potential customers, simple observers (lurkers) that appreciate the contents published by the hotel (for example, beautiful photos, interesting videos, information on the news of the city, etc.) and also various service providers who already work with the hotel or who would like to be noticed and to collaborate with the hotel in the future. Although the engagement in terms of "likes" and "shares" is important and sought after by hotels, several experts have stressed the importance of the "silent majority", or lurkers, who still see the posts published by the hotel and can also become potential customers, even without liking or sharing these posts.

The functions and challenges of the communication in social media are also different, depending on hotels and social networks. The financial and human resources of each property or group should be taken into consideration. Some hotels (especially upscale properties) or groups have specific positions of employees dedicated to the web communication management (web manager, community manager...), while in other properties this function can be part of the responsibilities of the front office manager, of the deputy general manager or of the general manager. Among the challenges of the social media communication, hoteliers cite the notoriety, the multiplication of points of contact with the existing and potential customers, and the strengthening of their engagement. In addition to the specific online consumer review sites, hotels also make themselves available to their customers (existing or potential) and all visitors to their profiles in the social networks to answer any questions, comments or complaints. Taking into account the cultural specificities of the international clients and an empathic approach are essential in this type of communication (especially in the social networks specific to certain countries or geographical areas).

Some hotels (especially in the upscale segment) work a lot with bloggers that are part of their communication strategies using the social media. Indeed, travel and "lifestyle" bloggers are opinion leaders with many fans and followers. Hotels have often requests by bloggers, including foreign ones, and they occasionally invite some of them to stay at the hotel and to have breakfast, lunch and/or dinner at the hotel's restaurant. Then, they expect, as a counterpart, some positive posts (a form of an implicit promotion) on blogs and profiles of these bloggers on social networks, to contribute to the reputation of the hotel. This collaboration is not official in terms of engagement, bloggers don't have any obligation to publish a post after their stay at the hotel, and some managers deplore it because sometimes they don't have any "return" from the blogger despite a free stay that a priori had been appreciated by the latter.

In this research note that is still a work-in-progress, we present only a part of our results (see Table 1), and a deeper and more detailed analysis will allow us to discuss other topics and issues related to the hotels communication in the social media. But we can already see that this communication differs, depending on the social media and the hotels types, and that it has specific issues and functions in the hospitality sector.

Table 1 Thematic content analysis of the expert interviews (abstract)

Thème	Sous-thème	Extrait de verbatim
Strategy of presence in the social media	Obligation of presence in the social media	"We worked in the social networks because *we had to do it* and we did not necessarily have a strategy behind it, to create pages (…) Because it's still good to be present, to occupy the space, in terms of branding too, pages that convey the image and the graphic design of the hotel" (E10) "I thought I had to be on Facebook because everyone was on Facebook, because everyone was present on Twitter, because everyone was starting to work, for example, on Instagram lately, in recent years" (E5)
	Youtube: large campaign in a long period = notoriety purpose	"We made a very large campaign on Youtube for a whole year, and you can see, we have a lot of notoriety thanks to our videos that we put on Youtube" (E5)
	Instagram: the power of the photo	"It is a social network that is very adapted to the hospitality sector, with clients that respond, that are quite engaged, that often like photos and comment them" (E3)
	Google +: search engine optimization	"You have to be in some social networks just for notoriety, this is the case of Google+. For example, I decided to stay on Google+ because it (…) has a system of algorithms that work on Google, and if you do not have (…) a Google tool, it will not refer you well. So basically, I keep my Google + page because I (…) want to be well referenced" (E5)

(continued)

Table 1 (continued)

Thème	Sous-thème	Extrait de verbatim
	Twitter: lack of engagement	"Twitter, I put a lot of things on it but there is not much engagement" (E2)
	Specific social networks in foreign countries (China: Weibo, Wechat): differences of practices	"Weibo or Wechat, in fact these are social networks that are Chinese, which work very well and (…) we decided to be present there. And it is true that the notoriety growth has been fast, so… and in fact, we post almost every day… we post in Chinese because we have somebody who is in charge of our Chinese social networks. And so it's completely different" (E6)
	Importance of the visual content	"It is very rare that I publish, in the past or now, posts without any visual content, there is often a picture or an illustration" (E5) "A post with just some text, I think it's not at all… it does not call people to… it's not exciting, it's not interesting for people" (E10)
Functions of the social media communication	*Minimal content*	"We made a little bit of content for people who want to go to our pages, to see that we publish things and that it is not empty" (E10)
	Answers to questions/comments	"We use (*our pages and profiles*) at least to answer people, because there are still potential customers or providers who contact us through the social networks. And you have to be present to answer them, to be there…" (E12)

(continued)

Table 1 (continued)

Thème	Sous-thème	Extrait de verbatim
	Cultural specificities to take into account	"(…) we are selling directly to Chinese agencies, for example… sometimes we have already asked if they are on Wechat or Weibo. And they are very happy and also very surprised that we are present in the social networks like these, and they immediately said: "oh yes, let's become friends" (E3)
Types of visitors/followers	*Regular customers*	"Here at the hotel N., Facebook functions because… oddly, it is especially people who come for years to the hotel N., who follow us, and they want to know… how to say… the news that we have at the hotel"(E5)
	Difficulties of the virality	"When we make content, we have customers who will like and who are happy, but it is hard to find a real virality" (E10)
	Providers/future cooperation	"The engagement (…) that we can have, can come rather from some service providers who might want to work with us later and who put stuff from time to time to remember our good service" (E7)
	Lurkers (« observers »)	"It is great, the likes, the shares… but there are much more people who will see a post, a photo or a video, even without liking… (…) they are also very important, even if they do not like… (E2)

(continued)

Table 1 (continued)

Thème	Sous-thème	Extrait de verbatim
Consumer review websites	*Negative review = sales opportunity*	"Basically, a bad comment must… well, me anyway, what I try to do is that I try to always bring it to further sales" (E6) "There is a part of the service, there is a part of sales, and we always consider very positively even the negative comments" (E2)
Bloggers	*Incentive for bloggers*	"On our website, we have a page that is dedicated to bloggers who have stayed here and who have written, who have published something (*on the hotel*)" (E5)
	Diversity of bloggers	"Every blogger, I know he or she can offer me something different" (E10) "(…) we'll see someone who specializes in the tea-time (…), the latter that we will see soon; another one, it's too funny, we'll see a blogger who… speaks of pet -friendly hotels" (E10) "there are a lot of mostly foreign bloggers who can therefore allow us to target American or British customers, but also customers from countries that are a little more" exotic "like Russia or that kind of things" (E6)
	Innovation ideas for the hotels	"Even if we were already a pet-friendly hotel, we want to develop it and we want to communicate about it" (E10)
	Experience effect, contribution to the notoriety	"(…) I can identify very very well who will give me far too much notoriety or who will not give me notoriety at all, that's the experience" (E9)

5   Limitations and Future Research

We realized twenty interviews with hospitality, communication and social media professionals in Paris and the Paris region. It would be useful to extend the sample to more experts and to other regions of France or other countries.

It also seems interesting to us, as a future research idea, to observe the real activities of the same hotels on different social media platforms and to compare them with the results of the interviews.

Moreover, our results could be compared with the different communication practices in social media in other sectors (tourism, cultural heritage, destination marketing…).

Finally, the customer comments and reviews on social networks constitute a very rich set of information that could be used by various hotels to realize market study and to improve their offers. Therefore, it would be useful to consider an in-depth analysis of these comments to identify needs for change and requirements for further evolution.

6   Conclusion

The findings of this research showed that the communication of hotels in social media is used differently by hotels. It depends on the level of commitment of professionals in this process and on the available means that are used for this purpose. Several interviewed hospitality professionals are aware of the importance of social media and of their effects on their businesses. So they often feel a sort of "obligation" to adopt this communication type. However, the investments and the available resources to build and realize an efficient social media communication strategy can be a problem for some properties and professionals.

The widespread use of social media is an important opportunity for the various tourism and hotel services providers. Communication in social networks would contribute to improve the attractiveness and competitiveness of hotels. Hence, it becomes extremely important for professionals in various businesses, and especially in tourism and hospitality, to learn how to use this method of marketing and communication. hospitality professionals become more and more vigilant to the quality and satisfaction of the customer needs, to get positive reviews and to avoid negative comments from customers. Indeed, these reviews become quickly visible on the Internet and the consequences could be dramatic for hospitality firms that fail to provide satisfactory quality of service to customers.

We believe that social media communication is an issue and an opportunity for hotels that wish to stand out from their competitors through the quality and customization of their offer and the satisfaction of the customers' needs.

The study and the analysis of comments in social networks could allow to hospitality professionals a deeper study of the needs of their customers. We believe that these social networks are not only a means of communication but also an opportunity and a new way of market research for hospitality professionals.

References

1. Dijkmans, C., Kerkhof, P., Beukeboom, C.J.: A stage to engage: social media use and corporate reputation. Tour. Manag. **47**, 58–67 (2015)
2. Hollebeek, L.D.: Demystifying customer brand engagement: exploring the loyalty nexus. J. Mark. Manag. **27**(7–8), 785–807 (2011)
3. Lee, J.-N., Choi, B.: Strategic role of IT and its impact on organizations. Inf. Manag. **51**, 881–882 (2014)
4. Vivek, S.D., Beatty, S.E., Morgan, R.M.: Customer engagement: exploring customer relationships beyond purchase. J. Mark. Theory Pract. **20**(2), 127–145 (2012)
5. Chau, M., Xu, J.: Business intelligence in Blogs: understanding consumer interactions and communities. MIS Q. **36**(4), 1189–1216 (2012)
6. Cui, G., Lui, H.-K., Guo, X.: The effect of online consumer reviews on new product sales. Int. J. Electron. Commer. **17**(1), 39–57 (2012)
7. Hennig-Thurau, T., Malthouse, E.C., Friege, C., Gensler, S., Lobschat, L., Rangaswamy, A.: The impact of new media on customer relationships. J. Serv. Res. **13**(3), 311–330 (2010)
8. Pagani, M., Mirabello, A.: The influence of personal and social-interactive engagement in social TV web sites. Int. J. Electron. Commer. **16**(2), 41–67 (2011)
9. Bronner, F., De Hoog, R.: Vacationers and eWOM: Who posts, and why, where, and what? J. Travel. Res. **50**(1), 15–26 (2011)
10. Harrigan, P., Evers, U., Miles, M., Daly, T.: Customer engagement with tourism social media brands. Tour. Manag. **59**, 597–609 (2017)
11. Leung, X.Y., Bai, B., Stahura, K.A.: The marketing effectiveness of social media in the hotel industry a comparison of Facebook and Twitter. J. Hosp. Tour. Res. **39**(2), 147–169 (2015)
12. Kaplan, A.M., Haenlein, M.: Users of the world, unite! The challenges and opportunities of social media. Bus. Horiz. **53**(1), 59–68 (2010)
13. Cabiddu, F., Carlo, M.D., Piccoli, G.: Social media affordances: enabling customer engagement. Ann. Tour. Res. **48**, 175–192 (2014)
14. Miguéns, J., Baggio, R., Costa, C.: Social media and tourism destinations: TripAdvisor case study. Adv. Tour. Res. **26**(28), 1–6 (2008)
15. Munar, A.M., Jacobsen, J.K.S.: Motivations for sharing tourism experiences through social media. Tour. Manag. **43**, 46–54 (2014)
16. Lin, H.F.: Understanding behavioral intention to participate in virtual communities. Cyber Psychol. Behav. **9**(5), 540–547 (2006)
17. Mabry, E., Porter, L.: Movies and Myspace: the effectiveness of official Web sites versus online promotional contests. J. Interact. Advert. **10**(2), 1–15 (2010)
18. Cheng, M., Edwards, D.: Social media in tourism: a visual analytic approach. Current Issues in Tourism **18**, 1080–1087 (2015)
19. Hudson, S., Roth, M.S., Madden, T.J., Hudson, R.: The effects of social media on emotions, brand relationship quality, and word of mouth: an empirical study of music festival attendees. Tour. Manag. **47**, 68–76 (2015)
20. Trusov, M., Bucklin, R.E., Pauwels, K.: Effects of word-of-mouth versus traditional marketing: findings from an internet social networking site. J. Mark. **73**(5), 90–102 (2009)
21. Dholakia, U.M., Bagozzi, R.P., Pearo, L.K.: A social influence model of consumer participation in network- and small-group-based virtual communities. Int. J. Res. Mark. **21**, 163–241 (2004)
22. Deighton, J., Kornfeld, L.: Interactivity's unanticipated consequences for marketers and marketing. J. Interact. Mark. **23**(1), 4–10 (2009)

23. Dwyer, P.: Measuring the value of electronic word of mouth and its impact in consumer communities. J. Interact. Mark. **21**(2), 63–79 (2007)
24. Bijmolt, T.H.A., Leeflang, P.S.H., Block, F., Eisenbeiss, M., Hardie, B.G.S., Lemmens, A., et al.: Analytics for customer engagement. J. Serv. Res. **13**(3), 341–356 (2010)
25. Goh, K.Y., Heng, C.S., Lin, Z.: Social media brand community and consumer behavior: quantifying the relative impact of user-and marketer-generated content. Inf. Syst. Res. **24**(1), 88–107 (2013)
26. Tuten, T.L., Solomon, M.: Social Media Marketing. New Jersey (2013)
27. Kumar, V., Aksoy, L., Donkers, B., Venkatesan, R., Wiesel, T., Tillmanns, S.: Undervalued or overvalued customers: Capturing total customer engagement value. J. Serv. Res. **13**(3), 297–310 (2010)
28. Sawhney, M., Verona, G., Prandelli, E.: Collaborating to create: The Internet as a platform for customer engagement in product innovation. J. Interact. Mark. **19**(4), 4–17 (2005)
29. Brodie, R.J., Iliic, A., Juric, B., Hollebeek, L.D.: Consumer engagement in a virtual brand community: an exploratory analysis. J. Bus. Res. **66**, 105–114 (2013)
30. Malthouse, E., Hofacker, C.: Looking back and looking forward with interactive marketing. J. Interact. Mark. **24**(3), 181–184 (2010)
31. Phang, C.W., Zhang, C., Sutanto, J.: The influence of user interaction and participation in social media on the consumption intention of niche products. Inf. Manag. **50**, 661–672 (2013)
32. Hollebeek, L.D., Glynn, M.S., Brodie, R.J.: Consumer brand engagement in social media: conceptualization, scale development and validation. J. Interact. Mark. **28**(2), 149–165 (2014)
33. Brodie, R.J., Hollebeek, L.D., Juric, B., Ilic, A.: Customer engagement: Conceptual domain, fundamental propositions, and implications for research. J. Serv. Res. **14**(3), 252–271 (2011)
34. Blau, P.M.: Exchange and power in social life. Wiley, New York (1964)
35. Thibaut, J.W., Kelley, H.H.: The social psychology of groups. Wiley, New York (1959)
36. Van Doorn, J., Lemon, K.E., Mittal, V., Nab, S., Pick, D., Pirner, P., et al.: Customer engagement behavior: theoretical foundations and research directions. J. Serv. Res. **13**(3), 253–266 (2010)
37. Foa, E.B., Foa, U.G.: Resource theory: inter-personal behavior as social exchange. In: Gergen, K.J., Greenberg, M.S., Willis, R.H. (eds.) Social Exchange: Advances in Theory and Research. Plenum Press, New York (1980)
38. So, K.K.F., King, C., Sparks, B.: Customer engagement with tourism brands: scale development and validation. J. Hosp. Tour. Res. **38**(3), 304–329 (2014)
39. Filieri, R., McLeay, F.E.: WOM and accommodation: an analysis of the factors that influence travelers' adoption of information from online reviews. J. Travel. Res. **53**(1), 44–57 (2014)
40. Forbes: TripAdvisor's growth plans for 2015 and beyond. Forbes.com. Available at: http://www.forbes.com/sites/greatspeculations/2015/03/06/tripadvisorsgrowth-plans-for-2015-and-beyond/. Accessed 15 Nov 2016
41. Arthur, C.: What is the 1% rule? In: The guardian. UK: Guardian News and Media (2006)
42. Bishop, J.: Increasing participation in online communities: a framework for human–computer interaction. Comput. Hum. Behav. **23**(4), 1881–1893 (2007)
43. Beaudoin, M.F.: Learning or lurking? Tracking the "invisible" online student. Internet High. Educ. **5**(2), 147–155 (2002)
44. Nonnecke, B., Preece, J.: Lurker demographics: counting the silent. In: Proceedings of the SIGCHI Conference on Human Factors in Computing Systems, pp. 73–80. ACM (2000)
45. Rau, P.L.P., Gao, Q., Ding, Y.: Relationship between the level of intimacy and lurking in online social network services. Comput. Hum. Behav. **24**(6), 2757–2770 (2008)
46. Küçük, M.: Lurking in online asynchronous discussion. Procedia. Soc. Behav. Sci. **2**(2), 2260–2263 (2010)
47. Fan, Y.-W., Wu, C.-C., Chiang, L.-C.: Knowledge sharing in virtual community: the comparison between contributors and lurkers. In: The 9th International Conference on Electronic Business, pp. 662–668. Macau (2009)
48. Kollock, P.: The economies of online cooperation. Communities in cyberspace, **220** (1999)
49. Leshed, G.: Posters, lurkers, and in between: A multidimensional model of online community participation patterns. In: Salvendy, G. (ed.) Proceedings of the 11th HIC International Conference. Lawrence Erlbaum Associates Inc., Las Vegas (2005)

50. Tedjamulia, S.J., Dean, D.L., Olsen, D.R., Albrecht, C.C.: Motivating content contributions to online communities: Toward a more comprehensive theory. In: System Ssciences, 2005. HICSS'05. Proceedings of the 38th Annual Hawaii International Conference on IEEE, pp. 193b–193b (2005)
51. Kollock, P., Smith, M.: Managing the virtual commons. Computer-mediated communication: linguistic, social, and cross-cultural perspectives, pp. 109–128 (1996)
52. Morris, M., Ogan, C.: The internet as mass medium. J. Commun. **46**(1), 39–50 (1996)
53. Rheingold, H.: The Virtual Community: Homesteading on the Electronic Frontier. MIT Press (2000)
54. Wellman, B., Gulia, M.: Net surfers don't ride alone: virtual communities as communities. Networks in the Global Village, pp. 331–366 (1999)
55. Van Mierlo, T.: The 1% rule in four digital health social networks: An observational study. J. Med. Internet Res. **16**(2) (2014)
56. Nonnecke, B., Andrews, D., Preece, J.: Non-public and public online community participation: needs, attitudes and behavior. Electron. Commer. Res. **6**(1), 7–20 (2006)
57. Wichmand, M., Jensen, S.S.: Small is beautiful-lurkers engaging through micro-contributions. In: 4th European Communication Conference (2012)
58. Lave, J., Wenger, E.: Legitimate peripheral participation. Learners, learning and assessment. The Open University, London (1999)
59. Zhang, W., Storck, J.: Peripheral members in online communities. In: Proceedings of AMCIS 2001 the Americas Conference on Information Systems (2001)

Antecedent Factors in Adolescents Consumer Socialization Process Through Social Media

Aarthy Chellasamy and Jessy Nair

Abstract The research paper attempts to find the antecedent factors that influence in adolescents consumer socialization process through social media and its impact on family purchase. Consumer socialization of adolescents through social media has become a key indicator in the area of marketing because of predominant online interaction of consumer. Socialization process framework is adopted to investigate among 254 respondents. The results show there is positive influence of antecedent variables like age, social media and peer identification on Purchase Intention and the variable social media also influences Product Involvement in family decision making. The outcome of this research benefits the academicians and marketers to explore the impact of social media on adolescent in their family decision making.

Keywords Adolescent · Social media · Peer group · Purchase intention · Product involvement

1 Introduction

Social media has given internet a whole new perspective in creating marketing opportunities for business. It is both a communication and sales tool that drives the organizations. These online platforms are used by individuals to share opinions, thoughts experience and insights. Advancement of technology is revolutionizing the communication process among individuals [1, 2]. Facebook, Hi5, LinkedIn, Instagram are few examples of social media which are empowering global societies by creating opportunities for marketers to promote and influence family purchase decision. Social media has brought a radical change in the traditional marketing system [3].

A. Chellasamy (✉)
School of Business Studies and Social Sciences, Christ (Deemed) University, Bangalore, India
e-mail: aarthy.c@christuniversity.in

J. Nair
Department of Management Studies, PES University, Bangalore, India
e-mail: jessynair@pes.edu

© Springer Nature Switzerland AG 2020
Y. Baghdadi et al. (eds.), *ICT for an Inclusive World*,
Lecture Notes in Information Systems and Organisation 35,
https://doi.org/10.1007/978-3-030-34269-2_15

Over a decade it has been observed that the time spent by adolescents on social media has tripled [4]. The popular acceptance of internet has created a new segment called "net generation or cyber teens" [5]. According to UNICEF India, there are around 243 million adolescents and teenagers in India. Among them 70.2 million teenagers (30%) are from the rural part of the country and the remaining 70% being 163.8 million children from urban India are active internet and social media users [6].

A survey by Tata Consultancy Service reveals that awareness and time spent on social media are 93% and 63% respectively [7, 8]. Social networks like Facebook, Twitter have changed the way youths live, socialize and interact with each other about their recent purchases. Youngsters connect with friends and unknown people through social networking sites [9]. Hence marketers are recognizing the opportunity and potential strength of social media as a tool for influencing the purchasing decision making process.

The higher the solicitude and interest parents show, the greater the children have alternatives to choose from. Children find security in attachment to objects associated with brand logo, a brand name or a product from a particular brand. So the question of children being brand loyal can easily be determined. Marketers are focusing on how to create an impact through adolescents to talk about products with their peers. Globalization plays a major role which has transmuted consumerism as a religion and children as the devoted convert [10]. This is because of the shift in status of children from just being a part of the parent purchasing decision to the complete purchase itself. According to Belch et al. [11], the adolescents have greater interest in the internet and greater access to market information; however, it is yet to be investigated what impact this might have on the teen influence in family purchase [12].

Social media is a place for marketers and advertisers to connect and communicate with its consumers and influence their purchase decisions [13]. Furthermore, it allows users to connect with peers by adding them to a network of friends, which facilitates communication among the peers [14, 15]. Social media has emerged as the new unconventional channel for consumer socialization through internet [16–18]. Ward [19] defines consumer socialization as a process by which individual consumers learn skills, knowledge and attitude from others which assist them in playing a role of consumer in market. The traditional socialization process occurs through family, media, colleagues, relatives, friends and neighbors [20, 21]. Although peer communication is widely acknowledged factor in consumer socialization process [22–24], peer communication through social media and its impact on family purchase has received less attention. To fill this gap we investigate the consumer socialization process of adolescent's through social media and its impact on family purchase.

2 Theoretical Background

2.1 Consumer Socialization Through Social Media

Consumer socialization theory states that communication among consumers affects their cognitive, affective and behavioral attitudes [19]. The two theoretical perspectives of consumer socialization are cognitive development and social learning theory [22]. Cognitive development focus on psychological process which occur between infants and adults [25] and social theory focus on agents like peers who transmit norms, values and attitude to learners [20, 23]. On the basis of socialization theory and literature the researchers established consumer socialization model [22] to explain social learning process through social media, peer communication and children's influence in family decision making along with the antecedents (Fig. 1).

2.2 Antecedents

Social structural variables and learning variables are the antecedents taken for study. Social structural variable is the environment within which learning takes place [26]. The social structural variable include gender, family, number of peers and social class with which adolescents belong to. The learning variables comprise of age, position in family and choice of social media usage. The degree of a child's influence on family purchase varies with age, gender, social class, number of siblings, family income, and

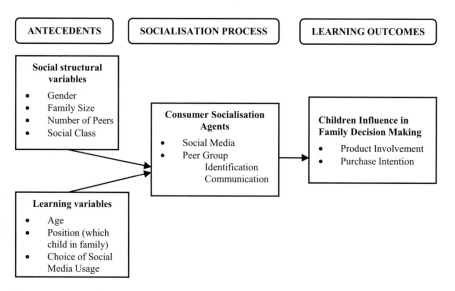

Fig. 1 Antecedent factors for consumer socialization through social media

education [10, 27–29]. The usage of social media may vary with respect to gender, family size, number of friends they have and also upon social class. Social structural and learning variables may have direct or indirect effect on learning process.

2.2.1   Age

Age is an important variable that determine the extent of influence children have in family decision making [30]. Older children had greater influence than younger children in search and decision stage [31–34]. Research shows that younger children spend more time with family and older children spend more time with peers [29, 35–40]. Research by Sondhi and Basu [10] Grant and Stephen [41] states that today's children especially older ones possess more economic influence than their predecessor and have more demands particularly in developed western markets.

2.2.2   Concept of Position of Children

Later born or only child has more influence on certain purchases than first born [42, 43]. Number of siblings and birth order of child may also reflect the extent of child's influence [44].

2.2.3   Gender

Gender of child has substantial influence in family purchase decisions [45]. Gender has also been shown to be a distinguishing factor with boys being more informed, receiving more pocket money, knowing more brands and using internet more frequently [12, 46]. Female children have greater influence than male children only for large purchases and food categories [47]. Male children had greater influence in initiation stage while female had greater influence than male in search and decision making stages [32]. Dotson and Hyatt [40] stated that boys are exposed to slightly more media per day than girls which will have greater impact in their purchase decisions. Boys are observed more knowledgeable and hence more favorable towards consumption. Girls on the other hand are more media focus [44]. Flurry [31] add that boys have greater influence than girls in purchase of food for family. On the contrary it is found that girls have more influence on family purchase [34]. Thus numerous differences are noted while comparing children's impact on purchase decision between different genders of children [48].

2.2.4 Family Income/Social Status/Family Type

Family influence in consumer socialization of children was studied by Robertson and Rossiter [49] found that social status of family also had a role in consumer socialization of adolescents. Those from dual income households and from single parent households spend less time interacting with their parents and in many cases spend more time interacting with peers [40]. Family income was found to be positively related to child influence [50]. Adolescents from well-educated families are able to perceive persuasive intent in advertisement very easily [45]. Moschis and Churchill [22] found out that child from families with higher socio economic set up were found to socialize faster. Roopnarine et al. [51] states that joint family system have been a major influence on socialization of children in India. Adolescents in single parent family had more influence over family purchase than children in other family type [32]. Also there has been a shift in society from joint family setup to nuclear family and rise in parental income. Until few years ago decision making was dominated by parents, today the role of adolescents cannot be ignored [30].

3 Socialization Process

Social media provides a virtual space for people to communicate through internet which also might be an important agent of consumer socialization [15–17, 23, 52]. Social media encourages online consumer socialization among peers through blogs, instant messaging and social networking sites. They all serve as a communication tool making socialization process easy and convenient [17]. Increasing number of consumers visit social media websites to communicate with others and find information to help them make various consumption related decisions [52]. Taylor et al. [53] found that online consumer attitude towards social network greatly depends on socialization factors. In 2016, 24% of Indian population accessed internet via mobile phone and the trend is predicted to grow at 37% by 2021 [54]. Key Facebook users from India are aged between 18 to 20 years [54] making India second largest online market after China.

India's digital advertising market has grown at 33% annually between 2010 and 2016. Social media also facilitate education and information as they feature multitudes of friends and peers who act as socialization agents and provide vast product information and valuation quickly [53, 55]. Ramnarai and Govender [13] and Lueg and Zachary [52] reveals that online peer communication can influence consumers and in turn they convert others into internet shoppers. Social contact has a comparative higher weightage than any other source on the web [56]. India's digital advertising market has a constant growth at 33% annually between 2010 and 2016. 77% of online users buy products exclusively on social media. The sale of physical goods via digital channels in India amounted to $16.8 billion in revenue. Internet usage is growing in India at the rate of 90% while global average is just 19% [57, 58]. Suggested that since social media is about providing space for consumers to influence each other during purchase process, the objective should be to encourage consumers to positively influence each other. Thus it can be noted that social media has brought about several changes in consumer behavior, especially among youth since it has inter-alia, afforded them the opportunity to more actively engage marketers of brand and products online, hence empowering the consumers.

H1: Social Media has significant influence on social structural and learning variables.

3.1 Peer Group Communication as a Socialization Agent

Peers act as significant transmitters of attitudinal or behavioral norms or standards by which one's own belief and actions may be adjusted [22, 59]. Relation with peers not only helps to compare products but also provide way of learning how to respond to consumption related activities. Consumer socialization literature indicates that peers are primary socialization agents beyond family members [22–24]. Consumers tend to interact with peers about consumption matters which greatly influence their attitudes towards products and services [22, 60]. In social media setting the consumer learns attitudes and purchase behaviors through written messages that peer send [21]. The peer pressure can force the consumer to like and/or purchase a product which can prompt rewards and acquainted relations from peers; whereas lack of purchase lead to punishment like exclusion from group. In summary; consumer becomes socialized to adopt some product that is new to him/her; peer being the socializing agent also provides models to be matched; rewards to be pursued and punishment to be avoided [21].

Peer group influence is defined as the amount to which peers exert influence on the assertiveness, feelings and behavior of person [61]. Peers offer distinctive background within which children develop social skills and cognitive talent [62]. Peers moreover play a significant role in imparting the knowledge of style, brand, and consumption pattern to children [22]. Studies say that Indian children are generally influenced by peer group, workmates and influence of peer group reaches peek during a child's adolescent age [45]. Wang et al. [21] states that peer communication through social media depends on tie strength of peers and identification with the peer groups. Tie strength with peers is defined as the degree to which a person is willing to maintain some relationship with peers through social media. Strong ties are more likely to transfer useful knowledge [63] and thus have more influence on receivers than weak ties [64, 65]. Therefore, in the context of social media, a strong tie between an individual and his peers is more likely to lead to communication about a product than a weak tie. Peer interaction can provide the child with non-rational sources of consumer socialization [66] where peers can influence children that parents may not be able to. With Socialization theory as a base, the authors say that peers act as socialization agents through social media and the adolescents are influenced by peers through communication.

H2: Peer group communication has significant influence on adolescents through social structural and learning variables.

3.2 Children's Influence in Family Decision Making

Children role in family decision making is essential to examine because they act as an influencer in family related consumption decisions. Kuhn and Eischen [67] highlighted that child rather than the parent maybe in many instances is the primary decision maker. Children have low influence in selecting in sub-decision regarding color, mode and brand choice [11, 12, 68–71]. Other factors affecting children influence relate to demographic variables like family, income, child's age and gender [12]. The importance of effects of the internet on adolescent life and its subsequent effects in family purchase decision can no longer be denied [8]. Internet influence may rearrange the decision making dominance in family members [12]. There arises a need for comprehensive study about consumer behavior of children other than US since majority of study is done on US children [72]. India has a suitable environment because of rapid socio-economic changes that have taken place in last 10 years [73]. Indian consumers exhibit a behavior change in spending and consumption pattern change, the family decision making too. It is going through a metamorphosis such as witnessing an increased level of children's participation in family decision making. These aspects have hardly been investigated empirically in the context of Indian families.

H3: Adolescent's influence in family decision making has significant influence on social structure and learning variables.

4 Analysis and Results

A structured questionnaire comprising of four sections; demographic factors, Peer Identification (PI) [21], Peer Communication (PC) [12, 21], Social Media influence [73], Product Involvement (PRI) and Purchase intention (PUI) [13] was designed. The respondents are adolescent school students in south Bangalore, a metropolitan city of India in the age group of 12–16 years [22] and the data was collected during the period February to April, 2017. The number of usable questionnaires was 254 of the total 264 distributed among school going adolescents. The demographic profile of the respondents is illustrated (see Table 1 in Annexure). The data was analyzed using SPSS 20.

A five point Likert scale is used in the questionnaire and its values range from 1-strongly agrees, 2-agree, 3-neutral, 4-disagree and 5-strongly disagree. From the study it is noted that an overwhelming majority (74%) of respondent's access internet every day which indicates that they use social media platforms to search for information and advice on products which may directly influence their purchase behavior.

Table 1 Demographic variable for study

Variables	Percentage
Age	
12 years	7
13 years	48
14 years	36
15 years	8
16 years	1
Gender	
Male	47
Female	53
Social class	
Upper class	11
Middle class	86
Lower class	3
Family size	
Nuclear	75
Joint	20
Single parent	5
Position in family	
Younger	34
Elder	34
Middle	5
Single	27
Usage of social media	
Facebook	96
Youtube	2
Instagram	2

Modern-day consumers highly value pre-purchase assistance and actively search for information on social media [74]. The demographic variables of the study (Table 1 Annexure) reveals that majority of respondents are female (53%) who are in the age group of 13 (48%) and they all belong to middle class (86%). The study supports the literature [22, 30, 32, 40, 45, 49–51], majority (75%) of respondents belong to nuclear family and either younger or elder children plays a role in major decision making (Table 2).

Correlation and multiple regression analyses were conducted to examine the relationships between the explanatory variables (age, gender, social class, family size, number of friends, position in family, social media use, SM, PI and PC) and the predictors (PRI and PUI). The partial correlation coefficients between the measures of consumer socialization agents and learning outcomes measured with respect to

Table 2 Descriptive statistics antecedent factors (Social structure and learning variable) and socialization agents

Variables	Mean	Standard deviation
Age	1.89	0.94
Gender	1.52	0.51
Social class	1.91	0.37
Family size	1.31	0.57
Number of friends	2.63	0.72
Position in family	2.25	1.18
Social media use	1.05	0.30
PI	3.52	0.91
PC	3.01	0.80
SM	3.48	0.74

an adolescents influence in decision making during product involvement and purchase intention (see Table 3 in Annexure). Partial correlation coefficient measures the association between two variables after controlling or adjusting for the effects of one or more additional variables. Gender is correlated to age ($r = -0.23, p < 0.001$), number of peers is correlated to gender ($r = -0.19, p < 0.002$), position in family is correlated to age ($r = -0.153, p < 0.15$), social media use is correlated to gender ($r = 0.14, p < 0.029$) and position in family ($r = -0.139, p < 0.028$). Among the consumer socialization agents, Peer Identification is correlated to adolescent age ($r = 0.23, p < 0.001$), social class ($r = -0.14, p < 0.03$) and number of peers. Peer Communication is correlated to age ($r = 0.28, p < 0.0001$), gender ($r = -0.15, p < 0.019$) and PI ($r = 0.35, p < 0.0001$). Social Media (SM) as an agent is correlated to age ($r = 0.17, p < 0.009$), PI ($r = 0.39, p < 0.0001$) and PC ($r = 0.41, p < 0.0001$).

Influence of explanatory (independent) variables with predictor variables are summarized in Table 4. In model 1, the influence of explanatory variables on Product Involvement (PRI) is analyzed. Only one independent variable, Social Media (SM) explains 28% ($b = 0.40, p < 0.0001$) of the variance in product involvement (PRI).

In model 2, the influence of independent variables on Purchase Intention (PUI) is analyzed. Three independent variables (age, social media and peer identification) have a relative contribution of 21% on PUI. Age ($b = 0.14, p < 0.05$), Social Media (SM) explains ($b = 0.26, p < 0.0001$) and peer identification (PI) ($b = 0.15, p < 0.05$) of the variance in Purchase Intention (PUI).

The study finds that social media is an important agent in consumer socialization process [15–17, 23, 52]. 50% of shoppers buy product online based on recommendation through social media networks and 74% customers rely on social media for making their purchase decisions. Exposure of adolescents to this social medium lead to various learning aspects of consumption [22] and the study also shows positive correlation between the social media and peer group influence (PI against age $r = 0.234$, sig < 0.01). This study identifies that peer group identification and communication has greater role in socialization process beyond family members.

Table 3 Inter correlation items of explanatory variables

		Age	Gender	Social class	Family size	Number of peers	Position in family	Social media use	PI	PC	SM
Age	Pearson correlation	1									
	Sig. (2-tailed)										
Gender	Pearson correlation	−0.226**	1								
	Sig. (2-tailed)	0.000									
Social class	Pearson correlation	−0.085	−0.012	1							
	Sig. (2-tailed)	0.179	0.850								
Family size	Pearson correlation	−0.028	−0.083	0.033	1						
	Sig. (2-tailed)	0.658	0.190	0.606							
Number of peers	Pearson correlation	0.041	−0.192**	−0.092	0.091	1					
	Sig. (2-tailed)	0.512	0.002	0.147	0.149						

(continued)

Table 3 (continued)

		Age	Gender	Social class	Family size	Number of peers	Position in family	Social media use	PI	PC	SM
Age	Pearson correlation	1									
	Sig. (2-tailed)										
Position in family	Pearson correlation	−0.153					1				
	Sig. (2-tailed)	0.015									
Social media Use	Pearson correlation	0.034	0.138*	−0.104	0.118	−0.115	−0.139	1			
	Sig. (2-tailed)	0.590	0.029	0.100	0.062	0.069	0.028				
PI	Pearson correlation	0.234**	−0.040	−0.136*	0.020	0.162	−0.054	−0.026	1		
	Sig. (2-tailed)	0.000	0.531	0.031	0.747	0.010	0.395	0.675			
PC	Pearson correlation	−0.278**	−0.148	0.057	0.021	−0.016	−0.045	0.082	0.350**	1	
	Sig. (2-tailed)	0.000	0.019	0.371	0.741	0.805	0.481	0.195	0.000		
SM	Pearson correlation	0.165**	−0.120	−0.066	−0.016	0.010	0.075	−0.003	0.388**	0.410**	1
	Sig. (2-tailed)	0.009	0.057	0.298	0.805	0.880	0.235	0.957	0.000	0.000	

PI Peer Identification; *PC* Peer Communication; *SM* Social Media Influence

**Correlation is significant at the 0.01 level (2-tailed)

*Correlation is significant at the 0.05 level (2-tailed)

Table 4 Regression result for PUI and PRI

Model 1 PRI (DV)	Standardized Beta	Sig.	Collinearity Statistics		Model 2 PUI (DV)	Standardized Beta	Sig.	Collinearity statistics	
			Less than 0.10	s above 0.10				Tolerance	VIF
(Constant)		0.00			(Constant)		0.05		
Age	−0.02	0.78	0.83	1.20	Age	0.14	0.03*	0.83	1.20
Gender	−0.10	0.10	0.86	1.16	Gender	0.01	0.82	0.86	1.16
Social Class	0.03	0.62	0.93	1.07	Social Class	−0.03	0.67	0.93	1.07
Family Size	−0.03	0.56	0.95	1.05	Family Size	0.11	0.07	0.95	1.05
Number of Friends	0.06	0.33	0.90	1.11	Number of Friends	−0.07	0.27	0.90	1.11
Position in Family	0.00	0.94	0.92	1.09	Position in Family	−0.03	0.58	0.92	1.09
Social Media Use	0.08	0.15	0.92	1.09	Social Media Use	0.00	0.95	0.92	1.09
SM	0.40	0.000*	0.74	1.35	SM	0.26	0.000*	0.74	1.35
PI	0.06	0.32	0.74	1.35	PI	0.15	0.02*	0.74	1.35
PC	0.12	0.07	0.73	1.38	PC	0.08	0.25	0.73	1.38

(continued)

Table 4 (continued)

Model 1 PRI (DV)	Standardized	Sig.	Collinearity Statistics		Model 2 PUI (DV)	Standardized	Sig.	Collinearity statistics	
	Beta		Less than 0.10	s above 0.10		Beta		Tolerance	VIF
Multiple R			0.28		Multiple R			0.21	

*Correlation is significant at the 0.05 level significance (2-tailed)

The peer group teaches consumers about consumption pattern and literature also supports that Indian children are greatly influenced by peer and reaches peek during child's adolescent age [30] and these peers can influence children that parents may not be able to do so. Thus the peers act as an important socialization agent through social media.

5 Discussions and Implications

The results show that adolescents belonging to middle class in nuclear family have more influence in purchase decision and irrespective of their position in family i.e. either younger or elder have equal say in their family purchase decision. What is more important to acknowledge is changing mindset of parents. Parents of today have no hesitation to take advice from their children and they take pride in admitting that they get advice from their children for shopping [75]. Adolescent's receive personal enjoyment by surfing internet and use their virtual market knowledge to contribute in family decision making. Revolution in technology and dual working families has changed the direction of decision making process within the family [11].

This research model supports the antecedents and outcomes of peer communication through social media from the proposed framework. The results of the study support the hypotheses and these findings provide unique insights about consumer socialization of adolescents through social media and its impact on family purchase. Previous researches have mainly focused on socialization agents like parents, mass media and school [21, 22] and less attention is given to peer communication. The main contribution of our finding is consumption related peer-communication through social media are becoming increasingly relevant for consumer socialization process and can significantly influence family purchase.

Mersey et al. [76] says that social media provides an opportunity for business to engage and interact with potential consumers thereby increasing sense of intimacy with consumers by building good relation. Marketers should utilize this active communication to strengthen their relationship. Social networking websites should not only allow consumers to exchange information but should engage them in participating and socializing experience. In addition, leveraging social media platform requires marketers to be more transparent, honest, interactive, guiding and contributing to the co-creation of user generated content, since consumers are actively turning to different social media platforms in search of product information [13].

The study establishes the significant role of social media in supporting consumer socialization process of adults. Internet to children is what television used to be for children of yesteryears. Apparently adolescents market should not be neglected as many of them nowadays have become tech savvy. This internet has given birth to many consumer generated media like blogging, social network sites like FB, You tube, Twitter, Instagram, Myspace etc., which are prevalent in world wide web [77]. Marketers who use social media tools should monitor and audit the effectiveness of peer communication and ensure that it spreads positive word of mouth. Experienced employees may be engaged in dealing with negative opinions or failures. Social media operators should understand the importance of both social and informational functions and provide additional support for enhancing website design. They should ensure that their forums offer credibility, relevance and evoke empathy through Word of Mouth. With the help of advanced technology and security mechanism, social media operators can ensure high quality peer communication and trust based interactions among peers.

6 Conclusion

A preliminary attempt is made in this study to provide an insight into the possibilities of adolescents consumer socialization process with the antecedent variables. There is no sparse literature concerning the consumer socialization of adolescent's especially through social media in Indian context and this article enriches our understanding of this issue. Today adolescents have taken an important place in the society than their parents ever had. They are not only consumers but have considerable influence in the decision making with the influence of peers and social media and also a shift in Indian culture like increase in nuclear families, dual income parents, hyper parenting and exposure to media. The study has a limitation like it has been conducted in only two public schools in south Bangalore region and the results can't be generalized to other regions of India. Future research may consider testing the learning outcomes of the socialization model.

Annexure

See Tables 1 and 3.

References

1. Boyd, D.M., Ellison, N.B.: Social network sites: definition, history, and scholarship. J. Comput.-Mediat. Commun. **13**(1), 210–230 (2007)
2. Mulhern, F.: Integrated marketing communications: from media channels to digital connectivity. J. Mark. Commun. **15**, 2–3 (2009)
3. Carter, J.: Social Media Strategies in Small Businesses, Manchester Metropolitan University, pp. 1–28 (2014)
4. Kaiser Family Foundation: Generation M2: Media in the lives of 8–18 years old. http://www.kff.org
5. Lee, C., Conroy, D., Hii, C.: The Internet: a consumer socialization agent for teenagers. In: ANZMAC 2003 Conference, pp. 1–3 December (2003)

6. Human development Report 2016. https://www.scribd.com/document/342707758/2016-human-development-report-pdf
7. TCS: urban students are digital natives. https://www.tcs.com/urban-digital-natives-tcs-generation-web-2-0-survey
8. Moscardelli, D., Liston-Heyes, C.: teens surfing the net: how do they learn to protect their privacy. J. Bus. Econ. 2(9), 43–56 (2004)
9. Siddiqui, S., Singh, T.: Social media its impact with positive and negative aspects. Int. J. Comput. Appl. Technol. Res. 5(2), 71–75 (2016)
10. Sondhi, N., Basu, R.: Role of children in family purchase across Indian parental clusters. Young Consum. 15(4), 365–379 (2014)
11. Belch, M.A., Krentlera, K.A., Willis-Flurry, L.A.: Teen internet mavens: influence in family decision making. J. Bus. Res. 569–575 (2005)
12. Kaur, A., Medury, Y.: Impact of the internet on teenagers' influence on family purchases. Young Consum. 12(1), 27–38 (2010)
13. Ramnarai, Y., Govender, K.K.: Social media browsing and consumer behavior exploring the youth market. Afr. J. Bus. Manage. 7(18), 1885–1893 (2013)
14. Ahuja, M.K., Galvin, J.E.: Socialization in virtual groups. J. Manag. 29(2), 161–185 (2003)
15. Zhang, J., Daugherty, T.: Third-person effect and social networking: implications for online marketing and word-of-mouth communication. Am. J. Bus. 24(2), 53–63 (2009)
16. Lueg, J.E., Ponder, N., Beatty, S.E., Michael, C.: Teenagers' use of alternative shopping channels: A consumer socialization perspective. J. Retail. 82(2), 137–153 (2006)
17. Muratore, I.: Teenagers, blogs and socialization: a case study of young French bloggers. Young Consum. 9(2), 131–142 (2008)
18. Okazak, S.: The tactical use of mobile marketing: how adolescents social networking can best shape brand extensions. J. Advert. Res. 49(1), 12–26 (2009)
19. Ward, S.L.: Consumer Socialization. J. Consum. Res. 1, 14–21 (1974)
20. Moschis, G.P., Moore R.L., Smith R.B.: The impact of family communication on adolescent consumer socialization. In: Kinnear, T.C. (ed.) NA—Advances in Consumer Research, vol. 11, pp. 314–319. Association for Consumer Research, Provo, UT (1984)
21. Wang, X., Yu, C., Wei, Y.: Social media peer communication and impacts on purchase intentions: a consumer socialization framework. J. Interact. Mark. 26(4), 198–208 (2012)
22. Moschis, G.P., Churchill Jr., G.A.: Consumer socialization: a theoretical and empirical analysis. J. Mark. Res. 15(4), 599–609 (1978)
23. Clemens, K., Andrew, R.: Ruyter ko de, Wetzels Martin: return on interactivity: the impact of online agents on newcomer adjustment. J. Mark. 75(2), 93–108 (2011)
24. Soyeon, S.: Adolescent consumer decision-making styles: the consumer socialization perspective. Psychol. Mark. 13(6), 547–569 (1996)
25. Kim, C., Lee, H., Tomiuk, M.A.: Adolescent's perceptions of family communication patterns and some aspects of their consumer socialization. Psychol. Mark. 26(10), 888–907 (2009)
26. Moschis, G.P., Moore, R.L.: Anticipatory consumer socialization. J. Acad. Mark. Sci. 12(4), 109–123 (1984)
27. Chaudhary, M., Gupta, A.: Children's influence in family buying process in India. Young Consum. 13(2), 161–175 (2012)
28. Jayantha, S.: Wimalasiri: a cross-national study on children's purchasing behavior and parental response. J. Consum. Mark. 21(4), 274–284 (2004)
29. Haynes, J.L., Burts, D.C., Dukes, A., Cloud, R.: Consumer socialization of preschoolers and kindergartners as related to clothing consumption. Psychol. Mark. 10(2), 151–166 (1993)
30. Ali, A., Batra, D.K., Shoiab Ur Rehman, R.N.: Consumer socialization of children: a conceptual framework. Int. J. Sci. Res. Publ. 2(1), 1–5 (2012)
31. Flurry, L., Veeck, A.: Children's relative influence in family decision making in Urban China. J. Macro Mark. 29(2), 145–159 (2009)
32. Beneke, J., Silverstone, G., Woods, A., Schneider, Greg: The influence of the youth on their parents 'purchasing decisions of high-technology products. Afr. J. Bus. Manage. 5(10), 3807–3812 (2011)

33. Martensen, A., Grønholdt, L.: Children's influence on family decision making. Innov. Mark. **4**, 4 (2008)
34. Thomson, E.S., Laing, A.W., McKee, L.: Family purchase decision making: exploring child influence behavior. J. Consum. Behav. **6**(4), 182–202 (2007)
35. Liang, Y.-W.: Children's influence on purchasing tourism products via the internet: parental power versus children's power-the social power perspective. J. Travel. Tour. Mark. **30**(7), 639–661 (2013)
36. Zeijl, E., Poel, Y., Bios-Reymond, M., Ravesloot, J., Meulmann, J.J: The role of parents and peers in the leisure activities of young adolescents. J. Leis. Res. **32**(3), 281–302 (2000)
37. Swinyard, W.R., Peng Sim, C: Perception of children's influence on family decision processes. J. Consum. Mark. **4**(1), 25–38 (1987)
38. Mangleburg, T.F., Grewal, D., Bristol, T.: Family type, family authority relations, and adolescents' purchase influence. Adv. Consum. Res. **26**, 379–384 (1999)
39. Laczniak, R.N., Palan, K.M.: Under the influence. Mark. Res. **16**(1), 34–39 (2004)
40. Dotson, M.J., Hyatt, E.M.: Major influence factors in children's consumer socialization. J. Consum. Mark. **22**(1), 35–42 (2005)
41. Grant, I.J., Stephen, G.R.: Buying behavior of "tweenage" girls and key societal communicating factors influencing their purchasing of fashion clothing. J. Fash. Mark. Manag.: Int. J. **9**(4), 450–467 (2005)
42. Batounis-Ronner, C., Hunt, J.B., Mallalieu, L.: Sibling effects on preteen children's perceived influence in purchase decisions. Young Consum. **8**(4), 231–243 (2007)
43. Signs You're Dealing With a Youngest Child: https://www.huffingtonpost.com/lian-dolan/28-signs-youre-dealing-with-a-youngest-child_b_4227594.html
44. Chaudhary, M., Gupta, A.: Use of influence tactics by children in India. Jindal J. Bus. Res. **1**(1), 115–125 (2012)
45. Ali, A., Mustafa, Z., Batra, D.K., Ravichandran, N., Rehman, S.U.: Examining the children's influence in family decision making in Delhi (India), **3**(2), 614–619 (2012)
46. Halling, J., Tufte, B.: The gender perspective: children as consumers in Denmark. Young Consum. **3**(4), 61–75 (2002)
47. Chavda, H., Haley, M., Dunn, C.: Adolescents' influence on family decision-making. Young Consum. **6**(3), 68–78 (2005)
48. Ali, A., Batra, D.K.: Children influence on parents buying decisions in Delhi (India). Eur. J. Bus. Manag. **3**(11), 19–28 (2011)
49. Robertson, T., Rossiter, J.R.: Children's attributions of intent in television commercials. J. Consum. Res. **1**, 13–20 (1974)
50. Foxman, E.R., Tansuhaj, P.S., Ekstrom, K.M.: Family member's perceptions of adolescent's influence in family decision making. J. Consum. Res. **15**(4), 482–491 (1989)
51. Roopnarine, J.L., Talukder, E., Jain, D., Joshi, P., Srivastav, P.: Personal well-being, kinship tie, and mother-infant and father-infant interactions in single-wage and dual-wage families in New Delhi. India. J. Marriage Fam. **54**(2), 293–301 (1992)
52. Lueg, J.E., Finney, R.Z.: Interpersonal communication in the consumer socialization process: scale development and validation. J. Mark. Theory Pract. **15**(1), 25–39 (2007)
53. Taylor, D.G., Lewin, J.E., Strutton, D.: Friends, fans, and followers: do ads work on social networks? J. Advert. Res. **51**(1), 258–275 (2011)
54. Latest Social Media Facts and Stats from India-2016. http://www.soravjain.com/social-media-facts-and-stats-india-2016
55. Gershoff, A.D., Johar, G.V.: Do you know me? consumer calibration of friends' knowledge. J. Consum. Res. **32**, 496–503 (2006)
56. http:// www.slideshare.com
57. The latest numbers on web, mobile, and social media in India. https://www.techinasia.com/india-web-mobile-data-series (2016)
58. Kumar, A.K.: Term paper: online advertisement, Hochschle Furtwangen University (2008)
59. Bush, A.J., Smith, R., Martin, C.: The influence of consumer socialization variables on attitude toward advertising: a comparison of African-Americans and Caucasians. J. Advert. **28**(3), 13–25 (1999)

60. Mukhopadhyay, A., Yeung, C.W.M.: Building character: effects of lay theories of self-control on the selection of products for children. J. Mark. Res. **47**(2), 240–50 (2010)
61. Bristol, T., Mangleburg, T.F.: Not telling the whole story: teen deception in purchasing. J. Acad. Mark. Sci. **33**(1), 79–95 (2005)
62. McGuire, K.D., Weisz, J.R.: Social cognition and behavior correlates of preadolescence chum ship. Child Dev. **53**, 1478–1484 (1982)
63. Levin, D.Z., Cross, R.: The strength of weak ties you can trust: the mediating role of trust in effective knowledge transfer. Manage. Sci. **50**(11), 1477–1490 (2004)
64. De Bruyn, A., Lilien, G.: A multi-stage model of word-of-mouth influence. Int. J. Res. Mark. **25**(9), 151–163 (2008)
65. Smith, D., Menon, S., Sivakumar, K.: Online peer and editorial recommendations, trust, and choice in virtual markets. J. Interact. Mark. **19**, 15–37 (2005)
66. Dholakia, R.R.: Intergeneration differences in consumer behavior: Some evidence from a developing country. J. Bus. Res. **12**(1):19–34 (1984)
67. Kuhn, M., Eischen, W.: Leveraging the aptitude and ability of eight year-old adults and other wonders of technology. In: European Society for Opinion and Marketing Research Conference Proceedings (1997)
68. Darley, W.K., Lim, J.-S.: Family decision making in leisure-time activities: an exploratory investigation of the impact of locus of control, child age influence factor and parental type on perceived child Influence, in NA, Advances in Consumer Research, 13, eds. Richard J. Lutz. pp. 370–374 (1986)
69. Jenkins, R.L.: The influence of children in family decision-making: parents perceptions. In: Wilkie, W.L. (ed.), vol. 6, pp. 413–416. Association for Consumer Research (1979)
70. Nelson, J.E.: Children as information sources in family decisions to eat out. In: Wilkie, W.L. (ed.) Advances in Consumer Research, vol. 6, pp. 419–423. Association for Consumer Research, (1979)
71. Szybillo, G., Sosanie, A.: Family decision making: husband, wife and children. In: Perrault, advances in consumer research, vol. 4, pp. 46–49. Association for Consumer Research, Atlanta, GA (1977)
72. McNeal, U.J., Yeh, C.-H.: Development of consumer behavior patterns among Chinese children. J. Consum. Mark. **14**(1), 45–59 (1997)
73. Kaur, A., Medury, Y.: SEM approach to teen influence in family decision making. Contemp. Manag. Res. **9**(3), 323–342 (2013)
74. Sheth, N.J., Mittal, B.: Consumer Behavior: A Managerial Perspective, 2nd edn. South Western Publishing Company, New Jersey (2004)
75. Sharma, A., Sonwaney, V.: Int. J. Mark. Bus. Commun. **2**(2), 32–43 (2013)
76. Mersey, R.D., Malthouse, E.C., Calder, B.J.: Engagement with Online Media. J. Media Bus. Stud. **7**(2), 39–56 (2010)
77. Ahmad, M., Sidin, S.M., Omar, N.A.: A preliminary investigation of adolescents' perception of the role of internet in parent consumer socialization. IUP J. Mark. Manag. X **3**, 7–17 (2011)

Social Media Patient Engagement in Healthcare: An Italian Case Study

Marta Musso, Roberta Pinna, Pierpaolo Carrus and Giuseppe Melis

Abstract The purpose of this paper is to analyse how health organizations use social media to engaging patients in the process of their health, care, and treatment and how this platform can facilitate the value co-creation processes in healthcare context. In order to understand how healthcare organizations are adopting social media technologies to address the challenges they face, the paper presents the results of a content analysis of comments, information and videos posted on the Facebook pages of an Italian healthcare organization. Although there are high expectations that the use of social media will provide more patient centred care, there is currently little evidence within the academic literature showing the health benefits of the use of social media by patients and healthcare institutions. The findings of this study have important implications for public healthcare organizations in order to understand how implement social media engagement and establish procedures to facilitate the process.

Keywords Value co-creation · Social media · Patient's engagement · Public health communication

1 Introduction

The idea that patients should be at the centre of the health-care system has become a topical issue and The Service Dominant logic (S-D logic) paradigm [1, 2] theorizes the joint role of organizations and customers in the value co-creation process [3]. S-D logic posits that these actors represent dynamic, operant, and active resources, enabling reticular/networked interactions [4] centred on many-to-many organizational relationships in which value co-creation is not limited to the supplier

M. Musso (✉) · R. Pinna · P. Carrus · G. Melis
Department of Economics and Business, University of Cagliari, Cagliari, Italy
e-mail: musso@unica.it

© Springer Nature Switzerland AG 2020
Y. Baghdadi et al. (eds.), *ICT for an Inclusive World*,
Lecture Notes in Information Systems and Organisation 35,
https://doi.org/10.1007/978-3-030-34269-2_16

and the customer but involves an entire network of stakeholders. Patient engagement is the process that promotes the centrality and the participation of the person in path health, enhancing conscious choices, priorities welfare, and the context of family life.

In the last few years, healthcare institutions are recognizing the power of the social media as a platform for co-creating value with their audiences [5]. Social media platform allow health organizations to engage in conversations with citizens through unique interactive feature, such as sharing videos, photos, commenting on platforms like Facebook or Twitter. Patients appear to become more engaged with their care in general, and one of the many results is that they are increasingly using the Internet to share and rate their experiences of health care [6, 7]. They are also using the social media to connect with others having similar illnesses, to share experiences, and beginning to manage their illnesses by leveraging these technologies. Starting from these reasons, recently the national and local governments in Italy is doing pressure on health care organizations to understand how well they can promote the health of their population and to reconfigure their service delivery processes [8, 9] by the use of the information and communication technology (ICT).

Starting from the growing use of social media in healthcare, the purpose of this paper is to examine how the use of the most widespread platforms, as Facebook, to communicate with their key publics, influences the ability of health care organizations to create opportunities for engage patients but also families and citizens in an active process health. Specifically, we explore how these tools are used by healthcare organizations as a mechanism for engaging audiences in true multi way conversations and interaction. Specifically, the paper aims to investigate the following research questions:

1. Do the healthcare institutions developed the ability, using social networks, to engage with its audiences?
2. How social media platforms allow value co-creation among participants?

To reply to the research questions, an explorative qualitative analysis, was carried out through the content represented by texts, and videos posted on the Facebook pages of an Italian healthcare organization. In particular, we analyzed the postings of a University Hospital, in relation to some of the objectives pursued by this communication, to analyze their ability to generate engagement by users, measured in terms of likes, sharing of posts and comments to post.

The rest of the paper is organised as follows. First, the theoretical background of the study is explained along with a review of relevant literature and proposed hypotheses. Next, the research methodology employed is detailed. Finally, we provide a summary of the key findings and discuss the implications for healthcare organizations.

2 Theoretical Background

2.1 Value Cocreation in Healthcare

One of the main challenges in healthcare sector is to create and properly deliver value for patients. In this context, Service dominant logic (SDL) proposed by Vargo and Lusch [1] sheds more light on patient inclusion in the service production and creation of value. Consequently, the actors' knowledge in the service exchange and sharing of information is central to SDL and value co-creation [9–11]. In such an information intensive field as healthcare it can be understood how important could be to exploit patient and actors' resources in co-creation perspective and which benefit can be reached. McColl-Kennedy and colleagues [12] define customer value co-creation as the "benefit realized from integration of resources through activities and interactions with collaborators in the customer's service network". Payne et al. [4] argue that, access to information, resources, individual knowledge and skills (competence), need assessment, and cognitive behaviours are some of the attributes to assist health operators to create value. The emphasis is upon the value (benefit to some party) that is co-created through the interactions and activities of patients with service providers. Resource integration is viewed as an opportunity for creating new potential resources, which during service exchange can be used to 'access additional resources' and create new resources (which can also be exchanged) through integration [2, 13–15]. Some scholars pointed out that the value co-creation depends on quality and diversity of personals experiences both past and present [4, 11, 16, 17]. Experiences that must be significant and able to meet the customer's needs. One systematic literature review found that patients with more experience in the health care setting were better able to navigate the interpersonal interaction between patient/family and provider [18]. These authors highlight the importance of the interactions about actors in order to create value [19]. In this perspective, an organization have to encourage the value creation by engagement platforms where the actors can interact and share their experiences. Gallan et al. [20] find that when a customer experiences greater levels of positivity, the customer engages in activities such as actively sharing information, providing suggestions, and engaging in shared decision-making. Some scholars [21, 22] point out that the interactions between professional healthcare and the patient provide opportunities for communication of essential information between the two parties and coproduction of positive outcomes. The success of co-creation is founded on the ability to create an environment of interaction in which participants feel free to engage in conversations and activities that are of personal interest and enabling them to develop their sense of belonging. In this context the value co-created comes from the perceived value by actors that interact each other through a deep dialogue, sharing information, being able to be responsible for the care path, and finally increasing the trust level by a even more clear relationship [23]. Remark 1. In the printed volumes, illustrations are generally black and white (halftones), and only in exceptional cases, and if the author is prepared to cover the extra costs involved, are colored pictures accepted. Colored pictures are welcome in the electronic version free of charge. If you send colored figures that are to be printed in black and white, please make sure that they really are legible in black and white. Some colors show up very poorly when printed in black and white.

2.2 Patient Engagement

In the last decade the concept of patient engagement is an increasingly important component of strategies to reform health care and has received a growing attention in managerial literature [24, 25], and it can be considered the foundational component of value co-creation. In particular, the concept of engagement describes the type of relationship that the patients (families and other citizens) establish—or may establish—with the health system of reference in the **various phases of its Care Path**. The Center for Advancing Health defines engagement as "actions individuals must take to obtain the greatest benefit from the health care services available to them". Engagement means that a person is involved in a process through which he harmonizes robust information and professional advice with his own needs, preferences and abilities in order to prevent, manage and cure disease. Some scholars defined patients' engagement as a psychological state, which occurs by virtue of interactive patient experiences with a focal agent/object within specific service relationships" [26]. Gruman et al. [27] defined patient engagement as "actions individuals must take to obtain the greatest benefit from the health care services available to them. This definition emphasizes the role of the individual independent of changes aimed at improving the effectiveness of the health care system. Graffigna et al. [28] has been defining patient engagement as "the multidimensional process that involves a cognitive, emotional and a behavioural dimension". Thus referring to an engaged patient, implies to have the complex psychosocial adaptation process that results from the joint activation at a cognitive, emotional and behavioural level. During the various stages of the engagement process, the relationship with the healthcare system evolves from a situation of pure passivity and delegation to a situation where the health care become personalized, in an effective and efficient way [29, 30]. The engagement implies an increase of their autonomy and responsibility in some of the crucial phases of health management. This means that an engaged patient is a person that is more attentive and awareness on the prevention process and more capable of modifying his own style of life. An engaged patient could be ambassador of good preventive practices for effective management of health at its proximal network of reference. Furthermore, he is able to mount properly at the first signs and symptoms of the disease, to get in contact with the health system in a timely manner and to benefit from the services offered in a more satisfactory way [31]. In order to create a positive engagement context, hospitals and healthcare systems are indeed deemed to directly engage patients in their health management. In general, the bulk of the literature on what providers can do to support engagement focuses on interactions. In healthcare, interactions between health care customers and health professionals play a key role. Interpersonal interaction increases open communication, in this way, patients and families are motivated to participate in engagement behaviours through encouragement from others, such as providers, and through positive feedback when they engage in these desired behaviours [32]. One review of the literature in this area found that patient participation increased in interactions with those health care providers who responded positively to patients' needs. Healthcare organizations have to encourage people to take an active role as key players in protecting their health and choosing appropriate treatments for managing their disease [33] for example through interventions direct at modifying patient medication compliance, chronic disease self-management, interventions directed encouraging patients to ask questions trough social platform and traditional behaviours associated with promoting health **and** preventing disease. Multifaceted information from healthcare providers includes verbal explanations, visual diagrams, pamphlets, book recommendations, credible online sources, question-and-answer sessions, and other creative avenues for information sharing.

2.3   Social Media and Patient Engagement

In the last few years, scholars have paid a growing attention to understand how the use of social media by healthcare organizations can support the need to be more engaged with their patients. The use of social media is part of a growing trend and is due to a realization that healthcare institutions need to be more engaged with their patients. In particular, the expanding use of social media enables new ways of creating, searching and sharing health information, accelerating collaborative health care opportunities.[1] Since then, the use of social media in the field of health has grown exponentially.[2] The term social media denotes highly interactive platforms via which individuals and communities share, co-create, discuss, and modify user-generated content [34]. Interactivity refers to "the condition of communication in which simultaneous and continuous exchanges occur, and these exchanges carry a social, binding force" [35]. Heldman et al. [6] defined social media engagement as "a multi-way interaction between and among an organization and digital communities

---

[1] Since the end of the 2000s, the practice of searching for information on the Internet has become increasingly widespread, and in this context social media has played an increasing role, including online forums and bulletin boards, used as sources of information on health and well-being. In this regard consider that according to a Pew Research Center survey, the "60% of US adults used the Internet to find health care information, and 10% used social media to follow their friends' health care experiences". Fox S. The social life of health information 2011. Pew Research Center. Available at: http://www.pewinternet.org/files/old-media/Files/Reports/2011/PIP_Social_Life_of_ Health_Info.pdf. Accessed May 13, 2017. Another study useful to take awareness of the phenomena is Elkin N. How America searches: health and wellness. iCrossing. Available at: http://www.rx-edge.com/research%20pdfs/How_America_Searches_ Health_and_Wellness.pdf. Accessed May 13, 2017.

[2] 30 facts & statistics on social media and healthcare. referralMD. Available at: https://getreferralmd. com/2017/01/30-facts-statistics-onsocial-media-and-healthcare/. Accessed May 14, 2017.

that could take many forms, using social media channels to facilitate that interaction". Health messaging is shared in a way that creates opportunities for information to be acted on by the audience, thereby opening a dialogue with the organization that allows both parties to work collaboratively to address issues affecting the health and well-being of the audience. From a health promotion perspective, these conversations can lead to varying levels of engagement. They can result in a range of outcomes, including increased awareness or knowledge of health-related information, feelings of belonging and social connection, and involvement with health promotion programs. Feedback mechanisms, such as buttons or quizzes, facilitate more participation from users of social media and encourage a discussion among users with relatively few access or content creation barriers.

Clearly, the use of social media within a strategic plan, prepared by the various health organizations, presupposes the definition of specific objectives that then must be monitored and measured on the basis of appropriate indicators, such as, for example, reach, click-through rates, impressions, posts, and followers must be tracked, interpreted, and documented relative to targets for each initiative [7].

The Ministry of Health suggests to the local health institutions, within the guidelines for the on-line communication published in 2010, the use of social media platforms for planning communication activities more effective health promotion and to establish with the citizens' relations more engaging and dialogical. In the last few years, an increasing number of health organizations in Italy have come up with Facebook health applications for facilitating brand awareness and promoting brand engagement [34]. In particular, healthcare organizations in Italy use social media as part of various community engagement activities, such as fundraising, customer service and support, the provision of news and information, patient education, and advertising new services. Social media represent a critical innovation for the healthcare sector not only because they allow informational exchanges among patients and affect the health professional and patient relationship, but also because they promote online partnerships and engage communities in a value co-creation process. Patients can be involved in co-creation of value in care processes in several ways. Some scholars [35] argue that the use of social networks will lead to a more patient-centred healthcare system that will improve communication and information flow between patients and the institutions. Studies have shown that patients through social media can, not only, to share their experiences through discussion forums, chat rooms and instant messaging, or online consultation with a qualified clinician but to express themselves, share their stories, learn from others and spread health knowledge [14]. Kotsenas et al. [7] point out that "The patient experience often begins long before a patient arrives at a doctor's office. Social media can be an important tool to reach out to patients before their appointments to improve their experience and potentially decrease anxiety associated with their care". Fisher and Clayton [35] found that by social media is possible to improve participation, autonomy, motivation, perceived self-efficacy, and trust for patients. Clerici et al. [36] reported that it was easier for patients to describe their experiences and first hand impressions relating to their disease using YouTube. Patients could describe and share their emotional perspectives and provide necessary coping skills, support, and resources for other patients.

Heldman et al. [6] point out that Social media monitoring tools allow public health organizations to learn more about what diverse audiences are saying regarding public health topics, identify information gaps, and adjust messaging accordingly. Social media give us insights into what health information may be important and interesting to users, in the moment. This real-time aspect of social media is a key component to ensuring that the communication efforts are relevant, meaningful, and useful to our audiences.

Thus, the value of any experience is generated in the interaction between the actors and is affected by their ability to involve each other in a relationship. it can thus understand how social media can offer a great opportunity for the development of these relationships., They enhance the possibilities for dialogue, making it more intense and frequent, they encourage the sharing of information and knowledge, contribute to increase the trust deriving from greater informality and ease of relationships, not only between patients but also between these and the healthcare staff, creating in fact a cognitive and emotional context that allow patients to feel part of a community in which the disease is no longer lived in solitude, but as a moment of life that also involves others and that they want to fight together with others, creating in this way a community of destiny in which one encourages oneself, or rejoices in good results, or also shares sadness when someone does not make it, etc. In other words, it can therefore say that the use of social media, in a context such as healthcare, generates value from multiple points of view among which, the human is perhaps the most important [37].

3 Research Method

In this study, we (1) investigated how a healthcare institution uses social media in order to engage with its audiences and (2) explain how audiences co-create value for healthcare organization. A case study [38] was conducted to explore the research question of this study. The case under consideration is the Facebook page, as an online social platform, of an Italian healthcare organization located in Sardinian region. A content analysis has been developed and following Miles and Huberman [39], a list of codes was created prior to define the fieldwork to guide the analysis. Defining coding as the organisation of raw data into conceptual categories, each code is effectively a category or 'bin' into which a piece of data is placed.

3.1 The Case Study

Healthcare organization aims to make citizens, patients and their family members as protagonists within the health service with the aim to improve health outcomes and contributing to make the health system more effective. The healthcare organization analysed is the Azienda Ospedaliera of Cagliari (AOU),[3] which, in line with the European eGovernment Action Plan 2011–2015, since January 2017 it has implemented a communication Plan that concern a renovation of the main digital communication platforms, including the Facebook, Tweeter and Instagram profiles. The European Commission indeed, calls on public administrations of all levels to become open, accessible and transparent to citizens. There is a relevant commitment of the AOU regarding this aspect: the institutional website has been renewed, focusing on social media and it has integrated all the Digital Healthcare facilities. The goal of the organisation is to keep focusing on all these aspects, enhancing the information technologies tools and online services available to users. Specifically, referring to social media, the AOU's presence on social networks is very relevant. The Facebook page, is active, as well as Twitter page, Youtube channel and the Instagram profile. It is worth mentioning, that the Facebook page of the Azienda Ospedaliera was followed by 6567 in November 2016 fans reaching 9581 fans on November 2017 in only one year. Initially, the social media channel and, in particular the Facebook page of the Azienda Ospedaliera was simply used to promote health services or "administrative" information (press releases, news). It was not enough used for health promotion and disease prevention. Converserly, for the AOU, the communication with citizens is not just promotion about services and the company but rather health promotion after the implementation of the new communication plan in 2017.

Concerning the case study, it has been selected the Facebook page, and more specifically the content analysis has been conducted only on the Aou posted messages, with the aim to highlight the reaction of its audiences. The Facebook page has been chosen as the social media platform to analyse considering that in Italy, by 2015, 28 million Facebook users were active every month, 8 millions of Instagram users and 6.4 million Twitter users (Audiweb). In particular, several studies highlighted the importance of Facebook in promoting health constituting a valid and effective platform where patient search for health information [40, 41].

3.2 Data Collection and the Coding Procedure

Through NCapture, a browser application of NVivo software, has been used to collect all multimedia contents shared into AOU official Facebook page since the beginning of 2017. Thanks to this tool, we gathered a rich collection of data (see Table 1) from January to November 2017, which allowed us to analyse both the typology of different communication messages related to different purposes and which are the different ways that the company used with the aim to engage patient for health promotion. At first the posted messages by Aou has been coded in relation to the different

---

[3]The AOU is leader in Sardinian region in health communication, thanks to the number of online communication platforms it uses which the AOU has been able to integrate. AOU of Cagliari is the first in Sardinia and one of the first in Italy to use of all the devices (pcs, tablets and smartphones) for patient services: from the withdrawal report, going for online booking, and dialogue with the administration.

Table 1 Summary of data from the Facebook page

Data type	Quantity
Post content type	
Text	124
Video	23
Photos	1150
Link	
User engagement type	
Comments	3871
Likes	5843
Sharing	2906

communication purpose, then the posts belonging to the health promotion code have been analysed in relation to the different engagement actions. Data collected consist mainly in posts, photos, links, tags, videos, posted on the Facebook wall and the company's replies to its clients' comments. With reference to the users, at this step of the analysis, the focus was on the descriptive aspect of the different reactions. The number of the most relevant reaction indicators in terms of like, number of posts and sharing have been evaluated. [42].

All the post of the AOU on the Facebook page served as the coding units of analysis for this study. Before the actual content analysis, to avoid observation bias driven by a researcher's expectations, two trained coders, independently coded a sample of 113 Post in order to evaluate coherence between the coding processes performed by the two co-authors, and consequently evaluate the robustness of the analysis.

The coding categories were developed based on previous literature in health communication and management studies [43–45] and they were modified to fit the context of health communication in a Facebook page. More specifically, the coding procedure has been developed through a two-step path. In the first step the coding's procedure aim was to identify the different categories of messages describing the different communication purposes of the social media institutional Facebook page in healthcare. As several authors reported in literature how health related organisations make use of interactive features and social media channels on Facebook [43], five main purposes categories have been identified for this classification (Table 2).

The second phase concerned the identification of different categories of action implemented by the health structure with regards to the patient engagement perspective for health promotion purposes. It has been decided to choose this perspective because social media sites have become extremely important venues for seeking and exchanging health information, contributing to a tremendous amount of health information available online. Interaction is the conceptual basis of engagement, so in order to engage patient within the social network the organisation has to provide and differentiate interaction opportunity.

Table 2 Post communication purposes on Facebook institutional page

Category	Description	Expected
Health promotion information	Information dissemination about health and disease prevention, the purpose is to rising awareness of several chronic pathology or to improve patient education for healthy lifestyle, and complementary treatments	Post and link related to information about health and information post related to events for information dissemination about health.
Organisation services promotion	To inform audiences on services provided by the health organisation, particularly referring possibilities to manage medical appointment, exam, and new services on department	Post related to services provided by the health structure or news or advert for daily health service distribution
Organisation quality promotion	The promotion of excellence characteristics of the organisation, together with the promotion of excellence in services provided by the health structure	Storytelling about daily activities in the hospital, about experiences in the department
Information collection	Discussions on these Facebook walls could also provide insights	A Facebook "group" could also be created to acquire information from a segment of the population that has experience with a particular topic. For example, a question could be posted on an organization's Facebook wall requesting a response

Therefore, referring to coding, for this step of the analysis, a classification of engagement related action have been recognised inspired by literature. The classification useful for the health organisation is show in Table 3.

4   Results and Discussion

Looking at the texts, video, photos, and links, posted by AOU, it has been found out that messages were principally aimed to stimulate the active involvement of patients and users (Table 4). It has been possible to observe that the post related to the different communication purposes are quite balanced, but there is a predominance for health promotion and the organisation service promotion also in terms of reactions

Table 3 Patient Engagement action of the healthcare structure for health promotion purposes

Engagement action	Description	Expected
Involving influencer and key partners	Engaging key partners and public health influencers driving online conversations on health	Conducting outreach to discuss public health topics with high-level professionals that align with an organization's priorities
Responding to questions or comments channels	Responding to health-related questions and comments—both negative and positive—received through organizational social media channels	Intervention by the health structure social media manger in answering directly and immediately to comments on Azienda
Make chance of interaction between users	Create opportunities for users to engage with the organization, and for your users to engage with each other, and to encourage user generated content	Asking users to comment on social media material, or make storytelling about patients experiences
Making chance to make people participate to offline health related events or activities	Integrating the virtual and real world, and gives committed social media users the opportunity to gain access to events and opportunities	Promoting offline health related events on the Facebook page
Encouraging user generated content	Stimulate content created or suggested by users	Asking user to give opinion or answer to health related question through special post referred to crucial topic on health and treatment management

Table 4 Numbers of post divided by type

Objective categories	Text	Video	Photo	Link
Health promotion information	76	8	68	76
Organisation services promotion	39	6	33	39
Organisation quality promotion	28	7	21	28
Information collection	9	0	9	9
Total	152	21	131	152

of users. More specifically, it has been observed that the reactions of users related to information dissemination for health promotion is massive in consideration to the quantity of post sharing by users and patients: the sharing of post related to the other communication purpose show a lower level of the same indicator. Moreover, with regards to the organisation service promotion, a very interesting thing on the Facebook page happened. The level of interactivity for these type of comments was qualitative significant, to give an example, a patient comment about the post of the app for tickets and services was to show the difficulties for elderly people with technologies, and AOU immediate answer was "*Dear Cenza, offering an extra service does not mean taking something off to someone else. Today, technology offers us many possibilities. I'll give you an example: our company allows patients who do the analysis from us to download the report on your smartphone or PC, obviously to do so you need to have one of these two objects. Those who do not have them can still withdraw their report to the hospital, as has always been done. The same applies to the row at the ticket or for many other services … have a nice day!*"

Another important consideration that emerged from the dataset is related to the collection of information purpose: the attempts of the health structure to ask directly for information and opinion were not so numerous; they introduced some posts for the possibilities for patient to give opinion from the website tool. Unexpectedly, to give an example an user comment was, apparently criticizing the tool: "*It seems to me the classic paper questionnaire that is also found in shopping malls where everyone sees you if you take it, fill it and put it in the classic box. If you exceeded that fear of being in front of everyone, you would have earned the first place in the box. This certainly surpasses the fact of having to "put your face" but with the personal data does not change much. If your intent was to have data on the type of person who uses the service you could have inserted in the form some spaces such as: nationality, gender, age, qualification, etc. I would definitely remove the first and last name and leave the email as the only address*". However, the AOU immediately replied: "*Actually, the aim is to give people the opportunity to tell their opinion, give suggestions, express their evaluation or criticism (always constructive) in real time and having immediate feedback. Anyway thank you very much for your valuable suggestions!*". This interaction can show that users are more willing to give information or telling their experience in an indirectly way rather than to be asked directly to do it. Indeed, the number of reactions in terms of likes, share and comments was small compared to those observable for the other type of post. Concerning the aim to reach broader audiences it is useful to underline that every single post of the AOU was accompanied by multimedia contents, like photo, video, and audio related to daily events on the AOU or health related contents to stimulate the attention of the users.

For what concern the organisation quality promotion, several post on the Facebook page were dedicated to this aim, in particular aimed to communicate excellence characteristics of the Azienda Ospedaliera in the field of innovative treatments, surgery and professional competences. It has been observed that, despite the predominance of health promotion and service promotion post the reactions belonging to these type is relevant considering the number of sharing, like and comments of users.

Examples of post related to each category are shown on Table 5.

Looking at our database, it emerged the attempt of the health structure to stimulate the interaction and the engagement of users and patients. As mentioned before, through the coding it has been possible to classify different type of actions within the purpose of health care promotion. In particular, it has possible to observe the relevance of post related to involving influencer and key partners. Particularly referring to the dissemination of information about chronic disease with the contribution of

Table 5 Summery of post communication purpose

Category	Quotation	Reactions
Health promotion information	"Vaccinations, the guide prepared by the Ministry of Health is available. Every day, from Monday to Friday, from 10 to 16, you can get clarification by calling the number 1500" Back to school, pay attention to the backpacks too heavy. Expert advice to protect the health of our children. #AouCa # labuonasanità #rasciaascuola. Back to school, pay attention to the backpacks too heavy. Here are the expert advice against back pain—Cagliari University Hospital Find out more AOUCAGLIARI.IT	267 share 13 share 32 likes
Organisation services promotion	Here is the new app to cover the line for the ticket and health services at the Policlinico of Duilio Casula. Immediate queuing and reservation up to 30 days before the performance. #FilaVia #AouCa # labuonasanità #pasocial Ticket and health services, at the Policlinico with the app of the Cagliari AU the row is now just a memory—Cagliari University Hospital—Find out more AOUCAGLIARI.IT	198 likes 114 share 8 comments
Organisation quality promotion	At the Policlinico Duilio Casula comes the 3 T resonances, which is able to obtain images within a few seconds, reducing the time spent by the patient in the machine. The Aou will be the only public structure in Sardinia to have it. A great innovation together with the latest-generation First Aid Tac. #AouCa # labuonasanità Extraordinary intervention at the #Policlinico! The bilateral #inning of the #laringe to restore the vocal cords' mobility was carried out by Professor Roberto Puxeddu. #AouCa # labuonasanità Performed at the Policlinico Duilio Casula for the first time in Italy reinnervation of the larynx	226 likes 50 share 13 comments 570 likes 236 share 23 comments
Information collection	"Your opinion is important for us: you can help us to provide more advanced quality health care services! Click on the link below and write to us!"	27 likes

important professionals, it has been noticed that the reaction of patient is very significant considering the number of share and comments. Furthermore, another important aspect is linked to the direct interaction between patients (asking information directly) and the AOU (immediately answering) for example, about a post of the surgery services: *"The surgery is done every Tuesday from 10:30 to 13:30. Third floor building Q.* Allowing for real-time and two-way communication, social media can facilitate organisational communication practice by sharing information and building dialogic relationships. Indeed, Facebook platform allow health organisations to engage in conversations with its audiences through unique interactive features, such as sharing videos and photos, commenting on sharing post. Interactivity refers to the condition of communication in which simultaneous and continuous exchanges occur, and these exchanges carry a social, binding force. Interactivity enables social networking sites to facilitate consumers' understanding of health information, increases word of mouth among interpersonal networks, and improves consumers' self-management behaviours (Table 6). Furthermore, it has been observed that several posts of the institutional Facebook page of AOU were structured to stimulate the emotional dimension interacting with patient. We founded that there is a particular emphasis on emotional concepts like *love, passion, pride,* which trigger a process of value co-creation confirmed by the correspondent reactions of audiences also expressed by using the "like" and "heart" bottoms of Facebook. Significant moment of patient emotional engagement occurs when the AOU shares daily hospital life pictures, such as maternity ward, aimed at hitting patients' emotions: "A new life to celebrate! What a nice way to start the day! Happy Sunday to all mothers and all the dads", which provoke consistent reactions of audiences.

5 Conclusion and Managerial Implications

The results of this content analysis highlight the importance of Facebook in the patient engagement and value co-creation process. The flows of information, activities, data, researches, products, videos and feedbacks are able to improve the sharing interaction between patients and the healthcare institution. This can provide to the citizens different solutions to solve their problems with better services [45]. The results indicate that the community groups were most inclined to engage actively in posting health information and interacting via Facebook. Through Facebook the healthcare organization provide health information on a range of conditions to the general public, patients and health professionals. This communication provides answers to medical questions and services and makes available health information to audience with special need or similar health issues. Patients describe and share their emotional perspectives and provide necessary coping skills, support, and resources for other patients. The social media encourage the dialogue between patients and patients, and patients and health professionals. These groups simultaneously serve as promotional spaces, support communities and venues for the solicitation and provision of disease management-knowledge. These type of supports are not necessarily available through formal channels of professional consultations. Facebook is used by the general public

Table 6 Summary of patient engagement actions of the healthcare organization for health promotion

Engagement action	Quotation	Reaction
Involving influencer and key partners	"Breast cancer, the day for awareness on breast reconstruction at the Polyclinic was a success. Very many women who came to the Casula and received the information. Professor Andrea Figus tells us what happened. #AouCa # labuonasanità #Policlinicoperledonne #Braday"	5 comments 115 likes 71 share
	"Menopause, October 21 open day at the Policlinico Duilio Casula with personalized visits. Prof Gian Benedetto Melis, director of Obstetrics and Gynecology dell'Aou of Cagliari, explains why it is an important event. To learn more, read here https://goo.gl/wf4Rt2. #menopausa #AouCa # labuonasanità"	12 comments 84 share 173 likes
Responding to questions or comments generated by users	"Dear Patrizia, you must refer to the surgeons or the doctor who sent you in surgery. In any case, talk to your doctor who knows the case well and knows how to act.… The treating doctor always knows what to do because he knows his patients and knows the case well"	2 comments in a direct conversation on the Facebook page

(continued)

Table 6 (continued)

Engagement action	Quotation	Reaction
Make chance of interaction between users	"A sensor under the skin with a smartphone with blood sugar, a real breakthrough in terms of prevention and improvement of quality of life. A new technology that the University Hospital of Cagliari, among the first in Italy, has made available to its patients in the logical diabetic Center of St. John of God. The first five sensors have been successfully implanted today. #AouCa # labuonasanità #innovazione"	218 like 27 comments 123 share
Making chance to make people participate to offline health related events or activities	"A news for all future mothers: here is the schedule for preparatory conferences for childbirth-analgesia! Read here to learn more. #AouCa # labuonasanità Partoanalgesia, the calendar of preparatory conferences for the first half of 2018: here is the program" "Saturday 11 November appointment promoted by the Diabetes Zero Onlus association. To learn more read here. #AouCa # labuonasanità #stopdiabete Type 1 diabetes, chilling numbers but preventing you can: in Sardinia the world day for prevention"	47 likes 22 share 4 comments 39 likes 20 share 2 comments
Encouraging user generated content	"It is always nice and exciting to tell the stories of our patients. It is so special when these stories concern our little guests. Congratulations Chiara Gaia and a big hug to parents! #AouCa # labuonasanità	206 likes 1 share 4 comments

nowadays. Patients and health professionals use the platform to share their experience of disease management, exploration and diagnosis.

Although social media should not be viewed as a solution to the complexities of behaviour change and improved health outcomes [46, 47], its potential remains an opportunity for healthcare organizations to engage their communities. In this perspective, the healthcare institutions have to encourage the value creation by engagement platforms where the actors can interact and share their experiences in a very informal and easy way. The results show that engaging patients in activities, which develop their skills and trust in self-management, might be a strategic resource that could transform the quality and sustainability oh health system. All these considerations lead to the conclusions that public health communicators can learn more about the audiences by paying attention to social media conversations at the aggregate level. In order to advance practice of patients' engagement they can unfold and observe conversation in real-time, and they can use monitoring tools to make public health organizations learn more about what diverse audiences are saying regarding public health topics, identify information gaps, and adjust messaging accordingly. Indeed, through social media the health organization should identify what health information may be important and interesting to users, in a specific moment. This real-time aspect of social media is a key component to ensuring that the communication efforts are relevant, meaningful, and useful to the audiences.

The limitation of this research consists of the consideration of only one social media, Facebook, the world's largest social networking site, and no other sites such as Twitter, which might yield alternate results. Having carried out the survey only on a specific institution, while it would be useful to make comparisons with other health organizations both in the same territorial context and in other contexts constitutes a second limitation.

This descriptive study provides a foundational basis for further investigations of social media strategy for patient engagement and value co-creation process in health care and other fields. Such an understanding also enables hypothesis generation and identification of key variables for follow-up studies that want to examine the effects of message features on the different qualitative reaction of users, as well as provide insights into the uses, opportunities, and challenges associated with the adoption of and research on this popular medium in the health care sector. Therefore, future possible research are linked to the possibilities to code and analyse the different comments of user in relation to the different engagement activities of the organisation, and also analysis the different reaction in terms of like and share splitting those have particular emotional feature.

References

1. Vargo, S.L., Lusch, R.F.: Evolving to a new dominant logic for marketing. J. Mark. **68**(1), 1–17 (2004)
2. Vargo, S.L., Lusch, R.F.: It's all B2B... and beyond: Toward a systems perspective of the market. Ind. Mark. Manage. **40**(2), 181–187 (2011)

3. Bonomi, S., Zardini, A., Rossignoli, C., Dameri, P. R.: E-health and value co-creation: the case of electronic medical record in an Italian academic integrated hospital. In International Conference on Exploring Services Science, pp. 166–175. Springer, Cham (2015, February)
4. Payne, A.F., Storbacka, K., Frow, P.: Managing the co-creation of value. J. Academy Mark. Sci. **36**(1), 83–96.5 (2008)
5. Kaplan, A.M., Haenlein, M.: Users of the world, unite! The challenges and opportunities of social media. Bus. Horiz. **53**(1), 59–68 (2010)
6. Heldman, A.B., Schindelar, J., Weaver, J.B.: Social media engagement and public health communication: implications for public health organizations being truly "Social". Public Health Rev. **35**, 1–18 (2013)
7. Kotsenas, A.L., Arce, M., Aase, L., Timimi, F.K., Young, C., Wald, J.T.: The strategic imperative for the use of social media in health care. J. Am. Coll. Radiol. (2017)
8. Sorrentino, M., De Marco, M., Rossignoli, C.: Health care co-production: co-creation of value in flexible boundary spheres. In International Conference on Exploring Services Science, pp. 649–659. Springer, Cham (2016, May)
9. Zardini, A., Rossignoli, C., Campedelli, B.: The impact of the implementation of the electronic medical record in an Italian university hospital. In Organizational Innovation and Change, pp. 63–73. Springer, Cham (2016)
10. Lusch, R.F., Vargo, S.L.: The Service-Dominant Logic of Marketing: Dialog, Debate, and Directions. Routledge
11. Osei-Frimpong, K., Wilson, A., Owusu-Frimpong, N.: Service experiences and dyadic value co-creation in healthcare service delivery: a CIT approach. J. Serv. Theor. Pract. **25**(4), 443–462 (2015)
12. McColl-Kennedy, J.R., Vargo, S.L., Dagger, T.S., Sweeney, J.C., Kasteren, Y.V.: Health care customer value cocreation practice styles. J. Serv. Res. **15**(4), 370–389 (2012)
13. Vargo, S.L., Lusch, R.F.: The nature and understanding of value: a service-dominant logic perspective. In: Special Issue–Toward a Better Understanding of the Role of Value in Markets and Marketing, pp. 1–12. Emerald Group Publishing Limited (2012)
14. Lober, W.B., Flowers, J.L.: Consumer empowerment in health care amid the Internet and social media. Semin. Oncol. Nurs. **27** (3), 169–182 (2011)
15. Vargo, S.L., Lusch, R.F.: Service-dominant logic: continuing the evolution. J. Acad. Mark. Sci. **36**(1), 1–10 (2008)
16. Gentile, C., Spiller, N., Noci, G.: How to sustain the customer experience: an overview of experience components that co-create value with the customer? Eur. Manag. J. **25**(5), 395–410 (2007)
17. Prahalad, C., Ramaswamy V.: Co-opting customer competence. Harvard Bus. Rev. **78**(1), 79–88 (2000)
18. Corlett, J., Twycross, A.: Negotiation of parental roles within family-centred care: a review of the research. J. Clin. Nurs. **15**(10), 1308–1316 (2006)
19. Ballantyne, D., Varey, R.J.: Creating value-in-use through marketing interaction: the exchange logic of relating, communicating and knowing. Mark. Theory **6**(3), 335–348 (2006)
20. Gallan, A.S., Jarvis, C.B., Brown, S.W., Bitner, M.J.: Customer positivity and participation in services: an empirical test in a health care context. J. Acad. Mark. Sci. **41**(3), 338–356 (2013)
21. Hausman, A.: Modeling the patient-physician service encounter: improving patient outcomes. J. Acad. Mark. Sci. **32**(4), 403–417 (2004)
22. Street, R.L., Makoul, G., Arora, N.K., Epstein, R.M.: How does communication heal? Pathways linking clinician–patient communication to health outcomes. Patient Educ. Couns. **74**(3), 295–301 (2009)
23. Hibbard J., Green J.: Do increases in patient activation result in improved selfmanagement. Health Serv. Res. **42**, 1443–1463 (2007)
24. Armstrong, N., Herbert, G., Aveling, E.L., Dixon-Woods, M., Martin, G.: Optimizing patient involvement in quality improvement. Health Expect. **16**(3) (2013)
25. Bate, P., Robert, G.: Experience-based design: from redesigning the system around the patient to co-designing services with the patient. Qual. Saf. Health Care **15**(5), 307–310 (2006)

26. Brodie, R.J., Hollebeek, L.D., Jurić, B., Ilić, A.: Customer engagement: conceptual domain, fundamental propositions, and implications for research. J. Serv. Res. **14**(3), 252–271 (2011)
27. Gruman, J.R.M.: From patient education to patient engagement: implications for the field of patient education. Patient Educ. Couns. 350–356 (2010)
28. Graffigna, G., Barello, S., Riva, G.: Technologies for patient engagement. Health Aff. (Maggio) 1–1 (2013)
29. Graffigna, G., Barello, S., Triberti, S.: Patient Engagement: A Consumer-Centered Model to Innovate Healthcare. Walter de Gruyter GmbH & Co KG (2016)
30. Graffigna G., Barello, S.: Patient engagement come qualificatore dello scambio tra la domanda e l'offerta di salute: il caso della cronicità. Ricerche di Psicologia **3**, 513–526 (2015)
31. Coulter, A, Ellins, J.: Interventions—A Review of the evidence. Health Foundation, London (2006)
32. McColl Kennedy, H.S.: Creative customer practices: Effects of health care customer value cocreation practices on well-being. J. Bus. Res. 55–66 (2017)
33. Rafaeli, S., Sudweeks, F.: Networked interactivity. J. Comput. Mediated Commun. **2**(4) (1997)
34. Househ, M.: The use of social media in healthcare. Stud. Health Technol. Inform. 244–248 (2013)
35. Fisher, C.J., Clayton, M.: Who gives a tweet: assessing patients' interest in the use of social media for. Worldviews Evid Based Nurs. **9**(2), 100–108 (2012)
36. Clerici, C.A., Veneroni, L., Bisogno, G., Trapuzzano, A., Ferrari, A.: Videos on rhabdomyosarcoma on YouTube: an example of the availability of information on pediatric tumors on the web. J. Patient Focused Pediatr. Hematol. Oncol. **34**(8), 329–331 (2012)
37. Zhao, J., Wang, T., Fan, X.: Patient value co-creation in online health communities: social identity effects on customer knowledge contributions and membership continuance intentions in online health communities. J. Serv. Manag. **26**(1), 72–96 (2015)
38. Yin, R.K.: Case study research: design and methods. Sage Publishing, Thousand Oaks (2014)
39. Miles, M.B., Huberman, A.M.: Qualitative Data Analysis: An Expanded Sourcebook. Sage (1994)
40. Zhang, Y., He, D., Sang, Y.: Facebook as a platform for health information and communication: a case study of a diabetes group. J. Med. Syst. **37**(3), 9942 (2013)
41. AlQarni, Z.A., Yunus, F., Househ, M.S.: Health information sharing on Facebook: an exploratory study on diabetes mellitus. J. Infec. Public Health **9**(6), 708–712 (2016)
42. Jaakkola, E., Alexander, M.: The role of customer engagement behavior in value co-creation: a service system perspective. J. Serv. Res. **17**(3), 247–261 (2014)
43. Neiger, B.L., Thackeray, R., Van Wagenen, S.A., Hanson, C.L., West, J.H., Barnes, M.D., Fagen, M.C.: Use of social media in health promotion: purposes, key performance indicators, and evaluation metrics. Health Promot. Pract. **13**(2), 159–164 (2012)
44. Korda, H., Itani, Z.: Harnessing social media for health promotion and behavior change. Health Promot. Pract. **14**(1), 15–23 (2013)
45. Moorhead, S.A., Hazlett, D.E., Harrison, L., Carroll, J.K., Irwin, A., Hoving, C.: A new dimension of health care: systematic review of the uses, benefits, and limitations of social media for health communication. J. Med. Internet Res. **15**(4) (2013)
46. Park, H., Rodgers, S., Stemmle, J.: Health organizations' use of Facebook for health advertising and promotion. J. Interact. Advertising **12**(1), 62–77 (2011)
47. Bonomi, S., Zardini, A., Rossignoli, C., Dameri, P.R.: E-health and value co-creation: the case of electronic medical record in an Italian academic integrated hospital. In International Conference on Exploring Services Science, pp. 166–175. Springer, Cham (2015, February)

Adoption of Social Media for Public Relations Professionals in Oman

Ali Al-Badi, Ali Tarhini and Hajer Al-Bolushi

Abstract Social media is considered a powerful business communication tool in nowadays businesses. Most businesses are trying to utilize this tool in order to enlarge their customer outreach. Therefore, using social media networks will provide excellent opportunities and building relationships for Public Relation Professionals. Hence, this study aims to identify the main factors that encourage Omani public relations professionals to adopt and use social media based on the Unified Theory of Acceptance and Use of Technology (UTAUT). The proposed model of social media acceptance by public relations consists of seven variables, namely, six (demographic information, performance expectancy, effort expectancy, social influence, facilitating conditions and perceived enjoyment) are independent variables and seventh (behavioral intention) is dependent variable. Data was collected using an online survey from public relations professionals from both public and private sectors in Oman. The findings show that the tendency and general awareness of social media by public relation professionals is high and many organizations use or plan to use social media for the purpose outreaching target audience.

Keywords Social media · Public relations · UTAUT · Behavioral intentions · Technology adoption · Oman

1 Introduction

The past decade has seen the rapid development of social media in business [1, 2]. Concerns have been raised by several business departments. Seiple [3] defined the public relations as "the practice of managing communication between a particular

A. Al-Badi
Gulf College, Muscat, Oman
e-mail: aalbadi@gulfcollege.edu.om

A. Tarhini (✉) · H. Al-Bolushi
Department of Information Systems, College of Economics and Political Science, Sultan Qaboos University, Muscat, Oman
e-mail: ali.tarhini@hotmail.co.uk

© Springer Nature Switzerland AG 2020
Y. Baghdadi et al. (eds.), *ICT for an Inclusive World*,
Lecture Notes in Information Systems and Organisation 35,
https://doi.org/10.1007/978-3-030-34269-2_17

organization and its publics". Namely, any organization has external publics, such as prospects, customers, media, investors, and the government, and internal publics which are the employees. So that it is important to have public relations professionals in each business [4–6]. On the contrary, social media is defined in as internet-based applications that are driven by user-participation and user-generated content to facilitate social interaction [7–9]. Social media might be considered one of the major tools in public relations field [10–16]. Al-Badi et al. [17] and Leak [18] found that the social media have the potential to market the profession more global, strategic, two-way and interactive, symmetrical or dialogical, and socially responsible. Many studies have found that there are a lot of benefits of using social media in public relations practices. Certainly, social media provides excellent opportunities for public relations professionals to build relationships with strategic public [19–21]. Truly, there is a lot of challenges might be resulted from using social media in public relations. For instance, professionals need extra time and effort to update the organization's profile, monitor their clients online, manage the negative comments and prevent the travels of rumors. But, there are opportunities that practitioners have to be aware of, such as targeting wide audience, facilitating open communication and improving business reputation [22–27]. This paper seeks to achieve the following main objective: identify the factors that encourage Omani public relations professionals to adopt and use social media based on the Unified Theory of Acceptance and Use of Technology. It will also address the following aspects: (1) the general awareness and social media usage in public relations professions, (2) determine the tendency of public relations professionals to use social media in their job practices, (3) formulate and validate a research model of technology acceptance regarding the acceptance and usage of social media.

This paper has been divided into seven sections. The second section explains the theoretical background about the UTAUT and the research factors. The third section presents the research model which shows the relationships among the research factors. The fourth section describes the data collection methods and design. The fifth section provides the analysis of collected data. The sixth section offers explanation and discussion around the research findings and results. The last section presents a conclusion of the study.

2 Theoretical Background

This section will present an overview of the Unified Theory of Acceptance and Use of Technology (UTAUT) and explain the basic modifications proposed to cater for the adoption of social media especially in public relations context.

2.1 Unified Theory of Acceptance and Use of Technology (UTAUT)

UTAUT includes four key determinants: performance expectancy, effort expectancy, social influence, and facilitating conditions that influence the behavioral intention to use a technology. In this research, we adopt these constructs and definitions from UTAUT in order to explore the acceptability and use of social media by public relations. According to UTAUT, performance expectancy, effort expectancy, and social influence are theorized to influence behavioral intention to use a technology, while behavioral intention and facilitating conditions determine the use behavior. In addition, individual variables, including age, gender, and experience are theorized to moderate various UTAUT relationships. Voluntariness, which is part of UTAUT, has been dropped because it does not fit with this context [28] (Fig. 1).

2.2 Factors Influencing Social Media Acceptance

This research will use a model that includes many determinants to examine the acceptance and use of social media. Specifically, these determinants are divided into: (1) the direct determinants of intention (performance expectancy, effort expectancy, social influence, and facilitating conditions) and (2) indirect determinant of intention (perceived enjoyment) which are both considered as independent variables. In addition, the determinant behavioral intention is considered as the dependent variable in this context. While gender, age and Experience are external demographical variables.

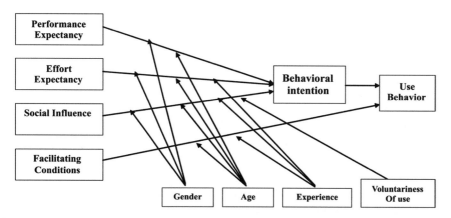

Fig. 1 The Unified Theory of Acceptance and Use of Technology

Performance Expectancy

Performance expectancy is defined in Venkatesh et al. [29] as the degree to which an individual believes that using social media will help him or her to attain gains in job performance. In a study conducted by Avery et al. [30], it was clearly highlighted that the adoption of social media by public relations professionals increases the power and influence of them within their organizations. Further, Alikilic and Atabek [10] mentioned that social media is expected to be the most important communication tool and it will improve the qualifications regarding the profession. In the study of Venkatesh and Morris [29], it was stated that gender differences indicate that men tend to be highly task-oriented and, therefore, performance expectancy, which focus on task accomplishment, are likely to be especially salient to men. In addition, Ameen and Willis [31] examined the use of mobile phones to support women's entrepreneurship in the Arab countries and found similar results to Venkatesh and Morris [29]. On the other hand, younger workers may place more importance on external rewards. Therefore, many studies of gender differences suggest that gender should be referenced to age in order to prevent the misleading.

H1: The influence of performance expectancy on behavioral intention will be moderated by gender and age, such that the effect will be stronger for men and particularly for younger men.

Effort Expectancy

Venkatesh and Morris [29] have defined the effort expectancy as the degree of ease associated with the use of social media. According to Eyrich et al. [32], the majority of public relations professionals stated that the social media have made their jobs much easier by reaching broader audiences. However, Wright and Hinson (2008) and Grunig [33] argued that using social media in public relations practices requires additional effort to manage and control the flow of information provided by publics. Specifically, some publics might harm the organization's reputation, so that the public relations have to be able to control this type of conversations. In fact, monitoring and following-up the social media communication channels is important for any modern public relations professional as stated in Seiple [3]. Effort expectancy is moderated by gender, age and experience [34]. In fact, Venkatesh and Morris [29] proposed that effort expectancy will be most salient for women, particularly those who are older and with relatively little experience with the system.

H2: The influence of effort expectancy on behavioral intention will be moderated by gender, age, and experience, such that the effect will be stronger for women, particularly younger women, and particularly at early stages of experience.

Social Influence

Social influence is the degree to which an individual perceives that important others believe he or she should use the social media, as defined in Venkatesh and Morris [29]. Three mechanisms that increase the impact of social influence on individual behavior: (1) compliance, (2) internalization, and (3) identification. The compliance mechanism causes an individual to simply alter his or her intention in response to the social pressure, while the internalization and identification altering an individual's belief structure and/or causing an individual to respond to potential social status gains [29]. A study conducted by Wang and Wang [35] suggested that women tends to be more sensitive to the influence of others and therefore social influence will be more salient when women form an intention to use social media. Nevertheless, older workers are more likely to place increased salience on social influences, with the effect declining with experience [29, 36]. Therefore, social influence will be most salient for older women who have little experience.

H3: The influence of social influence on behavioral intention will be moderated by gender, age, and experience, such that the effect will be stronger for women, particularly older women, particularly in mandatory settings in the early stages of experience.

Facilitating Conditions

Facilitating conditions are defined in Venkatesh and Morris [29] as the degree to which an individual believes that an organizational and technical infrastructure exists to support use of social media. In fact Avery, Lariscy [30], found that the high-technology organizations are among the earliest adopters of new technology tools. Furthermore, Dulle and Minishi-Majanja [37] clearly demonstrated that the age and experience were considered to play moderating roles on facilitating conditions towards usage of social media. Also, facilitating conditions have been established to impact actual usage of technology rather than behavioral intention [38]. Rather, facilitating conditions becomes insignificant in predicting intention, when both performance expectancy constructs and effort expectancy constructs are present [29]. Furthermore, older workers attach more importance to receiving help and assistance on the job. Accordingly, facilitating conditions will have a significant influence on usage behavior, when moderated by experience and age [29].

H4: The influence of facilitating conditions on usage will be moderated by age and experience, such that the effect will be stronger for older workers, particularly with increasing.

Perceived Enjoyment

In a study conducted by Park, Son [39], the perceived enjoyment was defined as the extent to which the activity of using social media is perceived to be enjoyable in its own right, aside from any performance consequences resulting from social media use. Moreover, it was defined in Liao, Tsou [40] as the degree to which a person believes that the adoption of social media is interesting and associates adoption with enjoyment. Park and Son [39] stated that people who experience enjoyment from using social media are more likely to adopt it. In fact, enjoyment lowers the cognitive burden associated with using social media, which in turn fosters favorable user perceptions, because it leads to underestimation of the level of difficulty associated with use of the social media and increases the willingness of users to put more effort into it.

H5: Perceived enjoyment positively affects behavioral intention to use social media.

Behavioral Intention

Behavioral intention is defined in [41] as "a measure of the strength of one's intention to perform a specified behavior". Venkatesh and Thong [28] found that behavioral intention has a significant positive influence on social media usage. Furthermore, Ameen and Willis [36] found that BI positively influenced actual usage of smartphone in the Arab countries. Hence, we propose the following hypothesis:

H6: Behavioral intention will have a significant positive influence on usage.

3 Research Methodology

Data were collected using an online survey using a convenience sampling techniques. More specifically, the survey was sent to 50 companies from private and public sectors. A 5 Likert scale ranging from 1-Strongly disagree to 5-Stongly agree was used to measure the items used in this study. Before the data was collected, the questionnaire has been explained on the arbitrators with a group of jurisdiction of the faculty members from number of professors of the Sultan Qaboos University, majoring in information systems, in order to ensure validity of the data collection, and after retrieving the survey items, the researcher conducting the proposed amendments of the arbitrators before being distributed to a sample study. After that, the survey was also tested with some potential respondents to check the survey items for content validity and to make sure that the tool that was used in this study actually measure what should be measured. This study seeks to identify the factors that encourage Omani public relations professionals to adopt social media based on the Unified Theory of Acceptance and Use of Technology (UTAUT). Eight hypotheses were driven from literature review as outline above and summarized in Table 1.

4 Data Analysis

Data were collected and gathered using Google forms. Google forms also provide the features of analyzing all data into graphical figures (Summary of responses) and excel sheet data (view responses). For this study, both features were used. The summary of responses was used to analyze the demographic information and organizations current status regarding the use of social media. While the view responses was used to compare and verify the eight hypotheses. Out of the returned survey, there was 66.7% Male, with age range between 20 and 50 years old. Most of the participants

Table 1 The proposed research hypotheses

Hypotheses
H1: Performance expectancy has an influence on behavioral intention
H1a: The influence of performance expectancy on behavioral intention will be moderated by gender
H1b: The influence of performance expectancy on behavioral intention will be moderated by age
H1c: The influence of performance expectancy on behavioral intention will be moderated by level of education
H2: Effort expectancy has an influence on behavioral intention
H2a: The influence of effort expectancy on behavioral intention will be moderated by gender
H2b: The influence of effort expectancy on behavioral intention will be moderated by age
H2c: The influence of effort expectancy on behavioral intention will be moderated by level of education
H3: Social influence has an influence on behavioral intention
H3a: The influence of social influence on behavioral intention will be moderated by gender
H3b: The influence of social influence on behavioral intention will be moderated by age
H3c: The influence of social influence on behavioral intention will be moderated by level of education
H4: Facilitating conditions has an influence on usage of social media
H4a: The influence of facilitating conditions on usage will be moderated by gender
H4b: The influence of facilitating conditions on usage will be moderated by age
H4c: The influence of facilitating conditions on usage will be moderated by level of education
H5: Perceived enjoyment positively affects behavioral intention to use social media
H6: Behavioral intention will have a significant positive influence on usage

were holds a Bachelor degree (73%) and working in private organizations (60%). In addition, Organizations current status regarding the use of social media in their practices has been investigated by a set of questions. (Are you interested in adopting the new technology in your work as public relation professionals, Are you using the social media in your work as Public Relation Professionals, for how many years you use social media in public relations, have you ever decided to stop suing the social media in public relation activities?) All Participants (100%) have stated that they are interested in adopting the new technology in their work as Public Relation Professionals. While (87%) of them are actually using social media in their profession. Moreover, nearly the half of respondents (40%) used the social media from 1 to 2 years and (23.3%) used it from 2 to 3 years. While only (13.3%) had stated that they used the social media from 3 to 4 years and (23.3%) used it for more than 4 years. Those organizations which use the social media for more than 4 years are mainly in the education, service and marketing sector. What is more important is all of them agreed that they never thought to stop using social media in their public relation activities. Table 2 shows the percentage of different social network have been used by these organizations.

Table 2 Networks
percentages of use

Network type	Percentage (%)
Aggregators	3.4
Blogs	31
Gaming	6.9
General social network	65.5
Live-casting	13.8
Micro-blogging/presences update	13.8
Mobile social network	65.5
New, News feeds, RSS and syndication	37.9
Online surveys	44.8
Photo-sharing	58.6
Podcasting	6.9
Presentations sharing tool	34.5
Project management, meeting and collaboration tool	44.8
Video-sharing	55.2
Virtual world	20.7
Wikis	3.4
Others	3.4

4.1   UTAUT Factors

This study aims to find the factors that encourage the Public Relation Professionals to use and adopt social media in their work. Therefore, UTAUT factors were used to build the proposed research model (Fig. 2) and research hypotheses (Table 1). To support and analyze these factors for our study, measurement items were built for the six variables (Performance expectancy, Effort expectancy, Social influence, Facilitating conditions, Perceived enjoyment, Behavioral intentions) based on Unified Theory of Acceptance and Use of Technology (UTAUT), while the demographical information are stated above. Table 3 shows the 6 variables and their measurement items in the research model. These measurements were used in the online survey which was categorized based on each variable.

Performance Expectancy

H1: Performance expectancy has an influence on behavioral intention.

The correlation between these two variables is equal to (0.436) with significance value equal to (0.016) which is less than 0.05 and therefore it can be concluded that there is a relationship between performance expectancy and behavior intention. The

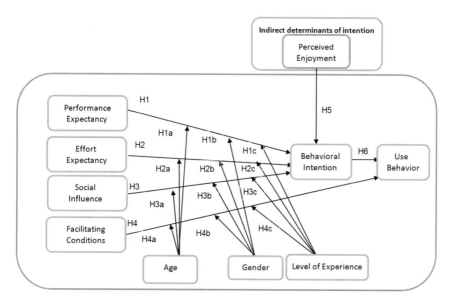

Fig. 2 The proposed theoretical framework

relation is investigated further to examine the effect of the three moderators' gender, age and level of education.

H1a: The influence of performance expectancy on behavioral intention will be moderated by gender.

The results show that performance expectancy has no significant effect on behavior intention for both sexes since the p-value is large and therefore there is no enough evidence to reject the null hypothesis

Male		Female	
F	Significance level	F	Significance level
1.567	0.225	1.545	0.318

H1b: The influence of performance expectancy on behavioral intention will be moderated by age.

Table 3 Constructs and measurement items in the research model

Construct	Items	
Performance expectancy	PE.1	I would find the social media useful in my job
	PE.2	Using the social media enables me to accomplish tasks more quickly
	PE.3	Using the social media increases my productivity
Effort expectancy	EE.1	My interaction with the social media would be clear and understandable
	EE.2	It would be easy for me to become skillful at using the social media
	EE.3	I would find the social media easy to use
Social influence	SI.1	People who influence my behavior think that I should use the social media
	SI.2	People who are important to me think that I should use the social media
	SI.3	The senior management of this business has been helpful in the use of the social media
Facilitating conditions	FC.1	I have the resources necessary to use the social media
	FC.2	I have the knowledge necessary to use the social media
	FC.3	The social media is not compatible with other media I use
Perceived enjoyment	PEN.1	I would use the social media in my profession, if I found it enjoyable
	PEN.2	I enjoy using the social media in my profession
	PEN.3	The enjoyment of using the social media in my profession encourages me to put more effort into it
Behavioral intention	BI.1	I intend to use the social media in the future
	BI.2	I predict I would use the social media in future
	BI.3	I plan to use the social media in the future

It was found that performance expectancy for those who aged above 30 years affect their behavior intention while it does not have an effect for those at smaller age.

20–29		30–49	
F	Significance level	F	Significance level
0.557	0.731	4.439	0.066

H1c: The influence of performance expectancy on behavioral intention will be moderated by level of education.

Due to the small number of respondents who have diploma or less and Master or Ph.D., the hypothesis for these levels of education could not be tested. The following table shows the results for the Bachelor degree. The result shows that there is no evidence that the influence of performance expectancy on behavioral intention will be moderated by level of education.

Bachelor	
F	Significance level
1.66	0.201

Effort Expectancy

H2: Effort expectancy has an influence on behavioral intention.
The correlation between these two variables is equal to (0.632) with significance value equal to (0.000) which is less than 0.05 and therefore it can be concluded that there is a relationship between performance expectancy and behavior intention. The relation is investigated further to examine the effect of the three moderators' gender, age and level of education.

H2a: The influence of effort expectancy on behavioral intention will be moderated by gender.
The results show that effort expectancy affects the behavior intention for male respondents only.

Male		Female	
F	Significance level	F	Significance level
3.48	0.028	1.859	0.237

H2b: The influence of effort expectancy on behavioral intention will be moderated by age

The results showed that performance expectancy for those who aged above 30 years affect their behavior intention.

20–29		30–49	
F	Significance level	F	Significance level
1.844	0.177	3.946	0.079

H2c: The influence of effort expectancy on behavioral intention will be moderated by education level

The results showed that there is no enough evidence that the relationship between effort expectancy and behavior intention is affected by level of education.

Bachelor	
F	Significance level
1.994	0.134

Social Influence

H3: Social influence has an influence on behavioral intention.

The correlation between these two variables is equal to (0.642) with significance value equal to (0.000) which is less than 0.05 and therefore it can be concluded that there is a relationship between social influence and behavior intention. The relation is investigated further to examine the effect of the three moderators' gender, age and level of education.

H3a: The influence of social influence on behavioral intention will be moderated by gender.

It was found that social influence affect behavioral intention for male respondents only.

Male		Female	
F	Significance level	F	Significance level
3.234	0.036	1.313	0.379

H3b: The influence of social influence on behavioral intention will be moderated by age.

The p-values are not significant for all age groups and therefore it can be concluded that the relationship between social influence and behavior intention is not moderated by age.

20–29		30–49	
F	Significance level	F	Significance level
1.512	0.253	3.103	0.120

H3c: The influence of social influence on behavioral intention will be moderated by level of education.

It was found that the behavior intention of respondents with Bachelor degree is influenced by their social environment at 10% significance level.

Bachelor	
F	Significance level
2.484	0.076

Facilitating Conditions

H4: Facilitating conditions have an influence on usage of social media.

The Chi squared value between these two variables is equal to (4.038) with significance value equal to (0.671) which is greater than 0.05 and therefore it can be concluded that there is no relationship between facilitating conditions and usage. The relation is investigated further to examine the effect of the three moderators' gender, age and level of education.

H4a: The influence of facilitating conditions on usage will be moderated by gender.

It was found that facilitating conditions do not have an effect on the usage for both males and females.

Male		Female	
F	Significance level	F	Significance level
2.166	0.904	4.444	0.349

H4b: The influence of facilitating conditions on usage will be moderated by age.

It was found also that facilitating conditions of all age groups have no effect on their usage.

20–29		30–49	
F	Significance level	F	Significance level
2.484	0.779	3.157	0.676

H4c: The influence of facilitating conditions on usage will be moderated by level of education.

It was found that the availability of facilitating conditions for those respondents who hold a Bachelor degree does not affect their usage.

Bachelor	
F	Significance level
3.838	0.699

Perceived Enjoyment

H5: Perceived enjoyment positively affects behavioral intention to use social media.

After applying the test, the F-value was found to be 5.957 with p-value $= 0.001$. Therefore, it can be concluded that perceived enjoyment positively affects behavior intention to use social media at 95% significance level.

Behavioral Intention

H6: Behavioral intention will have a significant positive influence on usage.

The relationship between behavior intention and the usage of social media was tested using Chi-square test since the usage here is a categorical variable. The chi-squared value was found to be (9.447) with significance level equal to (0.093) and therefore there is enough evidence to reject the null hypothesis at 10% significance level. It can be concluded that there is a relationship between behavior intention and the usage. More than the half (60%) had strongly agreed that they intend to use it and (26.7%) only agreed, while (13.3%) were neutral about it. However, (53%) of respondents predict that they will use social media in the future. While only (6.7%) disagreed. And what is more important is that more than the half had strongly agreed and agreed that they plan to use social media in the future (60% & 26%), while only (13%) were neutral.

4.2   Benefits Gained

When asked about the benefits that respondents gain from using social media, they stated that it is faster and easier to find what they look for and provide them more information in details. Some has indicated that it gives more options, free to use and it is a place where to get ideas to improve services or measuring work. What is more important that you can host anything you want and wait for feedback. In addition, it is considered as a marketing tool which can be used to engage people to be registered into company's database. Moreover, reaching more people though social media with different prospective and getting customer's feedback easily and directly. One of the respondents stated "make the internal and external stakeholders in particular and all people in general updated about my organization and build the positive repetition of my organization." Finally, it was stated that it has faster connection, wider influence and cheaper solutions. All that said and despite all the effort made to investigate the issue in hand, this study faced difficulty recruiting candidates due to the lack of response from the private sectors organizations.

5 Discussion of Findings

A study conducted by Cockerill [42] declares that the private sector is faster than the public sector in realizing the benefits of improved relationships via social media applications. Conversely, many government agencies rely on traditional communication tools which involve traditional transfer of information from the organization to publics. On the other hand, some organizations do not have a defined public relations department and they practice the public relations activities as a part of customer service or marketing activities. That is can be ensured in the study of Grunig [33] and Curtis et al. [43] who pointed out that the organizations which have a defined department for public relations are more likely to be excellent in handling the public relations practices through social media and achieve the organizational goals.

Regarding the objectives of this study, it was meant to identify the factors which encourage the adoption and use of social media by Public Relation Professionals, which it will come across in the end of this section. Moreover, the level of general awareness of public relation practitioners for using social media is high. Mostly all users know about social media importance in their career. (86.7%) of respondents agreed that they use social media, which means that 26 out of 30 organizations actually use social media in their public relation activities. While (23%) are using it for more than 4 years now. What is more important is that no one of these organizations want to stop using social media, if they do so it would be like separating themselves from the world. The Tendency to use social media by public relation practitioners is high as the findings that (86.7%) intend to use it in the future and (86%) plan to use it. So both findings show high tendency to use social media in their organizations. In addition, to verify the suggested hypotheses, we used the measurement items and the findings results to compare, analyse and confirm these hypotheses.

H1: Performance expectancy has an influence on behavioral intention.

It was found that there is a relationship between performance expectancy and behavior intention.

The relation is investigated further to examine the effect of the three moderators' gender, age and level of education. The results show that performance expectancy has no significant effect on behavior intention for both genders. It was found also that performance expectancy for those who aged above 30 years affect their behavior intention while it does not have an effect for those at smaller age. In addition to this, it can be concluded that the influence of performance expectancy on behavioral intention will be moderated by level of education.

The data shows positive results. More than the half of respondents were males (66.7%) and their ages were varying from 20 to 39 years. (43.3%) of respondents were 20–29 years while the other (23.4%) were 30–39 years. As they become older their performance expectancy gets lower. The younger males 20–29 years old choices were strongly 'agree' to the statements that indicate the usefulness, accomplishment, and productivity for using social media. While the older male 30–39 chose only to agree and some of them were neutral.

H2: Effort expectancy has an influence on behavioral intention.

It can be concluded that there is a relationship between performance expectancy and behavioral intention. The relation is investigated further to examine the effect of the three moderators' gender, age and level of education. The results show that effort expectancy affects the behavior intention for male respondents only. It was found also that performance expectancy for those who aged above 30 years affect their behavior intention and that level of education does not affect the relationship between effort expectancy and behavior intention.

H3: Social influence has an influence on behavioral intention.

It can be concluded that there is a relationship between social influence and behavior intention. The relation is investigated further to examine the effect of the three moderators' gender, age and level of education. It was found that social influence affect behavioral intention for male respondents only. Furthermore, it can be concluded that the relationship between social influence and behavior intention is not moderated by age and that the behavior intention of respondents with Bachelor degree is influenced by their social environment.

Older women 30–39 were only (6.6%) out of (33.3%) and the other (26.6%) of responders were 20–29 years. However, all respondents were educated and have an academicals degree. So we conclude that all participants are fully educated of social media importance in the work place. So the experience had an affect while the gender and Age didn't have any major effect on the choices of the respondents. The Male and Female whether they were older or younger, the perception of social influence were similar. The figures indicate that (40%) strongly agreed and the other (43%) only agreed, which means more than the half agrees that family and friends affect them to use social media. In addition, (56% & 33%) strongly agreed and only agree respectively that their managers think they should use social media in their jobs.

H4: Facilitating conditions have an influence on usage.

It can be concluded that there is a relationship between facilitating conditions and behavior intention. The relation is investigated further to examine the effect of the three moderators' gender, age and level of education. It was found that facilitating conditions have an effect on the behavioral intentions for both gender and that conditions on usage will be moderated by age It was found also that facilitating conditions of all age groups have an effect on their behavioral intention and that the availability of facilitating conditions for those respondents who hold a Bachelor degree affects their behavior intention.

Most of the respondents agreed that necessary resources they need to use social media are available for them in the work place. (50%) strongly agreed and (40%) just agreed to the later statement. Moreover, (86.6%) agreed that they have the knowledge needed for using social media. However, few people, (6.7%) indicated that they face difficulties to use social media and (16.7%) were neutral whether they find it difficult or easy to use. We can conclude that people vary on how to use social media. It may be resulted of the type of social media network used or experience and age as stated before. But the majority does not have any difficulties so we can say that this hypothesis is right.

H5: Perceived enjoyment positively affects behavioral intention to use social media.

It was found that the perceived enjoyment positively affects behavior intention to use social media at 95% significance level. The first statement was "I would use the social media in my profession, if I found it enjoyable". The second statement was "I enjoy using the social media in my profession" and the third one was "The enjoyment of using the social media in my profession encourages me to put more effort into it". As it was more than the half was strongly 'agree' in the 3 statements, we can say that this hypothesis is true and it does affect individual behavioral intention to use social media.

6   Concluding Remarks

Through this paper we raise the issue "Adoption of Social Media for Public Relation Professionals in Oman". We studied this issue in different aspect from the definition of Public relation till the challenges and opportunities gained. Moreover, an Online Survey was conducted in Omani organization from private and public sector. Then an analysis for the findings according to the objectives of this study was done. Though our observation, we found that the tendency and general awareness of Omani public relation practitioners to use social media is high. Moreover, there are some factors that affect the behavioral intentions of individuals to use social media, which are the preference expectancy, social influence and facilitating conditions, which the later can be affected by outside factors like age, gender and experience. In addition, there is an indirect determinate of intentions such perceived enjoyment. Each one has its own effect on Public relation practitioners as have been stated in the analysis section. To conclude, the Omani Public Relation Professionals are aware of the benefit and opportunities that social media gives, that why their positive responses were high.

References

1. Al-Badi, A., Tarhini, A., Al-Sawaei, S.: Utilizing social media to encourage domestic tourism in Oman. Int. J. Bus. Manag. **12**(4), 84–94 (2017)
2. Alalwan, A.A., Rana, N.P., Algharabat, R., Tarhini, A.: A systematic review of extant literature in social media in the marketing perspective. In: Conference on e-Business, e-Services and e-Society. Springer (2016)
3. Seiple, P.: How to Leverage Social Media for Public Relations Success. Using Social Media to Generate Media Coverage and Improve Brand Sentimen (n.d)
4. Al-Aufi, A.S., Al-Harthi, I., AlHinai, Y., Al-Salti, Z., Al-Badi, A.: Citizens' perceptions of government's participatory use of social media. Transforming Gov.: People Process Policy **11**(2), 174–194 (2017)
5. McDonald, P., Thompson, P.: Social media (tion) and the reshaping of public/private boundaries in employment relations. Int. J. Manag. Rev. **18**(1), 69–84 (2016)
6. Barnett, G.A., et al.: Measuring international relations in social media conversations. Gov. Inf. Q. **34**(1), 37–44 (2017)
7. Waters, R.D., Burnett, E., Lamm, A., Lucas, J.: Engaging stakeholders through social networking: how nonprofit organizations are using Facebook. Public Relat. Rev. **35**(2), 102–106 (2009)
8. Shoemaker, D., Natsev, P., Whalen, T., Xie, L.: Social Media Use by Government: From the Routine to the Critical. Minnesota University (2011)
9. Agostino, D., Arena, M., Catalano, G., Erbacci, A.: Public engagement through social media: the spending review experience. Public Money Manag **37**(1), 55–62 (2017)
10. Alikilic, O., Atabek, U.: Social media adoption among Turkish public relations professionals: A survey of practitioners. Public Relat. Rev. **38**(1), 56–63 (2012)
11. Al-Mukhaini, E.M., Al-Qayoudhi, W.S., Al-Badi, A.H.: Adoption of social networking in education: A study of the use of social networks by higher education students in Oman. J. Int. Educ. Res. **10**(2), 143 (2014)
12. Al-Salti, Z., Al-Badi, A., Al-Aufi, A., Al-Harthi, I., Al-Hinai, Y.: The presence of Omani government agencies on social media: an exploratory study. In: Proceedings of 2016 International Conference on Business and Information, 2–4 Feb 2016, Bali, Indonesia (2016)
13. Allagui, I., Breslow, H.: Social media for public relations: lessons from four effective cases. Public Relat. Rev. **42**(1), 20–30 (2016)
14. Moon, B.B., Rhee, Y., Yang, S.-U.: Developing public's information transmitting behavior (ITB) model in public relations: a cross-national study. J. Public Relat. Res. **28**(1), 4–18 (2016)
15. Protess, D., McCombs, M.E.: Agenda Setting: Readings on Media, Public Opinion, and Policymaking. Routledge (2016)
16. Charest, F., Bouffard, J., Zajmovic, E.: Public relations and social media: deliberate or creative strategic planning. Public Relat. Rev. **42**(4), 530–538 (2016)
17. Al-Badi, A.H., Al Hinai, Y.S., Al-Salti, Z.S., Al-Harthi, I.S., Al-Aufi, A.S.: Exploring the use of social media by governments worldwide. In: 25th International Business Information Management Association Conference-Innovation Vision 2020: From Regional Development Sustainability to Global Economic Growth in International Business Information Management Association, IBIMA (2015)
18. Leak, T.: Likes, Posts, and Tweets Oh My: Social Media and the Practice of Excellence in Public Relations Within Professional Sports Organizations. (Doctor of Philosophy), Georgia State University. http://scholarworks.gsu.edu/communication_diss/71/ (2016)
19. Wright, D.K., Hinson, M.D.: How blogs and social media are changing public relations and the way it is practiced. Public Relat. J. **2**(2), 1–21 (2008)
20. Cheng, Y., Huang, Y.-H.C., Chan, C.M.: Public relations, media coverage, and public opinion in contemporary China: testing agenda building theory in a social mediated crisis. Telematics Inform. **34**(3), 765–773 (2017)

21. Criado, J.I., Rojas-Martín, F., Gil-Garcia, J.R.: Enacting social media success in local public administrations: an empirical analysis of organizational, institutional, and contextual factors. Int. J. Public Sect. Manag. **30**(1), 31–47 (2017)
22. Gillin, P.: New media, new influencers and implications for the public relations profession. J. New Commun. Res. **2**(2), 1–10 (2008)
23. Al-Zedjali, K.H., Al-Harrasi, A.S., Al-Badi, A.H.: Motivations for using social networking sites by college students for educational purposes. World academy of science, engineering and technology. Int. J. Soc. Behav. Educ. Econ. Bus. Ind. Eng. **8**(8), 2577–2580 (2014)
24. Al-Harrasi, A.S., Al-Badi, A.H.: The impact of social networking: a study of the influence of smartphones on college students. Contemp. Issues Educ. Res. **7**(2), 129–136 (2014)
25. Guth, D.W., Marsh, C.: Public Relations: A Values-Driven Approach. Pearson (2016)
26. AlHinai, Y.S., Al-Badi, A., Al-Harthi, I., Al-Aufi, A., Al-Salti, Z.: Rethinking IT-governance: analytical review of IT governance for social media based on the COBIT standard. Int. J. Serv. Econ. Manag. **7**(2–4), 124–153 (2016)
27. Hon, L.C., Grunig. J.E.: Guidelines for Measuring Relationships in Public Relations, pp. 107–108. Gainesville (2017)
28. Venkatesh, V., Thong, J.Y., Xu, X.: Consumer acceptance and use of information technology: extending the unified theory of acceptance and use of technology. MIS Q. **36**(1), 157–178 (2012)
29. Venkatesh, V., Morris, M.G., Davis, G.B., Davis, F.D.: User acceptance of information technology: toward a unified view. MIS Q. 425–478 (2003)
30. Avery, E., et al.: Diffusion of social media among public relations practitioners in health departments across various community population sizes. J. Public Relat. Res. **22**(3), 336–358 (2010)
31. Ameen, N.A., Willis, R.: The use of mobile phones to support women's entrepreneurship in the Arab countries. Int. J. Gend. Entrepreneurship **8**(4), 424–445 (2016)
32. Eyrich, N., Padman, M.L., Sweetser, K.D.: PR practitioners' use of social media tools and communication technology. Public Relat. Rev. **34**(4), 412–414 (2008)
33. Grunig, J.E.: Paradigms of global public relations in an age of digitalisation. PRism **6**(2), 1–19 (2009)
34. Ameen, N., Willis, R.: Towards closing the gender gap in Iraq: understanding gender differences in smartphone adoption and use. Inf. Technol. Dev. 1–26 (2018)
35. Wang, H.-Y., Wang, S.-H.: User acceptance of mobile internet based on the unified theory of acceptance and use of technology: Investigating the determinants and gender differences. Soc. Behav. Pers. Int. J. **38**(3), 415–426 (2010)
36. Ameen, N., Willis, R., Shah, M.H.: An examination of the gender gap in smartphone adoption and use in Arab countries: a cross-national study. Comput. Hum. Behav. **89**, 148–162 (2018)
37. Dulle, F.W., Minishi-Majanja, M.: The suitability of the Unified Theory of Acceptance and Use of Technology (UTAUT) model in open access adoption studies. Inf. Dev. **27**(1), 32–45 (2011)
38. Harfouche, A., Robbin, A.: Inhibitors and enablers of public e-services in Lebanon. J. Organ. End User Comput. **24**(3), 45–68 (2012)
39. Park, Y., Son, H., Kim, C.: Investigating the determinants of construction professionals' acceptance of web-based training: an extension of the technology acceptance model. Autom. Constr. **22**, 377–386 (2012)
40. Liao, C.-H., Tsou, C.-W., Shu, Y.-C.: The roles of perceived enjoyment and price perception in determining acceptance of multimedia-on-demand. Int. J. Bus. Inf. **3**(1) (2008)
41. Abdulwahab, L., Dahalin, Z.M.: A conceptual model of Unified Theory of Acceptance and Use of Technology (UTAUT) modification with management effectiveness and program effectiveness in context of telecentre. Afr. Sci. **11**(4), 267–275 (2010)
42. Cockerill, C.H.: Exploring social media obstacles and opportunities within public agencies: lessons from the Ohio Division of Wildlife. Int. J. Bus. Soc. Sci. **4**(2) (2013)
43. Curtis, L., et al.: Adoption of social media for public relations by nonprofit organizations. Public Relat. Rev. **36**(1), 90–92 (2010)

Impact of Innovative Technologies in Developing Countries

An Insight into Concepts of Technology Transfer and Its Role in the National Innovation System of Latvia

Viktorija Stepanova

Abstract The modern world is based on data and information flows, and information and communication technologies (ICT) are ubiquitous in the modern digital age. They are tailored to meet the needs of different industries. Technology transfer is an essential factor in the national innovation system of the country and in the society as a whole. It contributes to sustainable development, improvement and knowledge building; moreover, it is one of the main drivers of growth and competitiveness. In the authors' efforts to improve the innovation indicators of Latvia in terms of knowledge and technology results, statistical data have been aggregated and scientific literature reviewed with the aim of evaluating relevant concepts of technology transfer, as well as its role in the national innovation system of Latvia. Through the research conducted and the results obtained, the authors of the research have substantiated the need to develop a new information technology model based on information technology standards, marketing and commercialisation processes, as well as technology transfer handbooks.

Keywords Technology transfer · Commercialisation · Information and communication technologies

1 Introduction

"Technology transfer is the transfer of certain technologies (knowledge, production skills, facilities) from one technology user to another; technology developed in one place is exploited in another place with the aim of creating new products, processes or services" [1]. Technology transfer and scientific and technical cooperation are the basis for the country's economic development and rapid growth. The transformation of scientific knowledge into innovation is one of the aspects of the innovation process,

V. Stepanova (✉)
Faculty of Computer Science and Information Technology, Riga Technical University, Riga, Latvia
e-mail: viktorija.stepanova@rtu.lv

© Springer Nature Switzerland AG 2020
Y. Baghdadi et al. (eds.), *ICT for an Inclusive World*,
Lecture Notes in Information Systems and Organisation 35,
https://doi.org/10.1007/978-3-030-34269-2_18

during which innovation evolves from an idea to a specific product ready to be introduced into the intended market.

The research approach that was followed for the purpose of this article was the data collection and data analysis. According to an inductive approach, the author decided to find the answer to the specific research questions:

Question 1: What are key terms and concepts in technology transfer?
Question 2: What are the main innovation indicators and factors that influence the technology transfer process?
Question 3: What is the role of technology transfer in the innovation life cycle?
Question 4: What is the existing state of innovation in the world?
Question 5: What is the role of Latvia in the subject of innovation and technology transfer?

Within the framework of the research, the Global Innovation Index (GII) and economic indicators such as public expenditure on R&D have been aggregated, the concepts of technology transfer have been defined, and the role of technology transfer in the innovation life cycle has been identified.

2 Related Research

To enable the effective functioning of the innovation system in a country, i.e., where new companies are operating and being established, the exchange of knowledge and experience takes place among research organisations, universities and industry, there is a need for a balanced interaction of the following factors:

- Education;
- Research (science, creativity);
- Business;
- Financial system;
- Legislation.

The operation of the national innovation system is clearly reflected by the Global Innovation Index (GII), which covers more than 100 countries and is based on the comparison of countries according to the seven criteria groups or pillars [2], taking into account factors influencing 81 parameters. The GII is designed to facilitate understanding of the country's innovation policy and its results, which allows assessing the overall situation and comparing the results with the indicators of other countries. The GII report provides a comprehensive collection of data on education indicators, research and development outcomes, lending, investment, creative industry products and services.

As far as technology transfer is concerned, it is important to evaluate the sixth pillar of GII "Knowledge and Technology Outcomes", which covers the following factors that characterise innovation:

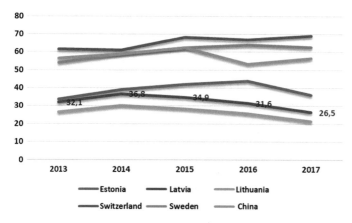

Fig. 1 Global innovation index. Knowledge and technology outcomes. Pillar 6

- Knowledge creation, which includes the number of national patents, the number of patent applications, the number of scientific publications and the number of citations;
- Impact of knowledge, which includes statistics on labour productivity growth in micro- and macro-economics, number of new enterprises and total production output;
- Knowledge diffusion, which includes data on the high-tech sector: ICT service exports, revenues from royalty and license fees, as well as foreign direct investment.

However, the statistics do not indicate that Latvia is moving in an innovative way (see Fig. 1).

The research conducted has shown that Switzerland, Sweden and China have achieved better results in terms of knowledge and technology over the past five years, while Latvia has been ranked 48th out of 127 countries in the world in 2017.

In the report drawn up by the European Commission [3], one of the main causes is the public funding for research intensity.

The state does not invest sufficient funds to conduct research in a wide range of disciplines. Lack of funding hinders the emergence of new discoveries, publishing of scientific articles and introduction of new products into the market.

According to the Europe 2020 headline target [4],—to invest 3% of the European Union's gross domestic product (GDP) in R&D,—Latvia has set a quantified target of increasing investment in R&D to 1.5% of GDP in Latvia by 2020, and up to 3% by 2030. In 2015, this indicator was 0.6% (see Fig. 2) of the GDP in Latvia, which was considerably lower than the average of the European Union member states over the last five years, i.e., 1.81 (see Fig. 3).

A low percentage of government funding leads to very low scientific performance and, in general, adversely affects the economic growth and economic development of Latvia.

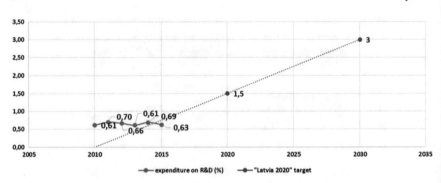

Fig. 2 Latvia's expenditure on R&D (%) from 2010 to 2030

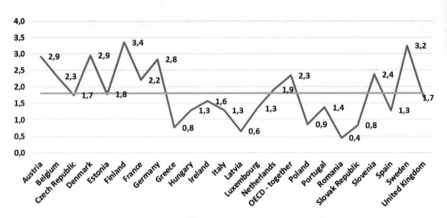

Fig. 3 Average % of GDP from 2010 to 2015 in the EU Member States

It is therefore necessary to raise additional financial resources in order to re-establish the existing situation and find ways to improve the innovation performance.

3 An Insight into the Concepts of Information Transfer

ICT industry is rapidly developing all over the world and in Europe, and many achievements directly depend on a technological solution that addresses the problem faster by saving time, money and energy. Often entrepreneurs cannot afford to invest their money and time in developing a new solution and experimentation. At the same time, Latvian higher education institutions and developers of new information technologies are struggling to find buyers for the prototype of the information system. Scientists in most cases have no knowledge of business, marketing and commercialisation processes.

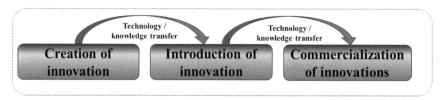

Fig. 4 Innovation life cycle

Therefore, in addition to looking for financial resources, it is necessary to study the concepts of technology transfer and find the way (in a model) for its activation.

Thus, the technology transfer should be considered one of the aspects of the innovation life cycle (see Fig. 4).

The concept of innovation life cycle is the process of transforming scientific knowledge into innovation that can be illustrated as a series of events, in which innovation matures from an idea to a certain product, technology or service and is distributed in practical applications.

Thus, the creation and implementation of innovations in the market directly involves the transfer of technology and knowledge from one participant to others (technology developers, technology owners, intermediaries, government agencies, investors and potential buyers).

By analysing various sources [5–14], the following common technology transfer components (elements) can be identified:

- the transfer object;
- at least two individuals or functional entities involved in the technology transfer process;
- the transfer method or means for information transfer;
- environmental factors and obstacles that may affect the technology transfer process.

The general technology transfer model is represented in Fig. 5 and can serve as a basis for the development of information technology transfer model and further practical application.

The successful and productive technology transfer process is influenced by several factors:

- *Participants' motivation*, which encourages a person to set aims and tasks, make efforts and show a particular attitude towards work;
- *The quality of technology*, which determines the ability to meet end user requirements and creates a positive image of the technology developer;
- *Marketing activities* that promote the distribution, sale and introduction of the technology into the market;
- *Provision of human resources* to direct the technology process towards the aim;
- *Budget*—the revenue and expenditure plan drawn up to achieve the aim of technology transfer;

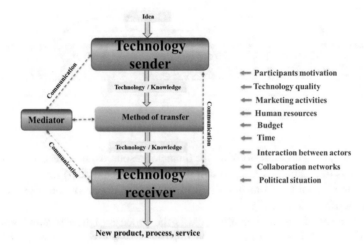

Fig. 5 General technology transfer model

- *Lead time* that determines the duration of the technology transfer process from aim setting to technology transfer;
- *Interaction among participants*—the interaction of people that may lead to changes in the status;
- *Collaborative networks* that provide a secure communication channel for information exchange and the fastest access to new knowledge;
- *Political situation* that determines the role of technology transfer in the country and its support.

The four most common technology transfer scenarios can be distinguished, where different participants/agents play the role of the initiator of the technology transfer process (see Table 1).

Two types of communication models can be distinguished from the described technology transfer scenarios [15]:

- *Linear communication model* (one way), in which the sender of the information encodes knowledge in a certain way and sends it to the recipient using any channel (speech, written message, etc.). This model envisages a one-way communication process with no feedback and in case the recipient receives a message, communication is considered successful. In the linear communication model, the scientific literature and teaching aids, standards, patent descriptions, encyclopaedias etc. serve as a transfer object. This model does not typically envisage revenue generation from the technology transfer process.
- *Interactive communication model*, in which the main element is feedback and the recipient's reaction to a message. In interactive models, communication is taking place in a circle: the beginning of each new circle is the end point of the previous cycle and the sender of the information changes with the recipient all the time. In an interactive communication model, an invention patent, design, license, computer

Table 1 Technology transfer scenarios

	Initiator	Description of technology transfer scenario
1st	Technology developer (technology provider)	First, a product or service is developed. Then the ways to commercialise the product are being sought. The developer him/herself is looking for alternatives to sell his/her invention and encourages the end-user (technology receiver) to use it This scenario involves a large amount of knowledge from the technology provider and a small amount of knowledge from the technology receiver. Technology developer can also involve a third party (intermediary) in the transfer process, who can accelerate this process using his/her own experience and contact networks
2nd	Technology end user (technology receiver)	Some organisations need a new solution to fulfil their functions and, therefore, are looking for a developer who could create it. This scenario assumes that the customer has certain requirements and a large amount of knowledge about the end product, but the developer collects it during the lead time and fulfils the requirements of the customer. Similar to the first scenario, this scenario does not preclude the intermediary's participation in the process
3rd	Intermediary (broker)	An intermediary or a broker implements a dialogue between technology developers and end-users. This scenario is directly related to the cooperation that takes place between the parties involved. The intermediary carries out the demand/supply market analysis and constructs his/her database for further transmission of information and initiation of technology transfer. An intermediary usually has a small amount of knowledge about technology, but has good communication skills and a large contact base, which the majority of technology developers often do not have
4th	Driving force of technology	The driving force of technology is the person who creates a technology transfer cycle from technology creation to its transfer to the end-user, including marketing managers, potential users, developers, investors and other participants involved in the process. The role of the driving force of technology can be played by the state through the introduction of a national innovation programme or strategy

prototype, materials for product development and any other technical knowledge can serve as a transfer object. This model is typically used to generate revenue from the technology transfer process.

4 ICT Technology Transfer

To promote technology, transfer and scientific performance for economic growth and national economy development, one of the solutions is to focus on the sector of Information and Communication Technology, which is rapidly developing world-wide and in Europe. As the modern world is based on data and information flows, information systems are ubiquitous in the modern digital age. They are tailored to meet the needs of different industries. Examples of such systems are business infor-mation systems, management information systems, transaction processing systems, geographic information systems and others. The factsheet issued by the European Commission shows that 75% of Europeans believe that digitisation has a positive impact on the economy, and 44% of current employees think that their work can be done at least partially by robots or artificial intelligence [16]. Recent studies [17] demonstrate that in 2016 more than 8 million people from the 28 EU Member States were employed as ICT specialists, accounting for 3.7% of total employment (see Figs. 6 and 7).

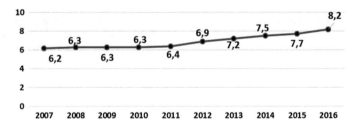

Fig. 6 Number of ICT professionals in the 28 EU Member States

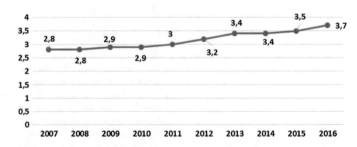

Fig. 7 The proportion of ICT professionals per total persons employed in the EU Member States

Moreover, the achievements in the Digital Single Market (DSM), which aim at eliminating national barriers to online transactions and have been recognised as one of the 10 political priorities by the European Commission since 2015 [18], could contribute to € 415 billion per year (GDP) to the economy of the EU 28 Member States and create hundreds of thousands of new jobs. At present, the ICT sector and the European Digital Agenda were recognised as one of the seven pillars of the Europe 2020 strategy [19].

In order to accelerate the development of information technology and its commercialisation, it is necessary to increase the income of research organisations and to promote cooperation between higher education institutions and industry by developing a new technology transfer model aimed at accelerating and improving the technology transfer process taking into account environmental factors and conditions.

To generate income from the technology transfer process, an interactive communication model should be used, where the prototype of computer systems can serve as a transfer object, research organisations play the initiator's role, and the end-user represents the industry. New information technology transfer models should be based on information technology standards, marketing and commercialisation processes and technology transfer handbooks. The development of models should combine knowledge of the creation, implementation and commercialisation of information technology for further practical application. For this purpose, within the framework of the further research the authors will develop a process-oriented information technology transfer model that will allow testing, evaluating and completing IT development and commercialisation processes before successful commercialisation and gaining profitability from the introduction of IT solution into the market.

5 Conclusions

As a result of the research, it has been concluded that for the efficient operation of the innovation system in the country the technology transfer process should be promoted from research institutions to the industry, with particular attention drawn to the ICT sector, which could generate € 415 billion per year (GDP) in the economy of the 28 EU countries and create hundreds of thousands of new jobs.

Within the framework of the research, the information on the main innovation indicators and factors that influence the technology transfer process has been summarised and structured. Using the results obtained in the research, the authors have substantiated the need to develop new information technology models based on information technology standards, marketing and commercialisation processes and technology transfer handbooks. For this purpose, the authors' further research will be devoted to the development of process-oriented information technology transfer model that will allow testing, evaluating and completing IT development and commercialisation processes before successful commercialisation and gaining profitability from the introduction of IT solution into the market.

Acknowledgements This study was partly supported by Latvian National Research Programme "Cyber-physical systems, ontologies and biophotonics for safe & smart city and society" (SOPHIS) Project No. 2 "Ontology-based knowledge engineering technologies suitable for web environment".

References

1. Latvian National Development Plan 2007–2013. In: Program for the Promotion of Business Competitiveness and Innovation for 2007–2013, National Program for the Development of SMEs, Riga (2006) (in Latvian)
2. Cornell University, INSEAD, and WIPO: The Global Innovation Index 2016: Winning with Global Innovation. ANNEX 1. In: The Global Innovation Index (GII) Conceptual Framework. pp. 49–56. Geneva (2016)
3. European Commission: Commission Staff Working Document, Country Report Latvia 2016. Brussels (2016)
4. European Commission: Communication from the Commission. Europa 2020 Strategies for smart, sustainable and inclusive growth. Brussels (2010) (in Latvian)
5. Goodman, J.: Industry partners: a technology transfer model for academia. In: OCEAN 75 Conference Proceedings, pp. 850–854. IEEE (1975)
6. Herron, C., Hicks, C.: The transfer of selected lean manufacturing techniques from Japanese automotive manufacturing into general manufacturing (UK) through change agents. In: Robotics and Computer-Integrated Manufacturing, vol. 24, Issue No. 4, pp. 524–531. Elsevier (2008)
7. Rao, E., Remer, J., Bauer, D.: A model for development, transition and technology transfer leading to commercialization of security technology. In: International Carnahan Conference on Security Technology (ICCST) Procceedings, pp. 1–5. IEEE (2015)
8. Taylor, H., Artman, E., Woelfer, J.P.: Information technology project risk management: Bridging the gap between research and practice. In: Journal of Information Technology 27(1), pp. 17–34. JIT Palgrave Macmillan (2012)
9. Duarte, C., Gorschek, T.: Technology transfer—requirements Engineering research to industrial practice an open (ended) debate. In: 2015 IEEE 23rd International Requirements Engineering Conference (RE) Proceedings, pp. 414–415, IEEE (2015)
10. Diebold, P., Vetro, A., Fernandez, D.: An exploratory study on technology transfer in software engineering. In: 2015 ACM/IEEE International Symposium on Empirical Software Engineering and Measurement (ESEM) Procceedings, pp. 86–95. IEEE (2015)
11. Wiratmadja, I.I., Sunaryo, I., Syafrian, R.N., Govindaraju, R.: The measurement of humanware readiness in a technology transfer process: case study in an electrical machinery company. In: 2014 2nd International Conference on Technology, Informatics, Management, Engineering & Environment Procceedings, pp. 32–325. IEEE (2015)
12. Wang, B.: Requirements traceability technologies selection for industry. In: IEEE 24th International Requirements Engineering Conference Procceedings, pp. 450–455. IEEE (2016)
13. Sun, Q., Feng, H.: innovating the new model of academy-locality cooperation. In: International Conference on Industrial Economics System and Industrial Security Engineering (IEIS) Procceedings, pp. 1–4. IEEE (2016)
14. Saini, A.K., Khurana, V.K.: ICT based communication systems as enabler for technology transfer. In: 3rd International Conference on Computing for Sustainable Global Development (INDIACom) Procceedings, pp. 90–99. IEEE (2016)
15. Grushevitskaya, T.G., Popkov, V.D., Sadokhin, A.P.: Fundamentals of Intercultural Communication: A Textbook for High Schools. http://www.countries.ru/library/intercult/mkmod.htm (in Russian)

16. European Commission: Digital Single Market: Commission calls for swift adoption of key proposals and maps out challenges ahead. https://ec.europa.eu/digital-single-market/en/news/digital-single-market-commission-calls-swift-adoption-key-proposals-and-maps-out-challenges
17. Eurostat: Employed ICT specialists—total. http://appsso.eurostat.ec.europa.eu/nui/show.do?dataset=isoc_sks_itspt&lang=en
18. European Commission: Commission and its priorities. 10 priorities. https://ec.europa.eu/commission/priorities/digital-single-market_en
19. European Commission: Strategy. Digital Single Market. Europe 2020 strategy. https://ec.europa.eu/digital-single-market/en/europe-2020-strategy

Moderating Effects of Age and Gender on Social Commerce Adoption Factors the Cameroonian Context

Paul Cedric Nitcheu Tcheuffa, Jean Robert Kala Kamdjoug and Samuel Fosso Wamba

Abstract The popularity and massive adoption of Web-based social networking has given rise to new opportunities for online commerce. Researchers and companies have been recently paying much attention to social commerce, which can be seen as a combination e-commerce and social media. And such euphoria has spanned virtually all regions of the world, including African countries. It is in this light that this paper aims to determine the factors influencing the adoption of social commerce in Cameroon. To this effect, the authors have designed a research model inspired by TAM2 and the trust theory. Data were collected from 404 internet users in Cameroon. Our results found that the perceived ease of use, perceived usefulness and trust have a significant effect on the intention to use social commerce. In contrast, concerning the moderating effect, only the group age is being proved to have a significant effect specifically on the relationship between perceived usefulness and the intention to use social commerce. This study ends with the implications for practice and research.

Keywords Social commerce · Trust · TAM2 · Cameroon

1 Introduction

The concept of social commerce (S-commerce) emerged in 2005 as part of the growing use of social networks and many other social media sites for commercial purposes [1]. It can be seen as a new form of e-commerce that involves a comprehensive

P. C. Nitcheu Tcheuffa · J. R. Kala Kamdjoug (✉)
Université Catholique d'Afrique Centrale, FSSG, GRIAGES, Yaoundé, Cameroun
e-mail: jrkala@gmail.com

P. C. Nitcheu Tcheuffa
e-mail: paulnitcheu5@gmail.com

S. Fosso Wamba
Toulouse Business School, Toulouse, France
e-mail: s.fosso-wamba@tbs-education.fr

Université Fédérale de Toulouse Midi-Pyrénées, 20 Boulevard Lascrosses, 31068 Toulouse, France

© Springer Nature Switzerland AG 2020　　　　263
Y. Baghdadi et al. (eds.), *ICT for an Inclusive World*,
Lecture Notes in Information Systems and Organisation 35,
https://doi.org/10.1007/978-3-030-34269-2_19

approach to social media in order to provide assistance in the context of buying and selling products and services online [2]. In this context, social commerce is a technology imposing itself on all companies and organizations seeking to survive in an increasingly competitive commercial environment; and Cameroon-based companies should follow this trend and spare no effort for their competitiveness, brand image and sustainability.

InternetLives study of 2016 make evidence that Cameroon totals about 4.3 million Internet users for a penetration rate estimated at 18%, which seems very much higher than the statistics of 2011 where the number of internet users was estimated at 1.055 million with a penetration rate of 5% [3]. The growing use of the Web can also be observed through social networks. Indeed, in 2017, about 2.8 million people are social media users in Cameroon [4], compared to 1.5 million in 2016 [5].

The main objective of our research is to determine the factors that influence the adoption of social commerce by consumers. To achieve this objective, we are going to answer the two following research questions: (1) what are the key determinants of social commerce in Cameroon? (2) What are the moderating effects of age and gender on social commerce adoption? It should be noted that this subject has been treated by many researchers, like Beyari and Abareshi [6], inter alia. Greater part of our background research therefore draws on most of these studies and proposes a research model inspired by TAM 2 [5] to which we add the variable Trust and moderating variables such as Age and Gender, in order to highlight difference between categories. The experience field for this study was acquired by interviewing users of social commerce in Douala and Yaoundé, the main cities of Cameroon.

2 Theoretical Background

Because it is characterized by a combination of economic, social, and technological aspects, social commerce has been at a center of different research disciplines, from information systems to marketing, or sociology [7]. In this study, we adopt the definition of Wang and Zhang and consider social commerce as a form of e-commerce that combines commercial activities and social media to enable consumers to actively participate, interact and communicate in the sale and purchase of products and services online [8].

Drawing on these prior studies, we propose the research model below (Fig. 1). The variables used are as follows: Perceived ease of used, Perceived usefulness, Image, Intention to use from TAM 2, Trust from Hajli [9], Hasan Beyari and Ahmad Abareshi [6]. We have added to our research model the moderating effect of age and gender to test their variability on the intention to use social commerce (Table 1).

As social commerce is considered a subset of electronic commerce, which consumers usually associate with technology use, theories explaining technology acceptance might be adapted to social commerce acceptance explanation [13]. Behavioral

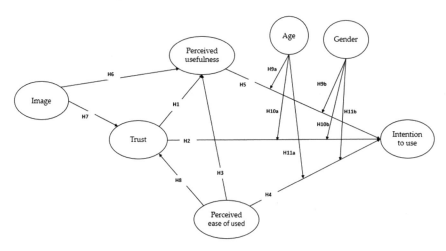

Fig. 1 Research model

theories such as the Theory of Reasoned Action (TRA), the Theory of Planned Behavior (TPB), the Technology Acceptance Model (TAM) or Unified Theory of Acceptance and Use of Technology (UTAUT) have been often used by many researchers to help understand the adoption of social commerce [10, 13, 14]. Nevertheless, our research is based mainly on the theory of trust and the technology acceptance model by Venkatesh and Davis [5].

The theory of trust studies the behavioral and computational trust among people, organizations, computers and networks [15]. Trust is a central issue in most economic and social transactions, especially in an online context where there may be lots of uncertainty [16]. Indeed, with the increase of social technologies and interconnectivity of people on the Internet, there is a need for some sort of trust and security that will allow the two parties to reduce their perceived risk in transactions [17]. A good number of studies show that trust has a close connection with the intention to use social commerce [6, 18]. According to H. Beyari and A. Abareshi, a consumer with a successful online shopping experience usually enjoys a high level of trust and will likely repeat the experience. Similarly, a lower level of trust makes a customer less likely to shop online [6]. All of these reasons led us to regard trust as a factor that could influence the adoption of social commerce. Therefore, we will test the following hypotheses:

H1: Trust has a positive influence on the perceived usefulness of S-commerce platforms.

H2: Trust has a positive influence on the intention to use S-commerce platforms.

The TAM is one of the most successful theories for examining technology acceptance [19]. This theory aims to link external factors, perceptions, attitude and the intention to study the behavior toward adopting or rejecting a technology, from the individual point of view. In its first version, the technology acceptance model is

Table 1 Construct operationalization

Constructs and definitions	References	Measure indicators
Image. It is defined as the extent to which the use of an innovation is perceived by the individual as an improvement to their position in a social system	[5]	(i) The extent to which the people in your community who use this type of tool have a more prestigious reputation than those who do not (ii) The extent to which the people in your community who use this type of tool have superior profiles (iii) The extent to which usage of this type of tool is a status symbol in your community
Trust. It refers to a sensation of security and the intention to rely on someone or something	[10]	(i) The degree to which you believe that S-commerce platforms will keep the promises and commitments they make (ii) The degree to which you believe S-commerce platforms are trustworthy (iii) The degree to which S-commerce platforms are honest (iv) The degree to which you believe that S-commerce is responsible (v) The degree to which you have confidence in S-commerce platforms
Perception of Ease of Use. It is defined as the degree to which a person believes that using a particular system would be free of effort	[11]	(i) Ease of learning (ii) Understandable (iii) Effort to be skillful (iv) Mental effort (v) Easy to use
Perceived usefulness. It is defined as the degree to which a person believes that the use of this system will improve performance at work	[11]	(i) Increase productivity (ii) Effectiveness (iii) The degree to which the use of S-commerce to make online purchases helps you (iv) The degree to which the use of S-commerce to make online purchases is beneficial
Intention to use. It refers to the perceived probability of a person or of the subjective probability of a person to engage in a particular behavior	[10, 12]	(i) Use S-commerce in the future (ii) Recommend to use S-commerce (iii) Intention to use S-commerce in the future

based on the perceived usefulness and the perceived ease of use to explain the user's attitude, intentions and adoption behavior.

H3: Perception of Ease of use has a positive influence on the perceived usefulness of S-commerce platforms.

H4: Perception of Ease of use has a positive influence on the intention to use S-commerce platforms.

H5: Perception usefulness has a positive influence on the intention to use S-commerce platforms.

The strength of this model resides mainly in its ability to explain up to 40% of the variance with the intention to use and 30% of the use of the system [20]. Otherwise, Davis and Venkatesh identified that TAM had some limitations in explaining why a person would perceive a given system useful, and so they proposed a new version of the technology acceptance model known as TAM 2 [5].

In the TAM2 version, the authors have incorporated variables of cognitive and social influence under the assumption that they may influence the beliefs related to the perceived usefulness. The variables that they add to this model are: subjective norm, voluntariness, image, experience, job relevance, output quality, and result demonstrability. Then we can formulate these hypotheses:

H6: Image has a positive influence on the perceived usefulness of S- commerce platforms.

H7: Image has a positive influence on the trust in S- commerce platforms.

H8: Perception of Ease of use has a positive influence on the trust in S- commerce platforms.

Understand influence of gender and age in individual technology adoption and usage decisions have been identified as a significant issue in the technology acceptance literature [5]. Concerning gender, several studies found that there are differences between males and females in their technology-related variables including adoption. For example a study made in Cameroon shows that males have more favorable attitudes towards technologies than females. Females generally experience greater computer anxiety and negative perceptions than males [21]. However, other studies found no significant difference between men and women regarding perceptions and usage of IT. Several studies suggest that age and gender are important demographic variables that have direct and moderating effects on the behavioral intention, adoption and acceptance of technology [22, 23]. This led us to formulate the following hypotheses:

H9 (a–b): Age and gender have a moderating effect on the relationship between the perceived usefulness and the intention to use.

H10 (a–b): Age and gender have a moderating effect on the relationship between trust and the intention to use.

H11 (a–b): Age and gender have a moderating effect on the relationship between the perception of Ease of Use and the intention to use.

3 Methodology

To meet our research objective, an approach based on instruments or quantitative research techniques for data collection has been adopted. It results in figures that make descriptive analyzes, tables and graphs, statistical analysis of research links between the variables or factors, correlation analysis and association. This approach allowed us to gather clear and observable data to test the assumptions of our theoretical model.

We have used a questionnaire to collect data. All items in our questionnaire were assessed on a Likert scale with seven levels [24]. In this research, all internet users in Cameroon were considered as the research population. Snowball sampling technique was considered in data collection, and consisted in sending the research questionnaire to family members, friends, peers, and so on, and in inviting them to resend it again for their acquaintances, in order to reach a highly representative sample size. Our investigation began on July 10 and ended July 22, 2017 (a period of 13 days). At the end of this survey, we obtained a total of 404 respondents.

For the purpose of this study, we used mainly two software applications for the collection, processing and analysis of the data collected. The online application Google forms was used for the development of the questionnaire and for the compilation of the descriptive statistics of our sample. The Smartpls-3.2.6 software allowed us to assess the adequacy of the theoretical model and to verify its hypotheses.

4 Results

This section presents the results of our study, following a proper processing of data collected in the field. The use of tables may have the advantage of presenting the results in a clearer and more understandable way.

4.1 Demographic Information

The demographic profile of our survey's respondents is presented in Table 2. This table shows that respondents are made up of 60.6% men and 39.4% women. It is important to note a high level of education in our study population. Of all respondents, about 88.1% have been at the university, 53.7% of whom obtained a master's degree and more. The high level of education of respondents can be justified by the fact that they have quickly become aware of the benefits and facilities offered by social commerce and are therefore better received. Concerning age, our population is young because 90.8% of it is in the age group of 18–34 years.

4.2 Demographic of Respondents

Table 3 presents the factor-loadings, the Cronbach's values alpha, composite reliability and average of the extracted variance of the model. All the values in the table stand above the thresholds of acceptability, normally at 0.6, 0.7, 0.7 and 0.5 [25, 26]. This clearly supports the relevance of the constructs used in our theoretical model.

Table 2 Demographic characteristics of respondents

Dimension	Category	Frequency	Percentage (%)
Gender	Male	245	60.6
	Female	159	39.4
Age	At least of 18 years old	6	1.5
	18–24 years old	175	43.3
	25–34 years old	192	47.5
	35–44 years old	28	6.9
	45 years old and more	3	0.7
Education	No formal qualification	1	0.2
	Primary school qualification	1	0.2
	Secondary	17	4.2
	Technical	29	7.2
	Bachelor's degree	139	34.4
	Master's degree and more	217	53.7

Table 3 shows that the Rho value of D.G varies from 0.805 to 1.000 > 0.7 and that Cronbach's Alpha of the construct ranges from 0.780 to 1.000 > 0.7, which indicates a strong internal consistency and reliability of our constructs. As for AVE, their value varies from 0.540 to 1.000 > 0.5. Based on these previous findings, we can conclude that the convergent validity is insured. Regarding the HTMT ratios of correlation between the constructs, the different corresponding values are set forth in Table 4. Such values are acceptable because they are below the threshold of 0.90 [27]. On the basis of the findings, both the reliability and validity of the constructs are guaranteed.

The Bootstrapping method allows testing the significance of the relationship between the constructs featuring in the model through the interpretation of the t-statistics, as well as the correlation between these constructs by looking deeply on the values of the path coefficient. To express some significance, the t-statistics must be greater than 1.96 [24]. Table 5 summarizes these values.

Table 5 shows that all t-statistics are greater than 1.96, but also that all the hypotheses were considered significant. The intention to use social commerce is positively influenced by PEOU ($\beta = 0.367$), PU ($\beta = 0.319$), TR ($\beta = 0.261$). In addition, Table 6 shows that the coefficient of determination R^2 that is being obtained is 0.605 for the IU social commerce, thus suggesting a good fit of the data with our proposed model [27].

Multigroup Analysis (MGA). The multigroup analysis assesses whether predefined data groups present significant differences for the group-specific model estimations. For this purpose, we decided to use the PLS-MGA approach (Partial Least Squares Multigroup Analysis). It focuses on the bootstrapping results for each construct [28]. The PLS-MGA method [29] represents an extension of Henseler's MGA [28]. This method is an important non-parametric test for the comparison of the

Table 3 Factor loadings, Cronbach's alpha, Rho de D.G. (ACP) and AVE of the model

Constructs	Indicators	Factor-loadings >0.6	Cronbach's Alpha >0.7	Rho de D.G. (ACP) >0.7	AVE >0.5
Image (IMG)	IMG1	0.847	0.832	0.835	0.748
	IMG 2	0.883			
	IMG 3	0.864			
Trust (TR)	TR1	0.771	0.907	0.910	0.732
	TR2	0.854			
	TR3	0.908			
	TR4	0.890			
	TR5	0.848			
Perceived ease of used (PEOU)	PEOU1	0.787	0.780	0.805	0.540
	PEOU2	0.800			
	PEOU3	0.805			
	PEOU4	0.519			
	PEOU5	0.723			
Perceived usefulnesss (PU)	PU1	0.823	0.832	0.833	0.665
	PU2	0.863			
	PU3	0.813			
	PU4	0.761			
Intention to use (IU)	IU1	0.912	0.908	0.909	0.845
	IU2	0.926			
	IU3	0.920			

Table 4 Heterotrait-monotrait ratio (HTMT)

	Intention to use	Image	Perceived ease of use	Perceived usefulness	Trust
Intention to use					
Image	0.279				
Perceived ease of use	0.787	0.260			
Perceived usefulness	0.748	0.344	0.695		
Trust	0.638	0.386	0.551	0.545	

Table 5 Structural model testing hypothesis using boostrapping

Hypothesis		Path coefficient (β)	Standard deviation (STDEV)	T statistics (IO/STDEVI)	P values	Hypothesis testing result
H1.	TR → PU	0.229	0.048	4.750	0.000	Accepted
H2.	TR → IU	0.261	0.039	6.607	0.000	Accepted
H3.	PEOU → PU	0.444	0.051	8.662	0.000	Accepted
H4.	PEOU → IU	0.367	0.052	7.040	0.000	Accepted
H5.	PEOU → IU	0.367	0.052	7.040	0.000	Accepted
H6.	IMG → PU	0.118	0.042	2.798	0.005	Accepted
H7.	IMG → TR	0.251	0.045	5.609	0.000	Accepted
H8.	PEOU → TR	0.409	0.043	9.412	0.000	Accepted

Table 6 R-square and R-square adjusted

Latent constructs	R square	R square adjusted
IU	0.605	0.602
PU	0.398	0.393
TR	0.273	0.269

group-specific bootstrapping PLS-SEM results. The fact that the p-value is smaller than 0.05 or is larger than 0.95 indicates a significant difference from the probability of 0.05 [30, 31].

For the sake of simplifying our study, we decided to restrict analyses to only the two groups relating to Group_age 18–24 versus Group_age 25–34. We considered the other values irrelevant. Table 7 shows only one completely different relationship across the two groups, namely the relationship PU ↛ IU (p-value = 0.01 < 0.05). The analysis of the values of each group path coefficient—Group_age 18–24 (path coefficient = 0.168) and Group_age 25–34 (path coefficient = 0.434)—reveals that the second group is stronger than the first group, which means that respondents' age

Table 7 Multigroup analysis of the group "age"

	Group_age 18–24		Group_age 25–34		Group_age 18–24 versus Group_age 25–34		
	p (1)	Se (p (1))	p (2)	Se (p (2))	I p (1)–p (2) I	t-value	p-value
PEOU → IU	0.47	0.073	0.286	0.066	0.185	1.892	0.059
PU → IU	0.168	0.076	0.434	0.070	0.266	2.592	0.010
TR → IU	0.276	0.056	0.262	0.057	0.014	0.173	0.863

p (l) and p (2) are path coefficients of Group_age 18–24 and Group_age 25–34, respectively; Se (p (1 1) and se (p (2 1) are the standard error of p (l) and p (2), respectively

Table 8 Multigroup analysis of the group "gender"

	Group_gender (F)		Group_gender (M)		Group_ gender (F) versus Group_ gender (M)		
	p (3)	Se (p (3))	p (4)	Se (p (4))	I p (3)–p (4)I	t-value	p-value
PEOU → IU	0.374	0.069	0.384	0.073	0.010	0.098	0.922
PU → IU	0.285	0.065	0.329	0.074	0.044	0.415	0.678
TR → IU	0.296	0.056	0.220	0.056	0.077	0.927	0.354

p (3) and p (4) are path coefficients of Group_gender (F) and Group_gender (M), respectively; Se (p (3) and se (p (4) are the standard error of p (3) and p (4), respectively

range 25–34 has a more significant effect on that relationship than the age bracket 18–24.

Table 8 shows that the two gender groups are not significant for any of the relationships (because no p-value meets the condition). This suggests that gender has no influence on the relationships PEOU → IU, PU → IU, TR → IU.

5 Discussion and Conclusion

S-commerce is more and more drawn to the attention of researchers and companies not only because of the volume of sales such channel and tool triggers, but also for the evolution that is expected from it [10]. Impact analyzing of S-commerce on the intention to purchase products and services have been carried on, based on a behavioral model from a prior literature review. Therefore, we have proposed a research model explaining why and how social commerce is adopted by consumers. Mainly by the TAM 2 [5], such research model has been enriched through an integration of the variable Trust.

The results of our study have shown that trust has a positive influence on the intention to use social commerce, which confirms several similar studies [18, 25, 26]. In other words, S-commerce platforms should be environments where consumers can sell or buy safely.

Another finding is a significant relationship between the perceived ease of use and the intention of consumers to use S-commerce. This means that easiness in handling and navigating processes are determinant criteria in the adoption of social commerce platforms.

Our study reveals also that the perceived usefulness has a positive influence on the intention to use social commerce, thereby implying that a potential buyer acts favorably only when he/she perceives to the usefulness of their act. Benefits in terms of performance and efficiency may further motivate the use of social commerce by a buyer. Furthermore, it has been established that age has a significant moderating effect on this relationship. Indeed, the MGA test showed that the group of users aged between 24 and 35 years old finds social commerce more useful than the group of users aged between 18 and 24. More exactly, based on the segments resulting from the application of the moderating effect of age among users, companies will be able to define strategies adapted to consumers. If an organization targets a young audience, her social commerce platform should be able to offer facilities to these consumers, for example the means of payment on the platform must be diversified [32].

By contrast, the gender factor has been proved to have no significant effect on all of the relationships being examined. This finding contradicts with others studies as the one from Onguéné et al. [21] where they found that, in the population of secondary school students in Cameroon, there is not an interaction between gender and IT adoption.

There are some limitations of our study which may provide interesting opportunities for future research. First of all, using only a cross-sectional design and a longitudinal approach [to test both the robustness of the relationships and the evolution of the moderating variables (gender and age)] seems restrictive. Further investigation may well think about curbing such shortcomings. Secondly, we failed to consider other important variables, such as experience and culture, in this research. The impact of such factors on the adoption of social commerce may be another interesting research topic.

Finally, it should be noted that by mastering consumers' behavior toward s-commerce and the enabling factors for purchasing through this emerging technology, managers would be more inclined to develop effective strategies for increased online consumer purchase.

References

1. Curty, R.G., Zhang, P.: Website features that gave rise to social commerce: a historical analysis. Electron. Commer. Res. Appl. 12(4), 260–279 (2013)
2. Shen, J.: Social comparison, social presence, and enjoyment in the acceptance of social shopping websites. J. Electron. Commer. Res. 13(3), 198 (2012)
3. Internet Lives Stats: Cameroon Internet Users. Online. Available http://www.internetlivestats.com/internet-users/cameroon/. Accessed 21 Aug 2017
4. Smart Insights: Global Social Media Statistics Summary 2017. Online. Available http://www.smartinsights.com/social-media-marketing/social-media-strategy/new-global-social-media-research/. Accessed 21 Aug 2017
5. Venkatesh, V., Davis, F.D.: A theoretical extension of the technology acceptance model: four longitudinal field studies. Manag. Sci. 46(2), 186–204 (2000)
6. Beyari, H., Abareshi, A.: The conceptual framework of the factors influencing consumer satisfaction in social commerce. J. Dev. Areas 50(6), 365–376 (2016)
7. Zhou, L., Zhang, P., Zimmermann, H.-D.: Social commerce research: an integrated view. Electron. Commer. Res. Appl. 12(2), 61–68 (2013)
8. Wang, C., Zhang, P.: The evolution of social commerce: the people, management, technology, and information dimensions. CAIS 31, 5 (2012)
9. Hajli, M.: A research framework for social commerce adoption. Inf. Manag. Comput. Secur. 21(3), 144–154 (2013)
10. Liébana-Cabanillas, F., Alonso-Dos-Santos, M.: Factors that determine the adoption of Facebook commerce: the moderating effect of age. J. Eng. Technol. Manag (2017)

11. Davis, F.D., Bagozzi, R.P., Warshaw, P.R.: User acceptance of computer technology: a comparison of two theoretical models. Manag. Sci. **35**(8), 982–1003 (1989)
12. Venkatesh, V., Davis, F.D.: A model of the antecedents of perceived ease of use: development and test*. Decis. Sci. **27**(3), 451–481 (1996)
13. Gatautis, R., Medziausiene, A.: Factors affecting social commerce acceptance in Lithuania. Procedia-Soc. Behav. Sci. **110**, 1235–1242 (2014)
14. Gefen, D., Karahanna, E., Straub, D.W.: Trust and TAM in online shopping: an integrated model. MIS Q. **27**(1), 51–90 (2003)
15. Gligor, V., Wing, J.M.: Towards a theory of trust in networks of humans and computers. Secur. Protoc. **XIX**, 223–242 (2011)
16. Pavlou, P.A.: Consumer acceptance of electronic commerce: integrating trust and risk with the technology acceptance model. Int. J. Electron. Commer. **7**(3), 101–134 (2003)
17. Hajli, N., Lin, X.: Exploring the security of information sharing on social networking sites: the role of perceived control of information. J. Bus. Ethics **133**(1), 111–123 (2016)
18. Hajli, M.: Social Commerce Adoption Model., Presented at the UKAIS, p. 16 (2012)
19. Hernández, B., Jiménez, J., Martín, M.J.: Customer behavior in electronic commerce: the moderating effect of e-purchasing experience. J. Bus. Res. **63**(9), 964–971 (2010)
20. Dash, M., Mohanty, A.K., Pattnaik, S., Mohapatra, R.C., Sahoo, D.S.: Using the TAM model to explain how attitudes determine adoption of Internet banking. Eur. J. Econ. Finance Adm. Sci. **36**(1), 50–59 (2011)
21. Onguéné Essono, L.-M., Béché, E.: Genre et TIC dans l'école secondaire au Cameroun: Au-delà des progrès, des disparités. Educ. Afr. (2013)
22. Tarhini, A., Hone, K., Liu, X.: Measuring the moderating effect of gender and age on e-learning acceptance in England: a structural equation modeling approach for an extended technology acceptance model. J. Educ. Comput. Res. **51**(2), 163–184 (2014)
23. Noutsa Fobang, A., Fosso Wamba, S., Kala Kamdjoug, J.R.: Exploring factors affecting the adoption of HRIS in SMEs in a developing country: evidence from cameroon. In: Baghdadi, Y., Harfouche, A. (eds.) ICT for a Better Life and a Better World, Lecture Notes in Information Systems and Organisation, vol. 30. https://doi.org/10.1007/978-3-030-10737-6_18
24. Gagné, C., Godin, G.: Les théories sociales cognitives: Guide pour la mesure des variables et le développement de questionnaire. Groupe de recherche sur les aspects psychosociaux de la santé, École des sciences infirmières, Université Laval (1999)
25. Hajli, N.: Social commerce constructs and consumer's intention to buy. Int. J. Inf. Manag. **35**(2), 183–191 (2015)
26. Akman, I., Akman, I., Mishra, A., Mishra, A.: Factors influencing consumer intention in social commerce adoption. Inf. Technol. People **30**(2), 356–370 (2017)
27. Hair, J.F. Jr., Hult, G.T.M., Ringle, C., Sarstedt, M.: A Primer on Partial Least Squares Structural Equation Modeling (PLS-SEM). Sage Publications (2016)
28. Sarstedt, M., Henseler, J., Ringle, C.M.: Multigroup analysis in partial least squares (PLS) path modeling: Alternative methods and empirical results. In Measurement and Research Methods in International Marketing. Emerald Group Publishing Limited, pp. 195–218 (2011)
29. Henseler, J., Ringle, C.M., Sinkovics, R.R.: The use of partial least squares path modeling in international marketing. In: New Challenges to International Marketing. Emerald Group Publishing Limited, pp. 277–319 (2009)
30. Chin, W.W.: The partial least squares approach to structural equation modeling. Mod. Methods Bus. Res. **295**(2), 295–336 (1998)
31. Fornell, C., Cha, J.: Partial least squares. Adv. Methods Mark. Res. **407**(3), 52–78 (1994)
32. Chendjou, K.: Etats des lieux d'Internet et des réseaux sociaux au Cameroun – 2016 – Le Storytelling du Community Management au Cameroun. Online. Available https://histoiresdecm.com/2016/02/03/etats-des-lieux-dinternet-et-des-reseaux-sociaux-au-cameroun-2016/. Accessed 6 Aug 2017

Mobile Commerce Adoption in a Developing Country: Driving Factors in the Case of Cameroon

Frank Wilson Ntsafack Dongmo, Jean Robert Kala Kamdjoug
and Samuel Fosso Wamba

Abstract In line with steady improvements in wireless communications, the number of people using mobile devices has skyrocketed globally while bringing about a veritable breakthrough in the use of mobile commerce (m-commerce). Against a backdrop of fast-evolving mobile commerce (including in developing countries), this study seeks to investigate factors predicting the consumer's intention to adopt m-commerce in Cameroon, but also the moderating effects of the demographic variables on such prediction. Data were collected from 262 Cameroonian respondents aged less than 45, as this age category accounts for the bulk of unconditional IT users in the country. Then, a quantitative approach analysis based on the PLS-SEM algorithm was used to test the research model. Results showed no significant moderation effect of gender and age when verifying the following hypotheses: (1) A variety of services positively influence the consumer intention to adopt m-commerce; and (2) Behavioural intention positively influences the consumer intention to adopt m-commerce. Findings of this research are expected to help companies and organizations dealing with m-commerce to better develop marketing strategies, applications and services likely to attract more users.

Keywords m-commerce · Consumer intention · Demographic variables · UTAUT · TAM · Adoption factors · Cameroon

F. W. Ntsafack Dongmo · J. R. Kala Kamdjoug (✉)
Université Catholique d'Afrique Centrale, FSSG, GRIAGES, Yaoundé, Cameroon
e-mail: jrkala@gmail.com

F. W. Ntsafack Dongmo
e-mail: ntsafackf@yahoo.fr

S. Fosso Wamba
Toulouse Business School, Toulouse, France
e-mail: s.fosso-wamba@tbs-education.fr

Université Fédérale de Toulouse Midi-Pyrénées, 20 Boulevard Lascrosses, 31068 Toulouse, France

© Springer Nature Switzerland AG 2020
Y. Baghdadi et al. (eds.), *ICT for an Inclusive World*,
Lecture Notes in Information Systems and Organisation 35,
https://doi.org/10.1007/978-3-030-34269-2_20

275

1 Introduction

The development of m-commerce is globally considered the most spectacular in the era of Information and Communication Technologies (ICTs). Both in developed and developing countries, people are becoming more and more dependent on this technology, which is virtually indispensable for their daily activities. Numerous authors have proposed definitions of mobile commerce [1]: To Yang, it is a set of transactions conducted through a variety of mobile media through a wireless telecommunication network [2]. Feng et al. argue that m-commerce is more than an extension of e-commerce because of its affordance (value chain, variety of usage models and interaction styles, etc.), which enables the technology to provide a new business model with features such as mobility and accessibility [3]. Tarasewich defines it as any activity related to a (potential) commercial transaction, carried out through communication networks using wireless (or mobile) devices [4]. A more comprehensive definition comes from Tiwari & Buse for whom m-commerce implies any transaction involving transfer of ownership or rights for goods and services, through computerized networks connecting electronic devices such as a Personal Digital Assistant (PDA) or a smartphone [5]. Better still, m-commerce represents m-business and should not be limited to transactions of monetary value, thereby neglecting other m-commerce activities such as after-sales services and the sending of games or free music to users [5]. As for Tiwari & Buse, they indicate that m-commerce does not necessarily need to operate through a wireless telecommunication network [5]. For the purpose of this research work, we adopt the definition by Chong, as it encompasses previous definitions: "any transaction involving the transfer of ownership or rights to use goods and services which is initiated and/use of mobile access to computerized networks with the help of mobile support" [6].

Numerous studies are been concerned with mobile commerce adoption in developing countries like the one from Islam et al. in two major cities in Bangladesh: Dhaka and Chittagong. The results suggested that pricing and cost, rich and fast information, and security and privacy are significant predictors of the adoption of m-commerce. Self-efficacy is found to be a moderating factor for the adoption of m-commerce services [7]. Sadi and Noordin tried to identify some factors that affect the adoption of m-commerce in Malaysia based on traditional technology models and theories such as Theory of Planned Behavior (TPB), Theory of Reasoned Action (TRA), Technology Acceptance Model (TAM) and Diffusion of Innovation Theory (DOI). The results show that the thirteen (13) factors (*Perceived usefulness, perceived Ease of use, perceived trust, personal innovativeness, perceived cost, subjective norms, perceived behavioral control, facilitating conditions, self-efficacy, attitude towards use* etc.) used were statistically significant and can affect the m-commerce adoption [8].

However, it is important to note that many other authors have addressed the issue of the adoption of m-commerce, by studying the barriers that would oppose it in a given population. Moorthy et al. explored the resistance factors to understand the reasons for this low adoption among generation X in Malaysia. They used Innovation Resistance Theory (IRT) and Valence Framework to examine the barriers, including usage, value, risk, tradition, image, and perceived cost barriers. They found that, except the cost barrier, all other barriers significantly affect the mobile commerce adoption [9]. Mahatanankoon and Vila-Ruiz studied why consumers won't adopt m-commerce in a context of developed country like United States of America, where applications are being implemented for mobile services. Through an explanatory analysis, they found five majors factors that impede the applicability of mobile commerce: device inefficiency, unawareness, interoperability, conventional transactions and personalization needs [10]. Li and McQueen examined and categorized the country-level adoption barriers of mobile commerce services, and tests those barriers in the case of New Zealand [11].

Finally, in a global world where local enterprises are directly in competition with local and foreign competitors, m-commerce appears to be an essential instrument to get a competitive advantage. Statistics on the development of ITs in Cameroon confirm that m-commerce is a great opportunity for enterprises. In fact, the Cameroon's population is estimated at some 23,924,407 inhabitants in 2016 [12]; the number of mobile telephony users is estimate at 16,331,852 (2016), for a penetration rate of 68.267%. Moreover, a study made by InternetLives (2016) shows that the country totals about 4.3 million Internet users, for a penetration rate of about 18%. This rate seems very much higher than the statistics of 2012, where the number of internet users reached around 1.234 million with a penetration rate of 5.7% [13].

In this context, the objective of this study is to determine the factors that influence the adoption of m-commerce in Cameroon. To achieve this objective, the two following research questions will be answered: (1) What are the key determinants of m-commerce in Cameroon? and (2) what are the moderating effects of age and gender on m-commerce adoption? Our research model has been developed drawing on theories and models such as the Technology Acceptance Model (TAM) [14], the Innovation Diffusion Theory (DOI) [15], the Theory of Reasoned Action [16], the Theory of Planned Behavior [17] and the Unified Theory of adoption and Use of Technologies (UTAUT) [18], which provided two major constructs, namely Social influence and Perceived cost. Two other contracts (Social influence and Behavioral intention) have been added. Finally, age and gender are used to moderate the effects of previous constructs on the Intention to adopt m-commerce. The remainder of this paper is structured as follows: The theoretical background aiming to define the research model is presented, followed by the methodology that is being adopted. Finally, data analysis is explained and the results are discussed, together with some limitations to the research.

2 Theoretical Background

Our structural model for this research process is made of four constructs: Variety of service, Social influence, Perceived cost, and Behavioural intention. These constructs have been already used by numerous authors on theories and models such as the Technology Acceptance Model (TAM) [14], the Innovation Diffusion Theory (DOI) [15], the Theory of Reasoned Action [16], the Theory of Planned Behaviour [17], and the Unified Theory of Adoption and Use of Technologies (UTAUT) [18].

2.1 Variety of Services (VS)

Variety of Services is a concept already used to capture the users' willingness to adopt a technology; for instance, Chong et al. have resorted to it to carry out a study in the Malaysian context [19]. The role of this construct in explaining technology adoption has been evidenced in several industries including entertainment, mobile ticketing, mobile banking [20]. With regard to m-commerce specifically, the big challenge lies in the variety of services that the companies having integrated such a commercial communication channel can deliver. So it may be assumed that the attractiveness of m-commerce platforms depends on their ability to offer such a wide variety of services. Therefore, we hypothesize that:

Hypothesis 1: Variety of services positively influences the consumer intention to adopt m-commerce.
Hypothesis 2: Variety of services positively influences behavioral intention.

2.2 Social Influence (SI)

Chong et al. define social influence as the degree to which an individual user perceives the importance that others believe that he or she should use an innovation [21]. The basic assumption for this construct is that: the influence of peers, family members, and even the media such as television, radio, and the Internet, may encourage users to use m-commerce. This is well explained in the Theory of planned behavior (TPB), by Fishbein and Azjen, which establishes that behavioral intention is a resultant of attitude and subjective norms (social influence) [16]. Hence the following hypothesis:

Hypothesis 3: Social influence positively influences behavioral intention.

2.3 Perceived Cost (C)

Generally, the customer perception of excessive costs limits the level of adoption of ITs, the perceived cost being defined as the degree to which an individual perceives that the use of IT is costly [20]. In others words, low costs encourage greater use of the service [22]. As far as m-commerce is concerned, a number of research works justify why the costs of acquiring and integrating such a technology do matter; they include a study by Dai and Palvi on the comparison between China and US consumers [23]. Therefore, we hypothesize that:

Hypothesis 4: Perceived cost positively influences behavioral intention.

2.4 Behavioural Intention (BI)

Behavioral intention can be defined as the strength of one's intention to perform a specific behavior [24]. While it measures the likelihood for a person to adopt the application, the TAM rather resorts to the actual usage to represent a self-report measure of time or frequency of adopting the application [25]. Behavioural intention has a positive direct effect on the usage of mobile devices [26]. Therefore, we set forth this hypothesis:

Hypothesis 5: Behavioral intention positively influences the consumer intention to adopt m-commerce.

2.5 Control Variables (Gender, Age)

The effects of both the Variety of services and Behavioural Intention on the Consumer intention to adopt m-commerce would be significantly different for each specific group of moderators.

Hypothesis 6(a–b): Age and gender are significantly different for both the relationship between Variety of services and Consumer intention to adopt m-commerce and the relationship between Behavioral intention and Consumer intention to adopt m-commerce.

Hypothesis 7(a–b): Age and gender are significantly different for both the relationship between Variety of services and Consumer intention to adopt m-commerce and the relationship between Behavioral intention and Consumer intention to adopt m-commerce.

Then, we conceptualize the research model (Fig. 1).

3   Methodology

The population of this study is various Yaounde-and Douala-based universities students who use smartphone with a Wi-Fi or 4G connection. Data collection has been carried in two phases. First, a developed survey questionnaire was used to make a pre-test with 8 young university students (in journalism, management of information

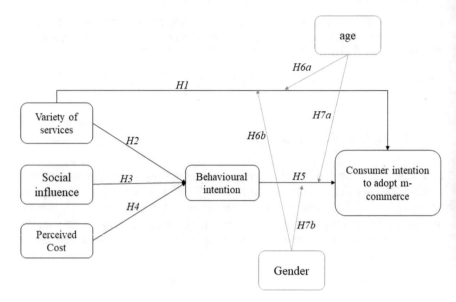

Fig. 1 Research model

system, accounting) and 8 young professionals (education, information system). Second, once this pre-test proved the stability of the research model, the questionnaire was widely administered via an Internet link (google forms) and physically at various Yaounde-and Douala-based universities (University of Yaounde 1, UCAC and University of Douala) and in workplaces. We obtained 55 answers online. Concerning the physical questionnaire, we distributed 295 and received 241 of them filled-in, 34 of which were unusable (not completely answered etc.). Overall, we obtained a total of 262 usable surveys for this study, giving a return rate of 77.06%.

Consistent with previous technology adoption studies, the independent and dependent variables used in this study are derived from the existing literature [27]. A total of 14 items were used to measure the 4 independent variables, and 2 items were used to measure the dependent variable. Besides the demographic profiles (age, gender), all items were measured on a 7 point Likert Scale ranging from 1 (strong disagree) to 7 (strongly agree).

In this study, we used the smartpls-3.2.6 software for the processing and analysis of the data collected. This allowed us to assess the adequacy of the theoretical model and verify its hypotheses.

4 Data Analysis and Results

This section presents the results of our study following a proper processing of the collected data.

Table 1 Demographic characteristics of respondents

Profile	Description	Frequency	Percentage
Gender	M	140	53.44%
	F	122	46.56%
Age	Less than 18 years	7	2.67%
	18–25	187	71.37%
	26–35	64	24.43%
	36–45	4	1.53%
	Over 45 years	0	0

4.1 Demographic Information

The demographic characteristics of our respondents are shown in Table 1.

Of the 262 respondents, 140 were men (53.44%), which is a fairly average distribution. Concerning age, the majority of respondents (95.8%) were aged between 18 and 35 while those aged between 18 and 25 accounted for 71.37%. This is actually the participants' average age, which corresponds to the individuals' incline to use mobile services intensively.

4.2 Demographic of Respondents

Measurement Model. To assess the measurement model, the internal reliability and a convergent and discriminant validity are used [28]. For each construct, the internal reliability is measured (Composite Reliability and the Cronbach's Alpha). The acceptable value of these measures must be greater than 0.70 [28, 29]. As for the convergent validity measured by the Average Variance Extracted (AVE), the preferred value is greater than 0.50 [28, 30]. Cross loading and correlations between constructs are also key measures for the convergent validity, because they ensure that the items being used match their correspondent constructs and that these constructs are independent. Concerning the outer loadings, Hair et al. [28] pointed that further analysis should be carried out for values between 0.40 and 0.70 and that items below 0.40 should be removed.

The results of the CR, Cronbach's Alpha and AVE are shown in Table 2.

Table 2 shows that the CR value ranges from 0.7614 to 1.0989 > 0.7, and that the Cronbach's Alpha of the constructs range from 0.7048 to 0.8741 > 0.7, which indicates a strong internal consistency and reliability of the constructs of our research model. As for AVE, their value ranges from 0.5366 to 0.8003 > 0.5. Based on these previous findings, we can conclude that the convergent validity is insured.

With regard to the HTMT ratios of correlation between the constructs, the different corresponding values are set forth in Table 3. Such values are acceptable because they

Table 2 Constructs reliability and validity

	Cronbach's alpha	rho_A	Composite reliability (CR)	Average variance extracted (AVE)
Variety of services	0.7173	0.8269	0.8705	0.7714
Social influence	0.7516	0.7610	0.8891	0.8003
Perceived cost	0.7048	1.0989	0.7614	0.5366
Behavioural intention	0.8741	0.8752	0.9026	0.5698
Consumer intention to adopt m-commerce	0.7471	0.7558	0.8873	0.7975

Table 3 Heterotrait-monotrait ratio (HTMT)

	Variety of services	Social influence	Perceived cost	Behavioural intention	Consumer intention to adopt m-commerce
Variety of services					
Social influence	0.0568				
Perceived cost	0.1302	0.1008			
Behavioural intention	0.3453	0.3603	0.2055		
Consumer intention to adopt m-commerce	0.1962	0.2217	0.1221	0.6877	

are below the threshold of 0.90 [28]. On the basis of the findings, both the reliability and validity of constructs are guaranteed.

Structural Model. The Bootstrapping method allows testing the significance of the relationship between the constructs featuring in the model through the interpretation of the t-statistics, as well as the correlation between these constructs by looking deeply on the values of the path coefficient (Table 5).

To express some significance, the t-Statistics must be greater than 1.96. Table 4 summarizes these values.

Table 4 shows that the relationships *Behavioural Intention* → *Consumer Intention to adopt m-commerce* ($t = $ **9.6952**), *Variety of Services* → *Behavioural Intention* ($t = $ **4.4492**), *Perceived Cost* → *Behavioural Intention* ($t = $ **2.5749**) and *Social Influence* → *Behavioural Intention* ($t = $ **4.6336**) have significant effects on the adoption of m-commerce. Hence, these findings support hypotheses H2, H3, H4 and H5 (Table 5).

Table 6 shows the value R^2 and R^2 adjusted of the latent constructs "Behavioural

Table 4 Structural model testing hypothesis using boostrapping

Hypothesis		Original sample (O)	Sample mean (M)	Standard deviation (STDEV)	t-statistics |O/STDEV|	p-values
H1	Variety of services → consumer intention to adopt m-commerce	0.0054	0.0058	0.0573	0.0935	0.9255
H2	Variety of services → behavioural Intention	0.2587	0.2641	0.0581	4.4492	0.0000
H3	Social influence → behavioural Intention	0.2697	0.2717	0.0582	4.6336	0.0000
H4	Perceived cost → behavioural intention	−0.1550	−0.1654	0.0602	2.5749	0.0103
H5	Behavioural intention → consumer intention to adopt m-commerce	0.5570	0.5641	0.0575	9.6952	0.0000

Table 5 Hypothesis testing results

Hypothesis		p-values	Test results
H1	Variety of services → consumer intention to adopt m-commerce	0.9255	Rejected
H2	Variety of services → behavioural intention	0.0000	Accepted
H3	Social influence → behavioural Intention	0.0000	Accepted
H4	Perceived cost → behavioural Intention	0.0103	Accepted
H5	Behavioural intention → consumer Intention to adopt m-commerce	0.0000	Accepted

Table 6 R-square and R-square adjusted

Latent constructs	R square	R square adjusted
Behavioural intention	0.1830	0.1735
Consumer intention to adopt m-commerce	0.3120	0.3067

Intention" and "Consumer Intention to adopt m-commerce". The variable "Behavioural Intention" is explained at 18% by the variables "Variety of Services", "Social Influence" and "Perceived Cost", but in turn it explains at 31% the variance of the variable "Consumer Intention to adopt m-commerce". Specifically in the case of the consumer intention to adopt m-commerce, $R^2 = 0.3120 > 0.25$. According to Hair et al., we can then conclude that our model is quite good and interesting [28].

Multigroup Analysis (MGA). The multigroup analysis assesses whether prede-fined data groups present significant differences for the group-specific model esti-mations. For this purpose, we decided to use the PLS-MGA approach (Partial Least Squares Multigroup Analysis). It focuses on the bootstrapping results for each group [31]. The PLS-MGA method [32] represents an extension of Henseler's MGA [31]. This method is an important non-parametric test for the comparison of the group-specific bootstrapping PLS-SEM results. The fact that p-value is smaller than 0.05 or is larger than 0.95 indicates a significant difference from the probability of 0.05 (Table 8).

Table 6 shows no significant difference between the two groups of gender as it may appear in the relationships "Behavioural Intention $\rightarrow$ Consumer Intention to adopt m-commerce" (p-value = 0.3090 > 0.05) and "Variety of Services $\rightarrow$ Con-sumer intention to adopt m-commerce" (p-value = 0.4853 > 0.05). Moreover, the path coefficients' values for each gender group are fairly equal in absolute terms (path coefficient = $0.5917 - R^2 = 0.3495$ for Female and path coefficient = $0.5344 - R^2 = 0.2837$ for Male for the relationship "Behavioural Intention $\rightarrow$ Consumer Intention to adopt m-commerce" and path coefficient = $-0.0013 - R^2 = 0.3495$ for Female and path coefficient = $-0.0098 - R^2 = 0.2837$ for Male for the rela-tionship "Variety of Services $\rightarrow$ Consumer Intention to adopt m-commerce"). These values reveal that the female group is sensibly stronger than the male group, which means that female respondents sensibly have more effect on "Behavioural Inten-tion $\rightarrow$ Consumer Intention to adopt m-commerce" than males. We also notice that for the same gender group, these values are greater for the relationship "Behavioural Intention $\rightarrow$ Consumer Intention to adopt m-commerce" although their contributions to R^2 are fairly equal.

As for Table 7, there is no significant difference between the two groups of age as regards the relationships "Behavioural Intention $\rightarrow$ Consumer Intention to adopt m-commerce" (p-value = 0.0869 > 0.05) and "Variety of Services $\rightarrow$ Consumer intention to adopt m-commerce" (p-value = 0.4124 > 0.05). Moreover, the path coefficients' values for each age group are different in absolute terms (path coefficient = $0.5962 - R^2 = 0.3704$ for age 18–25 and path coefficient = $0.3730 - R^2 = 0.1389$

Table 7 Multigroup analysis of the group "gender"

	Path coefficients-diff (|GROUP_Gender (F)-GROUP_Gender (M)|)	*p-value* (GROUP_Gender (F) vs. GROUP_Gender (M))
Behavioural intention $\rightarrow$ consumer intention to adopt m-commerce	0.0573	0.3090
Variety of services $\rightarrow$ consumer intention to adopt m-commerce	0.0085	0.4853

Table 8 Multigroup analysis of the group "age"

	Path coefficients-diff (|GROUP_Age (18–25)–GROUP_Age (26–35)|)	p-value (GROUP_Age (18–25) vs. GROUP_Age (26–35))
Behavioural intention → consumer intention to adopt m-commerce	0.2233	0.0869
Variety of services → consumer intention to adopt m-commerce	0.0359	0.4124

for the age range 26–35 for the relationship "Behavioural Intention → Consumer Intention to adopt m-commerce" and path coefficient = $0.0346 - R^2 = 0.3704$ for the age range 18–25 and path coefficient = -0.0013, $R^2 = 0.1389$ for the age bracket 26–35 for the relationship "Variety of Services → Consumer Intention to adopt m-commerce"). These values reveal that age group 18–25 is sensibly stronger than one ranging from 26 to 35, which means that younger respondents sensibly have more effect on "Behavioural Intention → Consumer Intention to adopt m-commerce". The same phenomenon is observed as regards the relationship "Variety of Services → Consumer Intention to adopt m-commerce" (Table 8).

Based on these findings, it appears that the hypotheses H6a, H6b, H7a and H7b are not supported.

5 Discussions and Limitations

Our study certainly contributes to enriching the literature on IT adoption research, especially by disseminating a relevant experience from the developing country context. The relevant literature on the development of such technology in sub-Saharian African countries, for instance, is still a little bit poor, whereas gigantic strides are steadily made in other regions about the subject. Furthermore, by proposing a research model integrating variables from TAM and UTAUT and by adding other variables such as the Perceived cost and the Variety of services, we have been able to identify the influence of such variables on the intention to adopt m-commerce, which is a major contribution to the extant literature. Findings of our research can be summarized as follows: (i) Social influence and Variety of services positively influence Behavioral intention while the Perceived cost negatively influences Behavioral intention; and (ii) factors such as age and gender are not significantly different between the relationship "Behavioural Intention → Consumer Intention to adopt m-commerce" and "Variety of Services → Consumer Intention to adopt m-commerce".

Out of the driving factors that can predict the adoption of m-commerce among Cameroonian consumers, our study has revealed that the variety of services, social influence and the Perceived cost significantly influence behavioural intention, and therefore the consumer intention to adopt m-commerce.

In terms of implications, this study has driven some of them: Firstly, the perceived cost has a negative influence on the behavioural intention to take adoption decision. Therefore, the increase in mobile service costs could discourage young people who are price conscious. In reaction to this, telecoms companies and others businesses investing in m-commerce in Cameroon should develop good pricing strategies and creative promotional activities to attract young customers. Secondly, the variety of services is found to positively influence behavioural intention, but does not influence directly and significantly the consumer intention to adopt m-commerce. In consequence, businesses investing in m-commerce in Cameroon should make more efforts to offer a greater variety of services and applications. Thirdly, the results also show that demographic variables of respondents (like age and gender), in general, are not good predictors of m-commerce adoptions. There were no significant difference between groups of respondents according to age (GROUP_Age (18–25) vs. GROUP_Age (26–35)) and gender (GROUP_Gender (F) vs. GROUP_Gender (M)). Finally, this research has contributed to the literature, by providing information of interest about some factors that can influence the adoption of m-commerce in a developing country like Cameroon.

The present study bears a number of limitations in this study. The first one is that the cultural values of respondents were not taken into account. Future studies may consider measuring this aspect of the survey's population. The second limitation relates to the geographical restriction of the study area to only Douala and Yaoundé, whereas more Cameroonian towns (Maroua, Ngaoundere, Buea, Bamenda or Dschang) could well be involved. This is a setback to be considered in future research attempts. Lastly, additional adoption factors, such as trust, innovativeness, and compatibility, could also be integrated with the research model, and researchers should think about it.

References

1. Zhou, T., Lu, Y., Wang, B.: Integrating TTF and UTAUT to explain mobile banking user adoption. Comput. Hum. Behav. **26**(4), 760–767 (2010)
2. Yang, K.C.: Exploring factors affecting the adoption of mobile commerce in Singapore. Telemat. Inform. **22**(3), 257–277 (2005)
3. Feng, H., Hoegler, T., Stucky, W.: Exploring the critical success factors for mobile commerce. In: ICMB'06. International Conference on Mobile Business, pp. 40–40 (2006)
4. Tarasewich, P., Nickerson, R.C., Warkentin, M.: Issues in mobile e-commerce. Commun. Assoc. Inf. Syst. **8**(1), 3 (2002)
5. Tiwari, R., Buse, S.: The mobile commerce prospects: a strategic analysis of opportunities in the banking sector, Hamburg University Press (2007)

6. Chong, A.Y.-L.: Mobile commerce usage activities: the roles of demographic and motivation variables. Technol. Forecast. Soc. Change **80**(7), 1350–1359 (2013)
7. Islam, M.A., Khan, M.A., Ramayah, T., Hossain, M.M.: The adoption of mobile commerce service among employed mobile phone users in Bangladesh: self-efficacy as a moderator. Int. Bus. Res. **4**(2), 80 (2011)
8. Sadi, A., Noordin, M. F.: Factors influencing the adoption of M-commerce: an exploratory Analysis. In: International Conference on Industrial Engineering and Operations Management, pp. 492–498 (2011)
9. Moorthy, K. et al.: Barriers of mobile commerce adoption intention: perceptions of generation X in Malaysia. J. Theor. Appl. Electron. Commer. Res. **12**(2), 37–53 (2017)
10. Mahatanankoon, P., Vila-Ruiz, J.: Why won't consumers adopt M-Commerce? An exploratory study. J. Internet Commer. **6**(4), 113–128 (2007)
11. Li, W., McQueen, R.J.: Barriers to mobile commerce adoption: an analysis framework for a country-level perspective. Int. J. Mob. Commun. **6**(2), 231–257 (2008)
12. CIA: The World Facebook—Africa : Cameroon, Government Printing Office(2016)
13. Internet lives stats: Cameroon Internet Users. 10 Jan 2017
14. Davis, F. D.: A technology acceptance model for empirically testing new end-user information systems: Theory and results (Sloan School of Management, Doctoral Dissertation), Cambridge, MA, Massachusetts Institute of Technology, (1986)
15. Rogers, E.M.: Diffusion of Innovations: modifications of a model for telecommunications. Die diffusion von innovationen in der telekommunikation 25–38 (1995)
16. Fishbein, M., Ajzen, I.: Belief, attitude, intention, and behavior: An Introduction to theory and research. Addison-Wesley Pub. Co. - Psychology - 578 (1975)
17. Ajzen, I.: The theory of planned behavior. Organ. Behav. Hum. Decis. Process. **50**(2), 179–211 (1991)
18. Venkatesh, V., Morris, M.G., Davis, G.B., Davis, F.D.: User acceptance of information technology: toward a unified view. MIS Q. 425–478 (2003)
19. Chong, A.Y.L., Darmawan, N., Ooi, K.-B., Lin, B.: Adoption of 3G services among Malaysian consumers: an empirical analysis. Int. J. Mob. Commun. **8**(2), 129–149 (2010)
20. Wei, T.T., Marthandan, G., Ooi, K.-B., Arumagan, S.: What drives Malaysian m-commerce adoption? An empirical analysis. Ind. Manage. Data Syst. **109**(3), 370–388 (2009)
21. Chong, A.Y.L., Darmawan, N., Ooi, K.-B., Lin, B.: Adoption of 3G services among Malaysian consumers: an empirical analysis. Int. J. Mob. Commun. **8**(2), 129–149 (2010)
22. Min, Q., Ji, S., Qu, G.: Mobile commerce user acceptance study in China: a revised UTAUT model. Tsinghua Sci. Technol. **13**(3), 257–264 (2008)
23. Dai, H., Palvi, P.C.: Mobile commerce adoption in China and the United States: a cross-cultural study. ACM SIGMIS Database **40**(4), 43–61 (2009)
24. Chew, A.A.: The adoption of M-commerce in the United States. Unpublished Honors Thesis California State University, Long Beach CA (2006)
25. Davis, F.D.: Perceived usefulness, perceived ease of use, and user acceptance of information technology. MIS Q. 319–340 (1989)
26. Carlsson, C., Carlsson, J., Hyvonen, K., Puhakainen, J., Walden, P.: Adoption of mobile devices/services—searching for answers with the UTAUT. In: Proceedings of the 39th Annual Hawaii International Conference on System Sciences, HICSS'06, vol. 6, pp. 132a–132a (2006)
27. Chong, A.Y.L., Chan, F.T., Ooi, K.-B.: Predicting consumer decisions to adopt mobile commerce: cross country empirical examination between China and Malaysia. Decis. Support Syst. **53**(1), 34–43 (2012)
28. Hair, J.F. Jr., Hult, G.T.M., Ringle, C., Sarstedt, M.: A primer on partial least squares structural equation modeling (PLS-SEM). Sage Publications (2016)
29. Chin, W.W.: The partial least squares approach to structural equation modeling. Mod. Methods Bus. Res. **295**(2), 295–336 (1998)

30. Fornell, C., Cha, J.: Partial least squares. Adv. Methods Mark. Res. **407**(3), 52–78 (1994)
31. Sarstedt, M., Henseler, J., Ringle, C.M.: Multigroup analysis in partial least squares (PLS) path modeling: Alternative methods and empirical results. Measurement and research methods in international marketing, Emerald Group Publishing Limited, pp. 195–218 (2011)
32. Henseler, J., Ringle, C.M., Sinkovics, R.R.: The use of partial least squares path modeling in international marketing. New challenges to international marketing. Emerald Group Publishing Limited, pp. 277–319 (2009)

The Information and Communication Technologies (ICT) in Leadership—Case of Lebanese Public Sector

Dina Sidani and Bissane Harb

Abstract The management is both a product and a process of and in its environment. The managerial thought is evolving and developing to adapt itself with new challenges both cultural and technological to meet different needs of the company. Today, the leader is characterized by his capacity to be in interaction with his environment to serve it better. Through a qualitative study and based on seven interviews conducted with superior person in charge of the Lebanese Public Sector, this article searches to analyze how the role of the leaders of public sector evolves in view of technological transformations resulting from the adoption and the diffusion of information and communication technologies (ICT) in their institutions. To face these new technological challenges, the person in charge of the public sector must exceed his role of a traditional manager to the role of a transformational leader. Hence the necessity of an adaptation, and a mutation in the organizational structure to give an intermediary role to the computer scientists specialist of data and information in the public institutions.

Keywords Leadership · Public sector · Information and communication technologies (ICT) · Transactional leadership · Transformational leadership

1 Introduction

The management is both a product and a process of and in its environment. The managerial thought is evolving and developing to adapt itself with new challenges both cultural and technological to meet different needs of the society [1]. In fact, every new contribution completes the precedent though by searching a better comprehension of the objectives of management, a better organizational performance and a better equilibrium between the individual needs and those of the organization

D. Sidani · B. Harb (✉)
Faculty of Business and Management, Saint Joseph University of Beirut, Beirut, Lebanon
e-mail: bissan.harbbaghdadi@usj.edu.lb

D. Sidani
e-mail: dina.sidani@usj.edu.lb

© Springer Nature Switzerland AG 2020   289
Y. Baghdadi et al. (eds.), *ICT for an Inclusive World*,
Lecture Notes in Information Systems and Organisation 35,
https://doi.org/10.1007/978-3-030-34269-2_21

as well as the establishment of a link between the organization and its environment. The leader is today characterized by his capacity to be in interaction with his environment to serve it better. From the Scientific Organization of Work to the transactional and transformational leadership, passing by the movement of human relations, the researches carried out since the beginning of the twenty first century reflect a call to human competencies rather than the technical capacities as well as the valorization of the sentiment of the group memberships and the social solidarity (communityship). Far from opposing, the concepts of manager and the leader complete each other; the leadership constitutes only the logical evolution of the concept of management according to the adaptation of the transformations of the organizational context and of the technological evolutions. In this context, the leadership in the public sector always arouses the interest of the researchers and the practitioners [2]. This could be attributed to the generalized diffusion of public administration reforms and to the general abandonment of managerialism for the profit of "leaderism" [3].

In fact, the public leaders occupy key positions in the public sector and are responsible for the engagement, the mobilization of persons and for the achievement of results. At the same time that they have to handle the current tasks and to familiarize with the changes that the modernization of the State consists, they must assimilate the new principles of leadership and be adapted to the mutations resulting from the New Information and Communication Technologies (NICT). Thenceforth, it seems legitimate to wonder about the specificities and the issues of the leadership in the public sector. Our problematic appears under the form of the following question: How did public leaders use the technological mutations in the domain of information and communication to play their role and to make a difference within the public sector in Lebanon? The choice of the Lebanese public sector as a framework of our field study seems both essential and original. Essential because the study of the relation between the 3 concepts—public sector, leadership and ICT—finds its pertinence in the vital sector that faces the technological mutations resulting from the ICT that are now unavoidable and part of our social and daily life. The introduction of ICT in the public administration is registered in the general problematic of the reform of the State and represents an important lever of these reforms [4]. In fact, given the technological gap in an organizational structure (so) hierarchical and compartmentalized within the public sector [5], these transformations arouse a particular interest. Original, because the question of leadership, within the Lebanese context, was rarely treated by previous researches particularly by the point of view of the impact of ICT on the roles of public leaders. Yet, these latter are strongly involved in the public reforms programs that depend largely on the adoption and the exploitation of ICT in the public administrations.

After tracing the evolution of the managerial though through the history, we will apprehend the concept of leadership by exposing its different evolutions in the theories within the organizational context, to focus at last on the concept of leadership in the public sector by approaching it from the perspective of the challenges of using information and communication technologies in this public sector. In a second time, we will expose the empirical study carried out among public managers who work in the public sector in Lebanon.

2 From the Managerialism to the Leaderism

2.1 The Evolution of the Managerial Though: From the SOW...

Considered as one of the first consultants in management, the engineer Frederick Taylor played an essential role in the development of the managerial thought by proposing the concept of the scientific organization of work (SOW), concept that relies on the decomposition of work into elementary, chronometric and organized gestures rationally to form a chain of production within an objective of efficiency. Then, Henri Fayol created a general theory of management by showing that the organizational success depends more on the managerial skills of a leader, as he is considered as a good administrator, rather than his technical capacities. Fayol describes the functions of managers: to plan, to organize, to direct, to coordinate and to control. Henry Mintzberg bounces on these four functions of managers and notes that these principal activities correspond a little to the daily reality of what managers do [6–8]. For [6, 7], the profession of a manager is divided among the interpersonal roles, the roles related to the information and the decisional roles. The managers do not give the same interest to each one of these roles which form a gestalt, a whole integrated and which are in fact inseparable.

2.2 To a Harmonious Development of Organized Worlds: The Human Relations

The evolution of the managerial thought continues its path and marks the 1930s as an exceptional period, a period based on the cooperation of syndicates and the participation of workers in the decision-making. Therefore this epoch involves our comprehension of persons in work, with authors like Georges Elton Mayo, Mary Parker Follett, Chester Barnard and others.

Concerning Mayo, the management must concentrate its efforts to maintain the integration, the cohesion and the solidarity of the group, which will permit to the organization to withstand the disturbances of external constraints. Concerning Follet, to establish good human relations relies on the necessity to create a work spirit with others rather than to work without the power of someone. Therefore, the authority resides in the situation and not in the position; it applies through the knowledge and the experience.

In his famous work, The Functions of the Executive, [9] defines an analysis of the formal organization by tracing the role of the informal organization, through its social interactions, to maintain the equilibrium. According to [9], the informal organization constitutes also a necessary part of the formal organization and assures three functions that he considers universal: the communication, the upkeep of the cohesion and the feeling of integrity and the self-respect in the organization. The ideas of Barnard are the precursor of the organizational equilibrium notion which constitutes a fundamental element of the organization effectiveness.

2.3 The Leadership in the Managerial Though

In fact, from Barnard's works, the study of organizations adopted a new way [1] which takes into consideration the social interactions between the individuals as an essential element of the organizational equilibrium. [10] poses the problem of the actualization and the adaptation of the individual to the exigencies of the organization, searching for a model of the organizational human being more than human, and a harmony between the individual and the organization, in other terms, an integration of both [1, 11].

Douglas McGregor marked the organizational behavior by proving that the management and the leadership style is influenced by the people's perceptions of human nature, summarizing thus two contradictory points of view of managers. The theory X concerns the leaders preferring the autocratic style, and the theory Y for the leaders preferring the participative style, which integrates the individual goals in the organization goals, extolling more participation and a spirit of cooperation from the managers. Its influence is found in the works of Robert Blake and Jane Mouton which develop the model of the leadership behaviorist [11], a graphic representation permitting to situate the leadership styles adopted in function of degree of interest brought to the imperatives of management (vertically) and of degree of interest brought to the human problems (horizontally) [12]. In 1981, William Ouchi develops this theory based on the consensual management [8].

3 The Leadership

3.1 Are the Managers and the Leaders Different?

The starting point of this question relies on the conclusion of the precedent part: "The best leaders are first and foremost efficient managers" [13]. The authors who were interested particularly in the functioning of the enterprises give a new perspective of the leadership [14–19]. In 1977, Abraham Zaleznik, professor at the Harvard Business School, published in the Harvard Business Review his innovative article Managers and Leaders are they different? During this period, the management was centered on the structure, the organizational processes, the control and the equilibrium of power.

According to the point of view that [19] supports, the half of the image which represents the essential elements of leadership like inspiration, vision and human passion leads to the success of the enterprise. He compared the leader to an artist who uses the creativity and the intuition to navigate his way through the Chaos, while the manager is perceived like the one who resolves the problems based on the rationality and the control [17, 18]. The article of Professor John Kotter What leaders really do shows that the managers support the stability while the leaders insist on the dynamic change. He considers that the management and the leadership are different but also complementary, and that in a changing world, one cannot function without the other [17]. "As a leader, I ask myself if the conduct of change implies obligatorily the change of the conduct".

According to [20], the difference between the management and the leaders relies on an orientation towards change. The leadership encourages a change of the orientation of the bureaucratic inflexible processes that characterize the management, to processes more strategic and dynamic which constitute the leadership [17–19, 21]. According to [16], the mechanism and the organicism determine the way from which we discern the management and the leadership. The leaders are considered as dynamic persons, charismatic, with a capacity of inspiring others (organicist or institutional leader), while the managers are seen like bureaucrats who pay attention only to the tasks (mechanism and administrative management). According to [6], the communityship requires another form of leadership that we name engaged or distributed management, valorizing mostly the collective citizenship. An organization must be and will be considered as a community to which a person belongs but which does not belong to any individual. The persons engaged in a community organization are considered as citizen rather than employees and follow together a common goal.

3.2 The Evolution of the Concept of Leadership upon the Theories in the Organizational Context

Despite the seniority of the notion of leadership-, it is present in the different cultures regardless of their economic or social configuration [22], it remains a complex concept that researchers always face. In the literature, there are as many definitions of leadership as there are researchers studying the concept [23]. The fundamental element on which relies the existence and the success of the leadership is an efficient management. As underlined [13]: "the best leaders are first and first of all effective managers". Thus, the leadership finds its identity on the organizational context and completes the management. According to [13], the organization is a social entity that contributes to the development of the society. The employees become partners in the management of the enterprise. The participative management is booked as an effective approach to motivate the employees. "Without the management, there will be only a crowd of persons rather than an institution; and without an institution, there will be no management" [13].

As underlined by [24], the first definitions identified the leadership as the center of the group process and its movement, personality in action, through which persons are led by the leader and commit themselves in a specific direction. The second type of definitions considered the leadership as the art of leading others with respect to obligations. In the sixties, the definitions defined it in terms of influent relations and of power differentials.

The leadership is judged as the action of leaders in the groups and the authority, which is accorded to them by the members of these groups. In the sixties, the leadership was an influence exercised by the leader on others to bring them to take a shared direction. The latest definitions of the eighties and nineties conceptualize the leadership as an inspiration for others to take definite measures, and it is defined in term of the influence exercised by the leader and the followers who agree to do real changes which reflect their common goals. The concept of leadership integrates all these elements.

3.3 Theory of Transactional-Transformational Leadership

During the second half of the twentieth century, [25] opened the domain of leadership research to new theories and new perspectives. More particularly, the analysis of leadership's behavior to the detriment of the study of the leaders' traits [26] brings the researchers to be interested in the compatibility between the leader's style and the internal context of the organization.

The situational theory and the contingence theory suppose that a given leader does not have chances to be effective in different situations unless he is flexible enough to assume the style of leadership the most adapted to each situation [27–30]. It is only by 1978, that they began to talk about the transactional and transformational leadership in the literature [31]. These two styles of leadership complete each other more than they oppose. (Annex: recapitulative table of the evolution of the concept of leadership according to the schools of thought).

The transactional leadership supposes that the alignment between the chief and the executants is done by the strategic use of financial incentives (rewards and sanctions), while the transformational leadership is often associated with the leaders who define a vision and objectives for an organization, who communicate constantly this vision and who motivate their executants by non-financial incentives (calls to the moral or to the ethic, persuasion and inspiration) [32].

4 Leadership and the Public Sector

The leadership is an ancient subject of research in the public organizations and the decisional latitude of the persons in charge of the public sector and it is studied since the first half of the twentieth century [33]. According to [2], this subject made the object of are newed interest among the researchers and the practitioners, because of the generalized diffusion of reforms of the public management in Europe and in the

United States and because of the general abandon of managerialism for the profit of leaderism [3].

4.1 The Specificities of the Public Sector

According to [33], the interest in the question has appeared again in parallel with the debate on the transactional/transformational leadership in the eighties and lately has reached its paroxysm in the nineties, when the studies on public management began to be interested in the differences between leadership in public administration and leadership in the private sector, particularly when, among others, the links between leadership and the values of the public service are envisaged. [33] defines the leadership of the public sector as the process that permits:

- To reach the results required by the authorized processes in an efficient, effective and legal manner.
- To develop and to support the executants who obtain these results.
- To adapt the organization to its environment.

The definition of Van Wart constitutes a definition of reference. Later, other authors proposed their own definitions like [34, 35]. In parallel, questions arise on the manner to consider the users, the general interest and to conjugate administrative efficiency, public service and ethic. The specific characteristics of the public sector organizations (like the process of complex planning, the biggest complexity and the particular values of the persons in charge of the public sector) drove the researchers to ask if a "new" style of leadership was in the process to appear. On this basis, [33] has pinned out four principal domains for a closer study:

- The complexity and the ambiguity of objectives characterizing the organizations of the public sector were confirmed on the rhetoric plan [36].
- The formalization and the "paper work": the public organisms are characterized by rules that are more formal and by higher levels of paper work regarding the organizations of the private sector [36].
- The satisfaction at work: a large number of studies related to the satisfaction about work realized before 2003 shows lower satisfaction among the public managers regarding their homologues of the private sector [33].
- The motivation: the responders of the public sector give more value to work that benefits to other and to the society, the devotion, the responsibility and the integrity [37].

4.2 Serving Leadership and Ethic: Two Inseparable Concepts of Public Services

For the leaders of the public sector, it is necessary to insist on the spirit of public service. Robert K. Greenleaf is the father of "serving leadership". For [38], it is not the charisma that founds the authority of the leader, but the fact that he "serves" the persons around him. The notion of service is thus at the heart of this vision of leadership. Greenleaf reverses as well the paradigm of the management by making from the manager, not the leader, rather the servant of his collaborators. He invalidates consequently the notion of authority founded on the respect of the hierarchy to prefer the hierarchy founded on the moral mission, the devotion and the authenticity, the service like the purpose and the stowage with the ethic.

In this optic, the humility appears thus as a quality, and a virtue to develop to incite the leader to not commit an abuse in the exercise of his functions. The public manager is asked to use a form of discretionary power in the management of public resources, in the relation with other functionaries and with the citizens and the elaboration of the public politics. In this optic, the ethic appears as a counterbalance limiting the arbitrary character of this discretionary power. Two fields of studies are to be considered about the relation between the leadership and the ethic: the conduct of the leaders and their character.

The conduct of leaders may be envisaged under two aspects, on one hand under the angle of consequences: what is the aim sought by the action: the justice, the liberty, and the equality, the maximization of individual or collective merits, of his own interests or of other's interest? On other hand, under the deontological angle, that is to say in virtue of duties and responsibilities that oblige each leader to give the good actions in the cadre of his functions. The theories related about the character of leaders are attached to his moral character, his virtuous disposition to make the good, his honesty, his sense of justice, his sociability, etc.

4.3 The Technologies of Information and Communication in the Public Sector

The technologies of information and communication (ICT) constitute one of the major technological innovations of this century. After establishing the fast changes in the way that persons communicate and work, the ICT cause deep modifications in the public administration. In fact, the innovative application of ICT in the private sector has put the pressure on the organizations of the public sector and pushed them to think again about their models of hierarchic and bureaucratic organizations [39]. According to these two authors, the application of TIC in the public sector appeared as a revolutionary mechanism for the management of public organizations worldwide, and as a change of the paradigm where the citizen-user is positioned at the heart of the public organization. This phenomenon was adopted by the developed countries and the developing countries [39]. Thus, the public sector, in most of the countries of the world, continues to invest in the advanced information and communication technologies [40, 41]. The use of these technologies aims to develop, on one hand, the internal functioning of the administration, and on the other hand, the relation with citizens and the enterprises [40]. Therefore, the development of ICT constitutes an orientation to the quality of service and to the performance and represents an essential lever of politics of modernization of the public function [42].

Otherwise, this integration of technologies of information and communication in the public administration has a considerable impact on the models of responsibility and management. In fact, the traditional models of responsibility are based on the idea according to which the direction comes from above and it is related to the process, which consists of giving a mandate to subordinates, and make them responsible for the results [43]. The integration of ICT in the public sector undergoes significant changes because a great part of the management of public innovation projects rises from the skill of the functionaries who are at the beginning of their career and deal with the public. The senior managers are often less experienced and less competent in this domain, and their new role consists of approving and permitting the authority exercised by the personal of inferior rank [43].

Furthermore, this orientation to ICT implies that the public leaders, especially the senior managers, understand clearly their roles, perceive the transversal nature of information and communication techniques, and understand how these changes could help to ameliorate the public sector in general [44]. They must put compatible politics with the technological evolutions, must know to coordinate the programs related to the digital development and fight against the numerical fracture. Finally, we can deduce that the information and communication technology is a "disruptive technology". It contributes to change the functioning and the organization of the administration, the distribution of power or its control and the sharing of the information and its protection. It permits also the transformation of the public administrations from command and control organizations to learning organizations, based on knowledge and networking.

The public leaders must face these transformations and guide the public administrations in this way. The management of network government requires different internal capacities of the public leaders and demands skills that are in short supply in the public sector. These skills, to name only a few, are the management of projects, the contractualization, the negotiation, the mediation among the different partners, etc. Thus, the public leaders must establish and inspire the trust, assure the collaboration, analyze and manage the risks relative to the operations on line, and at last work across borders. These skills are also scarce in the public sector. Recruiting and formation Strategies, and cultural transformations prove to be necessary to remediate this situation [44].

5   Empirical Study

5.1   Methodology of the Research and Positioning

The specificity of our object of research will be taken into account through a qualitative methodology by the nature of data. Our research has for objective the understanding and analyzing the impact that ICT can have on the characteristics and the roles of Lebanese public leaders. Thus, we registered our study in an inductive approach consisting of the comprehension of facts by relying on the lightning procured by back and forth movement between the collected theoretical elements and our exploratory study.

Thus, we will adopt an exploratory approach to analyze in a dynamic manner the challenges of use of information and communication technologies by public leaders in Lebanon. Before making our field survey, we resume a review of several works and reports effectuated on the historic of the public administration in Lebanon, its specificity and its actual challenges, to have a clear and thorough idea of the context of our research.

5.2   Choice of the Field

Our methodology relies on the collect and the analysis of qualitative data. These data were collected by a set of semi-directive interviews of 7 public managers (G1, G2, G3, G4, G5, G6, and G7). We took a field of convenience upon the following criteria:

- One of the two authors occupies a post of an Executive in a public administration, and can have easy access to different senior managers and of the Lebanese public administration.
- The interviewees were chosen in function of their (good) reputation in the administration as young and effective managers.
- These interviewees occupy all a key positions: three general directors and four chiefs of department. We met them by the intermediary of other people (technique of the snowball).

5.3   Source and Mode of Data Collection

Semi-directive interviews were conducted with 7 managerial staff and directors of the Lebanese public administration. The persons were met and interviewed face to face, in their place of work. The duration of the interviews varies between 45 min and one hour. We had difficulties in meeting some of the interviewees who occupy important position in the public sector, and who were totally overflowing with their daily tasks

Table 1 Guide of the interview

(1) What is your actual mission? How do you assure the management of your unit?
(2) What are the problems that you face in the management of your unit? How do you align with the organizational objectives?
(3) What do you do to motivate your collaborators and to help them to develop themselves?
(4) In your opinion, on what must the public leaders focus? (Performance technique, development of persons, organizational alignment)
(5) In your opinion, what is the most appropriate style of leadership for the public sector?
(6) Is the leader able to make difference in the public? Up till which degree? How he could guide the necessary changes?
(7) In what the information and communication technologies affect your role as a leader?

and persecuted, on one hand, by the citizens who reclaim them information on their formalities, and on the other hand, by the minister and the politicians who contact them permanently for the following up of delicate files. The collection of data spread over three months.

The information collected during the interviews, combined with the data relative to the concept of leadership, show a saturation starting from the seventh interview, which denotes that the collected information reflect in a loyal way a good comprehension of the phenomena of the study. The guide of the interview (cf. Table 1) contains seven questions that articulate around the following themes: the missions of leaders in the public sector, the problems that they face in accomplishing their tasks and the impact of ICT on their work. The centered semi-directive interviews permit us to collect data adapted to the case-study [45]. To the data collected by the interviews, we will add secondary data of several written sources (laws, periodic) or oral (discussions with managers working in the public organisms of control).

This step will permit us to better assimilate the specificities of the concept of leadership in the public sector and to focus more on the roles that the public leaders could exercise to face the multiple issues of the public sector. The principal objective of our research is to identify, in the era of the numerical revolution, the characteristics and the roles of these men of bureaucracy, presiding over the destinies of the Lebanese public administration, to understand how to realize the necessary changes and the transformations to make the public administration more efficient and more modern.

5.4 The Context of the Study and the Public Administration in Lebanon

The public administration in Lebanon is the product of the foreign heritage, especially the French. However, it reflects the problems of the society that accompanied the formation of the Lebanese State. Thus, it always represented a pole of attraction for politicians and a theater for their conflicts and quarrels.

During the period of the civil war (1975–1990), it knew remarkable paralysis and regression. Since the nineties, the reformist measures started and, in 1995, the Lebanese government created the office of the minister for the administrative reform. The objective was to conceive and to implant a modern public administration, to find solutions to these diverse problems and to make from the public administration an efficient tool in the hands of the government, especially that no serious and exhaustive reform was effectuated since the last project of reform and development of the administration in 1959 (Office of the Minister of State for Administrative Reform-Lebanon). The administrative reforms are also achieved under a vast project of reconstruction aiming to promote the growth and the prosperity of the country, after the end of the civil war. Actually, the administration suffers from the consequences of an excessive budget deficit that reached 4.94 billions of dollars in 2016 (The Commerce of Levant, March 8, 2017). The public debt reached 74.5 billion dollars end of October 2016, that is to say 139% of the PIB (L'Orient-le-jour, September 14, 2017). The rate of the economical growth in 2016 did not exceed 1% (Cofaces, economical studies).

Regarding public managers, they rise from a special statue. The public service is different from other jobs. It reposes on fundamental principles as the principles of equality, neutrality; continuity and mutability, like it is stipulated by the article n.111 of the legislative decree (legislative decree no. 111 of January 12, 1959) concerning the organization of the public administrations. The public service fills an essential social function and is moved by the general interest. For this purpose, the administration must be able at any moment, in a unilateral way, to modify its officials situation. According the general statute of public servers, the public function is founded on several fundamental principles: workers placed in a legal and regular situation, very derogatory compared to the common law of work, and a specific framework of rights and duties.

The present statute is applied on persons who are nominated in a permanent job in the public administrations. These persons are divided into five categories:

The workers of the first category like general directors and the mayors.
The workers of the second category like head of department.
The workers of the third category like chiefs of a section.
The workers of the fourth category.
The workers of the fifth category.

The functions of management are reserved to holders of the three first categories. The system of public servants recruitment in Lebanon has not had considerable changes since the public servers was promulgated in 1959, while the recruitment is an essential aspect of the management of the human resources because it defines the level of the future managers of the public administration. Influenced by the French model, the system of recruitment in Lebanon is a system based on the rank and not on the position. The candidates are recruited upon their diplomas, in a category and not for a determined post where the skills are identified. There are few links with the profile needed by the post itself. The modalities of recruitment are strictly defined. The general conditions to present oneself to a public function are specified in article 4 of the law of public servants.

6 Analysis and Discussion of Obtained Results

To understand deeply the issues related to the integration of TIC by the leaders of the public sector in Lebanon, interviews were made with the objective to understand and to analyze the role of ICT in the public administration in Lebanon. The themes below were cleared.

6.1 The Influence of the Administrative Bureaucracy

All the interviewers suffer from the administrative paper work that absorbs their time and their energy. The rigor of procedures and the high degree of the bureaucracy reigns always in the public administration in Lebanon.

"The administrative part occupies an important place in my work. I sign annually and I control the papers of 10 thousand associations in order to approve their registration. I pass more than 4 h per day to sign necessary papers and to decide the questions attached hereto" (G5).

"There is an administrative part which encompasses the daily tasks. I perform my duty, put the annotation and make my conclusion then I transfer the file to the minister, either he approves it or he refuses it. Even if he refuses my point of view and he contradicts it, he is obliged to put my conclusion in the file" (G2).

These heavy administrative tasks prevent these well-trained young leaders to profit from the technological advances introduced in their administration (like the case of the minister of finance) to emphasize their leadership, and to prove more creativity, rapidity and performance in their work. "We use two important software for the management of the public debt. The World Bank developed these two programs and they are my subordinates who work on it. I do not have time to profit from them because I have many administrative tasks to accomplish every day. However, the informatics and the technological important innovations in this domain might be enormously useful for my work as a chief of this department" (G1).

Otherwise, the problem is that the majority of the interviewees does not accept the delegation of the administrative routine tasks and desires to control all. The time is lacking to make important changes and to try out strategic missions "I intervene in all the aspects of work, I supervise everything, all the details from A to Z, because I do not have so much confidence that things will go on in a good way, will be done properly, without my intervention" (G2, G3, G5, G7).

6.2   The Principal Roles Observed with the Public Leaders

Concerning the roles exercised by the public leaders in Lebanon, the results of the interviews confirm that leaders are always cantoned in their traditional roles. The public leaders in Lebanon invest principally in three roles:

The Role of Organizer or Guardian of Process—The leaders assure first the functioning of the public administrations and ensure the respect of rules, procedures and laws. "I manage a unit upon the reality of the administration and upon the texts that regulate its activity" (G1, G2). "Everyone must exercise his role in the process of the functioning of the administrative work in accordance with the laws and regulations in force to avoid any failure in the administrative chain" (G3). They are still far from the concept of the transformational leader or the servant leader [14, 38]. These two concepts represent outcomes of the evolution of the theories on the leadership.

The Role of Guarantor of the General Interest—"I am the guarantor of the general interest, it is my duty stipulated in article 14 of the public servant law, and I cannot neglect this essential part of my function. Otherwise, I am affected by my respect of oneself and by the dignity of the public function" (G2, G3, G4, G6, G7). "I am the guarantor of the interests of the company and of the role of the administration. My objective (objective of each public servant) is the realization of the general interest in the most optimal way, upon the most appropriated conditions and norms, and all this is in the interest of our country" (G2).

The Role of the Controller of Execution—"I control the formalities of the public establishment placed under tutelage. This work absorbs an important part of my timetable. I must be extremely vigilant in the exercise of my control to avoid waste and infractions of laws and to save the establishment placed under my tutelage" (G2). However, the transformational practices appear timidly among the public leaders in Lebanon. According to [46], the components of the transformational leader are the process of moral influence, the personal motivation that inspires others, the intellectual stimulation and the particular attention to others individually. The first component of a transformational leader requires from the leader that he incarnates a model of engagement and of morality arousing respect and trust at the same time. "To prove that I can make difference, I work night and day to be able to encounter and to continue. Thus, my motivations are my morals and my dignity, and I do not aspire to any personnel favor and I do not covet anything. So, they cannot touch my conscience" (G2).

The third component appears also in two cases. According to [46], the intellectual stimulation invites the leader to be active, to propose new solutions to resolve the problematic situations, and to shove the received ideas. "We can transform the function of the public purchase of a bureau from a marginalized post office to an administration of a very good reputation. The personality of the general director influences and he can change things around him. However, there are still essential points that he cannot change and that require the intervention of the legislator" (G3). "Personally, I could create a new mode of behavior in the administration. In the relations with politicians, I added the equation of the power conciliating the interests of the politicians and the ministers all respecting the legislation" (G7). Otherwise, the leader servant as he was described by Greenleaf does not exist in the public administration in Lebanon.

6.3 The Challenges of Public Leaders in Lebanon

According to the experiences of our interviewees who faced multiple challenges during their professional career, it seems that it is pertinent to make, in the first degree, certain compromises between the interests of the politicians and the respect of laws and regulations in force. "He must conciliate between the application of the laws and the interests of the politicians. It is the challenge to be raised to succeed in his work of leadership in the cadre of the public administration in Lebanon" (G3). "He must reconcile between the politics and the laws. Furthermore, it must not be communal, and he must stand at an equal distance away from everyone, and welcome people in his bureau and listen to their complaints and try to help them whatever was their communal and religious appurtenance" (G5).

Otherwise, the major challenge consists of the conciliation between the rigid nature of the administrative work and the exigencies of change and development that imply more flexibility and rapidity. "In the realization of new projects of development, to ameliorate the situation of public finances in the country, it is necessary to conciliate among several contradictions. On the one hand, the development requires the flexibility and the rapidity, and on the other hand, in the public sector, there are a lot of procedures that we cannot surpass" (G4).

Finally, the support of stakeholders is a necessary condition. "The public leader cannot make big changes alone, specially at the level of positions of the second and third category. He needs support from the administration for his projects. The minister must adopt his project. The minister must be persuaded about the necessity to make this project. At the Ministry of Finances, we have always the support of successive ministers to develop the ministry. The strategic support is so important for the leader" (G5).

To succeed in their mission and to realize their projects, the public leaders must acquire and master the art of managing all these paradoxes.

7 Conclusion

The results of our exploratory study permit us to put in evidence the limited influence of ICT in the daily work of the leaders of the Lebanese public sector. Furthermore, the must observed the behaviors settle with the expectations, and are rather focused on the traditional roles of the manager evoked by the classical theories of management. The public mangers prove to be effective managers, but they seem also cantoned by the traditional roles and are also far from the modern concept of leadership, like the transformational leader [14] or the servant leader [38].

The notion of the general interest is present in the public sector in Lebanon. On the other hand, the notion of public service is missing. The relations of leaders with their subordinates are founded on the respect of the hierarchy. The hierarchic distance is strong. This is related to cultural values of the Lebanese. Otherwise, the integration of TIC in the public sector entrains the re-engineering of administrative processes and contributes to rethink about models of management and the existing responsibility [43]. According to [44] the public leaders are asked to assure the management of capacities of networks (network governance capabilities), to reorganize the administrative mechanism and to guide the way to the transformations relevant to ICT.

Our results showed that the Lebanese public leaders do not participate in the integration of TIC to their work. They are also unconscious of the importance of technological innovations to ameliorate the efficiency of the administrative action. In fact, the senior managers, (the general directors and the head of department) are not in the measure to collaborate with the computer scientists and to profit from their expertise to develop their methods of work and to do the necessary changes. Furthermore, the law of the administrative organization in Lebanon does not provide positions for computer scientists in the public sector. These computer scientists are recruited by contract. Several administrations became fields of conflicts between those who hold the knowledge and those who hold power. Otherwise, the integration of ICT implies a permanent follow up and a change of adopted methods of work. At the level of the organizational structure, a change is necessary: to create an intermediate level for experts or computer scientists, to integrate them in the structure to have access there and to use data that they manipulate.

Finally, we can say that there is still a big gap between the roles exercised actually by the public leaders in Lebanon and the managerial skills required to guide the development of the application of technologies of information and communication in the public sector. To fill this gap, the public administrations must elaborate new strategies of recruitment and formation, and also a cultural transformation seems necessary. This can constitute the object of our next survey.

Magazines

The Commerce du Levant, March 8, 2017.
L'orient le-Jour, September 14, 2017.

Annex: Recapitulative Table of the Evolution of the Concept of Leadership in Function of the School of Thought

Classic school	Frederic Taylor	Scientific organization of work
	Henri Fayol	Administrative function of the manager
School of human relations	Elton Mayo	Cohesion and solidarity of group
	Mary Parker Follet	Good relationship in the workplace
	Chester Barnard	Notion of the organizational equilibrium through the social interactions
Leadership in the managerial thought	Chris Argyris	
	Douglas Mac Gregor	Theory X and Theory Y
	Robert Blake and Jane Mouton	Model of behaviorist leadership, in function of the organizational context
	William Ouchi	Consensual management
Leadership	Abraham Zaleznick	Creativity and intuition of leader
	John Kotter	Leaders: dynamic changes
	Robert Terry	Institutional leader
	Henry Mintzberg	Communityship
	Peter Drucker	Success of leadership is an effective management
	James Burns	Transactional leadership and transformational leadership

References

1. Wren, D.A., Bedeian, A.G.: The Evolution of Management Thought, 6th edn. Wiley, Hoboken, N.J. (2009)
2. Orazi, D.C., Turrini, A., Valotti, G.: Public sector leadership: new perspectives for research and practice. Int. Rev. Adm. Sci. (2013). (Research Article)
3. O'reilly, D., Reed, M.: Leaderism: an evolution of managerialism in UK public service reform. J. Public Administration **88**(4), 960–078 (2010)
4. Anderson, J.E.: Public policy making, 4th edn. Houghton Mifflin Company, Boston (2000)

5. El Khoury, G. (2015): The NICT Between the Private Sector and the Public Sector: A Lever for the State Reform, Proche Orient Magazine, Faculty of Business and Management. Saint Joseph University
6. Mintzberg, H.: The manager's job: folklore and fact. Harvard Bus. Rev. **68**(2), 163–176 (1990)
7. Mintzberg, H.: The Management: Travel at the Center of Organizations (trans. From English Behar, J.M.). 2nd edition reviewed and corrected. Editions of organization, Paris (2006)
8. Kennedy, C.: All the Theories of Management: the Essential Ideas of Authors the most Mentioned. [Trad. Derville, S., et al.] 3rd augmented edition. Maxima, Paris (2003)
9. Barnard, C.: The Function of the Executive. Havard University Press, Cambridge (1938)
10. Argyris, C.: Personality and Organization, the Conflict Between System and Individual. England Harpers, Oxford (1957)
11. Aktouf, O.: The Management Between Tradition and Renewal, Revised edn. Gaëtan Morin, Montreal (1989)
12. Martinet, A.-Ch., Silem, C., et al.: Lexica of Business, 5th edn. Dalloz, Paris (2000)
13. Drucker, P.F., Maciariello, J.A.: Management, Revised edn. Collins, New York (2008)
14. Bass, B.: Leadership and Performance Beyond Expectations. Free Press, New York (1985)
15. Bryman, A.: Leadership and Organizations. Routledge & Kegan Paul, London (1986)
16. Terry, L.: Leadership of Public Bureaucracies: The Administrator as Conservator. Sage Publications, Thousand Oaks, CA (1995)
17. Kotter, J.P.: What leaders really do? Harvard Bus. Rev. **79**(11), 85–96 (1990, 2001)
18. Zaleznik, A.: Managers and leaders are they different. Harvard Bus. Rev. **82**(1), 74–81 (1977, 1992, 2004)
19. Bennis, W., Nanus, B.: Leaders: Strategies for Taking Charge, 2nd edn. HarperBusiness, New York (2007)
20. Bolden, R.: What is Leadership? (on-line). United Kingdom: University of Exeter. Center for Leadership Studies, 35p, Research Report 1 (2004). Access 23/11/2010. http://centres.exeter. ac.uk/cls/lsw/internal1.pdf
21. Bennis, W., Biederman, P.W.: The Essential Bennis: Essays on Leadership by Warren Bennis with Patricia Ward Biederman, 1st edn. Jossey-Bass, San Francisco (2009)
22. Trottier, T., et al.: Reinforcing the need for more sophistication in leadership studies in the government sector. Public Adm. Rev. **68**(6), 1172–1174 (2008)
23. Stogdill, R.M.: Towards a contingency theory of leadership based upon the consideration and initiating structure literature. J. Organ. Behav. Hum. Perform. **12**, 62–82 (1974)
24. Bass, B.M., Stogdill, R.M. (eds.) Handbook of Leadership- Theory, Research and Managerial Applications, 3rd edn. The Free Press, New York (1981)
25. Stogdill, R.M.: Personal factors associated with leadership: a survey of the literature. J. Psychol. **25**, 35–71 (1948)
26. Black, R.R., Mouton, J.S.: The Managerial Grid. Houston, Gulf (1964)
27. Tannenbaum, R., Schmidt, W.: How to choose a leadership pattern. Harvard Bus. Rev. **36**(2), 95–101 (1958)
28. Fiedler, F.: A theory of Leadership Effectiveness: A Review and Conceptual Framework. McGraw-Hill, New York (1967)
29. Adair, J.: Action-Centered Leadership. McGraw-Hill, New York (1973)
30. Hersye, P., Blanchard, K.H.: So you want to know your leadership style? Training Dev. J. 1–15 (1974)
31. Burns, J.M.: Leadership, 1st edn. Harper & Row, New York (1978)
32. Bass, B.M., Avolio, B.J. (eds.): Improving Organizational Effectiveness Through Transformational Leadership. Sage, Thousand Oaks, CA (1994)
33. Van Wart, M.: Public sector leadership theory: an assessment. Public Adm. Rev. **63**(2), 214–228 (2003)
34. Getha-Taylor, H., et al.: Focusing the public leadership lens: research propositions and questions in the minnowbrook tradition. J. Public Adm. Res. Theory **21**(1 (Supplement 1)), i83–i97 (2001)
35. Ospina, S., Foldy, E.: Building bridges from the margins: the work of leadership in social change organizations. Leadersh. Q. **21**(2), 292–307 (2010)

36. Rainey, H.G., Bozeman, B.: Comparing public and private organizations: empirical research and the power of the a priori. J. Public Adm. Res. Theory **10**(2), 447–469 (2000)
37. Kakabadse, A., Korac-Kakabadse, N., Kouzmin, A.: Ethics, values and behaviors: comparison of three case studies examining the paucity of leadership in government. Public Adm. **81**, 477–508 (2003)
38. Greenleaf, R.K.: The Servant as Leader, The Robert Greenleaf Center, Indianapolis, (originally published in 1970). (Scholar Google) (1991)
39. Halque, S., Pathrannarakul, P.: E-Government towards good governance: a global appraisal. J. E-Gov. **36**, 25–34 (2013)
40. Harfouche, A., Robbin, A.: E-Government implementation in developing countries. In: From Information to Smart Society, Springer, pp. 315–327 (2015)
41. Harfouche, A., Robbin, A.: Inhibitors and enablers of public e-services in Lebanon. J. Organ. End User Comput. **24**(3), 45–68 (2012)
42. Leisein, O.: Modernization of the Interface Citizen-Public Function: To a Reflected Integration of TIC, Review of Center of Research in Public Administration, vol. 7 (2003)
43. Brown, D.: The electronic government and the public administration. Int. Rev. Adm. Sci. **71**, 251–266
44. Hanna, N.K.: Transforming Government and Building Information Society. Springer Science & Business Media (2011)
45. Roussel, P., Wacheux, F.: Management des Ressources Humaines: Methodes de Recherches en Sciences Humaines et Sociales. De Boek Superieur (2005)
46. Maltais, D., Leclerc, M., Rinfret, N.: Le «leadership administratif» comme concept utile à la modernisation de l'administration publique. Rev. Fr. d'Adm. Publique **3**(123) (2007)

E-Banking Users' Profiles in Lebanon Exploration of the Role of Socio-Demographic Factors

Bissane Harb and Mariam Saleh

Abstract Referring to the model developed by Rogers [8] on the diffusion of innovations and that of Venkatesh and Morris [9], this article aims to explore and identify the role of the socio-demographic factors in the adoption of e-banking by the clientele of a big commercial bank operating in Lebanon. The analysis and processing of data emanating from the bank through the SPSS software allow us to draw representative profiles of customers based on their socio-demographic criteria. The obtained results are consistent with previous researches and confirmed the impact of age, income, educational level and profession on the adoption of e-banking by the Lebanese consumer. These results provide an in-depth understanding of the role of socio-demographic characteristics in the use of electronic distribution channels and help Lebanese banking institutions better establish strategies for promoting online banking services in the future.

Keywords Diffusion of innovations · Adoption of e-banking · Socio-demographic characteristics · Banking sector in Lebanon

1 Introduction

As the human species evolves over time, technological progress and the desire to create new technologies go hand in hand. Dependence on technology has become unavoidable. It is currently considered a fourth necessity in life after air, water and food. Thus, in the current era of technology revolution, no industry in the world is untouched to the use of Information systems, and Banking Industry is no exception [1].

Indeed, the banking sector has often been exposed to technological innovations as a result of development in the field of information and information technology.

B. Harb (✉) · M. Saleh
Faculty of Business and Management, Saint Joseph University, Beirut, Lebanon
e-mail: bissan.harbbaghdadi@usj.edu.lb

M. Saleh
e-mail: mariam_saleh@hotmail.com

© Springer Nature Switzerland AG 2020
Y. Baghdadi et al. (eds.), *ICT for an Inclusive World*,
Lecture Notes in Information Systems and Organisation 35,
https://doi.org/10.1007/978-3-030-34269-2_22

E-banking represents the latest initiative in the range of innovative banking services. Since their first introduction in four major New York banks in 1981, e-banking solutions have grown in importance and variety [2].

E-banking presents a general term used to refer to the process by which customers manage their banking transactions 24 h a day, 7 days a week, through a banking website [3, 4].

There are different definitions related to e-banking found in the literature. In this research, it could be defined as a concept referring to any banking transaction using electronic medium. It now covers various initiatives such as internet banking, telephone banking and PC banking [5]. These transactions can be done electronically and without the need to visit a branch. The integration of electronic distribution channels in the banking sector represents multiple benefits for both the bank and the customer [6].

This research is an extension of two previous researches conducted by the authors of this article [7] on e-banking. If the first two researches have addressed the issue of e-banking from the bank's point of view, this article aims to identify the socio-demographic factors that affect the adoption of e-banking by the clients of a large Lebanese commercial bank, based on the model of Rogers [8] on the diffusion of innovations and on that of Venkatesh and Morris [9]. We will try to find an answer to the following question: Who is the client using e-banking in Lebanon? Representative profiles comprising information of the different distinctive groups of e-banking users will be set up. Thus, we will be able to identify the most important socio-demographic characteristics that describe and define these clients to finally detect the main socio-demographic factors that affect the use of e-banking services in Lebanon.

Therefore, as a first step, we will review the literature to establish the relevant theoretical framework for our research. First, we will explain Rogers' model [8] on the diffusion of innovations, then we will discuss the relationship between socio-demographic factors and the diffusion of innovations in general by referring to the model of Venkatesh and Morris [9]. Finally, we will present the findings of the previous researches dealing with the relationship between socio-demographic factors and the adoption of e-banking. In a second step, we will present our methodology and expose our findings. And finally, we will discuss the obtained results, the contributions of our research and its limitations.

2 Literature Review

2.1 Rogers' Theory [8] on the Diffusion of Innovations

This article is based on Rogers' theory of diffusion of innovations [8]. This theory was developed by Rogers in 1983, from the synthesis of a large number of previous studies on this subject. [8] defines diffusion as the process by which an innovation is communicated across certain channels over time and among members by a given social system. It results from the acceptance or the penetration of new ideas, behaviors, or physical innovations. The Rogers model [8] can also be applied to the behavior of the adoption of innovations at the individual level. He illustrated this process by a diffusion curve that distinguishes between the different profiles of adopters corresponding to the different phases of the adoption process (Fig. 1).

Indeed, Rogers [8] divides the adopters into five categories that differ in terms of innovativeness, which could affect the adoption of technological innovations. The five adopter categories are: innovators, early adopters, early majority, late majority and laggards. Innovativeness could be defined in the field of information technology as the willingness of an individual to try out any new information technology [10]. Rogers suggests that new products and services should be targeted at innovators category when launching new products and services as they will begin the diffusion process by communicating to other adopter segments [11]. According to Rogers [8], the youngest ones with a high level of education and income are the first adopters of innovations.

Rogers also analyzes the behavior of these different types of adopters and suggests a process which he describe as a decision-making/innovation process. This process helps to explain the phenomenon of adoption of innovations within different organizations. It consists of five stages: knowledge, persuasion, decision, implementation and confirmation [12].

- Knowledge: During this stage, individuals learn about the existence of innovation and look for relevant information.

Fig. 1 The curve of diffusion of innovations

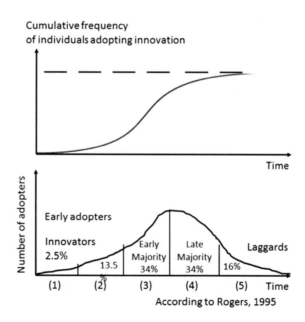

According to Rogers, 1995

- Persuasion: This stage occurs when the individual adopts a negative or positive attitude towards innovation, but this attitude does not lead directly to the rejection or the acceptance of this innovation.
- Decision: The decision to adopt or not the innovation occurs during this stage. If the innovation is adopted, it will be tested by the adopter before generalizing its adoption. On the other hand, the decision not to adopt can be made at any stage of the decision/innovation process.
- Implementation: innovation is now active. Its novelty raises uncertainty towards the results expected during the diffusion process. Its implementation will depend on the level of technical assistance mobilized to reduce this uncertainty.
- Confirmation: the decision of innovation has already been made and the adopter seeks the reinforcement of his decision. The adoption of the innovation will be confirmed or rejected according to the adopter's ability to bring other stakeholders to its decision.

Rogers also discusses the different attributes of innovation that may affect whether or not to adopt innovation. According to him, innovation is characterized by the following attributes: relative advantage, accounting, complexity, observability and testability. Relative advantage is the perception by consumers that innovation is better or more efficient than existing solutions. Compatibility is the degree of consistence with the existing values and past experiences of potential consumers and those needed for the use of innovation. The complexity of the innovation perceived by potential consumers can also be a barrier to its diffusion. The trialability of innovation can facilitate its appropriation by users and thus promote word of mouth and reduce uncertainty and therefore the risk that surrounds it. Finally, the observability of results or the rapid visibility of results is also a determining factor in the diffusion of innovations as it makes it easier to prove the advantage or advantages of innovation.

Roger's model (Fig. 2) provides a basic reference for several models that have addressed the theme of adoption and diffusion of innovations and technologies. These models have attempted to explain the decision to adopt or not one or more technologies by one or more users, by focusing on the explanatory factors of this decision. Some models have been particularly interested in the role of personal demographic characteristics of potential users of an innovation such as that of [13].

2.2 Socio-demographic Factors and Diffusion of Innovations

[13] proposed a development of the original model proposed by [14] in order to explain the determinants of technology acceptance by information system users. According to Davis et al. [14], the behaviors of user acceptance of technology are based on two types of beliefs: perceived usefulness and perceived ease-of-use. [9] add two other constructs: social influence process and cognitive instrumental process. The first construct refers to subjective norms, voluntariness and image, while the second

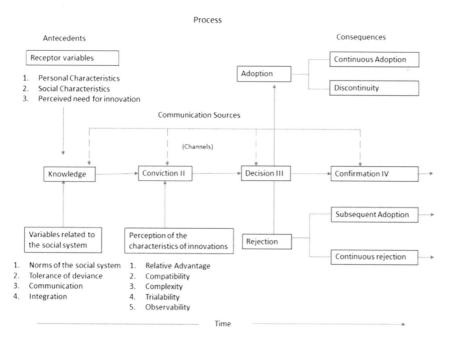

Fig. 2 Roger's model

relates to job relevance, output quality and result demonstrability, in addition to the traditional perception of ease-of-use.

[9] studied the impact of demographic factors on the diffusion of innovations. They found that gender plays a decisive role in the adoption and use of technology. In this respect, in a survey conducted in Germany and England in order to explore the relationship between gender differences and the percentage of technology adoption, the authors found that the percentage of men who adopt and use technologies is higher than that of women. In addition, they found that age differences influence the new technology acceptance. According to them, the first adopters are revealed to be young in the case of most technologies.

Thus, based on the theoretical contributions of Rogers' theory and the model of Venkatesh and Morris [8, 9], we will review the literature dealing with the impact of socio-demographic factors, in the specific context of online banking.

2.3 Socio-Demographic Factors and Adoption of E-Banking

The demographic factors that will be examined are age, gender, level of education and income. These factors were chosen because they are the main demographic factors examined in previous researches [9, 15–19]. These researches have evaluated and measured the impact of these factors by mobilizing different c. However, most of these studies have been conducted in developed countries [20].

Age

The influence of age on the adoption of e-banking has been detected in previous researches. Wood [21] found that young people under the age of 25 are more interested in adopting any new technology than older people. In addition, according to a survey conducted in Malaysia, [11] have found that mobile banking is more popular among younger consumers. Older clients fear the use of e-banking and find it much more stressful [22].

[23] also show in their survey a steady decline in the percentage of preference for e-banking as the age group increases. This means that the percentage of preference for e-banking for the 18–25 years age group is greater than the percentage of preference for e-banking for the above 60 years age group.

Recently, [24] see that older people are less likely to use e-banking systems because they suffer more from health problems (vision, mental reflex, patience, memory, etc.). These problems exacerbate their anxiety toward the use of online banking services. In addition, younger clients are more likely to be familiar with the latest developments in mobile technology [25], and have a high level of education and experience [15]. Thus, in general, in previous researches, the innovative consumer tends to be younger.

In addition, some researches have pointed out that age does not have a significant influence on the adoption of internet banking [26]. It is especially in developed countries that age is not considered a critical variable for banks planning to offer electronic services.

However, in the Middle East the situation is different since the majority of potential users of mobile banking range between 17 and 35 years [15]. So the 7 banks need to target this category of their customers in the strategies developed to increase the rate of adoption of e-banking.

Education

The education (the highest degree obtained by the client) is one of the most decisive socio-demographic factors affecting the adoption of e-banking. Indeed, a high degree allows the client to have the necessary skills to use the computer and interact with the computer environment [19]. Moreover, when a person has a high intellectual level, he becomes more open to any form of new technology [27].

According to [28], the level of education is among the social factors that have favored the adoption of information technologies by Arabs. They also found that the level of education has an influence on organizational behavior, especially in terms of adoption of new technologies.

Furthermore, [17] pointed out that clients who are more educated and younger are significantly more exposed to banking innovations than other members of the social system. In another important research conducted in Malaysia, [11] resulted in the following findings: 2.9% of the interviewees who have a secondary education degree at most are among the adopters, while 75% of the adopters have a higher educational level (university level). In fact, higher qualifications are positively associated with increased attention to online banking.

More recently, [29] also found that consumers' level of education and knowledge of ICT influences their acceptance of e-banking services. Furthermore, according to [30, 31, 32], the level of education does not have a significant influence on the e-banking adoption behavior of clients.

Income and Professional Activity

Several researchers have linked these two factors in order to show the socio-economic status of e-banking users. However, the socio-economic status may depend on several variables such as occupation, level of education, income, wealth and residency [33]. Thus, according to [16, 24], income and occupation influence the use of e-banking.

Several researchers have also shown that the adoption of mobile banking is common among high-income earners [11, 15, 18]. This may be justified by the fact that high-income households are positively correlated with computer possession, internet access and high educational level [34].

[24] see that the nature of the profession and its characteristics in terms of schedules, payment methods, programming of transfers for employees affect the use of online banking services. According to the same authors, clients who occupy interesting positions are more familiar with technological innovations and are more likely to take advantage of their multiple benefits such as the speed that best suits their agenda. In addition, according to [35], clients' financial well-being makes them less concerned about losing money.

As for the relationship between the type of profession and the adoption of e-banking, [32] found that the adoption of e-banking was more obvious for public employees than for other employees. In addition, according to [36], high-income earner public employees who have a bank account, preferably in government banks, are more likely to use e-banking services.

Contrary to these results, [37, 38] find that the profession does not affect the adoption of e-banking. According to these authors, the profession does not play a role in the adoption of e-banking by customers, so clients in different professions have the same practices of adoption or use of e-banking.

Gender

Some researchers have pointed out that men are more interested in the use of different types of technologies because they are more likely to take risks and try new technological products than women [11, 19, 26, 35].

Moreover, others have realized that the influence of gender on the use of e-banking is insignificant [39]. It seems limited in contexts characterized by a rigid division of work between women and men and low participation of women in the labor market.

Finally, referring to Roger's model [8] and based on our review of the literature, we might conclude that the main socio-demographic factors that affect the adoption of e-banking in previous researches are age, educational level, nature of occupation and income (Table 1).

Table 1 The previous studies related to the impact of demographic factors

Study	Country	Age	Gender	Education	Income
Greco and Fields [40]	USA	✓	×	✓	✓
Rogers [8]	–	✓	×	✓	✓
Venkatesh and Morris [9]	Indonesia	✓	×	×	×
Lee et al. [30]	–	✓	×	✓	✓
Karjaluoto et al. [18]	Finland	×	×	✓	✓
Sulaiman et al. [11]	Malaysia	✓	✓	✓	✓
Baker et al. [41]	Saudi Arabia				×
Harma and Dubey [17]	India	✓	×	✓	✓
AbuShanab et al. [20]	Jordan	✓	✓	✓	
Alafeef et al. [15]	Jordan	✓	✓	✓	✓

✓ (Reviewed by the study), × (not reviewed)

3 Methodology

We adopt an exploratory method as we try to explore the socio-demographic characteristics of e-banking users. Our work aims to deeply understand the role of socio-demographic factors in motivating clients to use online banking services. We chose these characteristics because they were considered in the literature as important determinants of e-banking users' profiles. Indeed, many researches advocate the use of socio-demographic characteristics to determine the reasons for the adoption of e-banking as these factors are considered as very influential components of consumer behavior.

Our goal is to build representative profiles of clients who conduct banking transactions over the Internet. These profiles will include more specific information on the most important socio-demographic characteristics describing and defining these clients. Our job is therefore to examine the link between these variables and the use of e-banking. It is also a question of examining the significance of the association between several socio-demographic variables and the orientation towards online banking services. Our work could be synthesized in the following research model (Fig. 3).

3.1 Data Collection

We had access to an internal database belonging to a large commercial bank operating in Lebanon. The information we processed was collected by the bank itself and relates to the following: the client's age, his level of education, income, occupation, frequency of his visits to the bank, the average number of his online interactions with

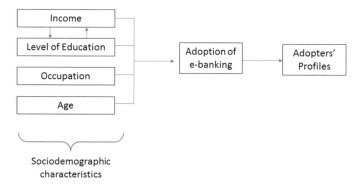

Fig. 3 Research model of the study

the bank and the nature of the transactions executed through electronic distribution channels.

The data obtained from the bank were carefully observed in order to better interpret the results. The data analysis and processing was performed by the SPSS software.

3.2 Characteristics of the Chosen Sample

The general information collected by the bank cover a large population of 300,000 clients. We decided to restrict our sample to 3000 clients (10% of the bank's clients) which is considered sufficiently representative for our exploratory study. Only 2361 out of the 3000 interviewed clients responded to the survey. The relevant information will be presented as follows:

3.2.1 Age

The age of the studied population ranges between 18 years and 80 years (Table 2).

Table 2 Age groups of the sample

From 18 to 23 years	3%
From 23 to 35 years	35%
From 35 to 45 years	29%
From 45 to 65 years	30%
65 and more	3%

Table 3 Categories of
Income

Less than 1000 $	11%
1000 $–2000 $	22%
2000 $–4000 $	20%
4000 $–7000 $	12%
7000 $–10,000 $	6%
10,000 $ and more	8%
No answer	20%

3.2.2 Income

We worked on a range of monthly income ranging from less than $1000 to over $10,000 (Table 3).

3.2.3 Socio-Economic Status

The clients will be divided into 4 economic statuses: status A, B, C and D. The determination of the economic status of the client depends on the association of three socio-demographic criteria: the nature of the profession, the level of education and the amount of annual income.

A score model has been developed in order to assign to each client a particular status among the 4 socio-economic statuses: (A, B, C, D). The number of scores awarded to each criterion varies between 0 and 10. For example, the client who has a Master degree and higher is granted a 10 for the criterion of level of education as it is the highest level of education. The income criterion has received a higher weighting (double the other two criteria), given its importance in the banking sector (refer to Tables 4 and 5).

3.2.4 Type and Frequency of Operations Executed with the Bank

In addition to these socio-demographic data, we were able to collect information that will be useful for our research:

- The average customer visits to the bank is estimated at 8.77, about 9 visits per year.
- The average interaction with the bank (number of login and ATM visit) via the electronic distribution channels is about 26.
- The average monthly income of the studied population is $348/-.

Table 4 Socio-economic status

Profession	Scores	Income	Scores	Level of Education	Scores
Professionals Managers	10	More than 500 K $	20	Master degree and higher	10
Liberal professions Business owners B Professionals	9	200 K$–500 K$	18	Bachelor degree	8
Employees	8	100 K$–200 K$	15	Technical Diploma	5
Men of religion	7	75 K$–100 K$	10	Baccalaureate	3
C Professionals Artists	5	25 K$–75 K$	7	Secondary degree and lower—illiterates	0
Agriculturers Laborers	3	Less than 25 K$	3		
Students-inactive-retirees	0	Inactive	0		

Table 5 Classification of socio-economic status

Scores	Socio-economic status
31–40	A
21–30	B
11–20	C
0–10	D

4 Analysis and Discussion of the Findings

4.1 Identified Groups

The description of the groups was made on the basis of the SPSS output analysis. Clients were divided into 5 groups: frequent users (11%), personal contact seekers (24%), independent clients (16%), passive clients (35%) and inactive clients (15%).

Group 1 (Frequent users)

They are those who deal frequently with the bank. They often visit the branches and at the same time they use the electronic distribution channels. 41% of this group is between the ages of 18 and 35, and only 4% are over the age of 65.

The average monthly income for this category is $ 758 while the average monthly income for all the customers of the bank is $ 348. Knowing that, according to a study conducted by the Ministry of Finance in 2017, 57% of the Lebanese citizens attain a monthly income below $ 833.[1]

---

[1] Income inequality: Lebanon is ranked 129th among 141 countries, Report published by the Ministry of Finance and the United Nations Development Programs, 2017.

This group has the highest concentration of income because 50% of its members earn more than $25,000 per year, while only 33% of the bank's clients do so. Similarly, 42% belong to socio-economic B category and 6% to socio-economic A category. This group is composed of a good number of A level (17%) professionals and managers (10%). 65% of the customers classified in this group use online banking. We could conclude that this category comprises high-income individuals belonging to a more or less affluent class and holding important managerial positions and responsibilities in companies.

Group 2 (Personal contact seekers)

They are the clients who prefer to visit the branches and interact with an advisor in order to manage their banking operations (95% of them go personally to the bank). 63% of them have never used online banking.

The average monthly income for this category is $ 492. However, 40% of prestigious customers (holders of large bank accounts and those who generate most profits) of the bank still belong to this group.

13% of the members in this category are older than 65, and only 20% are between 18 and 35 years old. 35% of the members of this group are generally retired or do not work at all.

Group 3 (Independent clients)

This group is not interested in human contact with their bank and does not frequent the branches, but rather prefers to manage its accounts and banking transactions remotely. It is dominated by a young and adult population, aged between 18 and 35 years old. The average monthly income of this population is $ 236. In this group, there is the lowest concentration of clients belonging to the socio-economic A category (2%), and at the same time a low presence of clients of the economic D category compared to other groups (28%).

More than half of this group uses online banking. 40% of the clients who have domiciliated their salary at the bank are self-employed. It is clear that the population belonging to this category is the youngest but not necessarily the most affluent. Indeed, in the highest socio-economic category, clients tend to be less independent and often use their banker to provide effective management for their huge bank deposits.

Group 4 (Passive clients)

This group visits rarely th Lebanon e bank, in order to recuperate their interests, for example. The average monthly income for this category is $ 287. 40% of this group's members are workers. They represent 10.2% of the total workforce in Lebanon.[2]

---

[2]Multiple Indicators Cluster Survey, 2012 Report of the Central Administration of Statistics, volume 3, p. 76.

Groupe 5 (Inactive Clients)

They never come to the bank. They opened bank accounts and deposited money and since then they did not make any physical or virtual contact with the bank. 16% of inactive people are older than 65, thus in this group, we find the highest concentration of older clients. The average monthly income for this category is $ 90. We also observe the lowest concentration of prestigious customers in this category (8%). Currently, older people who are over 65 represent 7.8% of the total population in Lebanon.[3] On the other hand, inactive people in Lebanon who are over 15 years old and do not work represent 52% of the total population in this age group.[4]

4.2 The Average Usage of Internet Banking Per Group

In group 1, individuals made an average of 25 visits to the bank and 108 online transactions (logins). Online transactions mainly involve internal and external transfers, payment of invoices, checking of bank accounts and wedding lists.

Group 2 includes individuals who made an average of 18 visits to the branch per year and 4 logins. As for group 3 members, they made an average of 4 visits to the bank per year and 71 online interactions. Finally, for group 4, the average number of annual visits to the bank is 3 while the average number of logins is 6.

4.3 Analysis of Findings

The results show that e-banking customers mainly belong to two groups: frequent users and independent users.

From the analysis of the socio-demographic characteristics of these two groups, we could conclude that clients who virtually deal with the bank are generally younger, more educated, and hold positions of responsibility in the private or public sector. They also earn above-average annual income. These young executives who are overwhelmed by their daily professional obligations, prefer to deal with their bank through virtual distribution channels. Their high level of education (their majority holds a university degree) facilitates their understanding and their proper use of online banking. In addition, their relatively high income enables them to broaden and diversify their banking interactions and to benefit more from the latest banking innovations.

---

[3] Idem, p. 26.
[4] Idem, p. 70.

Indeed, Lebanon is among the developing countries that show the most satisfactory results in terms of quality of education and schooling[5] (the enrollment rate was 86% in 2013).[6] Thus, we are witnessing a growing massive integration of well qualified and highly educated young people into the labor market. According to the latest report published by the Central Administration of Statistics, university graduates are the most economically active ones with an activity rate of 58%.[7] In addition, senior executives and managers account for 14.1% of the total active population, the liberal professions 12.1%.; knowing that 50% of the active population are employees, 30% work for their own account and 4.7% are employers.[8]

However, the wealthiest clients such as entrepreneurs and owners of large companies and businessmen who represent the most active population of the bank always refer to the physical branch, as they are generally older, and are already accustomed to privileged personal treatment from the bank. Thus, they rarely use e-banking. This wealthy category is more and more decreasing among the active population in Lebanon. According to recent statistics, people who earn more than $40,000 a year represent 6.3% of the active population, while those who earn an annual income of more than $ 80,000 represent only 1.4% of the active population.[9]

5   Conclusion

This article provides an interesting overview of the e-banking distribution process. It delivers a better understanding of the role of socio-demographic factors in the adoption of e-banking by the Lebanese consumer.

The review of the literature has shown how socio-demographic factors affect the adoption of e-banking. Our methodology has attempted to explore and identify the socio-demographic characteristics of e-banking users in a large financial institution operating in Lebanon. Our results have identified several client profiles and examined the links between these profiles and the use of e-banking.

Thus, according to Roger's and Venkatesh and Morris models [8, 9], we found that the youngest clients, with a high level of education and income, are more likely to adopt technological innovations such as e-banking. However, in the framework of the Lebanese context, the holders of high fortunes are reluctant to opt for virtual channels and still prefer to maintain a distinguished personal relationship with their bank.

---

[5]Daccache, Salim, The Lebanese Educational System: an overview of realities, problems and challenges, Colloque Fondation Oasis, Maison de la montagne, Lebanon, 2012.

[6]World Data Atlas.

[7]Multiple Indicators Cluster Survey, 2012 Report of the Central Administration of Statistics, Volume 3, p. 70.

[8]Idem, p. 72.

[9]Income inequality: Lebanon is ranked 129th among 141 countries, Report published by the Ministry of Finance and the United Nations Development Programs, 2017.

This could be attributed to the historically privileged treatment of large depositors by Lebanese commercial banks, and also to cultural reasons related to the specific structure of the Lebanese society.

The nature of the profession also represents an important factor of the use of electronic distribution channels. This finding is in line with the results reported by [24, 32, 35]. Indeed, senior professionals and managers represent a good part of e-banking users in our sample.

These results have multiple managerial implications. The banking sector could use them to improve the dissemination of information on e-banking, and to develop advertising policies that are compatible with the profiles identified to attract the potential users of e-banking. Thus, the banks will have to choose the communication style that is appropriate to the detected socio-demographic criteria in order to increase the percentage of adoption of electronic banking innovations at the level of each group.

Finally, this study presents limitations. It allows to identify the users of e-banking services based only on their socio-demographic characteristics. However, the analysis of some non-demographic personal factors such as innovativeness, openness to experience, the perceived need for innovation, or the level of social influence [42], seems interesting and could be the subject of a future research. Another limitation is that the processed and analyzed data in the exploratory study comes from a single bank. It seems appropriate to be able to expand this research to other banking institutions in Lebanon.

References

1. Choudhury, D., Dibyojyoti, B.: Impact of socio economic factors on adoption of e-banking amongst salaried employee. Int. J. Res. Manag. 2321–3264 (2015)
2. Osho, G.S.: How technology is breaking traditional barriers in the banking industry: Evidence from financial management perspective. Eur. J. Econ. **11**, 15–21 (2008)
3. Sharma, M.C., Sharma, A.: Role of information technology in indian banking sector. Int. J. Multi. Acad. Res. **2**, 1–12 (2013)
4. Thulani, D., Tofara, C., Langton, R.: Adoption and use of internet banking in Zimbabwe: an exploratory study. J. Internet Bank. Commer. **14**(1) (2009)
5. Kurnia, S., Peng, F., Liu, Y.R.: Understanding the Adoption of Electronic Banking in China, HICSS, IEEE Computer Society, pp. 1–10 (2010)
6. Angelakopoulos, G., Mihiotis, A.: E-banking: challenges and opportunities in the Greek banking sector. Electronic Commer. Res. **11**(3), 297–319 (2011)
7. Chedrawi, C., Harb, B., Saleh, M.: The e-banking and the adoption of innovations from a perspective of the transactions cost theory: case of the biggest commercial bank in Lebanon. In: ICT for a better life and a better world. Youcef Baghdadi and Antoine Harfouche, Springer (2019)
8. Rogers, E.M.: Diffusion of Innovations. New York Free Press, New York (1995)
9. Venkatesh, V., Morris, M.G.: Why don't men ever stop to ask for directions? Gender, social influence, and their role in technology acceptance and usage behavior. MIS Q. **24**(1), 115–140 (2000)
10. Agarwal, R., Prasard, J.: A conceptual and operational definition of personnel innovativeness in the domain of information technology. Inf. Syst. Res. **9**(2), 204–2015 (1998)

11. Sulaiman, A., Jaafar, N.I., Mohezar, S.: An overview of mobile banking adoption among the urban community. Int. J. Mobile Comm. **5**, 157–168 (2007)
12. Rogers, E.M.: Diffusion of Innovations, 5th edn, p. 2003. Free Press, New York (2003)
13. Morris, M.G., Venkatesh, V.: Age differences in technology adoption decisions: implications for a changing work force. Pers. Psychol. (2000)
14. Davis, F., Bagozzi, R., Warshaw, P.: User acceptance of computer technology: a comparison of two theoretical models. Manage. Sci. **35**(8), 982–1003 (1989)
15. Alafeef, M., Singh, D., Ahmad, K.: Influence of demographic factors on the adoption level of mobile banking applications in Jordan. J. Convergence Inf. Technol. **6**, 107–113 (2011)
16. Antonny, G.: Commercial banks put vendors to the test. National Mortgage News (11) (2011)
17. Harma, M.K., Dubey, R.: Prospects of technological advancements in banking sector using mobile banking and position of India. In: Proceedings of the international association of computer science and information technology spring conference, Singapore, pp. 291–295 (2009)
18. Karjaluoto, H., Koivuma, T., Salo, J.: Individual differences in private banking: empirical evidence from Finland. In: Proceedings of the 36th Hawaii International Conference on System Sciences (HICSS), Big Island, Hawaii, p. 196 (2003)
19. Harfouche, A., Robbin, A.: Antecedents of the digital divide at the Macro level. In: Mediterranean Conference on Information Systems Proceedings, p. 83 (2011)
20. AbuShanab, E., Pearson, J.M., Setterstrom, A.J.: Internet banking and customers' acceptance in Jordan: the unified model's perspective. Common. AIS **26**, 493–524 (2010)
21. Wood, S.L.: Future fantasies: a social change perspective of retailing in the 21st century. J. Retail. **78**, 77–83 (2002)
22. Im, S., Bays, B.L., Mason, C.H.: An empirical study of innate consumer innovativeness, personal characteristics and new product adoption behavior. J. Acad. Mark. Sci. **31**(11), 61–73 (2003)
23. Yitbarek, T., Zeleke, S.: Analysis of factors influencing customers' intention to the adoption of e-banking service channels in Bahir Dar city, Ethiopia: an integration of TAM, TPB and PR. Eur. Sci. J. **9**, 402–417 (2013)
24. Bellahcene, M., Khadem, M.M.: The factors influencing the adoption of e-Banking by the customers of Algerian banks. Economiet Soc. (12) (2016)
25. Mattila, M.: Factors affecting the adoption of mobile banking services. J. Internet Bank. Commer. **8**, 14–15 (2003)
26. Mirza, A.P., Beheshti, M.T.H., Wallstromet, A., Mirza, O.P.: Adoption of internet banking by Iranian consumers: an empirical investigation. J. Appl. Sci. **9**, 2567–2575 (2009)
27. Beladi, M.: Determination of Internet banking users' profiles in Quebec, Ph.D. Thesis, University of Quebec in Montreal, 2010
28. Hill, C.E., Loch, K.D., Straub, D., El-Sheshai, K.: A qualitative assessment of Arab culture and information technology transfer. J. Glob. Inform. Manag. **6**, 29–38 (1998)
29. Edwin, M.A., Ailemen, I.O., Okpara, A., Mike, O.A.: Impediments to e-banking services marketing in developing economies—a case study of Nigerian banks. Eur. J. Bus. Soc. Sci. **3**, 228–248 (2004)
30. Lee, E., Jinkook, L., David, E.: A two-step estimation of consumer adoption of technology-based service innovations. J. Consum. Aff. **37**, 256–282 (2003)
31. Annin, K., Adjepong, O.M., Senya, S.S.: Applying logistic regression to e-banking usage in Kumasi metropolis. Ghana. Int. J. Mark. Stud. **6**, 153–162 (2013)
32. Alagheband, P.: Adoption of electronic banking services by Iranian customers. Master Thesis, Lulea University of Technology, Sweden (2006)
33. Hirsh, E., Kett, J.: The New Dictionary of Culture Literacy. Houghton Mifflin Harcourt (2002)
34. Lohse, G.L., Bellman, S., Johnson, E.J.: Consumer buying behavior on the Internet: findings from panel data. J. Interact. Market **14**, 15–29 (2000)
35. Alafeef, M., Singh, D., Ahmad, K.: The influence of demographic factors and user interface on mobile banking adoption: a review. J. Appl. Sci. **12**(20), 2082–2095 (2012)

36. Mohammed, S.: Factors affecting ATM usage in India: an empirical analysis. UTMS J. Econ. **3**, 1–7 (2012)
37. Ismail, M.A., Osman, M.A.: Factors influencing the adoption of e-banking in Sudan: perceptions of retail banking clients. J. Internet Bank. Commer. **17**, 1–16 (2012)
38. Sheshadri, P., Rani, S.S.: The influence of demographic variables on customer adoption of e-banking services. Int. J. Sci. Res. **3** (2014)
39. Debaillon, L., Rockwell, P.: Gender and student status differences in cellular telephone use. Int. J. Mobile Commun. **3**(1), 82–98 (2005)
40. Greco, A.J., Fields, D.M.: Profiling early triers of service innovations: a look at interactive home video ordering services. J. Serv. Market. **5**, 19–26 (1991)
41. Baker, E.W., Al-Gahtani, S.S., Hubona, G.S.: The effects of gender and age on new technology implementation in a developing country: testing the Theory of Planned Behavior (TPB). Inform. Technol. People **20**, 352–375 (2007)
42. Harfouche, A., Ezzeddine, S., Kosremelli Asmar, M.: Religiosity, hedonism, social Image and e-banking acceptance in Lebanon. In: D'Ascenzo, F., Magni, M., Lazazzara, A., Za, S. (eds.) Blurring the Boundaries Through Digital Innovation. Lecture Notes in Information Systems and Organisation, vol. 19. Springer (2016)

The FDI-Economic Growth Nexus: A Human Resource Management Perspective—The Case of the ICT Sector in Sub-Saharan Africa

Aïcha Hammami and Cinzia Dal Zotto

Abstract How can foreign direct investment (FDI) in Sub-Saharan Africa better benefit host economies? Here, we consider the role of human resource management, taking the information and communications technology (ICT) sector as a case study. Our concern is to assess how human resource management can contribute to the success of FDI in the ICT sector in Sub-Saharan Africa in terms of human capital development and economic development. The paper thus provides a human resource management perspective on the FDI-economic growth nexus in that empirical context.

Keywords Economic growth · Foreign direct investment · Information and communication technology · International human resource management · Sub-Saharan Africa

1 Introduction

In the last decades, the information and communications technology (ICT) sector has witnessed a substantial growth both globally [1] and in African countries [2]. Empirical evidence suggests a strong positive relationship between the development of the ICT sector, foreign direct investment (FDI), and economic growth [1, 3]. The causality behind the positive relationship between ICT and FDI may vary across countries, with Gholami et al. [4] finding that investments in ICT increase FDI flows in developed countries, whereas increasing FDI flows increase ICT investment in developing countries. Studies addressing the human dimension of ICT sector development have focused on ICT use and access rather on its implications for human capital development, with a few exceptions [5]. Even then, however, little attention has been given to the role of human resource management (HRM) in the interplay between

A. Hammami (✉) · C. D. Zotto
University of Neuchâtel, Avenue du 1er-Mars 26, Neuchâtel 2000, Switzerland
e-mail: aicha.hammami@unine.ch

C. D. Zotto
e-mail: cinzia.dalzotto@unine.ch

© Springer Nature Switzerland AG 2020
Y. Baghdadi et al. (eds.), *ICT for an Inclusive World*,
Lecture Notes in Information Systems and Organisation 35,
https://doi.org/10.1007/978-3-030-34269-2_23

FDI, ICT, and economic development. Rapid population growth and urbanization in many African countries offer good reasons to conduct HRM research and identify how organizations can better contribute to human capital development in African countries, particularly in the less developed economies.

The aim of this paper is to understand how human resource management can contribute to the success of FDI in the ICT sector within Sub-Saharan African (SSA) countries, both in terms of human capital development and economic development. It is based on a review of the academic and professional literature, analysis of secondary data, and a few semi-structured interviews with practitioners and experts in the domain. The interviews were conducted face to face during the Mobile 360 GSMA conference that took place in Dar El Salam, Tanzania, on July 2017. Experts include chief strategy officers and managing directors of foreign MNCs investing in the SSA ICT sector. We thus first review the general context of FDI in Africa, addressing trends, policies and institutions, as well as outcomes. Then, we focus on the specific features that characterize FDI in Sub-Saharan countries in the ICT sector. Finally, we offer an HRM perspective on the interplay between FDI, ICT, and economic development in the African context. Accordingly, we outline opportunities for future research.

2 FDI in Africa

2.1 FDI Trends

Africa is often called 'a rising star' [6], 'the continent of the future' [7], 'a hopeful continent', 'the China of tomorrow' [8], and has one of the fastest growing economies in the world [9]. Its GDP grew at an average rate of 4.9% per year between 2000 and 2008. However, between 2010 and 2015, the growth rate dropped to 3.3% [10]. This is apparently due to a general decrease of FDI in Africa following the political uncertainty that emerged after the Arab Spring revolution in Tunisia, Egypt and Libya. Uncertainty in North Africa redirected some of the FDI injection towards SSA countries, even though Morocco was the second-largest FDI recipient economy [2]. Growth in Sub-Saharan Africa is expected to pick-up to 3.4% in 2019, rising to an average of 3.7% in 2020–2021 [11]. According to UNCTAD data [12], FDI inflows to Africa, at $54.1 billion, remain at about a tenth of those of developing Asia, at $540.7 billion. FDI flows to Africa dropped 21% between 2016 and 2017, notably because of weak oil prices and repercussions from the commodity bust, with flows to diversified exporters remaining more resilient, which points to the need for proactive policy to enhance structural economic transformation, beyond the focus on economic growth [13].

Since the 1980s, many governments in Sub-Saharan Africa have introduced structural adjustment programs under the influence of the World Bank and International Monetary Fund, with the expectation of stabilizing the economy and setting the bases of sustainable economic growth [14]. Measures such as financial and trade liberalization and the privatization of state-owned companies were expected to attract Foreign Direct Investment (FDI) in various sectors. Indeed, FDI flows have always been responsive to various factors such as exchange rates—considered as a barrier to capital movements [15–17]—or low production costs, as well as low-income levels.

FDI inflows vary across African sub-regions [18]. In 2017 [13], the African continent had a FDI inward stock of $866.8 billion, with the majority distributed across North Africa ($275.1 billion) and Southern Africa ($235 billion). West Africa had a FDI inward stock of $186.3 billion, whereas the stock in Central Africa was $87.8 billion and East Africa $82.6 billion. FDI also varies across industry sectors. In recent years, it has broadened beyond the earlier focus on extractive industries such as coal, oil, and natural gas, which accounted for about 13.3% of FDI investments in 2016 [2]. Prominent sectors now include real estate, hospitality, and construction at 40.6%, transport and logistics at 13.4%, and clean tech at 9.5%, with technology, media, and telecommunications at 3.4%.

The factors influencing foreign direct investment in Africa are interrelated and complex, including the origin of investments, post-colonial effects, culture, democracy, sectors, and policies. Indeed, changes in FDI flows not only depend on the economic and political situation of the investor country and the development stage of each economic sector per se. They are also impacted by the economic policies of recipient countries, particularly those related to creating a favorable and attractive investment climate [19], such as fostering the privatization of several sectors [20]. In recent years, such policies have differed from the reforms adopted during the 1990s, which primarily addressed poverty reduction rather than economic growth.

2.2 FDI Policies and Institutions

Asiedu [21] has noted that since the African economy—because of its highly diverse regional characteristics—is different from other emerging economies, successful policies to attract investors to Sub-Saharan Africa should be specific to the African market. According to Darley [22], the fact that the United Kingdom and France are among the top five investing countries shows that until now investments in SSA countries are mostly based on 'colonial ties' rather than 'strategic motivations.' The United States joined the ranking of top investors in Africa in 1996 [23] after major efforts coming from the African American community. The 'rising superpower' of Chinese multinational companies in some of the poorest African countries explain the connotation of Chinese investments in Africa as a new form of colonialism.

To attract foreign direct investments in SSA countries, Malikane and Chitambara [24] suggest firstly strengthening the democratic institutions and the governance structure. There are challenges regarding the quality and comparability of FDI data, notably because of the lack of information and transparency about the implemented policies to attract FDI [25]. In addition to macroeconomic fundamentals, factors such as geopolitical uncertainty and risk aversion can have an important influence on investor sentiment [2]. Some of the specific factors that appear to enhance FDI inflows towards Sub-Saharan economies are for instance conflict resolution for a more stable political environment [26], a predictable and consistent policy and macroeconomic environment; the successful implementation of privatization; efforts in regional integration, aggressive investment promotion; good infrastructural facilities and sound human capital development [25].

The fluctuation of FDI flows thus partly reflects different investment strategies at firm level, with a differing impact of globalization on both emerging and developed markets. Multinational corporations' (MNCs) entry strategies rest on the foreign market entry mode (e.g., acquisitions, joint ventures or Greenfield expansions), the appropriate timing and location such as low-cost production countries [27]. FDI strategies can be classified as market-seeking, efficiency-seeking, or resource-seeking [16]. The latter can be further distinguished into natural-resource seeking and strategic-asset seeking, with natural-resource seeking strategies not creating value added activities. Market-seeking strategies substitute exporting and consist on responding to the demand of local or adjacent markets. Efficiency-seeking and strategic-asset seeking are quite similar strategies as they both create assets in the host economy. Efficiency-seeking investments aim to enhance economies of scale by exploiting cross-border specialization through the relocation of manufacturing activities abroad. Asset-seeking involves acquiring competitive advantages through for instance R&D capabilities available in the host countries [28]. Asset-seeking investment motives have also been labeled as knowledge-seeking asset augmenting or resource augmenting [29–32]. MNCs choose their strategies depending on the industry sector and macro-economic factors such as market size or exchange rates [33].

In this regard, it is interesting to study how the choice of the host country and the investment strategies change depending on the origin of the investor. FDI inflows categories to Sub-Saharan African economies are split into two clusters according to the origin of the foreign direct investment: south-south FDI inflows particularly originated from South African—considered as intra-African investment [34]—Chinese and Indian MNCs, and north-south FDI inflowing mainly from Western countries such as European countries and the United States. In contrast to Western countries, China's investment strategy in SSA economies remains on a project-by-project basis [35]. Further, according to Gu [36], Chinese FDI into SSA focus particularly on the mining, infrastructure and technology sectors with less regard to issues such as corruption, crime and bureaucracy [36]. On the other hand, Western Economies' investments depend on a "general policy" basis. For instance, the US investment in Sub-Sahara Africa was for the most part resource-driven in mining and extractive industries rather than manufacturing [34].

2.3   FDI Outcomes

FDI has a complex relationship with economic growth. Over the last decades, world FDI flows have risen much faster than world gross domestic product (GDP) and world trade [37], especially within developed countries [38]. It is thus natural to wonder if FDI positively affects economic growth in host countries and/or if it effectively substitutes or complements domestic investment. Already back in 1993, Oxleheim considered that FDI had become the prime engine to foster growth and facilitate internationalization of formerly sheltered areas during the 1980s. In addition, according to the OECD [39] foreign direct investment is a catalyst for economic development within developing and transition countries, beyond bringing social and environmental benefits. However, research disagrees on the existence of a direct relationship between FDI and economic growth [40].

Contrary to the period prior to the mid-1980s, the focus of research on endogenous growth in international economies has shifted from quantitative to qualitative issues: whereas earlier attention went to the effects on physical capital accumulation and based on the marginal productivity of capital, there has since been increasing focus on knowledge accumulation. This untraditional non-competitive approach encompasses technological externalities and human capital accumulation through knowledge spillovers such as labor training, skills acquisition, alternative management practices, and organizational arrangements [41, 42].

There is evidence to suggest that FDI contributes to productivity and income growth [43], GDP growth [44], and poverty reduction [45]. Inward FDI reinforces cross-border transactions and integrates the host economy within global trade flows. Openness to international trade is thus one of the determinants of FDI attraction. We know that for instance in Singapore and in Ireland local suppliers managed to become global exporters thanks to FDI spillovers [45]. According to the OECD [39], technology transfers are the most important of MNCs' externalities in the recipient economy. Liang [46] further argues that the diffusion of technology and know-how to local firms is more effective in the presence of (a) strong industrial and vertical linkages between local firms and investors, (b) high firm's absorptive capacity (in terms of new technologies' adoption), and (c) low geographic distance between domestic firm and the source of knowledge (the FD Investor).

FDI can also contribute to human capital development. It can do so directly, either through measures such as training and learning on-the-job that can subsequently lead to developed employees moving to domestic firms or becoming entrepreneurs, or indirectly through government policies efforts to upgrade human capital to attract foreign investments. FDI may also influence competition in the host country, and thus contribute to sustainable economic growth by improving productivity and efficiency [45]. To synthesize, FDI seems to impact on economic growth through five main aspects: trade, technology, human capital, competition and domestic firms [39, 41].

FDI can however also harm the host economy through several negative effects. To attract foreign direct investment, governments can introduce reforms and provide incentives to MNCs such as favorable taxation or tax exemptions [43, 44, 47], and this at the expense of local firms. In addition, by reducing domestic firms' market share and providing high quality labor, FDI can hamper growth and competitiveness of domestic investments and firms in the short-term [46]. Furthermore, FDI inflows can bring inappropriate social and cultural norms to the host economy [47].

Hence, because of mechanisms leading to both positive and negative effects at the same time, the FDI-Growth nexus remains ambiguous [44]. Accordingly, to ensure a positive impact and maximize the benefits from FDI, both foreign investors and local actors need to collaborate, ideally on the basis of common objectives, such as diffusing MNCs' knowledge in the host country, implementing effective policies to develop national strategic sectors, and creating technology-oriented educational programs to improve the technological capabilities of human capital and the absorptive capacity of domestic firms. With the advent of digitization [48], MNCs are particularly well placed to help develop the local digital technology capability of FDI recipient countries, as we discuss next.

3   The Importance of ICT

3.1   FDI in the ICT Sector

Since the digital age, Information and Communications Technology (ICT) has been key to globalization, with the global economy being reshaped and shifted from an industrial to an information and communication-based system. This shift and the spread of the Internet has affected the flow of foreign direct investment, and thus its determinants, with factors attracting FDI flows in the past decades no longer being significant nowadays [4].

The development of ICTs has helped to make them more affordable, and thus to rapidly widen access to them in developing countries, as well as to raise economic productivity by enhancing technological upgrading and innovation within firms [49]. In this regard we can say that FDI in the ICT sector can contribute to each of the 17 Sustainable Development Goals (SDGs) of the 2030 UN Agenda for sustainable development [50].

Ketteni et al. [3] have suggested that there is a positive interaction between FDI and ICT investments that enables productivity and economic growth, and thus improving country performance. Other studies, however, show no direct correlation between economic development and the development of the ICT sector. ICT-based FDI picks up local firms' absorptive capacities of spillovers. Thus, ICT-based FDI seem to foster growth only if host countries offer an adequate level of human capital, financial resources and technological infrastructure [40]. Within least developed countries, including in SSA, FDI can contribute to the development of technological infrastructure and of human capital to ensure the base of absorptive capacity needed for FDI in the ICT sector to be worthwhile.

There are obstacles, however, to FDI growth in the ICT industry. Many developing countries are afraid of opening their economies to foreign investments in critical industries such as telecommunications because of its impact on national sovereignty (e.g. national security, social stability and economic development). In terms of control, the ownership of the ICT sector in developing countries ranges from state monopolies to foreign ownership, with the wave of privatization since the 1980s contributing to a shift from the former to the latter [51]. Foreign direct investors have contributed to technological spillovers, an increase of competition in the market, and the improvement of telecommunication infrastructures [52]. This phenomenon has attracted the interest of researchers in terms of impact on access and use of ICTs as well as on economic growth. A few studies have focused on the democratic impact that FDI in ICT can have in developing countries.

Interviews with key informants highlighted that FDI in the ICT sector of SSA came in response to the liberalization of the sector about two decades ago. Several informants considered that the foreign investment boom began in the early 2000s in response to the liberalization of the telecom sector, led by big operators such as Airtel, MTN, Orange and Vodacom. Two informants noted that:

«2000–2001, when the liberalization of the telecom sector arrived in sub-Saharan Africa, the first thing was big operators investing in Africa.» (Expert 1)

«In the early boom of mobile technology in the region, between 2000 and 2002, there was a big boost of foreign investors thanks to the friendly investment environment.» (Expert 2)

Key informants agreed that a significant, optimum and sustainable market structure should rest on stable political and economic environment, and thus on investor friendly regulations. Moreover, as Sub-Saharan African countries progressively become experienced and mature markets, mobile operators have to go beyond the role of voice and data providers, to turn into a catalyst of growth by investing in the mobile financial market, content, energy and e-commerce.

These findings seem part of a larger change in FDI motives in developing countries. Over the past decades, FDI motives in developing countries have shifted from natural resources seeking and railways building to knowledge-intensive activities [45] and market-seeking [27] FDI in developed countries has become increasingly resource-seeking, in contrast with the earlier focus on seeking markets [53].

To conclude we can consider that the spillover effects and infrastructure level improvements that took place thanks to the wave of liberalizations in the ICT sector, start to represent a sufficient base to justify FDI in the ICT sector and to expect potentially positive effects on the development of societies as well as on the overall economic growth of SSA countries. In the next sections, we will thus focus on the specificities and determinants of FDI in the ICT sector within Sub-Saharan African countries.

3.2   Trends, Policies, and Challenges Related to the ICT Sector

In the 1990s, apart from a few countries such as Ethiopia, most African countries developed ICT policy frameworks either by adopting existing international standards or by introducing specific national policies through their government agencies. Over the past decade, ICT regulation reforms were introduced in Africa, however they differed from country to country based on the social, economic, and political context, as well as on internal and external market forces. The impact of these reforms also differed.

The telecom sector in particular is facing several challenges: administrative difficulties, high infrastructure costs and the scarcity of local talents. Despite the progress achieved after the spectrum liberalization in the african continent, when expanding in a new country, telecom companies have to collaborate with governments and regulators to purchase licences and negotiate taxes. Informants revealed that when dealing with African governments, their organizations faced difficulties to find agreements in terms of connectivity and territory coverage.

Furthermore, an informant revealed that for his organization, infrastructure investment is considered as a real estate investment. Thus, as soon as they implement the infrastructure they sell it. Moreover, several of the interviewed experts agreed that there is a need to share the burden between telcos, governments and donors to reduce infrastructure costs and provide mobile broadband to people in rural areas. Indeed, network deployment can be not profitable due to the scattering of populations and their low consumption. For this reason, telecom companies have to collaborate with institutions such as the World Bank or the African Development Bank through equity models. This was highlighted by two participants:

> «IFC is the private bank of the World Bank. While the World Bank lends to governments, the IFC lends to private companies. In the telecom, they have a model through companies' equity or private equity funds… which works quite well.» (Expert 1)

> «Then, we do a lot of collaboration with the GSMA to open-up new areas … we believe strongly in providing mobile broadband to people, which will significantly change their lives.» (Expert 3)

The development and support of ICT policies have contributed to ICT development, as captured for instance by the penetration rates of mobile and fixed telephone and declining communication costs. Mobile phone development can further contribute to financial inclusion, notably in terms of number of deposits and loans per head, which favors economic growth. The positive correlation between mobile phone penetration and financial inclusion has been found to be significant in growth regression analyses. Although the rollout of mobile banking is still at its early stage, the evidence suggests that in countries where such financial services are available, the joint impact of financial inclusion and mobile phone diffusion on growth is stronger. Given the low coverage of banks in African countries, by facilitating the provision of cost-effective financial services, mobile phone diffusion can potentially boost financial inclusion. Even though the challenges and security concerns posed by mobile banking need to be addressed, policies promoting ICT adoption in the banking sector could improve mobile banking. Previous experiences in Kenya, Zambia, and South Africa have illustrated how mobile financial services can help reduce the infrastructure gap and thus the lack of access to financial services [54].

Despite the fear and resistance to initiate an independent regulatory system, some African countries have opened-up the ICT sector to foreign investments. It is worth recalling here that the concentration of foreign direct investments in Africa is no longer oriented to the primary sector but rather to services and manufacturing [18, 25]. In 2014, SSA countries such as South Africa, Nigeria and Kenya doubled their foreign investments' projects in the telecommunication industry with a focus on mobile phone and data traffic, "opening up opportunities to supply education, banking and health care via internet, adding to the sector's appeal" [55]. As a result, during the first decade of this century the average growth of the Kenyan ICT sector reached 20% a year, accounting for 24% of GDP growth.

More generally, the growth rate of mobile telecoms in Africa averaged 42% between 2006 and 2008, the rate lowered though to 21% from 2009 to 2011. In 2015, mobile technologies and services generated 6.7% of Africa's GDP. Recently, 94 mobile phone operators launched the 4G LTE services (high-speed wireless standard for mobile phones and data terminals) in 42 countries [56]. However, it is not clear or obvious whether these new technologies are going to impact development and even are going to be adopted by communities. Considering that SSA countries are anyhow still among the least performing and least connected of all, FDI appears to be one of the main reasons why the ICT sector experienced such a rapid growth in some specific countries. The other drivers most probably being the high consumption rates and the truly "vital" function of mobile services [55].

To better understand the effective impact of FDI in the ICT sector on economic growth in SSA, it is critical to explore the potential spillover effects that can stem from the practices chosen by MNCs to implement their FDI strategies. In the next sections, we will thus particularly focus on the implementation of human resource management (HRM) practices which we assume can directly impact on human capital development, one of the basic conditions to improve the absorptive capacity of the country, catalyze further FDI and thus engender economic growth.

4   A Human Resource Management Perspective

4.1   Human Resource Management in Context

MNCs face several challenges when they operate abroad. In Africa one of the most important challenges is represented by the weak domestic skill base and the lack of managerial capabilities [57]. The problem worsened after the deregulation trend and the opening of markets to international competition [58]. Brain drain has become a concern for the continent, too. For instance, Asia Pacific and the Middle Eastern regions have been attracting African skilled workers and professionals in response to the need for talent triggered by globalization. Major reforms in the human capital formation system, encompassing education, training and health systems are necessary to produce a sufficient stock of skilled workers in the near future [58].

Apart from the lack of skills and managerial capabilities, cultural differences represent another major challenge for foreign investors in Africa. According to Horwitz [59], African indigenous culture systems are characterized by high collectivism and group solidarity tendencies. HRM practices such as team working based on group behavior and norms are efficient, especially if performance management is linked to group-oriented rewards systems [60]. Giving feedback on performance has also to be done in a certain way when operating in Africa. In this perspective, academics [61] suggest the use of a team-based feedback that is not confrontational. In the specific case of Mozambique, employees were afraid to give their views and opinions directly to their superior, a phenomenon that might be explained by the long history of autocratic but paternal management.

Some studies found that the relationship between applicant and the current employees influenced selection decisions [62, 63]. Workforces rely more on word of mouth and internal recruitment with a tendency to favor relatives above outside applicants [61]. MNCs need to consider these trends when implementing recruitment and selection policies to employ the most qualified person.

Furthermore, scholars have highlighted that multinational companies from developed economies tend to implement in their African subsidiaries practices that they apply in their home country, without enough consideration of the local specificities [64]. For instance, Sartorius et al. [61] have noted the tendency of contract-focused HRM programs based on merit, authority, and individualism which totally clash with the collectivist-humanist culture of local African employees. In addition to the frustration that might arise among employees, this can become detrimental to the development of indigenous local African-style HRM practices [65]. It has also been highlighted that MNCs from emerging markets—mainly Chinese and Indian firms –import home-country practices, too, tending to invest in economies with low wage and labor standards, and insufficiently considering local skills gaps. This mirrors the common trend of relying on expatriates, a practice that engenders several challenges in terms of overall HR management. The capacity of emerging market MNCs to use labor substitutability strategies is with some variation, a characteristic of MNCs HR policy in African countries [59].

4.2 FDI and International Human Resource Management

International human resource management (IHRM) practices can represent a critical factor for the success of FDI. If chosen and applied appropriately, they can for instance positively impact on wages and income distribution; the diffusion of knowledge and technology, or the emergence of entrepreneurs, represent further potential indirect spillovers [37].

The relation between FDI, employment and wages in SSA has been the object of numerous studies. As the African labor force is rapidly growing, there is a strong need for job creation to decrease both unemployment and underemployment [66]. FDI can bring solutions to this issue of high political relevance by directly creating new job opportunities and/or better skilled jobs [67]. Coniglio et al. [66] suggested that foreign investments generate a higher amount of jobs compared to domestic ones. Yet attracting foreign investments of MNCs that adopt a low-income entry strategy—as it is the case of Nigeria, for instance—can harm employment practices. This effect, combined with the neglect of international labor standards, may lead to nonstandard forms of employment—casual, contract and outsourced workers—and to exacerbated unemployment.

With respect to wages, FDI can positively impact income levels by offering wage premiums. This depends, however, on the origin of investment. For instance, according to Coniglio et al. [66], Southern investments such as those of Chinese holdings are usually generating low wages, even lower than domestic firms' wages, and thus attracting blue-collar workers, whereas Northern or Western investments are more likely to offer premium wages and skilled job opportunities.

As FDI in Africa is growing, rivalry among competing investors is increasing, too. For foreign MNCs to succeed, and thus to engender positive effects in the economic system of the host company, they have to effectively manage their investment. One of the critical success factors when investing in a foreign country is related to how investors manage their human resources. In this regard, various studies have considered which among the convergent, divergent, and hybrid approaches to HRM practices would be most appropriate in the African context [14]. This question is extremely important considering the highly diverse cultural characteristics of the African continent [68] that may easily lead to misunderstandings, conflicts, missed goals, and thus jeopardize the FDI. In this regard, research needs to focus on the influence of culture on HRM practices implemented by foreign investors.

While considering the indirect effects of FDI, several externalities such as knowledge and technology transfer appear to increase human capital development, and thus the economic growth of host countries. Effective human resource practices such as training and continuous learning within MNCs can contribute to the spread of knowledge and technology to local firms. It is though unclear whether foreign companies invest enough in training, or if they rather restrict access to training out of fear of labor turnover [37]. This can depend on the country from which the foreign investment originated, as we already mentioned. Gomes et al. [65], for instance, noted that Indian MNCs invest less in training than European ones.

As HRM practices of foreign owned companies can vary according to the country of origin, the effects of FDI can also vary. To ensure human capital development, and thus economic growth, policy makers must pay attention to the different HRM practices that MNCs put in place and try to incentivize those firms that enhance skilled jobs creation and training programs.

4.3 The Promise of Good IHRM Practices

Nowadays HRM is expected to play a strategic role by implementing HR strategies and practices in accordance with the corporate and business strategy of an organization, and thus ensuring a competitive advantage [69–71]. In the 21st century, it is essential for organizations to be able to operate globally [70] as worldwide economies are becoming progressively integrated [72], MNCs need thus to effectively manage people across international boundaries. In order to transfer competencies and capabilities across their subsidiaries, MNCs look for appropriate policies and implementation practices [73]. In this regard, international HRM appears to be crucial and much more complex than domestic HRM. Indeed, HR managers have to deal with varying cultural and legal issues and thus adopt different approaches to HRM practices according to different country contexts [72]. IHRM in the context of multinational companies refers to several policies and practices serving to attract, recruit, select, train, develop, compensate, evaluate and retain the right talents to fill into international assignments.

Recruitment and selection are among the main HR functions and play essential roles in the performance of MNCs, as «talent has become a precious resource fought over by competitors in a global war for talents» [74]. According to Tarique et al. [72], recruitment involves the research and the attraction of qualified applicants to create a candidate pool from which employers could hire for open positions.

Training and Development (T&D) are defined as planned activities designed to promote the acquisition of knowledge and the development of skills and attitudes [75]. To ensure effective T&D, not only opportunities to learn and practice but also timely diagnostic feedback about employees' performance need to be provided [76]. At the international level, companies might fail to achieve the required T&D objectives because they simply transfer a program conceived at headquarters to another country, without taking cultural specificities into account [72]. Accordingly, on the one hand, leveraging organizational capabilities worldwide offers competitive advantage for MNCs [77]. On the other hand, local firms can benefit from spillover effect of T&D programs in the host countries. MNCs can play an important role in developing managerial competence within the local workforce; yet they may also lead to brain drain from host countries to investing countries [78]. Thus, investments in workforce development through training are often seen as a primary mechanism for national economic development [79].

Finally, employee retention is an important HR issue encompassing the practices aiming at enhancing job satisfaction and intention to stay over a long period in the organization. Retention of employees is valuable to organizations' knowing that they spend money on recruitment and training but also, because losing the best individuals is something they aim to avoid, to maintain a competitive advantage [80]. To reduce turnover and foster retention, organizations can influence organizational commitment and job satisfaction [81] through training, challenging work, opportunities for advancement, high compensation package, and learning opportunities [82, 83]. Good relationships between employees and supervisors can also positively affect talent retention. Adding to that, scholars have found that work-life balance practices along with a supportive organizational culture [84, 85] and flexible working opportunities [86] improve job satisfaction and reduce intention to leave. In addition, MNCs are attracting talents from diasporas [87]. Studies suggest that Diaspora members are more skilled than locals as they are able to push technology and knowledge transfer and promote institutional reforms in their countries. They can be thus highly valuable for higher positions within MNCs [88, 89].

5 Toward A Research Agenda

The first objective of this paper was to understand the interplay between FDI and economic growth in the ICT sector. At this stage, the literature review on the FDI-economic growth nexus demonstrates both positive and negative impacts depending on several factors such as the country of origin of the FD Investor, host-country characteristics such as openness to international trade, absorptive capacities and technological capabilities of the local human capital. This supports the view that the HRM practices applied by the FD investor can be a critical factor for both the success of the investment and for its impact on economic growth in the host-country. Indeed, such practices can contribute not only to bridge knowledge and cultural differences but also to develop the absorptive capacities and technological capabilities needed to catalyze further investments, and thus engender growth. The second objective was to understand more clearly the HRM challenges related to FDI in Sub-Saharan countries to suggest the most appropriate approach to African HRM for enabling economic development. We identified three main issues that involve choices in terms of HRM: the employment and wage levels, the convergence or divergence of HRM practices, and the knowledge and technological transfer. However, research in this field remains limited and a literature review could not allow us to fulfill our second objective.

To get a deeper understanding of the HRM challenges related to FDI in SSA countries, it is thus necessary to conduct an empirical study of the HRM practices adopted by different foreign MNEs in their foreign subsidiaries. We believe that case studies will be the most suitable method to apply for this purpose [59]. A major question is about the extent to which MNCs consider the potential externalities of their investments on human capital competencies and absorptive capacities [3]. Within the ICT sector, the telecommunications sector seems of particular interest since investments in this field are directly related to government decisions on information and communication policies and thus can have an impact on the economic development of the country. Considering the influence that the country of origin of the foreign investor can have, we need to consider two regional clusters of foreign subsidiaries: the cluster representing recipients of north western FDI and that including recipients of south FDI. The study will be based on in depth interviews with FDI representatives both at the headquarters of the foreign MNCs and at the African subsidiaries. Representatives will include persons in charge of the development and implementation of FDI strategies as well as of HRM. The main questions to be addressed are the following:

- Which HRM practices do foreign MNCs apply and how can those practices contribute to the success of FDI in SSA countries?
- What are the spillover effects that HRM can engender in the host country and how?
- Do FDI driven ICT improvements have an impact on human capital development and how?
- Do FDI spillover effects have a positive impact on access and use of ICT, and thus create a more informed society, in the host country?

Acknowledgements This study was conducted thanks to the financial support of the Swiss Network for International Studies (SNIS). We further thank Mansour Omeira for reviewing this paper and for his valuable comments.

References

1. ITU: Measuring the Information Society Report (2016)
2. Ernst & Young: EY's Attractiveness Program Africa: Connectivity Redefined (2017)
3. Ketteni, E., Kottaridi, C., Mamuneas, T.P.: Information and communication technology and foreign direct investment: interactions and contributions to economic growth. Empirical Econ. **48**(4), 1525–1539 (2015)
4. Gholami, R., Lee, S.Y.T., Heshmati, A.: The causal relationship between information and communication technology and foreign direct investment. World Econ. **29**(1), 43–62 (2006)
5. Asongu, S.A., Le Roux, S.: Enhancing ICT for inclusive human development in Sub-Saharan Africa. Technol. Forecast. Soc. Chang. **118**(May), 44–54 (2017)
6. Taylor, I.A.N.: Is Africa rising? Brown J. World Aff. **21**, 143–161 (2014)
7. French Government. http://www.gouvernement.fr/en/africa-is-the-continent-of-the-future. Last accessed 02 May 2018
8. The Economist: A hopeful continent. http://www.economist.com/news/special-report/21572377-african-lives-have-already-greatly-improved-over-past-decade-says-oliver-august (2013). Last accessed 01 May 2017
9. Deloitte: The future of Telecoms in Africa: the "blueprint for the brave" (2014)
10. McKinsey Global Institute: Lions on the Move II: Realizing the Potential of Africa's Economies (2016)
11. World Bank: Africa's Pulse: An Analysis of Issues Shaping Africa's Economic Future. Washington, DC (2018)
12. UNCTAD: Foreign Direct Investment: Inward and Outward Flows and Stock, Annual, 1970, 2015. Geneva (2017)
13. UNCTAD: World Investment Report 2018. Geneva (2018)
14. Kamoche, K., Debrah, Y., Horwitz, F., Muuka, G.N. (eds.): Managing Human Resources in Africa. Routledge, London (2004)
15. Hymer, S.H.: The International Operations of National Firms: A Study of Direct Foreign Investment. Massachusetts Institute of Technology, Cambridge, MA (1976)
16. Oxelheim, L.: The global race for foreign direct investment: prospects for the future. Springer-Verlag, Berlin (1993)

17. Yan, G., Li, S., Lin, Y.Q., Li, J.: Real effective exchange rate and regional economic growth in China: evidence from provincial Data. China World Econ. **24**(6), 43–63 (2016)
18. Anyanwu, J.C., Yaméogo, N.D.: Regional comparison of foreign direct investment to Africa: empirical analysis. Afr. Dev. Rev. **27**(3), 345–363 (2015)
19. UNCTAD: Economic development in Africa: rethinking the role of Foreign Direct Investment. Geneva (2005)
20. Wei, Y., Balasubramanyam, V.N.: Foreign direct investment: six country case studies. Edward Elgar, Cheltenham, UK (2004)
21. Asiedu, E.: On the determinants of foreign direct investment to developing countries: Is Africa different? World Dev. **30**(1), 107–119 (2002)
22. Darley, W.K.: Increasing Sub-Saharan Africa's share of foreign direct investment: public policy challenges, strategies, and implications. J. Afr. Bus. **13**(1), 62–69 (2012)
23. UNCTAD: The World Investment Report. Geneva (2002)
24. Malikane, C., Chitambara, P.: Foreign direct investment, democracy and economic growth in Southern Africa. Afr. Dev. Rev. **29**(1), 92–102 (2017)
25. Olatunji, L.A., Shahid, M.S.: Determinants of FDI in Sub-Saharan African countries: a review of the evidence. Bus. Econ. Res. **5**(2), 22–34 (2015)
26. Ezeoha, A.E., Ugwu, J.O.: Interactive impact of armed conflicts on foreign direct investments in Africa. Afr. Dev. Rev. **27**(4), 456–468 (2015)
27. Estrin, S., Meyer, K.E. (eds.): Investment Strategies in Emerging Markets. Edward Edgar, Cheltenham, UK (2004)
28. Narula, R., Dunning, J.H.: Industrial development, globalization and multinational enterprises: new realities for developing countries. Oxf. Dev. Stud. **28**(2), 141–167 (2000)
29. Chung, W., Alcacer, J.: Knowledge seeking and location choice of foreign direct investment in the United States. Manage. Sci. **48**(12), 1534–1554 (2002)
30. Narula, R., Zanfei, A.: Globalization of Innovation: The Role of Multinational Enterprises. DRUID, Copenhagen Business School, Department of Industrial Economics, Department of Business Studies and Strategy/Aalborg University (2003)
31. Meyer, K.E., Wright, M., Pruthi, S.: Managing knowledge in foreign entry strategies: a resource-based analysis. Strateg. Manag. J. **30**(5), 557–574 (2009)
32. Meyer, K.E.: What is "strategic asset seeking FDI"? Multinational Bus. Rev. **23**(1), 57–66 (2015)
33. Sethi, D., Guisinger, S.E., Phelan, S.E., Berg, D.M.: Trends in foreign direct investment flows: atheoretical and empirical analysis. J. Int. Bus. Stud. **34**, 315–326 (2003)
34. Ntembe, A., Sengupta, S.: The contribution of US Foreign direct investments to economic growth in Sub-Saharan Africa: evidence from panel data. J. Northeastern Assoc. Bus. Econ. Technol. **19**, 55–71 (2016)
35. Ado, A., Su, Z.: China in Africa: acritical literature review. Crit. Perspect. Int. Bus. **12**, 40–60 (2014)
36. Gu, J.: China's private enterprises in Africa and the implications for African development. Eur. J. Dev. Res. **21**(4), 570–587 (2009)
37. Farole, T., Winkler, D.: Making Foreign Direct Investment Work for Sub-Saharan Africa: Local Spillovers and Competitiveness in Global Value Chains. World Bank, Washington, DC (2014)
38. Markusen, J.R., Venables, A.J.: Foreign direct investment as a catalyst for industrial development. Eur. Econ. Rev. **43**(2), 335–356 (1999)
39. OECD: Foreign Direct Investment for Development: Maximizing Benefits, Minimizing Costs. Paris (2002)
40. Gönel, F., Aksoy, T.: Revisiting FDI-led growth hypothesis: the role of sector characteristics. J. Int. Trade Econ. Dev. **25**(8), 1144–1166 (2016)
41. de Mello, L.R.: Foreign direct investment-led growth: evidence from time series and panel data. Oxford Econ. Pap. **51**(1), 133–151 (1999)
42. Grossman, G.M., Helpman, E.: Globalization and growth. Am. Econ. Rev. **105**(5), 100–104 (2015)

43. Borensztein, E., De Gregorio, J., Lee, J.W.: How does foreign direct investment affect economic growth? J. Int. Econ. **45**(1), 115–135 (1997)
44. Moura, R., Forte, R.: The effects of foreign direct investment on the host country's economic growth: theory and empirical evidence. Singapore Econ. Rev. **58**(03), 1350017 (2009)
45. Velde, D.W.T.: Foreign Direct Investment and Development: An Historical Perspective. Overseas Development Institute, London (2006)
46. Liang, F.H.: Does foreign direct investment improve the productivity of domestic firms? Technology spillovers, industry linkages, and firm capabilities. Res. Policy **46**(1), 138–159 (2016)
47. Mah, J.S.: Foreign direct investment inflows and economic growth: the case of Korea. Rev. Dev. Econ. **14**(4), 726–735 (2010)
48. Arthur, W.B.: The second economy. McKinsey Q. **4**, 90–99 (2011)
49. ITU: SDG Mapping Tool (2017)
50. ITU: Fast-forward progress: leveraging tech to achieve the global goals (2017)
51. World Bank: Africa's ICT Infrastructure: Building on the Mobile Revolution. Washington, DC (2011)
52. Lin, C.H.: Role of foreign direct investment in telecommunication industries: a developing countries' perspective. Contemp. Manage. Res. **4**(1), 29–42 (2008)
53. Napshin, S., Brouthers, L.E.: Intermediary products: FDI strategies, imports, exports, and trade balances in developed economies. Thunderbird Int. Bus. Rev. **57**(4), 311–322 (2015)
54. Andrianaivo, M., Kpodar, K.: ICT, financial inclusion, and growth: evidence from African countries. Int. Monetary Fund, Washington, DC (2011)
55. Ernst & Young: EY's attractiveness survey Africa 2015: making choices (2015)
56. Balancing-act: Afrique: 94 opérateurs mobiles ont lancé des services 4G-LTE dans 42 pays. http://www.balancingact-africa.com/news/telecoms-fr/40459/afrique-94-oprateurs-mobiles-ont-lanc-des-services-4g-lte-dans-42-pays (2017)
57. Sydhagen, K., Cunningham, P.: Human resource development in sub-Saharan Africa. Hum. Resour. Dev. Int. **10**(2), 121–135 (2007)
58. Cooke, F.L., Wood, G., Horwitz, F.: Multinational firms from emerging economies in Africa: implications for research and practice in human resource management. Int. J. Hum. Resour. Manage. **26**(21), 2653–2675 (2015)
59. Horwitz, F.: Human resources management in multinational companies in Africa: a systematic literature review. Int. J. Hum. Resour. Manage. **26**(21), 2786–2809 (2015)
60. Horwitz, F.: Evolving human resource management in Southern African multinational firms: towards an Afro-Asian nexus. Int. J. Hum. Resour. Manage. **23**(14), 2938–2958 (2012)
61. Sartorius, K., Merino, A., Carmichael, T.: Human resource management and cultural diversity: a case study in Mozambique. Int. J. Hum. Resour. Manage. **22**(9), 1963–1985 (2011)
62. Carmichael, T., Rijamampianina, R.: Managing Diversity in Africa. In: Luiz, J. (ed.) Managing Business in Africa: Practical Management Theory for an Emerging Market, pp. 161–187. Oxford University Press, Cape Town (2007)
63. Dimba B., K'obonyo P.: Influence of culture on strategic human resource management (SHRM) practices in multinational companies (MNC) in Kenya: a critical literature review. In: Working Paper. College of Humanities and Social Sciences, University of Nairobi, Kenya (2007)
64. Wood, G., Mazouz, K., Yin, Y., Cheah, J.: Foreign direct investment from emerging markets to Africa: the HRM context. Hum. Resour. Manage. **53**, 179–201 (2014)
65. Gomes, E., Sahadev, S., Glaister, A.J., Demirbag, M.: A comparison of international HRM practices by Indian and European MNEs: evidence from Africa. Int. J. Hum. Resour. Manage. **26**(21), 2676–2700 (2015)
66. Coniglio, N.D., Prota, F., Seric, A.: Foreign direct investment, employment and wages in Sub-Saharan Africa. J. Int. Dev. **27**(7), 1243–1266 (2015)
67. Javorcik, B.S.: Does FDI bring good jobs to host countries? World Bank Res. Obs. **30**(1), 74–94 (2015)
68. Kamoche, K., Siebers, L.Q., Mamman, A., Newenham-Kahindi, A.: The dynamics of managing people in the diverse cultural and institutional context of Africa. Pers. Rev. **44**(3), 330–345 (2015)

69. Storey, J.: Human resource management: acritical text. Thomson, London (2001)
70. Brewster, C., Sparrow, P., Harris, H.: Towards a new model of globalizing HRM. Int. J. Hum. Resour. Manage. **16**(6), 949–970 (2005)
71. Boxall, P.: Mutuality in the management of human resources: assessing the quality of alignment in employment relationships. Hum. Res. Manage. J. **23**(1), 3–17 (2013)
72. Tarique, I., Briscoe, D., Schuler, R.: International Human Resource Management: Policies and Practices for Multinational Enterprises, 5th edn. Routledge (2016)
73. Farndale, E., Scullion, H., Sparrow, P.: The role of the corporate HR function in global talent management. J. World Bus. **45**(2), 161–168 (2010)
74. Cheese, P., Thomas, R. J., Craig, E.: The Talent Powered Organization: Strategies for Globalization, Talent Management and High Performance. Kogan Page Publishers (2007)
75. Salas, E., Tannenbaum, S.I., Kraiger, K., Smith-Jentsch, K.A.: The science of training and development in organizations: what matters in practice. Psychol. Sci. Publ. Interest **13**(2), 74–101 (2012)
76. Salas, E., Cannon-Bowers, J.A.: The science of training: a decade of progress. Annu. Rev. Psychol. **52**, 471–499 (2001)
77. Nohria, N., Ghoshal, S.: The Differentiated Network. Organizing Multinational Corporations for Value Creation. Jossey-Bass Publishers, San Francisco (1997)
78. Cox, A., Warner, M.: Whither 'training and development' in Vietnam: learning from United States and Japanese MNCs' Practice. Asia Pacific J. Hum. Resour. **51**(2), 175–192 (2013)
79. Aguinis, H., Kraiger, K.: Benefits of training and development for individuals and teams, organizations, and society. Annu. Rev. Psychol. **60**, 451–474 (2009)
80. Poudel, H.: A plead to Nepali Diaspora: an urge for homecoming. Repositioning **1**(1), 73–80 (2016)
81. Allen, D.G., Bryant, P.C., Vardaman, J.M.: Retaining talent: replacing misconceptions with evidence-based strategies. Acad. Manage. Perspect. **24**(2), 48–64 (2010)
82. Steel, R.P., Griffeth, R.W., Hom, P.W.: Practical retention policy for the practical manager. Acad. Manage. Exec. **16**(2), 149–162 (2002)
83. Govaerts, N., Kyndt, E., Dochy, F., Baert, H.: Influence of learning and working climate on the retention of talented employees. J. Workplace Learn. **23**(1), 35–55 (2011)
84. Cegarra-Leiva, D., Sánchez-Vidal, M.E., Cegarra-Navarro, J.G.: Work life balance and the retention of managers in Spanish SMEs. Int. J. Hum. Resour. Manage. **23**(1), 91–108 (2012)
85. Tlaiss, H.A., Martin, P., Hofaidhllaoui, M.: Talent retention: evidence from a multinational firm in France. Empl. Relat. **39**(4), 426–445 (2017)
86. Idris, A.: Flexible working as an employee retention strategy in developing countries: Malaysian bank managers speak. J. Manage. Res. **14**(2), 71–86 (2014)
87. Bücker, J.: Cultural intelligence as a key construct for global talent management. In: Al Ariss A. (ed.) Global Talent Management, pp. 65–78. Springer
88. Contractor, F.J.: "Punching above their weight" the sources of competitive advantage for emerging market multinationals. Int. J. Emerging Mark. **8**(4), 304–328 (2013)
89. Kshetri, N.: The Diaspora as a change agent in entrepreneurship-related institutions in Sub-Saharan Africa. J. Dev. Entrepreneurship **18**(03) (2013)

Traditional Banks and Fintech: Survival, Future and Threats

Nada Mallah Boustani

Abstract The FinTech(s) is an economic sector involving a number of enterprises that use technology to offer more efficient financial services. These startups disrupt the classical financial system namely commercial banks by modifying the payments and debts mechanism. Their technology offers opportunities in terms of enhancing the current financial services and widening the consumers' choices. In this paper, the author assesses the different conditions and requirements for the survival of the banking sector amidst the emergence of the Fintech startups worldwide and specifically in Lebanon. In this paper, the author explains the emergence and positioning of Fintech firms before developing a research model for this end. The model shall be based on the behavioral and innovation theories in finance, will be tested on site using structured interviews with banking specialists and officials, and will finally quantitatively be analyzed for research purposes.

Keywords Fintechs · Financial innovation · Banks · Technology

1 Introduction

Throughout history, the World has witnessed many changes that promised opportunities and enhancement: The invention of steam machinery by James Watt and the industrial revolution two centuries ago triggered a substantial swift in world economic models. In the 80s, computers were conceived, followed by the introduction of the internet 10 years later. The world became a global village thanks to the free flow of information. Nowadays, the internet and communication technology have become mandatory in our lives.

In all business sectors, innovation is running at high speed, hence imposing itself as a rule and a policy in any business. The widespread digitalization along with the intensification of data processing are all inducing industrial changes and change in

N. M. Boustani (✉)
Faculty of Business and Management, Saint Joseph University, Hjvelin Street, Mar Mikhael Beirut, PO. Box 17-5208, Beirut 1104 2020, Lebanon
e-mail: Nada.mallahboustany@usj.edu.lb

© Springer Nature Switzerland AG 2020
Y. Baghdadi et al. (eds.), *ICT for an Inclusive World*,
Lecture Notes in Information Systems and Organisation 35,
https://doi.org/10.1007/978-3-030-34269-2_24

the growth and type of companies. Such innovation has transformed the constituents of the ecosystem that have triggered economies of scale that contributed to modifying job profiles and increasing profit. Actually, no person was sufficiently aware of the impact of innovation on businesses and industries. As already said, the internet became mandatory, or has even become akin of raw material needed for the continuity, survival, growth and expansion of any business.

The financial sector and the industry are not excluded from such innovation and stand as no exception. On the contrary, they seem to be widely influenced by the latter due to the economy's digitalization and dematerialization. Classic banks, even the best positioned ones, have reshuffled their "business models" to partially align with the needs of innovation and specifically resist and counter attack the penetration of those newly conceived FinTech start-ups in the financial markets. The hypothesis of replacing classic banks with virtual banks "online" does not stop from spreading, and expanding among the stakeholders and players of the financial markets. In fact, conventional and classic bankers have a volatile and gloomy future ahead due to the invasion of finance technology.

FinTech firms with their new technology offer many substitutes to the classic financial products that help firms grow quickly and rise the appetite of large investors to venture in such firms with excessive financing amounts. With the supply of FinTech, clients tend more and more to demand digital financial products that are being considered a threat to the traditional system, business and market. The latest research has shown that more than 1400 FinTech enterprises are active on the market. In 2008, more than 100 million dollars have been invested in those firms; the total reached 19 billion dollars in 2015. FinTech firms are becoming a substantial source of influence and a driver of international financial institutions. Today, individuals can simply apply for a loan on the Internet; pay the installments using their mobile application and exchange virtual currencies. This so-called success is related to some factors that have facilitated and accelerated the rise of this innovative system:

1. The development and installation of cutting edge technology platforms to facilitate customers' relations management system and become closer to clients
2. The infiltration and acceptance of internet in the business arena
3. The mass usage of mobile telephones especially amidst the youth who seem highly dependent on such technology
4. The introduction of (3G and 4G) technology and more and more implementation of cloud computing projects
5. Changes in consumers' behaviors. Every day, they become more engaged with online purchasing and ultimately require that online banking and financial services are available 24/7
6. Markets are becoming more open due to the shrinking of Government barriers
7. Confidence in classic banks is constantly diminishing due to last decade's financial crisis and the result of Basel (1, 2, 3) that lead to imposing heavy regulations on financial institutions for risk containment purposes
8. Implementation of block chain and Big Data projects
9. Execution of artificial intelligence and business intelligence projects.

It is worth mentioning that every FinTech or finance technology company involves critical risks for.

1. The digitalization of financial market could cause damage to information security, for e.g. a hacking attack etc....Therefore, FinTech firms must introduce technology security systems to protect the privacy and confidentiality of their information and hence their clients'.
2. Some of the new electronic payment methods for e.g. the use of bitcoins, could also be considered as a risk factor due to its potential impact on the country's monetary policy.
3. Clients can also invest in alternative services and products. For e.g. loans could be awarded based on timely information however, the latter may not be available or could be falsified which could lead to huge losses among investors.
4. Risk of losing a conventional banking job.

A major question arises: What would the Lebanese banks do to mitigate this threat? Today more than ever before, we are aware about the escalating war among FinTech firms and banks. Nowadays clients are becoming more and more demanding as they look for sophisticated products. FinTech firms are a source of innovation for banks; therefore, having them associated with banks could be beneficial for both. Historically, traditional banks have always been capable of creating and developing new products that respond to the needs of their clients. However, presently, clients become more demanding and rely more on digitalization, a technology service that banks cannot fulfill due to their rigidity in response and adaptability to market change.

In fact, with digitalization, banks should invest substantially in upgrading the infrastructure and mobilizing the needed skills. Therefore, the banks optimal solutions could be to collaborate with the FinTech startups and turn threat into an opportunity through potential association, a strategy of many shapes and types. Banks can choose a simple collaboration with a FinTech through a service agreement or also merge and acquire such firms. Banks strategy for merging with or acquiring FinTech firms can carry many consequences:

1. With the acquisition of shares, banks shall have the hands on experience of the acquired FinTech
2. Less time is required for the development of advanced and sophisticated products
3. Acceleration of the innovation process at the Bank.

2 Literature Revue

2.1 The Theory of Behavioral Finance

Though FinTech firms have been threatening banks all the way through, their success is mainly dependent on consumers' behavior not only banks. The theory of Behavioral

Finance, adopted by Kahneman and Tversky [1], is aimed at studying investors' decisions and behaviors. The main hypothesis of this theory is about the irrational status of the investor. Sometimes investment decisions and options are influenced by the investors' culture, background, emotional status like fear, anger, confidence, habit etc....

Researchers say that human psychology plays a crucial role in finance and many cognitive bias has been developed in this regard to back up this theory.

Below are some of the biases feeding the behavioral change of some consumers:

1. The bias of familiarity. An individual sometimes tends to favor one situation over another on grounds of familiarity.
2. The bias reliability. Persons speculate future events. Therefore, investors as well can over-estimate the re-occurrence of an event in the future.
3. The bias of confidence and trust. It has a serious influence on the consumers' reaction. In fact, investors would not invest in a location where confidence is extremely volatile.

2.2 The Theory of Innovation

2.2.1 Schumpeter Innovation's Theory

With reference to [2], (1912) radical innovations distress the economic balance. Indeed, they cancel the old and obsolete models or activities. "Innovate" is defined as "new consumer goods, new methods of production and transport, new markets, new types of industrial organizations". The foundations of innovation according to [2] remain applicable, even with the fall of capitalism and since the 1940s innovation represents the source of growth in all sectors.

For [2], innovation takes several types. It could be of a technical, commercial, organizational, social and financial nature. As for financial innovation, it results from the rise of FinTechs.

Financial innovation means according to [3] (1991) the introduction of new products and services on the financial markets or the modification of an existing product using all sorts of improvements.

It was not until the global crisis (2007–2009) that the United States realized the importance of financial innovation. The default of housing payments triggered a global crisis and the recovery was marked by financial innovations.

This tool of change continues to be considered an opportunity for any financial institution especially for banks allowing the following benefits:

Increase in profits
Financial risk reduction
Reduced costs of financial transactions
Implementation of products with a better consumer orientation.

For [1], financial innovation is about offering services and financial products with the purpose of facing financial competition. According to [4], there are 5 forces and competition is one. The company must know how to manage by creating innovative differentiation strategies. Banks are now looking for financial innovations by creating new, differentiated financial products.

Schumpeter [2] also distinguishes several types of financial innovations:

1. The innovation of products made by the research and development department for the implementation of new financial products and services to satisfy customers's needs and increase banking mediation. These institutions develop a wide range of products such as travel loans, personal loans, credit cards etc....
2. Process innovation through the use of new technologies to try to improve the production processes which will make it possible to obtain cost efficiency (Establishment of ATM). This innovation aims at immaterializing the financial sector and achieving better market competitiveness.

2.2.2 Financial Innovation for Lancaster, Silbert and Kane

As per [5] (1996), a financial product is purchased by a client with reference to its characteristics that push the individual towards favoring it to other products. Some of those characteristics are:
The impositioning of the product

The risk factor level
The availability
The product profitability level.

As per [6] (1983), financial innovation is a simple tool for entreprises; it allows for competition and stands against the risk of changing market regulations which makes the financial sector rigid.

As per [7] (1981), the regulations defined by the Government shall oblige banks and financial institutions to bend the laws and use innovations to enhance the financial sector.

All theorists agree that innovation shall bring transformation to enterprises. However, it is not risk free. Below are some of its cons:

The liberalisation of the financial markets that could lead to crisis and crashes
Risk of fraud, financial crime and tax evasion
Decrease in currency demand due to investments in projects that can replace real currency bills.

Financial innovation shall also contribute in cancelling all kinds of financial intermediary activities. For under developed countries, growth is a necessity and therefore liberalisation of the financial sector can help. In Lebanon, the liberalization of the sector is still questionable.

Financial market liberalization happens when some restrictive laws are cancelled and the sector becomes more flexible and competing. The purpose of cancelling any financial intermediation is to favor the financial market rather than developing a credit based one.

For [8], those changes shall be able to stand and hold against the lack of financial intermediation, which signifies a gap between earning on deposits and expenses on loans. Therefore, new products shall see the light and new sources of financing shall be developed which will lead to more profit.

What is the relationship between the concept of creative destruction announced by Schumpeter [2] and the Fintech? The new entrants take over old players and sometimes try to eliminate them definitively. The innovative services and infrastructure provided by FinTechs transform the traditional banking profession and take it to lose more grounds on the market. With reference to the increasing number of digital products delivered by those enterprises, the conventional agencies become less attractive for the end client.

3   Research Methodology

The research analysis in this paper is of a qualitative nature. The case subject of this paper sheds the light on multiple recurrent events in different situations. It is deemed useful in situations where attention is focused on a contemporary phenomenon in a real life context [9] (1989), and respond to an inductive logic. The analysis should help identify the recurrent phenomenon with their respective evolution. Research information is taken from different sources (exploratory approach), and the structured interviews were conducted with banking specialists and officials. The qualitative assessment method adopted in this study is usually the most recurrent in management science [10] (2005). The questionnaires were designed to cover multiple subject matters aligned with the main purpose of this paper and respective model:

(1)   The rationale behind banks investment in finance technology
(2)   The benefits of finance technology for banks
(3)   In house innovation or outsourcing finance technology firms
(4)   The future of hybrid banks
(5)   Robots as substitutes in CSO departments
(6)   The lure of tap2pay
(7)   The charm of mobile banking
(8)   The innovative applications and major fields
(9)   Threats of FinTech firms on banks using similar products and a more time and cost efficient service
(10) Future of material branches.

In addition to the structured questionnaire, a mass survey was conducted targeting 800 individuals. 168 candidates responded fully to the survey on banking innovation in relation to online banking services. This survey helped researchers assess the common knowledge about banking technology and Fintech enterprises.

4 Context of the Study

With today's advanced cyber technology, individuals no longer depend on material banks. Thanks to the web, smart mobiles, and advanced technology, they can easily conduct banking transactions and manage their time. Physical presence requirements for the conducting of financial transactions, is constantly diminishing.

These advancements have also reduced the role of banks as financial intermediary. Banks profit were mainly resulting from netting between interest revenues and expenses in addition to some increase in intermediary fees every time a new financial product and service is introduced. The current business model is changing and it is highly probable to witness a drastic change in the role and existence of banks. Many innovative financial institutions are penetrating the banking and financial market and offering clients an advanced technology that can support the Banks's virtual model.

The so-called «neo banks» or online banks are gaining ground and momentum as they offer clients quality and time efficient banking services and products that seem unavailable at conventional banks. Those <Neo Banks> compete with national banks as they touch the heart of a wide audience that is interested in services that could be tackled virtually using the cyber space. In general, technological advancement is killing the current business models everywhere.

4.1 Types of Fintech

4.1.1 The Crowd Funding

The most famous FinTech firms are the ones who belong to Crowd Funding. The latter is a means of financing a project or a venture by raising small amounts of money via a large number of people, typically via the internet. Crowd funding is a concept that is rampant worldwide as it offers more appropriate solutions. Many platforms have been conceived by enterprises whereby the entrepreneur is put in direct contact with the investors. This means that the entrepreneur is in direct contact with the funding crowd and does not have to go and chase banking institutions.

Crowd lending is a type of crowd funding, but in this case the money is lend to the entrepreneur against a well-defined monthly installment. Crowd equity is yet another form of crowd funding allowing the investor to purchase shares in the startups against financing, and in this case the entrepreneur would not bear the risk of committing to any monthly installment.

4.1.2 Payment's System Modification

The money market for payments and transfers is also witnessing some modifications by FinTech firms. All got started with the inception of a new payment platform that manage clients online purchasing and respective payments, by allowing clients to subscribe onsite and supply personnel information for better cyber security measures. Today, online payments with smart phones or watches are becoming possible and to the extent of questioning the use of plastic cards. It should also be noted that the four giant Web companies: Google, Apple, Facebook, Amazon (GAFA) position themselves on this smart niche segment. Indeed, Apple Enterprise also stands on this segment line by offering the Apple Pay platform that allows for the execution and management of money transfers through Apple i-message notification; while Android (by Google) is developing the Android Pay. These are all payments mechanisms used in the USA and affecting the operating profit of banks. Hence, mobile technologies have paved the way for the management of banking services that could be offered to a wide range of non-banking users.

4.1.3 The Advisors Robots

The advisors robots or else called "Consult Robot" are presented as technology platforms that can supply people with consulting services in finance and management of online investment portfolio including retirement plans and tax management. Today, people can resort to an effective cost efficient technology service hence, avoiding the burden of physical encounters. Such technology service is absent in conventional banks. Indeed, in France an "advisor robot" costs around 0.2% of the total client's outstanding balance while it reaches 2% with conventional banks. Moreover, in the future these Robots would become available 24/7 to respond to clients queries. In the US, the average standard fee of a Robot advisory service is about $5000 compared to $100,000 for conventional banks.

4.1.4 The Person to Person Loan (P2P)

The person-to-person loan permits individuals to borrow funds without resorting to any financial intermediary. Usually, the interests of P2P are higher than others because such loans are unique and cannot be provided by conventional financial institutions. This type of borrowing is also considered an alternative for banks products and provides for the impact of the innovative digital currency on P2P loans.

Table 1 The 2016 top 10 FinTech firms

Fintech	Countries
1. Ant financial—Ali pay	China
2. Qudian	China
3. Oscar	USA
4. Lufax	China
5. ZhongAn	China
6. Atom	UK
7. Kreditech	Germany
8. Avant	USA
9. Sofi	USA
10. JD finance	China

4.2 FinTech Worldwide Ranking

As already stated, FinTech firms are turning the financial sector industry upside down. The most lucrative firms are the ones who have the ability to change the payment system and project financing principles. In 2016 [11] KPMG ranked the FinTech firms from most to the least lucrative. And as result, the 2016 top 10 FinTech firms are as follows (Table 1).

China is currently a major player in FinTechs and has overturned the US in terms of the investment scale in finance technology platforms. Indeed, Hong Kong is a great potential and holds the necessary finance tools and resources to help FinTech firms prosper and grow [12]. The enterprise "Ant Financial" [13] known as "Alipay" was founded in 2014 and considered an affiliate to the Chinese group of Alibaba that was established in 2004. "Alipay" provides financial services to 450 million people including payments and insurance management. On the Chinese market, mobile payment is more substantial compared to the US. In the US, Paypal, the subsidiary of Ebay provides services for 150 million users only [14].

4.3 The FinTechs in the Arab World

Banks in the Arab world should confront the serious competition of FinTech firms. In this part of the world, finance technology is rapidly growing although it is still considered pre-mature compared with other developed countries. However, there are solid business foundations, especially with the increased usage of smartphone in this region. The Arab population is demanding more solutions, an increased usage of mobile payments and many other innovative mobile electronic financial services and products. It is worth noting that while observing FinTech evolution in this region, encouraging signs float in the horizon with regard to prosperity of FinTechs in the future. In fact, innovative plans are in place to boost such industry in Saudi Arabia and other countries. In Lebanon, the banking sector is reputed for its stability, so time will judge whether this will tone down the competition of FinTech and the challenge they constitute to Lebanese traditional banks.

4.4 Research Model

This research is of a qualitative nature and is aimed at reaching a global understanding of the impact of financial related innovations on the market. Indeed, financial innovation is becoming a very sensitive subject for conventional banks. Therefore, substantial interviews are conducted with banking specialists and banks officials to better understand their attitudes. A mass survey was administered to seek individual and public feedback and try to appraise the viability of the below model that aims

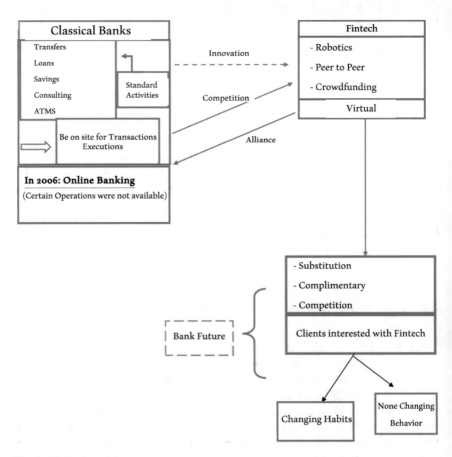

Fig. 1 Research model

at testing the potentiality of collaboration among between banks and FinTech firms along with their continuity and survival (Fig. 1).

5   Research Findings

5.1   Interviews with Banks Officials

The Lebanese Banks officials' responses have converged into admitting the necessity of expanding financial investment to improve the presence of banks on the markets and help them grow further. Banks aim at developing advanced and innovative technology finance products and services to meet and stand up against competition. This is a must to counter the threat caused by technology-leading firms. Banks need to appeal to young generations and advanced finance technology organization that can offer efficient and effective financial products and services to them.

As a matter of fact, one of the interviewee precised that a digital bank shall: "Embrace cutting-edge technology to help the financial product expand, avoid its rapid maturity, enlarge profit, and immerse clients with new experiences by providing customizable products and services, being present everywhere, and enhance business transparency and quality. He also stressed on 3 major objectives:

1. Positioning the bank as a modern bank of a prime choice
2. Recognizing the bank as a provider of quality and innovative products and services
3. Assisting clients with efficient customized offers and personalized services.

As to the robotization of the banking advisory business, the interviewees had different opinions. Bank (2) interviewee claims that robots could, on the short and medium terms, assist the CSO department to a certain extent. On the long run, robots cannot replace humans because in general people and clients prefer human contact when it comes to the management of their financing. Bank (3) candidate stresses on the fact that in addition to Tap2pay and mobile banking. Robots have already been installed and replaced the "sales & CSO" departments while human financial consultants are still gaining ground. Obviously, more technology products will be marketed subject to the new regulations of the Central Bank of Lebanon.

Finally, and based on the 3 banks officials responses, it seems that Lebanese banks can innovate internally or enter into a partnership with technology finance firms to produce and offer the most compliant product and service.

In fact, the threats and competitions launched by FinTech firm shall be a shock to Banks who should, their turn re-organize and upgrade their business model and operating mechanism. Therefore, Banks shall keep operating but differently. With the use of advanced technologies, they shall provide customized innovative financial products to meet the requirements of the different market segments.

Obviously, Lebanese banks are aware of their need to innovate and the impact of FinTech firms on them. As a counter attack, they are already determined to collaborate with technology companies to technically assist in the creation of innovative banking products.

The weaknesses and threats of Lebanon are serious barriers to the development and growth of FinTech firms. Despite Lebanon's weak Internet, communication and technology infrastructure, the banking sector pursues its outstanding performance, whilst technology startups still have a long way to go. Moreover, other obstacles forbid the further growth of those startups in Lebanon. As expressed earlier, Banks are in continuous collaboration with technology firms to develop innovative products, hence Banks can absorb the competition of those startups and sometimes eliminate them due to banks excessive financing capabilities.

However, the Lebanese in general are educated people and the young generation is dramatically active on the internet, smart phones and tablets. This is to say that the market segment is vast and diversified: 44.44% of Lebanese are aged between 25–54 years and 74% of the total population uses the internet despite of its poor current condition. As the rates of un-employment escalate in Lebanon, technology oriented start-ups could be an optimal solution as well because it helps hiring fresh graduates and junior professionals [15]. Despite the above, development of start-ups remains in an unstable environment. The attitude of the end user is crucial to test the future tendency acceptance.

5.2 Questionnaire Analysis

An internet survey was conducted with a random sample of 800 persons whereby 168 were marked as respondents. The survey included 16 questions to test citizens' knowledge level on subjects related to FinTech and try to understand their perception, attitude and behavior with respect to such enterprises. Are they aware of finance innovation? Would they be willing to drop conventional banks for FinTechs and related?

The random sample was varied enough and consisted of the following:

- 84% of candidates were aged between 18 and 50 years of age
- about 50% of respondents were females
- 95% of respondents had a bank account
- 57% of respondents visit their banks branches up to 2–5 times a month to:

  - deposit funds (57%)
  - withdraw funds (22%)
  - seek Bank advices (11%)
  - wexecute transfers (10%).

Internet banking is used by 58% of our sample but also those persons visit their branches from time to time to conduct operations. In fact, 80% of interviewees have claimed to have this habit of visiting their agency.

However, 69% of the sample is unaware of internet banking and has no idea about the meaning of peer to peer, crowdfunding and robots' advisors.

It also seems that clients are not satisfied with the cost or quality services provided by their banks, and they are ready to leave their financial institutions to collaborate with the innovative start-ups.

On the other hand, 33.33% do not wish to work with FinTechs due consumer behavior. Hence, 39.78% claim the necessity of physical interactions when it comes to banks related financial consultation. According to them, human encounter and cooperation is crucial in this regard.

Finally, it looks like 21% of the sample people are ready to work with robots' advisors for consulting purposes. But 72% of them also did not doubt about the continuous presence of banks despite future technological advancements.

The above is in line with what has been previously expressed by banks officials.

The current findings confirm that the Lebanese in general are unconscious about FinTech presence and business model. However, approximately half of the young persons have a certain tendency to quitting traditional banks to collaborate with start-ups whose services and products should be appealing.

Reference to this survey, the following relationships have been proven:

- Age is a crucial factor in changing the habit of dealing with financial firms
- Alliances among banks start-ups is mandatory for innovation growth and fulfilment of market needs.
- Some banks collaborate with FinTechs others prefer to compete.

6 Conclusion

The rapid technological advancement along with the digital revolution are changing factors that are disturbing all business sectors and especially finance. During the past decade, financial innovation encouraged the modification of financial services and products.

When banks adopt financial technology, they will be able to promote themselves as innovators, reduce operations cost, guarantee a better client retention, expand their market share and satisfy their clients by providing to them the required products and services. The future belongs to virtual banks and hybrid-banking structure could be defined as transitory only.

Schumpeter [2] exposes the theory of "innovation cluster". For him, through the process of "creative destruction", the new entrants on the market try sometimes to wipe off current players. Therefore, with the arrival of those start-ups accompanied with their innovative financial products, the financial industry sector is witnessing radical changes. Innovative financial services shall not stop from widening. Clients shall have a huge portfolio of innovative financial services and banks shall be obliged to re-consider and launch their self-transformation to preserve their continuity and survival.

The innovative financial applications could be used for payments, digital wallets, artificial intelligence, robotics, block chain, crypto-currency, and shadow banking etc. Today, most of financial services are provided by non-banking institutions, and the end consumer is the sole beneficiary. With more transparency, choice, flexible technology and better induction, consumers can even be more satisfied in the future.

Lebanon is still lagging behind due to lack of regulations, old rooted habits and confidence in cyber technology... Generally, Lebanese still prefer to visit material banks maybe because the internet and mobile banking is not yet well developed. Moreover, public 3G and 4G infrastructure remains weak, poor and of moderate quality! For this reason and to provide compensation, some Lebanese Banks collaborate with finance technology firms to boost innovation and related tendencies.

It is necessary to consider and observe the banking transformations that are happening elsewhere. FinTechs should become more present on the Lebanese market because they should not really be considered a threat but an opportunity. Their role is to integrate with banks but not replace them. But the threat that should not be neglected is the one that comes from the giants like Facebook, Uber, Google & Amazon because the financial power they hold can rapidly transform their companies into banks or simply establish new banks. This way, they would secure the coverage of all financial services and products that are related to finance technology and conventional banking at the same time.

In conclusion, Lebanese banks seem to seriously consider FinTechs potential threats along with other virtual platforms that are increasingly introduced to the market. It looks like in the years to come physical branches are going to be visited less and less by clients as they will be conducting most their banking transactions online using mobile applications.

References

1. Kahneman, D., Tversky, A.: Prospect theory: an analysis of decisions under risk. Econometrica **47**, 263–291 (1979)
2. Schumpeter, J.A.: Tenth Printing, The Theory of Economic Development. Transaction Publishers, New Brunswick, New Jersey (2004)
3. Gowland: Innovations Financière Et Investissement. Par Rogerio Sobreira (1991)
4. Porter, M.: The five competitive forces that shape strategy. Harvard Bus. Rev. **86**, 78–93 (2008)
5. Lancaster, K.J.: A new approach to consumer theory. J. Polit. Econo. **74**(2), 132–157 (1966). The University of Chicago Press, National Center for Biotechnology Information. http://www.ncbi.nlm.nih.gov
6. Silber, W.: The processsus of financial innovation. Am. Econ. Rev. **73**(2) (1983)
7. Kane, E.: Accelerating inflation, technological innovation, and the decreasing effectiveness of banking regulation. J. Finan. **36**, 355–367 (1981)
8. Goodhart, C.: Problems of Monetary Management: The UK Experienced and Courakis, Inflation, Depression and Economic Policy in the West. Mausell, Londres (1981)

9. Eisenhardt, K.M.: Building theories from case study research. Acad. Manage. Rev. **14**(4), 532–550 (1989)
10. Romelaer, P.: L'entretien De Recherche. In: Dans Roussel, P., Wacheux, F. (eds.) Management Des Ressources Humaines: Methodes De Recherche En Sciences Humaines Et Sociales, pp. 101–137. De Boeck (2005)
11. Fintech 100: KPMG présente le nouveau classement 2016 des leaders mondiaux de la Fintech. https://home.kpmg.com/fr/fr/home/media/press-releases/2016/10/fintech-100-nouveau-classement-2016.html
12. Hangzhou, China, January 24, 2017 – Alibaba Group Holding Limited (Nyse: Baba) Financial Results For The Quarter Ended December 31, 2016. https://www.alibabagroup.com/en/news/press_pdf/p170124.pdf
13. Lu, L.: Ant Financial Claims Doubling Of Daily Users- Financial Times- Mai 2017
14. Thomas Kaeb Les Banques Et Les Fintech: Quel Avenir Pour Le Secteur Bancaire ? 22/10/2016- Economie Matin https://www.economiematin.fr/news-lesbanques-et-les-fintech-quel-avenir-pour-le-secteur-bancaire-
15. World Factbook-Lebanon. https://Theodora.Com/Wfbcurrent/Lebanon/Index.html

ICT and the Performance of Lebanese Banks: A Panel Data Analysis

Amal Dabbous

Abstract This study explores the impact of information and communication technology (ICT) on the performance of 25 Lebanese commercial banks for the period between 2000 and 2014. Unlike previous studies, this study uses a panel data analysis to assess the effect of the number of Internet users and domain registrations in Lebanon on the performance of the banks. Results reveal that there is a positive statistical significant relationship between ICT and the performance of the banks. Moreover, the capital adequacy ratio, the size of the bank, the growth rate of the gross domestic product and the lending interest rates were found to have a positive impact on the performance. We conclude that a higher level of ICT use is an important factor that determines commercial banks' profitability as it supports the commercial work of the banks and enables them to achieve a better performance.

Keywords ICT · Bank performance · Lebanon

1 Introduction

The banking sector is considered one of the main sectors where technological improvement is closely monitored and widely adopted. Information and communication technology (ICT) presents the possibility for banks to create new systems and innovative products that satisfy a broad range of customer needs. Moreover, technology based financial products and applications such as Internet and mobile banking bring tremendous advantages to both customers and financial institutions. Technological innovation is reshaping the banking industry through offering most of the banking services and products at lower operational costs for 24 h and 7 days, which decreases the dependency rate on physical branches and raises the bank profitability. In light of the importance of ICT in the banking industry, previous literature presented a wide range of studies that tackle the positive relation between the use of ICT and the banks' performance (Binuyo and Rafiu Adewale [1], Onay and Ozsoz

A. Dabbous (✉)
Faculty of Business Administration, Saint-Joseph University of Beirut, Beirut, Lebanon
e-mail: amal.dabbous@usj.edu.lb

© Springer Nature Switzerland AG 2020　　　　　　　　　　　　　　　　　361
Y. Baghdadi et al. (eds.), *ICT for an Inclusive World*,
Lecture Notes in Information Systems and Organisation 35,
https://doi.org/10.1007/978-3-030-34269-2_25

[2], Hernando and Nieto [3], DeYoung et al. [4], among others). Banks adopt ICT in an attempt to increase the efficiency of the services they offer and to enhance their business processes, particularly with the high level of competition which drove banks to search for innovations and development that will increase their customers' loyalty. As a result, ICT is considered a major enabler for improving the banking sector performance in today's rapid pace of change and highly competitive environments.

Lebanese banks are not an exception. Despite the fact that the Lebanese banking industry was greatly affected by the civil war during the years 1975–1990, the Lebanese banking industry is now considered among the 87 banking systems with a "low level of potential vulnerability" according to Fitch rating agency in its semi-annual report that assesses the risk of 115 banking systems operating in advanced and emerging economies [5]. This is considered the highest category on Fitch Macro Prudential Indicator (MPI). In fact, the Lebanese banking industry applies and uses new technologies at different levels: managerial, transactional and executive. The majority of commercial banks operating in Lebanon consider ICT as the main tool to succeed in this new dynamic world where institutions must strive to lower their transactional costs and to provide innovative activities that ensure their competitiveness. Hence, ICT has an impact on all processes that shape the modern banking industry from daily routines to strategic decisions.

All these features encouraged Lebanese banks to offer electronic-based services for their customers and to make for themselves high standard of excellence in terms of technology use and adoption. Lebanon was the first country in the Levant that used Internet for commercial purposes since 1995 [6]. The number of Internet users reached 3.6 million by July 2015, which accounts for an 86% penetration rate compared to 40% in 2010 [6]. Moreover, in 2015, Lebanon ranked fourth in the Arab region after Bahrain, United Arab Emirates (UAE) and Qatar [6]. These technological changes helped the Lebanese banks to maintain their position as top operating institutions and to enhance their performance.

The Lebanese banking system is considered one of the strongest in the Middle East and North African (MENA) region with consolidated total assets of commercial banks reaching 310,176 billion Lebanese pounds (USD 205.8 billion) at the end of March 2017, hence increasing by 0.7% from end December 2016 according to the Lebanese Association of Banks in Lebanon March 2017 report [7]. Moreover, 10 Lebanese commercial banks are considered among the top 1000 banks in the world according to the 2017 survey of the best 1000 banks in the world [8]. The survey is conducted by the Banker magazine and the ranking is based on the level of the bank's Tier One capital in US dollars by the end of the previous year.

Finally, one has to mention that the ICT sector in Lebanon is also currently considered as one of the fastest growing sectors in the Lebanese economy. According to a report published by the Investment Development Authority of Lebanon [9], the ICT sector is expected to reach a compound annual growth rate (CAGR) of 9.7% by 2019 compared to 7% in 2016 and it contributed to 3% of Lebanon's GDP in the year 2013.

The main purpose of this study is to ascertain the level of use of ICT on the banking sector performance in Lebanon. Considering ICT as a key factor for higher banking performance, this study uses an unbalanced panel of 25 commercial banks operating in Lebanon for the period between 2000 and 2014 to investigate the impact of ICT use on the banks' performance measured by the return on assets (ROA). Unfortunately, data for the use of ICT and for ICT expenditures and adoption on the bank level was not available for the Lebanese commercial banks. Hence, we modeled the level of ICT use in Lebanon using two proxies, the number of Internet users per 100 people and the number of Lebanese domain registrations. In fact, Internet users per 100 people is a very well established indicator for the level of ICT use in the literature. Moreover, in 1993, the .lb domain name was first allocated by the operator of the Internet Assigned Number Authority (IANA) to the American University of Beirut (AUB). AUB was the first institution that acquired a .lb domain name. By the end of year 2015, the Lebanese domain name registry had approximately 4000 registered .lb domains [6]. The author believes that the adoption of online channel both by users and institutions, will eventually save time and costs in processing administrative and financial transactions. As a result, this operating costs reductions will increase the efficiency of the financial system, leading to a better financial performance. In fact [3], argue that the most important benefit that arises from the use of ICT by banks is the reduction in overhead expenses. ICT use can reduce the costs related to the maintenance of physical branches and can also decrease the marketing and labor costs. Moreover [1], conclude that the contribution of ICT to a bank performance comes essentially from information and communication technology cost efficiency compared to investment in ICT.

This study makes several contributions to the literature. First unlike previous studies this is the first study that conducts a quantitative analysis using secondary data to investigate the impact of ICT use on the performance of Lebanese banks. Second, to the best of our knowledge this is the first paper that addresses this issue in Lebanon using a panel data analysis. Previous studies conducted in Lebanon, Hilal [10], Sarji [11] among others, used primary data collected through the use of survey questions.

The remainder of this study is organized as follows: Sect. 2 presents the literature review, Sect. 3 explains the methodology and data, Sect. 4 discusses the empirical results and Sect. 5 concludes.

2 Literature Review

2.1 ICT and Bank Performance

Internet use and online presence of companies and banks is undoubtedly considered as one of the most important driving factors affecting the banking industry and changing banks' performance and activities. This study assesses the impact of Internet use and domain registration presence on the performance of commercial banks operating in Lebanon. Numerous studies in the literature investigate the impact of Information and communication technology (ICT) on the banking sector performance and efficiency. The first strand in the literature confirms that Internet adoption as an additional distribution channel has a positive impact on the profitability. DeYoung et al. [4] find that Internet adoption as a delivery channel improved US community bank profitability. This enhancement is mainly driven by increases in non-interest income from service charges on deposit accounts. Hernando and Nieto [3] assess the effect of adopting a transactional Website on the financial performance of commercial banks operating in Spain. Results show that the adoption of the Internet offers gradual reduction in overhead expenses. This cost reduction will eventually lead to an improvement in the banks' profitability and turns to be highly significant after one and a half years in terms of ROA. Ciciretti et al. [12] find a significant positive relation between offerings of Internet banking products and bank performance in Italy. Onay and Ozsoz [2] use a panel of 18 retail banks operating in Turkey for the period of 1990–2008 to assess the impact of internet adoption on the banks' profitability. Results indicate that Internet banking adoption has a positive effect on per-branch profitability. However, this impact becomes negative after 2 years of adoption as Internet banking increases competition, hence yielding lower interest income.

In the context of Lebanon [10], uses a survey to investigate the opportunities, motivations and effects of the implementation of NICTs for Lebanese commercial banks. She concludes that NICTs are playing an increasing role in the evolution of banking businesses and that the use of this NICTs improves the productivity of banks. Sarji [11] uses a questionnaire survey to assess the banking customers' perception in Lebanon regarding the provided banking service. His study shows that most Lebanese banks have benefited from ICT to improve their operations and that IT has a significant impact on Lebanese banks.

Moreover, previous studies in the literature investigated the relationship between ICT investment and the bank performance. Berger [13] examines technological progress and its effects in the banking industry. Results show that ICT investment generate improvements in costs and that technological progress increases overall productivity. Kozak and Eyadat [14] suggest that increasing ICT investment is associated with an increase in the value of return on assets for the US banking sector. Binuyo and Rafiu Adewale [1] investigate the impact of ICT on bank performance of South African banking industry for the period 1990–2012. Findings reveal that the use of ICT increases return on capital employed as well as return on assets. However, the study reveals that most of the contribution to performance comes from ICT cost efficiency rather than being the result of ICT investment.

2.2 Factors Affecting Bank Performance

In addition to the impact of ICT use on the banking sector performance, other internal and macroeconomic factors have been depicted to have a significant effect on this performance. Determining the factors that affect banks' performance has been widely tackled in the literature. Moreover, this has been a topic of interest for both developed and developing countries. Researchers investigated the effect of several candidate variables on bank performance. Previous empirical studies have related the bank performance to internal or microeconomic determinants as well as external factors that reflect the macroeconomic environment in which the bank operates. However, the literature reveals mixed results on the impact of these factors on the bank performance.

Among the internal factors, we use the size of the bank, the capital adequacy ratio and the ratio of operating expenses to total assets. The effect of the size on the bank performance is a subject of debate in the literature. Some advocate that size has a positive effect, others show that its impact on the performance is negative. Bikker and Hu [15], Pasiouras and Kosmidou [16] and Aladwan [17] among others, show a positive impact of size on performance. The second group suggests that a negative relation exists between the two variables [18–20]. Finally, some researchers did not find a statistically significant impact of size on the performance of banks [21, 22].

Regarding the level of capitalization, the Capital adequacy ratio (CAR) has been mostly used in the literature as an internal factor affecting the bank performance. A higher ratio reduces the risk incurred by banking activities and sends a positive signal to the market on the degree of the bank solvency, which improves the performance of the bank. Moreover, several empirical studies show the positive relation between CAR and the bank performance. Among others we cite [23–25]. However, some researchers such as [26] find that CAR has a negative impact on performance. In fact, a higher level of capital adequacy ratio will lead to an increase in the variable costs which might not generate a higher profitability. In addition, when capital levels are high, this result in a lower level of leverage and risk which do not really translate in a higher profitability as some argue that shareholders' profit is usually higher when equity level is reduced and risk raises.

The third internal factor used represents efficiency and it is measured by the ratio of operating costs to total assets. It is argued that higher expenses will generate lower profits. Previous studies show that banks that have lower expenses for a certain level of output are highly efficient, hence they have a higher profitability. Hong and John [24], in their study for Japanese banks find that there is a negative relation between the ratio of costs to income and the bank performance. Moreover [21, 27], establish a significant positive impact of efficiency on profitability.

For external variables, we use the Gross domestic product (GDP) annual growth rate and the lending interest rate. Economic theory suggests a positive impact of economic growth on bank profitability. In fact, when bad economic conditions persist the quality of the loan portfolio decreases, generating larger credit losses. As a result, banks increase the provisions for non-performing loans which decreases their profitability. A better economic situation will improve the solvency of borrowers, resulting in an increase in the demand for credits and improving the profitability of banks (Athanasoglou et al. [21], Calza et al. [28], Beckmann [29] among others).

In addition, lending rates is considered as an important external factor as it is associated with the macroeconomic instability which affects the profitability of the banks. As argued by Njuguna and Ngugi [30], macroeconomic environment is considered as a cause and a consequence influencing lending interest rates. Higher level of macroeconomic instability and a decrease in economic growth, increase investors' uncertainty towards their returns on investments which in turn increases the lending interest rates. At the same time, we argue that banks usually prefer higher lending rates as higher rates yield more returns. In fact, an increase in lending rates will generate more revenues as interest rates on loans and other investments increase. Aydemir and Ovenc [31] investigate the effect of the short-term interest rate and the slope of the yield curve on banking profitability in an emerging market. Results reveal that while their impact on bank profits is negative in the short-run, the effects of these variables on the profitability turn out to be positive in the long run. Maigua and Mouni [32] assess the impact of interest rate determinants on the performance of commercial banks in Kenya. Results show that higher levels of discount rates, inflation rates and exchange rates lead to higher performance in commercial banks in Kenya. Khan and Sattar [33] examine the effect of interest rates changes on the profitability of commercial banks operating in Pakistan. They find a strong and positive correlation between interest rate and commercial banks' profitability.

Finally, for the bank performance proxies, most of the empirical studies measure bank performance using return on assets (ROA), return on equity (ROE) or the net interest margin (NIM). ROA has been most widely used in the literature as a metric to measure bank performance and it was validated for its usefulness as a proxy for the bank profitability [34]. There are many reasons that make ROA a good proxy for the bank performance. ROA does not vary when the level of leverage changes as it is the case with ROE [35]. Moreover, as mentioned by Olson and Zoubi [36] assets can indicate the levels of income and expenses simultaneously. ROA is a financial ratio used to show how well a bank uses it assets to generate earnings. Among others, we cite [37, 38] who use ROA to estimate the profitability and performance of Indonesian and Nigerian banks respectively.

3 Methodology and Data

3.1 Model and Estimation Technique

Our linear model aims to explore the impact of ICT use on the performance of 25 commercial banks operating in Lebanon for the period between 2000 and 2014. We follow previous studies in the literature and model the performance of the bank as a function of both internal or microeconomic variables and external or macroeconomic factors. In addition, we consider that the performance of the bank is also affected by the level of ICT use proxied by the number of Internet users (per 100 people) and the number of Lebanese domain registrations. Hence, the empirical panel data model for the bank performance is specified as follows:

$$ROA_{it} = \beta_0 + \beta_1 OP_{it} + \beta_2 CAR_{it} + \beta_3 Size_{it} + \beta_4 GDP_{t-1}$$
$$+ \beta_5 LI_t + \beta_6 INT_t + \beta_7 DR_t + e_i \tag{3.1}$$

where, $i = 1, \ldots, N$ shows the subscript for each bank in the panel, $t = 1, \ldots, T$ indicates the time period and eit denotes the random error term which represents white noise characteristics. ROA_{it} the dependent variable, denotes the performance for the bank i in year t. It is measured by the return on assets. OP_{it} represents the operating costs ratio for the bank i in year t, as a proxy we use the ratio of the non-interest expenses to total assets. CAR_{it} refers to the capital adequacy ratio for the bank i in year t. $Size_{it}$ indicates the size of the bank i in year t and as a proxy we use the logarithm of the total assets of the bank. GDP_{t-1} refers to the lag of the annual growth rate of the GDP in Lebanon. It is known in the literature that a growth in the GDP does not affect the performance contemporaneously, it usually takes time for the effects to show. Therefore, we use the lag of the growth rate of the GDP. LI_t is the lending interest rate in Lebanon. Finally, ICT use is proxied by the number of Internet users (per 100 people) in Lebanon denoted by INT_t and the number of Lebanese domain registrations represented by DR_t.

In this study, the model in Eq. 3.1 is estimated using the fixed effects (FE) estimator. This method along with the random effects (RE) estimator technique are widely used in panel data analysis. The FE model considers exogenous variables as non-random. Moreover, the FE model assumes that the slopes of the regression lines are the same across the banks. The RE model in contrast considers that explanatory variables are driven by random movements. In an attempt to select the appropriate model to use the Hausman test is performed. The Hausman test statistic obtained is H = 167.789 with p-value = prob(chi-square (7) > 167.789) = 7.34042e − 033. This very low p-value counts against the null hypothesis that the RE model is consistent, in favor of the FE model. Thus this result shows that the FE model is the appropriate model to use. The FE model presents many advantageous, it fully captures the time constant omitted variables, hence removing any heterogeneity across the banks and avoiding misspecification error. The fixed effect model is represented as follows:

$$ROA_{it} = \beta_0 + \beta_1 OP_{it} + \beta_2 CAR_{it} + \beta_3 Size_{it} + \beta_4 GDP_{t-1}$$
$$+ \beta_5 LI_t + \beta_6 INT_t + \beta_7 DR_t + \alpha_i + u_{it} \tag{3.2}$$

where, the error term is decomposed into two error components, the individual specific component α_i and the traditional disturbance term u_{it}.

3.2 Data Source and Descriptive Statistics

The main goal of this empirical research is to assess the impact of ICT use on the performance of commercial banks operating in Lebanon while including the largest possible number of banks and covering the longest time period. However, the number

Table 1 Descriptive statistics

Variable	Mean	Std. dev.	Minimum	Maximum
ROA	1.05	1.35	−2.10	7.84
OP	2.15	2.83	0.77	33.19
CAR	7.48	2.73	0.68	18.58
Size	3.64	0.82	3.60	6.68
GDP	4.48	3.25	0.90	10.30
LI	10.59	3.43	7.25	18.15
INT	31.58	24.52	22.53	74.70
DR	144.53	28.32	142.50	205.00

of banks included in this study and the choice of the time period were dictated by the data availability. Annual data for ROA, non-interest expenses, total assets, capital adequacy ratio for the 25 Lebanese commercial banks included in this study, for the period between 2000 and 2014 were retrieved from the Bankscope database. Annual data on Internet users (per 100 people) and GDP growth rate were downloaded from the World Bank's World Development Indicators. In fact, Internet users (per 100 people) is the most widely used proxy for ICT in the literature. The data for the lending interest rate was obtained from the Global Financial Development Database. Finally, data for the number of Lebanese domain registrations was collected from the business handbook issued by InfoPro.SAL [6]. Due to lack of long time series for all the variables considered in this study, we ended up with an unbalanced panel and a total of 299 observations.

The descriptive statistics: the mean value, the standard deviation, the minimum and the maximum value for the different variables for the panel are presented in Table 1.

We notice that Internet users (per 100 people) and the number of Lebanese domain registrations have the highest standard deviations higher than 0.9 which reflects a high level of volatility over the years 2000–2014. These figures are expected particularly with the growing usage of ICT over these years. Other factors have almost the same volatility with a standard deviation ranging between 2.8 and 3.43. The performance indicator ROA have the lowest volatility with a standard deviation of 0.2. This result is expected particularly that commercial banks included in this sample have maintained a satisfying level of profitability over the course of the period 2000–2014.

4   Empirical Results

The results for the estimation of our fixed effects model presented in Eq. (3.2) are reported in Table 2.

Table 2 Fixed-effects model estimation output

Variable	Coefficient	Std. error	t-ratio	p-value
const	− 0.27	0.23	− 1.189	0.23632
OP	0.05	0.03	1.54	0.1235
CAR	0.20	0.099	2.05	0.0409**
Size	0.23	0.13	1.78	0.0755*
GDP_1	0.13	0.03	4.18	0.0000***
LI	0.29	0.11	2.67	0.0079***
INT	0.14	0.05	2.74	0.0065***
DR	0.23	0.13	1.71	0.0887*

Dependent variable ROA
*, **, *** Indicate that the estimated coefficients are statistically significant at the 10%, 5% and 1% significant levels respectively

Furthermore, in order to check the validity of our model, the F-Test was carried out. The F-Test for individual effects statistic is $F(24,267) = 89.9888$ and has a very low p-value, way less than 0.0001 which indicates that we reject the null hypothesis that individual effects are equal to 0 and confirms the fact that each bank has a different intercept. This result shows that the fixed effects model is the appropriate model to use as we need to model individual heterogeneity, we cannot simply pool the data.

Empirical results presented in Table 2 show that with the exception of operating costs to total assets ratio, all the exogenous variables have a statistical significant impact on the Lebanese Banks performance to a varying degree. The coefficient for Internet users is positive and statistically significant at the 5% significance level, showing that as the number of Internet users in Lebanon grows, the performance of the banks increases. Moreover, the coefficient for the number of domain registrations in Lebanon is also positive and statistically significant at the 10% significance level. Thus, as the number of domain registrations increases, the use of the Internet channel increases in Lebanon which positively influences the performance of the banks. These results highlight the fact that as the adoption of the Internet channel among Lebanese increases, the performance of the banks will be enhanced, particularly that almost all the banks included in our study are using the Internet channel. The results are in line with the studies conducted by Hilal [10] and Sarji [11] in the context of Lebanon that assess the impact of ICT and technological progress on the productivity and performance. Both studies conclude that ICT has a significant positive impact on the performance of the Lebanese banks.

In addition, the estimation results in Table 2 reveal that the coefficients for the capital adequacy ratio and the size of the bank are both positive and statistically significant at the 5 and 1% significance levels respectively. These results are in line with the strand of literature that established a positive relation between the size of the bank and its performance [15–17]. They also match the results of several empirical studies that show the positive relation between CAR and the bank performance

[23–25]. As for the macroeconomic factors, the coefficient for the lag of the GDP growth rate is positive and highly significant as expected since a better economic situation will improve the bank performance. This result is similar to the one obtained by Athanasoglou et al. [21], Calza et al. [28], Beckmann [29], among others. The lending interest rate coefficient is also positive and significant at the 1 significance level confirming the results of Maigua and Mouni [32], Khan and Sattar [33] among others who find a positive impact of interest rate on the bank performance. Finally, the coefficient of the ratio of operating costs to total assets is positive and not statistically significant, this result is not expected as usually the CAR is considered as one of the internal factors that influence the performance of the bank.

5 Conclusion

This paper examines the impact of the progress in the use of Internet among Lebanese and the higher number of domain registrations on the performance of 25 commercial banks operating in Lebanon for the period between 2000–2014. We tried through this paper to assess the impact of the ICT on the banking business, particularly that the ICT sector is now one of the fastest growing sectors in Lebanon and that the Lebanese banking industry is considered as one of the main sectors where technological innovations are widely adopted.

Our objective is to empirically test the relationships between the level of use of Internet channel among Lebanese, the online presence of firms, banks and institutions operating in Lebanon and the commercial banks' performance. Towards this end we use two proxies for the level of ICT use in Lebanon, namely the number of Internet users (per 100 people) and the number of domain registrations per year. The model was estimated using the fixed effects method and the results confirm the presence of a positive and statistically significant relation between ICT use and the Lebanese banks' performance.

Our empirical results suggest that a higher level of ICT use supports the commercial work of the banks, enables them to develop new distribution channels particularly through the use of Internet which as a result will lead to a reduction in costs and an increase in profits. Internet has become an integral part of the banking business, as the number of Internet users and domain registrations increases, performing banking operations online will become easier and more convenient particularly since online users are now familiar with this channel. The Lebanese banking industry should profit from this fact to offer a wider range of services and to enhance its ability to integrate financial products. Such practices in the online environment will yield major advantages in terms of cost reductions, efficiency and better performance.

These results provided us with an empirical evidence that depicts the importance of ICT use in enhancing the performance for the Lebanese banking sector considered as the back bone of the Lebanese economy. The implication of these findings underscores the need for banks' owners and policy makers to promote policies that enhance the optimal use of ICT without compromising information security, particularly that the rapid growth of ICT use by the banking system gave rise to a higher level of theft and fraud as more personal and financial information are becoming digitized.

Finally, one has to note that this study might suffer from some limitations regarding the number of banks included in the sample. Moreover, and due to data unavailability on the level of ICT investments or expenditures per bank, we were not able to model the level of ICT use and adoption as an internal factor, rather we considered the level of ICT use in Lebanon as an external factor affecting the performance of the banks. However, despite the fact that this research might suffer from some limitations, empirical results remain adequate and statistically significant and highlight the importance of the use of ICT on the profitability and performance of commercial banks operating in Lebanon. One possible extension of this study would be to perform it using ICT as an internal factor determining the bank performance as data for ICT on the bank level becomes gradually available. Another possible future work would be to conduct a similar study in the context of the MENA region.

References

1. Binuyo, A., Rafiu Adewale, A.: The Impact of information and communication technology (ICT) on commercial bank performance: evidence from South Africa. Probl. Perspect. Manage. **12**, 59–68 (2014)
2. Onay, C., Ozsoz, E.: The impact of internet-banking on Brick and Mortar branches: the case of Turkey. J. Finan. Serv. Res. **44**(2), 187–204 (2013)
3. Hernando, I., Nieto, M.J.: Is the internet delivery channel changing banks performance? The case of Spanish banks. J. Bank. Finan. **31**(4), 1083–1099 (2007)
4. DeYoung, R., Lang, W.W., Nolle, D.L.: How the internet affects output and performance at community banks. J. Bank. Finan. **31**(4), 1033–1060 (2007)
5. Byblos Bank: Lebanon this week letter. Technical Report 514, Byblos Bank SAL (2017)
6. Lebanon Opportunities: The Business Handbook. InfoPro.SAL (2016)
7. Lebanese Association of Banks in Lebanon: The economic letter. Technical Report March 2017. Association of banks in Lebanon, Research and Statistics Department (2017)
8. Byblos Bank: Lebanon this week letter. Technical Report 503, Byblos Bank SAL (2017)
9. Investment Development Authority of Lebanon (IDAL): Investment opportunities in the ICT sector 2016. Technical Report. IDAL (2016)
10. Hilal, M.: Technological transition of banks for development: new information and communication technology and its impact on the banking sector in Lebanon. Int. J. Econ. Finan. **7**(5) (2015)
11. Sarji, M.: Information technology and its influence on the Lebanese banking sector. IOSR J. Bus. Manage. **19**, 19–28 (2017)
12. Ciciretti, R., Hasan, I., Zazzara, C.: Do internet activities add value? Evidence from the traditional banks. J. Finan. Serv. Res. **35**(1), 81–98 (2009)
13. Berger, A.N.: The economic effects of technological progress: evidence from the banking industry. J. Money Credit Banking **35**(2), 141–176 (2003)
14. Kozak, S., Eyadat, M.: The role of information technology in the profit and cost efficiency improvements of the banking sector. J. Acad. Bus. Econ. **5**(2) (2005)
15. Bikker, J., Hu, H.: Cyclical Patterns in profits, provisioning and lending of banks and procyclicality of the New Basel capital requirements. Banca Nazionale del Lavoro Q. Rev. **55**(221), 143–175 (2002)

16. Pasiouras, F., Kosmidou, K.: Factors influencing the profitability of domestic and foreign commercial banks in the European union. Res. Int. Bus. Finan. **21**(2), 222–237 (2007)
17. Aladwan, M.S.: The impact of bank size on profitability: an empirical study on listed Jordanian commercial banks. Eur. Sci. J. **11**(34) (2015)
18. Kosmidou, K., Tanna, S., Pasiouras, F.: Determinants of profitability of domestic UK commercial banks: panel evidence from the period 1995–2002. In: Economics, Finance and Accounting Applied Research Working Paper Series (2005)
19. Kasman, A., Tunc, G., Vardar, G., Okan, B.: Consolidation and commercial bank net interest margins: evidence from the old and new European union members and candidate countries. Econ. Model. **27**(3), 648–655 (2010)
20. Saddique, A., Ahmad, M., Mumtaz, R., Arif, M.: The effect of financial variables on bank performance pre and post financial crisis'. J. Finan. Acc. **4**(6), 378–382 (2016)
21. Athanasoglou, P., Brissimis, S., Delis, M.: Bank specific, industry specific and macroeconomic determinants of bank profitability. J. Int. Finan. Mark. Inst. Money. **18**(2), 121–136 (2008)
22. Micco, A., Panizza, U., Yanez, M.: Bank ownership and performance. does politics matter? J. Banking Finan. **31**(1), 219–241 (2007)
23. John, G., Philip, M., John, W.: The profitability of European banks: a cross-sectional and dynamic panel analysis. Manchester School. **72**(3), 363–381 (2004)
24. Hong, L., John, W.: The profitability of banks in Japan. Appl. Finan. Econ. **20**, 1851–1866 (2010)
25. Saeed, M.S.: Bank-related, industry-related and macroeconomic factors affecting bank profitability: a case of the United Kingdom. Res. J. Finan. Acc. **5**(2) (2014)
26. Curak, M., Poposki, K., Pepur, S.: Profitability determinants of the macedonian banking sector in changing environment. Proc. Soc. Behav. Sci. **44**(Supplement C), 406–416 (2012)
27. Dietrich, A., Wanzenried, G.: Determinants of bank profitability before and during the crisis: evidence from Switzerland. J. Int. Fin. Mark. Inst. Money **21**(3), 307–327 (2011)
28. Calza, A., Manrique, M., Sousa, J.: Credit in the Euro area: an empirical investigation using aggregate data. Q. Rev. Econ. Finan. **46**(2), 211–226 (2006)
29. Beckmann, R.: Profitability of Western European banking systems: panel evidence on structural and cyclical determinants. SSRN Electron. J. (2007)
30. Njuguna, N., Ngugi, R.: Banking sector interest rate spread in Kenya. Technical Report. Kenya Institute of Public Policy Research and Analysis (2000)
31. Aydemir, R., Ovenc, G.: Interest rates, the yield curve and bank profitability in an emerging market economy. Econ. Syst. **40**(4), 670–682 (2016)
32. Maigua, C., Mouni, G.: Influence of interest rates determinants on the performance of commercial banks in Kenya. Int. J. Acad. Res. Acc. Finan. Manage. Sci. **6**(2), 121–133 (2016)
33. Khan, W., Sattar, A.: Impact of interest rate changes on the profitability of four major commercial banks in Pakistan. Int. J. Acc. Finan. Rep. **4**(1), 142–154 (2014)
34. Nippani, S., Green, K.W.: The banking industry after the Riegle Neal-act: re-structure and overall performance. Q. Rev. Econ. Finan. **42**(5), 901–909 (2002)
35. Golin, J., Delhaise, P.: The Bank Credit Analysis Handbook: A Guide for Analysts, Bankers and Investors. Wiley, New York (2013)
36. Olson, D., Zoubi, T.A.: Efficiency and bank profitability in MENA countries. Emerging Mark. Rev. **12**(2), 94–110 (2011)
37. Asutay, M., Izhar, H.: Estimating the profitability of Islamic banking: evidence from bank Muamalat Indonesia. Rev, Islamic Econ. **11**(2), 17–29 (2007)
38. Beck, T., Cull, R., Jerome, A.: Bank privatization and performance: empirical evidence from Nigeria. J. Bank. Finan. **29**(8), 2355–2379 (2005)

The Challenges Faced During the Implementation of Smart Schools in Oman

Ali Al-Badi, Ali Tarhini and Hajer Al-Mawali

Abstract Teaching today relies a great deal on IT resources and there are many schools opting to digitize they curriculum i.e. change the traditional style to what has recently been coined as "Smart School" style, in which ICT plays a significant role. The Smart School initiative seeks to enhance education in a smarter and more innovative way using ICT. The purpose of this study is (1) to explore the challenges faced during the implementation of smart schools from the perspectives/viewpoints of the service provider, teachers and school IT administrators; and (2) to provide a set of recommendations to minimize such challenges. In order to achieve the research objectives two case studies were conducted among schools that had already started implementing the process of becoming smart schools. Both case studies included a set of interviews with schoolteachers, the people in charge of the proposed project, school IT administrators and a service provider. In addition, there were sets of classroom observations conducted in the respective schools. Study results and the examination of data analysis revealed that there are many challenges faced by the perspective parties and these challenges are discussed in some detail. The researchers then provided a set of recommendations to minimize, or indeed to overcome the challenges encountered in becoming a Smart School in Oman.

Keywords Smart school · Information and communication technology · Technology adoption · Implementation · Qualitative · Observation · Oman

A. Al-Badi
Gulf College, Muscat, Sultanate of Oman
e-mail: aalbadi@gulfcollege.edu.om

A. Tarhini (✉) · H. Al-Mawali
Department of Information Systems, College of Economics and Political Science,
Sultan Qaboos University, Muscat, Sultanate of Oman
e-mail: alitarhini@squ.edu.om

© Springer Nature Switzerland AG 2020   373
Y. Baghdadi et al. (eds.), *ICT for an Inclusive World*,
Lecture Notes in Information Systems and Organisation 35,
https://doi.org/10.1007/978-3-030-34269-2_26

1 Introduction

Over the past few years the traditional learning model has been considered an instructional tool in which students need to be loaded with information without a deeper understanding of such information. According to this approach the role of the teacher is mainly to dispense the knowledge, whereas the role of the student is to receive and repeat the received information [1, 2]. This method emphasizes individual work; as less collaborative students get few opportunities to practice within groups. Such a learning approach can be described as one-way communication between the teacher and students, and limits the interactive learning environment of both teachers and students. Nowadays, due to the massive technological growth, the environment is getting smarter about offering new opportunities to people. Technology has been integrated into our lives progressively, and it is proliferating in different domains such as lifestyle, health, education, communication, economics, social skills etc. [3].

Education is one of the areas that has been greatly impacted by the emerging technology, which has changed the way people learn, work and communicate. Information and Communication Technology (ICT) explores the concepts of communication and technology together by exchanging information rapidly through the use of technological devices. The next generation suggests that Information Technology (IT) and Communication Technology cannot work in silos any more. Gaining knowledge of ICT is crucial for organizations in order to improve their business processes, productivity, efficiency and competitiveness [4–6]. It has been expanding rapidly and spreading into educational institutions as an integral part of education [7] and it is now considered to be an indispensable tool for successful educational reform. However, ICT is not only a successful element in this, but is also a contributor in shaping student-centered learning environments, which is crucial for better education [4]. Therefore, educational institutions have to take advantage of technological services by adopting the new model for education called Smart Schools, by utilizing the relevant ICT infrastructure.

The Smart School initiative is intended to integrate ICT into education [8], as it is considered to be a key component in facilitating enhanced technology, by creating what is called student-centered educational environment [9]. The idea is to improve the quality of teaching and learning processes by introducing new methods of teaching through ICT [10]. Oman is considered to be one of the developing countries that has started to embrace ICT in different government sectors as a step towards moving towards a strategy of e-government (and e-society) in Oman. The e-government initiative is directed by His Majesty and aims to enhance and digitalize government services for its citizens and residents [11]. The e-education initiative is one of the tasks in the e-government transformation plan. E-education aims to utilize ICT to support the academic domain and promote learning for both teachers and students in Oman [12]. One of the leading telecommunications companies in Oman has created a digital education bundle in partnership with Education as a Service (EaaS) leaders. This telecommunications company created this package in order to complement the government efforts towards endorsing Oman's entry into the digitalization era. Only a few schools in Oman have started moving towards their transformation into smart schools. However, the transition from traditional educational approach to the advanced Smart School educational system is not an easy or smooth process. It involves a drastic change in the educational culture and attitudes of both teachers and students, who are the direct stakeholders of this program. Thus, this paper sheds light on the challenges faced during the implementation of Smart Schools in Oman, in order to provide a set of recommendations to minimize and overcome the challenges. Specifically, this study has two main questions: (1) What are the challenges that smart schools face during their implementation in Oman?; and (2) How can these challenges be overcome during the implementation of smart schools in Oman?

The rest of the paper is organized as follows: the next section provides a detailed literature review about smart schools. The third section describes the data collection methods and conceptual framework. The forth section provides the analysis of the data collected. The fifth section offers an explanation and discussion around the research findings and results. The last section presents a conclusion to the study.

2 Literature Review

2.1 What Is a Smart School?

A Smart School is a new paradigm concept [13] in the educational domain and is defined as a teaching-learning institution based on technology that is designed to provide a standard teaching-learning environment in order to improve the preparation of children for the information age. Smart schools need qualified human resources and well-designed teaching and learning concepts in order to achieve a high standard in education [14]. In their paper El-Halawany and Huwail [15] define 'smart schools' as a new learning community that encourage an active thinking process to solve problems with confidence and prepare students to be ready and fully responsible in the global economy by applying the appropriate knowledge and technology. Smart schools are schools that are equipped with various ICT requirements including computers, software [16], smart boards and network facilities which can be used for interactive teaching purposes and for encouraging self-paced learning [17]. Smart schools seek to democratize education, to provide more opportunities to improve individuals' skills and abilities, to help them develop an awareness of, and give them exposure to technology, in order to prepare a well skilled workforce for the information age and prepare them for the challenges, and to stimulate student creativity skills and critical thinking. Over time smart schools will develop their professional personnel and principals, their administrative and management processes and their educational resources [14]. Smart schools attempt to transform the education system by focusing on the development of individuals using a holistic approach, thus creating high-value based education available to all those when and where they need it [18].

Omidinia et al. [14] highlight the fact that schools will require changes in their current policies, practices and procedures to transform themselves into a smart school, as it is not an easy task.

So what does 'smart' mean? Zhu et al. [19] present in their paper the meaning of 'smart learner'. It is the ability to apply intelligence quickly and behave appropriately in different contexts. The use of the word 'smart' in educational technology means 'the ability to achieve one's goals and objectives in an efficient and effective manner where adaptive and innovative use of technology is needed [Spector, 2014]. The term 'smart educational environment' refers to an environment that facilitates learning by building on the learning experience of the learner efficiently [19]. Spector [20] highlights further that the learning environment is considered to be 'smart' if it achieves its desired outcomes.

2.2   ICT Adoption in Education

Information and Communication Technology (ICT) is a combination of technology and resources that have been collected together and utilized to communicate. It includes hardware, software, and media for collecting, storing, processing, transmitting and presenting the information in different forms such as text, voice and images [21]. It also includes broadcasting (television), the internet, computers (PCs), and projection devices. These different ICTs are currently used in the education sector [7]. Sarkar [21] indicates the importance of ICT's role in education, which will keep growing in the 21st century. Obviously, this can be proved simply by the fact that it has transformed the nature of education. It certainly has the power to transmit knowledge from teachers to students, and it transforms daily teaching practices [22].

UNESCO, at the World summit on the information society (WSIS) conducted in Switzerland in 2003, stated that ICT should be used to improve education systems because it encourages the creation of new learning methods and it helps to drive innovations and training. Furthermore, the summit emphasized ICT as being a key enabler in delivering developing counties into the age of information and knowledge [23]. It enables people to benefit fully and to make use of the new opportunities offered by ICT. A number of previous studies have shown that ICT is considered a powerful tool in extending educational opportunities. Cheung and Slavin [24] examine the impact of ICT on enhancing educational outcomes in mathematics in K-12 classrooms. Their meta-analysis summarizes the results from 74 qualified studies. They find that ICT impacts positively but modestly on mathematical achievement compared to conventional methods [24]. The outcome of this study is similar to the study conducted by Garcia and Pacheco. A case study was conducted for sixty students in third grade to study the effectiveness of using computer simulation tools on mathematics. Based on the researcher's exploratory study, the results indicated that computational tools improve students' engagement and collaboration when integrated with traditional teaching methods, and it enabled children to build on their own knowledge [25].

Integrating ICT in education has witnessed a transformation in existing learning activities into a student-centered education and self-directed learning. Fu [7] states that students' skills in building new knowledge become more accessible and students become more capable of using information and data from a variety of sources through ICT integration. Livingstone [26] further illustrated the same concept by citing some cases. Students can search online for homework without having to go to the library to get the book, and students can also 'ask for expert opinions' besides asking advice from parents.

2.3 Worldwide Smart School Initiatives

Smart learning needs to prepare the workforce, and to train them to work effectively and with competence, in order to meet the immerse demands of the 21st century [19]. Many countries have taken the opportunity of transforming their schools into smart schools, leveraging the power of ICT in education and focusing on smart learning. Malaysia is one of the leading countries regarding smart schools, this initiative having become operational in 1999. With the advancement of ICT, the Smart school project in Malaysia aims to achieve the Malaysian National Philosophy of Education to foster learners' knowledge and produce children able to solve problems and to be more responsible [18]. In 2004 a smart school was launched in Iran following the Malaysian approach of integrating ICT into their schools [16]. New York recognized the importance of integrating technology into their schools to enhance teaching and learning practices and to develop a knowledgeable workforce in order to compete worldwide. In 2014 two billion dollars was allocated to prepare New York State schools with educational tools and to promote students to master the skills of the 21st century economy, and they proposed seven keys changes in order to have a successful smart school [27]. The United Arab Emirates (UAE) initiated a Smart Learning Program (SLP) in 2012. This program aims to enrich learner-centric education supported by the latest technology such as interactive smart boards, tablets and high speed 4G networks. Also, teachers are equipped with laptops and offer them with specialized training programs to ensure the success of the program. Their learning environment empowers students to become proactively engaged and interactive in the learning process [28].

The Utah State Office of Education in the United States (US) initiated a Smart School Technology Project in three schools for the academic year 2012–2013. Students at GVES School are adept at using the iTV, iPod and various apps. In one of the schools, classrooms are supported with Apple iTV and HDTV attached to iTV. Students are also supported with iPods and various educational apps. For administrators, faculty and staffs are supported with iPods, MacBook and Pro laptops. Professional development projects are also provided to them [29].

2.4 Benefits of Smart Schools and Integration of ICT in Education

Engaging and leveraging technology in education enhanced the educational achievement of learners, teachers and schools. A lot of studies and research assert that ICT mediated education had a significant impact. According to Galil [28], by investing in a Smart Learning Program (SLP) in the United Arab Emirates (UAE), schools contributed a new learning environment and delivered high quality education not only in English Language but also in their learning process of engaging students and teachers. The study showed that smart learning methods are more motivating and interesting to students than the traditional learning activities. In the new environment the role of teacher has become less teacher-centred, enabling teachers to prepare and plan for their lessons more smoothly [28]. A case study called the Flipped Classroom Pilot Project, conducted in a middle school in north China, stresses the importance of having a smart learning environment where learners are supported by tablets for learning purposes. The present instructional environment needs to be changed. This means that new instructions will be created by teachers and taken home in the form of video-based interactive lessons. Study results indicate that students can benefit from a broad range of learning styles and their awareness of the problems they might encounter will be further promoted. Teachers' attention can be focused more on building students' knowledge and skills. Thus the school can ensure the quality of the teaching will improve [19].

The research findings of Taleb and Hassanzadeh [8] show that evolving educational technology in Iranian smart school s leads to a greater improvement in the learning and retention of mathematics than the traditional learning method. The results of this study are similar to the findings of a study conducted by Cabus et al. [30] on the effectiveness of using educational technology such as Smart boards for teaching Maths. The experiment was done for Grade seven in the Netherlands. According to the findings of this experiment, the Smart board contributed significantly in increasing the students' performance, and particularly for low performing students [30]. Utah State Office of Education reported the role that iPads played in their smart schools. The data analysis of the academic year 2012–2013 is used to generate benchmark assessment to measure students' achievements and engagement in the following years. The report shows that teachers who use iPads in their teaching will notice the difference in school management and instruction. The analysis showed a significant positive impact on improving students' learning opportunities through the use of educational technology [29].

2.5 Challenges of Implementing Smart Schools

Although it has been demonstrated that there are many benefits to implementing smart schools and adopting ICT in education, barriers and challenges have been encountered. In their research study, Ong and Ruthven [31] conducted a study to evaluate the student outcomes in teaching science in a smart school by comparing two schools, a smart school with a traditional one. Even though the Malaysian smart school initiative is intended to prepare students in a developing economy and to enhance their scientific and technological knowledge, the study results show that student outcomes are not as expected [31]. Ming et al. [32] indicates this to be due to the lack of teacher training and professional development. Consistent results were obtained from another study conducted by Majeed and Yusoff [33], who highlight that teachers encounter a lack of access to training and professional development to improve their ICT skills. Besides not being provided with regular training, teachers are also challenged by a lack of school management support, which is not a top priority for the school, and time constraints that prevent them from exploring ICT tools [33]. In this regard Omidinia, Masrom [14] conducted a case study to identify the success factors for smart schools in Malaysia. They reported that teachers in Selangor progressed slowly during their training.

School principals are expected to be proficient in enhancing their competencies in ICT and they should act as role models for their staff in the use of ICT. Ibrahim et al. [17] analyzed much research in Malaysia and they found that teachers did not receive the required support from their school principals or heads.

The study of Ali et al. [34] about smart schools reveals that teachers were facing difficulties during the process of integrating ICT into their school. Difficulties include the time constraints, unrelated course content and technological issues such as server failure. In addition, teachers claimed that they could not prepare their lessons due to the insufficient time available to integrate ICT into these (lessons, and also, teaching time was shortened because the students took about five minutes to start their computers and more time was wasted if technical problems occurred, this study also demonstrates the absence of any school practices that involve teachers in the use of ICT in teaching. There were issues related to the accessibility of ICT equipment, teachers' willingness to change, teacher's confidence in innovation and teacher's knowledge of the use of ICT for teaching, and all these had an impact on the integration of ICT into the curriculum. Attaran et al. [16] have come to similar conclusions. According to their research interviews and observations, technical issues and wasting about twenty minutes of classroom time every lesson were also observed.

Dissertation research indicates that Southern Gulf Coast states have different challenges in equipping classrooms with interactive smart boards. Pourciau [35] in her study, identifies the challenges, which are (a) technical malfunctions, (b) lack of appropriate training and professional development, and (c) issues related to finding or create resources or materials for the smart board to use interactively with learners.

Efficiency and availability of ICT resources, and a lack of basic infrastructure and connectivity are considered to be other challenges faced during incorporating ICT into education. Obviously, without these facilitating conditions the integrated system, including web-based courseware and online management tools will not be accessible to the people concerned [32]. Fu [7] carried out a study on the challenges faced in the use of ICT in education. The researchers categorized the challenges or barriers into three groups: from a student's perspective; from a teacher's perspective;

and from an administrative and infrastructure perspective. His thorough literature review on a significant number of studies finds many challenges from a teacher's perspective, such as what the teacher's view is on the benefits of ICT use in the classroom is uncertain, and teachers' lack of clear ideas on how integrating ICT will affect students' learning. Furthermore, Kler [36] identifies resistance to change and having a negative attitude as one of the barriers from the teacher perspective. This is due to teachers' strong feelings and beliefs about their conventional teaching method. Hence, this resistance hampers the integration of ICT into education. However, Fu [7] further indicates that teachers' positive attitudes towards ICT are critical and act as a predictor of the degree of success achieved in integrating technologies.

A recent study was conducted by Kadhim [37] to measure the readiness of Iraqi schools for being transformed into smart schools by embracing ICT in schools. The study used a mixed quantitative and qualitative approach using teachers and staff from secondary schools of the General Directorate of Education in Babylon. The results reveal that transforming traditional schools to smart schools is not useful due to various challenges such as a lack of ICT and network infrastructure (Internet connection, local area network); teachers lack ICT competence to use software and communication tools; there is a lack of technical support, inadequate educational budgets allotted and lack of a proper comprehensive plan to standardize different educational projects to have smart Iraqi schools [37].

In addition to this research, in their paper, Khan et al. [38] discover what is hindering the integration of ICT into education in Bangladesh, an example of another developing country. Lack of ICT-supported infrastructure, lack of equipment resources, high cost, the absence of a proper plan and vision, teachers' acceptance, attitudes and beliefs towards the use of ICT and teachers' lack of skill and knowledge are some of the barriers. Definitely, developing and integrating ICT into the curriculum and learning environment is time-consuming.

3   Research Methodology

This study aims to explore the challenges the school and service provider faced during the implementation of an ICT bundle to transform schools into smart schools and to give some recommendations about overcoming the challenges encountered. The researchers applied the inductive approach to building theory from the data gathered through observations, interviews and intuitive understanding [39]. The purpose of an inductive approach is to gain a better understanding of the nature of the problem, with an emphasis on why an event occurs rather than describing what happens [40]. Therefore, the researchers used the inductive approach to build an understanding of the meaning of the challenges faced during the implementation of smart schools in Oman. They also explored the issues facing schools after implementing the Smart School Initiative. An exploratory study was also conducted which aimed to gain knowledge of the participant's perceptions, views about the challenges of integrating an ICT curriculum into smart schools. The output from the exploratory study was used as the initial data to build a research conceptual framework.

This research uses qualitative case study strategy. Saunders et al. [40] highlight the difference between qualitative and quantitative study design. 'Qualitative' refers to non-numerical data and 'quantitative' refers to numerical data. Furthermore, Kumar [41] argues that qualitative study design is more suitable if the research intends to explore, understand and simplify a group of people's concerns about their beliefs and experience. A case study is mainly one of the study designs in qualitative research. However, it can also be used in quantitative research [41]. A case study helps to give a richer understanding of the studied research context by collecting data through multiple techniques or sources such as interviews, observations and documentary analyses [40].

This research uses the multi-method case approach in both schools. Methods include face-to-face semi-structured interviews with the person in charge of the Smart School Project in both schools and with the project manager from a service provider of a reputed telecom company. According to Hyland [42] interviews offer an interactive way of gathering information in order to understand people's experience and attitudes and it provides a greater flexibility for explanation. Semi-structured interviews are conducted to gain an essential insight into the research context and are useful in exploring the research questions and objectives in more depth by asking additional questions, as opposed to structured interviews [40], which are more rigid. The research was carried out using in-depth face-to-face interviews with selected teachers in order to provide a deep understanding and seek a wide viewpoint on the difficulties experienced in integrating ICT in each of the two schools. This technique helps to promote researchers' understanding and to explore the interviewees experience and opinions in regard to the challenges they faced [43].

3.1 Classroom Observation Protocol

In addition to the research conducted in the classroom, non-participant observations with teachers and students were also carried out in order to evaluate the use of ICT in teaching and to identify the challenges faced during the class. Kumar [41] defines 'non-participant observation' as a state where the observer behaves like a passive listener, watching a particular situation without involving themselves in the group activities and without taking notes and drawing conclusions on the observed object.

After collecting all the information from the above-mentioned methods, the researchers conducted an analysis of all the data collected during the interviews and observation in order to draw conclusions and give recommendations to overcome the challenges. This information is recorded using a tape recorder and taking notes, and is also obtained from the minutes of the meetings.

3.2   Research Conceptual Framework

An intensive literature review was carried out to understand the concept of smart schools and the challenges faced during their implementation in Oman, and particularly regarding the adoption of ICT in education. An exploratory study was also conducted to explore the challenges, from the school side and from the service provider, in the implementation of smart schools. Based on these investigations a research conceptual framework is built as shown in Fig. 1.

4   Data Analysis

Different methods were used in this research project. In the qualitative approach a researcher can look for data in terms of "patterns, themes, categories and regularities" [44] collected from the participants to elaborate their experiences and to provide a better understanding of the research studied. A thematic approach was applied during the research to sort out the responses provided by the teachers, person in charge, service provider and school IT administrators. Data sets generated by interviews and classroom observations were collected and arranged manually in accordance with the themes on different perspectives such as the teachers and person in charge, service

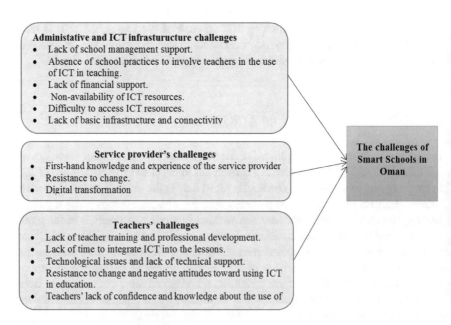

Fig. 1 Research conceptual framework

provider and school IT administrators. The researchers categorized the main themes and analyzed each one separately.

5 Results and Discussion

This section presents the analysis of the fieldwork conducted at a school that has implemented a Smart School Project and the service provider for the implementation of smart schools. The purpose was to investigate Research Question 1, namely: What challenges could the smart schools face during their implementation in Oman? The process began with interviews with the service provider project manager, the person in charge and the school IT administrators. The field work was concluded with in-depth interviews with the Science, IT, Maths and Social Studies teachers who were involved in the smart schools' project, followed by classroom observations in each of those subjects.

5.1 Understanding the Challenges of Smart Schools: Interview with the Person in Charge

The person in charge of the Smart School Project was interviewed to obtain information about the challenges of implementing the smart schools project in the school concerned. A number of detailed results are drawn from the outcome of the interview with the person in charge through four themes that reveal the aims of the interview.

Professional Training
The person in charge emphasized the importance of providing enough professional training to the teachers so that they could gain confidence and skills. She pointed out that the element of confidence and training should be linked with other competencies to use ICT. Thus, providing enough training is essential in order to increase the teachers' confidence and satisfaction in the integration of ICT into education effectively.

Technical Issues
Technical issues are another factor hindering the implementation of ICT into the curriculum. This problem is stressed by the person in charge to be one of the most important factors limiting the continued viability of ICT in the teaching and learning process, as it hinders the smooth delivery of the lesson.

Financial Support
The person in charge also stressed the importance of financial support for the smooth functioning of the smart schools. She elaborated that the integration of ICT depends on the financial capabilities of supporting its use in an effective and sustainable

manner. For instance, funds are essential to meet Smart School Project expectations, support existing IT assets and invest in new ones.

Resistance to Adopting the Use of ICT in Education
There were few instances of teachers' unwillingness to adopt technology in connection with the implementation of smart schools. Teachers' lack of knowledge and competencies in integrating ICT into education could be one of the reasons for an unwillingness to change things

5.2   Understanding the Challenges of Smart Schools: Interviews with the Service Provider and Manager of the Smart Schools Project

The service provider was interviewed to obtain information about the challenges faced from their perspective. The interview revealed three themes that investigated the service provider's perceptions and views towards challenges hindering smart school integration.

First-Hand Knowledge and Experience of the Service Provider
This is considered to be the biggest challenge faced by the service provider in the implementation of smart schools. The service provider has no prior experience in the education sector and he is quite unaware of the problems to be faced during the implementation since this project of smart schools is a new and unique one. No such service was offered by anyone before in Oman. As indicated by the interviewee, this was the challenge when they started working on the project.

Resistance to Change
Everyone finds change hard to accept. This is what the service provider encountered during the implementation of the project. The Smart School Project will require changes in the school environment, as it is considered to be one of the digitalization transition processes for the school to go through. Indeed, the service provider did experience some resistance from the teachers, and especially those who had been working using the conventional model for a very long time. Service provider and smart school manager explained this by saying:

> It took some time before the teachers accepted to be given training. (Service Provider Interview: Respondent 1)

Digital Transformation
The service provider and manager of the smart school demonstrated that transformation of a school or a teaching infrastructure is considered to be a challenge because it cannot be done all of a sudden. It has to be set up for transformation. He commented that the school should introduce steps for the change one by one. It will work as a gradual process. He supported this by saying:

By putting everything digital smart boards, devices and content it will not work. (Service Provider Interview: Respondent 1)

5.3 Understanding the Challenges of Smart Schools: Interviews with IT School Administrators

The IT administrators also mentioned the challenges that they faced during the implantation of ICT in smart schools. Some of the students could not remember their confidential password and had to reset the passwords again and again. Sometimes they faced a lot of problems due to the operational failure of electronic devices.

5.4 Understanding the Challenges of Smart Schools: Interviews with Teachers

The result of this study shows the different challenges faced by the teachers of the school where the Smart School Project is implemented. The researchers discovered technical, professional and management issues. The detailed outcomes are described in the subsections below through two themes. The researchers also noticed some issues related to the students' attitude towards teachers and learning during the integration of the ICT curriculum.

Technical Issues
In-depth analysis of the teachers' interviews highlighted many issues related to the connectivity of Wi-Fi in smart schools, and there were also issues with devices' battery charging. License-related issues for the smart board device were also reported. Lack of availability of electronic devices was another issue. Some teachers pointed out the irresponsive nature of the students during the course of study. Many students were reluctant to bring their iPads regularly and some of them were not charging them properly. There were also instances of losing devices or damaging them. Upgrading or updating operating systems of software is often time-consuming and this disrupts the teaching and learning transactions.

Professional and Management Issues
The second major issue pointed out by teachers is the lack of proper training on how to integrate the technology effectively. The teachers received only basic training to use software and tools like smart boards. Some of the teachers were exposed to self-learning, and they collaborated with each other to cascade learning objectives. Most of the teachers suggested that school management should provide them with professional training. One of the Maths teachers found it difficult to use the iPad for the classes assigned to her due to workload. Furthermore, she found it difficult to

complete the syllabus using an iPad since it was too time-consuming due to technical issues. So she experienced the shortage of time to integrate ICT during the lesson delivery. An instance was also reported by one of the students who refused to use an iPad, although most of them were used to use the new technology.

Issues such as lack of professional training can hinder ICT integration into the teaching process. Most of the teachers, however, were willing to use ICT creatively in the teaching process because it expanded the students' knowledge and enabled them to become more independent.

5.5 Classrooms Observations

Classroom observations were conducted at the school in five different classes: for Science, IT, Social Studies and for two Maths classes. The observations were made without disrupting the learning environment. Two themes are drawn to summarize the results of the classroom observation.

Technical Issues
During the classroom observation one of the teachers was forced to use the white board since the smart board was not working properly due to technical issues. The researchers noticed that one student was using the teacher's iPad since his electronic device was not working due to a technical issue.

Students' Conduct and Behavior
Some of the students were not attentive towards the teacher during the lesson delivery. In particular, it was observed that a few of the students were busy with their iPads, browsing the internet while the teacher was explaining the syllabus. On the other hand, the observation indicated that most of the students tended to be more dedicated towards learning when using smart boards and using their iPads to do their assignments.

6 Conclusion

This research aimed to explore the challenges faced during the implementation of the Smart School Initiative in Oman. The research investigated the viewpoints of the service provider, teachers, person in charge and school IT administrators. The main findings that were revealed from this research are as follows:

- Results indicate that teachers integrate ICT into education with diverse degrees of effectiveness despite the challenges that impede such integration (e.g., technical, professional and managerial issues).

- Most of the people in charge highlighted the challenges of changing a traditional school into a smart school which can be categorized into professional, technical and financial levels. They also pointed out that there was a certain amount of resistance to using ICT in education. However, the school management is highly excited about converting their school into a smart school as it will be beneficial for the status of education, preparing the students for the 21st Century and helping them to become more independent.
- The results from the interviews indicate that service provider faced some challenges in implementing the smart school at the operational level due to the first-hand knowledge and experience and the parents' unwillingness to adapt to the new digital system.
- School IT administrators also encountered some challenges such as creating so many student accounts and keeping on having to reset the students' passwords every time they forgot them.
- Technical issues and the students' negative attitude are the two challenges noticed with regard to classroom observation.

After identifying the challenges that were encountered during the implementation of smart schools, the researchers recommend the following actions for the effective functioning of smart schools in Oman:

- Enhance teachers' ICT competencies and skills by providing ongoing training on how to integrate ICT into education, such as how to use smart boards, educational software and classroom management software.
- Provide teachers with sufficient time so that they can learn and plan efficiently to integrate ICT effectively into teaching and learning processes.
- Provide teachers with professional development training in classroom management.

The study faced one main limitation, which was the small sample size, i.e. two case studies of smart schools in the Muscat area, which might affect the research findings. Therefore, further studies are recommended, in which a larger sample size should be used in order to obtain a holistic picture and make it possible to generalize results regarding the challenges of implementing smart schools in Oman.

References

1. Bimbola, O., Daniel, O.I.: Effect of constructivist-based teaching strategy on academic performance of students in integrated science at the junior secondary school level. Educ. Res. Rev. **5**(7), 347–353 (2010)
2. Ameen, N., Willis, R., Shah, M.H.: An examination of the gender gap in smartphone adoption and use in Arab countries: a cross-national study. Comput. Hum. Behav. **89**, 148–162 (2018)
3. Ameen, N.A., Willis, R.: The use of mobile phones to support women's entrepreneurship in the Arab countries. Int. J. Gender Entrepreneurship **8**(4), 424–445 (2016)

4. Iniesta-Bonillo, M.A., Sánchez-Fernández, R., Schlesinger, W.: Investigating factors that influence on ICT usage in higher education: a descriptive analysis. Int. Rev. Public Nonprofit Mark. **10**(2), 163–174 (2013)
5. Ameen, N., Willis, R.: Towards closing the gender gap in Iraq: understanding gender differences in smartphone adoption and use. Infor. Technol. Dev. **2018**, 1–26 (2018)
6. Maitlo, A., Ameen, N., Peikari, H.R., Shah, M.: Preventing identity theft: Identifying major barriers to knowledge-sharing in online retail organisations. Inf. Technol. People (2019)
7. Fu, J.S.: ICT in education: a critical literature review and its implications. Int. J. Educ. Dev. Inf. Commun. Technol. **9**(1), 112 (2013)
8. Taleb, Z., Hassanzadeh, F.: Toward smart school: a Comparison between smart school and traditional school for mathematics learning. Procedia Soc. Behav. Sci. **171**, 90–95 (2015)
9. Vanderlinde, R., Aesaert, K., Van Braak, J.: Institutionalised ICT use in primary education: a multilevel analysis. Comput. Educ. **72**, 1–10 (2014)
10. Pineida, F.O.: Competencies for the 21st century: integrating ICT to life, school and economical development. Procedia Soc. Behav. Sci. **28**, 54–57 (2011)
11. ITA, O.: eGovernment Transformation Plan (2012). Available from http://www.ita.gov.om/ITAPortal/Pages/Page.aspx?NID=820&PID=3330&LID=163. Cited 7 October 2016
12. e.oman.: COMEX 2013 continues with daily various activities and workshops (2013). Available from: http://www.eoman.gov.om/wps/portal/!ut/p/a1/hVDLjoJAEPyW_QDT7TD4OI7L4hM5zK7rcDG9MCJGBlQg8e93IF48qJ2-VKWqq9IQwRYiQ02WUpUVhk4tjgY7B6eI4XgecLnpI1v4njuSQzblaAXKCvDJCHz0L78DgczZ-IvxauB4Hr_7Xwje5P9C1EleNXjXQdkOwx1nX6I_-cRlKByOQvIwCP0ZQ-Qg2xvXi_PqkldVYUBJTVd4kPLn2t9uYHSPZ3Ucfe3li0p1aC68LjIczKJjbGAkoZMrC3a0-mqocx_tnh0y2bt2k0__gEdS2Nh/dl5/d5/L2dJQSEvUUt3QS80SmlFL1o2XzMwRzAwTzlJTTR0CUUQwMkoySzVTQTMTMyMFM0M0/?WCM_GLOBAL_CONTEXT=/EN/site/home/news/come2013. Cited 7 October 2016
13. Choi, Y.-C., Lee, J.-H., Lee, H.-J.: Prioritizing major policy issues regarding the smart schooling system using the AHP method. Education **9**(5) (2016)
14. Omidinia, S., Masrom, M., Selamat, H.: Determinants of smart school system success: a case study of Malaysia. Int. J. Acad. Res. **4**(1) (2012)
15. El-Halawany, H., Huwail, E.I.: Malaysian Smart Schools: a fruitful case study for analysis to synopsize lessons applicable to the egyptian context. Int. J. Educ. Dev. Inf. Commun. Technol. **4**(2), 117–143 (2008)
16. Attaran, M., Alias, N., Siraj, S.: Learning culture in a smart school: a case study. Procedia Soc. Behav. Sci. **64**, 417–423 (2012)
17. Ibrahim, M.S., Razak, A.Z.A., Kenayathulla, H.B.: Smart principals and smart schools. Procedia Soc. Behav. Sci. **103**, 826–836 (2013)
18. Ali, W.Z.W., Nor, H.M.: The Implementation of ICT Integration in Malaysian Smart Schools. InTech Open Access Publisher (2010)
19. Zhu, Z.-T., Yu, M.-H., Riezebos, P.: A research framework of smart education. Smart Learn. Environ. **3**(1), 1 (2016)
20. Spector, J.M.: Conceptualizing the emerging field of smart learning environments. Smart Learn. Environ. **1**(1), 1 (2014)
21. Sarkar, S.: The role of information and communication technology (ICT) in higher education for the 21st century. Science **1**(1), 30–41 (2012)
22. Elsaadani, M.A.: Exploring the relationship between teaching staff age and their attitude towards information and communications technologies (ICT). Online Submission **6**(1), 216–226 (2013)
23. UNESCO.: Education and Knowledge Societies (2003). Available from http://unesdoc.unesco.org/images/0014/001485/148576eb.pdf. Cited 10 Oct 2016
24. Cheung, A.C., Slavin, R.E.: The effectiveness of educational technology applications for enhancing mathematics achievement in K-12 classrooms: a meta-analysis. Educ. Res. Rev. **9**, 88–113 (2013)

25. Garcia, I., Pacheco, C.: A constructivist computational platform to support mathematics education in elementary school. Comput. Educ. **66**, 25–39 (2013)
26. Livingstone, S.: Critical reflections on the benefits of ICT in education. Oxford Rev. Educ. **38**(1), 9–24 (2012)
27. Canada, G., Evelyn, C., Schmidt, E.: New York Smart Schools Commission Report (2014). Available from https://www.ny.gov/sites/ny.gov/files/atoms/files/SmartSchoolsReport.pdf. 6th January 2017
28. Galil, T.E.A.: The Mohammed Bin Rashid's Smart Learning Program (SLP) Initiative in the Ministry of Education and its impact on English language performance in Cycle 2 classes, in the United Arab Emirates (UAE) (2014)
29. Education, U.S.O.: Smart School Technology Program (2013)
30. Cabus, S.J., Haelermans, C., Franken, S.: SMART in mathematics? Exploring the effects of in-class-level differentiation using SMART board on math proficiency. Br. J. Educ. Technol. (2015)
31. Ong, E.T., Ruthven, K.: The distinctiveness and effectiveness of science teaching in the Malaysian 'Smart school'. Res. Sci. Technol. Educ. **28**(1), 25–41 (2010)
32. Ming, T.S., Hall, C., Azman, H., Joyes, G.: Supporting smart school teachers' continuing professional development in and through ICT: a model for change. Int. J. Educ. Dev. Inf. Commun. Technol. **6**(2), 1B (2010)
33. Majeed, Z.S., Yusoff, Z.S.: Are we 'smarter' now? Case study of smart school implementation in a developing nation. J. Stud. Educ. **5**, 236–258 (2015)
34. Ali, W.Z.W., Nor, H.M., Hamzah, A., Alwi, N.H.: The conditions and level of ICT integration in Malaysian Smart Schools. Int. J. Educ. Deve. ICT **5**(2) (2009)
35. Pourciau, E.L.: Teaching and Learning with Smart Board Technology in Middle School Classrooms (2014)
36. Kler, S.: ICT Integration in Teaching and Learning: Empowerment of Education with Technology (2015)
37. Kadhim, T.A.: Gauge the readiness of transformation to smart schools for Iraqi schools. Technology **6**(9), 47–57 (2015)
38. Khan, M., Hossain, S., Hasan, M., Clement, C.K.: Barriers to the introduction of ICT into education in developing countries: the example of Bangladesh. Online Submission **5**(2), 61–80 (2012)
39. Merriam, S.B.: Qualitative Research: A Guide to Design and Implementation, vol. 3. Jossey-Bass, Somerset, US (2009)
40. Saunders, M.N.K., Lewis, P., Thornhill, A.: Research Methods for Business Students, 6th edn. Financial Times Prentice Hall, Harlow, England (2012)
41. Kumar, R.: Research Methodology: A Step-by-Step Guide for Beginners, 3rd edn: SAGE, London (2010)
42. Hyland, K.: Methods and methodologies in second language writing research. System **59**, 116–125 (2016)
43. Kamaruddin, N.: Interface Design in Interactive Science Courseware for the Malaysian Smart School Project. Queensland University of Technology (2012)
44. Cohen, L., Manion, L., Morrison, K.: Research Methods Educ. Routledge (2013)

Big Data in the Banking Sector from a Transactional Cost Theory (TCT) Perspective—The Case of Top Lebanese Banks

Charbel Chedrawi, Yara Atallah and Souheir Osta

Abstract The Voluminous data are being exchanged during banking transactions internally and externally. In the current information era, big data can help firms reveal hidden information and achieve competitive advantages, translating into higher productivity, lower operating costs, and a greater supply curve shift. In fact, the integration of big data analytics in the banking operations in England and Singapore enhanced customer services' efficiency, reduced transaction costs, increased number of users, and boosted demand. This article discusses challenges and role of Big Data in the banking sector through the transaction cost theory approach of Williamson [1]. Following a qualitative approach, this paper reveals the actions currently undertaken by the two leading banks in the Lebanese market in order to optimize big data integration in their internal and external transactions.

Keywords Big data · Transactions cost theory · Banking sector · Lebanon

1 Introduction

The world is currently enduring the fourth industrial revolution causing disruption on various economic and societal pillars [2]. The rapid growth of technologies like Internet of Things, Big Data (BD), Artificial Intelligence and Cloud Computing have disrupted many traditional industries, bringing forth new opportunities; the financial industry is not an exception [3]. Today's organizations have access to an innumerable amount of information, devoting huge efforts to find ways to use the available data [4]. In fact, big data's market has grown by US $48 billion in the last 5 years [5] producing 2.5 Billion gigabytes of data every day. For [6] every dollar spent on BD has an average return of 55 cents.

As sources and volume of information increase, the expectations in utilizing those large volume of data is to reduce costs, boost outcomes, and improve treatment [7].

C. Chedrawi (✉) · Y. Atallah · S. Osta
Faculty of Business and Management, Saint Joseph University, Mar Mikhael Beyrouth,
BP 17-5208, Beirut 1104 2020, Lebanon
e-mail: charbel.chedrawi@usj.edu.lb

© Springer Nature Switzerland AG 2020
Y. Baghdadi et al. (eds.), *ICT for an Inclusive World*,
Lecture Notes in Information Systems and Organisation 35,
https://doi.org/10.1007/978-3-030-34269-2_27

391

However, for [8], for successful developments and applications of big data, we have to consider existing and potential challenges. These challenges include: funding needs, infrastructure and related factors, knowledge and research evidence, leadership and governance, security and interoperability, and socio-cultural and technological environments. The most fundamental challenge of big data is to explore large volume of data's and extract the useful information or knowledge [9].

With this regard, banks, the main pillar of the economy, reap their primary edges from massive, quickly extracted and converted information [10]. In fact, financial services firms are leveraging BD to transform their processes, their organizations, and the entire industry [11]. Today, banks are no longer questioning the benefits of BD, they believe that BD analytics offer them a significant competitive advantage [12]. Lebanese banks are no exception.

However, transaction costs [1, 13, 14] are the main reason that innovation causes pain for companies implementing new technologies: training, proficiencies, and standards are the main costs of innovation. In fact, the transaction cost theory (TCT) supposes that companies try to minimize the costs of exchanging resources with the environment and that companies try to minimize the bureaucratic costs of exchanges within the company; therefore, the key feature of technological innovations is the possibility to reduce transactions' costs [15]. This is what makes the TCT a solid theoretical framework for our research.

In this context, we have chosen to proceed with a case study in order to carry out a fine collection of practices revealing all the complexity of the above-mentioned concepts. In fact, semi-structured interviews with General Managers, CIOs and several other managers allowed us to diagnose top Lebanese bank's strategic orientation of innovation and BD challenges and roles within a transactional cost approach.

In reference to the above, and in order to highlight the role of BD in the banking sector from a TCT perspective, our research questions are the following: "What are the main challenges of Big Data in the Lebanese Banking Sector? What role does Big Data play in reducing the transactional cost of the two leading banks in Lebanon?".

The choice of Bank Audi and BLOM Bank as a framework for our field study is valid; in addition of being the two leading banks in Lebanon with more than 30% market share, recognized at both national and regional levels, they are well known from the authors having worked there for several years.

Hence, we will firstly introduce the theoretical perspectives of BD exposing its various definitions, characteristics challenges and role in the banking sector. We will then elaborate with input of the TCT. In a second phase, we shall present the empirical study carried out among directors and managers working in the two leading Lebanese banks. And finally, we will reveal the main contributions of this article by gathering the elements that are prone to answer our research questions.

2 Literature Review

2.1 Big Data and Banks: Challenges and Opportunities

For [16], the BD revolution has found a resonance with financial service firms, considering the valuable data they've been storing since many decades. In fact, the potential unlocked by BD analytics exceeds any expectation. BD is generated from multiple increasing sources including internet clicks, mobile transactions, user-generated content, and social media as well as purposefully generated content through sensor networks or business transactions such as sales queries and purchases [17].

BD is defined by finance industry experts as the tool which allows an organization to create, manipulate, and manage very large data sets in a given timeframe and the storage required to support the volume of data, characterized by its Vs to help improve enterprise transparency and auditability [16]. This data has now unlocked secrets of money movements, helped prevent major disasters and thefts, and understand consumer behaviour. Banks reap the most benefits from BD as they now can extract good information quickly and easily from their data and convert it into meaningful benefits for themselves and their customers [16]. According to [18], banking is as much an information business as it is a financial business. In fact, banks have a vast variety and amount of customer data due to an increasing number of transactions through various devices, but they are only using a very tiny proportion to generate insights and enhance the customer experience [5], thus the potential benefits is very high.

BD was originally characterized by the 3Vs model representing its dimensions [19]; the Volume refers to the magnitude of the data generated and collected; the Velocity refers to the increasing rate of generation of data and the need for such data to be processed and analysed in near real-time to make informed decisions [20, 21] and to offer personalized services to the customers; finally the Variety refers to different types of data that are being generated and captured (structured, semi-structured and unstructured data). Later, few more dimensions have been added; the Veracity refers to the unreliability associated with the data sources [21] and relates to quality, relevance, predictive value, and meaning of data [22]. Precisely, this feature ensures the degree of trusts to the leader of an organization to make decision. As for Variability, it refers to inconsistency and variation in flow rate of data [20] and to the increasing complexity in managing data ranging from transactional data to BD. The last characteristic is the Value which represents the worth of information to various stakeholders and decision makers [22].

For [23], there are many motivating factors for engaging in BD technology with regards to retail banking, among which the ease and affordability of executing financial transactions and the availability of new data sources such as data from social media, blogs, and other news feeds that offer significant new opportunities. With this regards, there are a number of potential application areas for BD in retail banking; for instance, BD can screen new account applications for risk of default; it can identify high-risk borrowers for auto loans, and reduce cost. Therefore, it is highly crucial that appropriate guideline be set to prevent any privacy, security, and ethical issues.

However, BD projects are being held back by the high cost of setting up infrastructure to support the capturing of potentially hundreds of millions of data points each day. A lack of a business case and the need to integrate data sources are also holding back adoption [24]. In fact, the most fundamental challenge of BD is to explore large volume of data and extract the useful information or knowledge [8]. Furthermore, BD requires careful data management including data governance of the data sources, data quality, data content, data access and security, data consistency, and user training [25] in order to provide authentic, accurate, and reliable data essential for good decision making in the banking sector.

In addition, with the increased number of personal devices that can be traced through the Internet of Things, personal privacy remain an important issue to be considered. The data heterogeneity and diverse dimensionality issues become one of the major challenges if we are enabling data aggregation by the combination of data from all sources. In fact, as the volume of BD increases, the complexity and the relationships also increases [8].

Apart from the challenges of adopting BD, **the benefits are endless**. Effective integration of such data using data mining and informatics may result in lower costs and improved customers' services via well informed decision making [26]. In fact, for [27] BD analytics may influence cost reduction. According to the [28], banks that apply analytics to customer data have a 4% point lead in market share over banks that do not (acquisition and retention) improving bank's conversion rate [29]. Banks need to understand the benefits of BD analytics and assess their BD Maturity in order to make the prospects of gaining insights faster in a cost effective way.

2.2 Transaction Cost Theory in the Banking Industry

The term "Transaction cost" refers to the cost of carrying out a transaction by means of an exchange on the open market [13]. They are the cost of engaging in a commercial transaction and compensating for any market imperfections [30]. They are mainly made up of information acquisition costs and negotiation costs [14]. According to [1] transaction costs are the resultant friction that arises in undertaking transactions among exchange parties; such frictions are mainly caused by opportunistic behavior that usually arises when two parties in an exchange fail to fulfill their obligations [31].

There exist two types of transaction costs, ex post and ex ante costs in financial exchange. Ex ante transaction costs are incurred to build and establish credit relationships contracts such as costs of collecting information to make agreements. Ex post costs are incurred to minimize the chances of default such as the costs of recovery and the bonding costs of effecting secure commitments [1]. Both types of costs are critical in operation of financial intermediation services [32].

For [31], the most critical factors influencing transaction costs are the kind and type of lending product and the degree of uncertainty associated with the transaction [1]. These costs fall into two broad categories: the opportunity cost of time spent by borrowers and depositors as they negotiate financial contracts and the explicit expenses incurred by all participants to form, fulfill and enforce these obligations. To the above, we can add the costs of gathering and processing information required by lenders to screen potential borrowers, process loans and associated collateral, costs of monitoring loans and expenses generated by loan collection or collateral seizure.

In fact, financial intermediaries incur numerous transaction costs that may include search costs, screening costs, training and counseling, credit education costs, monitoring and enforcement costs, to control possible opportunistic behavior of clients (moral hazard) and adverse selection [33]. One can denote these types of transaction costs as information costs. Hence, information costs, defined as the cost incurred to ensure that borrowers adhere to terms of the loan, impact the operating costs in lending, and determine the successful completion of a financial transaction [34]. The use of information costs can create a screening effect that can improve the risk assessment of loan applicants, thereby raising portfolio quality (since it prevents uncreditworthy borrowers from penetrating into the Bank), which in turn reduces the loss rates on portfolio. In fact, information advantage available to the bank would control the opportunistic behavior of borrowers and require less monitoring and enforcement.

Therefore, information costs may be considered equivalent of what [1] suggests in his definition of transaction costs, as the costs of safeguarding contracts and the bargaining and haggling costs of moving contracts from one point to another [31]. Transaction costs may thus be classified as follows: the cost of drawing up contracts, which is related to the cost of research and information; the cost of signing contracts, which is related to negotiation and decision-making costs; and the cost of monitoring and enforcing contracts [27].

In their research, [35] argue that ICT lowers transaction costs because technology allows information to be communicated in real-time and at much lower costs, thereby reducing the costs required in order to find a particular good (the focus of the transaction). In fact, ICT which are substantially implemented to transmit, exchange, store, and process information [36] can lower search costs only if the increased amount of information and/or speed in its exchange is balanced by an equal increase in its ability to manage, process, and evaluate that information [37]; this is exactly the case of BD in banks.

BD can also be a solid answer to the characteristics of a transaction described by Williamson [38] in terms of asset specificity, frequency, and uncertainty. In fact, asset specificity (specialized investment that cannot be redeployed to alternative uses or by alternative users without a loss in productive value) can be resolved through the investment in BD analytical tools; this specialized investment can be redeployed on daily basis without any loss in its value, on the contrary it will evolve; furthermore, the frequency of the transactions that reduces transaction costs due to the ability to re-deploy knowledge and benefit from standardized processes and contracts is totally the case of BD. As for uncertainty, it will be reduced by BD whether the internal uncertainty that covers the complexity and tacit nature of the tasks performed internally by the firm or the external uncertainty, which includes technological, legal regulatory, fiscal and competitive uncertainty.

Finally, for [38], agents have bounded rationality, they have limited cognitive abilities and cannot contemplate all possible events and fully calculate the consequences of their decisions; BD analytics can solve this problem as well.

2.3   Big Data, TCT and Banks

Since the global financial crisis of 2008, financial services firms have been trying hard to re-invent themselves and to find new ways to establish sustainable competitive advantages [35]. Banks and other financial services firms are undertaking the transformation to a BD driven enterprise, broadening the effective frontier of financial services and providing a new path for the implementation of financial inclusion [3].

In fact, information asymmetry is the key cause for the restriction of traditional financial institutions providing financial services to small and micro businesses. BD technology provides a new solution, replacing the traditional ways such as collateral and guarantee. Through the correlating of multidimensional information, BD technology is capable of characterizing fine portraits of each customer. The analysis of massive and dynamic data can reveal the nature of the data behind the phenomenon; comprehensively describe the features of each individual such as creditworthiness, preferences, behaviour patterns, habits and other characteristics; and eventually financial service will be offered to clients precisely and fairly.

From a TCT perspective, [14] concluded that the elimination of negative externality will contribute to achieving effective allocation of resources, increase efficiency, and eventually reduce transaction costs. The high transaction costs of finance are mainly because financial institutions have to put in a lot of time and manpower into investigation and process of every business, which generates a lot of operation costs. The application of BD technology offers a new effective approach for reducing transaction costs. BD credit investigation makes measuring the default rate of a credit applicant in few minutes a reality. It can also give an interest rate recommendation based on that default rate (risk-based pricing). It can eliminate information asymmetry in the credit business with a lower cost. Credit applicants no more need to deal with complicated application process and prolix documents filling [3].

Sarrocco et al. [35], found that new techniques and technologies used with BD allow CFOs to gain useful information at a much lower cost due in part to greater scalability but also due to flexibility in the data analysis. BD allows banks a simplified and cost effective way to source their data and convert it into usable information. In fact, BD technology, can help generate important cost advantages due to a higher level of scalability and large volumes of data managed at a lower cost per unit. By using automated and sophisticated analytical tools that can store and analyse data faster and more easily, CFOs can reduce the overall cost to serve in relation to data elaboration [35].

Table 1 presents the major cost benefits for Big Data in the banking industry.

BD tools can shift through all the data and provides solely the desired information, while enabling banks to contour work processes, and saving time and prices. After getting access to huge amount of data, containing needs of different customers, banks can offer those needs in a meaningful way providing exactly the information

Table 1 Big data benefits for banking and its impact on cost

Big data benefits in banks	Description, details, example	Impact on cost reduction
Business profitability	BD help in identifying the services that customers want, price points for new services and helping customize services to drive new customer demands	BD increases customer acquisition and revenue per customer. It decreases costs to retain and reduces customer attrition
Customer acquisition costs	Banks can use customer data insights to build effective and targeted promotions by correlating customer purchase history, customer profile data and customer behavior on social media that indicate areas of interest. These customers can then be offered special promotions specific to them [39]	Big data help reduce Marketing and sales costs The strategy for saving cost is through identifying and targeting the right customer
Anti-money laundering	Standard Chartered was fined $340 million for anti-money laundering failings. Deloitte was fined a $10 million and a one-year ban on all consulting work at NYDFS-regulated firms	BD analytics enable a much more efficient ingestion, analysis, and visualization of large, diverse and constantly changing data sets so they can be harnessed in the fight against Anti-Money Laundering
Reduce data warehouse costs	An EDW (Enterprise Data Warehouse) is critical in generating operational reports for banks. But as the volume, variety, veracity and velocity of data increases, traditional systems can no longer run with efficiency. Hadoop overcomes this challenge by enabling the system to 'Scale-up' to any volume and store, combine, integrate and analyze all data types to generate insights	BD help banks by offloading expensive analytics and data preparation, discover the data and deal with various types of data

required by the customer instead of any other information. Customer segmentation, customer feedback examination and big knowledge analytics are being enforced across numerous spheres of banking sector helping those delivering higher services to their customers in a costly effective way [40].

3   Research Methodology

Our research follows a qualitative interpretive case-study approach; in fact, different trends in research topics and philosophical perspectives have prompted the rise of qualitative designs in information systems research [41, 42] and case study research figures among those [43, 44].

We have adopted an interpretivist position because we consider that there are multiple realities that make measurement difficult, and we can only seek to understand real-world phenomena by studying them within the context in which they occur. As for the case study, it is investigated to highlight all the complexities paused by different studied concepts [45].

This article aims to identify the above mentioned subjects concerning BD and TCT in the two biggest banks in Lebanon. However, any finding or conclusion in a case study is likely to be much more convincing and accurate if it is based on several different sources of information; such process is called triangulation [46]; therefore a triangulation of data was made using several sources (written, reported, and verbal) especially published reports concerning BD, information technologies and costs in an attempt to understand BD main challenges and role in reducing the transactional cost of the two leading banks in Lebanon.

Thus, our methodology is based on the collection and analysis of qualitative data collected through semi-structured interviews with General Managers (GM1, GM2), Chief Information Officers (CIO1, CIO2) and other managers whose work are related to big data, ICT and cost (D11, D12, D13, D21, D22 and D23) in both banks. Data collection took place between June and December 2017; Data consolidation and analysis was carried out using *NVivo*.

3.1   The Context of the Study: Big Data in Lebanese Banks

The banking industry today is in a state of flux, with multiple technologies regulatory and demographic factors impacting the way banks conduct their business in order to meet increasing customer expectations and improve profitability. BD is about to enhance every aspect of banking. Caused by the proliferation of mobile devices (equipped with multiple sensors, cameras, GPS, etc.) that facilitated the interaction with social media, BD is becoming more and more abundant. The amount of data created during the last 2 years is equivalent to all data generated from the beginning of creation of computers. According to [28], 60% of financial institutions in North America believe that BD analytics offers a significant competitive advantage.

Although it's the main holders of the local currency debt with about 83% of the total outstanding amount [47], the Lebanese banking sector is financially sound and stable. It plays a key role in the Lebanese economy where banks are major providers of credit to individuals, businesses, and the government. The sector is currently witnessing a big data and ICT revolution especially among top banks in order to sustain providing high quality services to customers and competing on an equal base with foreign banks. With this regard, new information systems were adopted and developed in order to reduce staff expenses which constitute a large part of the operating costs and to restructure bank's processes. Furthermore, the banking industry is undergoing transformation pressures as customers demand more intensive and engaging ways to interact with their bank and their loyalty becomes a function of convenience, gratification, and value in every interaction.

The consolidated assets of alpha banks exceeded $230 billion at the end 2017. Alpha banks represent the 14 largest banks in Lebanon with over 1200 branches and more than 31,000 employees (end of 2017). The gross doubtful and substandard loans as a percentage of gross loans rose from 6.8% in December 2016 to 7.8% in December 2017, a very alarming figure.

3.2   The Context of the Study: Top 2 Alpha Banks, BLOM and Audi

Incorporated in 1962, Bank Audi has one of the largest branch networks in Lebanon, with 85 branches and more than 3300 employees. At the ICT level, Bank Audi is in the process of implementing multiple transformational business and technology projects across many of its affiliates. Customers are served through an Omni-channel network of more than 450 advanced self-service machines (ITM, ATM, and Novo) and through digital channels (online and mobile). The number of transactions on bank Audi's mobile app have reached 41% of the total banking transactions in 2017.

Founded in 1951, BLOM Bank is a leading Lebanese bank recognized at the regional and international level. It devotes a huge budget to launching new online services designing and launching his own innovative products. BLOM Bank has won the "2017 Global Finance World's Best Consumer Digital Bank in Lebanon" award. In fact, more than 50,000 clients have made their transactions on mobile app in 2017 reaching 60% of total transactions.

As shown in Table 2, the choice of our sample of the two leading banks operating in Lebanon, strongly reflects the general state of the banking sector; it shows the main characteristics of our sample.

Table 2 Key figures on the sample of selected banks in Lebanon (2017) compared to the total banking sector in Lebanon (2017)

Bank name (values in US $ million)	Rank	Total assets	Customers' deposit	Shareholders' equity	Net profit
Bank Audi Sal	1	44,682	35,749	3807	437
BLOM Bank Sal	2	31,800	26,884	2874	357
Total sample		76,482	62.633	6.681	794
Total banking sector		226,981	181,815	20,811	1984
% of sample from total sector		33.7	34.5	32.1	40

4 Analysis and Discussion of the Results

The results of our exploratory study conducted within Bank Audi and BLOM Bank enabled us to better define the main challenges of big data in the Lebanese banking sector integrating the major role played by big data in reducing transactional costs. The results provide a significant insight on these subjects.

Big Data challenges within the Lebanese Banking Sector

The first noted conclusion is that BD technology can play a crucial role in facilitating the banking behavior and in strengthening banks' positioning.

In fact, both banks created their electronic platforms enabling customers to make online transactions and collecting data all along. "ICT plays a key role in the development of big data at our bank (CIO2)". "We have created our own information systems and databases to strengthen our local and regional position" (D21).

The first challenge identified was the big investments needed in order to benefit from BD: "increased competition necessitate the focus on innovation investments to retain and enhance competitive differentiation" (GM2); "we are currently witnessing a major transformation program reinforcing the Bank's positioning as a technology-driven retail bank built on a digital foundation." (CIO1); "and this is costing us a huge investment" (GM1). "There is a continuous need for investing in digital transformation, BD and modern core banking solutions" (D11).

With this regard, CIO2 added that "even though we are developing our core banking systems internally, it is costing us a fortune". "In fact, we have invested a lot in our Core Banking Application that is built around an Enterprise Service Bus (ESB) which centralizes BD based on customer's data and interactions thus driving efficiency, productivity and speed to market"(D3).

The second biggest challenge of BD is exploring large unstructured volume of data in order to extract the useful information or knowledge, confirming the work of [8]. In fact, "the most critical part is how to extract and analyze data from multiple sources" (CIO1, CIO2); [18] confirms that BD necessitates good analytics tools to bring large amounts of data from different sources together and serve up usable data. "The different data sources and the growing Internet of Things require advanced analytics and augmented intelligence; hence, data analytics is one of the most demanded specializations nowadays (D12).

The third challenge identified concerns having the skilled human resources to cope and analyze the extracted data and to transform it into beneficial knowledge to the bank: "so far we did very well on the development part and we intend to do the same with our own internal human resources (CIO2); "however it's not that obvious" (D21), "we need lots of investment on the training level, maybe it's better to outsource it" (D22). "With this regard, optimizing our costs is a better strategy" (D23). "Acquiring the appropriate talents and skills is a continuous challenge" (GM1).

The fourth challenge raised was Privacy concerns: "the use of customer data raises privacy issues" (D12), "privacy concerns may limit the adoption of BD analytics" (D13). "In fact, by uncovering hidden connections between seemingly unrelated data, BD analytics could potentially reveal sensitive personal information which could hinder the main BD benefits" (CIO1).

The role played by Big Data in reducing transactional cost of the bank

Our second conclusion concerns the role of Big Data in reducing transactional cost of the bank. "In today's world, each individual is generating data that, when combined, can allow us to predict accurate future consumer behavior" (GM1); "BD technologies are vital to making product and service improvements (D11); data analytics will allow a comprehensive 360° customer view that would allow us to offer personalized services to our customers while economizing time and effort and increasing efficiency and return" (CIO1). "BD technology is helping us in reducing the cost of transactions because it delivers efficient processes and eliminates time-consuming and time-costing tasks" (CIO2).

"A data driven approach to decision-making allows us to leverage idle data to take informed, pertinent, and timely business decisions through heavy usage of advanced forecasting, deep analysis, identification of patterns and trends, real-time prediction of customer needs and behavior, etc." (GM2).

Despite the increasing volume, variety, and velocity of data that banks have about their customers, banks start using this data to generate insights that enhance the customer experience" (D21).

In fact, top Lebanese banks will continue to leverage digital technologies to enhance customer experience. Saving on personnel and branch infrastructure costs by providing better digital experience via enhanced mobile platforms. "Cost strategy is always built on multiple factors among which BD: (CIO1); "While moving into the digital world, cost efficiency could certainly help in shaping tomorrow's strategy and direction" (D11). "The biggest banks in the world are trying to benefit from big data to maximize customers' experience with the lowest cost. There is a very big opportunity for the Lebanese banking sector. The more we refine data, the more it becomes useful and the more value we can retrieve from it. So we need to process data that leads to insights. Insights and intelligence are what our business need" (D21).

In addition, data analytics are playing a major role in modeling operational, market and credit risks and in predicting failures and defaults: "the first input of BD was the reduction of credit risks" (D11); "the screening effect is optimizing our portfolios' risk especially regarding SME loans: (CD13); confirming the work of Bag [31], the use of information costs can create a screening effect that can improve the risk assessment of loan applicants, reduces the loss rates on portfolio.

"We didn't dare to launch SME products and services because we were afraid of the high risk in these companies, now with BD, we are more confident because risk is reduced and therefore our non-compliance rate will begin to shrink" (GM1). "Information asymmetry was reduced as a direct impact of big data" (D11), "which reduced our cost" (D12).

Furthermore, Lebanese banks are focusing on financial inclusion and awareness for business growth and customer engagement, BD plays a major role in this: "BD provides more accurate visibility on current situation and future trends, therefore reduces cost of ineffective actions/decisions" (D11); "It increases customer retention and facilitates acquisition of new customers" (D12).

Moreover, BD is helping top Lebanese banks to comply with international regulators in a cost effective manner: "Business analysis can help gather, analyze and compile data to make regulatory compliance easier especially regarding (FATCA, GATCA, CRS, etc.).

As per [48], most of the banking executives surveyed (75%) believed that big data would give large global and national banks a competitive edge over smaller banks. Large banks have more data to leverage and more resources to put toward projects, but finance institutions of all sizes can benefit from analyzing big data. This was confirmed by our interviewees.

Finally, inspired by the work of [38] on TCT characteristics and BD characteristics, we have tried to combine and test these characteristics on our sample, Table 3 shows the main results regarding the improvements' input.

Table 3 TCT versus BD characteristics in our sample

		Transaction cost characteristics		
		Asset specificity	Uncertainty	Frequency of transactions
Big data characteristics'	Volume	Improvement	High improvement	High improvement
	Velocity	Improvement	Minor Improvement	High improvement
	Variety	Improvement	Minor Improvement	High improvement

5 Conclusion and Recommendations

Digital transformation and technology continue to heavily influence the banking industry. BD technologies and analytics are playing a vital role in the economy and especially in the banking sector. It is reshaping many aspects of the world's economies, governments, and societies. Lebanese banks are more and more oriented to automation, digitization and electronic transactions and are developing strategies for integrating the latest BD technologies in order to be in line with the current world's direction.

In this framework, we examined the main challenges of big data in the Lebanese banking sector in addition to their role in reducing transactional cost. Banks in Lebanon should invest more in BD analytics in the current data-driven economy. Analytics should be more considered to improve decision-making, uncover unseen innovation opportunities and improve compliance within a more stringent regulatory environment. Cloud computing could be a good solution in reducing the investment cost of top Lebanese banks; encouraging incubators and startups could also be a solution for the need for skilled people or the developers of new software and tools that enhance the extraction and analysis of BD. BD initiatives are typically time, resource and skills-intensive. To pave the way for a smooth implementation, banks should rather focus on continuous improvement.

The qualitative study enabled us to verify the relevance of some factors and variables derived from the literature on the challenges and roles of BD technology in the Lebanese context. Our research has a methodological limit in terms of the generalization of results in the Lebanese banking sector or in other banks operating in the same context (medium or small banks). In fact, the results provided in this research depend heavily on the two biggest Lebanese banks' context. Generalizing the results requires some further research, either in the same context, or in other banks.

References

1. Williamson, O.E.: The economic institutions of capitalism. The Free Press, New York, NY (1985)
2. Chedrawi, C., Howayeck, P.: Artificial intelligence a disruptive innovation in higher education accreditation programs: expert systems and AACSB. In: ICT for a Better Life and a Better World, pp. 115–129. Springer, Cham (2019)
3. Dawei, L., Anzi, H., Gen, L.: Big data technology: application and cases. In: Handbook of Blockchain, Digital Finance, and Inclusion, vol. 2, pp. 66–82. Elsevier Inc. (2018)
4. Saba, M., Bou Saba, P., Harfouche, A.: Hidden facets of IT projects are revealed only after deployment: the case of French agricultural cooperatives. Inf. Technol. People 31(1), 239–255 (2018)
5. Somal, H.K.: Big data & analytics: tackling business challenges in banking industry. Bus. Econ. J. 8(2) (2017)

6. Coumaros, J., Buvat, J., Auliard, O., Roys, S., Kvj, S., Chretien, L., Clerk, V: Big data alchemy: how can banks maximize the value of their customer data. Banks have not fully exploited the potential of customer data. Digital Transformation Research Institute and Capgemini Consulting: Paris, France (2014)
7. Fdez-Arroyabe, P., Royé, D.: Co-creation and participatory design of big data infrastructures on the field of human health related climate services. In: Internet of Things and Big Data Technologies for Next Generation Healthcare, pp. 199–226. Springer (2017)
8. Abinaya, K.: Data mining with big data e-health service using map reduce. Int. J. Adv. Res. Comput. Commun. Eng. **4**(2), 123–127 (2015)
9. Harfouche, A.L., Jacobson, D.A., Kainer, D., Romero, J.C., Harfouche, A.H., Scarascia Mugnozza, G., Moshelion, M., Tuskan, G.A., Keurentjes, J., Altman, A.: Accelerating climate resilient plant breeding by applying next-generation artificial intelligence. Trend. Biotechnol. **37**(11), 1217–1235 (2019)
10. Kathuria, A.: Impact of big data analytics on banking sector. Int. J. Sci. Eng. Technol. Res. **5**(11), 3138–3141 (2016)
11. Turner, D., Schroeck, M., Shockley, R.: Analytics: the real-world use of big data in financial services. IBM Glob. Bus. Serv. **27** (2013)
12. Bedeley, R., Iyer, L.: Big data opportunities and challenges: the case of banking industry. In: Proceedings of the Southern Association for Information Systems Conference, Macon, GA, USA (SAIS), pp. 1–6 (2014)
13. Coase, R.H.: The nature of the firm. Econ. New Ser. **4**(16), 386–405 (1937)
14. Coase, R.: The problem of social cost. J. Law Econ. **3**, 1–44 (1960)
15. Ciborra, C.U.: Teams Markets and Systems. Cambridge University Press (1993)
16. Srivastava, U., Gopalkrishnan, S.: Impact of big data analytics on banking sector: learning for indian banks. Procedia Comput. Sci. **50**, 643–652 (2015)
17. OECD: Exploring the economics of personal data: a survey of methodologies for measuring monetary value. In: OECD Digital Economy Papers, No. 220 (2013)
18. Yurcan, B.: Why Barclays sees banking's future as an information business. https://www.americanbanker.com/news/why-barclays-sees-bankings-future-as-an-information-business (2016)
19. Bhadani, A., Jothimani, D.: Big data: challenges, opportunities and realities. In: Singh, M.K., Kumar, D.G. (eds.) Effective Big Data Management and Opportunities for Implementation, pp. 1–24. IGI Global, Pennsylvania, USA (2016)
20. Singh Singh, S.N.: Big data analytics. In: International Conference on Communication, Information & Computing Technology (ICCICT), Mumbai 2012, pp. 1–4 (2012)
21. Gandomi, A., Haider, M.: Beyond the hype: big data concepts, methods, and analytics. Int. J. Inf. Manage. **35**(2), 137–144 (2015)
22. Haas, L.: In: HISA Big Data 2013 Melbourne Presentation. IBM Almaden Research Centre (2013)
23. Gutierrez, D.: Big Data and Retail Banking, Inside BIGDATA Guide to Big Data for Finance. https://insidebigdata.com/2014/09/22/insidebigdata-guide-big-data-finance (2014)
24. Telsyte: Australian BD and Analytics Study. www.telsyte.com.au (2014)
25. Shaw, C: The big hole in big data. https://beyondphilosophy.com/the-big-hole-in-big-data/ (2013)
26. Sun, J., Reddy, C.: Big Data analytics for healthcare. In: Tutorial presentation at the SIAM International Conference on Data Mining, Austin, TX (2013)
27. Davenport, T.: Big Data at Work: Dispelling the Myths, Uncovering the Opportunities. Harvard Business Review Press, USA (2014)
28. Capgemini: World Retail Banking Report 2016. https://web.uniroma1.it/dip_management/sites/default/files/allegati/World%20Retail%20Banking%20Report%202016.pdf (2016)
29. Armah, N.: Big Data analysis: the next frontier. Bank Can Rev **2013**, 32–39 (2013)
30. Robins, J.: Organizational Economics: notes on the use of transaction-cost theory in the study of organizations. Admin. Sci. Q. **32**(1) (1987)
31. Bag, D.: Transaction costs and efficiency. Intermediat. J. Serv. Res. **13**(1), 95–109 (2013)

32. Stiglitz, J.E., Weiss, A.: Credit rationing in markets with imperfect information. Am. Econ. Rev. **71**(3), 393–410 (1981)
33. Gray, R.: Transaction costs and new institutions: will CBLTs have a role in the Saskatchewan land market? Can. J. Agric. Econ. **42**, 501–509 (1993)
34. Cole, R.: The importance of relationships to the availability of credit. J. Bank. Finan. **22**, 959–977 (1998)
35. Sarrocco, F., Morabito, V., Meyer, G.: Exploring the Next Generation Financial Services: The Big Data Revolution. Retrieved from https://www.accenture.com/t20170314T051509__w__/ nl-en/_acnmedia/PDF-20/Accenture-Next-Generation-Financial.pdf (2016)
36. Chedrawi, C., Osta, S.: ICT AND CSR in the Lebanese banking sector, towards a regain of stakeholders' trust: the case of bank audi. Int. J. Serv. Stand. **12**(2), 205–219 (2018)
37. Malone, T.W., Yates, J., Benjamin, R.I.: Electronic markets and electronic hierarchies: effects of information technology on market structure and corporate strategies. Commun. ACM **30**, 484–497 (1987)
38. Williamson, O.E.: Transaction Cost Economics: The Natural Progression Nobel Lecture. Nobelprize.org, Nobel Foundation, Stockholm (2009)
39. MacDonald, T.J., Allen, D.W., Potts, J.: Blockchains and the boundaries of self-organized economies: predictions for the future of banking. In: Banking Beyond Banks and Money, pp. 279–296. Springer, Cham (2016)
40. Kathuria, A., Saldanha, T.J.V., Khuntia, J., Andrade Rojas, M.G.: How information management capability affects innovation capability and firm performance under turbulence: evidence from India. In: ICIS 2016: 37th International Conference on Information Systems. Association for Information Systems. AIS Electronic Library (AISeL) (2016)
41. Liebenau, J., Lee, A.S.: Information systems and qualitative research. In: Lee, A.S., Liebenau, J., De Gross, J.I. (eds.) Information Systems and Qualitative Research. IFIP Advances in Information and Communication Technology, pp. 1–10. Chapman & Hall, London, UK (1997)
42. Trauth, E.M.: The choice of qualitative methods in IS research. In: Qualitative Research in IS: Issues and trends, pp. 1–19. IGI Global (2001)
43. Benbasat, I., Goldstein, D.K., Mead, M.: The case research strategy in studies of information systems. MIS Q. 369–386 (1987)
44. Klein, H.K., Myers, M.D.: A set of principles for conducting and evaluating interpretive field studies in information systems. MIS Q. **23**(1), 67–93 (1999)
45. Chedrawi, C., Howayeck, P., Tarhini, A.: CSR and legitimacy in higher education accreditation programs, an isomorphic approach of Lebanese business schools. Q. Assur. Educ. **27**(1), 70–81 (2019)
46. Jick, T.D.: Mixing qualitative and quantitative methods: triangulation in action. Adm. Sci. Q. **24**(4), 602–611 (1979)
47. Chedrawi, C., Howayeck, P.: La Conjoncture Economique, Passage Obligé A Tout Investissement Au Liban. Proche Orient Etudes en Management **28** (2016)
48. Shumway, R., Kearn, T.: Transforming Big Data into Competitive Advantage in the Banking and Finance Industries. Cocero Institute (2016)

Urban Concentration in Lebanon: The Need for Urban Observatories

Abdallah Nassereddine and Amal Dabbous

Abstract Urbanization has become the norm of life of the twenty first century. It requires serious planning that feeds into decision making, which in order to be effective, must be based on consistent data collection of development indicators. Urban observatory provides an excellent technology to make use of the data and visualize it in a way that allows tracking the development process. This paper highlights urbanization in Lebanon and the challenges it faces. The paper shows that poor data collection in Lebanon and the lack of serious plan to calculate, monitor, and improve urban indicators put the future of urban quality of life in Lebanon at risk. The paper uses as a case study in Lebanon, the Tripoli Economic and Development Observatory (TEDO). Using original visual maps from TEDO, the case shows how urban observatories can be used to detect critical problems and their underlying causes and how they help in delivering effective solutions leading to better sustainability assessment.

Keywords Urbanization · Sustainable development · Lebanon · Urban observatories

1 Introduction

Urbanization is a key aspect of development since 1950 with an increasing share of the world's population living in cities. According to the Economic and Social Affairs of the United Nations, in 2014, 54% of the world's population live in urban areas. This number shows a major increase compared to 1950 when only 30% of the world's population lived in cities. The future prospects show a continuing increase with urbanization expected to reach 66% in 2050. In actual numbers, the people living in cities grew from 746 million inhabitants in 1950 to 3.9 billion in 2014, a fivefold increase. Large cities have become the norm of today's life. For example,

A. Nassereddine (✉) · A. Dabbous
Faculty of Business Administration, Beirut Arab University, Beirut, Lebanon
e-mail: a.nassereddine@bau.edu.lb

A. Dabbous
e-mail: a.dabbous@bau.edu.lb

© Springer Nature Switzerland AG 2020
Y. Baghdadi et al. (eds.), *ICT for an Inclusive World*,
Lecture Notes in Information Systems and Organisation 35,
https://doi.org/10.1007/978-3-030-34269-2_28

Tokyo, the world's largest city, has alone 38 million inhabitants, and so is the case in Delhi (25 million), Shanghai (23 million), and other cities such as Mexico City, Mumbai, Sao Paolo, which has each over 20 million inhabitants. By 2030, the world is projected to have 41 mega-cities with more than 10 million inhabitants [1].

Lebanon is no exception to the above worldwide trends and urbanization in Lebanon is even more severe. For instance, almost 88% of the Lebanese population lived in urban centres in 2014, compared to 83% in 1990. This share is expected to rise to 92% by 2050. In actual number, almost 4.4 million inhabitants live in cities in Lebanon. Lebanon is composed of six administrative areas (or Mohafaza) namely Beirut, Mount Lebanon, Bekaa, North Lebanon, Nabatieh, and South Lebanon. In Mount Lebanon alone, 40% of the urban population are concentrated. In addition, according to the United Nations, Lebanon population density reached 485.93 inhabitants per km^2 in 2015 to be the 22nd most populated in the world [2].

As the world continues to urbanize, maintaining the standard of living and the quality of life has become more challenging in cities. It is true that urbanization has improved livelihoods and contributed toward poverty reduction. Cities are also engines of opportunities, jobs and wealth as well as innovation and creativity. However, without careful urban planning, urbanization (mainly in large urban centres) has caused deterioration in the quality of life due mainly to enormous strains on resources and shortage of public services. As a result, social problems arise, unemployment increases, poverty becomes widespread, insecurity grows, and the environment suffers [3].

As such, urban planning becomes of major importance to achieve sustainable development in urban centres and policy makers cannot take the right decisions without consistently measuring and tracking economic, social, and environmental indicators. The application of Information and Communication Technology (ICT) brought about innovative solutions to the abovementioned challenges and lead to new urban economies including the digital economy, the green economy, the health & care economy, and the collaborative economy. These new concepts have greater chance of promoting equitable, efficient and sustainable human settlements and leading cities to prosperity [4].

In order to make urban centres liveable, measures to monitor and improve the quality of life needs to be adopted. Urban Observatories with the aid of Information and Communication Technology (ICT) derive local solutions where there is a need to identify local issues and evolve a strategy to ensure collection, compilation and analysis of data pertaining to urban centres in a systematic manner and on a regular basis which will, in turn facilitate effective decision support as highlighted in the conceptual model of sustainability assessment [5]. Therefore, the establishment of urban observatory at the local, national, and regional levels through collection, storage, comparison, analysis, and management of the data related to urban development, provides a key solution to decision makers for achieving sustainable development [4].

In Lebanon, the challenges related to the deterioration of standard of living in urban centres have increased with the large influx of Syrian immigrants due to the civil war in Syria. However, way before that, the UN Habitat and since 2000, have assisted and supported several municipalities in Lebanon to implement local urban observatories in order to better achieve the Millennium Development Goals (MDG). This paper sheds the light on an excellent example of urban observatories in Lebanon: Tripoli Environment and Development Observatory. The paper takes on the challenging task of assessing the lack of data in Lebanon, which is considered as one of the major problems preventing the construction of urban observatories [6]. To our knowledge, this is the first paper in Lebanon that sheds the light on urban obervatories in the country and their importance in tackling the alarming increase in urbanization and population density in the country. One of the major contributions of this paper is the presentation of visual maps of TEDO that haven't been published before to illustrate how urban observatories can indeed identify needs and contribute in delivering effective solutions for achieving sustainable development.

2 Sustainable Development and Urban Observatories

Urban observatories play an important role in economic development and this role can be highlighted by looking at the most recent measures of economic development and the contribution of observatories in achieving sustainable development. When it comes to the measurements of standard of living, these can be divided into two main categories. The first category ranks the standard of living in countries and includes traditional measures such as the Human Development Index (HDI) compiled and published by the United Nations, and other measures such as the Quality of Life index (QL) by the Economist Intelligence Unit. Traditional measures of standard of living fail to account for all aspects of the Millennium Development Goals (MDGs) and to account for the urbanization aspect of modern life. As such, new measures of standard of living that are more adapted to the urbanization feature of economic development were developed. In this category, three main measures can be highlighted: the City Development Index, the Mercer Quality of Living Index, and the Smart City Index [7, 8].

City-ranking has become a central instrument for assessing the attractiveness of urban regions with regard to different economic, social and environmental indicators. At the time, with globalization and the enormous international exposure it provides, cities have devoted immense efforts to brighten their image and the quality of life it provides in comparison to other cities [9].

The City Development Index (CDI) is based on five Urban Indicators developed by the United Nations Human Settlements Programme (UN-Habitat). These indicators that aims to reflect urban development includes infrastructure, waste, health, education and city product (Global Urban Indicators).

The Mercer Quality of Living Index compares 221 cities based on 39 criteria. New York is given a baseline score of 100 and other cities are rated in comparison. Important criteria are safety, education, hygiene, health care, culture, environment, recreation, political-economic stability and public transportation. Mercer is also used to help municipalities to assess factors that can improve their quality-of-living rankings. Based on the Mercer Quality of Living Index in 2016, Beirut ranks 180 out of 230 cities worldwide.

Finally, based on the Smart City Index, a Smart City is one where the inhabitants make a rational use of technological advances to improve their quality of life and welfare. The Smart City Index is based on six indicators including smart people, smart economy, smart living, smart governance, smart mobility, and smart environment [10]. None of the Lebanese cities appears on the list of Smart cities ranking in the world.

On the other hand, the need for urban observatories is highlighted in the literature of sustainable development. The conceptual model developed by Mendes et al. [5] sheds the light on the importance of urban observatories in sustainability assessment. As shown in Fig. 1, the model is divided into two sets of questions: questions of sustainability and questions of assessment. The first set of questions refers to the uncertainty related to the lack of knowledge and information that prevents policy makers from achieving further development in areas such as poverty, environmental conditions, and quality of life measures. The blame here falls on researchers and scientists. It also refers to the ambiguity in the connections between the different

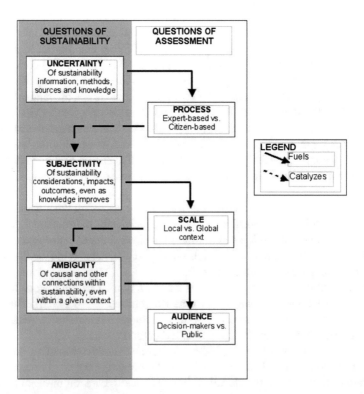

Fig. 1 Conceptual model relating key debates within sustainable development and sustainability *assessment. Source* Mendes et al. [5]

components of sustainable development which prevents policy makers from coming up with action plans that can make a real improvement to the quality of life of communities. Here, the blame falls on theorists, modelers, and leaders. Finally, the first set of questions refers to the subjectivity of defining and operationalizing the concept of sustainable development and as a result prevent policy makers from working with a coherent opinion about the concept of sustainability. The blame in the latter case falls on all those who use the sustainability term. The second set of questions refers to the process in engaging experts and citizens as a source of knowledge, and questions about the scale of the development indicators from the local to the global, as well as present questions related to the most effective audience.

In order to reduce uncertainty, implement rational sustainable development policy and calculate accurate urban indicators, better knowledge and more information is needed [11]. In this context, urban indicators become unbiased and policy makers can better make decisions. As such, urban observatories are crucially important to provide quality information about important indicators and achieve better sustainability outcomes. Moreover, urban observatories reduce the ambiguity associated with sustainability assessment. For instance, urban indicators as solid tools for decision making provide a practical plan to translate the large number of definitions about sustainable development. In addition, urban observatories are also important because they reduce subjectivity that results from the lack of a single definition about sustainable development. The sustainability term has many definitions proposed by many researchers and writers since it has become popular in the late 1980s. Finally, urban indicators on which urban observatories are based, help policy makers in positioning their communities for a better quality of life by attempting to improve these indicators.

In order to reduce uncertainty, knowledge and information must be based on experts and citizens together. Knowledge and information must also emanate from qualified scientists and community groups. In that sense, urban observatories must be based on information from the communities they serve. This makes them more effective at tackling development problems. In addition, sustainable development cannot be achieved without defining the scale and context of sustainability assessment. In this regard, urban indicators must be clearly differentiated between the local and global context. Hence, urban observatories need to be developed at the local and global levels. The question of ambiguity must take into consideration the audience of decision-makers and the public and the best way to motivate them. Urban indicators must enhance civic processes that value participation and community involvement in achieving sustainable development [12].

3   Urban Observatories and the Need for Data

Achieving a good ranking and a good standard of living based on the urban indices presented above is not possible without access to detailed, extensive, and standardized data. Urban Observatory with the aid of ICT presents data on urban development indicators using graphics, maps, and videos and makes it easier for policy makers to learn about their city and for ordinary citizens to be more aware of the progress of urban indicators in cities in which they reside. The Environmental Systems Research Institute (ESRI) makes tremendous efforts to develop the tools such as ArcGIS to visualize and better use an Urban Observatory [13]. This includes the use of Geographic Information System (GIS) and digital mapping. Geographical Information system is a geospatial platform which allows to visualize the urban indicators at the local level (Local Urban Observatory, LUO), national level (National Urban Observatory, NUO), regional level (Regional Urban Observatory, RUO), or global level (Global Urban Observatory, GUO). Without Urban Observatories, facing the increasing challenges related to slums and urbanization can be hardly managed. The inclusion of IT in the process of decision making related to improving the standard of living in cities becomes necessary [14].

Urban indicators are developed by UN-Habitat and divided into six categories: (1) shelter, (2) social development and eradication of poverty, (3) environmental management, (4) economic development, (5) governance, and (6) international cooperation. UN-Habitat aims to achieve sustainable development by measuring indicators in urban centres. These indicators aim to assess the quality of life and compare cities, regions, and countries. As such, Urban Observatories rely primarily on data to calculate urban indicators, and collecting this data and its storage can prove to be very challenging in some countries. Data can be obtained through governments various departments and ministries. When the data is not available, it must be collected through surveys. For that purpose, a special database and location web-based application were developed for the acquisition of information from both sources. Records in both databases are location-based, and they are considered the main sources to feed the GIS database [4].

By making these measures available at the local, national, regional, and global level, and with the aid of a geospatial platform, policy makers can better monitor progress toward achieving their development objectives. The UN Habitat provides the list of categories and subcategories of urban indicators as presented. By calculating these indicators, it becomes possible to provide a visual illustration of the development conditions at the local, national, and global levels. These indicators provide a roadmap for policy makers to track progress and as an accountability tool to monitor achievements. More importantly, these indicators can function at the municipality level and make the decentralization of economic development decisions more effective.

However, without data these indicators cannot be used to promote development. To be functional, urban observatories require the collection and calculation of a large set of data. Data remain one of the major constraints facing the development of urban indicators. For this reason, the UN-Habitat programme incentivizes countries and cities to collect data in order to compile the Urban Global Indicators. Data collections include 237 cities of 110 countries. Based on this data and on the GIS technology, UN-Habitat can calculate, visualize, and compare urban indicators around the world.

The list of the cities and countries included in the Global Urban Observatory are provided in the Urban Indicators report published by UN-Habitat. Lebanon and its major cities do not figure out in the Global Urban Observatory database and as a result, its urban indicators cannot be compared to other cities in the world. Despite major efforts to standardize data collection through the Central Administration of Statistics (CAS), data collection remains inconsistent and interrupted which prevents the ability to use it to conduct policy. As a result, there is a substantial amount of missing data.

Table 1 in the Appendix shows a list of available urban indicators in Lebanon. As the table indicates, the available indicators are poor in comparison to the UN-Habitat requirements. The data of urban indicators in the table are gathered from the Central Administration of Statistics (CAS). The CAS conducts several surveys with the United Nations Development Program (UNDP), the UNICEF, the World Bank, and the IMF. The CAS compiles a large amount of data from different ministries and directorates in Lebanon. This source is published in the CAS's webpage about the CAS cooperation with ministries [15–17]. However, it seems that this data is not consistent and is mostly collected in an irregular manner. For instance, 41.66% of data on shelter is not available, 33.33% of the data on social indicators and eradication of poverty is not available, 75% of the data on environmental management is not available, and 88.88% of data on economic development is not available. Filling this gap would need substantial efforts from municipalities in connected areas to join efforts to construct a common LUO. This is mainly observed during the last couple years where several indicators in the statistical yearbook were interrupted. The data compiled by the CAS is mostly regional, across Cazas in Lebanon. As such, based on the existent data, it is impossible to construct local urban observatories (LUOs) and this would need substantial efforts from municipalities in urban areas. Alternatively, Municipalities in connected areas can join efforts to construct a common LUO [18].

The missing data as highlighted in Table 1 may not necessarily be inexistent. For instance, this data might be available but need to be compiled. Some of the data is available at the UNDP, the IMF, and the World Bank, but for very few years. Potential sources of data need to be brought together on a national, regional, and across cities and Municipalities.

4   Example of Urban Observatories in Lebanon: TEDO

The Urban Community Al Fayhaa (UCF) was established in 1982 and located in North Lebanon. UCF includes four municipalities namely Tripoli, Mina, Bedawi, and Kalamoun. Tripoli is the second city after Beirut with a surface area of 30 km^2 and a population of 500,000 inhabitants (TEDO).

In September 1999, the Tripoli Environment and Development Observatory (TEDO) was established in Tripoli. TEDO is the only urban observatory in Lebanon mentioned on the Urban Observatories Program listing urban observatories in the Arab World. The Municipality in Sin El Fil is working on an Urban Observatory that still need tremendous efforts to be comprehensive [19, 20]. In that sense, TEDO is unique on the municipal level in Lebanon [21]. GIS was introduced to UCF since 2002 through TEDO which became a section in the engineering and technical department of the organizational structure of UCF since 2006 (TEDO).

4.1 Aims

TEDO aims to monitor the environmental trends as well as socio-economic development through the calculation, publication, and dissemination of a set of specific indicators. As such, the main aims of TEDO can be summarized as follows:

- Provides a more accurate vision on environmental trends in environment and socio-economic development in the municipalities of UCF.
- Fills the gaps, tackles the deficiencies, and prevents potential inconsistencies in collected data.
- Shares the information collected, facilitates the transmission and dissemination and makes it available to decision-makers at UCF.
- Establishes a dialogue and promotes coordination and cooperation between neighbouring municipalities.

4.2 Indicators of TEDO

TEDO calculates 26 indicators grouped around the following seven main themes as shown below.

- Socio-Economical (the population and population density; standard of living; the number of hospitals and beds)
- Urban planning and Land Use (the number of building permits and housing; the number of licenses settlement irregularities; the proportion of green space per inhabitant; cost of street cleaning)
- Water and Sanitation (the quality of drinking water; sewage)
- Solid Wastes (quantities issued by each municipality)
- Natural, Cultural, and Historical Heritage (the number of classified archaeological sites; the number of visitors to parks and historical sites visitors)
- Air Quality (emissions of particles of all kinds, sulphur dioxide emissions)
- Meteo Difficulties (wind speed, temperature, humidity).

As such, the main aim of TEDO is to help decision makers to access valuable information calculated, collected and organized by TEDO and to develop modern means of presentation and dissemination of information, such as Geographic Information System (GIS). The elaboration of a GIS application by TEDO allows users to search, query, and display results geographically. TEDO monitors the progress of indicators and highlights the cause of the changes that take place. TEDO collects, organizes, shares, and makes data and information accessible to a large number of stakeholders to improve planning and make decisions more efficient [21].

4.3 GIS Application and Database

TEDO uses the GIS to display complex and a substantial amount of information in simplistic visual images reflecting different values of the indicator, hence highlighting more easily the geographical location of these areas that are in serious need for improvement and tracking the progress that was achieved. As such, TEDO allows analysing information and presenting them in a way that facilitates awareness and communication with the public and other stakeholders. Besides, the GIS system plays an important role as a storage facility to deal with massive amount of data from municipalities. In 2002, some members of staff in the various municipalities of UCF were trained on the GIS system and more specifically on the ARC VIEW GIS [21]. Figure 2 illustrates the application of GIS to TEDO. A GIS database was created and includes: parcels, buildings, streets, units, blocks, infrastructure, permits, etc. TEDO was initiated and financed initially by the European Commission/LIFE Program DGX1. As any program funded, sustainability is a major issue at the end of the program. TEDO represents an excellent case at this level. It was institutionalized and became part of the organizational structure of Al Fayhaa Urban Community in 2006. TEDO is now legislated, has elected members and assists in the establishment of new observatories in the region.

One of the critical issues for the functioning of any Urban Observatory is the collection of data and information. In Lebanon, the issue of data collection and data

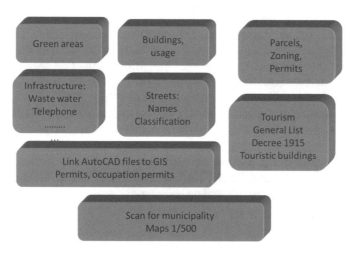

Fig. 2 GIS application and database. *Source* TEDO

availability is indeed a major impediment due to the fact that the government does not pay too much importance to National Statistics.

TEDO relies on several sources of data:

- Ministries i.e. Ministry of the Environment
- Elected Municipal Councils i.e. Tripoli Municipality
- National Scientific Research Council/Remote Censing
- NGO's
- Universities
- Central Administration of Statistics
- Directorate General of Urban Planning.

Some of the data used in the application is collected through field surveys for some activities and is used to update the GIS database.

4.4   Sample of TEDO Application: The Medical Campaign in Primary Schools

A visual illustration of the urban indicators listed in Sect. 4.2 is available but not presented due to the number of page restrictions. Among these indicators we mention the population density, the standard of living, solid waste, cultural heritage, air quality, and others. In this section, the Medical Campaign in Primary Schools will be presented as an illustrative example. The Medical Campaign in Primary School is used as a successful case in the context of TEDO and illustrates clearly how using a combination of urban indicators and GIS application to form an urban observatory allows us to detect the causes of severe problems and identify the areas to be acted upon. The campaign aims to collect information on existing diseases in primary schools and to the number of cases. The campaign in primary schools took three years in a row and collected data from surveys filled by the doctors of each school (kindergarten + primary). This data was then linked to the GIS system so that a database of students and diseases was elaborated in UCF. The first map in Fig. 3 provides a visual distribution of primary schools in UCF.

Figure 4 provides a visual illustration of the distribution of cases of diseases across geographic regions in UCF. The red circles for example reflect the largest number of cases.

The map shown in Fig. 5 allows us to locate on the same map Asthma cases and furniture painting activities. We can then conclude that 16.49% of Asthma cases are in one school near activities of furniture painting.

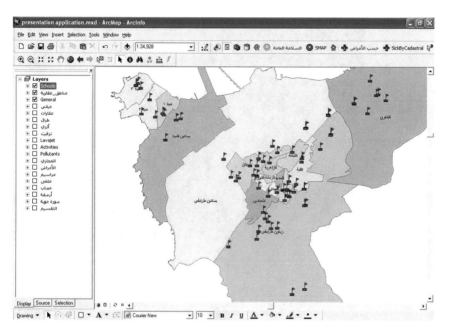

Fig. 3 Primary schools in UCF. *Source* TEDO

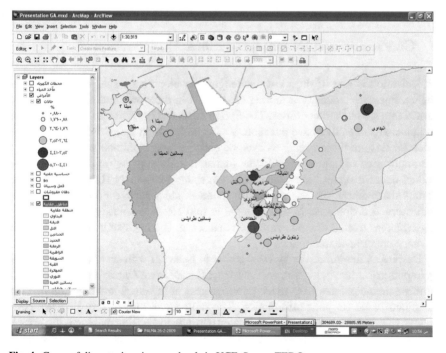

Fig. 4 Cases of diseases in primary schools in UCF. *Source* TEDO

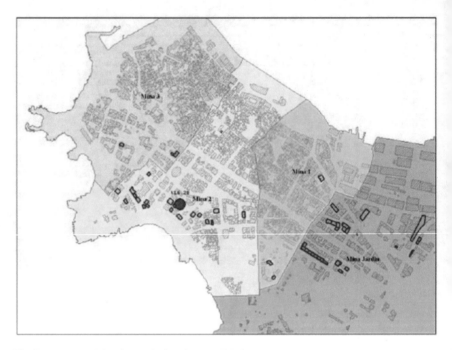

Fig. 5 Asthma and furniture painting. *Source* TEDO

5   Conclusion and Recommendations

Urbanization is one of the most challenging development issues that Lebanon is facing. Population density is among the highest in the word, and urban areas have turned into slums in major cities. The Syrian crisis and the influx of Syrian refugees to Lebanon since 2011 have put more strains on Lebanon cities' vulnerable infrastructure. Despite these negative developments, Lebanese officials are still ignoring the importance of improving National Statistics and imposing on municipalities to collect data for urban indicators as recommended by the UN-Habitat. This paper claims that without the use of ICT to monitor and visualize urban development indicators, decision makers will struggle to find effective solutions to the increasing problems related to urbanization. In that sense, Urban Observatories become of primary importance in Lebanon.

Despite all the initiatives by UN-Habitat in Lebanon with several municipalities to implement urban indicators and construct Local Urban Observatories, almost all of these municipalities have made poor progress at this level and decision making remained based on poor information. The only urban observatory that has been properly developed and that has contributed partially to decision making is the Tripoli Economic and Development Observatory (TEDO). Despite its coverage of a small number of urban indicators, TEDO provides an excellent opportunity to transfer its experience and know-how to other municipalities.

In urban cities, sustainable development has become crucial to preserve the standard of living. Sustainable development reinforces economic growth as can be seen in other cities in the region such as Dubai and Jeddah [22]. The major challenges such as poverty reduction, climate change, social disturbance, insecurity, poor housing, inadequate supply of infrastructures, water access, sanitation, and other urban services are faced by in Lebanon and will be faced further in the future if serious actions are not taken. Lebanon is turning into a one city country with deteriorating quality of life.

Therefore the establishment of urban observatories at the municipality level is very important to monitor the progress and to compare between data of different observatories in order to be able to group all this data into a centralized dataset to form a national urban observatory, given the absence of any recent census in Lebanon and the poor consistency of data. However, the lack of data is not the only impediment but also the lack of dissemination and the use of existing data in decision making which might be due to the fact that raw data needs to be visualized to facilitate its use and contribution to the decision making process.

One of the major mistakes that Lebanon is facing today is acting late and only when an indicator has reached an alarming sign of weakness. The garbage crisis is a good example. Using urban observatories ensures continuous monitoring of urban indicators and their progress hence enables us to tackle potential problems at early stages.

Acknowledgements The authors wish to acknowledge Eng. Amer Rafei, president of the Urban Community Al Fayhaa and Eng. Dima Homsi, director at the Urban Community Al Fayhaa for their valuable help in collecting data regarding TEDO urban observatory.

Appendix

See Table 1.

Table 1 Data availability of UN Habitat-Urban Indicators in Lebanon. *Source* Compiled by the author based on UN-habitat and CAS

Chapter/habitat agenda goals	Indicators	Data
1. Shelter		
Promote the right to adequate housing	Key Indicator 1.1: Durable Structures	The Census of Buildings, Dwellings and Establishments: 2004 (*CAS*), Regional Data
	Key Indicator 1.2: Overcrowding	**Not available**
	Key Indicator 1.3: Right to Adequate Housing	The Census of Buildings, Dwellings and Establishments: 2004 (*CAS*), Regional Data + Real Estate registry, *via CAS:* 2006, 2007, 2008, 2009, 2010, 2011, Regional Data
	Key Indicator 1.4: Housing Price and Rent-to-Income	**Not available**
Provide security of tenure	Key Indicator 1.5: Secure Tenure	The Census of Buildings, Dwellings and Establishments: 2004 (*CAS*), Regional Data
	Key Indicator 1.6: Authorized Housing	The Census of Buildings, Dwellings and Establishments: 2004 (*CAS*) Regional Data
	Key Indicator 1.7: Evictions	**Not available**
Provide equal access to credit	Key Indicator 1.8: Housing Finance	Housing Bank and Public Housing Institutions, *via CAS*: 2008, 2009, 2010, 2011, Regional Data + Potential: available
Provide equal access to land	Key Indicator 1.9: Land Price-to-Income	**Not available**
Promote access to basic services	Key Indicator 1.10: Access to Safe Water	Housing Characteristics: 2004, 2007, 2009 (*CAS*), Regional Data
	Key Indicator 1.11: Access to Improved Sanitation	Housing Characteristics: 2004, 2007, 2009 (*CAS*), Regional Data
	Key Indicator 1.12: Connection to Services	**Not available**

(continued)

Table 1 (continued)

Chapter/habitat agenda goals	Indicators	Data
2. Social development and eradication of poverty		
Provide equal opportunities for a safe and healthy life	Key Indicator 2.1: Under-Five Mortality	Living Conditions Survey: 2004, 2007 (*CAS*), Regional Data + Multiple Indicators Cluster Survey: 2009 (*CAS*), Regional Data
	Key Indicator 2.2: Homicides	UNDP, 2008–2012
	Key Indicator 2.3: Urban Violence	**Not available**
	Key Indicator 2.4: HIV Prevalence	**Not available**
Promote social integration and support disadvantaged groups	Key Indicator 2.5: Poor Households	Household Budget Survey: 2004–05, 2012 (*CAS*), Regional Data
Promote gender equality in human settlements development	Key Indicator 2.6: Literacy Rates Key Indicator 2.7: Gender Inclusion Key Indicator 2.8: School Enrolment	Living Conditions Survey: 2004, 2007 (*CAS*), Regional Data + Multiple Indicators Cluster Survey: 2009 (*CAS*), Regional Data
	Key Indicator 2.9: Women Councillors	**Not available**
3. Environmental management		
Promote geographically-balanced settlement structures	Key Indicator 3.1: Urban Population Growth	Living Conditions Survey: 2004, 2007 (*CAS*), Regional Data + Multiple Indicators Cluster Survey: 2009 (*CAS*), Regional Data
	Key Indicator 3.2: Planned Settlements	**Not available**
Manage supply and demand for water in an effective manner	Key Indicator 3.3: price of water	**Not available**
	Key Indicator 3.4: Water Consumption	Water Authorities, *via CAS*: 2008, Regional Data
Reduce urban pollution	Key Indicator 3.5: Wastewater Treated	**Not available**
	Key Indicator 3.6: Solid Waste Disposal	**Not available**
	Key Indicator 3.7: Regular Solid Waste Collection	Living Conditions Survey: 2004, 2007 (*CAS*), Regional Data + Multiple Indicators Cluster Survey: 2009 (*CAS*), Regional Data

(continued)

Table 1 (continued)

Chapter/habitat agenda goals	Indicators	Data
Prevent disasters and rebuild settlements	Key Indicator 3.8: Disaster Prevention and Mitigation Instruments	**Not available**
	Key Indicator 3.9: Houses in Hazardous Locations	**Not available**
Promote effective and environmentally sound transportation systems	Key Indicator 3.10: Travel Time	**Not available**
	Key Indicator 3.11: Transport Modes	**Not Available**
Support mechanisms to prepare and implement local environmental plans and local Agenda 21 initiatives	Key Indicator 3.12: Local Environmental Plans	**Not available**
4. Economic development		
Strengthen small and micro-enterprises, particularly those developed by women	Key Indicator 4.1: Informal Employment	**Not available**
Encourage public-private sector partnership and stimulate productive employment opportunities	Key Indicator 4.2: City Product	**Not available**
	Key Indicator 4.3: Unemployment	Living Conditions Survey: 2004, 2007 (*CAS*), Regional Data + Multiple Indicators Cluster Survey: 2009 (*CAS*), Regional Data
5. Governance		
Promote decentralisation and strengthen local authorities	Key Indicator 4.4: Local Government Revenue	**Not available**
	Key Indicator 4.5: Decentralization	**Not available**
Encourage and support participation and civic participation	Key Indicator 4.6: Citizens Participation	**Not available**
	Key Indicator 4.7: Voters Participation	**Not available**
	Key Indicator 4.8: Civic Associations	**Not available**
Ensure transparent, accountable and efficient governance of towns, cities and metropolitan areas	Key Indicator 4.9: Transparency and Accountability	**Not available**

References

1. Department of Economic and Social Affairs, Population Division. World Urbanization Prospects: The 2014 Revision, Highlights. United Nations, New York (2014)
2. UN-Habitat: Lebanon Urban Profile. UN-Habitat, Beirut (2011)
3. Henderson, V.: How urban concentration affects economic growth. In: World Bank Policy Research Working Paper 2326 (2000)
4. UN-Habitat: Urban Indicators Guidelines: Better Information, Better Cities. UN-Habitat, Nairobi (2009)
5. Mendes, W., Mochrie, C., Holden, M.: A resource guide on social sustainability for municipalities and their partners. Unpublished Report for the GVRD Social Action Team, Vancouver (2007)
6. World Bank and United Nations: Lebanon Economic and Social Impact Assessment of the Syrian Conflict. World Bank and United Nations, Beirut (2013)
7. Mercer: Quality of Living Worldwide City Ranking. Mercer (2016)
8. Economist Intelligence Unit: Liveability Report. http://store.eiu.com/Product.aspx?pid=455217630. Accessed 15 Feb 2016
9. Lora, E., Powell, A.: A new way of monitoring the quality of urban life. In: IDP Working Paper Series No. IDP-WP272, December 2011
10. Leichenko, F., Simon, D., Seto, K., Solecki, W., Sanchez-Rodriguez, R.: The green economy and the prosperity of cities. In: UN-Habitat Background Paper for the State of World Cities Report (2012)
11. Friedman, M.: The methodology of positive economics 259 (1953)
12. Jacob, A.L.: Creating sustainable cities: community-level sustainability indicators and public policy (1996)
13. Esri: ArcGis. http://www.esri.com/software/arcgis. Accessed 14 Mar 2016
14. Farah, J.: A draft for a typology of urban observatories. In: International Conference "Sustainable economics within the new culture of development". Liège: International Conference "Sustainable Economics within the New Culture of Development" (2011)
15. Central Administration of Statistics: Demographic and social. http://www.cas.gov.lb. Accessed 18 Feb 2016. http://www.cas.gov.lb/index.php/demographic-and-social-en
16. Central Administration of Statistics: Housing characteristics. http://www.cas.gov.lb. Accessed Feb 2016. http://www.cas.gov.lb/index.php/housing-characteristics-en
17. Central Administration of Statistics: Statistical Yearbook http://www.cas.gov.lb/i. Accessed 18 Feb 2016. http://www.cas.gov.lb/index.php/statistical-yearbook
18. Sankari, A., Jadayel, O., El Murr, N.: Urban noise mapping: the case of the city of El-Mina, North Lebanon. In: Middle East & North Africa Users Conference. ESRI, Tripoli (2010)
19. Sin El Fil Municipality: Sin El Fil. http://allegati.po-net.prato.it/. Accessed 20 Feb 2016. http://allegati.po-net.prato.it/dl/20080423121438300/sinelfil.pdf
20. Bedran, S., Zwein, V.: Local urban observatory at Sin El Fil municipality—Lebanon: challenges & Achievements. In: Map Middle East 2006. Map Middle East 2006, Dubai (2006)
21. TEDO: Application form for best practices criteria. http://www.medcities.org. Accessed 12 Mar 2016.http://www.medcities.org/documents/20544/37750/AF+Best+Practices.TEDO. Liban.pdf/ac0ca96b-337b-43fc-9772-922d2fe17fae
22. Abdulsalam, M., Dany, G.: Local urban observatory using GIS: Jeddah–KSA.www.khatibalami.com/.03March2016, www.khatibalami.com/gsi/PDF/JeddahUrbanObservatory.pdf

Cloud Computing and the New Role of IT Service Providers in Lebanon: A Service Dominant Logic Approach

Bachir El Zoghbi and Charbel Chedrawi

Abstract The ascent of Cloud Computing (CC) technology shall impact traditional IT and IT service Providers on many levels; for IDG Cloud Computing Survey [32], 60% of all IT infrastructure spending are Cloud-base, with both public and private cloud adoption growing. In fact, the world economy is moving from being products based to depending on services (Barqawi et al. in J Bus Ind Market 31(7):928–940 [10]) and CC confirms this trend by installing a service logic (Grönroos in Eur Bus Rev 20(4):298–314 [21]), in which the definition of "service" has evolved from a value offered to a value co-created. Therefore, the service dominant logic of Vargo and Lusch (J Mark 68:1–17 [12]) provides an excellent theoretical framework for studying the new role of IT service providers in the cloud era. Using qualitative interpretive multiple case study approach, this article discusses CC value co-creation opportunity for IT service providers in Lebanon by identifying their new role in fixing the CC roadmap from a service dominant logic.

Keywords Cloud computing · Service dominant logic · Value co-creation · IT service provider · Lebanon · CEDRE

1 Introduction

Whether public, private, community or hybrid, investments in Cloud Computing (CC) are booming: for [1], 80% of all enterprise workloads will move to the cloud by 2025; for [2], Worldwide Public Cloud Services Market and Revenue is projected to grow by 17.3% in 2019 (around USD 206 billion). However, such investment is not neutral since it reshapes the company's Information Technology (IT) landscape, strategy and performance [3].

B. El Zoghbi · C. Chedrawi (✉)
Faculty of Business and Management, Saint Joseph University, Mar Mikhael Beyrouth, BP 17-5208, Beirut 1104 2020, Lebanon
e-mail: Charbel.chedrawi@usj.edu.lb

© Springer Nature Switzerland AG 2020
Y. Baghdadi et al. (eds.), *ICT for an Inclusive World*,
Lecture Notes in Information Systems and Organisation 35,
https://doi.org/10.1007/978-3-030-34269-2_29

In fact, the impact of CC is not limited to benefits from IT cost savings [4], it is considered by Hashem [5] as one of the most significant shifts in modern IT and as a service for enterprise applications. Indeed, applications and software for major business applications such as Enterprise Resource Planning (ERPs), customer support, sales and marketing, have generally been run on premise on corporate servers, but now, vendors and cloud infrastructure providers provide it as an on-demand service.

With this regards, the value creation process is changing from linear to network, from centralized to decentralized [6] where customers are becoming co-creators [7], changing their role "from isolated to connected, from unaware to informed and from passive to active" [8] (p. 4). Furthermore, the local commercial added value of IT service providers is becoming obsolete with the ascent of CC, and their traditional role is being transformed with the increased adoption of CC [9]. In fact, the world economy is moving from being products based to depending on services [10, 11] and CC confirms this trend by installing a service logic.

In this context, the Lebanese government have signed off a list of structural reforms during the CEDRE international infrastructure investment conference held in Paris in April 2018; these reforms aimed at enhancing competitiveness, productivity and performance, among which a USD 200 Million "National Cloud Platform" with the ministry of telecommunications. Therefore, it is becoming urgent to explore the transformation caused by CC and affecting the role of IT service providers.

In fact, very limited research or literature has been found yet on the SDL especially on the new role of IT service providers in any developed or developing country as well as in Lebanon.

Henceforth, this article aims to identify the new role that CC imposes on IT service providers in Lebanon from a service dominant logic (SDL). An explanatory qualitative research methodology has been conducted between July and December 2017 targeting cloud services providers in Lebanon. To do so, this article tries to answer the following question: What will be the new role and the added value of IT service provider in the CC era?

The remainder of this article is organized as follows: the ascent of CC, its characteristics and possible architectures/services; followed by the transition from Goods Dominant Logic to Service Dominant Logic from a value co-creation perspective. Next, we review the literature of the Service Dominant Logic. A summary of the methodology and the context of the research will follow with a proper presentation of results discussion and findings. Finally, study conclusion, implications and limitations are presented.

2   Theoretical Background

The theoretical background of this paper is based on the Service Dominant Logic [12] and the co-creation theory of [8].

2.1 The Ascent of CC

For [13] CC is a type of "parallel and distributed system consisting of a collection of interconnected and virtualized computers that are dynamically provisioned and presented as one or more unified computing resources based on service-level agreements established through negotiation between the service provider and consumers" (p. 5). It's a style of computing in which scalable and elastic IT-enabled capabilities are delivered as a service to external customers using Internet technologies [2].

In fact, CC has five fundamental characteristics [13–16]:

- Client companies can unilaterally make use of technological resources on-demand in a self-service way (on a pay per use basis), without any human–human interaction.
- Client enterprise has a broad network access with a wide availability of computing resources over a network that can be accessed through all kinds of devices without any up-front commitment.
- CC resources are pooled on abstracted physical locations to serve multiple users. No physical server is needed by Client enterprise.
- CC services offer infinite computing resources and capabilities which can be elastically provisioned and released to match demand in an instant scalability, allowing companies to start small and increase hardware resources only when there is an increase in their needs.
- CC offers measured service, whereby advanced monitoring applications monitor, control and report the usage of computing resource providing transparency for both the CC service provider and the client company.

The power of the CC model gives access to anyone, anytime, anywhere allowing them to acquire better experience on the exciting offerings and to participate in the selection process of goods and services and even building them up. For [13], consumers' enterprises are attracted by the opportunity for reducing or eliminating costs associated with in-house provision of their IT services. The advantages include also virtualized resources, parallel processing, security and data service integration with scalable data storage [5]; in addition to the agility, scalability, pay-per-use and cost efficiency [17]. In fact, the service offered by cloud infrastructure providers is dynamically scalable because consumers enterprises only have to consume the amount of online computing resources they actually need [9], as this service is charged on a per usage basis.

With this regard, CC proposes three possible architectures/services for users [5]: (1) the Infrastructure as a Service (IaaS), (2) the Platform as a Service (PaaS) and (3) the Software as a Service (SaaS), among its four main types [14, 15, 18, 19]:

- Public Cloud ➜The cloud is made available in a pay-as-you-go manner to the general public; it can be accessed by any subscriber.
- Private Cloud ➜The cloud may exist on or off premise and could be managed by the organization itself or by a third party.

- Community Cloud ➔The cloud is shared, used and controlled by two or more organizations.
- Hybrid Cloud ➔It's a combination of public, private and community clouds.

However, the CC services do come with a number of potential risks regarding security, reliability, data privacy, regulatory compliance and data protection laws, etc. Hence, managers of consumers' enterprises should themselves evaluate the advantages associated with CC and compare them with any potential challenges or risks of such investment [9]; in this context, the role of the IT service providers is changing. In fact, IT service providers should be proposing a unique new values in order to survive and to justify their existence in the cloud era.

2.2 Value Co-creation: From Goods Dominant Logic to Service Dominant Logic

Co-creation, a new paradigm in the management literature, allows companies and customers to create value through interaction [8, 12]. From the co-creation perspective, suppliers and customers are no longer on opposite sides, but interact with each other for the development of new business opportunities [20].

Traditionally, a goods-dominant logic [12] has prevailed. However, the recent evolution occurring between companies and their customers allowed new mechanisms based on value co-creation to play a central role. In fact, for [10], the world economy is moving from being products based to depending on services [11]. CC confirms this trend by installing a service logic [21], in which the definition of "service" has evolved from a value offered to a value co-created.

Indeed, service has been defined as an economic movement and activity that does not lead to ownership and possession [11]; but value is created collaboratively in interactive configurations of mutual exchange between the service provider and the customer [22]. Therefore, service should be defined as per [23] as a series of interactions between IT service provider and clients that result in a visible output; such definition fits perfectly with our study context.

In fact, for [12], conventional goods-dominant logic is insufficient for understanding current markets and economic trade as it concentrates on "tangible resources, embedded value and transactions". New points of view that focus on "intangible resources, the co-creation of value, and relationships… are converging to form a new dominant logic, one in which service provision rather than goods is fundamental to economic exchange" [12] (p. 1). The Service Dominant Logic (SDL) is therefore, a service-focused alternative to the conventional goods-centered paradigm for understanding economic exchange and value creation.

SDL is a point of view on how, by embracing a service-based business logic, firms can incorporates interactions that happen between the firm, its clients and other stakeholders in its market offerings, while engaging itself in value co-creation opportunities with its customers [21]. Subsequently, it isn't the customer who turns into a value co-creator with a provider, rather, it is the provider which, provided that it adopts a service logic and develops firm-client interactions as part of its market offerings, can turn into a co-creator of value with its clients. In fact, adopting a service logic makes it possible for company to get involved with their clients' value-generating processes and, hence, also to actively take part in value fulfillment for clients.

Finally, for [10], SDL provides a theoretical establishment for CC; in fact, the shift to SDL is especially essential for IT service providers where organization's attention drifts away from hardware and software when they concentrate on conveying the services' their clients expect [24]. Thus, SDL is a very reasonable theory for studying the new role of IT service providers in the cloud era; its emphasis on service makes it a particularly fitting lens for studying the CC environment. It can help to understand intently how CC is forcing a new role for IT service providers to co-create value. In fact, interactivity and getting things done with the client as opposed to getting things done to the client is a sign of SDL.

3 Research Methodology

The research follows a qualitative interpretive multiple case-study approach because of its exploratory nature, which is appropriate for studying a phenomenon that is evolving and changing [25]. The case study was investigated to highlight on all the complexities paused by different studied concepts [26]. In fact, there is a developing convention to utilize qualitative research approaches to study information technology phenomena [27, 28] and case study research figures among those qualitative methods that have been perceived as having picked up acknowledgment over the previous decade in the IS field [29–31].

We are investigating the effect of CC implementation on IT server providers in Lebanon. In this way our main goal is to comprehend their direction and response on the best way to develop new roles ensuring business continuity and responding to the specific market needs for different cited points. This article, therefore, aims to identify the new role of the IT service providers in Lebanon from a SDL. It attempts to understand the rationale of Lebanese IT professionals in the new context of Cloud adoption. Hence, an explanatory qualitative research methodology has been conducted between July and December 2017 targeting cloud services providers in Lebanon.

Results are based on the analysis of evidence collected from ten semi-structured in-depth interviews targeting CEOs, General Managers and/or owners of vendors, cloud services providers, IT service providers and other industry leaders in Lebanon. We have maintained the anonymity of our informants by identifying them only with an alphabetic character and number (e.g., E1, E2, etc.). The interviews were recorded, transcribed and analyzed in an abductive way using the software Dedoose.

3.1   The Context of the Article

The forecasted trend in the MENA region, in term of both revenue and multifaceted cloud services, brings evidence on the transformation currently occurring. For [2] Worldwide and MENA Public Cloud Services Market and Revenue is projected to grow by 17.3 Percent in 2019.

According to [32], 60% of all IT infrastructure spending will be Cloud-base. For [1], 80% of all enterprise workloads will move to the cloud by 2025. The future of IT organizations lies therefore, in acting as a type of a service broker as part of a broader strategy, where IT has the ability to consume services, as well as provide cloud services by leveraging cloud-enabled technology.

In this context, the Lebanese economic situation is currently swinging both politically and economically [33]. However, the recently formed government along with the expected outcome of the CEDRE international infrastructure investment conference held in Paris in April 2018 constitute a major breakthrough in the current status-quo [34], mainly through the ministry of telecommunications USD 200 Million "National Cloud Platform" offering local and regional platforms to overcome business dependence on imported digital services. In fact, any ICT implementation would enable good governance [35] and reflects positively.

Finally, the Lebanese ICT market was valued by IDAL [36] at USD 436.2 million in 2016, of which more than 30% for services market; the demand for cloud services were estimated to upsurge as the telecom companies, the banking sector and the government's demand for technology products and services is rising; this market is expected to reach USD 600 million by 2020. In fact, many companies across industries in Lebanon are moving to the cloud.

4   Results and Discussion

Building on our qualitative empirical data collected from interviewing the decision maker of the ten case companies, this article shows that CC provides new avenues for interaction enabling IT companies to engage in co-creating value with each other while identifying a new role of IT service providers in Lebanon from a SDL. In fact, results of our qualitative field study identifies and conceptualizes the underlying IT service providers' roles and added values associated with the cloud computing era in Lebanon.

In the following we shall detail the transformation of IT service providers' roles in the CC era from a SDL, then we shall underline the important implication of IT service provider in fixing the CC road map. In fact, our results showed that in the CC era, the IT service provider plays a strategic role in helping client enterprises in fixing their CC roadmap. He is implicated at six different levels: (1) in assessing the workload for cloud migration; (2) in determining cloud delivery model; (3) in defining business value; (4) in establishing the CC architecture; (5) in implementing the cloud; and (6) in Optimizing cloud usage.

4.1 Transformation of IT Service Providers Role in the CC Era from a SDL

In the past, the traditional roles of IT service providers extending from consulting, design, implementation of solutions and IT infrastructure, hardware and software installation, upgrades, backup, data storage, security, to application maintenance and personalization, is changing as a result of CC concepts. New roles are emerging.

Before CC, the main players were network providers, hardware providers (producers), virtualization providers, platform providers, software producers, independent software vendors, IT service providers, hardware and software resellers, service mediators, system integrators, consultants and finally, client enterprises.

CC consists of a new paradigm that allows the use of all IT resources delivered as a service. Indeed, CC emerges as a meaningful access to the latest technology that could contribute to the optimization of each stakeholder's role by providing infrastructure, platform and software solutions for the whole chain via the Web.

This implies the metamorphosis of the traditional IT roles and the transformation of the relationships between various actors in the domain. Therefore, in the CC era, technical aspects related to the Cloud implementation are developed by the Cloud service provider and by vendors while creating their joint offer.

They are transparent to the client enterprise who's involved in the personalization phase, with the consultancy of the IT service provider. This allows the client enterprise to focus more on their business goals that can be obtained through the CC service. *"The need to consulting, negotiation, and analysis is filled by the IT service provider"* *(E4).*

The transformation and the change is not related to the fact that the infrastructure lays outside of the client enterprise; in the past, outsourcing models were proposing already externalized IT and managed by an external provider. However, CC is a revolution in terms of efficiency of outsourcing IT. The revolution is in the fact that IT is delivered as a service: *"clients plug their computers to the cloud on focus on their customers and how to satisfy their needs with the limited resources that they have"* *(E9).*

However, as CC is achieving increased popularity while linking directly cloud service providers with client enterprises, concerns are being voiced about the role of IT service providers. These local providers that were few years ago representing and selling vendor's software to local companies saw their role changing through the adoption of this radical technology.

The research results underline that, in the CC era, the IT service provider has an important implication in fixing the CC road map. In fact, the IT service provider plays a strategic role in helping client enterprises in fixing their CC roadmap at six

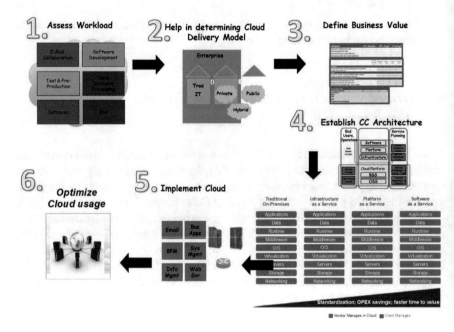

Fig. 1 The CC road map

different levels represented in Fig. 1: (1) in assessing the workload for cloud migration especially in assessing both the technical and business needs of the workload; (2) in determining cloud delivery model by evaluating regulatory constraints, performance concerns, data security and privacy risks, and the availability of existing infrastructure to propose the best cc delivery model between private cloud, public or hybrid model; (3) in defining business value with client companies based on planning the workload and evaluating its impact on their business; (4) in establishing the CC architecture between: PaaS, IaaS, SaaS… (5) in implementing the cloud by implementing the needed operating systems, databases, and application servers, database, and web server, the quantity of CPU, memory, network, storage, and software; (6) in optimizing cloud usage while helping client enterprises to fix their governance strategy that determines exactly how, when, where and by whom cloud services can be utilized.

4.2   CC Detailed Roadmap Levels

This section is reserved to explain the implication of IT service provider in each of the steps of CC road map. In fact, Interviews show that the evolution of the IT service provider role was triggered by CC, and that he plays a strategic role in helping client enterprises in fixing their CC roadmap; his implication in each of the steps of CC road map are detailed below:

First. Assessing Workload

In fact, performing initial groundwork is critical to determine the best underlying platform for migration. IT service providers can play a role in keeping the client enterprise on track with their cloud deployment efforts. He can help in *assessing both the technical and business needs of the workload*, then deciding which underlying platform offers the best fit. *"Assessing technical and business needs of a workload is the first step to ensure that client enterprise is making the right platform choice" (E7); "There is too many interconnecting parts before the workload can be made cloud-ready that are tough to identify without help from the IT service provider" (E4); "IT service provider has the experience to guide client companies in assessing workloads and placing them in the appropriate cloud environment. He proposes criteria that should be considered when determining what workloads are a good fit for the cloud environment, which can help client companies fulfill their cloud strategy" (E2).*

Second. Determining Cloud Delivery Model

In fact, determining the most appropriate cloud delivery model for client enterprise is a decision highly dependent on the client circumstance. IT service provider evaluates regulatory constraints, performance concerns, data security and privacy risks and the availability of existing infrastructure. He helps deciding if the client must *choose private cloud, public or hybrid model*. The three major cloud delivery models are widely used and each of the three approaches has pros and cons. The decision must balance performance, scalability and security. *"We need to help our clients in choosing the appropriate model that fits his profile" (E2); "private cloud enables the greatest control on the platform and data contained within; solutions can be tailored to suit specific business requirements. Public cloud model has lower capital expenditure since clients need only to pay for resources consumed. The hybrid solution provides flexible capacity and a cost-effective path for growth" (E5); "higher performance can be achieved with private clouds that are either on-premises of have dedicated network connectivity. However, private clouds require significant capital investment and incur ongoing static operational costs such a power, cooling and datacenter space. Public cloud reduces costs but lack transparency in security mechanisms implemented by cloud service providers; thus, we must aid our clients in choosing" (E9).*

Third. Define Business Value

The IT service provider analyzes the main consideration of the suitable Cloud delivery model. Both, client companies and IT service provider must *plan the workload and evaluate its impact on the business value*. *"We plan the workload and calculate the financial impact of CC on the business of our clients" (E6) "We help our clients defining the business value of the cloud" (E7); "we evaluate the implication of each possible solutions on the business of our client" (E8); "we check the suitability of the cloud model and its future implications" (E9).*

Fourth. Establishing the CC Architecture
Based on the previous three steps, the IT service provider *proposes a suitable CC architecture*. Therefore, he assesses client company needs to remove hard coded resource paths, to estimate the scaling considerations. He assesses the need to scale horizontally by adding capacity and instances or by adding more resource to a single instance. This work on the architecture is of high value for clients as they need to be consulted on this specific question. *"IT service provider provides the technologies and have the expertise to follow up the continually improved industry" (E3); "The different technologies that compose and support the cloud are constantly changing. The underlying infrastructure is critical, but it's not where client enterprises provide value. So, these clients are offloading that to IT service providers to take care of, so they can move faster in the areas where they provide value" (E4); "our value added remain in proposing the right architecture for the client needs" (E8).*

Fifth. Implement the Cloud
The IT service provider analyzes the needs in operating systems, databases, application servers and web server, the quantity of CPU, memory, network, storage and software. Finally, based on their specific needs, the IT service provider *implements one of these many architectures to clients: PaaS, IaaS, SaaS… "IT service providers will offer the appropriate cloud architectures, PaaS, IaaS, SaaS (E3); "if the client needs a CRM application, IT service providers should propose a SaaS architecture, but if he wants to develop a web application, then IT service provider must propose a PaaS architecture" (E7); "IT service provider must always make sure that the infrastructure is secure and maintained" (E9).*

Sixth. Optimize Cloud Usage
After the implementation of the Cloud, IT service provider can propose ways to optimize the CC usage. Indeed, cloud services are easy to consume. But they are also easy to leave running or underutilize. Periodically, IT service provider *reviews client cloud environment with the aim to keep costs down and applications secure.* *"IT service provider helps clients: maximizing the efficiency of their servers, storage and databases, reduce costs, increase uptime and reduce risks" (E7); "for an efficient cloud use, governance establishes protocols for utilizing and overseeing cloud resources throughout the organization. As a result, governance can cut down on inefficient instances of cloud use, ensuring that the resources are only utilized in a responsible sustainable way" (E1).*

Furthermore, IT service provider will *help client enterprises to fix their governance strategy*. The governance strategy will determine how the organization approaches and oversees its cloud solutions by establishing rules and policies. These policies ensure that the organization remains fully compliant with relevant regulatory measures. *"We help our client to establish a Governance protocol to determine who is authorized to access a given cloud service, what ways a cloud solution can be applied and so on. (E1); "we help our clients to fix rules, policies and road maps on how to use the cloud" (E8); "we help companies to remain compliant with Lebanese and international laws" (E5).*

In order for a client enterprise to *ensure that its cloud services operate efficiently*, IT service provider proposes means of determining exactly how, when, where and by whom cloud services are being utilized. Additionally, IT service provider proposes analysis on how the cost and use of a cloud service have changed over time. *"We offers indices, graphs and indicators to clients to help them optimizing their Cloud usage" (E10)"; "clients receive reports and analysis that can help them analyzing how their usage is evolving with time" (E7)*.

Therefore, we can conclude that client enterprise in Lebanon are provided with a sense of empowerment desiring a greater role in the exchange process with the IT service provider in fixing their CC roadmap.

5 Conclusion

Moving IT services to the cloud transforms the role of the main players imposing a logic of co-creation from a SDL.

The traditional IT model known as on premise obliged companies to buy assets and to build internally the IT infrastructure. They had the choice between having a single vendor or best of breed. Companies had also the choice to buy directly from a vendor (or many) or to choose to go through a local IT service provider. With CC, companies can choose their services directly through the cloud from vendors and from CC service provider or they can engage in a platform in which the IT service provider is playing a strategic role in helping client enterprises in fixing their CC roadmap.

Based on our study, we can conclude that through CC, IT service provider plays a strategic role in helping client enterprises in fixing their CC roadmap, in increasing value co-creation in businesses by reducing costs through the specialization of companies, partnerships and economics of scale and increase personalization for local companies while offering knowledge of the local market.

The first practical direct contribution of this article is that it maps the strategic role of IT service providers. For managers wishing to succeed the transition to the cloud, the implication of the IT service provider can help them as a client company optimizing the design of their needs.

To conclude, we would acknowledge that this study has some limitations inherent to the case study method and qualitative data collection procedures. In fact, since the findings are based on a ten purposeful sample of firms, hence, the study is naturally limited in terms of its statistical generalizability. Additionally, given the exploratory nature of our methodology, the interview participant's viewpoints are a reflection of a particular moment in time; as CC matures, these perspectives are also likely to transform with time. However, these limitations can be addressed in future research.

References

1. Oracle: Oracle's Top 10 Cloud Predictions. https://www.oracle.com/assets/oracle-cloud-predictions-2019-5244106.pdf (2019)
2. Gartner: Gartner Forcasts worldwide public cloud revenue to grow 17.3% in 2019. In: STAMFORD, Connecticut (2019)
3. Loebbecke, C., Bernhard, T., Ullrich, T.: Assessing cloud readiness: introducing the magic. MIS Q. Exec. 11(1) (2012)
4. Iyer, B., Henderson, J.C.: Preparing for the future: understanding the seven capabilities of cloud computing. MIS Q. Exec. 9(2), 117–131 (2010)
5. Hashem, I.A.T., Yaqoob, I., Anuar, N.B., Mokhtar, S., Gani, A., Khan, S.U.: The rise of "Big Data" on cloud computing: review and open research issues. Inf. Syst. 47, 98–115 (2015)
6. Kohler, T.: Crowdsourcing-based business models: how to create and capture value. Calif. Manag. Rev. 57(4), 63–84 (2015)
7. Lusch, R.F., Vargo, S.L., O'brien, M.: Competing through service: insights from service dominant logic. J. Retail. 83(1), 5–18 (2007)
8. Prahalad, C.K., Ramaswamy, V.: Co-creation experiences: the next practice in value creation. J. Interact. Market. 18(3), 5–14 (2004)
9. Gutierrez, A., Boukrami, E., Lumsden, R.: Technological, organizational and environmental factors influencing managers' decision to adopt cloud computing in the UK. J. Enterp. Inf. Manage. 28(6), 788–807 (2015)
10. Barqawi, N., Syed, K., Mathiassen, L.: Applying service-dominant logic to recurrent release of software: an action research study. J. Bus. Ind. Mark. 31(7), 928–940 (2016)
11. Spohrer, J., Maglio, P.P.: The emergence of service science: toward systematic service innovations to accelerate co-creation of value. Prod. Oper. Manage. 17(3), 238–246 (2008)
12. Vargo, S.L., Lusch, R.F.: Evolving to a new dominant logic for marketing. J. Mark. 68, 1–17 (2004)
13. Buyya, R., Yeo, C.S., Venugopal, S., Broberg, J., Brandic, I.: Cloud computing and emerging it platforms: vision, hype, and reality for delivering computing as the 5th utility. Future Gener. Comput. Syst. 25(6), 599–616 (2009)
14. Armbrust, M., Fox, A., Griffith, R., Joseph, A. D., Katz, R., Konwinski, A., Zaharia, M.A: View of cloud computing. Commun. ACM 53(4):50–58 (2010)
15. Mell, P., Grance, T.: The NIST Definition of Cloud Computing, Recommendations of the National Institute of Standards and Technology. National Institute of Standards and Technology, Information Technology Laboratory, Special Publication 800-145 (2011)
16. Bhaird, M., Lynn, C., T.: Seeding the cloud: financial bootstrapping in the computer software sector. Venture Capital 17(1–2), 151–170 (2015)
17. Oliveira, T., Thomas, M., Espadanal, M.: Assessing the determinants of cloud computing adoption: An analysis of the manufacturing and services sectors. Inf. Manag. 51(5), 497–510 (2014)
18. Zissis, D., Lekkas, D.: Addressing cloud computing security issues. Future Gener. Comput. Syst. 28(3), 583–592 (2012)
19. Gupta, V., Rajput, I.: Enhanced data security in cloud computing with third party auditor. Int. J. Adv. Res. Comput. Sci. Softw. Eng. 3(2) (2013)
20. Galvagno, M., Dalli, D.: Theory of value co-creation: a systematic literature review. Managing Serv. Q. 24(6), 643–683 (2014)
21. Grönroos, C.: Service logic revisited: who creates value? And who co-creates? Eur. Bus. Rev. 20(4), 298–314 (2008)
22. Vargo, L., Maglio, P., Akaka, M.: On value and value co-creation: a service systems and service logic perspective. Eur. Manag. J. 26(3), 145–152 (2008)
23. Harfouche, A., Robbin, A.: Inhibitors and enablers of public e-services in Lebanon. J. Organ. End User Comput. 24(3), 45–68 (2012)
24. Lusch, R.F., Nambisan, S.: Service innovation: a service-dominant logic perspective. MIS Q. 39(1)

25. Gephart Jr., R.P.: Qualitative research and the academy of management journal. Acad. Manag. J. **47**(4), 454–462 (2004)
26. Chedrawi, C., Howayeck, P., Tarhini, A.: CSR and legitimacy in: higher education accreditation programs, an isomorphic approach of Lebanese business schools. Q. Assur. Educ. **27**(1), 70–81 (2019)
27. Romm, C.T., Pliskin, N.: The office tyrant—social control through e-mail. Inf. Technol. People **12**(1), 27–43 (1999)
28. Trauth, E.M., Jessup, L.M.: Factors that influence the social dimension of alignment between business and information technology objective. MIS Q. **24**(1), 43–80 (2000)
29. Benbasat, I., Goldstein, D.K., Mead, M.: The case research strategy in studies of information systems. MIS Q. 369–386 (1987)
30. Klein, H.K., Myers, M.D.: A set of principles for conducting and evaluating interpretive field studies in information systems. MIS Q. **23**(1), 67–94 (1999)
31. Orlikowski, W.J., Baroudi, J.J.: Studying information technology in organizations: Research approaches and assumptions. Inf. Syst. Res. **2**(1), 1–28 (1991)
32. IDG Cloud Computing Survey. https://www.idg.com/tools-for-marketers/2018-cloud-computing-survey/ (2018)
33. Chedrawi, C., Howayeck, P.: La Conjoncture Economique, Passage Obligé A Tout Investissement Au Liban. Proche Orient Etudes En Management **28** (2016)
34. Chedrawi, C.: CEDRE 1,2,3… Go, the Lebanese Economic Spring. Research Gate Published Article (2019)
35. Harfouche, A., Robbin, A.: E-government implementation in developing countries: a neoinstitutional approach to explain failure. An example from Lebanon. In: MCIS 2012 Proceedings. Paper 21 (2012)
36. IDAL (Investment Development Authority of Lebanon) (2017)

Success and Failure of the Institutionalization of IS Dispositives Within Organizations: The Effect of External Pressures and the Role of Actors

Antoine Harfouche⊙, Jamil Arida, Mary Ann B. El Rassi, Peter Bou Saba and Mario Saba

Abstract Influenced by external pressures, organizations tend to adopt new IS management standards. This adoption is supported by institutional entrepreneurs who, because of their social position, are more attentive to their environmental global pressure. They are dis-embedded and working to drive adoption and acquire the implementation. Other actors which are embedded and conditioned by the old institutions, resist to this change. This study investigates the actors' role when faced with such a change by examining the differences in their reactions to it and how they could influence the success or failure of a new IS dispositive adoption in three different types of organizations.

Keywords Neo-institutional theory · IS dispositive management · IS adoption · Global pressures · Actor's role

1 Introduction

Today, the increasing globalization raises concerns about the environmental pressures that could drive organizations to adopt new management dispositives [1–3]. These pressures could have a direct influence on organizations as in the case of political or social pressures; furthermore, they may have indirect influence that reflects a mimetic behavior or a professional normative phenomenon [4]. When faced with

A. Harfouche (✉)
CEROS, Université Paris Nanterre, Nanterre, France
e-mail: antoineharfouche@icto.info; antoine.h@parisnanterre.fr

J. Arida · M. A. B. El Rassi
Université Saint Joseph, Beirut, Lebanon

P. Bou Saba
De Vinci Research Center – DVRC, Courbevoie, France

M. Saba
Cesar Ritz Colleges, Brig, Switzerland

Carson College of Business, Washington State University, Pullman, USA

© Springer Nature Switzerland AG 2020
Y. Baghdadi et al. (eds.), *ICT for an Inclusive World*,
Lecture Notes in Information Systems and Organisation 35,
https://doi.org/10.1007/978-3-030-34269-2_30

such pressures, organizations tend to increase their legitimacy in order to survive independently from the actual practices adopted [5]. In fact, external pressures drive actors within the organization to act according to their global vision especially when it comes to their organizations' constraints and contextual environment [6, 7]. Furthermore, these actors may also act based on their expectations and personal interests [8] which may lead a person to take a decision in accordance with his future ambitions, social position, capacities or resources [6, 7]. In this context, today, some organizations decide to adopt and spread the change by adopting the new management dispositive [9], while others may resist especially when their rationality is conditioned by old institutions which could create a resistance behavior among institutional entrepreneurs [10].

For the context of this study, we aim at answering the following questions: How institutional entrepreneurs succeed in the institutionalization of a new management dispositives? How will the other actors react to this set up? What are the potential reasons for the failure or success of the institutionalization of IS dispositives?

To answer these questions, we will explore the extended literature concerning the sociological neo-institutional theory which will allow us to highlight the importance of the external influence in an attempt to relate them to the actors within the organization. We will also take into consideration the economic, social and institutional factors that have a direct or indirect influence, whether triggered consciously or unconsciously, on the actors' behavior within an organization. This should help us to better understand the actors' role in the institutional analysis [8]. To fulfill this objective, this phenomenon will be explored in three different contexts while concentrating on analyzing the actors' behavior in those organizations.

The three cases studies are built based on semi-structured interviews conducted with different actors that have either a complementary role or sometimes an antagonistic behavior in the decision process. The first case study is related to the implementation of e-government process in Lebanon. Based on the nature of the study, the target population was employees, general managers, and ministers working in several ministries such as the Ministry of Economy, Justice, Public Health, Social Affairs, Finance and Administrative Reform. A total of 22 interviews were conducted. Ten out of these twenty-two interviews were conducted with employees who held middle and senior level positions; the other twelve interviews were conducted with ministers and general managers. The interviewees were considered as important actors and decision makers in their field.

The second case study is related to the ISO 14001 adoption in a large multinational Lebanese company that is specialized in producing cement. Six interviews were conducted with senior managers that were responsible for the ISO14001 implementation and six additional interviews were conducted with regular employees.

Finally, the third case study is related to the launch of an e-banking activity by a Lebanese bank. We have conducted three interviews with commercial managers and four with the Information System managers that were responsible for the e-banking implementation process.

The remaining of this paper is organized as follows. The next section presents the neo-institutional sociological theory contribution and its evolution as a theoretical framework and how it was approached in literature. This is followed by the research methodology that the study draws upon. The results of the data analysis and the evaluation of the hypotheses in light of the findings will then be reported and interpreted. Finally, the study implications, along with the limitations and the recommendations for future research will be presented.

2 Theoretical Framework: The Sociological Neo-Institutional Theory

The Neo-institutional theory is one of the major theoretical perspectives used in sociology and management that sheds the light on the role of the organizations' external environment. Drawing on the Neo-institutional theory, this research investigates the influential role of the global and the local environment that could possibility influence different actors within the organization taking into consideration both reactions: the voluntarisms' behaviors of institutional entrepreneurs as well as the alignments' or resistance's behaviors of the other actors. Therefore, our major concern is to focus on the differences that could possibly arise due to the paradox of change or resistance to change when implementing a new dispositive. Then, we will attempt to associate the expected results that could possibility arise from implementing or not implementing this new adopted dispositive.

The theoretical side of this work is studied in the following subsections by discussing the external influential factors that could influence any decision within an organization and the different reactions of the actors within an organization when faced with such pressures.

2.1 Management Dispositive and the External Pressures

In today's global competitive economy, implementing management dispositives has become a fundamental element in contemporary organizations [11, 12]. Financial norms, environmental and quality management solutions to an integrated management including information and management systems (such as supply chain management and customer relationship management) are the core of any organizations' operations. They are defined as "the new developed means that aim at planning, managing and controlling their function" [11, 12]. Nevertheless, this is a very broad concept and may include dispositives such as ISO, IAS/IFRS, Total Quality Management dispositives (TQM) and many other devices designed to organize work by prescribing and assigning tasks, controlling performance and/or staff evaluation. Thus, these dispositives have become a major part of the organization's governance system [13]. As a result, their implementation could directly influence the intra-organizational relationship (between the different actors within the same organization) and inter-organizational relationships (between the organization and their partners, suppliers, Parent Company, clients etc....).

As a matter of fact, adopting this new system (management dispositive) is not a new trend. It has been widely adopted since several decades in order to respond and adjust to any environmental and radical change [11, 12]. Today, and with global competitive pressure on organizations, it has become increasingly crucial for the organizations' survival. According to the neo-institutional literature, this pressure could be of two types: a global pressure or/and a local pressure. Global pressure mainly comes from other supranational organizations, competitive intensity of certain competitors in several countries, existence of a technological innovation, or a global need. Local pressure is related to the organizational local environment such as the country's economic-political pressure, local cultural pressure or other pressure due to their local market environment such as suppliers, customers, competitors, and others [14].

2.2   Actors' Reaction in an Organization

Beyond the neo-institutional deterministic vision, the extended vision of sociological neo-institutionalism adds more willingness to clarify the role that the actors play in the process of institutionalizing a new management dispositive [5, 15]. The major objective is to include all types of behaviors within the institutionalism, including those motivated by personal interests and the search for power [16]. According to this theory, some actors align and adjust to this change. They tend to adopt a new management dispositive and introduce the change within the organization [6, 7]. The decision to adopt a new management dispositive changes the work methods in an organization and leads the actors either to align or to resist especially when their rationality is conditioned by the other institutions [17]. Those who resist remain attached to their socio-political context and continue to protect their "taken-for-granted" routine.

2.3   The Institutional Entrepreneurs' Role

When the institutional entrepreneurs are influenced by their external environment change, they could possibly decide, at a certain moment, to change the rules of the game by institutionalizing new mechanisms and de-institutionalizing others [6, 7, 9]. In this case, the institutions lose their efficiency which makes the institutional entrepreneurs' interventions easier. Thus, and because this is considered against their institutional norms they initiate change with the actual model and thus, participate in creating new models and practices [6, 9, 18]. According to DiMaggio [5], in order to succeed in implementing these modifications, organizations should have access to resources and influential networks.

Once those institutions stop functioning, the dynamics of interpersonal relationships take place [19]. At this point, those who control the resources and the networks will be those who will maintain power in an organization [20]. Hence, institutional entrepreneurs must be able to take advantage of this at the right moment and convince other players to align with their project [9, 5], as their ability to control the access to those resources that are crucial to other actors will enable them to succeed. Their social level gives them the advantage over the others to detect any change in their environment. For example, the fact that they have been previously exposed to these dispositives in other organizations, international professional seminars, could lead them to better understand the environmental pressure [21]. Based on the literature review, there are two reasons why institutional entrepreneurs seek to introduce new management dispositives. First, they do it because they believe they can exploit the organizations for their own benefits [8, 22]. Second, because they try to leverage personal profit by changing the current operational system [11].

As a matter of fact, the application of new working methods will change the resource allocation rules. The institutional entrepreneurs will be at the heart of this strategic change and will attempt to manage this new management dispositive. This will allow them to gain power and profit as well [23, 24]. In fact, they can be even motivated by the values that these changes could carry to them [25, 26]. According to DiMaggio [23], the efforts deployed by those actors could lead them to improve the system.

2.4 The Role of Other Actors Within the Organization

The role of the other actors and the decision to set up the management dispositive comes downwards. Their reaction is a response to their personal situation, their visions and their contextual environment [27]. Therefore, and based on their objectives, social position, abilities and resources, they decide whether to accept or not the new dispositive which could eventually lead them to contribute to the organizational change and stability [28]. Eventually, each actor will use this flexibility to improve his situation. This flexibility could be detected at two levels: (1) accepting the new dispositive and therefore align with the institutional entrepreneurs' strategy or (2) resisting this new dispositive. Some actors that are influenced by the communication that develops around this new dispositive will support its implementation and will consider it as a credible solution to their problems [29]. They will eventually align with the institutional entrepreneurs' choice because they consider it more advantageous for them [30]. Some others will go so far as to creating new alliances with other institutional entrepreneurs in order to increase their own benefits and therefore defend its implementation and work with the other entrepreneurs to convince those that are still lagging behind indecisively. Nevertheless, other actors will not perceive this change positively and will resist eventually to its implementation and will keep their usual routine and habits. They do so unconsciously because they give great importance to organizational norms, structures and cultures that allow them to maintain the status-quo. They might also do it consciously because they fear losing the benefits that the old system offers them. In this case, adopting a new dispositive will create a conflict. For the purpose of our study, we have attempted to carry out longitudinal studies in three different sectors hoping that this could help us to better understand and answer the previously mentioned research questions.

3 Research Methodology: Three Longitudinal Studies

This paper addresses institutional change at the organization level, particularly during the change implementation phase. The paper further highlights cohabitation relationships between institutional entrepreneurs and agents' resistance to change within the same organization. To study any change within organizations, Barley and Tolbert [31] suggested a longitudinal perspective method. In our current research, and because we attempt to analyze dynamically the process of institutionalizing management dispositive within organizations, we decided to use a longitudinal qualitative approach. This type of approach favors the assessment of the related theory and field results. Thus, the case study methodology has emerged as the most appropriate approach to meet such an objective. The longitudinal vision of our study will enable us to analyze in depth an organizational phenomenon that extends over a certain period of time and would allow us to analyze the actors' reactions at different moments. This will allow us to observe their perception evolution and their behavior when faced with external pressures. According to Ménard [32], the data collected in a longitudinal study must relate to at least two distinct periods. We therefore decided to conduct interviews twice in the case of e-government and e-banking and three times in the case of ISO.

3.1 Method of Data Collection: Case Studies in Different Types of Organizations

The first case study is related to e-government implementation in Lebanon. We have conducted twelve interviews with Ministers and General Managers in several Ministries such as the Ministry of Economy, Justice, Public Health, Social Affairs, Finance and Administrative Reform in addition to ten other interviews with employees that also work in those administrations. The first stage began in August 2011. Our aim was to better understand the reasons behind the decision to adopt, the internal and external factors that influenced this choice, the way in which the public sector employees were informed, their reactions and the reactions of the General Managers. Hence, five years later, in June 2016, we interviewed the same people that we have already seen in 2011 or their successors. The objective of this step was to evaluate whether there is any progress, track any changes or evolution in their perception concerning the e-implementation, and better understand the new dynamic that has taken place.

The second case study is related to the implementation of ISO dispositive within a Lebanese multinational company. The first phase started in December 2012, which happened to be right after the initiation of the project and during the information and communication period that followed the decision. The interviews lasted for three months. We have interviewed decision-makers (6 senior managers) and 10 other employees that were recommended by other fellows on the basis of their experience and relativeness to this subject. The purpose of this step was, as mentioned previously, to better understand the reasons behind the decision to adopt, to investigate the internal and external factors that might have influenced this choice and observe the reaction of officials and employees once informed about the decision.

The second stage began seven months after the end of the first stage. We interviewed in September 2013 and for a period of three months, the same actors as in phase one. The objective of the second phase was to assess the implementation progress (what has been done and what should be done), track any changes or evolution in the managers' and employees' perceptions and understand the new dynamic that has taken place. The third and final phase began in July 2014, seven months after the end of the second phase. We again interviewed the same people of the first and second phases. The objective of this third phase was to evaluate the final implementation (what had worked out and what was discarded) and also to measure the perceived results by managers and workers.

The third case study is related to the establishment of e-banking within a Lebanese bank. The first phase started in January 2014. The interviews lasted for two months. We have conducted three interviews with commercial managers and four with the Information System managers that were responsible for the e-banking implementation process. The objective of this first step was to understand the origin and the reasons for this decision, the internal and external factors that influenced this choice, the reaction of the officials, and the reaction of employees as well as that of all the stakeholders. The second phase began a year after the end of the first phase. We interviewed in February 2015 and for a period of three months, the same people that were interviewed in the first phase. The objective of this stage was to evaluate any potential progress and understand the impact of the e-implementation in terms of operational change or in terms of the actors' perception evolution.

3.2 Method of Data Processing

The interviews recorded and transcribed were analyzed using the Dedoose software. We started from a list of themes to code all interviews in order to make our data collection easier.

4   The Results

Based on the above mentioned interviews, we present in the following section the results while focusing on the actors' role in implementing this new dispositive.

4.1   Implementation of e-Government in the Country of Cedars

Since the beginning of 2009, the e-government implementation project has become a major concern for the Lebanese government [33]. Indeed, the interviews reveal that the objective was to implement e-government in order to obtain grants and attract donors' support. The objective of the Lebanese government was not to set up public e-services. Its major objective was to privatize the entire public sector to repay part of the public debt, (Interviewee-EG11). Originally, it was the European Union which launched this project and provided €50 million for the administrative reform and for introducing the communication and information technologies, (Interviewee-EG2). The United Nations Development Program (UNDP), the World Bank and the International Monetary Fund (IMF) also played an important role. "*In 2006, the UNDP asked us to set up a national 'e-strategy' that can help establishing an e-government implementation*" (Interviewee-EG1). "*For this reason the UNDP has offered an open budget grant. However, once the credits are granted, the government has to present a project. This is how the e-government strategy' has been defined*" (Interviewee-EG4). Donors like the World Bank and the IMF have proposed their ideas. Yet, this project did not progress because it did not receive any support from the government. "*We have renovated the infrastructure, provided the equipment and trained the staff efficiently. Indeed, obstacles do arise at the time of the implementation of the e-services. Obstacles were of two types: lack of a political decision and employees' resistance who were probably afraid of losing their power*" (Interviewee-EG4).

Furthermore, the UNDP continued to impose rules to support the establishment of an e-government. Later on, the European Union (EU) has even gone so far as to using sanctions especially when the Lebanese government did not fulfill its commitments regarding the deadlines. "*As the current government at that time did not meet the requirements of the EU, the latter decided to withdraw the funds and grant them to Jordan. The amount was estimated to be around €30 million*" (Interviewee-E13).

"*That's when things started to move. I held several contacts and found interesting ideas*" (Interviewee-EG3). "*I dared to say aloud that the absence of a sharp political decision that supports e-government embarrasses us in front of the donors and weakens our credibility*" (Interviewee-EG18). "*We were running out of time and I had to move fast, otherwise the Europeans would withdraw their financial support…They made it clear that we had to finish within a certain time frame, otherwise they would send the money elsewhere*" (Interviewee-EG15).

The global pressure continued for years. But since donors did not know the Lebanese field, decision-makers in the Lebanese government have repeatedly managed to withdraw donations without any progress in the project implementation. The implementation of e-government has therefore become symbolic. *"We went to Paris-I conference with the administration modernization and adoption of e-government project. After receiving donations and aids, nothing was done. The results were disappointing. later on, and before attending Paris-II, the government tried to speed things up because we could not go back empty-handed. Donors asked for reports. Three weeks before Paris III, the government decided to accelerate the implementation"*, (Interviewee - EG12). *"Yet, alone, I could not do anything. I was only one minister out of thirty"* (Interviewee-EG2). *"Even if the country needed it, in compliance with the will of the Prime Minister, it was decided not to do anything and the money was invested elsewhere"*, (Interviewee-EG17). *The minister in charge at that time" had an army of advisors. When the project was proposed, it was directly transferred to the technology advisor. The latter has almost become a minister. He was really doing everything. Since this 'super advisor' in charge was not happy with the project, nor with those who brought it back, nor with those who did it, the project was not progressing."* As in many developing countries [34, 35], the implementation of e-government in Lebanon has failed. The adoption of e-government was slow and did not introduce any reforms or improvements in the quality of services. On the contrary, it created new problems. Thus, years after the launch of the project, the e-government services still did not exist [36]. Despite the efforts of institutional entrepreneurs and despite the existence of resources, the lack of power has hindered its establishment.

Today, therefore, the situation has not changed too much. For the majority of the Lebanese, the public administration continues to suffer from the same problems: poor quality of services, complicated administrative formalities, arbitrary measures, slowness and corruption.

4.2   Implementation of ISO 14001 Dispositives Within a Subsidiary

The implementation of ISO 14001 Dispositives was the result of the global pressure. It was the parent company that was responsible for the implementation of these dispositives. Indeed, as revealed in the interview with the CEO, *"The ISO 14001 quality certification project has been decided at an international level"* (Interviewee-IS1). *"Our subsidiary's business line generates CO_2 and emits greenhouse gaz. As a result, the group has asked its subsidiaries to become ISO 14001 certified"* (Interviewee-IS6). *"The subsidiary has no choice but to fulfill this obligation, despite the fact that this practice was not perceived as necessary by the Lebanese subsidiary"* (Interviewee-IS2). This context is similar to what Kostova and Roth [37] call 'institutional duality'. A work plan was quickly developed by the administration and several meetings were held to inform and prepare the employees for this change. *"These meetings have failed to clarify the issues for employees. The practical side of the dispositives was not very clear and therefore employees resisted the implementation process"* (Interviewee-IS1). In addition, this new dispositive generated changes in work practices. Some employees did not understand the value of such a change. After the first application, the results were disappointing. The system has become inefficient, which has increased bureaucracy. As for the employees, they thought that there is a downsizing project behind these practices, (Interviewee-IS7). Employees were organized to block the use of new dispositives. Some have even seen these practices as a personal danger. They have even gone far by mobilizing their political representatives or their political parties or even their religious leaders, (Interviewee-IS11). *"Faced with this resistance, the administration has remained unresponsive for about 1 to 2 months"* (Interviewee-IS8). Some administrative members managed to take a step back and disengage themselves from this context because they were convinced of the strategic importance of this project. They transformed themselves into institutional entrepreneurs and carried out the project by negotiating it with the company's administration committee and requested the support of the parent company. For example, *"a manager supported by local political forces, contacted the parent company"* (Interviewee-IS13) while another person stated that *"Following to my boss quick visit to Europe, he returned as a project manager. His first reaction was to call the unions to negotiate a redundancy plan"* (Interviewee-IS14). Shortly afterwards, a plan was developed. The plan contained two components: a collective redundancy plan and a training program to enable employees to learn how to use these dispositives effectively (Interviewee-IS16). Thus, thanks to their networks, institutional entrepreneurs have managed to gain the support of the parent company. They were able to find the resources and the necessary power to make this project a reality (Interviewee-IS14, 15, 16). When the procedures became formally established and documented, the employees followed them and have learned to value them.

4.3 Implementation of an e-Banking System

In 2010, the bank decided to invest in the implementation of an e-banking as only few Lebanese banks were offering this service. This decision came in response to clients' request residing abroad. Indeed, the international customer relations officers have referred to the general management a petition on the behalf of their clients in the diaspora, demanding an online remote monitoring which was also the need of some other local clients. Indeed, this new dispositive offered them several benefits: *"Clients can keep track of their accounts, personal loans, stimulate credits and other services on a daily basis"* (Interviewee-B05). *"E-services are faster. If they want to check their accounts, e-banking is faster than going to an agency. It's rather an easier way for the customer. It's much easier to connect and click online than to physically go to the bank, park the car, get off, take a ticket number, and wait half an hour before you can talk with an advisor. With e-banking, the customer can know everything in one click*" (Interviewee - B03). The institutional entrepreneurs who carried out the project did so because they considered that this type of service has great potentials. They did not want to lag behind in a potentially attractive market. "*For us, e-banking was a future project because we do not want to be the followers in this field. Our goal is to be the market leaders*" (Interviewee-B02). The project holders had the power and their decisions were supported. All the means have been put in place, to achieve timely implementation. "*From the outset, we carried out the necessary steps, in order to be fast and efficient. We did not want half-solutions. I had an approval on a large budget for the best possible results*" (Interviewee-B01). The bank has recruited highly competent professionals. "*We also funded training sessions for these new recruits and they were sent to attended training sessions abroad*" (Interviewee-B02). The stated objective of this project was "*the desire to offer more autonomy to customers*" (Interviewee-B03). A large internal and external communication plan accompanied the implementation. The project leader had the power to involve everyone. Indeed, all the components of the bank were mobilized in the implementation process. So when the e-service project was launched, everyone was waiting for the advanced e-banking service. Internally, the main message that accompanied the implementation is that these e-services allowed advisors to better succeed in their mission with customers. "*They will be able to sell more services and earn more commission*" (Interviewee - B03). "*E-banking can never replace agencies and human contacts. The objective is not to substitute the agencies by e-banking, nor to replace face-to-face contacts by e-services. We designed e-services to support the traditional service. There will always be physical bank services. Their numbers will even increase. The advisor will become a consultant who advises clients how to invest and/or place their money. He can help them in their choice. His role will improve and his salary will increase. Human contacts will remain a necessity. e-banking will help clients in their daily operations especially when they do not need an advisor*" (Interviewee-B01).

As a result, there was no resistance from the other actors because everyone wanted to be part of this revolution. The contact staff hoped to improve their relationship with clients. According to customers' advisors, customers who have tried the e-service found it useful with minor complications: "*To talk about the customers' reactions, we had positive feedbacks. The clients were not shocked by the e-service that we are offering and the site was judged to be friendly-user. They found it uncomplicated ...*" (Interviewee-B07). The results of the new implementations were positive. The bank considered this experience as a positive dispositive that had helped to increase their clients' satisfaction. "*We had to meet the expectations of the customers. In doing so, we were able to win their confidence. For example, now we can respond to customers' complaints in a timely manner. We can help the clients receive a response that meets their expectations which could lead them to appreciate our services and thus gain their confidence*" (Interviewee-B03). "*I have to note that this migration to the online platform didn't decrease our work, on the contrary, we have more to do now and we cannot complain as it had improved our performance and return on investment. We are able to conduct more analysis, surveys and adapted answers*" (Interviewee-B06). Table 1 resumes and compares all the findings.

Table 1 Overall results

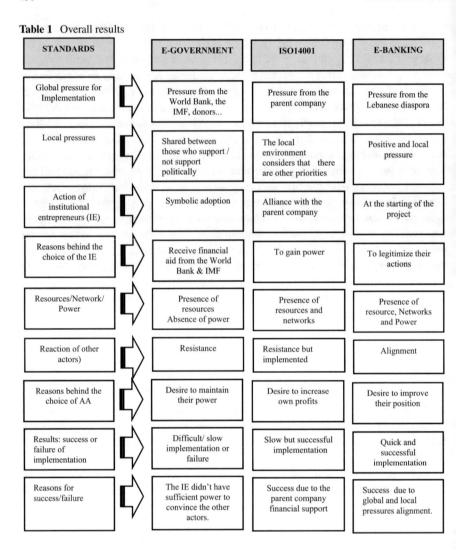

STANDARDS	E-GOVERNMENT	ISO14001	E-BANKING
Global pressure for Implementation	Pressure from the World Bank, the IMF, donors...	Pressure from the parent company	Pressure from the Lebanese diaspora
Local pressures	Shared between those who support / not support politically	The local environment considers that there are other priorities	Positive and local pressure
Action of institutional entrepreneurs (IE)	Symbolic adoption	Alliance with the parent company	At the starting of the project
Reasons behind the choice of the IE	Receive financial aid from the World Bank & IMF	To gain power	To legitimize their actions
Resources/Network/ Power	Presence of resources Absence of power	Presence of resources and networks	Presence of resource, Networks and Power
Reaction of other actors)	Resistance	Resistance but implemented	Alignment
Reasons behind the choice of AA	Desire to maintain their power	Desire to increase own profits	Desire to improve their position
Results: success or failure of implementation	Difficult/ slow implementation or failure	Slow but successful implementation	Quick and successful implementation
Reasons for success/failure	The IE didn't have sufficient power to convince the other actors.	Success due to the parent company financial support	Success due to global and local pressures alignment.

5 Interpretation and Conclusion

The introduction of a new management dispositive created an organizational dynamic characterized mainly by a support for change and/or resistance to change. The social context of certain actors allowed them to be more attentive to global pressures. These actors are more likely to act as institutional entrepreneurs [4, 11, 12] while the other actors can only perceive the pressures visible to everyone. When there is alignment between global external pressures and local pressures, institutional entrepreneurs encounter less resistance because a large majority of actors are aware of the need to change. Actors who perceive only local pressures tend to resist change, if the latter results from an overall external pressure not aligned with a local pressure. Institutional entrepreneurs who initiated the adoption of the new dispositive must mobilize resources, networks and power to successfully institutionalize it. Once institutionalized, the new dispositive will give power to those who implemented it. Thus, they will favor institutional entrepreneurs and their allies and disfavor those who resisted it [4, 11, 12]. The institutional entrepreneurs and their allies will acquire a central role within the organization which could offer them a privileged post at the expense of other actors. Through adoption, institutional entrepreneurs also seek to legitimize some of their actions in order to make people believe that they are acting to improve their organization's situation.

In conclusion, the broad sociological approach of the new institutionalism (neo-institutionalism) explains the actors' reactions to the new management dispositive. It opens up promising horizons for further research in this field. Most importantly, the role of all actors in the institutionalization's process should be defined. The second way is to strengthen the alliances created when introducing a new dispositive. And the third way is to study the conflicts that arise between embedded and dis-embedded actors and the potential methods of resolving those conflicts.

References

1. Greenwood, R., Hinings, C.R., Whetten, D.: Rethinking institutions and organizations. J. Manage. Stud. **51**(7), 1206–1220 (2014)
2. Höllerer, M.A., et al.: The consequences of globalization for institutions and organizations. Sage Handbook Organ Inst, pp. 214–242 (2017)
3. Meyer, J.W., Rowan, B.: Institutionalized organizations: formal structure as myth and ceremony. Am. J. Sociol. **83**(2), 340–363 (1977)
4. DiMaggio, P., Powell, W.: The iron-cage revisited: institutional isomorphism and collective rationality in organizational field. Am. Sociol. Rev. **48**(April), 147–160 (1983)
5. DiMaggio, P.: Interest and agency in institutional theory. In: Zucker, L.G. (ed.) Institutional Patterns and Organizations: Culture and Environment, pp. 3–21. Cambridge (1988)
6. Becker-Blease, J.R., Sohl, J.E.: New venture legitimacy: the conditions for angel investors. Small Bus. Econ. **45**(4), 735–749 (2015)
7. Zimmerman, M., Zeitz, G.: Beyond survival: achieving new venture growth by building legitimacy. Acad. Manag. Rev. **27**(3), 414–431 (2002)
8. Leca, B., Huault, I.: Pouvoir: une analyse par les institutions. Revue Française de Gestion **35**(193), 133–149 (2009)
9. Battilana, J., Leca, B., Boxenbaum, E.: How actors change institutions: towards a theory of institutional entrepreneurship. Acad. Manag. Ann. **3**(1), 65–107 (2009)
10. Scott, R.: Institutional theory: contributing to a theoretical research program. In: Smith, K.G., Hitt, M.A. (eds.) Great Minds in Management: The Process of Theory Development. Oxford University Press, Oxford, UK (2004)
11. Foucault, M.: Surveiller et punir. Gallimard, Paris (1976)
12. Maugeri, S.: Travail, dispositifs de gestion et domination. Communication aux XIes Journées de Sociologie du Travail, pp. 20–22, juin 2007
13. Charreaux, G.: Concilier Finance et Management, un problème d'architecture organisation-nelle. Revue Française de Gestion **8–9**(198–199), 343–368 (2009)
14. Prahalad, C.K., Doz, Y.L.: The Multinational Mission, Balancing Global Integration With Local Responsiveness. Free Press, New York; Collier Macmillan, London (1987)

15. Arida, J., Harfouche, A.: L'institutionnalisation des standards internationaux au sein de la filiale libanaise d'une multinationale: le cas des normes ISO et IFRS. Proche Orient Etudes en Manag. **23**, 1–24 (2011)
16. Holm, P.: The dynamics of institutionalization: transformation processes in Norwegian fisheries. Adm. Sci. Q. **40**(3), 398–422 (1995)
17. Scott, R.: Institutions and Organizations, 2nd edn. Sage, Thousand Oaks, CA (2001)
18. Zilber, T.B.: Institutionalization as an interplay between actions, meanings and actors: the case of a rape crisis center in Israel. Acad. Manag. J. **45**(1), 234–254 (2002)
19. Peng, M.W., Luo, Y.: Managerial ties and firm performance in a transition economy: the nature of a micro-macro link. Acad. Manag. J. **43**(3), 486–501 (2000)
20. Pfeffer, J., Salancik, G.R.: The external control of organizations: a resource dependence perspective. Harper et Row, New York (1978)
21. Boxenbaum, E., Battilana, J.: Importation as innovation: transposing managerial practices across fields. Strat. Organ. **3**(4), 1–29 (2005)
22. Leca, B., Naccache, P.: A critical realist approach to institutional entrepreneurship. Organization **13**(5), 627–651 (2006)
23. DiMaggio, P.: Constructing an organizational field as a professional project: U.S. Art Museums, 1920–1940. In: Powell, W.W., DiMaggio, P.J. (eds.) The New Institutionalism in Organizational Analysis, pp. 267–292. Chicago University Press, Chicago (1991)
24. Fligstein, N.: Social skills and the theory of fields. Sociol. Theory **19**(2), 105–125 (2001)
25. Rao, H.: Caveat emptor: the construction of nonprofit consumer watchdog organizations. Am. J. Sociol. **103**(4), 912–961 (1998)
26. Wade-Benzoni, K.D., Hoffman, A.J., Thompson, L.L., Moore, D.A., Gillespie, J.J., Bazerman, M.H.: Barriers to resolution in ideologically based negotiations: the role of calues and institutions. Acad. Manag. Rev. **27**(1), 41–57 (2002)
27. Bernoux, Ph.: Encyclopédie des Ressources Humaines. Paris; Allouche, J. (dir.), Gazier, B., Huault, I., Louart, P., Schmidt, G. (comité de pilotage), Vuibert (2003)
28. Demers, C.: De la gestion du changement à la capacité à changer: l'évolution de la littérature sur le changement organisationnel de 1945 à aujourd'hui. Gestion-revue internationale de gestion **24**(3), 131–139 (1999)
29. Midler, C.: Logique de la mode managériale. In: Annales des mines, gérer et comprendre, pp. 74–85 (1986)
30. DiMaggio, P., Powell, W.: The New Institutionalism in Organizational Analysis. Chicago University Press, Chicago (1991)
31. Barley, S., Tolbert, P.: Institutionalization and structuration: studying the links between action and institution. Organ. Stud. **18**(1), 93–117 (1997)
32. Menard, S.: Longitudinal Research. Sage Publications, Newbury Park (1991)
33. Harfouche, A., Robbin, A.: e-government implementation in developing countries: a neo-institutional approach to explain failure. Ex. Lebanon, MCIS2012, Proc. vol. 21 (2012)
34. Ciborra, C.: Interpreting e-government and development: efficiency, transparency or governance at a distance? Inf. Technol. People **18**(3), 260–279 (2005)
35. Ciborra, C., Navarra, D.: Good governance, development theory, and aid policy: risks and challenges of e-government in Jordan. Inf. Technol. Dev. **11**(2), 141–159 (2005)
36. Harfouche, A., Robbin, A.: e-Government implementation in developing countries. In: Mola, L., Pennarola, F., Za, S. (eds.) From Information to Smart Society: Environment, Politics and Economics. Springer's Lecture Notes in Information Systems and Organisation Series, vol. 5, pp. 315–327 (2015)
37. Kostova, T., Roth, K.: Adoption of an organizational practice by subsidiaries of multinational corporations: institutional and relational effects. Acad. Manag. J. **45**(1), 215–233 (2002)

Transformational Process of the Implementation of an Information System Dispositive in an Organization: The Role of Power and Interests from an Institutional Perspective

Antoine Harfouche⦿, Jamil Arida and Georges Aoun

Abstract This paper addresses the role of power and interests in implementing a new Information System (IS) in an organization. It examines how responses to external pressures and expectations can be led by powerful agents that can use resources, and their membership to relevant social and institutional groupings in order to generate a transformational process in their organization. To study these interactions, the paper adopts the Institutional Theory and more specifically the circuits of power introduced by Backhouse et al. [1]. Based on a case study of the implementation of an integrated IS in a private University in Lebanon, this paper portrays how the implementation of such dispositive results from the interactions of power among the different actors and stakeholders involved. The case study also shows how the different interests and objectives of actors and stakeholders were influenced by exogenous contingencies and institutional forces. It shows how IS can become a dispositive of power that can replace the chain of command and organizational structure authority. Finally, this paper discusses theoretical and practical implications for the future development of these results.

Keywords Institutional theory · Institutional entrepreneurs · Institutional change · Praxis · Power · Interests · Transformational process of IS

1 Introduction

The role of Information and communication technologies (ICT) in organizations has evolved from a technical support toward a strategic role [2]. Indeed, ICT has been recognized as an important catalyst of the organizational transformation. Transformational process in which the intra-organizational political dynamics can completely change the organization [3].

A. Harfouche (✉)
Université Paris Nanterre, Nanterre, France
e-mail: antoineharfouche@icto.info; antoine.h@parisnanterre.fr

J. Arida · G. Aoun
Université Saint Joseph, Beyrouth, Lebanon

© Springer Nature Switzerland AG 2020
Y. Baghdadi et al. (eds.), *ICT for an Inclusive World*,
Lecture Notes in Information Systems and Organisation 35,
https://doi.org/10.1007/978-3-030-34269-2_31

This change is embedded in multiple levels of interpenetrating, incompatible institutional arrangements and contradictions [4].

The aim of this paper is to explore the transformational process generated by the implementation of an integrated IS in organization used as a dispositive of power. We adopt the definition of dispositive proposed by Foucault [5] as "an heterogeneous ensemble consisting of discourses, institutions, architectural forms, regulatory decisions, law, administrative measures, scientific statements, philosophical, moral and philanthropic proportions-in short: the said as much as the Unsaid" [5]. The dispositive will be considered as a mode of comprehension, or a diagnostic tool that permits us to grasp emergent strategies as they are realized, traversed, and leave their mark on the organization [6].

In order to understand the recursive process that results from the implementation of this new system, we adopted an institutional perspective. Indeed, according to Nielsen et al. [7], the Institutional Theory has become a more dominant perspective in IS. It offers the possibility to explore the process of accommodating conflicting institutional demands and constraints [8].

While we acknowledge that individual preferences and choices cannot be understood apart from the larger cultural setting and historical period in which they are embedded [9], we also argue that power and interests play important roles in organizations decisions related to IS implementation. Therefore, we consider that the transformational process of IS in organizations is the outcome of a political struggle among multiple social constituencies with unequal power [4].

The empirical context for our research is the Lebanese higher education, a sector comprising organizations that serve important social values. Based on in-depth interviews conducted with key decision makers of a Lebanese private University, we describe how the introduction of an integrated IS in this University initially organized as a federation of schools and institutes changed the distribution of power in this institution. We analyze the effects of IS on the University's decision-making and process. We focus specifically on how power operates silently but relentlessly in the implementation and institutionalization of such dispositive, and brings to light valuable insights into the social and political processes accompanying the implementation. The case study shows that the IS can change the distribution of power beyond organizational authority and IS can become a dispositive of power that can replace the organization's chain of command

2   Institutional Embeddedness and Change

During the past decades, neo-institutional theorists have been able to offer interesting insights into the processes that explain how institutional pressures force organizations to adopt similar practices or structures [10] to gain legitimacy and support [11]. Indeed, in its early stages, the Institutional Theory started by focusing on the pressures and constraints of the institutional collective and interconnected environments that includes not only the governmental agencies, regulatory structures, laws, courts, and professions [12], but also interest groups and public opinion [13, 14].

Indeed, according to Suddaby et al. [15], the Institutional Theory offers a clear understanding of how individual perceptions are embedded in broader cognitive schemes [16], of the process by which "actors" and "actorhood" are socially constructed [17, 18], and of the role of social institutions in explaining how practices are maintained and reproduced [19].

In this context, much of organizational decision making was seen as based on myths and ceremonies elaborately constructed from prevailing and highly rationalized expectations of how an organization should function [20] in order to increase its legitimacy [21]. Institutions were defined as "socially constructed, routine-reproduced programs or rule systems" [22]. They were considered as firmly rooted in taken-for-granted rules, norms, and routines [23, 24].

But recently, the Institutional Theory has become a more dominant perspective in IS research through which processes of continuity and change are interpreted and understood [3]. In this context, institutions are not anymore considered as only constraints on action but also as the objects of constant maintenance or modification through action [25]. Indeed, according to Holm [26], institutions, while they are products of action, also constitute action. They are nested systems containing two kind of interconnected actions: (1) practical actions guided by the established institutional order, and (2) political actions geared toward creating new or changing old institutions. According to [26], the "practical" and "political" modes of action are not completely separate. On the contrary, "much of the dynamics of institutional processes can be traced to the interconnections between these two levels of action".

The important implication of this recursive intertwining is that we do not see these interdependent actions as occurring at different levels; practical actions do not occur at the user's level and then get transformed into taken-for-granted routines. Instead, practical actions must be aligned with political actions in order to create change.

Indeed, according to Seo and Creed [4], institutional contradictions initiate praxis and praxis mediates between institutional contradictions and institutional change with subsequent institutionalization of these changes. They propose that four factors compose the mediating construct of praxis: (1) potential change agents, (2) a reflective shift in consciousness, (3) actor mobilization and (4) collective action.

Based on this theory, we consider in this paper that inefficiency, non-adaptability, inter-institutional incompatibilities and misaligned interests inherent in existing institutions create institutional contradictions that set the stage for institutional change. When institutional contradictions create sufficient tension and when the mediating effect of praxis develops sufficient strength to modify existing institutional logics, embedded institutional entrepreneurs become change agents [27]. Perceiving these tensions, institutional entrepreneurs are collectively transformed from passive recipients of institutional direction to active actors [28] with motivation to mitigate tensions through resolution of institutional contradictions [4].

They engage in the articulation of a vision of change and the mobilization of allies to support this vision. They reconfigure systems of meaning and institutional logics [29] transform existing institutions and sometimes create new ones [30].

3 Power, Interests, and Transformational Process of IS

The role of power and interest in transforming organizations is an important topic in the Institutional Theory. The relationships between power, institutions, and organizational change are complex [31]. Indeed, power and institutions can affect each other. Actors can find it advantageous to change their organization to acquire more power, just as institutions limit what actors can do [32].

Backhouse et al. [1] adapted Clegg's [33] definition of power "as a force like electricity, which circulates through social relations and working practices". It may include the ability to directly influence others, set agendas, and become part of the unquestioned institutional order [34]. According to Backhouse et al. [1], there are three circuits of power: the episodic circuit, the social integration, and the systemic circuit. The episodic circuit emphasizes changes in the organizational context that are manifested when a certain person A makes another person B do something the latter would otherwise not do. The social integration circuit focuses on symbolic power associated with rules of meaning, status, organizational positions, and membership impacting on social relations, alliances, and necessary conditions that provide A with the legitimation, authority, influence, and access to resources to exercise power over B. The systemic circuit shows power circulating through techniques of production influencing working practices and enabling B's compliance.

From Lawrence and Suddaby [35] perspective, power is often acquired and expressed through episodes of institutional work.

Individuals rely on their networks to gather the financial and symbolic resources needed that they can use to wield power [31]. They can acquire the authority to influence events in the organization. They can create divisions or otherwise restructure an organization in order to increase their own power and that of their allies [36, 37].

4 Research Methodology

Data collection took place between Feb and May 2015. After a period of intensive e-mail exchange and telephone conversations, we developed an interview guide using the institutional theoretical framework (see Appendix A). Based on this guide, we conducted 9 one-on-one semi-structured interviews with key decision makers (see Appendix B) of a Lebanese private University. Each interview session lasted for about 50–55 min. After the interviews, e-mails were exchanged and Skype meetings were organized to explore issues that required further clarification. Besides the interviews, other documents and materials were analyzed during the period of the fieldwork (see Appendix C). The combination of data collected from interviews with other data from the organization's minutes of meetings and e-mail communications provided us with theoretical saturation. According to Eisenhardt [38], the theoretical saturation denotes confidence that the data collected constitutes a comprehensive picture of the phenomenon under study.

To manage the complexity of data, our analysis unfolded in stages. First, we read through the collected material to gain a chronology of major events [39]. We identified antecedent conditions and major events that took place between 1998 and 2008 related to the IS implementation within the private University. The next stage was more directly linked to our research question and our theoretical constructs. After coding the interviews, we identified four themes: the context of IS introduction and external pressures, the process of IT institutionalization in the organization, the role and reaction of different actors, and the effect of the organization's management.

5 Case Study—Implementation of an Integrated IS in a Private University in Lebanon

5.1 Universities in Developing Countries

Universities are widely regarded not only as teaching establishments but also as organizations that create new knowledge and support social communities. In developing countries, they are regarded as key institutions in processes of social change and development [40]. In Lebanon for example, after many years of war, universities played a key role in building new institutions of the society, in encouraging and facilitating new cultural values, and in training and socializing new elites.

Nevertheless, universities in developing countries have many disadvantages compared to universities in developed countries in terms of based knowledge, research, supporting tools, infrastructure and resources. The budget of universities in developing countries is a fraction of universities budget in developed countries. Under great institutional pressures, a number of universities have implemented strategies and procedures that improve their legitimacy and support.

5.2 The Historical Start

This private University started with three main schools (Medicine, law and engineering), each of these schools had a distinct strong identity and a separate administration. Later on, all the other schools and institutes followed these three by creating their distinct identity and by moving to separate campuses.

All of these institutes recruited student with the baccalaureate degree. They offered diploma similar to what was given at that time by French universities. After completing two years of study, students can have a first degree known as «Diplôme d'études universitaires générales» (DEUG), followed by a third year «Licence» which was the equivalent of the Bachelor's degree. Then, students had the choice to start working or to enter the «Maîtrise», which was a one-year Master degree. After the Maîtrise, they can choose to do a specialization known as «Diplôme d'études supérieures spécialisées» (DESS), or to do a one-year research degree known as «Diplôme d'étude approfondies» (DEA). The DEA was a preparation for the «Doctorat» which takes a minimum of three years of research; all the programs were following a yearly cycle. Some institutions dedicated to specific subjects offered also specific diploma such as «Diplôme d'ingenieur» that was awarded to students after five years of study of engineering and «Doctorat de pratique de Pharmacie» awarded to students after five years of study of Pharmacy.

5.3 The Adoption of the ECTS and the Need for Change

Historically, this private University had strong ties with France through the French Embassy in Lebanon. "In 1999, the French Ambassador in Lebanon informed the rector of the private University that through the Bologna Accords, Europe is adopting the European Credit Transfer and Accumulation System (ECTS). He expressed his fear that if the private University do not adopt quickly the ECTS this will curb its cooperation with France and Europe" E1.

But at that time, the Rector of this private University had no power to impose his vision on the independent faculties and institutions of this private University. Indeed, "every Faculty, School, and Institute had its own independent administration (budgeting, students' records, alumni, communication, social assistance, marketing, admission, program development, research…) with dedicated staff to run these operations" E1 and E4. "Every School and Institute had autonomy in strategic decisions such as purchasing, hiring and firing personnel and Faculty, managing its resources and setting its academic calendar. The Deans were considered as top managers of their institutions" E1.

"The Rector was a kind of a façade and a formal representative who had only to sign diplomas and documents" E2. The decision was in the hand of the Deans and Directors of independent faculties and Institutes. "Sometimes, if the Dean of a "strong" faculty takes a decision contradictory to the rules and status of the university, the Dean had to fill a form or a request, sign it, and ask for the signature of the Rector to get the decision done" E3. "The rector was member of the University Council", E1, "this council was composed of the University Rector, all vice-Rectors, and Deans and Directors of faculties and institutes". "It was considered as a federation with limited efficiency due to the large number of participants with divergent and sometimes contradictory objectives" E4. "For more efficiency in the coordination of the different components activities, the university created a restricted council for consultancy known as the University Board that was composed from the Rector, his vice-rectors, and one Dean from each Campus" E3.

At the beginning of 2002, with the ECTS pressures, the University council has nominated a "Council for Strategic thinking" for a mandate of 5 years (2002–2007) in order to prepare a strategic plan that takes into consideration the University future challenges while preparing a quick adoption of the ECTS. Indeed, during this period, the role of this private University was changing from an institution helping young generation to resist and to survive after a long war, to an institution that creates bridges between communities and fractions by delivering high quality teaching and training for the development of the country and the region. Therefore, there was a need internally to overcome the geographical, managerial, and organizational distances that separate its institutes and schools, and externally to protect its bridges with France, Europe, and the world. Therefore, on the internal organizational level, there was an urgent need for common rules and procedures to avoid subjectivity and to reduce the interference of personal considerations in decision-making. On the external partners' level, this university had to keep and protect its historical strong ties with France through the adoption of the ECTS.

5.4   From ECTS Implementation to the Implementation of an Integrated IS

The ECTS system was designed to promote the mobility of teachers, researchers and students, to ensure that teaching was of a high quality, and to embed a unified dimension into higher education. However, the resistance to change was very high due to the long tradition of institutions' full independence and their strong identity. "For people in strategic positions, there was a fear from full transparency and doubts from peer comparison" E6. "For most of employees, the ECTS bring them extra work without adding any academic or qualitative value" E5.

Therefore, after many technical, managerial, and human problems in the implementation of the ECTS, the Vice-Rector for Administrative Affairs found that it was nearly impossible to influence the ECTS implementation with his existing authority. Without additional effort, the Rectorate was an office with limited influence, and there were limits to his resources.

The vice-Rector for Administrative Affairs tried to acquire powers that would allow him to force the implementation of the ECTS. Therefore, he used the IS dispositive as a tactic to achieve his goal. The aim of the IS dispositive was to leverage normative resources into coercive resources. His strategy was implemented in three steps.

First, he used his position as member of the University Council to create the "Technology Committee" (was later transformed into the powerful "Steering Committee"). In composing this committee, he created a coalition by recruiting allies with key persons from all faculties, schools, and institutes. Indeed, this committee was composed of a selection of motivated Deans (one from each Campus) and a group of specialized persons with shared perception of the role of IS. The announced aim of the committee was to plan the implementation of an integrated IS at the University level. "A system that can connect the university components at all levels, to implement common procedures, to adopt a central students database with online students registration, and a common regulation for the Faculty of all Schools and Institutes" E1 and E6.

The ambitious, large-scale IS project was initiated in 2000. "The decision was to build an in-house platform instead of buying a standard system from SAP or Oracle and make adaptations" E6. The new platform was set up in sections allowing the users to use it gradually over 10 years (2000–2010), the structure and the processes were modified according to the decision of IT implementation and were in place a year later in 2001.

In its early stages, the new IS dispositive was criticized. "Some Deans complained about the Jacobinism of the vice-Rector for Administrative Affairs, and his IS dispositive" E4. But with time, the dispositive became a powerful vehicle for introducing new organizational methods, new academic agendas, and in the same time, for gaining specific experiences in designing and implementing integrated systems, and for gaining more legitimacy for the Central administration (Rectorate).

Second, after quick success in the implementation of an integrated IS, the Technology Committee was quickly transformed into a "Steering Committee". During eight years, this committee gained power by redesigning all the university processes and by developing new policies that redefined the role of the central administration (Rectorate). This redesign conducted the transfer of many administrative tasks from the institutions to the Central office (accounting, procurement, finance, human resources …).

Third, the coalition was extended outside the Steering Committee by the promotion of the most supportive members of this committee into the University's new leadership. Deans members of the Steering Committee were appointed vice-Rectors, and other specialists as Campus Administrators. The purpose was to have a dependable group of influencers and administrators who would support change.

Using the terminology of institutional work theory, the vice-Rector for Administrative Affairs combined vestment (attaching individuals to practices and rights) with an implementation of new controls [35] that allowed these actors to expand their power by acquiring the authority to coerce others and combining institutions.

6 IS as a Dispositive of Power

The IS dispositive was successfully used by the vice-Rector for Administrative Affairs by deploying his knowledge, skills, reputation, social connections, his membership to relevant social and institutional groupings, and other resources so that he could rewrite the chain of command and acquires more authority for the Central administration (Rectorate) through power transfer from the independent Faculties.

He acquired extensive powers by challenging the private University chain of command and its organizational structure authority. The path to more authority arrived by creating consistency that legitimizes itself through a "hybridized institutional regime" [31, 41] that merged old organizational structure authority (University Council and

University Board) with new structures (the Council for Strategic thinking and the Steering Committee).

The implementation of an integrated IS at the university level installed a systematic circuit of power. The consequences of the changes initiated by the systemic circuit of power that resulted from the implementation of the IS dispositive were directly related to the recruitment of the new administrative staff in the Central administration (Rectorate).

The size of the IT department in charge of designing, implementing, and maintaining the platform has increased and its role became more strategic. The intensive training of the users required increasing the size of the human resources department. The development of online courses in many programs changed completely the way things are done at the Faculties level.

The transformation of the "Technology Committee" into the "Steering Committee" created a social integration circuit of power. "Several changes in the decision making process were noticed with less delays in the decision making, better quality in decision making through professionalism and accurate information (past decisions, number of decisions, tools ...), better follow up of decisions and more participants in the process with higher involvement" E1.

Such results were impossible without the IS dispositive. After its institutionalization, most of the private University's actors took this fact for granted and did not even ask about how and why things have changed. The success of the transformational process is an example of the functioning of the episodic circuit of power.

Instead of counting on exogenous capacities for change, the IS dispositive offered an opportunity to change the circuit of power by installing new practices and thus made movement response an endogenous process.

7 Conclusion

The transformational process of the IS dispositive brings additional insight to studies of organizational change by providing crucial micro-foundations for the rise of new institutional orders.

The decisions about the implementation of an IS dispositive is not normally reached based on a rational-logical process, but are instead constructed through the constant realignment of interests among the actors involved. In this paper, our aim was to reveal how realignment reshape the power mechanisms in an organization. Indeed, the IS dispositive can create social coalitions among actors which can affect the structure of authority in an organization.

The motivation does not always arise from the economic or strategic incentives, but mainly from the influences of exogenous contingencies. The decision of the implementation of an integrated IS first requires decision makers to reach a consensus on a set of requirements. This is not possible if all members of the organization's authority do not share a common perception of the role of IS. As shown, the case study of the private University presents highly pertinent evidence about how key actors form alliances within the circuits of power and generate important dynamic of change by designing and implementing an IS dispositive. The systematic circuit of power resulting from the design and the implementation of new IS dispositive leverages normative resources into coercive resources. Indeed, the introduction of a new integrated IS will help institutional entrepreneurs obtaining sufficient support and resources that change the power structure and improve their social integration circuit of power in the organization. The transformational process created and institutionalized a new episodic circuit of power that led to the connection of the university components at all levels, the adoption of common procedures, the implementation of a central students' database, online students' registration, the implementation of common rules for the Faculty of all schools and institutes, the transfer of many administrative tasks from the institutions to the Central office (accounting, procurement, finance, human resources …).

This case study shows how power in organizations is enabled, shaped, and then constrained by shifting institutional regimes. It underlines the role played by the introduction of a new IS dispositive in obtaining sufficient support and resources that led to changing the power structure in an organization. Indeed, in our case, the new dispositive produced a transformational process in which the intra-organizational political dynamics changed the chain of command of the organization.

Appendix A: Interview Guide

Interview's objective/Presentation of research to stakeholders

Understanding the meaning of IS implementation project for key decision makers (Top Management/Rectorate, Deans, Directors (ex: financial, HR …), IT department …) at a Lebanese Private University and how it was implemented, how far and with which effects on the Organization's management.

QUESTION 1. Each unit (faculty) has its own distinctive strategy, aim, cultural that can have impact on the IS implementation. What do you think is the specificity of your unit (faculté)?

Theme 1: Your experience in the process of IS implementation

QUESTION 2. At the time of the introduction of a system integrator IS, in which of your responsibilities you had the occasion to address issues relevant to the IS implementation?

QUESTION 2 Up Question: in which position? When? Which project? Which internal political context? Which interlocutors?

QUESTION 2 Up Question: In which areas: finance, RH, program, administrative tasks …?

QUESTION 3 How do you define an integrated IS?

QUESTION 4 What was the result? What are the effects (negative, positive) of this project for the University: from an economic point of view, from strategic, organizational, and political points of view (such as functioning of institutions and relations between them and with the rectorate)?

QUESTION 5 What were/are the progress indicators of the IS implementation from the institutional point of view? What were/are the most relevant to you? Why?

Theme 2: the different actors of the process

QUESTION 6 Why the IS project has become strategic at the University level? Iin your unit?

QUESTION 7 At that time, what made this project important? New strategies/management? When? By whom?

QUESTION 8 Who financed?

QUESTION 8A Up question: It seems that it was a project supported by the rectorate, was it imposed from outside? Was there any specific commitment from the University? What was this commitment?

QUESTION 9 What was the influence of the "Recteur" in this process? When? Why?

QUESTION 9A Have you felt a kind of control from the rectorate? When and why did they do? How do you think it has been felt by your institution actors (prof, employees, students…)? How did they react?

QUESTION 10 Did you ask for any help from experts? Have they become important/influential? (Did they contribute to compromise)?

QUESTION 11 What was the role of the different actors in the process of IS implementation?

QUESTION 11A Up question: Have your team followed up the project? How? What were their effects on the process?

QUESTION 12 Y - Was there any compromise between the actors? Entities? Between the Rector and the faculties? Between IT and faculties?

QUESTION 13 At what level compromises were made in the areas targeted by the new IS? On what topics? When? Between whom?

QUESTION 13A Did you feel that there was failed compromise? When? Why? Between whom?

QUESTION 13B Did you make any compromises? Refused compromise? When? Why? With whom?

QUESTION 14 From a technological point of view, where the choice of material and technique was made? By whom?

Theme 3: The effects on the strategic, organizational, and administrative part

QUESTION 15 Ask questions about the centralization decentralization and its relationship with the project

QUESTION 16 Do you think that the places of power changed? In the context of this project, did you go in other places, meet other people? Who? Why? When? When did it change? Why? What were the consequences?

QUESTION 18 There are several stages of implementation of IS, what stage can the University reach, and why?

Appendix B: Interviewees

Position	Role	Interview method
Dean of the Business and Management Faculty	– Member of the University Council – Member of the University Board – President of the University Council for Strategic thinking	– Face-to-face interview – e-mail, – Telephone interview
Dean of the Engineering School	– Member of the University Council for strategic thinking – Member of the University Council – Member of the University Board	Face-to-face interview
Dean of the Dental School	– Member of the University Council – Member of the University Board	Face-to-face interview
Vice-rector for administrative affairs	– Member of the University Council – Member of the University Board – Founder of the "Technology Committee" that was transformed later to the "Steering Committee"	Face-to-face interview
Dean of human sciences faculty	– Member of the University Council – Member of the University Board	Face-to-face interview
Director of the IS Department	– Designer of the integrated system – Member of the "Technology Committee" and the "Steering Committee"	Face-to-face interview
Campus administrator	Director of a pilot campus	Face-to-face interview

Appendix C: Analyzed Documents

Documents
Minutes of the "Technology Committee" that was transformed later to the "Steering Committee"
Strategic Plan

References

1. Backhouse, J., Hsu, C., Leiser, S.: Circuits of power in creating de jure standards: Shaping and international information systems security standard. Manag. Inf. Syst. Quarterly **30**, 413–438 (2006)
2. Henderson, J.C., Venkatraman, N.: Strategic alignment -leveraging information technology for transforming organizations. IBM Syst. J. **32**(1), 4–16 (1993)
3. Mignarat, M., Rivard, S.: Positioning the institutional perspective in information systems research. J. Inf. Technol. **24**(4), 369–391 (2009)
4. Seo, M.-G., Creed, W.D.: Institutional contradictions, praxis, and institutional change: a dialectical perspective. Acad. Manag. Rev. **27**(2), 222–247 (2002)
5. Foucault, M.: Discipline and punish: the birth of the prison. Penguin Books, London (1977)
6. Raffnsøe, S., Gudmand-Høyer, M., Thaning, M.S.: Foucault's dispositive: the perspicacity of dispositive analytics in organizational research. Organization, pp 1–27 (2014)
7. Nielsen, J., Mathiassen, L., Newell, S.: Theorization and translation in information technology institutionalization: evidence from Danish home care. MIS Q. **38**(1), 165–186 (2014)
8. Pache, A.-C., Santos, F.: When worlds collide: the internal dynamics of organizational responses to conflicting institutional demands. Acad. Manag. Rev. **35**(3), 455–476 (2010)
9. Powell, W.W.: Expanding the scope of institutional analysis. In: Powell, W.W., DiMaggio, P.J. (eds.) The New Institutionalism in Organizational Analysis, pp. 183–203. University of Chicago Press, Chicago, IL (1991)
10. Meyer, J.W., Rowan, B.: Institutionalized organizations: formal structure as myth and ceremony. Am. J. Sociol. **83**(2), 340 (1977)
11. DiMaggio, P.J., Powell, W.W.: The iron cage revisited: Institutional isomorphism and collective rationality in organizational fields. Am. Sociol. Rev., pp. 147–160 (1983)
12. Scott, W.R.: The adolescence of institutional theory. Adm. Sci. Q. **32**, 493–511 (1987)
13. Scott, W.R.: Organizations: rational, natural, and open systems, 2nd edn. Prentice-Hall, Englewood Cliffs, NJ (1987)
14. Harfouche, A., Robbin, A.: E-government impletation in developing countries: a neoinstitutional approach to explain failure. An example from Lebanon. In: MCIS 2012 Proceedings. Paper 21 (2012)
15. Suddaby, R., Seidl, D., Le, J.K.: Strategy-as-practice meets neo-institutional theory. Strat. Organ. **11**(3), 329–344 (2013)
16. Johnson, S.C., Dweck, F.S., Chen, F.S.: Evidence for infants' internal working models of attachment. Psychol. Sci. **18**(6), 501–502 (2007)
17. Hwang, H., Colyvas, J.A.: Problematizing actors and institutions in institutional work. J. Manag. Inq. **20**(1), 62–66 (2011)
18. Meyer, J.W.: Reflections on institutional theories of organizations. Sage Handbook Organ. Inst., pp. 790–811 (2008)
19. Corradi, G., Gherardi, S., Verzelloni, L.: Manag. Learn. **41**(3), 265–283 (2010)
20. Brusson, N.: The Organization of Hypocrisy. Copenhagen Business School Press (2002)

21. Colyvas, J.A., Powell, W.W.: Roads to institutionalization: the remaking of boundaries between public and private science. Res. Organ. Behav. **27**, 305–353 (2006)
22. Jepperson, R.L.: Institutions, institutional effects, and institutionalism. In: DiMaggio, P.J., Powell, W.W. (eds.) The New Institutionalism in Organizational Analysis. University of Chicago Press, Chicago (1991)
23. Powell, W.W., DiMaggio, P.J.: The New Institutionalism In Organizational Analysis. University of Chicago Press, Chicago, IL (1991)
24. Tolbert, P.S., Zucker, L.G: Institutional sources of change in the formal structure of organizations: the diffusion of civil service reform, 1880–1935. Admin. Sci. Quart., pp. 22–39 (1983)
25. Barley, S.R., Tolbert, P.S.: Institutionalization and structuration: studying the links between action and institution. Organ. Stud. **18**(1), 93–117 (1997)
26. Holm, P.: The dynamics of institutionalization: transformation processes in Norwegian fisheries. Admin. Sci. Quart., pp. 398–422 (1995)
27. DiMaggio, P.: Interest and agency in institutional theory. In: Zucker, L.G. (ed.) Institutional Patterns and Organizations: Culture and Environment, pp. 3–22. Ballinger, Cambridge, MA (1988)
28. Battilana, J., Leca, B., Boxenbaum, E.: How actors change institutions: towards a theory of institutional entrepreneurship. Acad. Manag. Ann. **3**(1), 65–107 (2009)
29. King, B.G., Soule, S.A.: Social movements as extra-institutional entrepreneurs: the effect of protests on stock price returns. Adm. Sci. Q. **52**(3), 413–442 (2007)
30. Maguire, S., et al.: Institutional entrepreneurship in emerging fields: HIV/AIDS treatment advocacy in Canada. Acad. Manag. J. **47**(5), 657–679 (2004)
31. Rojas, F.: Power through institutional work: acquiring academic authority in the 1968 third world strike. Acad. Manag. J. **53**(6), 1263–1280 (2010)
32. Freeland, R.: The myth of the m-form: governance, consent and organizational change. Am. J. Sociol. **102**(September), 483–526 (1996)
33. Clegg, S.R.: Frameworks of Power. Sage Publications, London (1989)
34. Lukes, S., Power: A Radical View, 2nd edn. Palgrave (2005)
35. Lawrence, T.B., Suddaby, R: Institutions and Institutional Work. SAGE Handbook Organ. Stud., p. 215 (2006)
36. Pfeffer, J.: Power in Organizations. Pitman, London (1981)
37. Pfeffer, J., Salancik, G.: The External Control of Organizations: A Resource Dependence Perspective. Harper and Row, New York (1978)
38. Eisenhardt, K.: Building theories from case study research. Acad. Manag. Rev. **14**(4), 532–550 (1989)
39. Miles, M.B., Huberman, A.M.: Qualitative Data Analysis: An Expanded Sourcebook, Thousand Oaks. Sage, Calif (1994)
40. Brennan, J., Lebeau, Y.: The role of universities in the transformation of societies. In: An International Research Project, Paper Presented at the CHER 15th Annual Conference, Vienna, Austria, 5–7 Sept 2002
41. Washington, M., Ventresca, M.J.: How organizations change: the role of institutional support mechanisms in the incorporation of higher education visibility strategies, 1874–1995. Organ. Sci. **15**(1), 82–97 (2004)

MENACIS 2018

Individual Intention to Become an Entrepreneur: Technological Perspective

Mousa Albashrawi and Tawfiq Alashoor

Abstract Since entrepreneurs contribute to the economy of nations by creating new ventures and job opportunities, they are considered valuable assets. Entrepreneurship literature has given much attention to what drives individuals to become entrepreneurs from various perspectives, however, it is lacking with regard to IT cognitive and emotional factors that can influence individuals to become entrepreneurs. This research in progress sheds light on the technological perspective and develops a theoretical model that extends theory of planned behavior by incorporating IT factors into established entrepreneurial models. Particularly, the developed model explains how general computer self-efficacy and computer anxiety can determine entrepreneurial intention. SEM is used to test the developed model and preliminary results are presented. Potential contributions are communicated to both academia and industry.

Keywords Entrepreneurial intention · TBP · IT · General computer self-efficacy · Computer anxiety

1 Introduction

Anecdotal evidence suggests that IT skills can play a fundamental role in intention to become an entrepreneur (i.e. entrepreneurial intention) [1]. For instance, individuals skillful at computer use and basic software programs are likely able to find and exploit potential opportunities to start up an IT-related business [2]. No doubt that acquiring IT skills is critical to streamline the process of starting up an IT business. However, it is argued that acquiring such skills is even necessary for starting up a non-IT business, considering today's technological and highly competitive business environment. To the best of our knowledge, there is only one study [2] that has investigated the role of IT on entrepreneurial intention. This study has shown that personal innovativeness with IT and computer self-efficacy significantly explain intention to

M. Albashrawi (✉) · T. Alashoor
College of Industrial Management, King Fahd University of Petroleum and Minerals, University Blvd, Dhahran 31261, Saudi Arabia
e-mail: bishrama@kfupm.edu.sa

© Springer Nature Switzerland AG 2020   469
Y. Baghdadi et al. (eds.), *ICT for an Inclusive World*,
Lecture Notes in Information Systems and Organisation 35,
https://doi.org/10.1007/978-3-030-34269-2_32

start up an IT business [2]. However, the results from Chen's [2] study are limited to entrepreneurial intention in the context of IT business. Against the backdrop of limited research on this phenomenon, we will empirically test the role that IT skills play in entrepreneurial intention in a broader domain. In particular, we developed a theoretical model that explains the role of general computer self-efficacy and computer anxiety on intention to become an entrepreneur, regardless of the business domain. Our research question is: How do general computer self-efficacy and computer anxiety impact entrepreneurial intention? We draw upon theory of planned behavior (TPB) and the literature on IS and entrepreneurship to develop the theoretical model and build a set of hypotheses.

General computer self-efficacy is defined as an individual's judgment of his/her competency across multiple computer application domains while computer anxiety represents an emotional factor defined as an expressive state of apprehension and fear to use a computer [3]. As business is becoming heavily dependent on computer usage (manifested in various business activities ranging from writing a business report to conducting a business transaction.), studying individuals' cognitive and emotional state towards computer when engaging in business startups becomes a driving need. Hence, it is possible to say that individuals who like to start a new business could be influenced by the level of techno-competency and technophobia. These distinct technos can be represented by general computer self-efficacy and computer anxiety, which reflect IT-specific individual differences. Therefore, we integrate them into TPB to examine their impact on creating new ventures.

This research in progress is expected to contribute to the literature in several ways. First, it explores how IT can play a role in determining entrepreneurial intention using the theoretical lens of TPB. The IT role in developing future ventures is nascent; thus, it is important to be emphasized at both IS and entrepreneurship literatures. Second, integrating computer anxiety into the theoretical model can complement TPB by addressing its limitation with regard to emotional elements [4]. Third, the study results could identify important practical insights and hence be communicated to policy makers, especially in higher education, in order to reinforce the mindset of entrepreneurs. With the analysis of different groups of students and their IT-specific differences, we can advise on incorporating various types of learning experiences through the promotion of greater computer self-efficacy.

The rest of this paper is structured as follows: related work in section two, followed by hypotheses development in section three, then research method in section four, data analysis and results in section five, and lastly conclusion in section six.

2   Related Work and Hypotheses Development

Entrepreneurial intention has been examined in extant research from various aspects; for example, psychological [5–8], multi-national [9], educational [10, 11], social [12], regional [13], and cultural [14]. In the entrepreneurship literature, three models have been predominantly used to explain and predict entrepreneurial intention [15]: the model of entrepreneurial event [16], the model of entrepreneurial ideas implementation [17], and Ajzen's [18] theory of planned behavior (TPB). Bird's model has less validation while both models of Shapero and Sokol [16] and TPB are considered to be equally effective in organizations emergence [19]. But what makes TPB better compared to other models, is its consistency in prediction, and its coherence and generalizability as a theoretical framework [9] as well as its validity that has been shown by thousands of studies across different contexts [6, 9, 11, 20].

TPB developed by Ajzen [18, 21] suggests that an individual's behavioral intention is influenced by three major factors: attitude, subjective norms, and perceived behavioral control. Attitude indicates whether an individual has a positive or negative assessment toward a specific behavior [20]. Subjective norms indicate the degree of social pressure on an individual to perform or avoid a specific behavior while perceived behavioral control indicates the degree of perceived ease or difficulty to perform a particular behavior [6]. In the context of entrepreneurial intention, several scholars have adopted and supported the predictive power of TPB [13, 22]. However, some scholars have argued that TPB lacks sufficiency because it cannot completely explain an individual intention towards a particular behavior [23]. As well, TPB does not involve any emotional factors that may affect individuals' behavioral intention [4].

Chen [2] emphasized the important role of IT skills in the context of entrepreneurship and called for future research examining this phenomenon. In this study, we incorporate general computer self-efficacy (a cognitive factor) and computer anxiety (an emotional factor) into TPB to explain entrepreneurial intention. By doing so, we are able to extend TPB's explanatory power from an IT perspective while addressing its limited consideration of emotional factors. The following section briefly discusses the established linkages between the predictors of TPB and entrepreneurial intention while focuses more on theorizing and developing the novel hypotheses pertaining to the impact of general computer self-efficacy and computer anxiety on entrepreneurial intention. Figure 1 depicts our research model.

2.1 The Three Pillars of Theory of Planned Behavior

Our suggested hypotheses are developed based on prior research. According to Gird and Bagraim [6], the thinking process to start a new venture is a planned behavior. This behavior can be affected by having a positive attitude, perceiving the ease of this behavior, and receiving social support from close individuals. These three pillars of TPB can empirically determine entrepreneurial intention among individuals as suggested by the literature [11, 13]. Thus, we replicate the three hypotheses tested in prior research:

H1: Attitude is positively related to an individual's intention to become an entrepreneur.

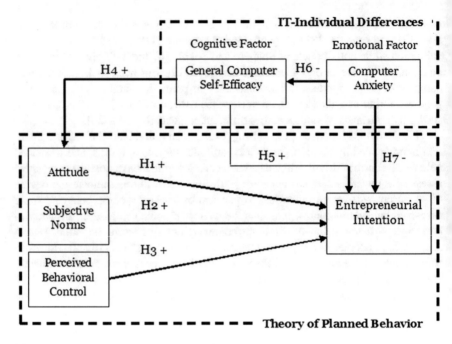

Fig. 1 Research model (*IT factors integrated to TPB*)

H2: Subjective norms are positively related to an individual's intention to become an entrepreneur.

H3: Perceived behavioral control is positively related to an individual's intention to become an entrepreneur.

2.2 General Computer Self-efficacy and Computer Anxiety

He and Freeman [3] illustrated that computer self-efficacy is a set of beliefs about having the capability to perform tasks using a computer; these beliefs can have either a direct or indirect effect through attitude on behavioral intention. Computer self-efficacy has been found to determine individuals' attitudes, particularly in the context of information systems [3] and Internet [24, 25]. Extending this to our context, those who are capable of interacting with various software applications and fixing common computer operational problems would be more likely to evaluate themselves positively and to show satisfactory attitude toward initiating a new business.

Individuals who show a high level of entrepreneurial self-efficacy will be more likely to engage in starting a new business [2]. Additionally, self-efficacy is considered to explain opportunity recognition and self-employment intention [19]. Hence, it can be argued that computer self-efficacy impacts entrepreneurial intention. For instance, individuals who possess good computer knowledge and skills are likely to show greater beliefs in their ability to develop a new enterprise. General computer self-efficacy, which is a special application of computer self-efficacy, has a tendency to influence one's career interests and choice [3]. According to the above discussion, we hypothesize that:

H4: General computer self-efficacy is positively related to an individual's attitude.
H5: General computer self-efficacy is positively related to an individual's intention to become an entrepreneur.

Computer anxiety reflects the affective components of "fear and apprehension, intimidation, hostility, and worries that one will be embarrassed, look stupid, or even damage the equipment" [26, p. 50]. Such a psychological state of affect can influence negatively general computer self-efficacy [27, 28]. He and Freeman [27] emphasize that female students feel more anxious towards using computers because they have a lower level of computer learning and experience compared to their counterparts of male students.

Computer anxiety can also have a negative impact on behavioral intention. According to Rana and Dwivedi [29], anxiety reduces adoption of e-government system. The psychological state embedded in computer anxiety can be extended to individual's behavioral intention in a different context. For instance, individuals who intend to be self-employed, but they are highly attached to old-fashioned ways to perform their job due to computer phobia. Intention to become an entrepreneur for these individuals can be significantly undermined because today's business world is highly dependent on computer and information technologies. This suggests a negative relationship between computer anxiety and entrepreneurial intention. According to the above, we hypothesize that:

H6: Computer anxiety is negatively related to an individual's general computer self-efficacy.
H7: Computer anxiety is negatively related to an individual's intention to become an entrepreneur.

3 Research Method

The targeted population for this study are college students. Students represent a good sample because they can be classified based on their study focus and accordingly provide us with groups of different levels of computer experience to compare. Two groups are included; the first group is computer-related major students and the second group is non-computer-related major students. We managed to recruit 90 students for our pilot. Structural equation modeling (SEM) are used to analyze the data via SmartPLS 3.0 software.

This study was conducted using a survey design. The survey had been developed from existing instruments in which all factors are well-established. Those factors were adapted from prior research but modified for the study context. Attitude, subjective norms, and perceived behavioral control were adapted from Vinogradov et al. [22]. Both general computer self-efficacy and computer anxiety were adapted from He and Freeman [3]. Intention to become an entrepreneur was adapted from Zhao et al. [30].

4 Data Analysis and Results

Students' demographics were analyzed and presented in the below table. The majority of the sample consisted of white, male students (69, 62%) who aged between 18 and 25 (64%) and completed high school (33%) as per Table 1 below.

Table 1 Participants demographics profile

Demographics	Frequency	Percentage (%)
Gender		
Male	56	62
Female	34	38
Age		
18–25	58	64
26–30	16	18
31–35	7	8
>35	9	10
Education		
High school graduate	30	33
Technical, trade, business after high school	3	3
Associate degree	20	22
Bachelor degree	29	32
Master degree	4	4
Ph.D.	1	1
Other	3	3
Ethnicity		
White	62	69
Black or African American	16	18
Asian	9	10
Native Hawaiian or Pacific Islander	1	1
Other	2	2

We followed a two-step process for analyzing our data; measurement model was firstly used to ensure reliability and validity of the used measures and structural model was secondly used to test the hypothesized relationships.

4.1 Measurement Model

The factors were evaluated in terms of their Cronbach's alpha (CA), composite reliability (CR), average variance extracted (AVE), variance inflation factor (VIF), and loadings (FL) as well as statistically described in terms of their means, and standard deviations (SD).

As per Table 2, all reliability and validity measures exceed the recommended thresholds. In particular, both CA and CR are greater than 0.7, thus good internal reliability is established. Also, satisfactory convergent validity is confirmed as both AVE and FL are greater than 0.5 and 0.7, respectively, except for the loading of PBC (0.686), which was removed in the structural model. Additionally, satisfactory discriminant validity is confirmed since the cross loadings indicate that the loadings on the intended constructs are greater than the loadings of other constructs. Lastly, there is no collinearity between the constructs because all VIF values are smaller than 5.

4.2 Preliminary Results and Discussion

As per Table 3, we conducted an incremental testing where we develop several regression models and add one more factor at a time. This helped to differentiate the various factors effects as per Fig. 2 below.

SEM-PLS results indicate that two TPB's pillars (attitude and perceived behavioral control) appear to significant determinants of individual's entrepreneurial intention. Similarly, general computer self-efficacy influences attitude positively. But surprisingly, the third TPB's pillar (subjective norms) appears to be insignificant determinant of entrepreneurial intention in all tested models. Hence, H1, H3, and H4 are supported but H2 is not.

However, general computer self-efficacy does not seem to predict the individual's intention to start a new business except for model 3; this implies that a standalone integration of general computer self-efficacy into TPB or can increase the intention to become an entrepreneur. When computer anxiety is related to general computer self-efficacy, a significant negative relationship may exist but when it is related to entrepreneurial intention, no relationship can exist (model 5). This means that computer anxiety has an indirect relationship with entrepreneurial intention instead. Overall, H5 is partially supported, H6 is fully supported, but H7 is not supported. The explained variance across the five models for entrepreneurial intention is considered very high (>74%), confirming the quality of our model.

Table 2 Constructs' reliability and validity

Constructs	Items	FL	Mean	SD	AT	SN	PBC	GCSE	CA	EI
Attitude (AT) CA = 0.935 CR = 0.951 AVE = 0.797 VIF = 2.014	AT1	0.791	4.844	1.452	**0.791**	0.488	0.505	0.358	−0.094	0.598
	AT2	0.944	4.900	1.713	**0.944**	0.489	0.567	0.339	−0.112	0.783
	AT3	0.889	5.000	1.732	**0.889**	0.451	0.575	0.247	−0.013	0.765
	AT4	0.925	5.144	1.589	**0.925**	0.471	0.586	0.185	0.025	0.738
	AT5	0.907	4.778	1.731	**0.907**	0.507	0.605	0.300	0.023	0.777
Subjective norms (SN) CA = 0.853 CR = 0.911 AVE = 0.773 VIF = 1.637	SN1	0.885	5.289	1.424	0.455	**0.885**	0.365	0.459	−0.161	0.411
	SN2	0.852	5.644	1.177	0.443	**0.852**	0.334	0.315	−0.068	0.393
	SN3	0.900	5.256	1.252	0.515	**0.900**	0.433	0.346	−0.061	0.480
Perceived behavioral control (PBC) CA = 0.915 CR = 0.934 AVE = 0.704 VIF = 1.753	PBC1	0.686	3.422	1.535	0.417	0.270	**0.686**	0.042	0.147	0.460
	PBC2	0.861	3.911	1.780	0.517	0.379	**0.861**	0.083	0.153	0.615
	PBC3	0.889	3.856	1.859	0.546	0.413	**0.889**	0.162	0.059	0.651
	PBC4	0.870	3.289	1.790	0.500	0.264	**0.870**	0.063	0.102	0.571
	PBC5	0.839	4.050	1.789	0.613	0.411	**0.839**	0.289	−0.069	0.696
	PBC6	0.873	3.922	1.695	0.583	0.410	**0.873**	0.188	0.037	0.628
General computer self-efficacy (GCSE) CA = 0.878 CR = 0.879 AVE = 0.623 VIF = 2.370	GCSE1	0.687	5.300	1.650	0.323	0.369	0.360	**0.687**	−0.413	0.366
	GCSE2	0.834	6.111	1.159	0.212	0.290	0.069	**0.834**	−0.562	0.222
	GCSE3	0.790	5.778	1.306	0.209	0.288	0.163	**0.790**	−0.491	0.242
	GCSE4	0.805	6.111	1.197	0.243	0.295	0.096	**0.805**	−0.576	0.274
	GCSE5	0.771	6.189	1.201	0.309	0.394	0.117	**0.771**	−0.517	0.338
	GCSE6	0.838	6.311	0.915	0.206	0.361	0.026	**0.838**	−0.560	0.176

(continued)

Table 2 (continued)

Constructs	Items	FL	Mean	SD	AT	SN	PBC	GCSE	CA	EI
Computer anxiety(CA)	CA1	0.787	2.889	1.773	0.002	−0.058	0.127	−0.497	**0.787**	−0.035
CA = 0.907	CA2	0.903	3.002	1.776	−0.050	−0.129	0.023	−0.572	**0.903**	−0.134
CR = 0.935	CA3	0.924	2.467	1.543	0.037	−0.053	0.118	−0.611	**0.924**	−0.046
AVE = 784	CA4	0.921	2.667	1.633	−0.110	−0.135	0.018	−0.648	**0.921**	−0.172
VIF = 1.969										
Entrepreneurial intention (EI)	EI1	0.910	4.833	1.881	0.849	0.466	0.633	0.415	−0.165	**0.910**
CA = 0.950	EI2	0.923	4.456	1.869	0.690	0.470	0.675	0.293	−0.112	**0.923**
CR = 964	EI3	0.949	4.585	1.962	0.783	0.428	0.677	0.276	−0.097	**0.949**
AVE = 0.870	EI4	0.948	4.522	1.916	0.741	0.463	7.727	0.293	−0.047	**0.948**
VIF = N/A										

Bold indicates factors loadings for each construct

Table 3 SEM-PLS regression analysis: the impact of GCSE and CA on EI (N = 90)

Variables	Model 1	Model 2	Model 3	Model 4	Model 5
H1: AT → EI	0.598*** (9.143)	0.597*** (9.051)	0.579*** (7.895)	0.580*** (8.283)	0.586*** (8.329)
H2: SN → EI	0.022 (0.317)	0.021 (0.305)	−0.018 (0.234)	−0.016 (0.228)	−0.004 (0.052)
H3: PBC → EI	0.339*** (5.390)	0.339*** (5.598)	0.345*** (5.539)	0.348*** (5.460)	0.357*** (6.119)
H4: GCSE → AT		0.332*** (3.695)	0.334*** (3.754)	0.319*** (3.150)	0.319*** (3.129)
H5: GCSE → EI			0.105* (1.660)	0.102 (1.488)	0.031 (0.403)
H6: CA → GCSE				−0.661*** (13.778)	−0.661*** (13.781)
H7: CA → EI					−0.093 (1.216)
R²	0.750	0.749	0.758	0.758	0.762
Adjusted R²	0.741	0.740	0.747	0.746	0.748

Note *$p < 0.10$, **$p < 0.05$, ***$p < 0.01$, *t-statistics inside the parentheses*

Fig. 2 PLS Analysis Results (*Model 5, t-statistics on arrows and R² inside circles*)

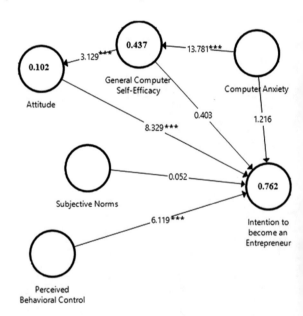

5 Conclusion and Future Steps

Entrepreneurs are perceived as valuable assets to any society as they contribute to the economy development by creating new ventures, which in turn leads to more job opportunities. Exploring IT role through general computer self-efficacy and computer anxiety is of a great value as it can help in determining whether individuals will become entrepreneurs. This study is one of the first attempts to test the relationship between IT-related factors and entrepreneurial intention; hence, the results may lend future research opportunities to build up on them. For example, investigating different but relevant IT-related factors on entrepreneurial intention may shed light on other important drivers to entrepreneurial development process.

We will attempt to recruit more sample for the full study and then divide the sample into computer-related and non-computer-related. This grouping will enable us to have a priori knowledge about the heterogeneity in the IT-related factors that can undermine the effect on the dependent variable (i.e. intentions). Such heterogeneity, if not accounted for, can lead to Type II error; in other words, even if there is an effect of the IT factors on entrepreneurial intention it may not be observed [31]. Adopting this grouping methodology will reduce the noise and increase the signal with regard to the relationships between IT factors and entrepreneurial intention.

References

1. Ndubisi, N.O., Kahraman, C.: Malaysian women entrepreneurs: understanding the ICT usage behaviors and drivers. J. Enterp. Inf. Manag. 18(6), 721–739 (2005)
2. Chen, L.: Understanding IT entrepreneurial intention: an information systems view. J. Comput. Inf. Syst., pp. 2–12 (2014)
3. He, J., Freeman, L.A.: Understanding the formation of general computer self-efficacy. Commun. Assoc. Inf. Syst. 26, 225–244 (2010)
4. Rapaport, P., Orbell, S.: Augmenting the theory of planned behaviour: motivation to provide practical assistance and emotional support to parents. Psychol. Health. 15, 309–324 (2000)
5. Bullough, A., Renko, M., Myatt, T.: Danger zone entrepreneurs: the importance of resilience and self-efficacy for entrepreneurial intentions. Entrep. Theory Pract. 38(3), 473–499 (2014)
6. Gird, A., Bagraim, J.J.: The theory of planned behaviour as predictor of entrepreneurial intent amongst final-year university students. South Afr. J. Psychol. 38(4), 711–724 (2008)
7. Hatak, I., Harms, R., Fink, M.: Age, job identification, and entrepreneurial intention. J. Manag. Psychol. 30(1), 38–53 (2015)
8. Kumara, S.P.A.P.: Undergraduates' intention towards entrepreneurship: an empirical evidence from Sri Lanka. J. Enterprising Cult. 20(1), 105–118 (2012)
9. Iakovleva, T., Kolvereid, L., Stephan, U.: Entrepreneurial intentions in developing and developed countries. Edu. Train. 53(5), 353–370 (2011)
10. Pihie, Z.A.L., Bagheri, A.: Students' entrepreneurial regulation and intention to become an entrepreneur: a comparison between public and private universities. South Afr. J. Bus. Manag. 44(4), 25–32 (2013)
11. Solesvik, M.Z.: Entrepreneurial motivations and intentions: investigating the role of education major. Edu. Train. 55(3), 253–271 (2013)
12. Xiao, L., Fan, M.: Does social network always promote entrepreneurial intentions? an empirical study in China. Neural Comput. Appl. 24(1), 21–26 (2014)

13. Kibler, E.: Formation of entrepreneurial intentions in a regional context. Entrep. Reg. Nal Dev. **25**(3–4), 293–323 (2013)
14. Solesvik, M., Westhead, P., Matlay, H.: Cultural factors and entrepreneurial intention: the role of entrepreneurship education. Edu. Train. **56**, 680–696 (2014)
15. Fayolle, A., Liñán, F.: The future of research on entrepreneurial intentions. J. Bus. Res. **67**(5), 663–666 (2014)
16. Shapero, A., Sokol, L.: Social dimensions of entrepreneurship. Encycl. Entrep., pp. 72–90 (1982)
17. Bird, B.: Implementing entrepreneurial ideas: the case for intention. Acad. Manag. Rev. **13**(3), 442–453 (1988)
18. Ajzen, I.: The theory of planned behavior. Organ. Behav. Hum. Decis. Process. **50**(2), 179–211 (1991)
19. Krueger, N.F., Reilly, M.D., Carsrud, A.L.: Competing models of entrepreneurial intentions. J. Bus. Ventur. **15**(5/6), 411–432 (2000)
20. Bergevoet, R.H.M., Ondersteijn, C.J.M., Saatkamp, H.W., van Woerkum, C.M.J., Huirne, R.B.M.: Entrepreneurial behaviour of dutch dairy farmers under a milk quota system: goals, objectives and attitudes. Agric. Syst. **80**(1), 1–21 (2004)
21. Ajzen, I.: The theory of planned behavior: reactions and reflections. Psychol. Health. **26**(9), 1113–1127 (2011)
22. Vinogradov, E., Kolvereid, L., Timoshenko, K.: Predicting entrepreneurial intentions when satisfactory employment opportunities are scarce. Edu. Train. **55**(7), 719–737 (2013)
23. Conner, M., Armitage, C.J.: Extending the theory of planned behavior: a review and avenues for future research. J. Appl. Soc. Psychol. **28**, 1429–1464 (1998)
24. Durndell, A., Haag, Z.: Computer self-efficacy, computer anxiety, attitudes towards the internet and reported experience with the internet, by gender, in an east european sample. Comput. Hum. Behav. **18**(5), 521–535 (2002)
25. Harfouche, A., Robbin, A.: Inhibitors and enablers of public e-services in Lebanon. J. Organ. End User Comput. **24**(3), 45–68 (2012)
26. Heinssen, R.K., Glass, C.R., Knight, L.A.: Assessing computer anxiety: development and validation of the computer anxiety rating scale. Comput. Hum. Behav. **3**, 49–59 (1987)
27. He, J., Freeman, L.A.: Are men more technology-oriented than women? the role of gender on the development of general computer self-efficacy of college students. J. Inf. Syst. Edu. **21**(2), 203–212 (2010)
28. Maricutoiu, L.P.: A meta-analysis on the antecedents and consequences of computer anxiety. Proc. Soc. Behav. Sci. **127**, 311–315 (2014)
29. Rana, N.P., Dwivedi, Y.K.: Citizen's adoption of an e-government system: validating extended social cognitive theory (SCT). Gov. Inf. Quarterly **32**(2), 172–181 (2015)
30. Zhao, H., Seibert, S.E., Hills, G.E.: The mediating role of self-efficacy in the development of entrepreneurial intentions. J. Appl. Psychol. **90**(6), 1265–1272 (2005)
31. Becker, J.M., Rai, A., Ringle, C.M., Völckner, F.: Discovering unobserved heterogeneity in structural equation models to avert validity threats. MIS Q. **37**(3), 665–694 (2013)
32. Bao, Y., Xiong, T., Hu, Z., Kibelloh, M.: Exploring gender differences on general and specific computer self-efficacy in mobile learning adoption. J. Edu. Comput. Res. **49**(1), 111–132 (2013)
33. Bandura, A.: Social Foundations of Thought and Action: A Social Cognitive Theory. Prentice-Hall, Inc (1986)
34. Carlson, R.D., Grabowski, B.L.: The effects of computer self-efficacy on direction-following behavior in computer assisted instruction. J. Comput.-Based Instr. **19**(1), 6–11 (1992)
35. Compeau, D.R., Higgins, C.A.: Computer self-efficacy: development of a measure and initial test. MIS Q. **19**(2), 189–211 (1995)
36. Downey, J., McMurtrey, M.: Introducing task-based general computer self-efficacy: an empirical comparison of three general self-efficacy instruments. Interact. Comput. **19**(3), 382–396 (2007)
37. Korzaan, M.L., Boswell, K.T.: The influence of personality traits and information privacy concerns on behavioral intentions. J. Comput. Inf. Syst. **48**(4), 15–24 (2008)

38. Lee, H., Choi, S.Y., Kang, Y.S.: Formation of e-satisfaction and repurchase intention: moderating roles of computer self-efficacy and computer anxiety. Expert Syst. Appl. **36**(4), 7848–7859 (2009)

39. Marakas, G.M., Yi, M.Y., Johnson, R.D.: The multilevel and multifaceted character of computer self-efficacy: toward clarification of the construct and an integrative framework for research. Inf. Syst. Res. **9**(2), 126–163 (1998)

40. Mishra, S.: Adoption of M-Commerce in India: applying theory of planned behaviour model. J. Int. Bank. Commer. **19**(1), 1–17 (2014)

41. Rashidian, A., Russell, I.: Intentions and statins prescribing: can the theory of planned behaviour explain physician behaviour in following guideline recommendations? J. Eval. Clin. Pract. **17**(4), 749–757 (2011)

42. Sivell, S., Elwyn, G., Edwards, A., Manstead, A.S.R.: Factors influencing the surgery intentions and choices of women with early breast cancer: the predictive utility of an extended theory of planned behaviour. BMC Med. Inform. Decis. Mak. **13**(1), 1–8 (2013)

43. Thatcher, J.B., Perrewe, P.L.: An empirical examination of individual traits as antecedents to computer anxiety and computer self-efficacy. MIS Q. **26**(4), 381–396 (2002)

44. Tolentino, L.R., Sedoglavicha, V., Lua, V.N., Garciab, P.R.J.M., Restubog, S.L.D.: The role of career adaptability in predicting entrepreneurial intentions: a moderated mediation model. J. Vocat. Behav. **85**(3), 403–412 (2014)

45. Weisheng, C., Kwang-Yong, L., Doyeon, W.: consumer behavior toward counterfeit sporting goods. Soc. Behav. Pers. **42**(4), 615–624 (2014)

Developing an IT Risk Management Culture Framework

Neda Azizi and Bruce Rowlands

Abstract The concept of IT risk management culture is an important topic in IS research because culture helps facilitate the successful implementation/adoption of ITRM frameworks. In this paper we develop an IT risk management (IT-RM) framework based on Cameron and Quinn's model involving four dimensions of culture. Each cultural dimension is described in terms of how they relate to the implementation of IT-RM initiatives. Our contribution is to illustrate the utility of the framework by linking the four general cultural dimensions to propose a conceptual model of IT-RM values and beliefs. By doing so we present a necessary step in developing the concept of IT-RM culture and moving frameworks such as COBIT5 towards a more comprehensive framework based on systemic empirical research.

Keywords IT risk management · Culture · Conceptual research/study

1 Introduction

Managing IT risks has become a vital part of regulations, standards, and best practices within organizations [1]. IT-RM is defined as the activities, and processes for identification, analysis, execution and monitoring of risks that arise in terms of information system (IS) use [2]. Indeed, IT-RM is a subset of broader IT governance (ITG), focusing on the identifying exposure to significant IT risks, and establishing responsibilities to manage these risks in the organization [3]. IT-RM process is quite well served through standards and guidance designed to provide structure and formal frameworks that can adopt and adapt to improve organizational performance. These include ISO 38500 and COBIT5 [2]. Thus these formal frameworks facilitate IT-RM implementation.

N. Azizi (✉) · B. Rowlands
School of ICT, Griffith University, Brisbane 4111, Australia
e-mail: neda.azizi@griffithuni.edu.au

B. Rowlands
e-mail: b.rowlands@griffith.edu.au

© Springer Nature Switzerland AG 2020
Y. Baghdadi et al. (eds.), *ICT for an Inclusive World*,
Lecture Notes in Information Systems and Organisation 35,
https://doi.org/10.1007/978-3-030-34269-2_33

COBIT5 for IT risk is designed to provide structure for identifying and controlling risks across the complete lifecycle of investment in IT [2]. COBIT5 for IT risk contains an acknowledgement that the effectiveness of IT-RM requires a holistic approach. The holistic approach takes into account several enablers: principles and policies, processes, structures, culture and value, information, services and people, skills and competencies [2]. Thus, organisational culture (an enabler) is underestimated as a critical factor to achieving effective IT-RM [2]. Given this acknowledgement, and the limited academic research that develops the concept of IT-RM culture as a unit of analysis, the aim of this research is to explore the concept of IT-RM culture and propose a model based on systemic empirical research.

This paper explores how various dimensions of organisational culture may influence the effectiveness of IT-RM. The paper's contribution is to develop an IT-RM culture framework involving the dimensions of culture that improve an IT-RM implementation initiative. This exploratory research proposes a two stage research design. In stage 1, we have identified from prior literature, there is a relationship between organizational culture and the effectiveness of IT-RM. In stage 2, three case studies will be conducted allowing for analytical generalization from empirical observation to theory. This framework considers a theoretically grounded basis so that future research concerning the role of culture in IT-RM implementation can be built.

The remainder of this paper is organised as follows. Section 2 provides background to essential factors that may influence effective IT-RM. A discussion of organisational culture in Sect. 2.1 is provided as the basis for developing IT-RM culture framework. Section 2.2 investigates the conceptual framework by over-viewing cultural terms, including an illustration of Cameron and Quinn's model of culture. We propose a research design in Sect. 3 based on the literature and an exploratory interview. The last section provides a short overview of our next stage of the research.

2 Background

Recently, researchers have been investigating the types of factors or mechanisms that influence the effectiveness of IT-RM [1, 4]. Because of the use of information technologies and that the resource of information is considered as an essential part of business, managing IT risks effectively becomes a strategic and competitive success factor in organizations [4]. COBIT5 for IT-RM includes the following processes: (a) Scope establishment process that illustrates the targeted information system, its limits, environment, and goals [2]. (b) Risk identification process specifies which risks might influence the outcomes of projects [2]. (c) Risk analysis process leads to the shift of risk data into decision making information [2]. (d) Risk response planning process facilitates the conversion risk information into actions and judgments [2]. (e) Execution process focuses on investigating or changing the recent execution plan, ending the risk and probably initiating a new plan (f) Risk monitoring is considered as a feedback process [2]. Thus, risk monitoring includes reviewing and updating the risk states and the RM context, assessing the effectiveness of risk behaviour, and seeking out new risks and sources.

COBIT5 consists of several enablers: principles and policies, processes, structures, culture and value, information, services and people, skills and competencies [2]. The unique property of each organisation will result in these enablers being implemented in a different approach to manage risk [2]. Similarly, Wilkin and Chenhall pointed out that effective IT-RM is defined as a mechanism of ITG, which may be deployed through a mix of structures, processes, and relational mechanisms [3]. Structures include explicitly defined roles and responsibilities for an especial organisational group. Processes provide formal processes of strategic decision making, planning, and monitoring for emphasising that IT objectives are according to business needs [5]. The relational mechanism of IT-RM which comprises vital factors such as communication and trust as well as how to "to encourage desirable IT behaviours" [6]. The key point is that the intra-organizational IT-RM framework has to incorporate relational mechanisms that play a vital role in fostering an effective collaborative partnership.

Additionally Jahner and Krcmar pointed out that organisational work systems are facilitated by two components: the soft behavioural component embodied in the organizational environment and culture, and the more concrete component embodied in the formal RM program that guides the enterprise [7]. These authors found that organizations tended to rely on socio-cultural aspects in the development of IS, after focusing on technical and procedural aspects in the 80 s and 90 s. The socio-cultural perspective is a tool for understanding the roles and significance of stakeholders and their information in the effectiveness of IT-RM.

To date, there is little understanding of what may influence the effectiveness of IT-RM in a collaborative or organisational context [1, 8]. In terms of culture, Cameron and Quinn found that culture at both the national or organisational level can influence organisations, also culture theory has been applied to illustrate a wide range of social behaviours and outcomes in organisational settings [9]. Organisational culture has also been identified to play an important role in IT-RM implementation [10], many studies have highlighted that cultural variables affect organisational performance [11]. Accordingly, this research therefore proposes to illustrate the role of cultural factors in the effectiveness of IT-RM in collaborative or organisational contexts.

2.1 Organizational Culture

The culture of an organization can be defined as beliefs, values, symbols, assumptions and even the style of dress of the individual who work for the organization [12]. Researchers provide various ideas as to whether culture is something an organization "has" or what the organization "is" [13]. Thus, it can be hard to alter a culture in a different way or to make major changes, although change is occurring all the time [14].

According to Schein organisational culture is considered as defined activities, such as the defined strategy by management and the different reactions that individuals represent through their behaviour [12]. Indeed, organisational behaviour is about what individuals do in an organisation and how their behaviour influences the organisational performance. Thus organisational culture that grows via the represented behaviour, is explicit in artefacts, values, and basic assumptions [12].

The artefacts can be referred as physical layout, the dress code, or annual reports, archival records and products. Values are norms, trust among individuals, ideologies, and philosophies. Basic underlying assumptions can be considered as historical events that determine perceptions, behavior and feelings [12]. According to Leidner and Kayworth, basic assumptions are invisible, thus it is difficult to study them. It is also difficult to study artefacts, while being visible, as they are not easily decipherable [15]. Hence, the majority of research aiming at analyzing culture emphasizes the respective group's values. This paper focuses on the Competing Values Framework (CVF) of organizational culture, developed by Cameron and Quinn as our theoretical lens. Because of the CVF provides a holistic view of culture and has been validated in both international and Australian contexts [9]. Indeed, Cameron and Quinn's model states that organizations often tend to establish a dominant culture over time rather than a single cultural type as they respond to the challenges in the surrounding environment [9]. Further, they represented their model by linking it to a set of values which demonstrating the fundamental of successful Total Quality Management (TQM) adoption. Thus, the successful implementation of TQM, as well as the resulting effectiveness of the organizational performance, depended on having the improvement strategies embedded in a culture change [9].

2.2 Cameron and Quinn's Model of Organizational Culture

The CVF considers an assessment of a company's dominant culture involving six key characteristics of overall organizational culture: (a) Dominant characteristics that refer most the prevailing characteristics within organization, such as orientation on production versus orientation on individual [9]. (b) Organizational leadership determines the leadership styles within organization, such as educators, and organisers [9]. (c) Management of employees provides the management methods within organization [9]. (e) Organizational glue is the bonding mechanisms that hold the organization together, such as loyalty [9]. (f) Strategic emphasis refers the main focus on factors such as human development, and actions; and (g) criteria of success includes the properties and standards based on which an organization defines success [9]. The CVF identified the complex concept of culture according to two main dimensions: internal/external focus and stability/flexibility structure. These two dimensions establish four quadrants including: Clan, Adhocracy, Hierarchy and Marketing [9] (see Fig. 1).

Further, the CVF focuses on both quantitative and qualitative methods. For example, it was noticed in [16] that much of the existing culture literature was integrated

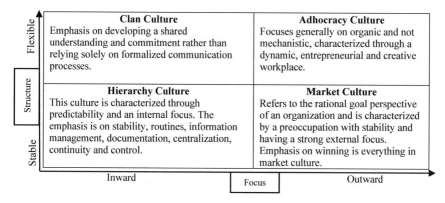

Fig. 1 The Competing Values Framework (CVF) [9]

into the four dimensions of Cameron and Quinn's model through a quantitative method for investigating their impact on knowledge sharing in organisations. Our research similarly focuses on CVF developed by Cameron and Quinn to improve IT-RM as previously described in Sect. 2.1.

3 Research Design

Although aspects of culture and their relationship to IT-RM have been identified [2, 7], we are not aware of any research specifically analyzing the relationships between IT-RM and Cameron and Quinn's model. It was noticed in [10] that researchers may wish to explore the effect of organizational culture on IT-RM, and in [8] that given the relatively immature state of study on IT-RM there is a requirement for qualitative research.

This exploratory research proposes a two stage research design (see Fig. 2). In stage 1, we have identified from prior literature, there is a relationship between organizational culture and the effectiveness of IT-RM. We interpret the four dimensions originally proposed by Cameron and Quinn to link them to the cultural values underlying IT-RM through exploratory interviews. At this stage, it is argued that a dominant culture is indeed needed and must be integrated effectively with IT-RM to ensure correct execution. To obtain the integration of cultural values with the IT-RM, the relationship between culture and risk has been examined to produce an integrated framework.

We consider that clan culture, as a dominant culture within the organization, supports two important IT-RM processes: risk analysis; and risk response planning. Clan culture provides a friendly place to work where individuals share a lot about themselves and their experiences. This culture facilitates information exchange among employees about IT risks that are produced externally or within the organization and

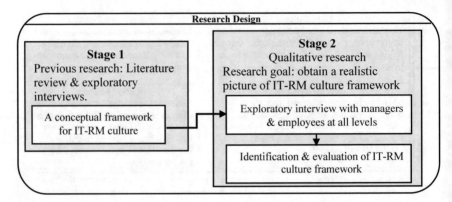

Fig. 2 Overview of research design

to document any newly identified risks. IT-RM in this culture is considered as iterative process for both, risk analysis and planning processes as during risk analysis, a new risk can reveal and requires collaboration to evaluate its impact and severity. Hence, IT project team can share their experience in the process, which will serve as an input to the risk analysis or the risk response planning for aim of modifying the sub-processes of both. Therefore, clan culture plays an important role in the IT-RM framework. There are needs to have a continuous communication on values and on processes that encourage transferring of information and knowledge and early identification of risks.

We also consider that market culture, as a dominant culture within the organization, supports two important IT-RM processes: risk identification and risk response. This culture focuses on transaction with external stakeholders to create competitive advantage. Indeed, market culture is defined as an environment that adopts any information from the external environment and transforms it into a representation that can be used within an organization. This involves identifying risk-related information from external sources, interpreting the identified information and risk response rapidly. Market culture dominated in three categories, Organisational Leadership, Management of Employees, and Organisational Glue [16]. In a hierarchy culture principles of stability, and formal rules are seen to hold the organization together. This culture focus on evaluating the risk execution progress, risk prioritization and risk control mechanisms continuously. However, IT-RM in this culture will act as a continuous process leading to either retiring an existing IT risk once a solution is achieved or identifying a new IT risk. Hierarchy culture dominated in two categories: Dominant Characteristics and Criteria of Success [16]. Finally, adhocracy culture that emphasizes on dynamic, and a creative workplace, supports two key IT-RM processes: risk identification and risk execution. The reason is that adhocracy culture tends to capture IT risk-related information and agile response to IT risks (see Fig. 3).

In stage 2, three case studies will be conducted allowing for analytical generalization from empirical observation to theory. Analytical generalization will be supported

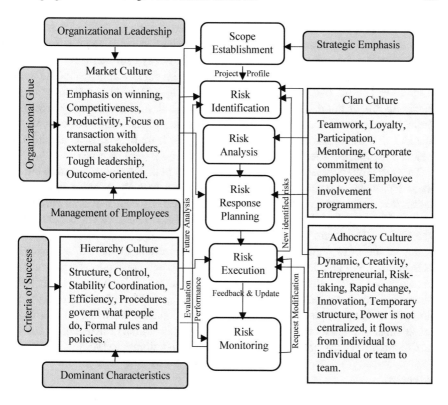

Risk Management Processes ☐   Organisational Culture ☐   Six Key Characteristics ☐

Fig. 3 A conceptual framework for IT-RM culture

by extensively profiling each case and by cross-case analysis. Reliability will be supported e.g. by a transparent process involving semi-structured instruments, and taped interviews, which will be transcribed and coded. Our triangulated research strategy will involve data triangulation (interviews with managers and employees at several levels, direct observations and archival data) and investigator triangulation. We suggest that the outcome of the experience of experts input significantly adds to our understanding of the IT-RM culture phenomenon.

4   Conclusion and Overview of Next Phase of Research

Risk management is a concept of growing significance that is continuously being evolved and improved to address the increasing complexity of the organizational environment. RM is an advantage that is particularly vital to organizations, institutions and industry due to the enhancing globalization and evolving regulatory requirements. Although RM has been widely studied in different fields such as health, finance, engineering, insurance as well as other business-specific areas, there is little research on the cultural aspects of RM in information system literature. Nevertheless, individual attempts are mostly seen to clash with organization's values in terms of effective IT-RM. Our exploratory research attempts to develop a framework for managing organizational IT risk and addresses a lack of a theoretically-grounded research to steer empirical studies that can contribute to the domain of culture. We consider that the proposed framework in Fig. 3 will be beneficial as a bridge to establish the link between organizational culture, and IT-RM research.

This research includes a two stage research design that was introduced in Fig. 2. Stage 1 provided a conceptual IT-RM culture framework by resource to previous literature and exploratory interviews. At this stage, it is argued that a dominant culture is needed and must be integrated carefully with IT-RM to ensure correct execution (see Fig. 3). Therefore, we demonstrated which IT-RM process can be supported by any of those for dominant culture within organization. In stage 2, a qualitative methodology will be introduced for evaluating proposed conceptual framework. At this stage, we will evaluate our IT-RM cultural framework by multi-case analysis, where each company (case) will be assessed in terms of where it fits in the cultural dimensions that took place during IT-RM implementation. We will then synthesise our findings through a cross-case analysis to illustrate which dimensions of culture best facilitate IT-RM processes implementation. By doing so we aim to present a necessary step in developing the concept of IT-RM culture based on COBIT5 framework.

References

1. Aven, T.: Risk assessment and risk management: review of recent advances on their foundation. Eur. J. Oper. Res. **253**(1), 1–13 (2016)
2. ISACA.: COBIT 5, an ISACA Framework, Rolling Meadows (2012)
3. Wilkin, C.L., Chenhall, R.H.: A review of IT governance: a taxonomy to inform accounting information systems. J. Inf. Syst. **24**(2), 107–146 (2010)
4. Wiesche, M., Schermann, M., Krcmar, H.: Understanding the enabling design of IT risk management processes. In: 36th International Conference on Information Systems, Fort Worth, TX, USA (2015)
5. Van Grembergen, W., De Haes, S.: Enterprise Governance of Information Technology: Achieving Strategic Alignment and Value. Springer, N.Y., New York (2009)
6. Weill, P., Ross, J.: IT Governance: How Top Performers Manage IT Decision Rights for Superior Results. Business Review School Press, Boston, MA (2004)
7. Jahner, S., Krcmar, H.: Beyond technical aspects of information security: risk culture as a success factor for IT risk management. In: Proceedings of the 11th Americas Conference on Information Systems, Omaha, NE, 11–14 Aug 2005
8. Darwish, S.Z.: Risk and knowledge in the context of organizational risk management. Risk **7**(15) (2015)
9. Cameron, K., Quinn, R.: Diagnosing and Changing Organizational Culture: Based on the Competing Values Framework. Jossey-Bass, San Francisco, CA (2005)
10. Alhawari, S., Karadsheh, L., Talet, A.N., Mansour, E.: Knowledge-based risk management framework for information technology project. Int. J. Inf. Manag. **32**(1), 50–65 (2012)

11. Wu, S., Straub, D., Liang, T.: How information technology, governance mechanisms and strategic alignment influence organizational performance: insights from a matched survey of business and IT managers. MIS Q. **39**(2), 497–518 (2015)
12. Schein, E.: Organisational Culture and Leadership. Jossey-Bass (1997)
13. Corriss, L.: Information Security Governance: Integrating Security into the Organizational Culture. In: Workshop on Governance of Technology, Information and Policies, ACM, New York, pp. 35–41 (2010)
14. Rowlands, B., De Haes, S. D., Grembergen, W.V.: Exploring and developing an IT governance culture framework. In: 35th International Conference on Information Systems, Auckland, NZ (2014)
15. Leidner, D., Kayworth, T.: A review of culture in information systems research: toward a theory of information technology culture conflict. MIS Q. **30**(2), 357–399 (2006)
16. Wiewiora, A., Trigunarsyah, B., Murphy, G., Coffey, V.: Organizational culture and willingness to share knowledge: a competing values perspective in Australian context. Int. J. Project Manag. **31**(8), 1163–1174 (2013)

Industry 4.0: Impact of New Technologies on Logistics Management

Selwa Elfirdoussi, Hamid Hrimech, Frederic Fontane and Hind Kabaili

Abstract In the context of Industry 4.0, new technologies have made it possible to face the challenges of the logistics sector. They have integrated smart models to improve the traceability and support logistics processes in real time while ensuring high accuracy and flexibility. In this article, we propose a study on the impact of new technologies on logistics issues in the context of Industry 4.0. We have relied on a set of works aimed at transforming the logistic process into a smart process, with a capacity for communication, perception, action, and management of the information available locally or through a network.

Keywords Industry 4.0 · SMART logistic · Web service · Cloud-computing · 3D printing · Internet of things · Artificial intelligence

S. Elfirdoussi (✉) · F. Fontane
EMINES, Université Mohammed VI Polytechnique, 43140 Ben Guerir, Morocco
e-mail: selwa.elfirdoussi@emines.um6p.ma

F. Fontane
e-mail: Frederic.fontane@emines.um6p.ma

H. Hrimech
Laboratoire d'analyse et modélisation de système pour l'aide à la décision Ecole Supérieure de Technologie, Université Hassan Premier, B.P 218, Berrechid, Morocco
e-mail: hamid.hrimech@uhp.ac.ma

F. Fontane
Mines ParisTech, Centre de Robotique, 60 Boulevard Saint-Michel, 75272 Paris Cedex 06, France

H. Kabaili
ISCAE Group, Information System and Decision Department, Km 9,5 Route Nouasseur, BP. 8114, Casablanca, Morocco
e-mail: hkabaili@groupeiscae.ma

© Springer Nature Switzerland AG 2020
Y. Baghdadi et al. (eds.), *ICT for an Inclusive World*,
Lecture Notes in Information Systems and Organisation 35,
https://doi.org/10.1007/978-3-030-34269-2_34

1 Introduction

Logistics can be defined as a process that groups together all the activities implemented to ensure the availability of a product or service in order to satisfy a customer's request. It also ensures optimal management of physical flows, from upstream
to downstream, quantity, time and cost, while integrating the human and material
resources of the company. In its simplest form (Fig. 1), logistics is a binding function
of transactions and various operations of the company. In the medium term, the process would aim not only to define the actions initiated but also to advise managers
on the choice of operations to be executed or outsourced to help optimize the cost
of the investment and the working capital. In the long term, the purpose of logistics
should help the organization to master the complexity, the uncertainty and the resulting delays by constantly updating the impacts on the operating costs to be proposed.
In this case, a competitive advantage through intelligent logistics called SMART
Logistics would be appreciated.

The logistics sector has endured profound changes over the last decade. Indeed,
it has evolved towards the concept of supply chain whose spirit is to coordinate
all flows of products, services and information. It has also allowed integration of
its various departments of the company and all the actors in the chain: from the
manufacturer to the final consumer [2]. As a result, Logistics Service Providers
(LSPs), whether internal or external to the organization, are totally exposed to inter-
organizational approaches that must guarantee the flexibility and reactivity of the
entire chain with stated objectives. Such as cost savings, time and customer service
[3]. These constraints obviously have an immediate impact on the profitability of
the entire chain, depending on the coordination between physical flows, information
flows and financial flows [4].

New technologies have made it possible to confront the issues and problems of
the logistics sector. They have played a leading role in the development of logistics innovations, such as just-in-time (JIT) [5] consisting of developing a set of
technologies dedicated to the management and exchange of information within the
chain logistics: EDI (Electronic Data Interchange) systems, planning software such
as ERP, MRP, identification and traceability technologies, mobility and geolocation
tools, etc. The main purpose of these applications is to automate, on the one hand,

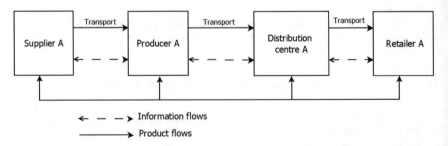

Fig. 1 Supply chain management schema [1]

the heavy administrative tasks necessary for the proper functioning of the logistics system. And secondly, the comprehensive planning models used in the development of appropriate logistics networks to support the company's overall strategies.

In the context of Industry 4.0, deployed technologies have integrated intelligent logistics models to improve traceability and support of logistics processes in real time, while ensuring high accuracy and flexibility. To adequately cover the different aspects of automation in the logistics sector, researchers used a classification of information into various categories to help structure data and guide operators to gaps in development and the need to follow [6]. Research has focused on modeling and optimizing the logistics process [7]. This has been implemented thanks to the use of existing technological approaches, which make it possible to ensure its interest and its starting from the best settings of the SMART logistics [8].

Recall that good supply chain management is an increasingly strategic issue for the organization in view of the diversity of products, stakeholders [3], globalization and competition. The supply chain is required to optimize all these processes and mainly its logistics insofar as the latter involves structuring choices for the organization in partnership with internal or external stakeholders. Indeed, logistic stakeholders are most often solicited in the context of logistical alliances between suppliers and customers. Their tasks consist primarily of supplying, distributing and transporting raw materials and final products. In addition, they are also involved in the management of intermediate operations in the production process for storage or transport.

From a perspective of transforming the logistics chain into a value chain [9], logistics is essentially concerned with ensuring operational flexibility within the supply chain. Given the variations in the level of activity and organization, logistics operators generally play the role of equilibration variable. As a result, these logistic operators have generally been taken into account on the basis of reasoning in terms of substitutability and quantitative management methods [10]. It would then be imperative to manage both the logistic activity (intra-organizational dimension), the information exchanges with the partners (upstream and downstream inter-organizational dimension) as well as the coupling of this information with the information systems (Double dimension intra and inter-organizational). In addition, logistics issues have a strong influence on the performance of the service itself, based on organizational or activity-related indicators [11], such as:

- Delay: This dimension represents the time required to complete a task in the logistics process, whether it is the transport time, the stock rotation or the production-related inactivity time.
- Cost: Each operation in logistics has a cost: storage, transport or loading and unloading operations.
- Information: The management of information is essential in this area. In fact, the logistician must be able to provide the right information at the right time in order to guarantee good management of the activity in real time.
- Process: The logistician must be able to implement methods that are both flexible and rational. They will allow him to situate his action within a global framework and to regulate the flow of the company by developing a logistics system and

efficient information networks. He must know the tools needed to optimize the quality and safety of physical and information flows.

– Quality of service: The logistics performance depends heavily on its quality of service and this can be qualified by the delivery time, the cost of storage or the coordination and communication between the different tasks of the process.

In this paper, we will propose a selection of research work based on some technological components of Industry 4.0 to optimize logistics. The research methodology that we followed consists of:

1. Defining the approach and its components,
2. Making a state of the art work done in the context of logistics,
3. Demonstrating the impact of technology on the process,
4. Making a synthesis of the study by proposing axes of researches.

After presenting the challenges of the logistics sector, we will comment on some of the work carried out, grouped by a technological approach, to demonstrate the impact of these tools on better modeling and optimization of the logistics process. These approaches are based on the technological advancements known to date in the context of Industry 4.0, particularly in the field of artificial intelligence, the Internet of Things, 3D printing, web technologies and the cloud-computing. And finally, we will discuss, in Part 7, a set of perspectives defined in the form of research axes to lead to a SMART Logistics.

2   Artificial Intelligence

Artificial Intelligence (AI) is a scientific discipline whose role is to increase knowledge in different areas of mental and social functioning [12], using computers as tools to experiment with models [13]. To this end, the IA approach operates in four main areas: understanding natural languages, artificial vision (associated with robotics), learning, and Expert Systems [14]. These are the first "smart" IT tools accessible to businesses, which are based on three main activities: observe, analyze and model as illustrated in Fig. 2.

Technological developments have allowed the IA to integrate into different sectors by promising new challenges for better optimization. For this purpose, the diffusion of the competence and the knowledge, allowed by the I.A., integrated in the logistic computer systems, can thus accompany the decentralization of the function of decision until the place where it must be exerted.

To this end, the work carried out was based on two approaches: The first one is used to define "strategic" analysis tools for managers, or systems that guarantee logistics quality for operational staff. And the second is to develop systems that assist in the implementation of complex procedures or the operation of the logistics process. These two approaches aim to limit the disturbances due to failures or malfunctions of equipment. Thus, they concern the maintenance activity: an essential activity for the reliability of logistics chains [15].

Fig. 2 The main activities
of AI

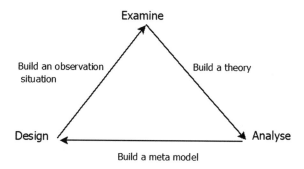

To address the problem of troubleshooting electric locomotives, RATP has developed several "models" of Expert Systems (SE). These tools have been applied in various fields to explore their potentialities and possible uses. The result of this research gave birth to the RUFUS system, capable of investigating the status of terminating RER trains and diagnosing possible failures [16].

A multi-agent model called EUROSIM proposed in [17] was designed to simulate the medium-term evolution of the European cities system from relatively regular and uniform rural planting. In [18], the team designed a multi-agent logistics system resulting from a dynamic vision of collective intelligence. This system will be implemented in two case studies: the phenomenology of artificial intelligence in swarm, relating to the behavior of ant colonies, and the formation of bird clouds.

INRETS addresses the problem of urban traffic, and defines a system to manage congestion processing from a permanent traffic analysis. By simulating situations, this tool evaluates the saturation state and proposes measures that can solve the problems [19]. We can also mention [20] which proposes a system allowing to control the fires. The algorithm is based on the traffic modeling, the regulation method, the performance evaluation, and the summary of characteristics and the traffic variables used. As part of the coordination of logistics operations, a modeling was carried out in [21] to coordinate the different collaborative parts both internal and external to the supply chain. The proposed models are based on Coalition Coordination of Multi-Agent Systems (MAS). IA approaches have resulted in remarkable convergence in the field of operations research. In logistics, the human understanding of the event to be launched by a process or the interpretation of a result is essential. Indeed, it will guide the further execution of different workflows in the supply chain. This approach can be based primarily on the implementation of an IA approach to achieve a logistics SMART, through the automation of the execution of processes without human intervention.

3   IoT: Internet of Things

According to the International Telecommunication Union (ITU) [22], the Internet
of Things (IoT) is a global infrastructure for the information society. It provides
advanced services by interconnecting objects (physical or virtual). These are based
on existing or evolving interoperable information and communication technologies
(Fig. 3).

Conceptually, the Internet of Things (IoT) refers to a set of physical objects that
have an identification number and are connected to a computer network. By using
the Internet, they are able to communicate with each other. As for the technical point
of view, the IoT consists in digitally and standardly identifying an object thanks to a
wireless communication system (Zigbee, Wi-Fi, RFID chip, Bluetooth or Infrared)
[24].

The integration of the Internet of Things (IoT) and the Internet of Services (IoS)
into the industrial manufacturing process has helped launch the fourth industrial revolution [25]. It has been characterized by the integration of digital technologies into
physical processes, thus favoring cyber-physical production processes in factories.
The main objective is to ensure better interaction between economic actors and their
customers, and a highly flexible and customizable production volume. The authors
of [26] designed a framework based on IOT to improve inbound and outbound operations in ERP for the apparel and footwear industry. Experimental research on supply
chain closed loop supply with the Internet of Things was conducted in [27]. The
authors proposed a profit-maximizing mathematical model (MILP) consisting of
different sales revenue and total cost to determine the valuation of returned products.
In the context of IoT-based virtualization, in [28], the authors conducted an analysis
of the concept of virtual food supply chains from an IoT perspective and proposes
an architecture to implement enabling information systems.

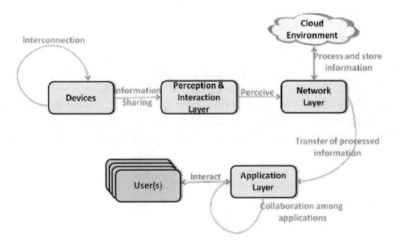

Fig. 3 Deployment diagram in IoT [23]

According to Rivera and Goasduff [29], the dramatic emergence of physical devices connected to the Internet by 2020 is likely to "significantly change the way the supply chain works". Specifically, how supply chain leader's access information. For better visibility of the supply chain, the IoT will offer "intelligent" solutions, connecting people, processes, data and objects using devices and sensors. Thus, collect information and store it using the Big Data approach [30]. These big data can provide decision makers with clues about consumer practices.

GPS, cloud computing and RFID are the backbone of IoT in the supply chain [31]. They can be used to collect data, and thus provide detailed visibility of an element during the manufacturer's journey phase. By putting for example an RFID chip in a pallet and a device in the transport vehicle, the data is transferred to the cloud. Thus, devices can identify the pallet, share its position using GPS coordinates. In addition, they will provide other data such as weather conditions, traffic conditions, and driving-specific data (driving model, average speed). The combination of real-time sensor data and environmental data can provide higher-order information to all players in the ecosystem. This study allows stakeholders to be socially aware in order to make effective decisions that boost overall productivity, and makes the logistics process proactive by providing information related to the unfolding of the entire activity. To summarize, IoT can help supply chain professionals in the following way (examples are not exhaustive):

– Reduce asset loss and know product issues in time to find a solution.
– Optimize fleet routes by monitoring traffic conditions (Reduce fuel costs).
– Ensure the stability of the temperature. Monitor the cold chain.
– according to the Food and Agriculture Organization of the United Nations, about a third of food perishes in transit each year.
– Manage inventory and monitor inventory to reduce out-of-stock situations.

4 Internet Technologies

In recent years, the emergence of Internet technologies has made it possible to share information in real time and pave the way for processes and exchanges of data between companies. The classic EDI standards adapt to Internet exchange standards, as evidenced by the development of web-EDI. For example, the creation of web portals allows customers to reach the carrier regardless of the device they use (Phone, GSM, Web, E-mail, Fax, PDA, etc.). These web portals provide immediate access to information for employees or business partners. A study in [32] suggests different web-based information practices for logistics service providers.

Thus, the integration of web technologies into supply chain management (SCM) enables information flow through strategic and reliable coordination of supply chain management [33]. It is based on research in the areas of scientific information management, supply chains and organizational innovation. An entire linear programming model was designed in [34] as an alternative to one of the traditional hardware

Fig. 4 Service web
architecture [36]

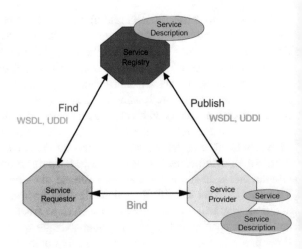

requirements of the Planning System (MRP), to extend the concept of supply chain synchronization upstream in the supply chain to multilevel supply.

Web services have also played a very important role in optimizing the logistics chain with a view to customer-supplier interactivity defined in their architecture (Fig. 4). In fact, the integration of web services into the supply chain allows for effective interaction between the various stakeholders. The authors of [35] propose a reconfiguration of its services to extend the logistics by exploiting complex computer systems, and by using interfaces allowing the modification of the operations provided and required for each one of them.

In [37], the authors examined the relationship between Internet-based supply chain integration strategies and performance in manufacturing and services. They summarize the literature on demand and supply integration and describe four online strategies on optimal pricing strategies for a monopoly intermediary implemented via web services. In the field of application, the authors of [38] proposed an automated control post system in transport. The architecture of the system is focused on SOA (Service Oriented Architecture). The system proposed allows collecting the information of opening and closing of door, the identification of vehicles, etc. These are stored in a BigData structure and analyzed later. As a result, web services present a promising technology in the industrial context and mainly in logistics.

Indeed, the logistics chain as we defined it at the beginning of this article consists of an interaction between several processes hosted on different platforms and different networks. This interaction can only be effective through the implementation of web services connected to each other to ensure the transfer of information while managing security aspects. From another point of view, and given the semantic layer [39], the information exchanged can be interpreted intelligently and thus respond to the SMART Logistics approach.

5 Cloud Computing

Cloud computing refers not only to the applications delivered as Internet services, but also to the hardware and software systems installed in the data centers that provide these services. The services themselves have long been called Software as a Service (SaaS) [40]. The cloud has the potential to transform much of the IT industry, making it even more attractive and thus operating in the way that the hardware is designed and purchased. Once the cloud is deployed, new applications with possibilities and usage patterns have been discovered that would not be done previously [41]. This has made the cloud a promising approach to implement the autonomous control of Logistics, and mainly logistics SMART. The cloud provides a scalable IT infrastructure on which logistics solutions are self-sustaining. These solutions are managed by intelligent software agents that coordinate across resources and can be deployed and analyzed [42] (Fig. 5).

Cloud services can range from a scalable hardware platform to complete the process control by the cloud service provider to new flexible and modern approaches for business entities [41]. In the latter case, the cloud service provider can become a fourth-generation logistics provider. Thus, logisticians no longer have to invest in IT infrastructure, they can flexibly acquire the required infrastructure [43]. Especially since the constraints imposed on applications, including ERP [44], must meet the 5 goals of security (i.e. availability, confidentiality, data integrity, control and audit). These constraints are well supported in the Cloud literature [45] in addition to optimizing logistics information systems in an environment ready to integrate them.

Research in [46] has been conducted to map the features available in the various software solutions on the market and to collect logistics information around the world. Analysis of this data showed that while the market was dominated by a few large software vendors, each client requested a customized set of IT applications that best fit their own processes.

In an article published by [47], the authors explore how the standard EPC electronic product code and its elements can be used to support controlled and autonomous logistics. The developed EPC global Framework provides technical and explicit support for the first type of autonomous logistic objects that defines the

Fig. 5 Cloud architecture [40]

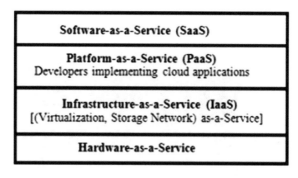

Software-as-a-Service (SaaS)
Platform-as-a-Service (PaaS)   Developers implementing cloud applications
Infrastructure-as-a-Service (IaaS)   [(Virtualization, Storage Network) as-a-Service]
Hardware-as-a-Service

individual physical entity. A multilevel system for collaborative management in the supply chain is proposed in [48]: the first level consists of defining a manufacturing structure consisting of a group of models that integrates the platform and the cloud resources, a framework logic to coordinate activities in real time, and a platform for cloud manufacturing services for a typical business combining theory with practice. Large industries are in great need of using cloud services to adapt collaborative operation and solve resource coordination problems based on information available everywhere and at any time. As a result, the cooperation of cloud manufacturing resources remains a complex project given the variety of models to be managed.

6 3D Printing

As an integral part of Industry 4.0, 3D printing or additive manufacturing [49] is a 3-dimensional solid object manufacturing process from a digital CAD file. This CAD file is created using a 3D modeling application or with a 3D scanner (to model an existing object). The creation of a printed 3D object is achieved using additive methods. In an additive process, an object is created by fixing successive layers of materials until the object is created. Each of these layers can be considered as a horizontal section in thin slices of the final object (Fig. 6).

3D printing is constantly evolving. According to [51], the worldwide 3D printing industry is expected to grow from \$3.07 B in 2013 revenue to \$12.8 B in 2018, and surpass \$21 B in revenue worldwide by 2020. 3D printing technology is designed to transform almost every major industry and change the way we live and work in the future [52]. As a result, it will significantly affect manufacturing and the supply chain [53]. The ability to create complex elements without the traditional manufacturing circuits of a traditional plant (Fig. 7) will make the supply chain more efficient, more local and globally connected.

3D printing could change the supply chain in the following way (non-exhaustive examples):

- Manufacturing lead times will be significantly reduced.
- Customer requests will be processed locally and more quickly.
- Printing will be on demand, this will mean that inventory levels will be reduced.

3D Printing Process

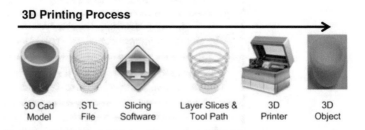

| 3D Cad Model | .STL File | Slicing Software | Layer Slices & Tool Path | 3D Printer | 3D Object |

Fig. 6 3D printing process [50]

Fig. 7 Impact of 3D printing on traditional manufacturing [54]

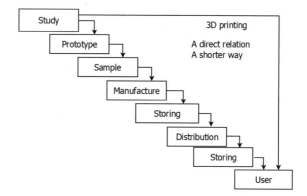

7 Discussions

The integration of different technologies presented in this article are some basic elements of Industry 4.0 to meet the concept of SMART Logistics, which aims to improve productivity, turnover, resources and investments as is shown for the case of German industries in [55]. In addition, setting up an intelligent industry relies mainly on real-time communication of industrial processes to monitor and act on the company's activities. Thus, connected systems can cooperate with each other, while integrating humans, products and machines via the new technologies proposed to date [56]. With this in mind, the concepts presented in this article can be combined to provide an intelligent, interconnected and value-added logistics chain. The perspectives that we can propose aim at transforming the classical processes of the material oriented logistics chain into an information-oriented connected approach. This will allow better integration of the supply chain in Industry 4.0 (Fig. 8).

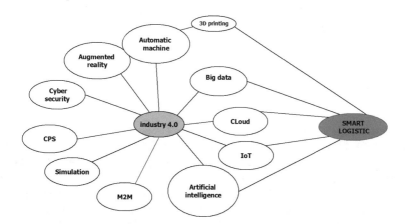

Fig. 8 Technologies used in industry 4.0 [56] and their integration on smart logistics

First, the components of the logistics process will be automated using an artificial intelligence-based system. The information collected using the "IoT" objects will be stored and exchanged via the cloud based on web services and composition algorithms for better orchestration that can integrate a 3D printing approach. With this in mind, we can propose some lines of research as follows:

– Modeling of the logistic process in the form of generic objects for a global structuring of the chain. The generic notion will thus make it possible to instantiate the objects according to several adjusted scenarios based on primary and dynamic variables.
– Definition of intelligent agents based on a set of processes for analyzing and observing the behaviors of the objects in the chain. These agents will thus make it possible to define an expert system of management of the process in its entirety to take charge of the management of all the resources. Different approaches can be used in this system, such as neural networks, machine learning and Bayesian networks.
– Simulation of the logistics process via 3D printing algorithms to build a logistics of the future. These simulation approaches can be defined as the virtual mirror of the entity concerned integrating all its human resources, material or more generally its logistics. Thus, this axis will make it possible to analyze the robustness of the process to be implemented while integrating the economic valuation and the quality of the service.
– Integration and composition of interconnected web services available via the cloud to connect and enable real-time access and communication of information to all internal and external entities of the chain and thus piloting the modeled objects. The required information can be processed on mass data management platforms using Big-data technologies such as (HPC—High Performance Computing, etc.)
– And finally, it would be wise to design a system based on DSS approaches to enable integrated and intelligent control of the chain for effective decision-making on the downstream and upstream while maximizing the use of information and defining management predictions with a Data Science approach.

8 Conclusion

To conclude, this article presents the challenges of logistics as well as the impact of the components of Industry 4.0 on the process to make it intelligent. We made a state of the art of the various works and studies in the framework of the implementation of an intelligent logistics by demonstrating for each technology its contribution to the SMART Logistics. Nevertheless, the smart logistics as defined, and which ensures an optimization of the workflows in the chain is practically not supported in every system proposed, and the combination of different technologies to ensure a complete automation of the chain remains limited. Which, thus, opens the door to several lines of research in the field of SMART Logistics that we have addressed in this article.

In addition, we did not discuss the economic impact of these technologies within the company [4]. Indeed, today's business model presents significant challenges for supply chain management that industries can effectively address by providing efforts to create a more agile supply chain and by applying certain key principles they can quite survive and prosper [9].

References

1. Ramirez, A.: Contribution à la Modélisation et à la Gestion des Interactions Produit-Processus dans la Chaîne Logistique par l'Approche Produits Communicants. Rapport de thése, Nancy (2006)
2. Durand, B., Faultrier, B.: L'impact de la supply chain sur les métiers de la logistique et des achats. Logistique Manag. 15(2), 55–70 (2007)
3. Camman, C., Livolsi, L.: Enjeux et difficultés de la gestion des cadres intermédiaires chez les prestataires de services logistiques. Logistique Manag. 15(2), 43–54 (2007)
4. Miloudi, F., Semma, H., Riane, F.: Enjeux financiers dans la gestion des chaînes logistiques. In: Conception et Production Intégrées, Tanger (2015)
5. Bardi, E.J., Raghunathan, T.S., Bagchi, P.K.: Logistics information systems: the strategic role of top management. J. Bus. Log., pp. 71–85 (1994)
6. Stenger, A.: Information systems in logistics management: past, present, and future. Transp. J., pp. 65–82 (1986)
7. Andre Langevin, D.: Logistics Systems: Design and Optimization. GERAD and Ecole polytechnique de montréal, Montréal (2005)
8. Uckelmann, D.: A definition approach to smart logistics. In: International Conference on Next Generation Wired/Wireless Networking, pp. 273–284 (2008)
9. Christopher, M.: Les enjeux d'une supply chain globale. Logistique Manag. 7(1), 1–7 (1999)
10. Colin, J., Guilhon, A.: Apport des politiques GRH aux activités logistiques et transport. In: Colloque du GRAAL, Bordeaux (1996)
11. Tang-Taye, J.-P., Picard, P.: Système d'information et supply chain management: rôle d'un prestataire de services logistiques. Logistique Manag. 8(2), 17–28 (2000)
12. Harfouche, A., Quinio, B., Skandrani, S., Marciniak, R.: A framework for artificial knowledge creation in organizations. In: ICIS 2017 Proceedings. Paper 15. http://aisel.aisnet.org/icis2017/General/Presentations/15 (2017)
13. Nicolle, A.: L'expérimentation et l'intelligence artificielle. GREYC, Caen (1996)
14. Marquis, P., Odile, P., Henri, P.: Panorama de l'intelligence artificielle, ses bases méthodologiques, ses développements, vols. 1, 2, 3 (2014)
15. Fabbes-Costes, N.: Vers l'intelligence des systèmes informatiques en logistique. L'emprise de l'informatique, Neuilly (Juillet 1990)
16. RATP: Les systèmes experts: expérimentations et réflexions, Paris (1988)
17. Sanders, L., Favaro, J.-M., Mathian, H., Pumain, D., Glisse, B.: Intelligence artificielle et agents collectifs: le modèle EUROSIM. Eur. J. Geogr., 392 (2007)
18. Charrier, R., Bourjot, C., Charpillet, F.: Un modèle connexionniste pour l'intelligence en essaim: le système multi-agent logistique. In: Colloque de l'Association pour la Recherche Cognitive, Nancy, pp. 19–31 (2007)
19. Bhouri, N., Boillot, F., Vinant, P.: Régulation multimodale du trafic routier et des transports en commun de surface. Recherche Transports Securite (98) (2008)
20. Boillot, F., Braban, F.: Les systèmes temps réel de commande de feux en milieu urbain. Synthése 44, INRETS, Arcueil (2003)
21. Anane, D., Aknine, S., Pinson, S.: Coordination d'Activités dans les Chaînes Logistiques: une Approche Multi-Agents par Formation de Coalitions. In: INFORSID, Fontainebleau, pp. 133–148 (2008)

22. UIT: UIT: Engagée à connecter le monde. http://www.itu.int/fr/Pages/default.aspx
23. Sehgal, V., Patrick, A., Rajpoot, a.: A Comparative study of cyber physical cloud, cloud of sensors and internet of things: their ideology, similarities and differences. In: IEEE International Advance Computing Conference, pp. 708–716 (2014)
24. Rabeb, S.: Modèle collaboratif pour l'Internet of Things. IoT), Québec (2016)
25. Henning, K.: Recommendations for Implementing the Strategic Initiative Industrie 4.0: Final report of the Industrie 4.0 Working Group. Technical report, National Academy of Science and Engineering, Germany (April 2013)
26. Aabid, A., Thashika, D.: Internet of Things (IoT) embedded future supply chains for industry 4.0: an assessment from an ERP-based fashion apparel and footwear industry. Int. J. Supp. Chain Manag. 6(1) (2017)
27. Turan, P., Ĝsmail, K., Hadi, G., Panos, M., Belkıs, T.: An experimental research on closed loop supply chain management with internet of things. J. Econ. Bibliogr. 3(1S) (2016)
28. Verdouw, C.N., Wolfert, J., Beulens, A.J.M.: Virtualization of food supply chains with the internet of things. J. Food Eng. 176, 128–136 (2016)
29. Rivera, J., Goasduff, L.: Thirty-fold increase in internet-connected physical devices by 2020 will significantly alter how the supply chain operates. In: Gartner. Available at http://www.gartner.com/newsroom/id/2688717
30. Harfouche, A.L., Jacobson, D.A., Kainer, D., Romero, J.C., Harfouche, A.H., Scarascia Mugnozza, G., Moshelion, M., Tuskan, G.A., Keurentjes, J., Altman, A.: Accelerating climate resilient plant breeding by applying next-generation artificial intelligence. Trend. Biotechnol. 37(11), 1217–1235 (2019)
31. Shoumen, P., Austin, D.: L'Internet des Objets: la troisième révolution industrielle. Logistique Manag. 23(3), 29–33 (2016)
32. Lynagh, P., Murphy, P., Poist, R., Grager, W.: Web-based informational practices of logistics service providers: an empirical assessment. Transp. J., pp. 34–45 (2001)
33. Ranganathan, C., Dhaliwal, J., Teo, T.: Assimilation and diffusion of web technologies in supply-chain management: an examination of key drivers and performance impacts. Int. J. Electron. Commer., pp. 127–161 (2004)
34. Mulaa, J., Lyonsb, A., Hernándezb, J., Polera, R.: An integer linear programming model to support customer-driven material planning in synchronised, multi-tier supply chains. Int. J. Prod. Res., pp. 4267–4278 (2014)
35. Talevski, A., Chang, E., Dillon, T.S.: Reconfigurable Web service integration in the extended logistics enterprise. IEEE Trans. Ind. Inf. 1(2), 74–84 (2005)
36. Kreger, H.: Web Services: Conceptual Architecture. IBM Software (2001)
37. Frohlicha, M., Westbrookb, R.: Demand chain management in manufacturing and services: web-based integration, drivers and performance. J. Oper. Manag. 20(6), 729–745 (2002)
38. Kumar, P., Punitha, F., Premlatha, D.: Automated check-post on cloud using bigdata analysis with web service security. Int. J. Comput. Appl. 113(3), 44–47 (2015)
39. Berners-Lee, T., Hendler, J.: Ora: the semantic web. Sci. Am. 5(284), 34–43 (2001)
40. EECS Department: University of California at Berkeley.: Above the Clouds: A Berkeley View of Cloud Computing. University of California at Berkeley, Berkeley (2009)
41. Gromoff, A., Kazantsev, N., Kozhevnikov, D., Ponfilenok, M., Stavenko, Y.: Newer approach to create flexible business architecture of modern enterprise. Global J. Flexible Syst. Manag. pp. 207–215 (2012)
42. Ye, N., Yang, S., Aranda, B.: The analysis of service provider-user coordination for resource allocation in cloud computing. Inform. Knowl. Syst. Manag., pp. 1–24 (2013)
43. Schuldt, A., Hribernik, K., Gehrke, J.D., Thoben, K.D., Herzog, O.: Cloud computing for autonomous control in logistics. In: GI Jahrestagung, pp. 305–310 (2010)
44. Symonds, M.: Cloud ERP meets manufacturing. Softw. Anal. 51(4), 40–43 (2012)
45. Zhou, M., Zhang, R., Xie, W., Qian, W., Zhou, A.: Security and privacy in cloud computing: a survey. In: Sixth International Conference on Semantics, Knowledge and Grids, Ningbo, China, pp. 105–112 (2010)

46. Kumthekar, N., Aserkar, R.: Study of current software trends of logistics service providers with feasibility of cloud computing as an alternative. Skyline Bus. J., pp. 41–50 (2011)
47. Hribernik, K., Hans, C., Thoben, K.: The application of the epcglobal framework architecture to autonomous control in logistics. Dyn. Logistics, pp. 365–374 (2011)
48. Yanga, X., Shia, G., Zhang, Z.: Collaboration of large equipment complete service under cloud manufacturing mode. Int. J. Prod. Res., pp. 326–336 (2014)
49. Laplume, A.O., Peterson, B., Pearce, J.M.: Global value chains from a 3D printing perspective. J. Int. Bus. Stud. **47**(5), 595–609 (2016)
50. Agence pour le Développement Économique et Culturel Nord-Sud: L'impression 3D [NL62]. Available at www.adecns.fr/limpression-3d-nl62/
51. Wohlers, T.: Wohlers Report, 3D Printing Additive Manufacturing, State of the industry. Wohlers Report 2001 Executive Summary, Wohlers Associates Inc, United States of America (2015)
52. Blum, G., Blois, M., Tadjine, N.: L'impression 3D: de l'émerveillement technique aux enjeux organisationnels, Économiques Et Sociétaux, 2017th edn. Wikimedia—Jonathan Juursema, Québec (Qc), Canada (2017)
53. Morand, P., Rosenberg, J., Turcq, D.: Fabrication additive: où en sommes nous? Réalités Industrielles, pp. 113–116, 122, 127–128, 134–136 (2017)
54. Rufer, S.: Quel est l'impact de l'impression 3D sur la supply chain?. Mémoire Université Paris Dauphine, Paris (2014)
55. Rüßmann, M., Lorenz, M., Gerbert, P., Waldner, M., Jan Justus, P.: Industry 4.0: The Future of Productivity and Growth in Manufacturing Industries. Boston Consulting Group, Boston (2015)
56. Pellerin, R., Rivest, L., Danjou, C.: Prendre Part À La Révolution Manufacturière? Du rattrapage technologique à l'Industrie 4.0 chez les PME. Rapport de comité de recherche, Polytechnique Montréal, École de technologie supérieure, Québec (2016)

Using Immersive Virtual Reality in Ancient Egypt's Giza Plateau

Dina Rateb, Hoda Hosny, Fayza Haikal and N. Azab

Abstract The aim of this research study is to adopt an innovative IT means for presenting the ancient Egyptian heritage to both the academics and tourists, remotely. Academic staff and students, tourists, tour agents/guides, and historians can all benefit from the online access to major Egyptian monuments using an advanced Immersive Virtual Reality (IVR) package, such as Second Life (SL). IVR is a form of technology that creates computer-generated worlds or immersive environments which people can explore and interact with. SL is a virtual game environment that has been used successfully in education and tourism. We had reported on the preliminary results of this research project in [1] where we compared what we did using SL with other tourism packages and games. With the success of the first stage of the research in the Giza plateau, we expect it to lead the way for further integration between IT and cultural heritage. It may very well be replicated for other historical locations in Egypt.

Keywords Immersive virtual reality (IVR) · Second life (SL) · Information technology (IT) · Ancient egyptian heritage · Virtual egyptian pyramids

D. Rateb (✉) · H. Hosny · F. Haikal · N. Azab
The American University in Cairo, AUC Avenue, New Cairo, Egypt
e-mail: DFR@aucegypt.edu

H. Hosny
e-mail: hhosny@aucegypt.edu

F. Haikal
e-mail: fhaikal@aucegypt.edu

Y. Baghdadi et al. (eds.), *ICT for an Inclusive World*,
Lecture Notes in Information Systems and Organisation 35,
https://doi.org/10.1007/978-3-030-34269-2_35

509

1 Introduction

1.1 The Giza Plateau

The Giza plateau has the pyramid of Khufu (Cheops), the oldest of the Seven Wonders of the Ancient World, and the only one remaining intact. The following details about the Giza plateau can be found in Refs. [2–5]. The Giza Plateau is an area of the Memphite cemetery which extends from Abu Rawash in the north to Saqqara in the south. The Memphite cemetery was the final resting place for the kings of the Old Kingdom and some of the kings of Middle Kingdom along with both elite and non-elite tombs dating mainly to that period. During the Late Period, several tombs were built among the Old Kingdom tombs in close proximity to the pyramids.

King Khufu, the second king of the 4th royal dynasty that ruled Egypt was the first king to build his pyramid complex in the area of the Memphite cemetery now called the Giza plateau. However, the Giza plateau was not a virgin ground, since jar seals were found in one of the tombs on the south part of the plateau dating to King Ninetjer of Dynasty 2 as well as another inscription in a tomb dating to king Wadj of Dynasty 1. King Khafre, King Khufu's son, also built his pyramid on the plateau, and despite the fact that it is smaller in size, the elevated spot on which the pyramid was built gave it the same sense of grandeur as the great pyramid of his father Khufu. Menkaure's pyramid is the smallest in scale. After the three kings of the 4th dynasty, the kings of the 5th dynasty chose a different location for their burials, in the area now called Abusir.

The most complete of these complexes in Giza is that of King Khafre and to a large extent King Khufu's complex as well. These types of pyramids are known as "True Pyramids" and they used the style of pyramid architecture of the 4th dynasty, as opposed to the other type which was popular during the preceding 3rd dynasty, the "Step Pyramids". The funerary complexes of the 4th dynasty were also different in their types of structures. The pyramid itself contained the burial chamber and the sarcophagus that contained the mummy of the king. The rest of the complex's structures were for sustaining the cult of the deceased king as a god. This was done by providing offerings to the statue of the king residing in the mortuary temple that was usually situated at the eastern side of the pyramid. Within the complex of Khafre there's also the Sphinx statue, which has the head of the king and the body of a lion. The symbolism of the Sphinx is related to the king equating himself with the sun god.

Another very important feature of the Giza plateau is that it's not an exclusive cemetery for royalty. Non-royal burials can be found in proximity to each pyramid complex. Such non-royal burials were composed of an under-ground burial chamber and a superstructure that resembles a huge rock-cut bench, hence they are called mastabas (an Egyptian term for bench). These mastabas have been granted by the king to the high officials of his court and for the priests responsible for maintaining the cult of the deceased king. The owners of those mastabas benefited from this proximity to the king's pyramid in two ways: first they receive a chance to spend eternity in the afterlife with the king and second they would benefit from the redistribution of offerings presented to the king.

Another very important discovery in the Giza plateau was the Khufu boat that was found dismantled in a rectangular pit on the southern side of the great pyramid of Khufu. The boat was found in the 1950s by the architect and Egyptology enthusiast Kamal El-Mallakh. There's another pit that contains a second boat which has been opened recently. The first boat that was discovered in the 1950s has been put together and erected in a specially built museum that covers the pit in which it was originally placed. The Giza plateau witnessed several other important discoveries especially by Selim Hassan and Reisner but much more of the site still remains unexcavated.

The unique nature of the Giza plateau is not only because of the impressive pyramids that are considered one of the best examples of pyramid architecture, or because the great pyramid is the only standing monument of the Seven Wonders of the World, but also because the Giza plateau was a cemetery for the period of the Old Kingdom and then for more than 1000 years it was not used as a cemetery until the 26th dynasty when it was reused as a cemetery once again. As for the New Kingdom structure it was mainly in the form of temple building in the area of the sphinx as well as some renovations of the monuments during the 21st dynasty. In other words, when it comes to funerary beliefs, the Giza plateau is almost a time capsule of a single period of Egyptian history.

1.2 Second Life in the Giza Plateau Project

Second Life (SL) is a popular 3D virtual platform that is used as an educational tool with social networking capabilities. Within this virtual environment, people can meet each other to interact with existing objects (such as the Pyramids), visit new places or restricted areas (such as the Sphinx); sit in forbidden areas (such as a tomb) and get to know new cultures. The game like set-up gives the visitor a feeling of the environment with one's avatar that can move, jump, and fly inside the virtual Egyptian Pyramids Plateau area. A plan is displayed outside and another plan at the entrance to explain what is there to see and experience. The actual photos are also displayed in different locations through a Horus like projector.

Interestingly when we tested one pyramid stone using 3DS Max and then uploaded it on SL the cost was 11 Linden dollars; but with 12 pyramid stones done using 3DS Max, the cost was 24 Linden dollars when uploaded on SL. In other words, there is no formula for calculating the cost of uploading. Additionally, we found that the objects done on 3DS Max looked much more professional than those done directly on SL. More importantly, 3DS Max helped us overcome a lot of the limitations/restrictions imposed on us by SL. Hence we decided to use 3DS Max first and then upload on SL.

The "Virtual Egyptian Pyramids" project on SL is an example of a large-scale virtual Giza Plateau with many opportunities for savoring heritage as well as social-izing. The SL Giza plateau includes a replica of the pyramids, the Sphinx and the tombs with the actual tunnel that takes you all the way to the King's chamber and the Queen's chamber. The whole project is breath-taking with every single monument replicated at the actual size and direction (e.g. all entrances of the three pyramids are facing North on SL just like the actual). Visitors can walk around or climb the pyramid and visit areas that could otherwise be difficult to go through in real such as the tunnel. In addition, there are numerous examples of rich media and interactivity, including a solar ship/boat that is used to teleport the visitors from one pyramid to the next. The pyramids were stacked on different virtual floors because no land on SL was big enough to allow for the display of all the pyramids with their actual sizes and actual distances from each other.

2 Literature Background

2.1 Immersive Virtual Reality (IVR) and Tourism

IVR is a form of technology that creates computer generated worlds or immersive environments which people can explore and in many cases, interact with [6]. As VR technology continues to evolve, the number and significance of such applications is expected to increase [7]. The increasing immersive VR technology is accorded with a creative economy, it aligns with the concept that relies mainly on using creativity as the main human production factor [8]. The immersive nature of 3D virtual worlds presents significant opportunities for the tourism industry as an optimal marketing platform as well as a useful management tool to develop brand awareness and gain competitive advantage in the global market [9].

Putro [8] reports on the growth of Indonesian tourism and creative industries. His research arrives at a wider possibility of using the VR application to promote Indonesian tourism and sees this as a great opportunity to enhance the competitiveness of Indonesian tourism in the global free trade [8].

The authors in [10] believe that IVR is going to change the way we visit a place, because it will be more immersive as the VR technology becomes cheaper. "Some people will use VR to evade tough reality, some people will confuse real and virtual, but some will use it to improve their culture and the way they work" [10].

Bulencea [11] predicted that the coming years are important for VR in which visitors will have access for the first time to a number of powerful headsets for viewing alternate realities in an immersive 3-D environment. Visitors can use Google Cardboard and Samsung Gear VR to watch them in a 360-degree view with the latest version of Chrome, Opera, Firefox or Internet Explorer on a PC. On a cell phone, the latest version of the YouTube app for Android or iOS [11] may be used. "Virtual reality is the most realistic experience you can have of a place without being there. It's powerful. It gets people excited and engaged and interested in having that experience in real life" [12]. In Australia, news reports in January 2016 [13] focus on promoting Australia's aquatic experiences with a VR and 360 mobile immersive display; while in South African Tourism on VISUALISE [14], a visit is filmed entirely in one location where the video was shot using a series of cameras in 3D printed mounts to create a full 360° effect.

The World Immersive Tour project [15] was founded to make full use of the technical potential of the web, which today is in a position to promote not just information but also emotions and sensations of holidays with great efficiency. The World Immersive Tour is a platform for tourist promotions based on dynamic 360° photographs of landscapes, cities and monuments. Virtual itineraries can be realized with advanced technologies to give the tourist an enthralling multimedia visit to selected destinations.

2.2 Second Life (SL) and Education

SL is a virtual world that can be used for educational purposes [16] as well. There are many virtual games on the internet, which are similar to the SL but only as a game. SL is a platform that helps reconcile the human experience using a computer. The use of avatars gives a feeling of proximity which makes the student's experience more real. The students are engaged with their avatars in an immersive way (as if they are the avatar), as well as in an augmentative way (for a real-world).

Deale [16] reports on the Scholarship of Teaching and Learning (SoTL) project which investigated the use of SL in online hospitality education as an integral learning tool. Her findings indicated that SL provides students and instructors with interesting learning opportunities and allows students to effectively engage with each other and work together on group projects. Stanford University is one of the many universities that use SL (a list of other universities that use SL can be found in [17]).

We refer to this as the "pedago-technical" approach in education. By this we aim to achieve joint optimization in the technical performance and quality of education. However, integrating technology and tools like SL with education is a must-have these days to catch up with the generation being taught and to speak their language. virtually going to restricted or dangerous areas such as climbing the pyramids; revision sessions either guided by the faculty or unguided at the pace of the student; extra "office hours" to increase the students' perception of support; eLearning opportunities; make-up classes that do not have to be physically carried out, to name just a few.

2.3 Second Life (SL) and Tourism

More recently, several travel and tourism organizations have used SL as a collaborative and commercial tool for communicating with travelers as well as tourism enterprises (e.g., Tourism Ireland; Philippines Department of Tourism; STA travel agents; Starwood Hotels; Crowne Plaza) [15]. The tour guide can point out all of the most popular places and direct the visitor to a fun activity [9]. Numerous examples of the museums and galleries in SL can be found in [18, 19]. The Second Louvre Museum is a popular example of a traditional museum installation displaying both classic and modern works of art in a setting specifically designed to replicate a wing of the Louvre Museum in Paris [18].

Challenges that need to be conquered were also identified, such as the sometimes cumbersome nature of the SL program and the time commitment involved with its use [16]. However, given the growth and potential of technologies within the tourism industry and particularly the rising interest in virtual worlds such as SL, a study by Yuchih et al. [1] focuses on the extent to which the virtual world of SL has been used in the tourism industry. Specifically, this study describes what types of spaces tourism businesses are creating or simulating and the types of tourism activities being conducted in the 3D virtual environment [15]. SL has often offered a very unique business opportunity in the tourist guide and travel guide [20].

"When you enter Second Life for the first time, you'll start on Welcome Island. This area is designed to quickly teach you the basics of Second Life, including: walking, zooming with your camera, chatting, standing/sitting, flying, and teleporting" [21]. Along the way, one may be rewarded with a few entertaining surprises. "Travel by foot, by flying, or else jump in a car, tank, plane or magic carpet. With infinite possibilities come limitless modes of transportation - why not drive a fancy car or sail a pirate ship? Or just spread your arms and take to the sky" [21].

Mauritius Island [22] has become virtual and offers a window of its charms on the new Internet frontier of SL. Tourism, culture or diving informs the visitor and tells him/her about the charms of this tropical paradise. The Visit Mexico Ruta Maya [5] is sponsored by the Mexican Tourism Board. A few years ago, the Netherlands Board of Tourism & Conventions [23] announced the launch of http://us.holland.com, a fully Web2.0 based site, as well as the official launch of the world's first National Tourism Board in SL. Justin Glow [24] mentions that Sweden opened an official embassy on SL and that avatars are organized to march for peace, big name companies like American Apparel, Reuters, and Pontiac have setup virtual real estate thus aiming to reach a new audience.

In Virtual Pilgrimage to Mecca [25], Building Dialogue with Avatar Advocates, the authors describe a SL avatar within a replica of Mecca on the path to the Hajj (Pilgrimage) in the virtual world. Sambhanthan and Good [26] report on their SL based virtual community model for enhancing tourism destination accessibility in developing countries. They anticipate that the implementation of their proposed community model can enhance the tourism destination accessibility for users of different categories. In 2014, the Arab Tourism Fair in SL [27] published a 5 min SL video that shows the major tourist attractions and cultures in 3 Arab Countries (KSA, Egypt and Morocco).

2.4   Why SL?

Other popular games when compared to SL:

IMUV [28] is basically an instant messenger for online chat. It has its own virtual currency and you can use it to buy anything to put in the online catalogue. However what you buy may not be traded back into real currency.

With Blue Mars players can travel to various "cities" to interact with other avatars, or create their own businesses and trade with Blue Mars Dollars [29]. You can use it to put on different clothes and see if they suit you or not [30].

The Sims [20] is a life simulation video game series.

Second Life (SL):

- SL is not only a game environment [31]. There's a lot more going on in SL than playing such as learning, teamwork, relaxation, and therapy [32].
- Actually Linden Labs insist that SL is not a game since it does not have any "manufactured conflict" and no "set objective" [33]. Technology & Engineering Emmy Awards for progressing the work of online sites was given to SL in 2008.
- IBM purchased 12 SL islands for "virtual training and simulations of key business processes" (also Reuters and BBC have a presence in SL)
- Entrepreneurial activities and economic opportunities are also potential on SL where one can sell one's own creation.
- SL has its own virtual currency which is the Linden Dollar (1 US$ = 250 L$) provided by Linden Lab, or by brokers or by other SL users. L$ could also be cashed back into US$.
- In 2006 Ailin Graef (avatar's name is Anshe Chung), started with only US $9.95 to buy and sell and even rent virtual real estate in SL; and now became the first in-world millionaire (also considered to be a real-world millionaire).
- It is a big world, not like separate chat rooms. You can teleport from one place to the other using landmarks (bookmarks), names of places, or a map.
- The SL Avatar looks like a human rather than a doll. Skin textures are much more defined and you can use your own face for your avatar.
- You can speak (using a microphone) with other people.
- You can buy things in SL as you would in the real-world. You can also browse the marketplace on the website.
- You can build anything anywhere but the place must be set for that.
- SL now has visually impaired users who move around their avatars using different vibrations; others such as the University of Nevada, IBM, and Max built upon that SL technology and made great improvements (Max is famous for its virtual guide dog).

3   The Technical Approach and Resolved Problems

First a professional photographer took pictures of the 3 Giza pyramids, the Sphinx and the inside of the Khufu pyramid. Using 3DS Max, those pictures were then modeled before being uploaded on SL with the exact size but because SL land was limited in size, Khufu was placed on the ground and the rest of the monuments were placed on the upper part of the virtual land. The net result is breath-taking with every single monument replicated with the actual size. Visitors can climb the pyramid and visit areas that could otherwise be difficult to do in real-world.

3.1   Getting Started with Second Life (SL)

Go to http://secondlife.com, click on Play for Free; choose an avatar; create a username; Select an account type (Select Free); download Second Life l.

3.2   Second Life (SL) Limitations (Very Important)

- The virtual land we bought for the SL project is a 65 km^2 island.
- SL sells only islands the maximum size of which is 65,536 m^2.
- Therefore our project was done on an island that is surrounded by water and the area of 65 km^2 is a restriction imposed by SL.
- Therefore we had to put each pyramid on a separate virtual floor (this way we avoided losing the actual size). We added a virtual elevator as a solar boat.
- SL naming island guidelines: 25 characters max, including up to 2 spaces.
- Virtual Egyptian Pyramids Plateau (the 4 words are not accepted).
- We cannot build with more than 3750 objects in one island.
- We could not upload Khufu as one object because of the 64 m restriction.
- For Khufu we used up a total of 48 objects as displayed in Fig. 1.
- Khufu was not uploaded in one piece as one object since we used the actual dimension of Khufu (sides are more than 64 ms).
- In SL an object is made up of more than one prim as can be seen in Fig. 2.

Fig. 1 Khufu has 48 objects uploaded on SL

Fig. 2   Object versus Prim (this Object is a Pyramid made up of 2 Prims (using SL terms)

- Since our work was done on 3DS Max and later uploaded on SL we did our "prims" on 3DS Max and then uploaded and used only objects (Fig. 1).
- In other words the stones in each numbered object in Fig. 1 were done on 3DS Max (i.e. each object is made up of more details and more stones).
- Had we attempted to do all the prims (stones) one by one on SL, we would have failed since Khufu has 2.3 million stones which is more than 3750 stones.
- 3DS Max was used to avoid a lot of the SL constraints and to get better resolution.
- The Maximum number of vertices per object is 64,000+ vertices (Fig. 3).
- The 64 m vertices restriction on SL is a restriction of the length of one object and when linking 2 objects together (i.e. if one object is 60 m and the other is 5 m we cannot link them together as the total is 65 m which is >64 m):
- Therefore we could not link our 48 objects of Khufu together due to this constraint of 64 m (see Fig. 4).
- We ended up with 2000+ objects when we finished the whole project (48 of which were in Khufu alone).
- All 2000+ objects are not linked together due to the SL constraint explained above.
- This is only problematic if we have to dismantle our objects and put them in Inventory and then assemble them back.
- We will need to dismantle our objects and put them in Inventory only if we do not possess the SL Island anymore.
- Another constraint in SL is the limited tools for creating 3D shape with a texture. Therefore, we created our 3D modeling by using 3DS Max and then uploaded to SL.
- The following Figure which displays one stone done on 3DS Max.
- Attempting to upload on SL goes through the following steps: SL converts the object into triangles (Fig. 6 on the left shows how the stone in Fig. 5 was converted into 13,776 triangles and 8568 vertices).Then SL takes that rendered object to see if all of it was converted into triangles; if not, the empty space in between the triangles is called hulls (the right side of Fig. 6 shows that it calculated 576 hulls).

Fig. 3   Vertices restriction of 64 m

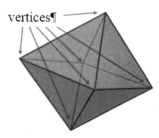

vertices¶

Fig. 4 Two different objects/pieces not linked

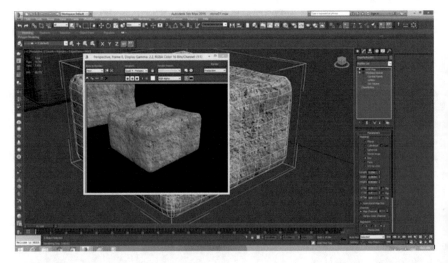

Fig. 5 One pyramid stone done on 3DS MAX

- The maximum number of vertices per object is 64,000+ vertices per object and 170,000+ triangles per object and 256 hulls per object (on the right side we see 576 hulls which is more than the maximum).
- Another restriction on SL is the max uploaded texture size for the real pictures; currently in SL it is 1024 × 1024 pixels (our photographer's pictures are 5616 ×

Fig. 6 Steps to upload a stone on SL

3744 pixels so we put all pictures on Photoshop to resize the image and decrease the pixels; and we lost some of the resolution in the process).

- Another restriction on SL is the avatar height; in our project we had one tunnel with height 1.05 m and according to the avatar height limitation we had to change the Tunnel height to let the avatar pass through the Tunnel and we added some effects to make it clear that it is not the actual height of the tunnel (Fig. 7).
- Another restriction on SL is the mesh but that was not problematic in our project: the maximum mesh (object/DAE file) size after compression is 8 MB and the maximum number of materials per mesh 8.
- When we upload a tunnel as a DAE file in SL with 27.003 m × 4.435 m × 3.032 m, the following message appears:
  "Upload failed because hulls exceeded (hulls number is 425)"
- SL also has Impact limitations.

  https://community.secondlife.com/t5/English-Knowledge-Base/Calculating-land-impact/ta-p/974163

Fig. 7 Tunnel height restriction

How it works

For each object in the Second Life world, Second Life compares three important performance factors: download weight, physics weight, and server weight. It then chooses the highest of these weights and assigns it to the object as that object's land impact rating.

Here's a very quick overview of the different weights; for more information on each, follow the links below:

- Download weight: Calculated by determining how much bandwidth is required to download and view the object. Larger and more visually complex objects have a higher download weight. You can reduce the download weight of complex objects by generating or uploading less complex meshes for differing levels of detail when you upload a model.
- Physics weight: Calculated by determining the complexity of the objects physics model. You can reduce the complexity of a mesh's physics model by using the analysis and simplification tools in the Upload Model window, by uploading your own less-detailed physics model, or by choosing a different physics shape type, such as Convex Hull, on the Features tab of the Build Tools window. Vehicles must have a physics weight of 32 or lower, but may have higher download or server weights.
- Server weight: Measures the impact an object has on Second Life's server resources. Objects that are composed of many prims and have physics enabled and/or contain scripts tend to have high server weights.

- Another restriction is that only 20 avatars can be invited to our island at the same time.
- Light limitation, "Me > Preferences > Graphics" advanced check on advanced lighting model. Therefore, you cannot change the light in specific areas.
- There is a limitation in Camera Angle: "Me > Preferences > move and view". You can change the angle and follow a distance there but with limits.

3.3 Screen Shots

Mr. Hisham Labin, our professional photographer, gave us 546 photos in total: on March 1st 2015 he took 160 photos; on March 17th 2015 he took 332 photos outside and 54 photos inside the Khufu.

We displayed the 546 photos and numbered each one and then saved them on Photoshop to decrease the resolution (Fig. 8) and then uploaded on 3DS Max (samples are shown in Figs. 9, 10, 11, 12).

After that we took all the 3DS Max work and uploaded it on SL (samples are shown in Figs. 13, 14, 15, 16, 17, 18).

When you click on the solar boat, the avatar will sit and the menu will appear in the right to navigate from floor to floor.

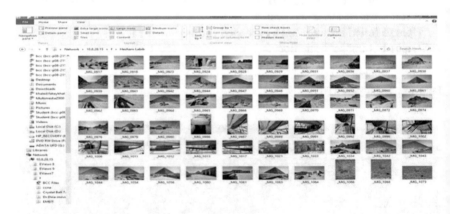

Fig. 8 Mr. Hisham Labib's photos: (total 546 photos)

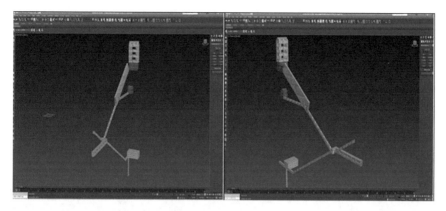

Fig. 9 Khufu pyramid tunnel (3DS Max)

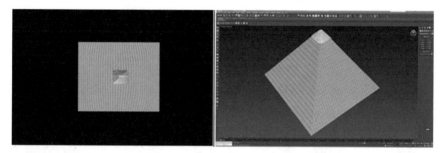

Fig. 10 Over view of the Khafura Pyramid (3DS Max)

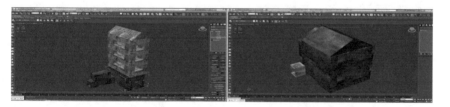

Fig. 11 The King's Chamber (3DS Max) and Queen's Chamber (3 DS Max)

4 The Socio–Economic Impact of the Project

From a socio-economic point of view, the beneficiaries from this research work will be threefold. The first is the local community in the surrounding areas of the monuments to be documented. Their contribution and stake in this project will ensure their cooperation, socioeconomic development, and their will for sustainable preservation of the cultural heritage surrounding them.

Fig. 12 The Sphinx (3DS Max)

Fig. 13 The Plan outside the Pyramid (SL) Zoomed in (left) and Zoomed out (right)

Fig. 14 Explanation outside the Pyramid (SL) Zoomed (left) and Zoomed out (right)

Fig. 15 Entrance explanation Zoomed in and explanation at the entrance zoomed out

Fig. 16 Khufu Pyramid entrance (SL) and the plan inside the great pyramid (SL)

Fig. 17 The solar boat as an elevator and the solar boat going up as an elevator (SL)

Fig. 18 The sphinx on the 4th virtual floor (SL)

The second beneficiary group is that of the academic researchers and scholars in various schools, including but not limited to tourism, business, and the social sciences.

The third beneficiary group is broader in scope and is professionally oriented: the tourism industry as well as the technology based public and private sectors.

5 Conclusion and Directions for Further Work

In the traditional tourist towns worldwide, visitors are greeted with racks of brochures promoting everything from tours and museums to restaurants and hotels. But in the world of portable computers, smart phones and tablets, where holidays are increasingly being chosen and organized on the internet, visitors are expecting new interactive centers where the emphasis is on a quality "high touch" as well as "high tech" experience that can make the discovery of information both fun and educational.

IVR offers tourism many useful applications. Some of the most significant recent ones are cited in the background section above. As IVR technology continues to evolve, the number and significance of such applications will undoubtedly increase. Heritage preservation, entertainment, education and accessibility are some areas of tourism in which IVR may prove particularly valuable.

The advantages of IVR in education and tourism are numerous, including little or no risk (e.g. in climbing the pyramid), remote access which saves time and money, as well as giving an innovative and enjoyable means for students especially for those studying at their own pace. Our tool could be used for eLearning and distance learning courses in Egyptology and Information Technology. The success of this pilot experiment will open doors for further investigations on the integration between the technology and cultural heritage. The study may now be replicated for other historical monuments/locations not only in Egypt but also in many other places worldwide.

On the other hand, the outreach of this online interaction or virtual visit can be reached by millions of remote visitors across the internet to satisfy the desire of those who are unable to visit at this point in time as well as those who could eventually be more encouraged and attracted to come and visit the actual site.

Acknowledgements This research project was supported in part by a university grant. The authors wish to acknowledge the support and permissions granted by the former Egyptian Minister of Antiquities Mamdouh el Damati. As for the technical work and reporting, the authors wish to thank the team who worked on 3DS Max (Gihan Assaad, Ahmed Mirabakhsh, Khaled Shaeishaa, Khaled Abdel Rasoul) and the team who worked on SL (Moataz Osman and Tamer Said). Additionally, we wish to thank Mr. Hisham Labib, the professional photographer as well as the SL experts (Eng. Mohamed El Fadly and Dr. Soumaia El Ayyat). Last but far from least, all the students (graduate and undergraduate) who participated in the SL design work.

References

1. YuChih, H., Backman, S.J., Mcguire, F.A., Backman, K.F., Lan Lan, C.: Second Life: The Potential of 3D Virtual Worlds in Travel and Tourism Industry. http://www.cabdirect.org/abstracts/20133398486.html;jsessionid=E7A1E5D271196E632261E2166099198C
2. Atiya, F.S.: Pyramids of the Fourth Dynasty. Farid Atiya Press, 6th of October City, Giza, Egypt (2004)
3. Baines, J., Jaromír M.: Atlas of Ancient Egypt. The American University in Cairo Press, Cairo (2005)
4. Ikram, Salima: Ancient Egypt: An Introduction. Cambridge University Press, New York (2014)
5. Second Life places: Visit Mexico Ruta Maya. http://www.engadget.com/2008/05/25/second-life-places-visit-mexico-ruta-maya/
6. Virtual Reality Site.: http://www.vrs.org.uk/
7. Guttentag, D.A.: Virtual Reality: Applications and Implications for Tourism.http://www.sciencedirect.com/science/article/pii/S0261517709001332. (2009)
8. Putro, H.T.: Immersive Virtual Reality for Tourism and Creative Industry Development. https://www.researchgate.net/publication/280244745_Immersive_Virtual_Reality_for_Tourism_and_Creative_Industry_Development
9. Tourism is Alive and Well in Second Life. http://www.secondlifeupdate.com/uncategorized/tourism-is-alive-and-well-in-second-life/
10. Immersive Virtual Reality and Tourism: The Kiss of Death. http://www.31december2099.com/2015/12/30/immersive-virtual-reality-and-tourism-the-kiss-of-death/

11. Bulencea, P.: How to Use Virtual Reality in Tourism. http://www.gamification-in-tourism.com/how-to-use-virtual-reality-in-tourism. Jan 2016
12. How Virtual Reality is Making Its Way Into Tourism Industry, AP. http://indianexpress.com/article/technology/gadgets/how-virtual-reality-is-making-its-way-into-tourism-industry/#sthash.3gm21wVY.dpuf. 24 Dec 2015
13. AdNews http://www.adnews.com.au/news/tourism-australia-launches-immersive-campaign-on-australia-day
14. VISUALISE, South African Tourism, Creating the World's First Virtual Tourism Experience. http://visualise.com/case-study/south-african-tourism
15. World Immersive Tour.: http://telecomdesign.it/technologies/world-immersive-tour/
16. Deale, C.S.: Practice Papers: incorporating second life into online hospitality and tourism education: a case study https://www.infona.pl/resource/bwmeta1.element.elsevier-f0863a64-572d-3a27-95f0-d6f7fa774521. J. Hosp. Leis. Tour. Edu., pp. 154–160 (2013)
17. Second Life Education Directory. http://wiki.secondlife.com/wiki/Second_Life_Education_Directory
18. Exemplars of Museums in Second Life. http://alex.state.al.us/librarymedia/Second%20Life%20Educational%20Places.pdf
19. Richard Urban, R., Marty, P., Twidale, M.: A Second Life for Your Museum: 3D Multi-User Virtual Environments and Museums. http://www.museumsandtheweb.com/mw2007/papers/urban/urban.html
20. The Sims.: https://en.wikipedia.org/wiki/The_Sims#cite_note-The_Sims_4_and_other_upcoming_games_to_watch-1
21. Virtual Tourism Research, About Second Life.: https://sites.google.com/site/virtualtourismresearch/secondlife
22. Mauritius Island is on Second Life. https://secondlifemauritius.wordpress.com/
23. Netherlands Opens Tourism Office in Second Life. http://happynews.com/news/8302007/netherlands-opens-tourism-office-second-life.htm. (2007)
24. Glow, J.: Second Life as Virtual Tourism http://gadling.com/2007/01/30/second-life-as-virtual-tourism/. (2007)
25. Virtual Pilgrimage to Mecca, Building Dialogue with Avatar Advocates. http://www.aspeninstitute.org/policy-work/communications-society/programs-topic/journalism/arab-us-media-forum/dead-sea-scrolling/virtual-pil
26. Sambhanthan, A., Good, A.: A Second Life Based Virtual Community Model for Enhancing Tourism Destination Accessibility in Developing Countries (2013)
27. Arab Tourism Fair in Second Life. https://www.youtube.com/watch?v=7MvRQ_E1Y0Q
28. IMUV.: https://en.wikipedia.org/wiki/IMVU
29. Blue Mars. https://en.wikipedia.org/wiki/Blue_Mars_(video_game)
30. Blue Mars Demo Movie.: https://www.youtube.com/watch?v=n8uqEcVlkyg. (2013)
31. Kalning, K.: If Second Life Isn't a Game, What is it? http://www.nbcnews.com/id/17538999/ns/technology_and_science-games/t/if-second-life-isnt-game-what-it/#.VvztD3DWiHl. (2007)
32. Paneque, C.: Second Life is Not a Game. http://www.hypergridbusiness.com/2011/12/second-life-is-not-a-game/. (2011)
33. Second Life. https://en.wikipedia.org/wiki/Second_Life. (2017)

Governance of IS Security in a Cloud Computing Ecosystem: A Longitudinal Approach

Wafa Bouaynaya

Abstract This research proposes an analysis of IS governance in three phases: pre-adoption, the adoption and post-adoption of cloud computing. This approach aims to highlight the different artefacts and key concepts of security governance in a cloud computing ecosystem. It is necessary to ask the question: Which solution to choose? It is also important to differentiate between three key artefacts: data as an asset, the cloud solution as a system, and the service provider as an actor to understand their relationship with the enterprise.

Keywords Cloud computing · Security governance SI · Reversibility cloud computing · Data outsourcing

1 Introduction

Cloud computing is defined by the National Institute of Standards and Technology (NIST) as "a model for enabling ubiquitous, convenient, on-demand network access to a shared pool of configurable computing resources (e.g., networks, servers, storage, applications, and services) that can be rapidly provisioned and released with minimal management effort or service provider interaction. This cloud model is composed of five essential characteristics, three service models, and four deployment models."

The impact of cloud computing in the Information Systems (IS) outsourcing process poses increasingly complex questions of both practitioners and theorists of the digital economy. Becoming a paradigm of organizational transformation, cloud computing already raises numerous security questions related to the confidentiality of outsourced data [1, 15]. Besides, the lack of maturity of several cloud computing services puts business leaders in doubt.

W. Bouaynaya (✉)
Graduate School of Management and CRIISEA research center, University of Picardy, Amiens, France
e-mail: wafa.bouaynaya@u-picardie.fr

© Springer Nature Switzerland AG 2020 527
Y. Baghdadi et al. (eds.), *ICT for an Inclusive World*,
Lecture Notes in Information Systems and Organisation 35,
https://doi.org/10.1007/978-3-030-34269-2_36

The cloud computing market is relatively youthful and very changing [12, 16]. Several start-ups end up disappearing after a few years, or even a few months, endangering the activity of their customers. The company must, therefore, reorient its information system to another provider or reintroduce its activity.

The bankruptcy risk of a cloud provider is not the only factor that drives a company to think about its use of cloud computing. Several organizational, technical or regulatory elements (opportunistic behavior on the part of the supplier, alignment with market offers, regulatory requirements, etc.) require the company to adopt an IS governance approach that starts before the project is launched and which lasts even in breach of the contract with the cloud provider. IS governance is a risk and resource management approach that allows the company to value its use of technology. It will, therefore, be interesting to propose guidelines based on a literature review that allows companies to implement inclusive and longitudinal cloud computing governance.

This work is structured in three parts according to a temporal approach: We begin, first, by studying the governance of the IS security before the adoption of cloud computing. We will then examine the adequacy of the IS governance standards with cloud computing. And in the last step, we will explore post-adoption IS governance of cloud computing through the study of the service reversibility.

2   Governance of IS Security in the Pre-adoption of Cloud Computing

The technological maturity of cloud computing solutions requires a redesign of the business process of each company [16] to be able to assimilate cloud computing into the common value chain. As part of the implementation of an information system, the concepts of Cloud Computing and Datacenters are embedded in a value chain, where the criterion of high availability becomes decisive in the choice of a solution.

Other than the availability of the service, a cloud-based information system must meet the objectives set as part of an overall corporate strategy. In a pre-adoption phase of cloud computing, it is important to ask the question: *Which solution to choose?*

The prospects for such a query go beyond the technical and functional aspect of the cloud solution to incorporate organizational circumstances such as the criticality of the data to be outsourced or the relationship with the supplier (auditability, service reversibility, etc.). At this point, it is necessary to differentiate three artefacts: data as an asset, the cloud solution as a system and the service provider as an actor to understand their relationship with the company. Therefore, we will try to examine each of its artefacts independently of the other two to define inclusive governance of IS security pre-adoption of cloud computing.

2.1　Criticality of Outsourced Data

The performance of inter-organizational information systems is often associated with the modalities of information sharing. Inter-organizational coordination that defines the interdependencies of activities can be analyzed through the process involved. We retain three modes of coordination of activities [7, 10] to characterize information exchange: alignment, flow and sharing.

Whatever the mode of coordination, cloud computing is a vector of ideal transmission of information within the information system. Moreover, although the development of total quality management after the Second World War has given importance to data quality and trade improvement [7]. The emergence of massive storage has altered the notion of data quality with its multidimensional posture (accuracy, temporality, security, reliability...): Each piece of information is likely to be important at any time.

It is however interesting to classify the information to be able to decide on its outsourcing. The probabilistic theory of information [11] defines information as a measurable quantity according to randomness. The information will be the uncertainty calculated from the probability of the event [11]: the more information is unlikely, the more important it is. A first classification of the information can thus be translated through the probability of the event. The company can outsource information with high certainty and internally manage the unlikely information which is an organizational asset and can provide a competitive advantage for the company.

By referring to the harmonized method of risk analysis (MEHARI, 2010), it is possible to distinguish between individually sensitive data that we can associate with the unlikely information [11] and the rest of the data. The distinction between isolated data and data sets is no longer sufficient to encompass the difference in impact on the information system. Therefore, the 2010 version of MEHARI considers individually sensitive data as a specific primary asset class. It is not advisable to outsource any type of primary asset. Only weakly specific assets can be outsourced [3].

It is also possible to specify the criticality of data based on the area of activity. A study conducted by Markess in 2010 showed that SaaS cloud computing applications are particularly relevant to enterprise collaboration, customer relationship management and human resources management. Few companies access to cloud solutions to outsource the core of their business or financial data.

2.2　Auditability of the Cloud Computing Solution

The assessment of the risks associated with the migration to a new information system necessarily involves an audit activity that affects, among other things, the control of the source code. This activity is even more crucial and acquires all its importance in IT outsourcing or operating a public cloud service.

The appreciation of the source code of an application is still not obvious in the case of the proprietary software industry because the provider reserves the right to provide part of the code to an external auditor. Note also that the appreciation of a part of a code, carefully chosen by its creator, cannot be accepted as a representative sample of source code. Only the open source software industry provides complete transparency in the audit [13, 14].

The most relevant argument presented in favor of open source security is the peer review process which necessarily involves an audit of the external code. This review systematically evokes the evaluation made in the academic community for criticism of research work. Therefore, the examination of source code by peers gives a competitive advantage to open source software by promoting objectivity and security transparency.

Although Richard Stallman, founding father of the free software movement, has strongly criticized cloud computing,[1] the open source alternative (OpenStack, Docker,...) has gained a significant share of the cloud market, after the security controversy launched by Edward Snowden in June 2013. These offers remain, however, ambiguous and raise several questions about their reliability. The transformation of the role of CIO within the company following the migration to a cloud solution results in a loss of its technical know-how and consequently a loss of expertise to audit outsourced information systems.

2.3   Relationship with Cloud Computing Provider

Data leakage under the multiplier effect of cloud computing has highlighted a mistrust of the services offered by several providers: seven out of 10 companies in Europe accuse their service providers of non-compliance with the current regulations on data protection.[2]

Trust appears as an old concern for the implementation of an information system [18, 20]. With the emergence of cloud computing, supplier confidence is influenced by the customer's perception of security practices [15]. Although businesses are often overwhelmed by multiple offerings and options, security issues remain high on the agenda. It is therefore important to ask questions about cloud provider security approaches and practices as well as internal risk tolerance.

A first question arises with respect to the location of the data. The difference in laws governing data access is a problem in outsourcing European data to a data center in the United States. The USA PATRIOT Act allows US security services to retrieve personal and business data without prior authorization and without informing users.

---

[1] "Cloud computing is a trap, warns GNU founder Richard Stallman" (2008), The Guardian: https://www.theguardian.com/technology/2008/sep/29/cloud.computing.richard.stallman.

[2] "Data Breach: The Cloud Multiplier Effect in European Countries" (2015), Netskope: https://resources.netskope.com/h/i/40485095-data-breach-the-cloud-multiplier-effect-in-european-countries/162467.

It is also possible that the cloud provider, although European, is outsourcing the data to another provider. We must, therefore, consider how it handles judicial requests for access to data and understands the process of their traceability.

A second question arises with regard to outsourced data access permissions. The distinction between virtual access and physical access is essential to understanding the rights to data manipulation. First, there is a need to define an exhaustive list of actors who benefit from virtual access to data as well as their reading, writing and excursion roles. Each level of actors must be associated with an adequate level of encryption.

Physical access control is also important to anticipate any unwanted intrusion. It is, therefore, important to have a clear idea about datacenters security procedures. The four-level certification issued by the uptime institute or the certification of the ISO 270xx series (ISO 27017 and ISO 27018, specific to cloud computing) can be sufficient security guarantees.

One last question is necessary with respect to the procedures of service reversibility. Although the problem is not much addressed by the literature, it is essential to anticipate the end of an outsourcing contract. A company must first make sure of the transferability of its data to another service provider at the end of the contract before signing it. It must, in addition, ensure procedures for deleting its data after recovery. Physical destruction of hard drives is, for example, desirable to ensure the confidentiality of its intangible heritage.

3   Governance of IS Security During the Adoption of Cloud Computing

Interest in IT governance has increased since the application of US Sarbanes-Oxley or HIPPA laws to mitigate the risks associated with IT [4]. Since then, the security of information is no longer limited to the operational dimension but also includes a strategic aspect. Numerous references have emerged and several researchers have examined the question [9, 19, 21] to frame the IS governance. Although no governance model covers all aspects of possible controls, each meets a number of requirements that affect the techniques, objectives and scope.

IT governance goes beyond the operational focus to offer a holistic view of information security management [2, 19]. It encompasses the issues and decisions made by senior management in a long-term strategic approach. The introduction of organizational culture is all the more necessary to involve employees in IT governance [17, 20].

In a cloud computing context, IT governance requires a new definition of organizational policies with an explicit description of roles and responsibilities for managing technologies, business processes, and applications. Indeed, the flight to a cloud service of the IT function [16] does not disrupt the objectives set by the IT governance standards. It introduces, however, a new relational element with cloud providers that must be included in the application of IT governance. Traditional IT governance models (COSO, CobiT, ENISA, ITIL and ISO) are therefore not affected by the implementation of cloud solutions, but they must be adapted to the new context.

Since 2011, the Information Systems Audit and Control Association (ISACA) has tried to adapt the Cobit repository to a cloud context by proposing a new reading of IT governance through the publication of "IT control objectives for cloud computing". The study describes the technological and organizational requirements of implementing the repository in cloud computing.

In addition, COSO has submitted an Enterprise Risk Management Framework (ERM framework) applicable for cloud computing governance through seven guidelines:

(1) Internal environment: perception of risks and controls;
(2) Objective: alignment of the objectives of the organization;
(3) Identification of the event: identification of opportunities or risks;
(4) Risk assessment—definition of the impact of risks;
(5) Risk treatment;
(6) Control Activities—definition of control responsibility;
(7) Information and communication—establish timely and accurate communication flows.

The framework can be tailored to the business process, deployment model, and cloud service model. It is clear that this framework can also be merged with the cloud cube model suggested by the Open Group (The Cloud Cube Model) to include the four characteristic dimensions of the service instead of the cloud options:

• Physical location of the data (internal/external)
• Technological ownership (owner/Open SOurce)
• Border between companies (configurable/deparameterable)
• Cloud service acquisition management (outsourced/internalized).

ISO has also published two new standards that are appropriate for cloud computing requirements: ISO/IEC 27017 and ISO/IEC 27018. The first provides guidelines for implementing information security controls for cloud services. In addition to the initial guide defined by ISO 27002, while the second includes best practices for the protection of Personally Identifiable Information (PII) in public cloud computing.

ISO/IEC 2700x standards are often associated with the harmonized risk analysis method (MEHARI), developed by CLUSIF. MEHARI offers an analysis of the business challenges of the company that reduces the risk exposure through customized measures. The method is in its sixth version and has marked an advanced stage of maturity in terms of risk management. It is easily applicable to the cloud computing context since it supports distributed data sites.

Regardless of the repository or security standard is chosen by the enterprise to manage its outsourced information system in cloud mode, it must have a sufficient degree of control [21] to reduce informational asymmetry with his supplier.

4 Governance of IS Security in the Post-adoption of Cloud Computing: Reversibility of Service

The cloud computing market is a relatively youthful and very changing market [12, 16]. Several start-ups end up disappearing after a few years or even a few months, endangering the activity of their customers. The company must then consider the reversibility of this service and, consequently, reorient its information system towards another supplier or re-internalize its activity.

The bankruptcy risk of a cloud provider is not the only factor that drives a company to think about the reversibility of the service. Companies can use reversibility for various organizational, technical or regulatory reasons: opportunistic behavior on the part of the supplier, alignment with market offers, organizational transformation. Reversibility is not always an alternative to failed outsourcing [8] but it can give the company new organizational perspectives.

It is true that there is a great deal of research into the adoption of cloud computing in companies, but few researchers have considered the reversibility of this service. The work on cloud computing addresses the irreversibility of the service as an obstacle to the development of the cloud without analyzing it.

The information systems security classically based on the integrity, confidentiality and availability triad is no longer able to meet the new requirements of a cloud-hosted IS. The reversibility of the information system in cloud mode should be seen as a new security axis [6]. Reversibility cannot be associated with data privacy, let alone with the integrity or availability of the system (Fig. 1).

Fig. 1 Tetrad security—information system hosted in cloud computing [6]

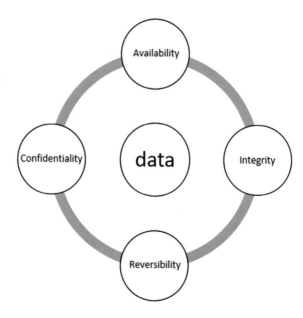

Although the outsourcing of information systems exists well before the adoption of cloud computing on a large scale, the cloud has revived old questions that affect both CIOs and departments concerned by the adoption/migration process. A deep reflection on what the company needs is required in order to be able to better manage the risks incurred either in relation to the cloud computing adoption or in relation to the reversibility of this service.

Reversibility is perceived as a transferability of the cloud service to another provider rather than a re-outsourcing. Therefore, reversibility is not a reintegration of the system internally but a new "flight" to the cloud [16]. The transferability commits the service provider to cooperate with a competitor for the transfer of the system or data of his client. However, the perception of this commitment has separated the experts [6]. This leads us to deduce that the cooperation of a supplier at the end of the contract is linked to several factors including the implementation of the cloud computing project. Although reversibility is explicitly written into the majority of cloud outsourcing contracts, the contract clauses are not sufficient to guarantee it. The reversibility of a process does not depend on the inventory of the existing at the end of the contract, but it must be taught through a plan detailing the conditions and resources put in place for its success from the signature of the contract.

Reversibility is defined as the resumption of a previous viable situation and thus avoid blocking the system. It ensures the autonomy of the company in relation to its supplier and consequently, guarantee the continuity of the service in case of bankruptcy of this one.

It is important to note that the complexity of a reversibility operation depends largely on the cloud service model. The PaaS/IaaS market, dominated mainly by four major players (Amazon, Microsoft, IBM and Google), imposes a technological dependence for these suppliers [5] and therefore limits the transferability of the service. The SaaS market, on the other hand, is much more heterogeneous and atomic, is available in several services and allows customers to reorient their choices according to their needs. It is, therefore, necessary to position oneself in relation to the market before starting a reversibility operation: it is not possible to transfer a service in PaaS/IaaS mode, but it is highly recommended to prepare a reversibility plan before to launch in a SaaS project, especially as the risk of bankruptcy is much greater for SMEs offering SaaS services.

Reorienting a cloud service to a new provider first and foremost requires interoperability between the old and the new system. Interoperability is defined as the ability of different hardware, software, or protocols to work together and share information, and includes the standardization of the exchange interfaces: the application programming interfaces (APIs).

Although the standardization of APIs appears to be an obligation to guarantee the reversibility of cloud services, it is only assured for public sector data. The private sector is still suffering from the fragmentation of standards due to lack of involvement by several key actors.

Nevertheless, to minimize the risk of blocking, it is always possible for a company to refer to a free and open format to retrieve its data at the end of the contract or duplicate them at home according to a business continuity plan. Salesforce Service

Provider, for example, agrees to deliver customer data in Comma-Separated Values (CSV) format with all attachments in the native format if the customer makes a request 30 days after the close of its service.

It is also possible to anticipate possible problems of reversibility at the supplier by setting up a punctual audit process. The CIO remains the key actor in controlling the vendor throughout the contract.

The irreversibility of a cloud service is an obstacle for the development of the sector but for a large number of companies, it does not determine the choice of provider [6]. It is possible that this is related to the lack of commitment of the general manager and that, consequently, the decision of migration to the cloud is taken arbitrarily by the only department concerned.

5 Conclusion

This work provides an analysis of pre-adoption IS governance during the adoption and post-adoption of cloud computing. It is necessary to ask the question: Which solution to choose? It is also important to differentiate between three key artefacts: data as an asset, the cloud solution as a system, and the service provider as an actor, and understanding their relationship with the enterprise.

Our cross-reading of risk management, notably based on a reference system used by computer science specialists, highlighted the adequacy of these standards with cloud computing as a new technological paradigm.

In the last step, and considering the absence of a formal and structured framework for the definition of the reversibility of a cloud computing service, we opted for an abductive approach. We have tried to define the conditions of application (When), the key actors (Who), the techniques of reversibility (How), and the objectives (Why) through a fragmentation of the theoretical context.

References

1. Armbrust, M., Fox, A., Griffith, R., Joseph, A.D., Katz, R., Konwinski, A., Zaharia, M.: A view of cloud computing. Commun. ACM **53**(4), 50–58 (2010)
2. Baskerville, R.: Information systems security design methods: implications for information systems development. ACM Comput. Surv. (CSUR) **25**(4), 375–414 (1993)
3. Barthélémy, J.: L'externalisation: une forme organisationnelle nouvelle. Communication à l'Association Internationale du Management Stratégique (1999)
4. Becker, J., Bailey, E.: A Comparison of IT Governance & Control Frameworks in Cloud Computing (2014)
5. Bouaynaya, W., Bidan, M.: Une exploration qualitative du rôle des opérateurs du Cloud Computing dans l'acheminement des données des PME. Manag. Avenir **3**, 65–83 (2017)
6. Bouaynaya, W.: Characterization of cloud computing reversibility as explored by the DELPHI method. Inf. Syst. Front. 1–14 (2019)

7. De Corbière, F., Durand, B., Rowe, F.: Effets économiques et environnementaux de la mutuali-
    sation des informations logistiques de distribution: avis d'experts et voies de recherche. Manag.
    Avenir **9**, 326–348 (2010)
8. Fréry, F., Law-kheng, F.: La réinternalisation, chaînon manquant des théories de la firme. Revue
    française de gestion **8**, 163–179 (2007)
9. Garigue, R., Stefaniu, M.: Information security governance reporting. Inf. Syst. Secur. **12**(4),
    36–40 (2003)
10. Malone, T.W., Crowston, K., Lee, J., Pentland, B., Dellarocas, C., Wyner, G., Klein, M.: Tools
    for inventing organizations: toward a handbook of organizational processes. Manage. Sci. **45**(3),
    425–443 (1999)
11. Shannon, C.E.: A mathematical theory of communication, part I, part II. Bell Syst. Tech. J. **27**,
    623–656 (1948)
12. Shivakumar, B.L., Raju, T.: Emerging role of cloud computing in redefining business
    operations. Glob. Manag. Rev. **4**(4) (2010)
13. Spinellis, D., Gousios, G., Karakoidas, V., Louridas, P., Adams, P.J., Samoladas, I., Stamelos,
    I.: Evaluating the quality of open source software. Electron. Notes Theoret. Comput. Sci. **233**,
    5–28 (2009)
14. Stamelos, I., Angelis, L., Oikonomou, A., Bleris, G.L.: Code quality analysis in open source
    software development. Inf. Syst. J. **12**(1), 43–60 (2002)
15. Stieninger, M., Nedbal, D., Erskine, M., Wagner, G.: The Adoption of Cloud Services in the
    Context of Organizations: An Examination of Drivers and Barriers (2014)
16. Tiers, G., Mourmant, G., Leclercq-Vandelannoitte, A.: L'envol vers le Cloud: un phénomène
    de maturations multiples. Systèmes d'information Manag. **18**(4), 7–42 (2013)
17. Van Niekerk, J.F., Von Solms, R.: Information security culture: a management perspective.
    Comput. Secur. **29**(4), 476–486 (2010)
18. Vermeulen, C., Von Solms, R.: The information security management toolbox–taking the pain
    out of security management. Inf. Manag. Comput. Secur. **10**(3), 119–125 (2002)
19. Veiga, A.D., Eloff, J.H.: An information security governance framework. Inf. Syst. Manag.
    24(4), 361–372 (2007)
20. Von Solms, B.: Information security–the fourth wave. Comput. Secur. **25**(3), 165–168 (2006)
21. Warkentin, M., Johnston, A. C.: Fear appeals and information security behaviors: an empirical
    study. MIS Q. 549–566 (2010)

Rate of Penetration (ROP) Prediction in Oil Drilling Based on Ensemble Machine Learning

Djamil Rezki, Leila Hayet Mouss, Abdelkader Baaziz and Nafissa Rezki

Abstract This work presents the prediction of the rate of progression in oil drilling based on random forest algorithm, which is part of the family of ensemble machine learning. The ROP parameter plays a very important role in oil drilling, which has a great impact on drilling costs, and its prediction allows drilling engineers to choose the best combination of input parameters for better progress in drilling operations. To resolve this problem, several works have been realized with the different modeling techniques as machine learning: RNAs, Bayesian networks, SVM etc. The random forest algorithm chosen for our model is better than the other MLS techniques. in speed or precision, following what we found in the literature and tests done with the open source machine learning tool on historical oil drilling logs from fields of Hassi Terfa located in southern Algeria.

Keywords Oil drilling · Rate of penetration · Prediction · Random forest · SVM · ANN · Machine learning · WEKA · KNIME

D. Rezki (✉) · L. H. Mouss · N. Rezki
LAP Laboratory, Batna 2 University, 05000 Batna, Algeria
e-mail: djamil.rezki@hotmail.com

L. H. Mouss
e-mail: hayet_mouss@yahoo.fr

N. Rezki
e-mail: nafissa_rezki@yahoo.fr

A. Baaziz
Institut Méditerranéen des Sciences de l'Information et de la Communication (IMSIC) — Université Aix-Marseille, Marseille, France
e-mail: abdelkader.baaziz@univ-amu.fr

© Springer Nature Switzerland AG 2020
Y. Baghdadi et al. (eds.), *ICT for an Inclusive World*,
Lecture Notes in Information Systems and Organisation 35,
https://doi.org/10.1007/978-3-030-34269-2_37

1 Introduction

The aim of drilling optimization is to minimize the overall cost of oil well drilling from the first one. Oil companies have always sought to reduce drilling costs mainly by increasing the rate of penetration (ROP). The most important operations to effectively optimize ROP are modeling and forecasting. Unfortunately, most of the existing ROP forecasting methods are based on physical field experiments. It is difficult to practice these methods on the site hence the need to find a convenient and relatively accurate ROP predicting method.

The key drilling variables that directly influence the rate of drilling penetration are not well understood and are often complex to model. In such situations, it's very difficult to find reliable mathematical models. In this context, intelligent methods such as random forests can be powerful tools to effectively predict the ROP and allow drilling engineers can make better decisions.

2 Literature Review

2.1 Related Works

As previously mentioned, the main drilling variables that directly influence ROP are often poorly understood, making it more difficult to find an adequate model to predict an accurate ROP. Several works based on artificial intelligence have been conducted to address this problem focusing on artificial neural network, fuzzy logic and other techniques. Moradi et al. [1] introduced a new drilling model using K-Means to simulate annealing and fuzzy logic to construct a fuzzy model for ROP prediction. The defined model gave good ROP accuracy. A study conducted in Kuwait [2], artificial neural networks are successfully used to predict drilling parameters. A similar application of artificial neural networks was successfully used for ROP prediction in an oil tanker field in southern of Iran. The obtained results show that the approach developed in these fields, is more efficient compared to conventional methods [3]. Edalatkhaha et al [4] proposed an approach using artificial neural networks to allow selecting the drill bit that provides a maximum ROP. In another study that deals with the optimization of drilling costs in an offshore field in Brazil [5], a combination of Bayesian inference approach and Neuro-fuzzy system, is used to predict ROP. This study showed the advantage of the neuro-fuzzy model to enhance the prediction quality. SVR (SVM for regression) was applied to predict drilling cost in one of Chinese oil fields [6], the experimental results show a good ROP accuracy of developed predicting model of the drilling cost.

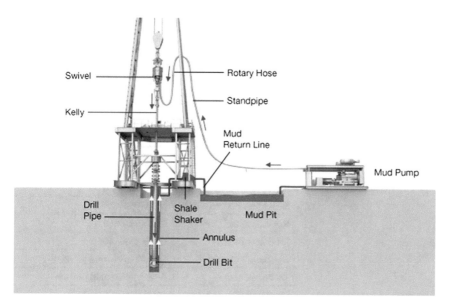

Fig. 1. Rotary drilling process[2]

2.2 Oil Well Rotary Drilling Process

Rotary drilling involves applying a force on a drill bit through a weight while driving it in rotation with a continuous injection of drilling mud to evacuate debris [7].

The rotary drill probe is a needed equipment to perform the three functions following (shown in Fig. 1):

- Weight on the drill bit,
- Rotation of the drill bit,
- Fluid injection.

2.3 Oil Drilling Parameters

The drilling parameters are the various mechanical and hydraulic factors that can influence the ROP [8]. The optimization of ROP is very important in the drilling process because it is directly related to the time spent in the drilling installation.

These types of parameters [9, 10] can be presented as in Table 1.

Table 1 Oil drilling parameters

The mechanical parameters	The hydraulic parameters
Weight on bit (WOB)	Mud type
Rotation speed (RPM)	Hydraulic flow and pressure
Torque on bit	Mud density

Table 2 Factors influencing ROP

Controllable factors	Environmental factors
Bit wear state	Depth
Bit design (Bit type)	Geological properties of the formation
Weight on Bit (WOB)	Mud type
Rotation speed (RPM)	Mud density
Mud flow rate	Other mud properties
Hydraulics of the bit	Overbalance mud pressure
Bit nozzle size	Bottom hole mud pressure
Engine/turbine geometry	Bit size

2.4 Factors Influencing the Rate of Penetration (ROP)

The factors which are influencing ROP can be classified in two main groups: controllable factors and environmental factors. The controllable factors can be altered more easily than environmental factors. Because of economical and geological conditions, the variation of environmental factors is impractical or expensive [11].

These factors can be presented as in Table 2.

2.5 Random Forest

The main of ensemble methods is to construct a collection of predictors, then aggregate the set in their predictions [12].

In a regression problem, aggregating the prediction of q predictors amounts to the average. For example, in classification, a majority vote among the classes provided by the predictors, for the purpose of more precision and efficiency in the product predictor, the combination of the predictor may be sequential, parallel or hybrid. These methods rely on several methods for induction such as Bagging, Boosting and Random Subspace, and Randomizing output.

Random forest is part of the family of ensemble methods that take the decision tree as an individual predictor generally the CART algorithm which is a statistical method introduced by Breiman in 2001 which constructs predictors by binary tree in regression and classification as well. They are based on the methods of Bagging, Randomizing Outputs and Random Subspace by excusing Boosting [13, 14].

3 Our Approach: Implementation, Experimentation and Results

Our main idea is to use the random forest algorithm, which is part of the methods set that build a predictor collection and to aggregate all their predictions. The use of ensemble methods ensures accuracy and efficiency [15].

Previous works have used artificial intelligence techniques such as artificial neural networks (ANN) that have given better results. Nevertheless, the latter remain less efficient compared to the "random forests" algorithm. This performance concerns both speed and accuracy. Indeed, following the tests that we carried out for ROP optimization (by using an open source machine learning tool) on drilling logs obtained from Hassi–Terfa field (located in the south from Algeria), we found that the random forest algorithm was more accurate and faster than other techniques such as SVM and neural networks.

This approach is implemented through the following steps (as shown in Fig. 2):

Fig. 2 A proposed approach to resolve ROP prediction problem

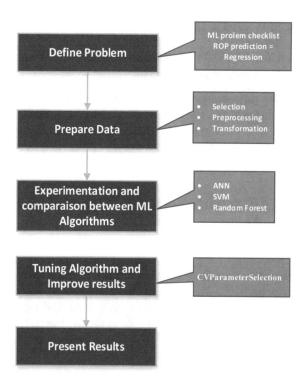

3.1 Define the Problem

It is very important to understand the problem before handling data or algorithms. The ROP prediction which is a real (continuous) value can be considered a regression problem.

3.2 Prepare Data

Preprocessing and data cleanup are important tasks that must occur before using a dataset for machine learning purposes [16]. Raw data is often noisy, unreliable and incomplete. In oil drilling, the data comes from several sources. They may contain anomalies or incorrect values that compromise data quality.

The main data of this study are obtained from vertical onshore wells drilled in the Hassi–Terfa field in southern Algeria in 2012 and our ROP prediction model is based on the following parameters:

- WOB: The weight on bit;
- RPM: Rotation speed;
- Flow in: Incoming mud flow;
- MWI: Mud density;
- SPP: Stand pipe pressure;
- Torque;
- UCS: Uniaxial Compressive Strength;
- ROP: Rate of penetration (meter per hour).

All parameters are surface measurements from the Mud Logging operations except UCS which is a bottom parameter that can be computed in laboratory tests from sonic logs (Gamma Ray), three databases have been prepared. The ROP (meter per hour) is the expected output parameter.

3.3 Experimentation and Comparison Between Machine Learning Algorithms

There are several machine-learning algorithms to handle regression problem, among them we have selected those who seem to be the best performers based on the results of experiments in the WEKA machine-learning tool and the works encountered in the literature. These include Artificial Neuronal Networks (ANN), Support Vector Machine (SVM) and random forest that will be the subject of our experimentation and comparison.

3.3.1 Artificial Neural Networks (ANN)

Neural networks are used in decision analysis in its data mining part for the prediction [15], classification and analysis of data. In this work, the chosen architecture is of the Multi-Layer Perceptron (MLP) type, the learning of the MLP classifier implemented on WEKA.[3] It consists of at least three layers of nodes. Except for the input nodes, each node is a neuron that uses a nonlinear activation function. MLP utilizes a supervised learning technique called backpropagation for training. The activation function is described by $y(v_i) = \tanh(v_i)$. The learning of the MLP classifier is optimized by minimizing the quadratic error added to a quadratic penalty with the Broyden–Fletcher–Goldfarb–Shanno method (BFGS) to solve a problem of nonlinear optimization without constraints.

The architecture of the obtained MLP is shown in Fig. 3.

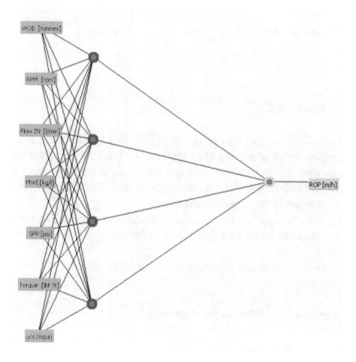

Fig. 3 The obtained ANN

---

[3]MLP classifier's implementation on WEKA. Visited on 05/07/2018 @ http://weka.sourceforge.net/doc.packages/multiLayerPerceptrons/weka/classifiers/functions/MLPClassifier.html.

3.3.2 Support Vector Machine SVM

SVM is a generalization of linear classifiers. It involves a set of supervised learning techniques for solving classification and regression problems.

The used classifier called Sequential Mininmal Optimization for regression (SMOreg)[4] implemented under WEKA, is an algorithm for solving the Quadratic Programming (QP) problem that arises during the training of support vector machines. It was created by Alex J. Smola and Bernhard Scholkopf who implements Support Vector for regression whose learning is carried out in using polynomial or RBF kernels. SVM is trained by solving quadratic problems which is expressed in the dual form as follows:

$$\max_{\alpha} \sum_{i=1}^{n} \alpha_i - \frac{1}{2} \sum_{i=1}^{n} \sum_{j=1}^{n} y_i y_j K\left(x_i, x_j\right) \alpha_i \alpha_j$$

$$\text{Subject to} : 0 \leq \alpha_i \leq C, \quad \text{for } i = 1, 2, \ldots, n \text{ and } \sum_{i=1}^{n} y_i \alpha_i = 0$$

3.3.3 Random Forest

Random Forest (RF) was formally proposed in 2001 by Leo Breiman and Adle Cutler [12]. It's a supervised learning algorithm that can be used for both classification and regression problems.[5] It performs learning on multiple decision trees trained on slightly different datasets to get a more accurate and stable prediction where the comparison criterion is the correlation rate.

The most important parameters: the default number of trees is 100, the number of parameters chosen randomly by default is (p/3) for regression (p is the total number of parameters).

Figure 4 show a part of our own random forest build model.

3.3.4 Evaluation and Selection of Algorithm

There are two modes of evaluation:

1) *Division in learning set and test set:* which consists of dividing the database into two parts, the first one (66%) for learning and the remaining part for testing.
2) *Cross-Validation:* a method for estimating the reliability of a model based on a sampling technique, dividing the original sample into k samples, then selecting

---

[4]SVM (SMOreg) classifier's implementation on WEKA. Visited on 05/07/2018 @ http://weka.sourceforge.net/doc.dev/weka/classifiers/functions/SMOreg.html.
[5]RF classifier's implementation on WEKA. Visited on 05/07/2018 @ http://weka.sourceforge.net/doc.dev/weka/classifiers/trees/RandomForest.html.

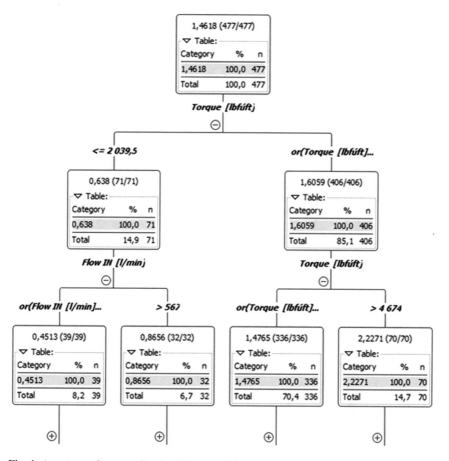

Fig. 4 An extract of our own Random Forest model

one of the k samples as the validation set and the (k−1) other samples will constitute the learning set.

The experiment was carried out with the following parameters:

- *10 control iterations,*
- *66% learning set and 34% test set,*
- *10 samples for cross-validation,*
- *The criterion of comparison chosen is the correlation rate.*

After the experiment with the first evaluation mode (train/test), the results are presented in the Table 3. With cross validation (10 samples), the results are presented in the Table 4.

The results of Tables 3 and 4 show that the random forest algorithm has the highest correlation rate. Then it is the best choice for support our prediction problem.

Table 3 Experimentation results in mode (train/test)

	ANN (MLP)	SVM (SMOReg)	Random forest
Database 1	0.48	0.52	0.74
Database 2	0.58	0.58	0.74
Database 3	0.72	0.61	0.81

Table 4 Experimentation results in mode cross-validation

	ANN (MLP)	SVM (SMOReg)	Random forest
Database 1	0.54	0.55	0.79
Database 2	0.51	0.56	0.74
Database 3	0.74	0.63	0.85

3.4 Tuning of Random Forest Parameters

The configuration of the parameters can have a significant impact on the accuracy of the prediction of the proposed model. The optimal parameter configuration is often different for each different data set. Therefore, they must be ordered for each data set. Since the training process does not define the parameters, there must be a process tuning parameter (Fig. 5).

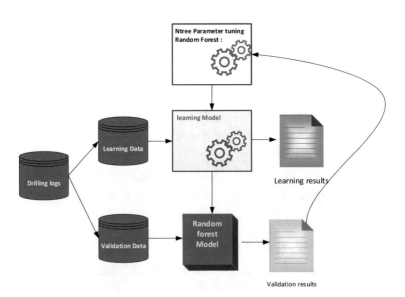

Fig. 5 Machine learning tuning

Targeting optimal parameters for a classifier can be a tedious process, WEKA offers some ways of automating this process through the following metaclassifiers[6]:

- CVParameterSelection: allows to optimize an arbitrary number of parameters by using cross-validation;
- GridSearch: allows the setting of the parameters used to construct and evaluate a model for each combination of algorithm parameters specified in a grid;
- MultiSearch: allows the optimization of any number of parameters.
- We used the metaclassifier CVParameterSelection to optimize the tree number parameter "ntree" in our Random Forest algorithm. The database 3 is used for evaluation after running the metaclassifier, we obtained a coefficient is 0.87 and the number of trees "ntree = 70".

3.5 Present Results in KNIME Platform

We load the database 3 (Well 3/6-inch phase) into our collected data. The target is an ORDOVICIAN reservoir and our predictor created with the random forest algorithm can predict the ROP with a very good accuracy (correlation coefficient = 0.87). The database is divided into two parts (66% for learning) and the rest for the test. After experimentation in WEKA tool, we developed a model workflow in the open source platform KNIME (Fig. 6) to validate and present the prediction results of the Random forest algorithm. The results is shown in Fig. 7.

Interestingly, even though our prediction model is still not perfect, as shown in Fig. 7, the predicted ROP is very close to the observed ROP and reflects the accuracy of our developed model.

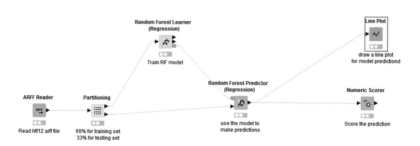

Fig. 6 Prediction random forest flow model in KNIME

---

[6]Optimizing parameters on WEKA, Visited on 05/07/2018 @ https://weka.wikispaces.com/Optimizing+parameters.

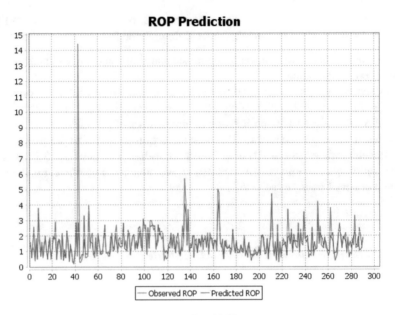

Fig. 7 Comparison between observed and predicted ROP

4 Conclusion

Most existing ROP prediction methods rely mainly on physical field experiments. It is difficult to play these methods on site, so it is necessary to find a convenient and relatively accurate ROP prediction method.

In this paper, we have developed of a model of prediction for the drilling speed using intelligent techniques and random forest. To validate our model, we have used a data from wells drilled in Hassi–Terfa field located in South of Algeria. The developed model can be used as a decision aid for drilling engineers to predict the ROP and plan drilling programs. It is also useful for adjusting the input parameters to predict the best ROP in order to reduce the drilling time.

References

1. Moradi, H., et al.: Drilling rate prediction using an innovative soft computing approach. Sci. Res. Assays **5**(13), 1583–1588 (2010)
2. Al-Rashidi, A.F.: Designing Neural Networks for the Prediction of the Drilling Parameters for Kuwait Oil and Gas Fields. Master thesis in gas and oil engineering. University of Virginia West, USA (1999)
3. Monazami, M., et al.: Drilling rate of penetration prediction using artificial neural network: a case study of one of Iranian southern oil fields. Electron. Sci. J Oil Gas Bus. **6**(6), 21–31 (2012)

4. Edalatkhaha, S. et al.: Bit selection optimization using artificial intelligence Syst. Pet Sci Technol. **28**(18) (2010)
5. Carlos, M., et al.: Optimization models and prediction of drilling rate (ROP) for the Brazilian pre-salt layer. Chem. Eng. Trans. **33**, 823–828 (2013)
6. Pan, H., et al: Drilling Cost Prediction Based on Self-adaptive Differential Evolution and Support Vector Regression. In: Intelligent Data Engineering and Automated Learning—IDEAL, Springer, Berlin, Heidelberg, pp 67–75 (2013)
7. Nguyen, J.P.: Techniques d'exploitation pétrolière le forage, Editions Technip (1993)
8. Tuna. E.: Real time optimization of drilling parameters during drilling operations, doctorate thesis in petroleum and natural gaz engineering. Middle East Technical University, turkey (2010)
9. Farage, A.: Commande non linéaire dans les systèmes de forage pétrolier: contribution à la suppression du phénomène de « stick-slip » , Ph.D. thesis, Paris Tech University, French (2006)
10. Amadou-Abdoulaye, A.: Contribution à la surveillance d'un processus de forage pétrolier, Ph.D. thesis, Paris Tech University, French (2010)
11. Osgouei, R.E: Rate of penetration estimation model for directional and horizontal wells, M.S. thesis, Middle east technical University (2007)
12. Breiman, L.: Random Forests, Statistics Department University of California Berkeley, CA, 94720 (2001)
13. Genuer, R.: les Forêts aléatoires: aspect théoriques, sélection de variables et applications, Thèse de Doctorat Mathématiques, Université de Paris-Sud XI (2010)
14. Gregorutti, B.: Forêts aléatoires et sélection de variables: analyse des données des enregistreurs de vol pour la sécurité aérienne, thèse de doctorat en Mathématiques (statistiques), Université de Paris 6 (2015)
15. Harfouche, A.L., Jacobson, D.A., Kainer, D., Romero, J.C., Harfouche, A.H., Scarascia Mugnozza, G., Moshelion, M., Tuskan, G.A., Keurentjes, J., Altman, A.: Accelerating climate resilient plant breeding by applying next-generation artificial intelligence. Trend. Biotechnol **37**(11), 1217–1235 (2019)
16. Harfouche, A., Quinio, B., Skandrani, S., Marciniak, R.: A framework for artificial knowledge creation in organizations. In: ICIS 2017 Proceedings. Paper 15. http://aisel.aisnet.org/icis2017/General/Presentations/15 (2017)

A New Model for Information Security Risk Management

Ali Shirazi and Mozaffar Kazemi

Abstract This article introduces a new risk management method for information security risk management, proposed and applied for the first time in the IT department of a telecommunication company in Iran. According to law requirements and security strategic plan, the mentioned company implemented information security risk management (ISMS). So one of the main phases of ISMS is the risk management. The results show that the methodology of the information security risk management containing the risk identification, risk analysis, risk evaluation and risk treatment, uses the frameworks of ISO 27005, ISO 27002, ISO 27011, OCTAVE and NIST 800-30 and OWASP standards. This new method is practical and accurate and is suitable for large scale organizations.

Keywords Information security · Risk assessment model · Security risk management · Risk management in ISMS

1 Introduction

In a large scale organization, risk assessment, risk analysis and risk treatment should be conducted in more than one phase. These phases can be defined in accordance with organizational processes or chart. In this case, the organization as a whole is divided into four parts. The criterion met in this division is the good match of organizational processes with organizational chart. One of these parts is the Department of Information Technology. Considering the legal requirements (AFTA document), senior management requirements (in the forms of project-based security strategy and ISO 27001 standard) as well as lack of knowledge about information security risk and insecurity and absence of a plan for risk management, there is need for a systematic information risk management to be implemented in the organization. In this

A. Shirazi (✉)
IT Management Department, Tarbiyat Modares University, Tehran, Iran
e-mail: shirazi@parsasharif.ir

M. Kazemi
Parsa-Sharif Research Center, Tehran, Iran

© Springer Nature Switzerland AG 2020
Y. Baghdadi et al. (eds.), *ICT for an Inclusive World*,
Lecture Notes in Information Systems and Organisation 35,
https://doi.org/10.1007/978-3-030-34269-2_38

research, a new method for information security risk management was introduced. Identification and valuation of assets, recognition of vulnerabilities and threats, and important risk scenarios which are the significant inputs of the risk treatment plan (RTP) process are the main outputs of the proposed method.

2 A Review of Literature

2.1 Information Security and Objectives

Information security is related to providing a secure condition, in which only those with the right of having access to the information can be able to read, hear, change, and broadcast it [1]. Thus, its major objective in an organization is maintaining confidentiality, integrity, and availability of information [2].

2.2 Definition of Risk

A risk is defined as the potential of the probable occurrence of an undesired event and its outcomes [3], through which an asset or a group of assets will be threatened to undergo a loss or damage due to their vulnerabilities [4]. An asset is any valuable thing to be protected in an organization [5].

There are 3 conditions known as risk factors (contextual problems) that can cause a risk: existence of a threat (hazard), an asset being exposed to the threat, and the asset's vulnerability [6]. A threat can be caused by a natural or man-made event incorporating potential individuals, entities, or actions to produce a disturbance in the information, environment, operations, and/or properties [2, 7]. There are 3 types of threat namely: deliberate, accidental, and environmental (natural) threats, which may lead to a damage or loss of crucial services [5]. Threatening actions can be intentionally undertaken by a capable adversary to jeopardize the interests of an organization [2]. The issue of information security exposure might be related to a system configuration, software mistake, or some reasonable security policies that allow an attacker to enter a system or network and find an access to information [8]. Vulnerability is the combination of a facility's attractiveness and the deterrence level of an existing countermeasure [9].

2.3 Risk Management Concept and Its Steps

Risk management helps an organization to meet its objectives of planning, decision-making, and performing productive activities by allocating resources [10]. Risk management deals with uncertainties, including the probable occurrence of harmful events and their resulting consequences in an organization, thus differing from other management activities [10].

Risk assessment and analysis are the two major activities of risk management [2, 11]. The former involves risk identification, characterization, and realization by studying, analyzing, and describing the probable outcomes for an effort [7, 12], while further identification of security risks and their magnitudes as well as the corresponding areas to be safeguarded are associated with the latter [4]. To reduce the risk level or eliminate it, countermeasures prove to be helpful as the most crucial steps in the establishment of ISMS. To address threats at all informational infrastructure layers, an effective overall security solution may be formulated by establishing security countermeasures [13]. Depending on the existing threats and exploitable vulnerabilities in computer and information systems, various information security mechanisms are selected [14].

Aimed at avoiding intrinsic damages to the risk factor or using organizational advantages, risk treatment selects and applies the most suitable risk security measures to modify it [12, 15]. Risk avoidance, acceptance, transference, and treatment are the 4 outstanding risk treatment strategies commonly utilized [2, 11]. In their method of selecting both technical and non-technical countermeasures, Kim and Lee (2005) considered the value of information, level of threat, and scope of security services [13].

2.4 Methods of Risk Management and Their Objectives

Several methodologies have been recognized for risk management [16]:

- Some have been issued by national and international organizations (ISO/IEC TR 13335, 1998; NIST SP800-30, 2002; AS/NZS 4360, 2004; HB231, 2004; BSI Standard 100-3, 2005; ISO/IEC 27005, 2008).
- Some others have been proposed by professional organizations (CRAMM, 2001; CORAS, 2003; OCTAVE, 2005; Magerit, 2006; Microsoft, 2006; Mehari, 2007).
- The other methodologies not accounted for by the first two procedures have been introduced by research projects (Kailay and Jarratt 1995; Smith and Eloff 2002; Robert and Rolf 2003; Karabacak and Sogukpinar 2005; Hoffanvik and Stolen 2006; Mayer et al. 2007).

All the above-mentioned approaches follow the common goals of prioritizing and estimating the risk value and suggesting the most proper plan to eliminate that risk or minimize it to an acceptable level [17]. Within a given organizational context, a risk management chooses its method based on its ability to appropriately understand and apply that method, the case which is difficult for the small-scale organizations due to the fact that they are constrained by resources and expertise [2]. ISO 27005 framework was selected by comparing it with those of some enterprises with general

Table 1 Comparison of information security risk management framework

Framework	Description	Target organization	Target level organization
ISO 27005	Complete process in generic manner	Governments, large companies, SME	Management, operational
OCTAVE	Self-directed approach	SME	Management, operational
NIST SP 800-53	Very detailed guidance and identifications	Governments, large companies, SME	Management, operational

information security risk management like NIST SP 800-30, Octave, and ISO 27005. The results of the comparison are shown in Table 1 as follows [18]:

The process of information security risk management can be applied to the whole or part of an organization, or any information system together with its existing aspects, or certain planned controls [5]. A summary of the mentioned process is displayed in Fig. 1 [5].

Establishment of the context: The context of this kind of risk management should be established to determine its necessary basic criteria, define its scope and boundaries, and appropriately organize its activities.

Risk assessment: This involves managers' qualitative risk measurement or description for a risk prioritization based on the seriousness perceived or other established criteria. Activities of risk analysis incorporating risk identification, estimation and evaluation will be plausible through risk assessment.

Risk treatment: The risk is selected to be reduced, maintained, avoided, or transferred and the plans are set accordingly. Based on the results of risk assessment and the expected costs and benefits, risk management options are selected and implemented.

Risk acceptance: This indicates an officially recorded decision to accept the risk and its responsibility.

Risk communication: This involves the activities between decision makers and other stakeholders to reach an agreement on how a risk management should be conducted by exchanging and/or sharing information about the risk.

Risk monitoring and reviewing: Risk is not static since threats, vulnerabilities, probabilities, and consequences can suddenly change with no signs. Therefore, a constant monitoring powered by an external service of providing information about new threats or vulnerabilities is required to detect these changes.

2.5 Qualitative and Quantitative Approaches of Risk Management

Based on the risk analysis and assessment applied, risk management follows a quantitative or qualitative method [19]. Detailed academic studies usually plunge into specific areas in an attempt to propose an effective solution to a specified problem

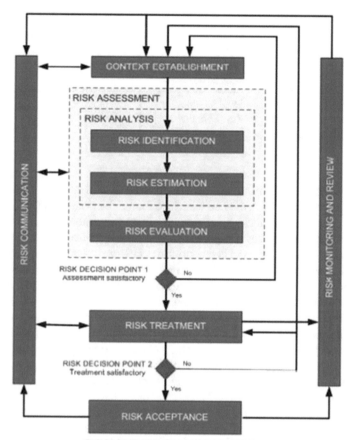

Fig. 1 Information security risk management process of ISO 27005

in the process of information security risk analysis through a number of quantitative methods. Yet, simpler and more generic and collaborative approaches are needed for public organizations [20]. Information security risk management is mostly based on the quantitative methodologies employed by financial institutions and insurance companies [2, 21]. Annualized Loss Expectancy (ALE) and Livermore Risk Analysis Methodology (LRAM) are among the popular examples of quantitative methods of risk analysis and assessment [2, 7] that use numerical results to express the probability of each risk factor and its effects on organizational objectives [19]. Therefore, the infrastructures of large information systems supported by reinforced human and financial resources are properly in need of quantitative methods [22], the objectivities of which are capitalized based on mathematical formulae that can be readily verified [2]. These methods depend on the estimations of probable damages to assets or loss of information systems [2, 23]. Rot [24] argues that generally more costs, greater

Table 2 Qualitative risk metrics

	Likelihood		
Consequences	Low	Medium	Low
High	M	H	H
Medium	L	M	H
Low	L	L	M
Key: H: high risk M: medium risk L: low risk			

experiences, and more advanced tools are involved in a quantitative method when compared with a qualitative method exercised for a risk management [25].

On the other hand, to make a decision on how to solve the potential risk factors, qualitative risk management is required to assess their identified effects on the assets of the information systems and create priorities [19]. Any available expertise in an organization can modify the qualitative methods for easy uses [22]. Due to their simplicity for using the very familiar 'jargon' for non-technical people, less time, finance, and effort are needed since risks can be expressed based on descriptive variables instead of accurate monetary terms [2]. They are further based on the risk management exercise conducted by the judgment, intuition and experience of an individual [21]. However, due to some complexities, serious problems are posed by some identified techniques of qualitative risk assessment and analysis. For instance, a highly trained technical team and strong financial basis are required to carry out risk assessment and analysis using Hazard and Operability study (HAZOP), Failure Mode and Effects Analysis (FMEA) or Failure Mode and Effects Criticality Analysis (FMECA), the Central Computer and Telecommunications Agency, and CCTA-Risk Analysis and Management Method (CRAMM), which are thus labor-intensive [25]. Of course, highly technical people or robust financial supports are not always needed for the techniques of qualitative risk assessment and analysis. For example, as any other easy, cheap, and viable methods, the Operationally Critical Threat, Asset, and Vulnerability Evaluation (OCTAVE) technique is conducted to achieve the same objectives [26]. OCTAVE as a most appropriate approach in organizations with no experts of information risk management is from among the common examples cited for qualitative risk management [22, 27]. An example of a qualitative risk metrics is shown in Table 2 [14].

2.6 Problems of Risk Management Approaches

Due to the lack of awareness, high cost, need of expertise, and long process, the present risk management methods have been demonstrated by various reports, surveys, and relevant literature not to be widely used within organizations so far despite the increasing number of standard and commercial ones [28].

Regarding the poor results, bulky confusing reports, and narrow technological scopes, these methods are less relied upon [29].

Any organizations willing to adopt one of these methods are confused by their huge numbers (more than 200 methods at present) while no agreeable benchmarks or comparative frameworks can be referred to for the evaluation of information security risks of enterprises and thus they are less practical [30].

As noted by Solms [31], information security is not a technical matter, but a social, business, and regulatory issue" protecting all the elements of an information system, including hardware, software, information, people, and processes [2]. These traditional methods focused generally on the technology and are used to manage risks and propose technical solutions to them within enterprises. Human, organizational, strategic, and environmental factors are seldom considered by most of them. Technology is not the only element to be recognized in this process, though it is a necessary consideration [32]. In an IT-based approach to security risk analysis, it is not so much necessary for business users to identify a comprehensive set of risks or promote security awareness throughout an organization [33]. A practical business continuity risk analysis should be adopted and applied to the business as a whole in a consistent, manageable, and cost-effective manner and not just to the IT department [34]. Some shortcomings of the traditional risk management approaches can be minimized via a holistic risk management method of information security as has been recently suggested by many authors [29, 35–37]. Small-scale organizations may surrender to unsanctioned methods or avoid practicing a complete risk management since its techniques are too difficult to understand [2, 26].

3   Theoretical Framework

Based on literature review, the theoretical framework for this research was conducted as shown in Fig. 2. Figure 2 illustrates the planning process of information security risk management by which the IT Department is influenced.

Figure 3 shows the process of information security risk management.

3.1   Context Establishment

Risk evaluation criteria: In this research, risk evaluation criteria are the impacts of losses of information confidentiality, integrity and availability (CIA) on the business.

Impact criteria: In this research, the impact of losses of CIA was examined in three dimensions of loss of financial value, service disruption and loss of image of the organization.

Risk Acceptance Criteria: in this research, risk acceptance criteria are based on comparison of impact of the security incident and cost of preventing that incident.

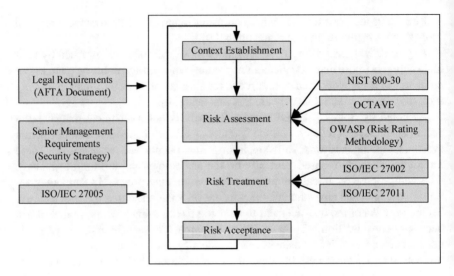

Fig. 2 Theoretical framework

Scope and boundaries: This research focused on the IT department because it is responsible for the storage, processing and transmitting of organization information.

Organization for information security risk management: In this research, the security department is responsible for the information security risk management process.

3.2 Information Security Risk Assessment

A. Risk identification

Risk identification includes three steps which are described as follow:

1. Identification of assets: Identification of the assets of IT department, identification of owner and location of asset.

    There are 4 main types of asset in this research:

- Information assets
- Assets that are carriers of information assets
- Infrastructure devices
- Intangible assets.

2. Identification of threats: Identification of the threat of every asset and the origin of the threat. There are 38 kinds of threats that can affect risks.
3. Identification of existing control: It is used to ensure that the controls are working correctly and avoid dispensable work or cost.

Fig. 3 Information security risk management planning process

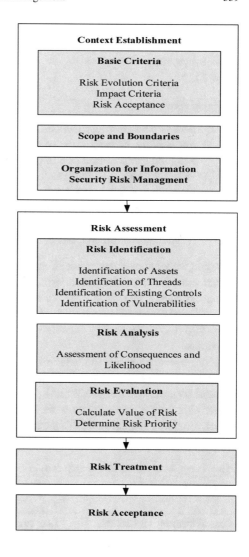

This identification is checked with the relevant personnel of the IT department and with the onsite review for the physical controls.

4. Identification of vulnerability: After identification of threats and existing controls on any asset, the vulnerabilities that may occur in them are identified. Vulnerabilities are identified by interviewing relevant staff, observations and using technical tools such as Nessus. Vulnerability may occur due to the lack of control or an existing control that cannot manage or reduce the threat that occurred. Types of identified vulnerabilities are listed as follow:

- Organization;
- Human resource;

- Network;
- Hardware;
- Software;
- Sites.

B. **Risk Analysis**

  1. Assessment of consequences: In this research, the assigned value to the assets is the consequences of an incident scenario. An incident scenario is defined as description of a threat exploiting a certain vulnerability or set of vulnerabilities in an information security incident [5]. The impact criteria of the context establishment activity are considered to determine the impact of these scenarios [5]. Value of each asset is determined based on the impact of loss of CIA and it is examined in three dimensions of loss of financial value, service disruption and loss of image of the organization (Table 3).

When we want calculate value of an asset, we should sum impact of loss of CIA of each asset in three dimension. For example, based on Table 3, if "Loss of financial value: Between X to Y dollars (5)", "Service disruption: between B to C minutes per year (5)" and "Loss of image of organization: at the national level (10)" then "Asset value = 5 + 5 + 10 = 20". So value of an asset can be 0 in minimum and 30 in maximum.

Then, because we use the value of the asset that is involved in an information security scenario for assessment of the consequences of that information security incident scenario, we can use Table 4.

For example, if value of an asset is 20, the consequences of the information security incident scenario that this asset is involve in, is High (=3).

Table 3 Impact of loss of CIA of each asset in three dimension

Dimension	Impact			
	0	1	5	10
Loss of financial value	Effect less	Less than X dollar	Between X to Y dollar	More than Y dollar
Service disruption	Less than A minutes per year	Between A to B minutes per year	Between B to C minutes per year	More than C minutes per year
Loss of image of organization	Effect less	At the organization level	At the customers level	At the national level

Table 4 Consequences of each information security incident scenario based on the value of the involved asset

Asset value	0	1–7	8–15	16–23	24–30
Consequence	Not important (=0)	Low (=1)	Medium (=2)	High (=3)	Very high (=4)

Table 5 Threat likelihood scale

Event recapitulation	Likelihood	Value[a]
More than 3 times a year	High	3
2 or 3 times a year	Medium	2
Maximum once a year	Low	1
This threat is not applicable	Not applicable	0

[a]In order to evaluate the likelihood of each threat easily, we assigned the value of 0–3 to them

2. Assessment of incident likelihood: In this research, two parameters of likelihood of threat and level of vulnerabilities form the likelihood of the incident scenarios. The previous experience of the events recapitulated in the IT department and interviews with relevant staff are the bases for assessment of each threat likelihood (Table 5).

Level of each vulnerability, is identified based on vulnerability factors, according to the Table 6.

Based on sum of numerical values assigned to each vulnerability, according to Table 6, we can categorize each vulnerability in one of the three categories below:

- Low: between 4 and 12,
- Medium: between 13 and 25, and
- High: between 26 and 36.

Table 7 gives an example for each level.

Table 6 Level of each vulnerability

Vulnerability factors	Description	Options
Ease of discovery	How easy is it for this group of threat agents to discover this vulnerability?	Practically impossible (=1), difficult (=3), easy (=7), automated tools available (=9)
Ease of exploit	How easy is it for this group of threat agents to actually exploit this vulnerability?	Theoretical (=1), difficult (=3), easy (=7), automated tools available (=9)
Awareness	How well known is this vulnerability to this group of threat agents?	Unknown (=1), hidden (=3), obvious (=7), public knowledge (=9)
Intrusion detection	How likely is an exploit to be detected?	Active detection in application (=1), logged and reviewed (=3), logged without review (=7), not logged (=9)

Table 7 Level of vulnerability

Vulnerability factors				Level of vulnerability
Ease of discovery	Ease of exploit	Awareness	Intrusion detection	
Practically impossible (=1)	Theoretical (=1)	Unknown (=1)	Active detection in application (=1)	Low (1 + 1 + 1 + 1 = 4)
Difficult (=3)	Difficult (=3)	Hidden (=3)	Logged without review (=7)	Medium (3 + 3 + 3 + 7 = 16)
Automated tools available (=9)	Automated tools available (=9)	Public knowledge (=9)	Not logged (=9)	High (9 + 9 + 9 + 9 = 36)

As mentioned before, the likelihood of the incident scenarios is the combination of two parameters: likelihood of threat and level of vulnerabilities. In this research, Table 8 was used to determine the likelihood of each incident scenarios:

C. **Risk Evolution**

In this research, calculation of value of risk is based on NIST SP 800-30 and ISO/IEC 27005, which have risk matrix as shown in Table 9 and below risk formula:

$$\text{Risk Value} = \text{Consequence} \times \text{Incident Likelihood}$$

Based on the results of calculation of risk values in Table 9, the risk priority is listed in four categories from the highest risk to lowest as shown in Table 10.

3.3   *Risk Treatment*

Identification of Risk Treatment: The risk treatment has four options: reduction, acceptance, avoidance and transfer [5]:

- Reduction: Appropriate and justified controls should be selected to meet the requirements identified by the risk assessment and risk treatment. This selection should take account of the risk acceptance criteria as well as legal, regulatory and contractual requirements. This selection should also take account of cost and timeframe for implementation of controls, or technical, environmental and cultural aspects. It is often possible to lower the total cost of ownership of a system with properly selected information security controls.
- Acceptance: If the level of risk meets the risk acceptance criteria, there is no need for implementing additional controls and the risk can be retained.
- Avoidance: When the identified risks are considered too high, or the costs of implementing other risk treatment options exceed the benefits, a decision may be made to avoid the risk completely, by withdrawing from a planned or existing activity or set of activities, or changing the conditions under which the activity is

Table 8 Likelihood of incident scenarios

Likelihood of threat	Not applicable (=0)			Low (=1)			Medium (=2)			High (=3)		
Level of vulnerability	Low (4–12)	Medium (13–25)	High (26–36)	Low (4–12)	Medium (13–25)	High (26–36)	Low (4–12)	Medium (13–25)	High (26–36)	Low (4–12)	Medium (13–25)	High (26–36)
Incident likelihood	1	2	3	2	3	4	3	4	5	4	5	6

Table 9 Value of risk

Incident likelihood (Table 8)	Consequence (Table 4)			
	Low (1)	Medium (2)	High (3)	Very high (4)
1	1	2	3	4
2	2	4	6	8
3	3	6	9	12
4	4	8	12	16
5	5	10	15	20
6	6	12	18	24

Table 10 Risk priority

Risk Score	Priority
1–5	Low
6–10	Medium
11–17	High
18–24	Very high

operated. For example, for risks caused by nature it may be most cost effective alternative to physically move the information processing facilities to a place where the risk does not exist or is under control.

- Transfer: Risk sharing involves a decision to share certain risks with external parties. Sharing can be done by insurance that will support the consequences, or by sub-contracting a partner whose role will be to monitor the information system and take immediate actions to stop an attack before it makes a defined level of damage.

For the sake of confidentiality agreements RTP is not presented.

4 Conclusion

The information security risk management method which is appropriate for IT Department of the telecommunication operator in Iran, covers the items listed below:

1. Context establishment based on ISO/IEC 27005, legal requirements (AFTA Document) and Senior Management Requirements (Security Strategy) includes definitions of risk evaluation criteria, the criteria of impact, risk acceptance criteria and organizational information security risk management.
2. Risk identification is done by identifying the assets, identification of threats which can cause harm to assets, identification of existing controls and the identification of vulnerabilities.

3. Risk estimation is accomplished by identifying the level of consequences and likelihood of risk level. Information security risk scenarios are divided into four levels: low, medium, high and very high.
4. Risk evaluation is done by calculating values of risk matrix and prioritizing the risks based on risk values from the highest to the lowest.
5. Risk treatment consists of four options: acceptance, reduction, avoidance and transfer. In order to reduce the risk the recommendations in accordance with ISO guidelines 27002 and 27011 are applied.

References

1. Elky, S.: An Introduction to Information System Risk (2006)
2. Karabacak, B., Sogukpinar, I.: ISRAM: information security risk analysis method. Comput. Secur. **24**(2), 147–159 (2005)
3. Dorian, L.: Risk Management: Understanding Industry Insights. http://www.ica.bc.ca/ii/ii.php?catid=17
4. Chen, M.T.: Information security and risk management. In: Encyclopedia of Multimedia Technology and Networking, 2nd edn. (2009)
5. International Standard Organization. ISO/IEC 27005:2008—Information Technology—Security Techniques—Information Security Risk Management. Switzerland (2008)
6. Siu, T. Information Security Risk management. http://wiki.edu/information_security_risk_kanagementOverarching_themes (2011)
7. Pare, G., Sicotte, C., Jaana, M., Girouard, D., Paré, G., Ph, D.: Prioritizing clinical information system project risk factors: A delphi study. Methods Inf. Med. **47**(3), 251–259 (2008)
8. Rainer, R.K., Snyder, C.A., Carr, H.H.: Risk analysis for information technology. J. Manag. Inf. Syst. **8**(1), 129–147 (1991)
9. Tiwari, A.: Information Security Risk Management: An Overview Risk Management: An Essential Guide to Protecting Critical Assets. http://www.suite101.com/profile.cfm (2010)
10. Renfroe, N.A., Smith, J.L.: Threat/Vulnerability Assessments and Risk Analysis. http://www.wbdg.org/resources/riskanalysis.php#top
11. Ciechanowicz, Z.: Risk analysis: requirements, conflicts and problems. Comput. Secur. **16**(3), 223–232 (1997)
12. Hicks, J., Craig, L., Shortreed, J.: Basic Frameworks for Risk Management. http://www.irrneram.ca/pdf_files/basicFrameworkMar2003.pdf (2003)
13. Kim, T.: Design procedure of IT systems security countermeasures. In: International Conference on Computational Science and Its Applications (ICCSA), pp. 468–473 (2005)
14. Beachboard, J., Cole, A., Mellor, M., Hernandez, S., Aytes, K., Massad, N.: Improving information security risk analysis practices for small- and medium-sized enterprises: a research agenda. J. Issues Informing Sci. Inf. Technol. **5**, 73–85 (2008)
15. Sosonkin, M.: OCTAVE: Operationally Critical Threat, Asset and Vulnerability Evaluation. http://isis.poly.edu/courses/cs996-management-s2005/Lectures/octave.pdf (2005)
16. Saleh, M.S., Alfantookh, A.: A new comprehensive framework for enterprise information security risk management. Appl. Comput. Inform **9**(2), 107–118 (2011)
17. Vorster, A., Labuschagne, L.: A framework for comparing different information security risk analysis methodologies. Inf. Secur. **193**(C), 95–103 (2005)
18. The European Union Agency for Network and Information Security (ENISA). Available: http://IIrm-inv.enisa.europa.euIcomparison.html
19. Mazareanu, V.: Risk Management and Analysis: Risk Assessment Qualitative and Quantitative. http://papers.ssrn.com/sol13/papers.cfm?abstractid=1549186 (2007)

20. Tong, C.K., Fung, K., Huang, H.Y., Chan, K.: Implementation of ISO17799 and BS7799 in picture archiving and communication system: local experience in implementation of BS7799 standard. Int. Congr. Ser. **1256**, 311–318 (2003)
21. Lo, C.C., Chen, W.J.: A hybrid information security risk assessment procedure considering interdependences between controls. Expert Syst. Appl. **39**(1), 247–257 (2012)
22. Panda, P. The OCTAVE approach to information security risk assessment. http://www.isaca. org.Journal/past-issues/2009/volume4/documents/jpdf09-OCTAVE.pdf (2009)
23. Ding, T.: Quantitative Risk Analysis Step-by-step. GSEC Practical Version. http://www.sans. org/reading_room/whitepapers/auditing/quantitative-risk-analysis-step-by-step_849 (2002)
24. Yeh, Q.J., Chang, A.J.T.: Threats and countermeasures for information system security: a cross-industry study. Inf. Manag. **44**(5), 480–491 (2007)
25. Rot, A.: IT Risk Assessment: Quantitative and Qualitative Approach. In Proceedings of the World Congress on Engineering and Computer Science (WCECS), pp. 22–24. San Francisco (SANS) (2008)
26. Alberts, C., Dorofee, A.: Managing Information Security Risks: The {OCTAVE} Approach. Addison-Wesley Anderson, Boston (2002)
27. Alberts, C., Dorofee, A.: An introduction to OCTAVE SM Method. http://www.cert.org/octave/ methodintro.htm/#intro (2001)
28. N.C.C. (NCC).: The Business Information Security: 2000 Survey. National Computing Center, UK (2000)
29. Spears, J.L.: A holistic risk analysis method for identifying information security risks. pp. 185–202 (2006)
30. Syalim, A.: Comparison of risk analysis methods : Mehari, Magerit, NIST800–30 and microsoft's security management guide. In: 2009 International Conference on Availability, Reliability and Security, pp. 726–731 (2009)
31. von Solms, B.: The 10 deadly sins of information security management. Comput. Secur. **23**(5), 371–376 (2004)
32. Werlinger, R., Hawkey, K., Beznosov, K.: An integrated view of human, organizational, and technological challenges of IT security management. Inf. Manag Comput. Secur. **17**(1), 4–19 (2009)
33. Lategan, N., von Solms, R.: Towards enterprise information risk management—a body analogy. Comput. Fraud Secur **2006**(12), 15–19 (2006)
34. Nosworthy, J.D.: A practical risk analysis approach: managing BCM risk. Comput. Secur. **19**(7), 596–614 (2000)
35. Zuccato, A.: Holistic security management framework applied in electronic commerce. Comput. Secur. **26**(3), 256–265 (2007)
36. Anderson, K.: Convergence: A holistic approach to risk management. Netw. Secur. **2007**(5), 4–7 (2007)
37. Huang, J.-W., Ding, Y.-S., Hu, Z.-H.: Knowledge based model for holistic information security risk analysis. In: 2008 International Symposium on Computer Science and Computational Technology. vol. 1 (2008)

Using Process Mining for Process Analysis Improvement in Pre-hospital Emergency

Peyman Badakhshan and Ahmad Alibabaei

Abstract Process management has been considered in many organizations. Finding improvement opportunities is an important part of process management. Process mining technique can be used for analyzing the processes and extracting improvement opportunities. Healthcare systems includes one of complicated processes between industries. In this paper, process mining techniques are used in order to analyze pre-hospital processes in emergency room. The process discovery phase is implemented based on 4 different states, which are introduced in this study to increase the accuracy of process analysis. After discovering the process model, conformance checking and enhancement are following steps that were done in this study. The data is extracted from the automation system of a pre-hospital emergency room, which is used as input event logs for process mining. Statistical records including control sheet of one year were provided by the organization. Control sheet and in consequence the P-control chart are used as supplement of conformance checking phase. Enhancement phase is based on two states, and used performance analysis by considering factors of output, cycle time/duration and costs, which helps the pre-hospital emergency room to improve their processes.

Keywords Process mining · Conformance checking · Enhancement · Healthcare · Pre-hospital emergency

1 Introduction

Processes in practice have become a critical success factor in organizations [1]. However, managing the process in organizations are difficult and related to different factors such as external/internal contextual factors [2, 3]. One of the important aspects

P. Badakhshan
University of Liechtenstein Institute of Information Systems, Vaduz, Liechtenstein

A. Alibabaei (✉)
Shahid Beheshti University of Medical Sciences, School of Management and Medical Education Sciences, Tehran, Iran
e-mail: a.alibabaei@sbmu.ac.ir

© Springer Nature Switzerland AG 2020
Y. Baghdadi et al. (eds.), *ICT for an Inclusive World*,
Lecture Notes in Information Systems and Organisation 35,
https://doi.org/10.1007/978-3-030-34269-2_39

567

of process management is finding improvement opportunities and weaknesses in the process in order to lead BPM to success. The BPM success can be evaluated based on BPM capabilities [4], ten principles of good BPM [5], critical success factors [6], etc. In addition, process mining can also be used for clarifying process performance.

Process mining is a field that is situated between Machine Learning and Data mining on the one hand and process modeling and analysis on the other hand. Process mining has three main domains including discovery, conformance checking, and enhancement, which aims to improve processes by providing techniques and tools for discovering knowledge about process, organization, and social structures from event logs that can be extracted from current systems [7–9].

Process Management initiatives can play an important role in different fields [10] such as healthcare that consider using information systems and Industrial engineering concepts in order to improve the performance and increase its customer satisfaction. One issue of healthcare is a multidiscipline environment that brings several challenges to related studies. These challenges include Ad hoc actions and process changes, proper data collection, data redundancy, as well as incorrect and insufficient data recording [1, 11–13].

The health and medication processes are assumed to be very complicated, which is caused by many factors such as complicated medical decision-making process, the huge amount of transferred data, and that patients and their medications are un-predictable. The medical decision-making process was developed through the interpretation of special data from the patient concerning medical knowledge. This decision-making process is the basis of clinical processes [14]. Also, medical environments are looking for improvement of their treatment quality and reducing costs with process optimization. Treatment quality is one important aspect of healthcare as the demand for medical services are increasing every day [12].

The quality of medical services is dependent on process execution. These processes contain set of activities including diagnosis, treat and prevent diseases to improve the patient's health and they are supported by clinical and non-clinical activities that can be performed by various resources [15].

2 Literature Review

There are existing literature that considered Process mining and its application in healthcare area such as Yoo et al. [16], which is focused on design, implementation and evaluation of mobile patient guide system to address the difficulties that outpatients would face in finding hospital facilities and recognizing their daily treatment schedule [17], or Yoo et al. [16], which used Process mining technology to analyze process changes based on environmental changes in hospital with the goal of measuring effects of changes in terms of consultation waiting time, time spent per activity, and outpatient care process [16].

"Pre-hospital emergency services" are also known as "emergency call services". In existing literature, papers with the topic of emergency medical services are mostly focused on emergency departments of hospitals such as Basole et al. [18], Kaymak et al. [19], Mans et al. [20], and Rebuge and Ferreira [14], and medical attention provided for a patient after he/she reaches the hospital, but there is a little attention to the other division of emergency medical services, which is pre-hospital care given to the patients.

Pre-hospital care processes includes first aid at the site of the ill or injured patient, plus most commonly services of the ambulances including transferring the patient to the medical facility or from one facility to another in times of need while providing the emergency services (Genesis), [21].

The literature existing in this division is about improving the management of emergency call center by combining Process mining and discrete event simulation approaches [22], which first use Process mining techniques to obtain knowledge about collaborative processes, then use a discrete event simulation approach to assess the efficiency of the management in the emergency call center.

Process Mining is a way to extract knowledge from events, which were recorded in any type of systems. These events include information about start and completion of process steps. The purpose of Process mining is discovering, monitoring and improving the real processes with a usage of knowledge extracted from events [12]. Figure 1 displays the position of three main domains of Process mining including discovery, conformance checking, and enhancement.

Discovery techniques get the recorded event logs from the system and produce a model without any need for a prior model [8]. For this purpose, it is needed to extract event logs from existing systems (ex. Office Automation, HIS, and etc.) and import the right format of the file into the software to view the initial process model. From existing Discovery techniques, Workflow Management, Fuzzy Miner, Heuristic Miner, Genetic miner, and, etc. can be addressed.

Conformance checking techniques investigate if real processes in organization match the initial model and vise-versa. Conformance checking will compare process model with event logs, identify deviations and measure the conformity. In addition,

Fig. 1 Overview of process mining types. Adopted from process mining: data science in action (p. 32), by Wil [25]

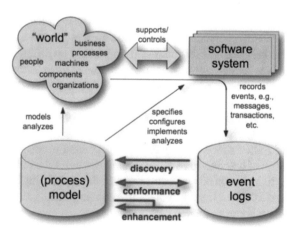

it compares the event logs with business rules and it's applicable to control the conformity of documented processes quality, identifying processes with the most deviations and investigating process goals [9].

Enhancement techniques help to improve the existing process model using information about the actual process. The objective of enhancement types including repair and extension is to extend or change the prior model using different techniques such as Decision Miner, Performance Analysis, Statistical Process Control, and etc.

In this paper we first provided some information about the background of the study, then we introduced the methodology used in each phase with providing the case study of pre-hospital emergency and illustrated the application of the presented method in reality. In the end, the discussion and conclusion section provided with several recommendations for future research.

3   Research Methodology

In this section, the methodology used in each phase of Process mining is described. The application of proposed methodology in each phase is presented based on the case study of this paper, which is a pre-hospital emergency in Iran and its process in patient admission, transfer and providing medical services.

3.1   Process Model Discovery

This paper has considered the "Ask for emergency and receive the service" from pre-hospital emergency processes in Iran, which is modeled and illustrated in Fig. 2.

As mentioned in previous parts of the paper, healthcare processes are complex and it's hard to understand and analyze them. In addition, when it comes to the execution, there are always variances between the model and the data recorded. To solve the issue of a complex process based on the recorded logs, it is suggested to consider four different states of the process such as Table 1 to have a better understanding of the process. The different states are based on different percentages of activities and routes, which are provided by Process Mining software. These states achieved by trial and error method for the case of this study and they can differ based on different event logs.

The model with 100% of activities and 0% of routes provide the model with most important routes between all activities. The model with 100% of activities and 50% of routes shows more paths that happened between all activities. The model with 50% of activities and 50% of routes includes the information about more important activities with 50% of paths between them and in the last model with 50% of activities and 100% of routes, shows the more important activities in the process with all the paths between them.

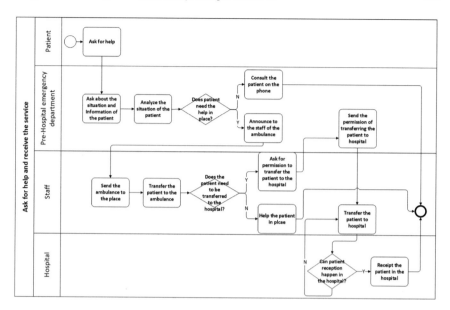

Fig. 2 The process of "ask for help and receive the service"

Table 1 Different state of process based on rate of routes and activities

n	Routes (%)	Activities (%)
State 1	0	100
State 2	50	100
State 3	50	50
State 4	100	50

　　To start the phase of Discovery, a set of event logs from one existing information system that had been recorded in 2009 were selected including 1013 events and 644 cases. Disco provides us with an overview of the process, and as mentioned in Table 1, four different states of the process were discovered based on different proportions of activities and routes. For instance, the discovered process for state 1 reported in Fig. 3.

　　Control sheet and P-Control chart in the sequence is used in this phase to check if the process is statistically under control or it faces special causes of variance, which means the process is not under control. If the process is acceptable by P-Control chart, then the method continues with conformance checking algorithm otherwise the process must be monitored for removing the special causes, record the data again then monitor the process statistically iteratively. This procedure must repeat till the process is statistically accepted. Control sheet includes the data recorded in 12 months about several defects and it's capable to check the number of each defect that happened in each month and in the end the number of each defect that happened

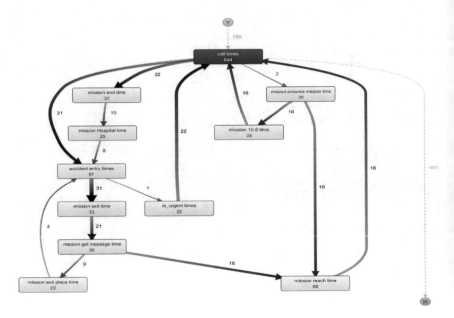

Fig. 3 Process model considering 100% Activities and 0% routes conformance checking algorithm

in 12 months. After analyzing the data, the data were plotted from Control sheet to the Control chart.

As the expectation of control chart is to control the service from pre-hospital emergency, the data that only reflects the patient's situation and it's out of the scope of analysis is eliminated from statistics. After this elimination, the data from Control Sheet were used and plotted to P-control chart that is 12 plotted points as it contains 12 months. Shaping the control limits inside the Control Chart enable the analysis to check if the process is under control or not. If one sample appears over the upper limit then the process has a special cause of variance, which must be investigated and removed. According to the case study and considering that SPC tools are used only as a supplement then the process is accepted if only one sample is out of control but for more than one sample over the upper limit, the process must be rejected and conformance checking procedure is not allowed to proceed.

The defect in the case study is a number of deaths caused by a problem in pre-hospital service, so the patient is dead or not. This description proves that the data has Bernoulli distribution so the P-control chart used for monitoring the process. The control limits including centerline, upper and lower control limits are computed based on the formula shown below [23]:

$$\text{UCL} = \bar{p} + 3\sqrt{\frac{\bar{p}(1 - \bar{p})}{n}}$$
$$\text{CL} = \bar{p}$$

$$LCL = \bar{p} - 3\sqrt{\frac{\bar{p}(1 - \bar{p})}{n}} \qquad (1)$$

And P-bar compute as below:

$$\bar{p} = \frac{\sum D_i}{\sum n_i} \qquad (2)$$

where "D" is the number of defects and "n" is the number of observations.

If the process gets accepted at this stage then the method continues with conformance checking phase.

3.2 Conformance Checking

In the algorithm developed for conformance checking by Haung et al. [24], Process mining techniques have been exploited for monitoring in Statistical Process Control. In this algorithm, only one state of the process model was considered, which does not lead clearly to an accurate answer. To prove this supposition, changing the percentage of activities and routes in Process mining software (with regard to observing the routes and activities which had the highest frequencies) were suggested. This change in the rate of activities and routes cause different answers for similarity level of the processes. It is recommended to use four different states of processes mentioned in Table 1. For this purpose, the second group of event logs extracted from the system and were compared to 4 models that discovered in Discovery phase.

The algorithm that is introduced for checking the conformity in this paper, is the development of the existing algorithm by Haung et al. [24], which tries to bring the more reliable answer. The model discovered in Discovery phase called model "a" and second event logs provided us with model "b". Considering four states, the algorithm developed as below:

$$D_{ab} = \frac{\sum_{1}^{4} \frac{A_{a \cap b} * N_{a \cap b}}{A_{a \cup b} * N_{a \cup b}}}{4} = \frac{D_{a1b1} + D_{a2b2} + D_{a3b3} + D_{a4b4}}{4} \qquad (3)$$

$$C_{ab} = \frac{\sum_{1}^{4} \frac{N_{a \cap b}}{N_a}}{4} = \frac{C_{a1b1} + C_{a2b2} + C_{a3b3} + C_{a4b4}}{4} \qquad (4)$$

where:

D_{ab} The ratio of similarity between two models

C_{ab} The ratio of similarity of existing relations between model b and a with respect to model a

$A_{a \cap b}$ The number of all similar activities in two models

$A_{a \cup b}$ The number of all existing activities in two models
$N_{a \cap b}$ The number of all similar relations in two models
$N_{a \cup b}$ The number of all the existing relations in two models
N_a The number of existing relations in the first model

In the Eq. (3), the number of consecutive activities and their relations are specified and the conformity level of two models are determined. In fact, the similarity of two models is determined. In the Eq. (4), the ratio of similar activities and relations are specified. In fact, the percentage of similarity of model b compared with model a. The Eq. (4) is a good evolutionary equation for Eq. (3) to focus on how much process models are similar to each other.

To execute this algorithm, the quantities of C and D must be calculated for all of the four states mentioned in Table 1. Then the average of these quantities is presented as an answer. It is worth to mention that these four states can be considered for every research and in fact, this consideration increases the accuracy of analysis in the conformity of process.

To apply what has proposed in this section, the control sheet of the process in one year is introduced in Table 2.

Based on the proposed control sheet, the control chart is created according to the Eqs. (1) and (2). The P-control chart is reported as Fig. 4.

It's concluded from P-control chart that process is statistically under control as no samples in this chart appeared out of control limits. Regarding the result from control sheet and in consequence the control chart as SPC tools, the phase of conformance checking can be started. For this phase of Process mining the case study must follow the developed algorithm that presented in this section, which shows how much is the reliability of the process. After discovering the four states for the second group of event logs, the two set of event logs were compared regarding four states.

The first step is to calculate D_{ab} and C_{ab} for each state, which is reported below:

- State 1 (100% Activities and 0% Routes): $D_{ab} = 0.684$, $C_{ab} = 0.81$
- State 2 (100% Activities and 50% Routes): $D_{ab} = 0.60$, $C_{ab} = 0.78$
- State 3 (50% Activities and 50% Routes): $D_{ab} = 0.451$, $C_{ab} = 0.645$
- State 4 (50% Activities and 100% Routes): $D_{ab} = 0.380$, $C_{ab} = 0.666$.

Considering only one state of the process model as presented by Haung et al. [24], errors occurred in the analysis. According to the results of D_{ab} and C_{ab}, it can be concluded that the state 1 shows the acceptable situation while the state 4 is unacceptable. Calculated values of D_{ab} and C_{ab} based on the algorithm proposed in this paper reported below:

$$D_{ab} = \frac{\sum_{1}^{4} \frac{A_{a \cap b} * N_{a \cap b}}{A_{a \cup b} * N_{a \cup b}}}{4} = \frac{D_{a1b1} + D_{a2b2} + D_{a3b3} + D_{a4b4}}{4} = \frac{0.684 + 0.600 + 0.451 + 0.380}{4} = 0.528$$

$$C_{ab} = \frac{\sum_{1}^{4} \frac{N_{a \cap b}}{N_a}}{4} = \frac{C_{a1b1} + C_{a2b2} + C_{a3b3} + C_{a4b4}}{4} = \frac{0.810 + 0.780 + 0.645 + 0.666}{4} = 0.725$$

Table 2 Control sheet of pre-hospital emergency

Defect description (death caused by …)	March	April	May	Jun	July	August	September	October	November	December	January	February	Sum
1) Ambulance lateness	6	6	7	7	4	9	4	4	5	5	8	4	69
2) Errors in, or breaking of equipment of an ambulance	0	0	2	1	0	1	0	0	0	0	0	0	4
3) Staffs mistakes	7	9	6	7	5	8	5	5	7	8	5	0	72
4) Lack of communication with doctor	1	2	0	1	0	0	1	0	1	2	0	0	8
5) Lack of equipment	0	0	0	0	0	2	0	0	1	0	0	0	3
6) Lack of medicine	0	3	0	1	1	0	1	0	1	1	2	0	10
Sum	14	20	15	17	10	20	11	9	15	16	15	4	166

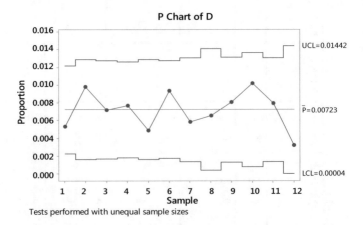

Fig. 4 P-control chart with variable "n" for initial process monitoring

Results of the algorithm prove that proposed algorithm in this paper provides a more reliable answer regarding the compliance of the process. The factor "D" is more than 0.5, and the factor "C" is a big proportion, which means the process is generally acceptable but there is a need for process improvement techniques to improve the level of compliance with optimizing the process. If the factor "D" were less than 0.5 or there was a huge difference between factor "D" and "C", then the conformity was not acceptable, which would end up to radical changes in the process.

Although the conformity is accepted, the factor "D" is on the border of rejection, so there is a need for improving the current situation and put effort for improving the performance of the model. For this objective, two actions took place. First, several processes have been designed in order to solve the defined defects (Table 2). These processes includes "Consumption of drugs and equipment monitoring", "Evaluation and determination of educational and skill levels", "Supply and distribution of medicines and medical supplies", "Developing and executing maneuvers and exercises", "Strategic Management over emergency services improvements", "Temporary relocation plan ambulances", and "Auditing and monitoring the bases and ambulances". Second, the enhancement phase, which is described in Sect. 3.2 for analysis and improving the process.

3.3 Analysis and Improvement

Enhancement is the third domain of Process mining. After understanding the process and the workflow, information about the time spent in different parts became under consideration and ended up into process performance evaluation. For this objective, the view in Disco as Process mining software changed to performance view that shows the time spent between activities. In this view, spent time is evaluated based on the identification of Total duration, Mean duration, Maximum and Minimum duration. In general, there are three basic factors to evaluate process performance including "Output", "Duration/Cycle time" and "costs". These factors can be evaluated at any process levels including the main process, sub-processes, activities, sequences and, etc.

The output is talking about the cases that were done in specific duration, which can be financial or non-financial. It must be accepted that event logs are providing proper feedback on the cases. One way to improve the capability of the process is understanding the outputs and limitations, which points to bottlenecks in the process.

Duration/Cycle time is talking about the time spent in the process from start to the end, which can be spent by one case or a group of cases. Generally, it must answer three questions in process regarding the time. First is to find out the whole time spent in the process. Then the time spent on activities which brings value and the last question is to find out the waste time.

Costs are about resources that were consumed by one case or a group of cases, which can be financial or non-financial. It must be noted that in many cases it's not necessary to use financial values and it's enough to investigate costs in the frame of resources from organization or social networking point of view. For organization analysis and social networking, it's enough to replace resources with activities in the event logs and discover the model.

Based on the initial data and using trial and error concerning the proportion of activities and paths, process performance chart must be reported in two states. One state reports 100% of activities with 0% of paths and the other one contains 100% of activities and 100% of paths. These reports will show the bottleneck and helps the evaluation of the performance according to time, cost and output factors. Based on the results of this phase and the help of SPC tools the ideas of improving the process will appear, for instance designing new processes, changes in resources and, etc. After changing the view point in software and applying the two mentioned states in performance view, the model is reported in Fig. 5. This stage of the process visualizes the complete paths and activities. The analysis of this stage alone is very time consuming and in most of the cases not feasible. Specifically when the process contains a lot of cases and activities, which forms spaghetti process.

It is concluded from models that the bottleneck is between "sending aid units" and "changing the ambulance and medical services" (which are mentioned in logs as "mission 10–8 time" and "mission announce mission time"), which takes 28.5 h in total duration. This performance is 106.9 min, 8.2 h and 71 s considering Mean, Max and Minimum of time.

Considering the process performance diagram with total duration, three questions that stated previously about duration/cycle time must be answered. The total duration time considering 644 cases is 3670.8 min. The total time for value activities is 1784.6 min and the total waste time is 1796.2 min. With calculating the proportion of waste time, the value of 0.49 has reached, which means a lot of loss in time. Based on this result and considering the bottleneck, a solution to change the process is needed in a way of removing this bottleneck. For this objective, the process must change or proper resources must be dedicated to the current process.

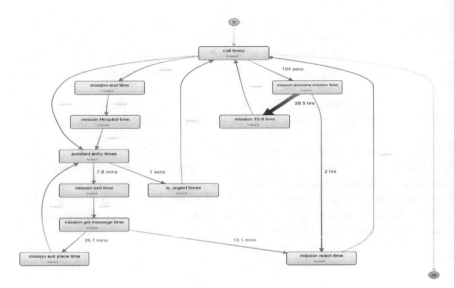

Fig. 5 Process performance with 100% activities and 0% routes considering total duration

After calculating the performance based on the factor of time, the focus should be on performance based on costs. As mentioned before, the cost is the way of using resources and in this paper, resources are considered as humans. Referring to the event logs and the overview of the software, it is realized that 15 resources are acting in the process. These resources have been used 4 times in minimum, 152 times in maximum and 68 times on average. Considering the bottleneck of the process, it is realized that there are 16 cases happening within the bottleneck, which they are assigned to 4 resources. This means that 26% of resources have been assigned to the activities that have the most process flow, while there are 4 other resources with the same skills existing in a place. According to this investigation among resources and their assignment to activities, it is recommended to use the other 4 resources in the bottleneck as well and economically. This action will help to improve the process and generally help the organization to prevent hiring costs. Also, it will bring a solution for the bottleneck, and improve the efficiency of resources as they will divide the huge amount of work between resources, and increase the cooperation among them.

4   Conclusion and Further Considerations

The purpose of this study was using Process mining in order to analysis pre-hospital processes. Therefore, this paper followed the techniques of Process mining from Discovery phase to conformance checking and in the end the phase of enhancement to provide the complete overview of one Process mining project. The methodology presented in the paper were applied step by step in a real case study in Healthcare area, which was a pre-hospital emergency process in Iran.

Disco was used in this study as a Process mining software, which means the use of fuzzy miner for Discovery phase and it is recommended to use and check the results from other Discovery models (i.e., Heuristic miner, Alpha algorithm, etc.). Also, one conformance checking algorithm was developed but it is recommended to use different algorithms and check the results. For process improvement, Enhancement phase of process mining was used next to designing new processes to solve the issues related to the defects that cause deaths of patients. In enhancement phase, the performance analysis was used, but in the cost analysis part, only the human resources were considered. It is recommended to use financial analysis for enhancement as well. And in general the methodology should be provided with more accurate logs with more information, so it can be used in any other departments of hospitals or other healthcare environments. For instance, in one hospital it's really important to find the relation between different departments.

Also considering the pre-hospital emergency problems, it can be useful to combine Process mining techniques with other tools of Information systems and Industrial Engineering field to reach strategic goals, for instance decreasing the time spent of being beside the patient in place and also increasing the level of services, etc.

References

1. Homayounfar, P. (ed.): Process Mining Challenges in Hospital Information Systems (2012)
2. Alibabaei, A., Bandara, W., Aghdasi, M.: Means of achieving business process management success factors. In: 4th Mediterranean Information System Conference. Athene, Greece (2009)
3. vom Brocke, J., Zelt, S., Schmiedel, T.: On the role of context in business process management. Int. J. Inf. Manage. **36**(3), 486–495 (2016)
4. Rosemann, M., vom Brocke, J. (eds.): The six core elements of business process management. In Handbook on Business Process Management 1, Springer, Berlin, Heidelberg (2015)
5. Vom Brocke, J., Schmiedel, T., Recker, J., Trkman, P., Mertens, W., Viaene, S.: Ten principles of good business process management. Bus. Process Manag. J. **20**(4), 530–548 (2014)
6. Trkman, P.: The critical success factors of business process management. Int. J. Inf. Manage. **30**(2), 125–134 (2010)
7. van der Aalst, W., van Dongen, B.F., Herbst, J., Maruster, L., Schimm, G., Weijters, A.: Workflow mining: a survey of issues and approaches. Data Knowl. Eng. **47**(2), 237–267 (2003)
8. van der Aalst, W.M.P.: Process Mining: Discovery, Conformance and Enhancement of Business Processes. Springer, Berlin, Heidelberg
9. Van Der Aalst, W.: Process mining: overview and opportunities. ACM Trans. Manage. Inf. Syst. (TMIS) **3**(2) (2012)
10. Alibabaei, A., Badakhshan, P., Alibabaei, H.: Studying BPM success factors differences in various industries. Int. J. Manag. Comput. Sci. **6**(1), 68–74 (2017)
11. Lenz, R.: A practical approach to process support in health information systems. J. Am. Med. Inform. Assoc. **9**(6), 571–585 (2002)
12. Mans, R.S., Schonenberg, M.H., Song, M., van der Aalst, W.M.P., Bakker, P.J.M. (eds.): Application of Process Mining in Healthcare-A Case Study in a Dutch Hospital. Springer, Berlin, Heidelberg (2008)
13. Gupta, S.: Workflow and Process Mining in Healthcare. Eindhoven (2007)

14. Rebuge, Á., Ferreira, D.R.: Business process analysis in healthcare environments: a methodology based on process mining. Inf. Syst. **37**(2), 99–116 (2012)
15. Mans, R.S., van der Aalst, W., Vanwersch, R.J.: Process Mining in Healthcare: Evaluating and Exploiting Operational Healthcare Processes. Springer, Berlin (2015)
16. Yoo, S., Cho, M., Kim, E., Kim, S., Sim, Y., Yoo, D., Hwang, H., Song, M.: Assessment of hospital processes using a process mining technique: outpatient process analysis at a tertiary hospital. Int. J. Med. Inform. **88**, 34–43 (2016)
17. Yoo, S., Jung, S.Y., Kim, S., Kim, E., Lee, K.-H., Chung, E., Hwang, H.: A personalized mobile patient guide system for a patient-centered smart hospital: lessons learned from a usability test and satisfaction survey in a tertiary university hospital. Int. J. Med. Inform. **91**, 20–30 (2016)
18. Basole, R.C., Braunstein, M.L., Kumar, V., Park, H., Kahng, M., Chau, D.H.P., Tamersoy, A., Hirsh, D.A., Serban, N., Bost, J., Lesnick, B., Schissel, B.L., Thompson, M.: Understanding variations in pediatric asthma care processes in the emergency department using visual analytics. J. Am. Med. Inform. Assoc. **22**(2), 318–323 (2015)
19. Kaymak, U., Mans, R., van de Steeg, T., Dierks, M. (eds.): On Process Mining in Health Care. IEEE, Seoul, Korea, 14–17 Oct 2012
20. Mans, R.S., van der Aalst, W.M., Vanwersch, R.J., Moleman, A.J. (eds.): Process Support and Knowledge Representation in Health Care: Process Support and Knowledge Representation in Health Care: Data Challenges When Answering Frequently Posed Questions. Springer, Berlin, Heidelberg (2013)
21. Ludík, T.: Process framework for emergency management in the Czech Republic. Doctoral dissertation, Masarykova univerzita, Fakulta informatiky (2015)
22. Lamine, E., Fontanili, F., Di Mascolo, M., Pingaud, H. (ed.).: Improving the Management of an Emergency Call Service by Combining Process Mining and Discrete Event Simulation Approaches. Springer International Publishing, Berlin (2015)
23. Montgomery, D.C. (ed.): Introduction to Statistical Quality Control. Wiley (2007)
24. Haung, Z.-C., Chen, Yun-Shiow, Chung, Yun-Kung (eds.): Statistical Process Monitoring by Using Process Mining. IEEE, China (2013)
25. van der Aalst, W.: Process Mining: Data Science in Action. Springer, Berlin (2016)

Digital Innovation in Manufacturing Firms: Why Smart Connected Products Become a Challenge?

Milen Ivanov

Abstract Digitalization is a phenomenon impacting all areas of our life. It opens a variety of opportunities for firms and individuals. At the example of manufacturing firms with a long tradition in physical product development, digitization is used to enhance product characteristics, to move the focus of the firm towards user-centricity and to integrate services into physical products. The research examines the emerging role of digital innovation in the context of traditional manufacturing firms. Throughout this paper, digital innovation refers to the innovation of smart connected products evolved from the symbiosis of physical products and digital components (digitization). The paper follows a case-study design with in-depth analysis of how manufacturing firms react on and define digital innovation. The study is exploratory and interpretative in nature and adopts the grounded theory approach. This research provides an important opportunity to advance the understanding of how digital innovation emerges in manufacturing firms.

Keywords Digital innovation · Manufacturing firms · Grounded theory · Smart connected products

1 Introduction

Following the digitalization trend and exploring new possibilities for competitive advantage manufacturing firms face the challenge of developing and offering new products based on the combination of physical products and digital components (smart products) also known as digital innovation [1]. Digital innovation provides promising opportunities for extending the life cycle of physical products [2] or offering new digital services. These advantages can be only leveraged if digital innovation is integrated into the existing processes and organizational arrangements.

In the extant literature, digitization is identified to be the enabler of digital innovation. Digitization is the process of "… encoding of analog information into digital

M. Ivanov (✉)
Vienna University of Economics and Business, Vienna, Austria
e-mail: milen.ivanov@s.wu.ac.at

© Springer Nature Switzerland AG 2020   581
Y. Baghdadi et al. (eds.), *ICT for an Inclusive World*,
Lecture Notes in Information Systems and Organisation 35,
https://doi.org/10.1007/978-3-030-34269-2_40

format" [1]. Digitization allows digitalized artifacts to replace previously existing analog artifacts in the social economic context and contributes to the creation of new social-technical structures. The transformation of the artifact itself and its context is defined as digitalization [3]. Hence, the impact of digitization goes beyond the technical transformation of analog data towards creating new or enhancing existing organizational structures, relationships, and business models. The contextual differentiation between digitization and digitalization is important to be given here since the broad use of the term digitalization is sometimes equated with digitization.

Digitalized physical products are characterized by enhanced functionalities making them programmable, addressable, sensible, communicable, memorable, traceable, and associable [4]. In this context, the paper takes the view of Yoo et al. considering digital innovation as a separate innovation type different to IT (Information Technology) innovation, due to its focus on product innovation [1]. IT is considered as an enabler (operand resource, tangible and static) and as a trigger (operant resource, rather intangible and dynamic) of innovation and impacts both the innovation process and the innovation outcome [5]. IT is a facilitator of the innovation process (e.g., providing platforms for "open" or "closed" innovation networks), IT is a significant factor when it comes to decision support in the area of innovation network governance structure and policies (centralized vs. decentralized governance structure). IT also considerably contributes to IT embedded services or software, since their introduction does not only impact the innovation outcome, but also the innovation processes and governance [5]. Digital innovation compared to IT innovation has different requirements on the organizing logic, the market dynamics and the architectural design [6].

Overall digital innovation "… referrers to the embedding of digital computer and communication technology into a traditionally non-digital product" [7].

In a broader sense, digital innovation can be defined as a digitization of artifacts across industries and organizations extending value propositions [3]. The new capabilities of smart products and the generated data are changing the competitive environment of manufacturing firms [8].

In a narrow sense, digital innovation is "the carrying out of new combinations of digital and physical components to produce novel products" [1]. In this context, digital components embedded into physical products are known as smart or intelligent products. All or some of the following characteristics belong to intelligent products; the product has an own identity, communicates with its environment, stores data, participates on decisions relevant to its destiny [9, 10]. Intelligent products interconnect with information sources across organizational boundaries and have a communication interface to information systems and users [11]. Three unique characteristics distinguish digital innovation: the reprogrammability, the homogenization of data and the self-referential character of digital innovation [1]. Reprogrammability allows the logical separation of physical and digital functions of products. Digital components can be instantly updated and improved, which can extend the product life cycle of products [2]. Data homogenization is based on the fact, that not analog but digital data are used by the digital devices. Standardized digital data content can be interpreted by multiple devices. Therefore, digital content can be used by different devices, since the content and the medium are de-coupled. The self-referential character of digital innovation means that the usage of digital technology is a prerequisite for enabling the digital innovation. That leads to multiple positive effects for the development and distribution of digital innovation, e.g. digital components get more affordable, relevant knowledge and ecosystems grow faster [3].

Considering the role of IT as the main driver of the evolvement of smart products [8] as well as the impact of IT on the performance of the firm [12] the paper adopts the lens of information system (IS) research, aware of the complexity and the interdisciplinary character of the research topic.

2 Theoretical Background

Triggered by the fast development of technology and embedded components digital innovation leads to transformation of multiple dimensions of the firm. Being an exogenous factor in the firm digital innovation would call for a theory which reflects the flexibility of the firm to rapidly react to environmental changes. One theory reflecting this ability is known as dynamic capabilities and defined as "...the ability to integrate, build, and reconfigure internal and external competencies to address rapidly changing environments" [13]. Dynamic capabilities are analytically divided into the capacity to sense and shape opportunities and threats, to seize opportunities and to maintain competitiveness through rearrangements of resources [14].

From organizational perspective the dynamic capabilities framework is based on three factors; assets (knowledge, organizational setup, technology) which should shape the potential of the company, processes (governance structure, management systems, resource management) which are related to the reconfigurability of capabilities and paths (commitments and investments conducted over time), which are responsible for the creation of the capabilities over time [15]. The dynamic capabilities framework is built on the concept of path dependencies: "...meaning what happens today is a function of what happened yesterday ..." [15]. From the perspective of path dependency, the actors are circumscribed in the legacy paths which have been established over time and locked in those in case an environmental is not causing a change [16]. For the determination of a path dependent process a set of criteria have been defined: weak initial conductions, contingent or chance events e.g. random unpredictable events, "self-reinforcing mechanism" and sticking to an existing path [16, 17].

Even though the dynamic capabilities of the firm are seen as a key to the innovation power of the firm in multiple studies it is still to be questioned if they can explain the evolvement of digital innovation in manufacturing firms keeping in mind their foundation built upon the concept of path dependencies.

The path creation concept is considered as an alternative view on the same problem [16] and has been applied in the context of digital innovation [7]. The concept of path creation has been introduced by Garud and Karnøe and refers to the main elements of the path dependencies concept – initial condition, contingencies, self-reinforcing and lock-in [16, 17] but considering the same context from a different perspective:

"…, initial conditions are not given, but rather constructed by actors who mobilize specific sets of events from the past in pursuit of their initiatives. Similarly, what is exogenous and what is endogenous is not given, but instead, depends on how actors draw and redraw their boundaries. Emergent situations are not 'contingencies', but instead afford embedded actors the possibilities to pursue certain courses of action while making others more difficult to pursue. Self-reinforcing mechanisms do not just exist, but instead are cultivated. Rather than lock-in, there is ever the possibility of creative destruction" [16].

Both path dependency and path creation are concepts related to innovation processes. While path dependency deals with organizational restraints emerged in the past which cannot be easily avoided, path creation puts a major focus on the role of actors in the innovation process, who proactively try to shape its outcome by "deviating from the existing path and creating an alternative future" [7]. Even contradictory both concepts fit well to the traditional manufacturing firms, which are historically closely bound to their innovation processes for physical products (path dependencies). On the other hand, path creation fits all their attempts to leave the traditional way of innovation in order to develop different innovation types e.g. digital innovation. The researcher acknowledges the importance of both concepts and considers them as a possibility to determine limitations hindering firms to implement innovations. However, in the context of the research, the goal is to go beyond these concepts and to provide a deeper understanding of the evolving digital innovation processes in manufacturing firms.

3 Research Problem and Research Question

A perspective considering the innovation outcome and the innovation process of digital innovation delivers six major dimensions: Convergence, digital materiality (innovation outcome) and generativity, heterogeneity, locus of innovation and pace (innovation process) [3]. The innovation outcome is determined by the integration of digital components into physical products in the socioeconomic environment (digital materiality). Consequentially convergence is reached by decoupling of digital content and digital infrastructure. The impact on the innovation process is characterized by lowing the boundaries for digital innovation. Hence, data and knowledge could be exchanged easily via different architecture layers (heterogeneity). That leads to the creation of product platforms which can be easily accessed by actors outside the company to which new components can be easily attached (generativity). The innovation process becomes unstructured and can be driven outside the boundaries of the firm. Manufacturing companies face another innovation dynamic not driven by incremental innovation as in the product development but by external actors. Various external actors could participate in the innovation process due to low communication costs and no geographical barriers (locus of innovation). All this combined with the characteristic of smart products e.g. reprogrammility, convergence ...etc. lead to the higher speed of digital innovation (pace) [3].

The new face of digital innovation and its flexible boundaries become a challenge for manufacturing companies since the shift towards digital innovation lead to an ultimate transformation of the integrated product-service design, strategy definition, organization structures, innovation processes, ecosystems and cognitive capabilities [8, 18, 19].

Tightly coupled with product innovation digital innovation could positively impact the performance of firms. It creates new product types, e.g. smart product but also offers possibilities for combining smart products with specific services increasing the added value of customer offerings. Technology-driven service innovation is considered as a powerful way of differentiation and there are multiple examples of service innovation enabled by high-technology service [20] e.g. new services related to transportation like trace and track of deliveries or systems for fleet monitoring [21].

Consequently, manufacturing firms are adding new services to their portfolios as part of a differentiation strategy [22]. The basis for differentiation is built on new offerings in which products and services are bundled together. That leads to unique customer value propositions. Differentiation strategies driven by the fusion of products and services are difficult to imitate and leads to hybrid value creation [23].

Following the discussion above developing and implementing digital innovation become a general challenge for manufacturing firms. Besides, additional challenges arise with regards to the role of IT and the resulting digitization of products since two innovation regimes IT and product innovation [6] have to be streamlined within the boundaries of the manufacturing firm. The research focuses on the intersection of digitization and product innovation defined as digital innovation and its impact on the organizational context known as digitalization, in which setting the rapid development of IT plays a significant role. Looking at that specific context and considering digital innovation and digital transformation in manufacturing firms as a strategic innovation choice with a direct impact on competitive capabilities and the financial performance of the firm, the research aims to understand:

RQ: What is the strategic role of diverse types of digital innovation in manufacturing firms?

The research question seeks to examine the emerging role of digital innovation in the context of manufacturing firms. The primary goal is to determine how digital innovation is understood and evaluated within the given context. In addition, this question should shed light on the distinct types of digital innovation. Considering the tension between IT innovation and product innovation based on the different characteristics of the hardware-based manufacturing paradigm and the service-oriented software logic [6, 24] a classification of digital innovation types shall draw the boundaries in which digital innovation co-exists in manufacturing firms. It is likely that across manufacturing firms, different understandings and categories of digital innovation exist which would have multiple effects on their motivation, characterized by perceived opportunities and challenges, regarding digital innovation.

4 Philosophical Stance and Research Method Choice

The study is exploratory and interpretative in nature and adopts the grounded theory approach. Considering the digital innovation as a sociotechnical issue, the grounded theory has been chosen as a feasible approach for understanding its dynamics in the given context [25, 26]. In this setup, the subjective experiences of the actors and their perception of reality play a significant role in the research, which is seen as a strength of the grounded theory [27].

A research adopting the grounded theory approach should answer the questions "what is going on there and how". Once these questions are answered theoretical concepts are derived and interlinked [26, 28]. The grounded theory approach is considered as a flexible research construct characterized. Firstly, due to the instant process of data analysis and data collection, a theoretical sampling can be applied. Means, the sample size, and scope are refined during the research process based on the data. Secondly, it allows starting a research with a high-level definition of the research problem, which is further concretized and shaped during the research process [28].

In the field of IS the paper from [29] has contributed to the wide acceptance of grounded theory as a research approach by showing that grounded theory is applicable in cases where the organizational context is crucial for the understanding of the phenomenon, where change management is involved and in areas where no or only limited theoretical knowledge exists [30]. As a consequence in the past years, the grounded theory approach has gained ground in the field of IS research [31] and leading IS journals [31, 32].

The research takes the interpretive philosophical stance. It subscribes to the interpretative view of the grounded theory paradigm promoted by Strauss and Corbin [33]. The following conclusive reasons led to this decision. Firstly, the research problem can be best explored by considering the view of the actors and understanding the context in which they interact. Using the Strauss and Corbin paradigm a conceptualization of the phenomenon can be achieved by focusing on the context and the dynamics within by building casual relationships [31]. Secondly, the major goal is to conceptualize the phenomenon of digital innovation by creating a substantive theory. The paradigm of Strauss and Corbin supports the creation of substantive theories by determining relationships between different theoretical categories [31]. Finally, along the overall acceptance of the grounded theory in the field of IS research [32] the paradigm of Strauss and Corbin has a strong support in the field of IS for the conceptualization of IT artifacts [31].

5 Research Process and Techniques

Data collection will be achieved by conducting an interpretative case study. An interpretative case study is seen as a feasible approach in the context of the grounded theory approach [34, 35]. Case studies are used for evaluating contemporary events, which require a different type of evidence [36]. In the context of digital innovation, these evidence can be for example decision processes, product developments or causal relationships. Since a case study is an empirical analysis which investigates present event the a real-life context [37], it provides the abilities to undercover exactly these aspects of the research [36]. Therefore, the case study approach is used as the main research technique. Data collection will be directed by conducting semi-structured interviews with decision makers and contributors in digital innovation projects in manufacturing firms. The semi-structured interview approach was chosen because of its ability to deliver a high level of data density [38].

The first step of the research process follows the suggestion for interdisciplinary triangulation [39, 40]. Triangulation is achieved by consolidating findings based on expert interviews and a preliminary literature screening. A preliminary interdisciplinary literature screening carried out at the beginning of a research is considered as …" a means to an end" for developing "…sharper and more insightful questions about the topic" [36]. Achieving a contextual theoretical awareness before applying grounded theory is a valid approach which has been supported by several scholars [27, 41] and defined as a theoretical sensitivity by [31, 42]. The results of the literature review are seed concepts as described and recommended by previous work [32, 42]. The seed concepts provide guidance for determining the substantive research area and influence the theoretical sampling [32].

Expert interviews with practitioners in the field of digital innovation have been used as additional "slices of data" [42] attached to the seed concepts in order to provide contextual insights. They improve the practical relevance of the research and provide guidance how to get a better understanding of the context in which digital innovation evolves. This input has been used to determine the direction of the research questions and ensure practical relevance of the research.

Following [42] the second stage of the research is the theoretical sampling which "… implies overlapping data collection and analysis…" [43].

The final phase of the research process is defined as a substantive theory creation. Main categories developed from the data are interlinked and causal relationships are determined. The main literature review related to the area of inquiry will be conducted in order to identify how the conceptualization of the research problem does fit to the existing body of knowledge in the main research domain [30]. Finally, the substantive theory and the area for which they are applicable will be presented.

6 Data Collection and Analysis

In the scope of the research are traditional manufacturing firms, which intend to develop or are already, developing digital innovation e.g. smart products. In this research, traditional manufacturing firms are defined as companies originally established to develop and produce physical products. The potential partners are not limited to their company size or the type of manufacturing industry if they are considered as traditional manufacturing companies and are not active in the automotive industry. This limitation is important since the automotive industry has its specific dynamics and product lifecycles which are beyond of the scope of the research. The geographical scope includes internationally operating manufacturing firms with solid tradition in physical product development with headquarters in Germany, Austria or Switzerland.

Business and IT decision makers, as well as experts in the field of digital innovation, are the target group for the semi-structured interviews. One main challenge of the research is to gain an access to the data of the target sample. Therefore, the first contact will be established with firms where personal relations with decision makers exist. A presentation of the objectives of the research will be used to lay out potential benefits of participating in the research project. The awareness of the reservations of companies and persons towards research projects is well known in terms of invested time, data confidentially and benefits for the organization. Therefore, during the data collection process, the names of the participants and the organizations they work for will be anonymized, in order to protect sensitive information. Once transcribed the audio recordings of the interviews will be sent back to the participants or deleted. A high-level description of the manufacturing firms and the position held by the interviewees will be disclosed. The aspect of ethics and trust during the research is crucial for gaining access to relevant data. Therefore, a transparent communication to the research partners on the process of data anonymization will be provided. The author believes that respecting the ethical aspect of the data collection will help to resolve concerns and overcome reservations from the research partners.

As a tool supporting the data analysis process NVivo 10 is used for classification of external sources e.g. literature review and interviews. Following the grounded theory approach the collected data from semi-structured interviews will be coded using open, axial and selective coding. The interviews will be recorded and immediately after transcribed and coded by applying open coding. The first step of theory generation, theoretical memos will be created during the coding process. Theoretical memos reflected the thoughts of the researcher on the data during the coding process and are the foundation for the later theory generation [43].

7 Research Contribution

The contribution of the research is twofold. Firstly, the selected research problem is a practical problem with high relevance for manufacturing firms. Considering the identified challenges of applying digital innovation in manufacturing companies, an assessment approach to understand the firm's capacity of practicing it will provide more transparency on the existing gaps and be a basis for defining an implementation strategy.

Secondly, the research is just scratching the surface of a complex topic in a specific industry. The substantive theory I intend to develop will provide a better contextual understanding of the process of digital innovation and can be used for further research in the same or similar substantive areas. Finally, the research should further promote the use of qualitative methods and especially the grounded theory in the research field of Information Systems.

References

1. Yoo, Y., Henfridsson, O., Lyytinen, K., Tiwana, A., Konsynski, B., Bush, A.A.: Research commentary—the new organizing logic of digital innovation: an agenda for information systems research. Inf. Syst. Res. **21**(4), 724–735 (2010)
2. Hylving, L., Henfridsson, O., Selander, L.: The role of dominant design in a product developing firm's digital innovation. J. Inf. Technol. Theory Appl. **13**(2), 5–21 (2012)
3. Yoo, Y., Lyytinen, K.: The Next Wave of Digital Innovation: Opportunities and Challenges: A Report on the Research Workshop 'Digital Challenges in Innovation Research. Available SSRN 1622170, No. October 2015, pp. 1–37 (2010)
4. Yoo, Y.: Computing in everyday life: a call for research on experiential computing. MIS Q. **34**(2), 213–231 (2010)
5. Nambisan, S.: Information technology and product/service innovation : a brief assessment and some suggestions for future research. J. Assoc. Inf. Syst. **14**, 215–226 (2013)
6. Svahn, F., Henfridsson, O.: The dual regimes of digital innovation management. In: Proceedings of the Annual Hawaii International Conference on System Sciences. pp. 3347–3356 (2011)
7. Henfridsson, O., Yoo, Y., Svahn, F.: Path creation in digital innovation: a multi-layered dialectics perspective. Assoc. Inf. Syst. **9**, 1–26 (2009). Working Paper
8. Porter, M.J., Heppelmann, J.E.: How smart, connected products are transforming competition. Harv. Bus. Rev. **92**(11), 64–88 (2014)
9. Wong, C.Y., McFarlane, D., Zaharudin, A.A., Agarwal, V.: The intelligent product driven supply chain. IEEE Int. Conf. Syst. Man Cybern. **4**, 6 (2002)
10. McFarlane, D., Sarma, S., Chirn, J.L., Wong, C., Ashton, K.: Auto ID systems and intelligent manufacturing control. Eng. Appl. Artif. Intell. **16**(4), 365–376 (2003)
11. Kärkkäinen, M., Holmström, J., Främling, K., Artto, K.: Intelligent products—a step towards a more effective project delivery chain. Comput. Ind. **50**(2), 141–151 (2003)
12. Sambamurthy, V., Bharadwaj, A., Grover, V., Sambamurthy, V., Bharadwaj, A., Grover, V., Sambamurthy, V., Bharadwaj, A., Grover, V.: Shaping agility through digital options: reconceptualizing the role of information technology in contemporary firms. MIS Q. **27**(2), 237–263 (2003)
13. Teece, D.J., Pisano, G., Shuen, A.: Dynamic capabilities and strategic management. Strateg. Manag. J. **18**(7), 77–115 (1997)
14. Teece, D.J.: Explicating dynamic capabilities: the nature and microfoundations of (sustainabile) enterprise performance. Strateg. Manag. J. **298**(13), 1319–1350 (2007)
15. Pisano, G.P.: A normative theory of dynamic capabilities: connecting strategy, know-how, and competition. Harvard Bus. Sch. Technol. Oper. **16–036**, 42 (2015). Working Paper
16. Garud, R., Kumaraswamy, A., Karnøe, P.: Path dependence or path creation? J. Manag. Stud. **47**(4), 760–774 (2010)
17. Vergne, J., Durand, R.: The missing link between the theory and empirics of path dependence : conceptual clarification, testability issue, and methodological implications. J Manage. Stud. **47**(4), 736–759 (2010)
18. Baines, T.S., Lightfoot, H.W., Benedettini, O., Kay, J.M., Authors, F.: The servitization of manufacturing: a review of literature and reflection on future challenges. J. Manuf. Technol. Manag. **20**, 547–567 (2009)
19. Porter, M.J.E., Heppelmann, J.E.: How smart connected products are transforming companies. Harv. Bus. Rev. **93**(10), 96–114 (2015)

20. Van Den Ende, J., Wijnberg, N.: The organization of innovation in the presence of networks and bandwagons in the new economy. Int. Stud. Manag. Organ. **31**, 30–45 (2001)
21. De Jong, J.P.J., Vermeulen, P.A.M.: Organizing successful new service development: a literature review. Manag. Decis. **41**(9), 844–858 (2003)
22. Gebauer, H.: Identifying service strategies in product manufacturing companies by exploring environment-strategy configurations. Ind. Mark. Manag. **37**, 278–291 (2008)
23. Velamuri, V.K., Neyer, A.-K., Möslein, K.M.: Hybrid value creation: understanding the value creating attributes. Multikonferenz Wirtschaftsinformatik MKWI **2010**, 399–400 (2010)
24. Svahn, F., Henfridsson, O., Yoo, Y.: A threesome dance of agency: mangling the socio materiality of technological regimes in digital innovation. Int. Conf. Inf. Syst. 1–18 (2009)
25. Fernández, W.D.: The grounded theory method and case study data in IS research : issues and design. Inf. Syst. Found. Constr. Crit. Work. Aust. Natl. Univ. **1**, 43–59 (2004)
26. Tan, J.: Grounded theory in practice: issues and discussion for new qualitative researchers. J. Doc. **66**(1), 93–112 (2010)
27. Suddaby, R.: From the editors: what grounded theory is not. Acad. Manag. J. **49**(4), 633–642 (2006)
28. Becker, P.H.: Common pitfalls in published grounded theory research. Qual. Health Res. **3**, 254–260 (1993)
29. Orlikowski, W.J.: CASE tools as organizational change: investigating incremental and radical changes in systems development. Misq **17**(3), 309 (1993)
30. Urquhart, C., Fernandez, W.: Grounded theory method: the researcher as blank slate and other myths. Inf. Syst. **12**(31), 456–464 (2006)
31. Seidel, S., Urquhart, C.: On emergence and forcing in information systems grounded theory studies: the case of Strauss and Corbin. J. Inf. Technol. **28**(3), 237–260 (2013)
32. Urquhart, C., Lehmann, H., Myers, M.D.: Putting the 'theory' back into grounded theory: guidelines for grounded theory studies in information systems. Inf. Syst. J. **20**(4), 357–381 (2010)
33. Strauss, A., Corbin, J.: Basics of Qualitative Research, vol. 15 (1990)
34. Walsham, G.: Interpretive case studies in IS research: nature and method. Eur. J. Inf. Syst. **4**(2), 74–81 (1995)
35. Urquhart, C.: Grounded Theory for Qualitative Research: A Practical Guide. Sage Publications Ltd (2013)
36. Yin, R.K.: Applications of case study research. Appl. Soc. Res. Methods Ser. **34**, 173 (2013)
37. Schramm, W.: Notes on Case Studies of Instructional Media Projects. Working paper for the Academy of Educational Development. pp. 1–43 (1971)
38. Corbin, J., Morse, J.M.: The unstructured interactive interview: Issues of reciprocity and risks when dealing with sensitive topics. Qual. Inq. **9**(3), 335–354 (2003)
39. Janesick, V.: The dance of qualitative research design: metaphor, methodolatry, and meaning. In The SAGE Handbook of Qualitative Research. pp. 209–219 (1994)
40. Kuechler, B., Park, E.H., Vaishnavi, V.: Formalizing theory development in IS design science research : learning from qualitative research. Am. Conf. Inf. Syst. 1–11 (2009)
41. Gasson, S.: Employing a grounded theory approach for MIS research. Handb. Res. Contemp. Theor. pp. 34–36 (2009)
42. Glaser, B.G., Strauss, A.L.: The Discovery of Grounded Theory: Strategies for Qualitative Research. vol. 1, no. 4 (1967)
43. Urquhart, C.: Grounded Theory for Qualitative Research: A Practical Guide. Sage Publications Ltd (2012)

A Dynamic System for Instabilities Prediction

Mohamed Amine ISSAMI

Abstract Targeting financial stability has become an important matter for central banks. This objective has considerable impacts on growth and reinforces the economic structure. During the last decades, the financial environment has suffered from different forms of instabilities. Turbulences, crashes, and bubbles are occuring frequently. The ability of modern economies to absorb shocks is questionned since their vulnerability is increasing. This situation is due mainly to the contraction of business cycles, fragility of financial institutions, and corporate debt. Within this scope, volatility clustering in the financial markets has been consistently observed. This paper aims to develop a dynamic system able to detect instantly different instabilities using ABM models. It consists of implementing a strategy-based prevention holistic and integrated.

Keywords Agent-based models · Financial stability · Holistic perspective · Integrated mode · Prudential regulation · Safety nets · Central authority · Strategy-based prevention

1 Introduction

A dynamic system for instability prediction is one of the alternatives for implementing self-fulfilling stabilization policies. This mechanism requires sophisticated tools, able to capture instantly the evolution of the financial system (i.e. a strategic watch).

Indeed, when prevention fails, the expertise of the supervisory authorities can trigger a recovery and adjustment procedures. Such capacity can only be capitalized if the monitoring mode is available in real time and the simulation models introduce the systemic component.

Nevertheless, the macroeconomic models are dedicated exclusively to the analysis of the real sphere and neglect the endogenous risks related to the financial industry.

M. A. ISSAMI (✉)
Professor of Finance, Groupe ISCAE, BP. 8114, Casablanca, Morocco
e-mail: aissami@iscaextra.net

© Springer Nature Switzerland AG 2020   591
Y. Baghdadi et al. (eds.), *ICT for an Inclusive World*,
Lecture Notes in Information Systems and Organisation 35,
https://doi.org/10.1007/978-3-030-34269-2_41

In addition, they are characterized by the dominance of linear specifications, whereas the contagion and interaction phenomena are rather nonlinear.

However, the advanced macro-financial models cover the economic and financial components. The major challenge of this technical breakthrough is the lack of significant information, which represents a major handicap for the calibration and accuracy of the findings.

In this regard, High Performance Computing (HPC) techniques and simulation efforts have become a pillar of the strategy-based prevention and a sophisticated tool for measuring the adverse effects of economic and financial turbulences. This analysis mode does extend beyond quantitative variables. It includes the testability of the payment and settlement system infrastructure as a main vector of financial stability. The size of the high frequency data and the common exposures on the interbank market represent a prime input for running models.

As a result, this article focuses primarily on the implementation of a dynamic instability prediction system. Our approach is in accordance with the following three axes: (i) real-time financial bubbles detection, (ii) use of multi-agent simulations, and (iii) creation of an observatory of financial stability. This perspective represents a relevant surveillance action and ricochet off to control the extent of idiosyncratic and systemic risks. Finally, using multi-agent systems, introducing simulators and platforms for financial services monitoring in real time or with a specific time lag are prerequisites in order to identify the stylized facts of financial markets.

2 Speculative Financial Bubbles Formation

A financial bubble[1] is an autonomous state of drift from the underlying structure of the price formation process [1, 2]. There are, moreover, several elements contributing to the amplification of this phenomenon. In this regard, the financial valuation (pricing) of assets is the main reason.[2]

2.1 The Reference Value Problem (Real or Fundamental Value)

The value of an asset is the discounted sum of the generated revenue streams. This formula ignores the impact of internal and external interactions in the business cycle. In addition, the diversity of valuation models for calculating asset growth has failed in the business valuation exercise.[3] This failure is related to the complexity of

---

[1] A bubble is recognized only after its burst, when the ascending phase was sufficiently continuous and did not reflect the real value of the asset.

[2] As well as the expectations of the economic agents.

[3] Asset-based approach, dynamic, and market value.

quantitative techniques and the effects of financial innovation (out-of-equilibrium dynamics).

For assets valuation, there are two main methods: one is real based on the fundamental value; the other one is financial: fair value is a valuation method introduced by the IAS/IFRS international accounting standards, which apply to the consolidated financial statements of listed companies. It is defined as "the amount for which an asset could be exchanged, or a liability settled, between knowledgeable, willing parties in an arm's length transaction".

2.2 The Detection of Speculative Bubbles in Real Time

The evolution of prices on the financial markets[4] is one of the most discussed essays in quantitative finance. On a preventive level, the monitoring of this stochastic process - usually autoregressive - allows to explain if the oscillations refer to a fundamental value (based on Discounted cash-flow method, "DCF") or the direction of variation follows a bullish or bearish trend. Thus, to rule on the corrections or if necessary, to predict stock market crashes[5] will be the subject of a continuous centralization of factual data. For this purpose, the price of a financial asset is defined according to the following formula:

$$\mathbf{P^a} = \mathbf{P^f} + \mathbf{B_t} + \boldsymbol{\varepsilon_t}$$

We consider: P^a a is the current price of the asset; P^f is the fundamental price of the asset[6]; B_t is the accelerator factor "financial bubble" and ε_t is the random term of the time series. To estimate the factor B_t, we refer to Sornette's model[7] [3].

$$\mathbf{B_t} = \mathbf{a_t B_{t-1}} + \mathbf{e^{rt} \varepsilon_t}$$

The parameters of this model are defined as follows: (i) B_t and B_{t-1} are components of a financial bubble at time t and t−1; (ii) a_t is the multiplying factor, can be estimated according to the following formula: $a_t = a_0 e^\sigma_{\eta t}$, σ represents the volatility of the asset and ηt is a Gaussian random variable; (iii) $e^{rt}\varepsilon_t$ is the exponential growth of the residuals and ε_t follows a uniform distribution.

---

[4]It is a channel where the transmission of signals and the effects of monetary policy are realized.

[5]Following a burst of a bubble or because of a sharp fall of the stock price.

[6]The fundamental value of a stock is the discounted sum of the company's future profits. There is a divergence between stock prices and this discounted sum of future profits, which is generally attributed to risk, and is represented by the equity risk premium.

[7]LPPL (Log Periodic Power Law), Sornette [3] "Slimming of power law by increasing market returns". The power law derives from a mathematical relationship between two quantities. If a quantity is the frequency of an event and the other one is the size of an event, then the relation is a distribution of the power law if the frequencies decrease very slowly when the size of the event increases.

For the calibration of the model, several steps are accomplished: the introduction of the constants (a_0, r, σ); creating a time vector t (time) from 1 to T; the development of a vector for ηt (random variable that follows a normal distribution); The calculation of the matrix vector at $t = 1, 2, ..., T$; the definition of a vector for e^{rt}; the assignment of a vector $ε_t$ (random variable of a uniform distribution); initial value $b_0 = 0$, with ($E[b_t] = 0$); The calculation of the second and the first order; Thus, we can extract the different paths of b_t.

However, the implementation of a dynamic system for instabilities prediction, using advanced models (multi-agent systems) and the extension to a holistic approach constitute a key performance vector to maintain financial stability. This further step will modulate economic and financial policies under a completely new concept.

3 Multi-agent Models Simulations "Agent-Based Models"

Agent-based modeling (ABM) is a dynamic technique that integrates at least two levels of micro and macrostructure entities that are in constant interaction. This property explains the interest of this method for modeling in financial economics (field where many phenomena have a multi-scale structure). This involves carefully examining the factors that contribute to the formation of systemic risks.[8]

3.1 A Literature Review of Multi-agent Models Applied to Finance

The multi-agent systems are based on the "individual-centered" and consider that the phenomena observed at a certain stage of organization arise from the interactions that occur between the elementary entities of the same level. The use of these simulations was quickly addressed in the field of social sciences as in other scientific disciplines.

Traditionally, evolutionary economics has brought together the ideas of several economists, such as Arthur [4]. Multi-agent models are implemented to promote interactions[9] between agents, or at least between agents and the environment [5, 6]. These interactions originate in cooperation between operators, directly or indirectly, and produce results that in turn modify their behavior [7].

In monetary economics, financial innovations play an important part in the prudential system. The forces conditioning the generation of these innovations play a

---

[8]This approach introduces a more explicit monitoring of interconnections at the financial system level and the feedback effects of the real and financial economy, in order to contain the development of financial imbalances.

[9]Non-linear.

decisive role in the dynamics of the financial industry. The behavior[10] of banks and firms (with different strategies) is one of these forces, but their analysis cannot ignore the external environment [8].

3.2 An Application of Multi-agent Models "Agent-Based Models"

The object-oriented programming applied to finance provides a broader range for the testability of complex problems. Indeed, multi-agent simulations[11] bring solutions to the limits of mathematical modeling (eliminate the hypothesis of looping of the model). This advanced technique is adopted by the Fed (Federal Reserve Board). It is a relevant tool for systemic measurement and is an indispensable instrument for the financial stability observatory.

The computer programs[12] used by central banks - notably the Bank of England - have multiplied and are interested in the simulation of interbank networks (Figs. 1

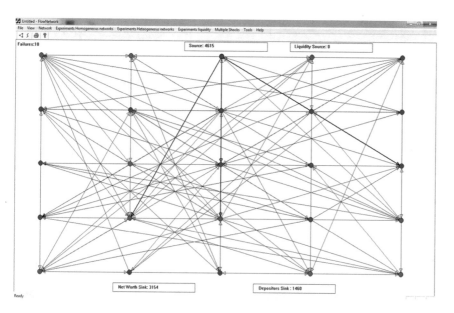

Fig. 1 Interbank system simulation with shocks transmission. *Source* author, from FlowNetwork software, (*Bank of England*)

---

[10]Three behaviors are presented in the form of three hierarchical modules: a first reactive module; a second module where learning is planned; and finally, a third cognitive level.

[11]http://www.agent-based-models.com et http://www3.imperial.ac.uk/complexityandnetworks.

[12]FlowNetwork software (*shareware*) and IPSS, Interbank Payment System Simulator (*open-source*).

and 2) and the evaluation of payment systems (Fig. 3).[13] In this context, multi-agent systems appear as a privileged tool, since they make it possible to model

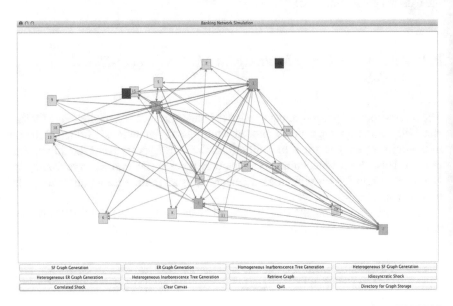

Fig. 2 Propagation of shocks simulation over banking industry. *Source* author, from FIN-STAB platform (open-source), http://www2.cs.uic.edu/~dasgupta/financial-simulator-files/

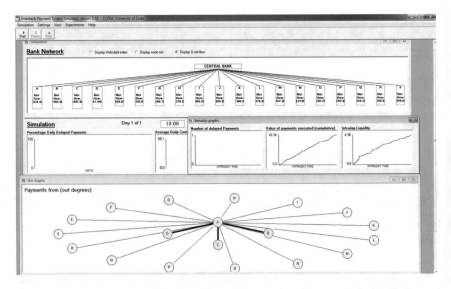

Fig. 3 Simulation of payment system resilience. *Source* author, from "IPSS, Interbank Payment System Simulator" software, Essex University (open-source)

---

[13]The simulations are based on synthetic data (incompatibility of data on a real payment system).

individual behaviors,[14] decision-making modes, exchanges and interactions between individuals and entities.

As such, the creation of a virtual stock market[15] opens a promising horizon in favor of stability (eliminating consideration of the balance that links the decision of the element and its action). This new computational technique "Agent-based models" strives to understand the behavior of economic agents when making decisions for the purchase and sale of financial assets[16] (trading strategies).

In order to create a dynamic system for predicting instabilities and as illustrated by the findings (Figs. 1, 2, and 3), the real-time financial bubbles detection model has been significantly improved. This monitoring mechanism is possible using Agent-based modeling (ABM). It is a dynamic technique that integrates at least two levels of micro features and macrostructures that are in permanent interaction. This property explains the interest of this tool for modeling in financial economics (field where many phenomena are of a multi-scale structure).

Consequently, the advantage of a multi-agent platform is its continuous and scalable capacity to simulate inter-temporal dynamics. Like financial markets, multi-agent systems put strategic alternatives into perspective in accordance with available resources, in a competitive process.

The guidance developed by the monetary and financial authorities has a positive effect on the resilience of the financial industry. For example, the introduction of a preventive approach implies an investment in the adoption of structured standards. In this respect, the scope of a self-fulfillment policy of the stability mechanisms is then extended to the interconnections linking all stakeholders and governing the interactions within the financial system concerned.[17] In addition, the preventive approach[18] offers the opportunity of extension to a holistic track (considering the whole). It appears that the viability of one approach cannot be asserted to the detriment of the other, hence the interest of integrating the two lenses into a common device, called "integrated approach".

Finally, the monetary authority has several instruments to calibrate the restore of equilibrium. The problematic issue that looms up at this level: if the central bank has an expanded mission, how risks will be managed within this organization? And what impact will it have on changing the expectations of economic agents, following a discretionary policy during periods of instability and crisis?

---

[14]Heterogeneous behaviors included.

[15]Issami M. A. et al. [9], http://www.multimedia.ethz.ch/misc/2012/abm.

[16]Integration of investment strategies, portfolio management, fundamental and technical analysis.

[17]An isolated financial system is not accepted as an assumption, the consideration of the external environment is essential for the determination of network linkage schemes and potential channels of contagion.

[18]The preventive approach is a preliminary step in the holistic perspective to prepare financial and non-financial companies for an integrated monitoring.

4 Financial Stability Observatory

In an economic and financial environment subject to increasingly complex and unpredictable risks, the monitoring of financial activity helps to cushion the magnitude of shocks. In this context, the setting up of an ad hoc structure will certainly reinforce the preventive mode. This exercise is an early warning system against any possible disturbances.

Traditionally, this entity will have the mission of gathering the analytical framework and scientific methodologies for measuring financial stability. This work can be done through an examination of the conditions of access to finance and the distribution of credits (e.g. the cost of capital). In addition, the monitoring of the indebtedness of non-financial enterprises and households will contribute to the definition of safety nets for systematically important financial institutions.

Given these elements, the monitoring of financial market developments (capital markets, derivatives, etc.), namely, the appreciation of financial assets is of primary interest, when detecting speculative financial bubbles. Securing mutual exposures of banks, including exposures related to holding other forms of equity instruments (and receivables) issued by financial actors in real time, through a computer-aided platform.[19]

In this perspective, it is thus necessary to monitor the operation of the payment system, settlement and delivery of the deviations. Essentially, the respect of the terms of the payment deadlines over a specific period and assessing their evolution according to multi-scales: sectors of activity, with emphasis on different deadlines for companies and not only their average levels, foreign trade, investments of industrial enterprises (whatever their size), group membership, public administrations. In addition, it is a question of carrying out these actions by:

The creation of network models (Network and graph theory) which formalize the interbank relations with the integration of liquidation of assets in the financial network.

The constitution of joint working groups composed of scholars, practitioners and experts in specialized organizations (dedicated to analysis and advice).

Broadening the scope of research on the theme of financial stability, integrating public finances (problems of fiscal sustainability and conditions of macroeconomic stability), harmonization of trade policies with the exchange rate regime.

A periodic publication (public information and factual data) of the findings and the comments of analysis.

---

[19]http://www.fna.fi/platform.

4.1 The Functions Assumed by the Financial Stability Observatory

The Financial Stability Observatory is a form of cooperation between financial and non-financial institutions and any stakeholder. The recommendations made by this entity are generally taken into account by decision makers. The independence of such a structure and the centralization of information offer opportunities to anticipate the behavior of economic agents (on-site system).

At the same time, the central bank[20] is confronted with a conflict of interest between several financial policies to be implemented (notably its monetary commitments) and the "stress" of arbitration in case of intervention (non-conventional measures).

4.2 The Externalities of the Financial Support Framework

The involvement of economic agents is a key success factor for the success of financial support phases (the transparency of financial transactions and their settlement). In addition, the expected benefits are mainly the proposal of preemptive actions in case of major deviation or turbulence. In this respect, the periodic publication of business continuity plan (BCP) reinforces the resilience of the financial industry (positive externality).

The monetary authority plays a fundamental role in the proper functioning of the financial system. However, the stability of the system depends on many other factors, including the strength of real counterparts, the changing environment and infrastructure.

Central banks (Central Bank of Luxembourg, Bank of Canada, Banque de France) set up their own "Financial Stability" department to monitor financial market trends, the positions of financial and non-financial institutions, expectations and investment capacities, savings of households, as well as the determination of possible contagion channels in the event of a crisis. The results are published periodically as a report or a review.

Furthermore, the research effort provided by an independent observatory requires more credibility and objectivity. The only problem for this structure is access to funding, without recourse to government assistance, in order to maintain the autonomous aspect of a non-profit entity. The recommendations made are not binding for economic agents to apply. In addition, there are currently several scientific laboratories at the level of the US and European universities, responsible for monitoring the state of the local financial system and its interconnections and the consequences of backing a structured network.

---

[20]Accumulation of functions.

After identifying the sources of systemic risk, the creation of institutional mechanisms strengthens security and resilience. This guidance combines the various crisis prevention and resolution guidelines with regulations that increase the cost of activities according to the risks that financial intermediaries generate.

However, the new challenges at this stage are the quality of the data collected and the analysis of economic and financial topics. Moreover, the lack of information quality on financial and non-financial institutions has had serious consequences during the financial crisis (2007–2008). In addition, the ability of the authorities to respond in a collective and timely manner has been hampered by the lack of a common database on banks (relating to concentration risk, market risk, financing risk, risk of contagion, and sovereign risk). Thus, new avenues for reflection and action are needed in the inquiry for a mode adapted to the systemic maintenance of stability (New deal/Reset).

5 Conclusion

The complexity of financial stability cannot be approached by a standard operating procedures or usual interventions. The construction of a resilient system depends mainly on the depth of its underlying structure and the support of competent authorities during the monitoring process.

Besides, the explicit nature of the policies sometimes adopted by the public authorities leads to the erosion of uncertainty towards the macroeconomic and financial perspective, and contributes partially to the consolidation of trust mechanisms. However, engaging in a discretionary policy for targeting financial stability is a relevant measure to avoid for economic agent the formation of moral hazard.

Generally, regulators expect from the decision-making entities of financial and non-financial institutions to adopt best practices in their integrated risk management agenda. This approach is based on the awareness of operators and the introduction of proactive actions in continuous and constant change.

Referring to the economic and social entity, the holistic approach presupposes the implementation of a method adapted to this particular process. The developed methods highlight the links between micro-stability and macroeconomic effects.

Thus, an integrated doctrine at the level of systemic surveillance is implemented to impregnate all stakeholders within the value chain of the financial system. This new framework is participative and leads to an implicit stabilization mechanism.

The central bank will not be able to ensure the stability of a financial system on its own. The success of a stabilization policy depends essentially on the collaboration of all stakeholders, including the government (e.g. through stimulus programs). Thus, the central authority is given a new form of horizontal exchanges.

Ultimately, the development of the national financial system is conditioned by the strengthening of competition and the regulation of financial innovations. In this context, stability has undoubtedly become a prerequisite and an inextricable condition for the sustainability of economic growth.

References

1. Minsky, H.P.: The financial instability hypothesis: a restatement. Thames papers in political economy (1978)
2. Kindleberger, C. P.: Manias, panics, and crashes: a history of financial crises. Basic Books, revised and enlarged, New York 1989, 3rd ed. 1996 (1978)
3. Sornette, D.: Why stock markets crash: critical events in complex financial systems. Princeton University Press, New Jersey (2003)
4. Arthur, W.B.: Complexity and the economy. Science **284**, 107–109 (1999)
5. Harfouche, A.L., Jacobson, D.A., Kainer, D., Romero, J.C., Harfouche, A.H., Mugnozza, G., Moshelion, M., Tuskan, G.A., Keurentjes, J., Altman, A.: Accelerating climate resilient plant breeding by applying next-generation artificial intelligence. Trend. Biotechnol. **37**(11), 1217–1235 (2019)
6. Harfouche, A., Quinio, B., Skandrani, S., Marciniak, R.: A framework for artificial knowledge creation in organizations. In: ICIS 2017 Proceedings. Paper 15. http://aisel.aisnet.org/icis2017/General/Presentations/15 (2017)
7. Treuil, J.P. et al.: Agent-based vs. PDE modeling of runoff dynamics: simulation experiments. Paper presented at the international symposium in memory of Michel Rieu, Bondy (FRA), 10/08-10 (2001)
8. Lo, A.W. et al.: A computational view of market efficiency. Papers 0908.4580, arXiv.org (2009)
9. Issami, M. A. et al.: The automatic Reverse engineering financial time series, Web interface V1.0, ETH Zurich (2011)

Printed in the United States
By Bookmasters